# HARMONIC
# EXPERIENCE

# HARMONIC EXPERIENCE

*Tonal Harmony from
Its Natural Origins to Its Modern Expression*

## W. A. MATHIEU

INNER TRADITIONS INTERNATIONAL
ROCHESTER, VERMONT

Inner Traditions International
One Park Street
Rochester, Vermont 05767
www.gotoit.com

LIBRARY OF CONGRESS CATALOGING-IN-PUBLICATION DATA
Mathieu, W. A.
Harmonic experience : tonal harmony from its natural origins to its
modern expression / W. A. Mathieu.
p.  cm.
Includes bibliographical references (p.  ) and index.
ISBN 0-89281-560-4
1. Harmony.  I. Title.
MT50.M48  1997
781.2'5—dc21        96-40069
CIPMN


Printed and bound in Canada

10  9  8  7  6  5  4  3  2  1

Text design and layout by Virginia L. Scott
This book was typeset in Goudy with Americana as the display typeface

Distributed to the book trade in Canada by Publishers Group West (PGW),
Toronto, Ontario

Distributed to the book trade in the United Kingdom by Deep Books, London

Distributed to the book trade in Australia by Millennium Books, Newtown, N. S. W.

Distributed to the book trade in New Zealand by Tandem Press, Auckland

Distributed to the book trade in South Africa by Alternative Books, Ferndale

All music composed by W. A. Mathieu except as otherwise noted.

*To Pandit Pran Nath*
*1918–1996*

# CONTENTS

# EDITOR'S PREFACE

MY WIFE TELLS ME that her adult music students often begin lessons with this request: "I want to play better, of course, but what I'm really hoping to learn is *how music works*." The wording may vary—some say they want to learn harmony, others music theory—but the underlying need is the same: A hunger to understand how music exercises its power over our psyches.

What those students are often surprised to learn is how many professional musicians feel the same hunger. Even after years of university or conservatory training, most musicians still sense that a large piece of musical understanding is missing. Conventional music theory courses have taught them how to label different musical elements, identify chord progressions, and notate what they hear. They may indeed have learned something valuable about how music works, but what remains missing is a clear idea of how their own perceptions and responses fit into the picture.

The insatiably curious among us begin to search outside the usual sources of instruction to find an answer to that question. In my own journey as a composer and performer, that search has included playing African *mbira* music, exploring European tuning systems that predate equal temperament, and cracking my skull on the esoteric writings of Pythagorean philosophers. Each of these sources has supplied another piece of the puzzle, but generally I've found myself on my own when it came to relating the useful bits and pieces to one another and to the actual music I want to make.

I had already spent a couple of decades in this search before I crossed paths with W. A. Mathieu, a musician who not only had covered much of the same lonely territory before me but had also managed to synthesize his knowledge into a teachable form. A pianist and composer in both jazz and classical traditions, as well as a longtime student of North Indian singing, Mathieu has developed an approach to self-training in harmony that focuses on the listener's response to combinations of tones. He takes as his starting point the phenomenon that comes closest to being a universal part of human experience: Our attraction to music that is in tune. That quality of being in tune is called *resonance*, and just as tones in correct relationships resonate together, so do we, as listeners and performers, resonate along with them. Mathieu shows us how, by singing and playing various combinations of notes in tune, we can learn to observe our changing responses and begin to develop an understanding of music's power based on what happens in our own bodies and minds.

*Harmonic Experience* begins with the fundamental building blocks of music—single tones, sung over a drone—and shows you how to examine in minute detail your own responses to pure resonance. As you gain a conscious appreciation of these responses, a map of music's inner geography starts to emerge. Once those responses are mapped, the same process of attentive listening and introspection is applied to the impure tunings of equal temperament, which we are able to accept as more or less reasonable facsimiles of the genuine article. The next step, then, is to examine how the ambiguities of equal temperament make possible a harmonic language of exquisite subtlety and beauty.

Such a regimen of careful listening reveals to us not only how music works but also how it works *in us*. The one prerequisite, beyond the ability to read music, is a willingness to do the practices. Reading the book will put ideas into your head; singing, playing, and listening will put knowledge in your heart.

Mathieu's approach is at once so simple and so profound that musicians working in any style and at any level can profit from it. Savvy readers may recognize elements of North Indian music theory and jazz theory in addition to orthodox classical ideas. That's not because his method is some sort of eclectic New Age blend. On the contrary: His theory embraces so many musical traditions because it takes as its starting point the essential physical and psychological facts common to all music. It seems fitting that such a book should appear at a time when many musicians are dissolving the artificial boundaries between musical styles; those musicians will find this book an invaluable tool in the conciliation of opposing views.

In a time when we are inundated with throwaway books, *Harmonic Experience* definitely falls in the category of durable goods—a book to return to again and again. The book's structure resembles a spiraling ascent up a mountain: The same vistas keep coming into view, but from successively higher vantage points. Once the journey has been made, you may choose to revisit parts of the mountain, avoiding the switchbacks and bushwhacking straight up to keep one vista constantly in sight. But any way you journey on this mountain, your relationship with music is certain to be illuminated and enriched by Mathieu's gentle wisdom.

Larry Hamberlin
Rochester, Vermont

# INTRODUCTION

HARMONIC EXPERIENCE DESCRIBES THE FULL RANGE of harmony, from its fundamental gestures to its most complex expressions, by means of the unifying principle of resonance. By harmony I mean not simply chord progressions but the relationships of all the notes in a piece both to the keynote and to each other. By resonance I mean those specially reenforcing combinations of tones that in their mutual resounding—their perfect in-tune-ness—evaporate the boundary between music and musician.

It is generally believed that there are two related but distinct and opposed systems of harmony: an ancient one based on a system of resonances, or "pure" tunings, called just intonation, and a modern one based on the equal division of an octave, but with "impure" tuning, called twelve-tone equal temperament. This book redefines the modern as an evolutionary transformation of the ancient and is allied with a comprehensive revival of ancient values that is already, at the turn of the twenty-first century, well under way.

## Two Reasons for Writing This Book

The chasm between music theory and music practice is immense. The way we *think* music is so greatly removed from the psychological reasons we *do* music that theory is more often a hindrance than a help. Students only gradually figure out what most specialists already know in their hearts but are not quick to advertise: there exists no satisfactory general theory of harmony. The central energies that define music are not conscious, much less articulated, in the culture. The universal acceptance of equal temperament in the West has resulted in a splendid body of music, but the accumulated result of centuries of impure, approximate tuning has given our ears a kind of jet lag, a condition of aesthetic depletion. We have no comprehensive music theory today because we are so removed from direct experience of the seed resonances that generated music in the first place. Equal temperament has been something

1

like electric light—highly useful, but alienating us from the basic rhythms of the sun and the moon, the purest phases of being.

It is astounding how thoroughly the resonances of just intonation have been submerged. Entire African villages sing nightlong rituals beautifully in tune, but Americans cannot sing "Happy Birthday" in tune in a restaurant. This raises the deeper issue of our separation from what is natural, and perhaps points to a more complete musical behavior. Maybe, as was thought by Pythagoras, musical harmony really *is* a model for harmony on a grander scale, and a clear model of our music can teach us something about our present state of separation and loss.

Until the present, just intonation and equal temperament have never been reconciled theoretically. They seem to be two sides of an issue whose adherents are at odds. This book shows how they are a single subject responding to a single theory, that they coevolved and can continue to do so, and that their future together is full of promise. The larger purpose of *Harmonic Experience*, then, is to bring a complete model of harmony into common practice.

I would like also to mention a more personal reason for writing *Harmonic Experience*. Ever since I was a teenager attracted to the perfectly tuned jazz chords of the Stan Kenton trombone section, I have wanted to understand harmony as part of my own psyche. During my subsequent apprenticeship to European classical music, however, I could not find—try as I might—the connection between classical theory and the palette of feeling that its music inspires. I need that connection because I do not mimic music easily. To learn music, my intuition needs help: At some point it needs to name the thing it is learning. Only after I have named a thing is my intuition free to take charge. The more I studied the concepts and nomenclatures of music theory, the less it seemed capable of addressing the psychological responses of the listener. Over many subsequent years of studying music that is not in equal-tempered tuning, including Medieval European music, African music, Middle Eastern music, and especially North Indian *raga*, I came to understand that the link missing from our culture's classical theory is not so much unknown as forgotten, and that it could be brought forward and described in contemporary terms. As I began to describe this to others, I found I could better describe it for myself. The personal reason for writing this book, then, has been to deepen my own absorption in harmonic language.

## How This Book Is Organized

The text is divided into four parts.

Part 1 shows how the simplest frequency ratios—perfect fifths and major thirds—are felt as resonances, and how these two resonances combine to organize the system of just into-nation. It goes on to describe how a lattice of perfect fifths and major thirds generates most of the world's musical modes, and asks you, the reader, to be an accomplice in eliciting these modes by singing them. It maintains that bodily understanding is crucial for authentic intellectual mapping, and guides you step by step in comprehending the harmonic relationships implicit in the melodies you sing.

Part 2 shows how the lattice of just intonation serves as the template for our modern system of twelve-tone equal temperament. In the beginning keyboard practices, the twelve tones of equal temperament stand unambiguously for the twelve least-complex tones of the just lattice. The text goes on to demonstrate how, under certain conditions, the twelve tones of the equal-tempered keyboard can stand for more than thirty tones in just intonation.

Part 3 examines in detail the musical responses that allow only twelve tones to stand for more than twelve. First, it shows how a single equal-tempered tone can be made to evoke either of two distinct just tones separated by a very small difference in pitch, called a comma. It then enumerates the behaviors of the various types of commas as they are perceived in equal temperament, thus accounting for all tonal harmony—modal, diatonic, and modulatory—that is available in the modern tuning system.

Part 4 presents a compendium of keyboard practices designed to place the language of tonal harmony simultaneously in the ears, in the intellect, and under the hands. These include diatonic and cadential formulas, tonal modulations, modal modulations, cyclic sequences, and symmetrical harmony. Various notations are offered, the better to visualize the harmonies. Analyses of pieces from the fourteenth to the twentieth centuries show how a resonance-based theory can enrich our understanding of a variety of musics.

There are many books that this book is not: it is not a book about counterpoint, or figured bass, or melodic or rhythmic structure, or compositional development, although all of those subjects come into play. It is a harmony book that is meant to reconcile and go beyond, but not supplant, traditional texts.

## The Method: Art over Science

From ancient times, theorists have tried to rationalize and objectify emotions into abstractions, called *affections*, that correspond to specific musical elements. In the same way that rhetoric was the systematic art of persuasion, various theories of affections determined how certain modes, rhythms, and melodic figures controlled the emotions of the listener. The relationship of specific musical elements to specific responses is, on one level, obvious: We hear an ascending melody and something within us rises also. But when you examine individual cases, nothing seems able to be pinned down. After all, who decides which responses we are supposed to have? Is there an Affection Police patrolling all listeners: "You there, with the paisley tie—are you properly feeling the anxiety of this augmented second?" The issue lies at the cusp where science and art meet. Science is primarily defined by its objectivity, art by its subjectivity. Are there strategies by which the two can be creatively conjoined?

I approach harmonic theory as an empirical art rather than an aesthetic science. I am led forward by subjective experience, ephemeral feelings of longing and aversion. Learning to hone and keen these, and to trust them, is my work. I can talk numbers and examine the responses of populations, but that will not tell me, finally, what I want to know. What I want to know is my own ear, because it is the only true path to yours.

Inner knowledge of harmony grows with creative use. You hear things, then you use them to construct the world. That is not a very scientific method: it won't produce repeatable experiments or objective data. As a musician I am fascinated by the objective quantification of experience only to the extent that it will increase my ability to use musical language as a resonator for my life's portion. Beyond that, the numbers are nonvital curiosities.

In traveling through these pages, I want you to cherish your inner responses, nurse and groom them, learn to believe them. Then, when the numbers shed light on them, fine. But never sacrifice your hearing for a name or a number; there is no music in that direction. True, I will say, "Such-and-such sounds like so-and-so," and I will describe numbers as having qualities; that is because words and numbers can point the way. But it takes authentic experience—the inside feeling of rightness—to validate concepts. You are the replete knower, and the method of your knowing is the self.

## Learning by Singing

Many if not most musicians in our culture have lost the basic act of singing in tune, the process by which the combinations of tones that organize our hearing and our music are internalized and authenticated. When these harmonic sources have been reclaimed and honored, the particular effects of equal-tempered harmony can be recognized, categorized, and creatively used, as we shall see. It is not enough to listen passively to pure harmonies, or learn to recognize them, or to combine them on an instrument. One has to connect them with one's feelings by placing them in the body. Sung harmony is embodied intelligence.

In *Harmonic Experience*, great emphasis is placed on singing over a drone. I want this to sound inviting and not the least bit forbidding, because everyone—no exceptions—is capable of singing perfectly in tune over a drone. The object is not to become a great singer, or a performer of any kind, necessarily. The object is to begin at the source, and then to carry the source resonances with you as you go along.

## What Is Theory For?

A good thing to remember about music theory is that it typically springs up decades, often centuries, after the birth of the music it describes. A book like this one could simply not have been written during the time its primary subject matter (twelve-tone equal-tempered tonal harmony) was being discovered and developed. The rules of sixteenth-century counterpoint were not definitively codified pedagogically until the eighteenth century (by J. J. Fux, still studied today). The behavior of just intonation itself has been most confusingly and inefficiently articulated by theorists for almost three millennia, right up to the present. And only in the present generation is the code of tonal harmony being cracked, well over a century after its art came into full bloom. Theory is the scat of music, what it leaves behind. Luckily for us, we don't make music by following rules. We don't *make* music at all, so much as find our way in it. Only after the way has been found can the maps be drawn.

But the maps exist, right alongside the music. And good maps can save you centuries, soldiers, ships, fortunes. The danger: sitting at home hunched over your map table with a fixed grin thinking you've been places you haven't. The balanced way is to study these maps while you cover the territory. By the time you know your way around the territory, the maps will have become torn and faded, and you won't have to look at them anymore because the territory is teaching you more than the maps ever could.

## Who Is Theory For?

The question cannot help but arise, "Don't some people get music naturally, without all of the discipline and commitment and analysis?" The answer is yes, some people do and so do you. We all do to some degree. Every action is partly intuitive and partly rational; the proportions change from action to action and from individual to individual. No one is entirely analytical in the process of learning music, and no one is entirely intuitive (although I've seen some serious contenders at both extremes). There is even a part of the psyche that actively seeks to *not* know. It wants sensual saturation and intuitive wholeness, the pure being of childhood, the animal self.

You have to work out your own recipe for learning, which includes your interaction with this book and the procedures outlined in it. A good guideline to remember is this: the rules of music—including the rules of counterpoint and harmony—were not formed in our brains but in the resonance chambers of our bodies. What feels right and good is what survives. The "rules," codified over many generations by musicians serving as teachers, arise to protect and disseminate the good vibrations. But every rule and formulation ever made burns away at the moment of music making. Ultimately everyone makes music intuitively; individual circumstances determine the point at which the music rises above the mind and the intuition takes over.

There is a population of musicians who are both intellectually aware and musically whole; at the same time there are millions among us who achieve a high level of musical creativity in a state of musical innocence: The lyrical jazz trumpet player Chet Baker comes to mind. The musically innocent know where they are in the music without possessing a naming language; they have an internal musical map with no proper place-names on it.

So if half the folks are striving to rise above names and the other half never learned any to begin with, why go about naming everything?

People name things because transcending knowledge is different from not having any. Intellectual transcendence is not the same as intellectual innocence. A woman who has transcended her intellect and is whole in the moment of music making is a different whole woman than she was when she was musically innocent. The issue is not who has the secret, the intellectually transcendent or the intellectually innocent. The issue is how intellectual or innocent you need to be to find your own musical completion.

The Sufi mystics say, "The mind is the willing slave of the heart." The key word is *willing*. The intellect that wills to be in the service of the intuition is powerful and mature—the kind of mind a musician needs in order not to be paralyzed by knowledge. The great fear, especially among singers but among many instrumentalists as well, is that analytical knowledge disables us at our core in the very act of making music. Yet that need not be true. Ideally, an intellectually awake musician is not analyzing while she is performing. She is complete in the moment of pure sound; no thinking is needed. However, she *has* thought, she *has* analyzed. The homework has been done, the dues paid, the mental discipline gained. The musical spirit is flying free, but it has been shaped by the work of the mind.

Music theory is not for everyone. I think each person's mind has a certain capacity for willingly serving his or her heart. Theory should be studied to the limit of that capacity but no more. When you stuff the mind with facts and rules beyond its power to yield, the mental slave rebels and fills the house with mental music, and your heart pines away.

Yet what if your heart is singing fortissimo and your mind is bored to tears?

Then you realize that your mind needs to sing too.

I think you find the balance between heart and mind by asking your heart what it really needs to become musically complete. If the question is clear, your answer will be clear too. Then your mind is finally free to offer service.

## For Whom This Book Is Written

These pages are looking for musicians within a very wide range of training, including near-beginners who really want to know how harmony works, as well as advanced composers and performers who feel the pinch of traditional concepts and need to redefine music in a whole-making way. Since most people are somewhere in between, let me say that the perfect reader is simply one who wants to know music intimately from the inside out. New paradigms of integrative experience operate at all levels of development: a new way of perceiving old ways can be useful at every stage of learning.

To benefit most fully from this work, however, you must bring to it certain skills. You need to be able to read music. For the last three parts you need to be able to play a keyboard instrument well enough to navigate at least most of the musical examples. It helps to have previously investigated the overtone series, or be ready to (the text helps you). Also, the more you are in the habit of listening to the music of the world's various cultures, the more insight you will bring to this study.

# How to Use This Book

I have tried to avoid the typical textbook tone and rhythm. I want to be in the same room with you, talking and showing you what I know so you can hear it for yourself. Then, since you have to *do* it for yourself, I say, "Now, sing (or play, or write) one of these on your own." "One of these" will not be a numbered exercise, and there will be no test on Wednesday. But if you take the suggestions for playing and writing as you go along, a new area of harmonic experience will become yours. If you defer too much for too long, your understanding will become increasingly mental and removed—which may be OK for a while. But how long is a while?

A question that always comes up is, "How much time should I spend on this before going on?" A book about harmony needs to be conceived in a more-or-less straight line, with a sensible organization and a cogent train of procedures. But you can't learn music linearly. Rather, you learn it all at once, a little at a time. You learn it like a ground-glass range finder focuses a distant image: at first everything is a blur, then you barely recognize the scene, then the detail clarifies, and finally everything comes into sharp focus, right down to the leaves. How do you read a book front to back while reading it all at once? You skim, then you read selectively, then you skim some more, settling down like a hawk on different branches of different trees, then up circling again. I suggest that you skim the book first, then peruse passages that seem most interesting, which might mean reading back to front (I, for one, cannot resist reading the end of a book first). Eventually choose a certain part to work your way through experientially, page by page. Sooner or later you will feel the through-line of the book. But—since you could spend your whole life on one page—always keep circling and skimming. Hawks need altitude.

How many passes can you expect to make over one exercise or paragraph? Perhaps one; perhaps thousands, since the work—especially the work of singing in tune—is never done. Certain singing practices become lifelong companions. When tones are in tune they are not merely vibrant; they seem as if they are separate, individual lives inside your own life, awake and singing inside your mouth. Over the span of years they become like friends whose faces you recognize in the dark.

Another tenacious question is, "How long is this going to take?" The subtext is fear: "I'll die before I get it," and images of your brief, unfulfilled career flicker across the screen. There are strategies for dealing with this. One of them is to recognize that you cannot learn faster than you can learn, and to accept that. Another is to realize that each person has his or her own special mixture of advantages and disadvantages. Everyone is an idiot savant in this work, half fast and half slow. Some jazz singers, indelibly in tune, cannot read music or spell chords. I'm a harmony nut who can scarcely waltz. You might give an arm for something of mine that I take for granted, and I might give my teeth for something of yours that you take for granted. My advice is to keep yourself intact and work with what you have.

Thankfully, one eventually learns how not to get bored with the routines of practice.

The first evening Adam resides in Eden, let's say, God makes a gourmet banquet for him, which Adam eats with pleasure.

"Did you like it?" asks God.

"Loved it," says Adam.

The next night Adam comes to supper, looks down at the feast God has prepared, then looks up at God:

"What? *Food* again?"

The secret lies in always going deeper into the simplest gestures, appreciating them as gifts instead of burdens.

A related strategy is to let go of any idea you have of yourself as an accomplished master and simply do the work. Whatever is yours to realize will come out of your work, not from a picture you put on your wall. The light around good work is itself achievement and contentment; the rewards of mastery come of their own when the work is true. This advice is easier to give than to follow, but maybe it can help transfer your work energy away from the future and into the present, in the sounding moment where it belongs.

## Tools

I have written two books that you may find useful as preparation or companions for this book: *The Listening Book* and *The Musical Life* (refer to the Sources section). The first one discusses listening in general, with emphasis on singing in unison with a single tone. The second contains a detailed, practical section devoted to the production and appreciation of the overtone series (pp. 139–210). In addition, the present book contains a glossary that may be especially useful during the early going, as well as a bibliography for further reading.

You will also need a tunable instrument capable of producing a sustained drone. Best among these is the tamboura, an instrument made in India, but unless you live near a large coastal city or have contact with musicians from India (or their students), these are difficult to obtain. Drones from reeds are also a good possibility. An accordion, which is beautiful but unwieldy, or a concertina, could work. Indian musicians often use a *sruti box*, which consists of a few drone reeds activated by a bellows and is much more portable and less expensive than a tamboura. An electronic instrument especially made for producing drones, or an electronic keyboard with a program for just intonation would be OK with the right choice of sound: no vibrato, clean, kind to the ear.

It is also convenient to have a "drone tape." Such a recording, which provides a continuous hour or so of uninterrupted tonic-and-dominant drone, usually in C, are often distributed privately by teachers of North Indian music. An especially sonorous one played on two huge, gorgeous tambouras is available for twelve dollars (plus appropriate postage) from Kirana-Kahn Music, 304 Devon Drive, San Rafael, California, 94903. Using the piano for a drone is OK but not as satisfactory as any of the above.

Probably the most versatile and available drone instrument is the guitar. Its dronal function is less satisfactory than that of an instrument made especially for the purpose, like a tamboura. But it has the advantage of offering four bass strings that can easily be tuned for a variety of dronal purposes. Many of the practices in part 1 depend on the availability of at least two tunable bass tones, and a guitar is often the most convenient solution. An inexpensive one will work fine; perhaps there is a neglected one near you with your name on it. A harp could also serve well. Instruments from the violin family work less well except in the case of trained musicians who can bow them expertly and effortlessly; their plucked sounds decay too rapidly.

For the last three parts of the book you will need a decent-sounding piano or electronic keyboard well tuned in conventional equal temperament.

Although you can make do nicely with less, the very best solution is to have three instruments: the most pleasing drone instrument you can find (for singing practice), a guitar (for versatility in tuning while learning theory), and a piano (for keyboard harmony).

## The Teacher Question

Is a living, personal teacher necessary in order to learn harmony? In the largest sense, sound itself is the teacher of sound. A living teacher is always preferable in any transmission, however, and music, which is a human use of sound, is ultimately passed from person to person, from heart to heart. Nonetheless, I want this book to be as far as possible a living paper teacher, a reliable guide through both subject and psyche, so that with its counsel, a few tunable strings, a voice, and a keyboard, you can go as far as you wish on your own.

# PART ONE

# HARMONIC PURITY: FEELING THE NUMBERS

# 1

# SEEING AIR AND TOUCHING SOUND

## Seeing

Harmony is about the agreement of things with one another. Among musicians, the term *harmony* usually refers to the way tones relate vertically—stacked up and sounding simultaneously as chords. But a broader musical definition involves the way the ear relates pitches to one another in every dimension, including the agreeableness of an entire piece of music.

When the sound waves that reach our ears are evenly spaced—periodic—we perceive the sound as musical: It is a "tone." If the waves produced by a harp string (for instance) were visible, your eyes would feast on global mandala patterns undulating outward in every direction. But when you crumple a piece of paper, the sound waves that are produced are aperiodic; we call them "noisy." If you could see those sound waves you would find no pattern in them; they would seem as random as windblown leaves.

What if the air were not only visible but also in slow motion? Imagine you are the size of a pollen grain; imagine as well that time moves at one-thousandth of the speed of human time (it takes the equivalent of ten minutes to nod "yes") and that the visible waves of air are glowing. The sound of crumpling paper is a moonscape, peaks and canyons scattered every which way. But when the harp string sounds you are inside a theater of dancing lace. Along every line of sight, geometric tessellations are sequencing gracefully through time. *Two* harp strings sounding together all but overwhelm the senses in a hall of shimmering mirrors. Now call yourself back to human dimensions. A harp string sounds; you say, "Harp." Two strings together: "Nice." The amazing thing is that the human ear does experience these almost unbearably beautiful displays simply as tone and the harmony between tones.

To get a fix on the nature of these patterns, let's consider some simple kinds of periodic motion. Motion moves through time, and we love our time periodic: We respond to the seasons, to the intrinsic polarity of summer and winter. Breath comes in and goes out, waves move up and down and back and forth in peaks and troughs; we walk left and right; we drum *boom* and *chick* in the everlasting holy backbeat. Of course we love other kinds of time too: the randomness of rain has its place. But to the human body, chaotic motion can all too easily become spastic motion; we prefer the periodicities of the dance.

The conscious appreciation of simple periodic motion in everyday life is a kind of musical practice, the care and feeding of a primary musical sensibility. To the ear, simple periodicity is the littlest brick needed to build a music mansion. By sensitizing ourselves to it we become like a builder who, by experiencing the essence of a brick, can envision a building.

## Touching

It would be fascinating to examine our responses to simple sound waves, but we cannot hear them in pure form. Although we can scrutinize the behavior of periodic waves, called sine waves, in the macroworld of jump ropes and pendulums, in the world of audible sound the naked sine wave is denied us. Why? Because waves make waves. A pebble dropped in a puddle makes ever smaller, ever finer waves. The same is true within the chambers and fluids of the ear. The very act of hearing even a simple thing involves complex waves-within-waves. Furthermore, vibrating bodies themselves do not vibrate as a single entity only; they split themselves up into many parts, each of which produces its own characteristic sine wave; in musical tone these are called overtones. If a sounding body has a sufficiently simple shape (a long string with a constant diameter, for instance) the many resulting overtones are related to one another in simple ways that we call harmonic and recognize as harmonious.

Overtones relate to the tone that generates them, and to each other, with various degrees of complexity. Generally speaking, the simpler the vibrational pattern the more we tend to term it "consonant"; the more complex the pattern, the more we use the term "dissonant." In the everyday world we can distinguish between a marching band, a riotous mob, and the many stages in between. But in the microworld of the ear and brain, the discriminations of musical harmony are effected in a realm almost too small and too fast to conceptualize. Almost, but not quite.

In describing the qualities of consonance and dissonance we usually use the sense of touch as an analogy: Certain harmonic combinations are smooth, others are rough. But I think the sense of touch is more than an analogy. Quite literally, music touches us.

A plucked harp string vibrates the air; the air vibrates the eardrum, which vibrates the tiny bones attached to it; these vibrate the fluid in the snail-wound cochlea of the inner ear. If the cochlea were stretched out straight, the basilar membrane, a kind of inner skin, would be seen to run the length of it. Up through this skin sprout thousands of the finest hairs. The vibrating fluid in the cochlea vibrates the basilar membrane, which vibrates its hairs, sending electrical pulses to the brain, where, by the greatest miracle of all, the pulses become our consciousness of a harp string. To experience sound with the same sensibility that your fingers experience the smooth and rough surfaces of the touchable world, try to feel the surface of your basilar membrane being excited as you listen to an ear-catching sound: a harp string, for instance, or a more everyday sound like birdsong or a whistling tea kettle.

Seem impossible? Maybe, maybe not. Perhaps we cannot reach that far inside. But a clear picture of the chain of energy transformations connecting a sound source in the outer world to a receiving station in the brain may help in imagining how sound touches our innermost skin.

## Numbering

All this talk of seeing air and touching sound is meant, of course, to increase your range of perception; the simplest facts of musical life can never be too vividly envisioned or deeply felt. But there is also another mode of perception: number.

When we study acoustics in books, the subject looks indeed like a swarm of numbers. Once we realize that the numbers stand for actual auditory experience, however, a new perception comes in: We are in awe of an ear that navigates by innate intelligence the unimaginably complex territory of periodic vibration. The numbers are there to help make the unimaginable imaginable. We can be just as stimulated by numbers as we are by images and sensations.

Because you can't put everything into one book, this book must assume that you have learned enough about the overtone series to recognize it. (If you haven't, try some of the sources listed in the back of the book.) But for reference, example 1.1 is a chart of the overtone series based on C. Reading from the bottom to the top, it includes:

- The letter names of the first five overtones of C
- The staff notation of the tones
- Their frequencies, assuming that C vibrates 128 cycles per second (the frequency of C is actually 126.2 at standard concert pitch)
- The frequency ratios of the overtones to the generating tone (C)
- Their frequency ratios if the generating tone is called *x*
- The scientific name (the generating tone is called the *first partial*)
- The names in common usage (*harmonics* or *overtones*)

Sooner than later you will need to be able to conceptualize the overtone series immediately from any pitch, so this is a good time to learn it as the keyboard chord shown in example 1.2.

| Common names: | Generating tone or fundamental | First overtone or first harmonic | Second overtone or second harmonic | Third overtone or third harmonic | Fourth overtone or fourth harmonic | Fifth overtone or fifth harmonic |
|---|---|---|---|---|---|---|
| Scientific name: | First partial | Second partial | Third partial | Fourth partial | Fifth partial | Sixth partial |
| If generating tone is $x$: | $1x$ | $2x$ | $3x$ | $4x$ | $5x$ | $6x$ |
| Ratio with C: | 1:1 | 2:1 | 3:1 | 4:1 | 5:1 | 6:1 |
| Cycles per second: | 128 | 256 | 384 | 512 | 640 | 768 |

Example 1.1.
The overtone series of C

| Letter names: | C | middle C | g | $c^1$ | $e^1$ | $g^1$ |

Even though the piano is not conventionally tuned precisely to the overtone series (as we will discuss in part 2), it is extremely valuable at this stage to learn to transpose this overtone chord at the keyboard chromatically. For the time being, think in terms of the spellings shown in example 1.3, which you should practice both ascending and descending.

Example 1.2

Example 1.3

As we shall see, it is not sufficient to know, for instance, that the fifth partial of A is C♯; you need also to be instantly clear that C♯ is the fifth partial of A. You need to know which overtone series a given pitch is part of. This will come more easily if you can put your hands on the overtone chords of each pitch.

Our work in part 1 of this book is to enter the heart of the harmony implicit in the overtone series, to pass conscious time there, and to grow gradually accustomed to the light it gives.

# 2

# SINGING UNISON WITH A DRONE

## Entrainment in Two Worlds

Grasp two wooden pencils, one in each hand, eraser ends away from you, as if they were drum mallets. Against the edge of a shelf or desk, strike the circular metal bands that hold the erasers so that each sound is crisp and clear. Now, striking both pencils simultaneously, try to synchronize your two hands so well that you hear only one sound. You will need lots of skill or luck to do so repeatedly. Typically there will be two sounds separated from one another by anywhere from $\frac{1}{10}$ to $\frac{1}{1,000}$ of a second, much like the click of a camera shutter. The word *click* itself might sharpen your ears: notice the doubleness of the initial hard *c* followed (after *li*) by the *ck*. A single sound would be closer to *kih*, or simply an aspirated *k* without the vowel. Try to make the two pencils go *k*, not *click*. Now do this in tempo, about one attempt per second. Strangely elusive, no?

Now for a more musical experiment. Set a metronome (an electronic one is preferable) at sixty beats per minute and try to synchronize the tapping of one pencil to it. Partly because of the clean sound of the metronome, the discrepancy between you and it will now be more clear. If you experiment at faster tempi you may notice that you can become entrained in a metric "groove" for a few beats; but soon you will stray to the early or the late side, then come to dead center again. This gradual, barely perceptible straying on either side of the tempo is often desirable in music, and good musicians can control it. In jazz it is a factor in groove aesthetics; in classical music it is one of the conditions of phrasing called *rubato*, which means "robbed"—in this context, continually robbing and paying back.

In the rapid-fire world of tone, where instead of a few strokes per second there are typically a few hundred cycles per second, the groove of entrainment produces the euphoric resonance of a true unison. Speeding and slowing (raising and lowering) of the true pitch a few times per second is called vibrato, and it is beautiful in the degree that it is intentional on the part of the musician, just as the speeding and slowing of the tempo of a piece is musical only to the degree that it is intentional.

The object of our pencil-and-metronome research is to examine more closely the experience of the groove of metric entrainment. It can be a frustrating experience, but it can also be compelling and uplifting. The word *yoga* is from Sanskrit; it means "to join," as a yoke joins and unifies the energies of two oxen. A little bit of metronome yoga is good for us; it allows us to experience in the measurable, countable realm of metric time what happens in the tonal world when we try to sing in unison with a string. A musical unison is nothing less than a metric groove, but faster—too fast to count, but not too fast for the ear to register as pitch. If our voices vibrate too slowly, our pitch is flat; too quickly, then we are sharp; just right, and we say, "Ah!"

What is this *ah*? What energies join in union? Maybe it is the will of the singer with the energy of matter. You *will* yourself in tune with the string. Your intention drives your voice, and as the union becomes real you say *ah*. When your unison with a string is true, you seem to merge into it, to disappear, and all your fantasies and financial statements disappear too, at least for a breath.

To learn how musical harmony behaves, it is crucial to clarify and retain this image of *one* vibration of a something per *one* vibration of something else, and to associate that image with your experience of singing the unison. The "one to one" of two things vibrating in unison is written 1:1. The difficulty at this point in the discussion is that the concept seems too simple. You nod and say, "Sure, of course." But the more complex ratios, like 3:2 and 16:9 (which will soon be introduced) all derive from the same basic process: *x* of these per *y* of those. So your internal picture of 1:1 can never be too vivid, nor your experience of it too deep.

## Singing *Sa*

Singing unison with a drone is such an intrinsic aspect of learning North Indian classical music—possibly the most pitch-sensitive music in the world—that serious students practice it with conscious devotion over many years. The first degree of a scale, which in European solfege is called *do*, in Sanskrit is called *sa*. I suggest using *sa* because it sings so well. The following description of singing in unison with a drone is adapted from *The Listening Book* (pp. 139–40).

Find a note you can sing comfortably, not too low. This generally falls around C, B, or A. Find a drone string (piano, guitar, harp, tamboura, etc.) or reed (organ, accordion, sruti box, etc.) that produces a full tone at your chosen pitch. You can sing sitting on a chair, or cross-legged on the floor, or standing, or in any comfortable position. Find your breath and even it out. Relax your jaw, stretch your spine a little. Get hollow. Sound the drone and listen for a full minute. Listening is the key. Let the expansiveness of the drone's sound, even if it is soft, fill you up. Take an ample breath and, using *sa* with the vowel wide open, sing the drone's pitch *within* the sound of the drone.

The idea is to sing and listen at the same time, with equal energy: receptively and expressively balanced. To perfect that balance, to own it and identify with it, is the essence of music practice. Each *sa* is a chance to go up on point and make a controlled turn. On each breath, inside meets outside; sea meets shore. Find the rhythm of your breath and repeat the pitch with increasing awareness.

Some practical hints:

> The less vibrato the better.
>
> The notes should be not too long, not too short.
>
> Let your breath determine the length of the notes, one breath per note.
>
> Let the back of your tongue fall into the back of the throat naturally.
>
> Try to begin each note at the *exact* pitch of the drone; don't slide up to pitch like a motor revving up.
>
> Give yourself a limit, and no further: Two minutes? Eleven breaths? Twenty-one breaths? Maybe three today.
>
> Keep track on your fingers, not in your mind.

## Simplicity

There is a relationship between mastery and simplicity. The greater the mastery one has in a subject, the more absorbed one can become in its most fundamental concepts and behaviors. Conversely, a beginner usually needs to skim the surface before being drawn in. A child is much more likely to be interested in learning "Greensleeves" or current pop music than she is in learning how to sing in unison with a string, or in recognizing the overtone series. It is natural to want to do something musical right away. But as you develop, you begin to hunger for what is beneath the surface, for the practices and concepts that deepen and widen your range of perception. Gradually, your capacity for elementary practice increases, and you find yourself moving slowly and listening deeply for the mere pleasure of it. Don't be too surprised or chagrined if at first you become easily bored singing unisons or doing the other practices in part 1 of this book. You need to practice only long enough to draw something from the moment. But keep coming back to the simple things. It may come to pass that what was once mildly interesting and marginally relevant has become a touchstone for your musical life.

# 3

# SINGING OCTAVES

## No Babies or Dogs

The next most complex integer after one is two. The ratio 1:1 is a unison. The ratio 2:1 is an octave. In the metric realm, 2:1 is two taps to one tap, or eighth notes to quarter notes, as shown in figure 3.1.

*Figure 3.1*

Exquisitely simple as 2:1 is, it is not a no-brainer; it requires discrimination. True, our bilateral form helps us along intuitively, not to mention the intrinsic duple nature of the up-and-down bounce of balls and the back-and-forth swing of pendulums. But it still takes a special state of consciousness to clap your hands twice as fast as you tap your foot. And even though the frequencies of a sung tone are too fast to count, we are able to sing octaves just as certainly as we are able to clap 2:1. This capability is peculiar to humans. You might get two dogs to sing at once, but not in octaves. Nor can infant humans discriminate octaves, though they learn to, often by age two and usually by age five. When grown men and women sing together they sing in octaves spontaneously. It is this special human capacity for learning that has enabled us to develop the labrynthine harmonic structures of our music.

To experience the nature of this specialness, try pretending that you are learning to clap 2:1 for the very first time in your life. How old do you think you might have been when you first clapped 2:1 with someone? How much more difficult is it, exactly, for a child to learn to clap 2:1 than to clap 1:1? How much more difficult is it to sing an octave than a unison? People who think they are tone deaf (no one is) find out that after they learn to sing unisons, octaves are the next hurdle to cross.

Try singing a perfect octave above your drone while grasping the quality of 2:1 consciousness in the mind of the ear.

# Nomenclature: Octave versus 2:1

The following paragraphs are adapted from *The Musical Life* (p. 164).

*Octave* means eight, as in *octopus*, *octagon*, and *October* (which was originally the eighth month). A musical scale can be seen as a ladder; in our culture there are seven distinct rungs in that ladder—seven scale tones—before the eighth tone of "starting over again" occurs. Culturally, Westerners prefer these seven-rung ladders. But other cultures prefer five rungs in their ladders, so in those cultures, the scale "starts over" on the sixth note; an "octave" would be the sixth note, and could be called a "sixth." Some twentieth-century music divides the musical ladder into twelve equally spaced rungs; in that twelve-tone system, the scale "starts over" on the thirteenth note; in this case an "octave" could justifiably be called a "thirteenth."

Regardless of how many rungs are on their musical ladders, all human ears recognize the doubled frequency as the place for starting over, but our word *octave* is culture-bound, appropriate to the music we Westerners are most familiar with. "Twice-as-fast" or "2:1" is the proportionate—or harmonic—name for the "starting over" effect, which is common to all people.

So is an octave a "two" or an "eight?" It is clear that the harmonic name, *2:1* (based on frequency ratio), and the interval name, *octave* (based on scale steps), refer to different aspects of the same thing. The distinction between the names does not seem terribly problematic in this simple case. But in more complex cases the competing nomenclatures create a murk so obfuscating that entire theory classes have been known to return home to mother. Again from *The Musical Life* (p. 190):

Even well-schooled musicians have rarely clarified this apparent contradiction for themselves. Distinctions between melody and harmony are typically ignored. So prevalent are the easier, melodic concepts of distance that the term *interval* has taken over musical thinking and practice, much to the detriment of both. Most people learn their way around the musical landscape by measuring the melodic distances only, by interval; and they think this describes what is going on. It is as if you asked someone, "How ya doin'?" and instead of hearing, "My girlfriend came back and I'm soaring," or "The rain is getting me down," you hear, "Seventeen feet from that rock over there, and six inches from your nose." Too bad, because clarity about the relationship between harmonic and melodic space is precisely what our music once had and has now lost.

Do your best to clarify the difference between the *ratio* of 2:1 and the *interval* of the perfect octave—between the harmonic name and the melodic name—now, while the going is still relatively easy.

# SINGING PERFECT FIFTHS

## Triple Nature

Triple time is as different from duple time as a triangle is different from a line. How do you experience the difference between the two kinds of rhythm in figure 4.1?

Threefold symmetry has always puzzled and absorbed the bicameral mind. I recall learning to waltz as a young child and having trouble toughing it out all the way to the third beat; even now I have difficulty detaching my body sufficiently from its bilateral symmetry to waltz without feeling one of the beats as extra. I remember the failures, so I don't take the apparent simplicity of a three-to-one for granted. The complexity that occurs immediately beyond duality is not obvious.

For the same reason that the second partial is called an octave, the third partial is called a twelfth (i.e., up the scale an octave, then four more notes). It can be closely approximated on the piano, as in example 4.1.

Although any in-tune piano will give some sense of the quality of the relationship of the fundamental to its tripling, it is much more purely produced as the third partial of a guitar string, as follows:*

*Figure 4.1*

**Example 4.1**

- To be consistent with the nomenclature of this book, tune the D string down a whole tone to C.
- Lay the guitar face up on the floor or on a table, keeping the fretboard on your left.
- Lightly place your left index finger exactly one-third of the way along the newly tuned string (over the seventh fret).

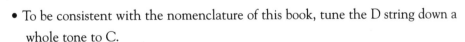

---

*Passages from *The Musical Life: What It Is and How to Live It* (W. A. Mathieu, © 1994) and *The Listening Book: Discovering Your Own Music* (W. A. Mathieu, © 1991) are reprinted by arrangement with Shambhala Publications, Inc., Boston.

- With a pick or your right index finger, pluck the string vigorously near the bridge of the guitar while leaving your left index finger in place.
- A half second after the pluck, take your left finger away. The third partial G will ring out.
- The longer you leave your left finger lightly in place, the more you will damp the generating tone, so with practice you can balance the loudness of the overtone G and the generating tone C as you please.

Unlike the fundamental and its doubling, the fundamental and its tripling sound essentially different from one another—at least more different than the same. There is an energy in their combination that is not in a unison or an octave, some new feeling imparted by this waltzing in the tone world. This perception is worldwide: Cultures that name scale tones assign identical or similar names to octaves (tenor C and alto C) but different names to twelfths (tenor C and alto G). The two tones C and G clearly belong together: They are placidly, eternally, and utterly consonant. But they are different specifically in that we do not perceive the musical scale as beginning again at the twelfth tone. We have gone past "starting over" into something new. As we shall see, this newness grows new newness, and gradually a musical structure of tones is built.

## Octave Reduction

In order to proceed we need to consider a few practical matters. First, two tones separated by more than an octave are often treated as if they were within the same octave. Hence a twelfth becomes a fifth (i.e., we throw out the bottom seven notes and start counting from what was the eighth, or octave). Two octaves and a third becomes, simply, a third. Getting rid of the unwanted octaves is called *octave reduction* and allows the relationships we are examining to be more easily sung. Although it might make a purist nervous, this process adroitly turns harmonic theory into melodic practice, because in actual music, melodies typically move by intervals smaller than an octave.

To experience the real difference between a twelfth and a fifth, consider for a moment the purist's view. The first three tones of the harmonic series are shown in example 4.2. First sing a twelfth, 3:1, above the drone. Then play the drone an octave higher and sing the same note, which now forms a fifth, 3:2, with the drone. (Do this at the piano if your usual drone instrument doesn't allow this octave switch easily.)

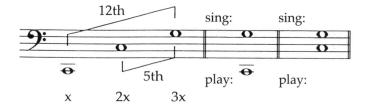

*Example 4.2*

In the macroworld, 3:1 (figure 4.2) is easily played. The more complex rhythm 3:2 (shown in figure 4.3) is also easily played if you know how, but you have to learn how. When you carefully balance the triple and duple elements, the result is neither a waltz nor a march, but a cross-rhythm, and it can be enormously beguiling. It seems to have some witchcraft in it, a kind of floating magic.

Figure 4.4 shows how to practice three against two.

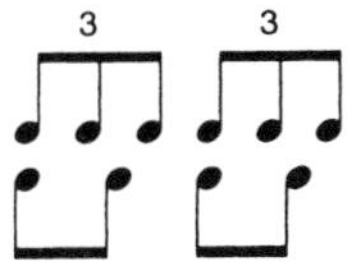

*Figure 4.2*

*Figure 4.3*

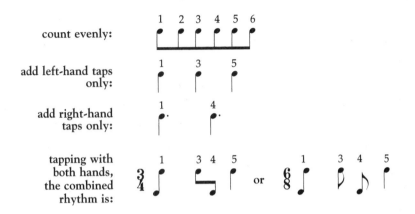

*Figure 4.4*

The meter of the combined rhythm varies, depending on your accent. If you accent the left hand, then the $\frac{3}{4}$ meter predominates; if you accent the right hand, $\frac{6}{8}$ predominates. Practice this until you can hear either meter at will and finally both equally. A new experience arises that is the result of both rhythmic feelings occurring simultaneously.

## The Rhythmic 3:2 versus the Harmonic 3:2

Imagine that you are, in addition to your normal-sized self, a very small person stationed at the surface of your own eardrum. As your large self is singing 3:2 with a drone, your small self is being choreographed by a cross-rhythm trampoline. What the ears of your large self hear is a familiar perfect fifth. "Oh, that," you say, while your small self is wildly dancing away. How to experientially connect the consonance of the perfect fifth with the physicality of the cross-rhythm?

Some composers have tried to make the connection by electronically doubling the speed of the cross-rhythm until it turns into audible pitches, and then precisely matching up the rhythm with the harmony it generated. But I suspect there is a perceptual canyon between rhythm and pitch we do not cross. The sense of pitch itself may be a breakdown in the ear's ability to process pulses as they become too rapid to perceive individually, much the same way that still images following one another more and more rapidly confound the eye and become, at a critical speed, a movie. "As above, so below" has its conditions: Certain dimensions are indeed similar between higher and lower orders; others change form. What we need to do now is plumb the numbers in our minds and wholly absorb the harmonies in our bodies and accept the mystery as nature presents it: When the numbers two and three get married, they produce harmonic and rhythmic offspring that, even if they don't look much like siblings, nevertheless do have the same parents.

We can now see just how much more complex 3:2 is than 3:1. In the process of octave reduction we accept the added richness of the complex version on the assumption that it does not alter the essential harmony of the simple version but merely presents it in a more usable from. Although in the practical world we accept the two versions as virtually equivalent, for the sake of a deeper understanding, be sure to appreciate the hierarchical difference between 3:1 and 3:2.

## Nomenclature: Reading versus Singing

One of the confusions of our musical nomenclature stems from the fact that we conventionally sing scales *up* and read text *down*. As children we learn our *do, re, mi* and count our scale degrees from the bottom up: A perfect fifth is the fifth scale degree up from the bottom. But we learn to read words from the top down:

E

A

T

Likewise, we read fractions from the top down: $\frac{3}{4}$ means "three over four" or "three quarters" or, in music, "three-quarter time," not "four under three," and so on. In terms of our present discussion, consequently, one says not only that the interval of five scale degrees from C up to G is a "perfect fifth" but also that the 3:2 ratio G makes with the C below it is a "three-to-two ratio." The full, maddening sentence is, "A perfect fifth is three to two," meaning that the interval of a fifth (counting up) stands as the proportion 3:2 (counting down).

Just as the distinction between the scalar name *octave* and the harmonic name *2:1* has been clarified in chapter 3, so also the various names for the third partial must now be reviewed and entirely understood.

The third partial is 3:1 harmonically, and it is also the twelfth scale degree above the fundamental. By octave reduction, 3:1 becomes 3:2, as in example 4.3.

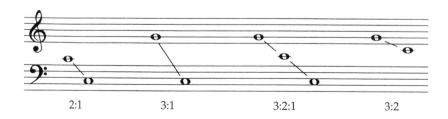

*Example 4.3*

2:1          3:1          3:2:1          3:2

Likewise, a scalar twelfth becomes a scalar fifth, as in example 4.4.

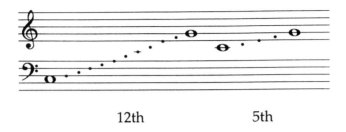

*Example 4.4*

12th                    5th

So by octave reduction, *a scalar fifth is harmonically 3:2.* Truly realize this, or the eyes are guaranteed soon to glaze. You must be satisfied in your mind that the numbers five and three are being used to measure different dimensions of the same thing. Which dimensions? The answer is "scalar distance and harmonic ratio." (This opens the larger question, "Why is scalar space additive and harmonic space multiplicative?" which is a question I cannot answer.)

## Naming Your Place: Solfege and *Sargam*

Another practical matter concerns naming pitches as you sing them.

*Solfege* (also called *solmization*) is the practice of applying syllables (rather than letters) to each of the seven degrees of the scale. *Do, re, mi, fa, sol, la,* and *ti* are the syllables most in use today. They date from medieval times and were derived from Latin to assist the memory and comprehension of the singer. Another system, called *sargam,* is derived from Sanskrit. It is used primarily in India not only to track and remember the vocal line but also to assist the singer in attaining optimal harmonic resonance. It is for singing as well as thinking. The vowels are more open and will guide you to the true qualities inherent in the music. The name *sargam,* incidentally, is a contraction of the first four syllables: *sa re ga ma.*

Table 4.1 lists the syllables of both solfege and *sargam.*

| TABLE 4.1 | | |
|---|---|---|
| SOLFEGE | SARGAM | DEGREE |
| do | sa | 8 |
| ti | ni | 7 |
| la | dha | 6 |
| sol | pa | 5 |
| fa | ma | 4 |
| mi | ga | 3 |
| re (ray) | re (ray) | 2 |
| do | sa | 1 |

The four degrees *re, ga, dha,* and *ni*—which correspond to the major second, the major third, the major sixth, and the major seventh—can be made minor by underlining them: <u>dha</u> for instance, is the minor sixth, called *komal dha.* (*Komal* means tender.) The fourth degree, *ma,* can be made augmented by adding a vertical stroke (ṁ) and is then called *tivra ma.* (*Tivra* means acute, or sharp.) When these names are used in singing practice, as they will be in the following chapters, the words *komal* and *tivra* are not articulated, so that, for instance, the syllable *ma* is used for both the perfect fourth and the augmented fourth.

I strongly suggest using *sargam* for the practices throughout this book. I know that means learning a new naming system while learning new concepts, perhaps not unlike taking a geophysics course in Turkish. But the rewards, in this case, are great.

## Singing *Pa*

sing:

play drone:

*Example 4.5*

When you hear a perfect fifth in tune, it is pleasing enough. But when you *sing* it in tune, it glows, and you glow along with it. Sing a perfect fifth over a drone as in example 4.5. Sing the syllable *pa,* with the vowel wide open, and with the steadiness of the sun at midday. Drop your jaw, relaxing its hinge muscles; relax the back of your tongue as well. (Might as well straighten your spine while you're at it.)

What is this shining in the tonal world? The exercise is to experience the harmonic feeling—howsoever it may be described or thought about—consciously, so that you not only have it but also know that you are having it. The singing part isn't so very difficult. Understanding the harmonic ratio 3:2 isn't so very difficult. The difficulty lies in putting both of these in the same breath, a sung breath of harmonic experience and understanding combined.

# SINGING
# MAJOR THIRDS

## Pentamerous Nature

Five is the next prime number after three. Just as three is an entire world more than two, five opens a new, "prime" realm of experience not definable by anything previous to it. Human thought is permeated with the five mystery. There are five elements—earth, air, fire, water, and the fifth, quintessence, the spirit of all the others. There are five directions—north, south, east, west, and center. A true five is a pentacle, a pentagon, a five-pointed star. Cut an apple or a quince through its equator and examine the fivefold symmetry of the seed cavity. Let your eye be drawn into a five-petaled wildflower. In pentamerous nature, the stability and purity of triple nature has been filled in by a fullness we can feel.

Johannes Kepler said that you can account for the nature of fruit blossoms not only by contemplation of their beauty but also by contemplation of the number five, which characterizes the soul of these plants. "The fruit from a pentamerous blossom becomes fleshy, as in apples and pears, or pulpy, as in roses and cucumbers, the seed concealed inside the flesh or pulp." He emphasizes the especially fecund quality of five by noting that from a hexamerous (six-sided) blossom "nothing is born except a seed in a dry cavity."*

One way of invoking pentangularity is to try to draw a pentagon with equal sides and angles, or trace one in the air. It is revealingly difficult. But to become truly grounded in pentamerous nature, we need to beat time. Most of what is *called* five in the metric world is not a true five, but an alternation between the lower primes, three and two. Fortunately, the perfect investigative tools are at our disposal: five-fingered hands. Try tapping on a tabletop, one finger after the other, calling your thumb one, and the succeeding fingers two, three, four, and five, counting smoothly and evenly and not pausing between five and the

*Kepler is cited in *Tone: A Study in Musical Acoustics* by Sigmund Levarie and Ernst Levy (Kent, OH: Kent State Univ. Press, 1968), who translated the passage from the German.

next one. Be sure not to emphasize the three (one-two-*three*-four-five) or the four (one-two-three-*four*-five). This is neither easy nor obvious, but if you stay with it you can feel your pentamerous self emerging.

More accessible and accurate, but slightly diluted, is the practice of walking while using your fingers to number your steps one through five. As you get into the feeling of your walk, five nature will take over. I say "slightly diluted" because this is really ten nature. Every other *one* will be on an alternate foot, and ten steps are needed for the five-times-two cycle to come around. All in all, though, this is the best way to feel convincingly pentamerous. A refinement: slightly flex each finger in turn as you step, without even thinking number names.

The ancient cross-rhythm between two (legs) and five (fingers), still common in India and the Middle East, is less obvious in cultures dependent on wheels (not legs) and calculators (not fingers). It is a lost world worth reviving because it is both elevating and reassuring. It keeps you spinning but grounds you before you spin away.

As for musical harmony, pentamerous nature generates in us deep and often elaborate responses. As usual, singing against a drone is the surest method for realizing this. If you can, find a trusted string that produces Great C, which is two octaves below middle C. The low string of a large tamboura is ideal if rare; a pedal harp Great C is also excellent. The lowest string of a guitar tuned down a third from E to C is OK, as is the Great C of an organ, electronic or otherwise. Beware the Great C of a piano—it is not so great for this purpose, unless you listen very selectively. The extreme tension under which piano strings are strung render their overtones progressively sharper as their partial numbers increase (this is called the *inharmonicity* of the string). So you can use the piano Great C only if you strike it very softly and trust your vocal intuition more than you trust the fifth partial sounding off the string, which will be mildly sharp.

If you are able to find the right Great C string, sound it, listen to it, and then sing its fifth partial (two octaves and a third higher), quietly mixing your note with the bass. Men can sing this note in falsetto if it is more comfortable. If you can, induce the fifth partial and let it guide your voice. (On the guitar, its appropriate node—for touching lightly as you pluck the string—is just shy of the fifth fret.)

If none of the above strategies seem to work, transpose the exercise in any way so that your voice comfortably rests two octaves and a major third above a supportive drone. Less good, but still useful, is to reduce by one octave so that you sing a major tenth above tenor C. Whatever your arrangement, keep in mind that it is ultimately a state of resonance—a kind of shelf of certainty—more than it is a sharpening or flattening of pitch that you will come to recognize as the experience of being "in tune." It is more a sympathy than a measurement of distance, a quality rather than a quantity. There is not enough paper in the universe to say this enough times.

Use the *sargam* syllable *ga*. Feel the current of your air column streaming against the back ridge of your soft palate. Sing softly, with no vibrato, until your voice seems to come out of the fundamental in the same effortless way the fifth partial does. Blend into the drone almost to the point of disappearing entirely, with no worries about coming back.

It may be that the sound of a pure third requires a subtle shift in your listening, and there may be a good reason. The kind of major third you are used to hearing from an equal tempered piano keyboard is about one-seventh of a semitone sharper than the fifth partial. That is quite an audible difference, and your piano ears may guide you into singing a bit sharp. Again, remember that it is primarily a resonance you are seeking rather than a pitch. Listen more to the drone than to your voice; the drone knows the answer and will tell you if you listen. After you practice this a few times you will hear and feel the rightness in it.

# The Concurrent Study of Just Intonation and Equal Temperament

The system of music based on the low prime-number resonances we have been studying is called *just intonation*. Some students are afraid that their growing sensitivity to just intonation will dampen their appreciation of equal-tempered music. Be assured, however, that no one ever really becomes too sensitive to what is naturally true; there is no reason not to learn pure harmony.  It is historically true that our culture has gradually—although conditionally—traded the beauty of just intonation  for another beauty, perhaps commensurate: the pleasure of modulation through many keys within a given piece.  In our modern tuning system, the deep, smooth pleasure of pentamerous harmony especially is sensibly compromised. The resultant sharpness of the major thirds is not enough to drive you crazy, but it is enough to make you restless, which is one of the reasons our music is restless. To compensate for this (and here is the "condition" of the trade mentioned above) when the harmony calms down and stays close to the tonic, sensitive singers and players of variable-pitch instruments adjust their pentamerous harmonies to agree with their innate pentamerous nature, and thus our ancient, patient ears are recompensed.

What actually happens to you when you experience the full beauty of just intonation—especially the richness of pure thirds—is that the exquisite finery of equal temperament becomes all the more mysterious and compelling. Ultimately, you come to understand precisely what equal temperament does that just intonation cannot do. Our aim is to heighten the appreciation of both tunings, and the real beginning is here in the task before us: living some long moments in the consonance of pentamerous harmony.

Whatever you do, don't try to get pentamerous religion by striking C and E together on the piano. Get it by letting the fifth partial guide your singing. As with duple and triple harmony, quintuple harmony is made real by understanding slow-motion experience (walking and beating rhythms), by internalizing the vibrational experience (listening and singing) and by the little darting leaps we make between these different ways of knowing.

# Octave Reduction of the Fifth Partial; Rhythmic 5:4 versus Harmonic 5:4

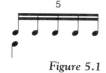

*Figure 5.1*

Once you have learned to use the fifth partial reliably as your guide to singing, it is time to examine the octave reduction that allows 5:1 to become 5:4, or in the rhythmic world, figure 5.1 to become figure 5.2.

In chapter 4 we saw how even though 3:2 is substantially more complex than 3:1 in the rhythmic world, the two ratios are nonetheless heard as having the same harmonic essence. We now will apply the same method to pentamerous harmony. For reference, example 5.1 shows again the overtone series.

*Figure 5.2*

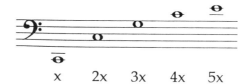

*Example 5.1*

Study the progressively more complex relationships shown in example 5.2.

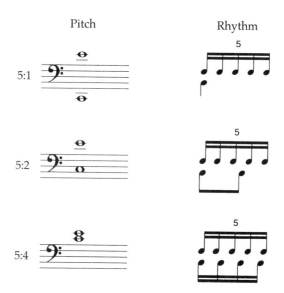

*Example 5.2*

If you thought 3:2 was a problematic cross-rhythm, 5:2 will be no easier. 5:4 is truly difficult, so much so, in fact, that one rarely hears it performed, apart from a few African drummers, fewer Indian tabla players, and specialists in twentieth-century concert music of the West. Contrast this with the fact that nearly everyone in every culture—most of the billions of us—has found 5:4 in the harmonic world to be a natural and intuitive musical given. 5:4 is an extremely rare rhythm yet an extremely common harmony. Our bilaterally symmetric, gravity-conditioned bodies do not easily cast off the duple dimension. For a dancer, 5:1 (five arm motions for one leg motion, for instance) is possible and perhaps beautiful, but 5:4 is extremely rare by virtue of its difficulty. Dancers simply don't *do* the rhythmic equivalent of octave reduction; that is, they don't transform 5:1 into 5:4. The aural brain, on the other hand, somehow minimizes, to a substantial degree, the effect of the duple dimension; in the harmonic world it reduces octaves effortlessly and with little change of meaning.

For those interested in learning the cross-rhythm 5:4 it is best to first practice, in one hand only, the straightforward rhythm in $\frac{5}{4}$ time shown in figure 5.3. Placing that rhythm in two hands as shown in figure 5.4 results in the right hand playing five beats while the left hand plays four.

*Figure 5.3*

Perhaps, for a student of harmony, it may be enough to appreciate that 5:4 feels relatively complex to us and leave it at that. After all, the harmonic ratios are certain to become even more

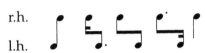

r.h.

l.h.

*Figure 5.4*

complex as we proceed, and we must be prepared to lose track of their rhythmic equivalents sooner or later. We surely will never make a viable cross-rhythm out of 16:15, which is a garden variety semitone in just intonation. Nevertheless, for the obsessive among us (count me in), 5:4 may not prove too difficult to learn after all, and might even prove musically useful. "Learning music is the art of turning the seemingly impossible into the familiar," said Easley Blackwood to me more than once.

If you can beat 5:4 fluently, do you have a better understanding of a pure third? A better *understanding,* yes. A deeper *experience*? You have to find that one out for yourself, gentle musician, and when you do, send me a postcard.

## The Three-and-Five Problem Summarized

To dispel some of the confusion in the nomenclature for harmonic and melodic space, especially in regard to the numbers three and five, table 5.1 is a comparative chart of terms used throughout this book.

| TABLE 5.1 | |
| --- | --- |
| HARMONIC SPACE | MELODIC SPACE |
| proportional | intervalic |
| multiplicative | additive |
| chordal | scalar |
| 1:1, unison, first partial, sa | unison |
| 2:1, duple nature, doubling, second partial | octave |

*(Table 5.1 continued on next page)*

| TABLE 5.1 (continued) | |
|---|---|
| HARMONIC SPACE | MELODIC SPACE |
| 3:1, triple nature, tripling, third partial, *pa*, Pythagorean (see chapter 6) | perfect twelfth, twelfth |
| 3:2 | pure fifth, just fifth; perfect fifth, fifth (these last two terms can also refer to their equal-tempered equivalent) |
| 5:1, pentamerous nature, quintupling, fifth partial, *ga* | two octaves plus a major third (major seventeenth) |
| 5:4 | pure third, just third; major third, third (these last two terms can also refer to their equal-tempered equivalent) |

**Note:** A system of tuning limited to triplings, quintuplings, and their octave reductions is called a five-limit system. Tones compounded from perfect fifths *and* major thirds (page 37) are called *ga*-blooded (introduced on page 70).

An empty shell for music is made by the doublings called octaves; within that shell, the interactions among the triplings (called perfect fifths) and the quintuplings (called major thirds) account for nearly all of the tonal music that exists. We have begun to experience the properties of these harmonic elements individually. Now let's find out how they combine to make music.

# A Map of Harmonic Relationships

HOW DO THE HARMONIC ELEMENTS—octaves, fifths, and thirds—combine to create music? How could such simple and common sounds generate a system of harmony so generous and elaborate?

## The Powers of Two as Sterile

Before going on, it would be good to clarify that the number two and its powers do not generate, by themselves, what we recognize as music. Example 6.1 shows Great C and its first five doublings.

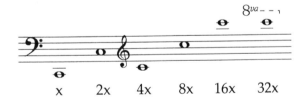

*Example 6.1*

The second partial (2:1) is an octave higher than the fundamental, the fourth partial (4:1) is two octaves higher, the eighth partial (8:1) is three octaves higher, the sixteenth partial (16:1) is four octaves higher, and the thirty-second partial (32:1) is five octaves higher. A piece of music starting on C and containing only doublings (or halvings) would have only C's in it. You can find every C on a piano and play octave music, like a kid who has just discovered that there are eight C's on a piano *and here they all are*. It's an eerie piece. The stack of octaves stands like the floors and ceilings of an empty building, an outline with nothing filled in. The duple world could be thought of as harmonically sterile in that it replicates itself only; it does not know how to make a new realm.

# The Powers of Three as Generative: Compounding

The powers of three are different; from them have come penetrating metaphors for our inner life of thought and spirit. Lao-tzu, around 600 B.C.E., wrote, "One has produced Two, Two has produced Three." A commentator explains, "These words mean that One has been divided into Yin, the female principle, and Yang, the male principle. These two have joined, and out of their junction has come a third, Harmony. The spirit of Harmony, as it condenses, produces all beings."*

In music we can observe how the third partial of C begets a new note, G (3:1). In turn, the third partial of G begets *another* new note, which is the tripling of the tripling: namely, D (9:1), as shown in example 6.2a.

With octave reduction, the perfect twelfths become perfect fifths, as seen in example 6.2b. (This harmonic generation is preserved in conventional classical nomenclature by the term "the dominant of the dominant," meaning the fifth scale degree above the fifth scale degree.)

If we leave out the middle term (the G) and further octave-reduce the C, the result is the whole tone shown in example 6.2c. Could this be what Lao-tzu's commentator meant when he refers to the "spirit of Harmony as it *condenses*"?

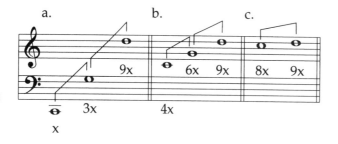

*Example 6.2*

The process of generating new, more complex tones (with high-number ratios) from simpler tones (with low-prime ratios) is called *stacking*, or *compounding*. The concept of compounding fifths is easy: They stack like Tinkertoys or Lego blocks; so do thirds, as we shall see, and fifths and thirds combine with themselves and each other, building out in any direction, as we shall also see. But the vibrational experience of singing compounded harmonies in tune is the crucial thing. Such experience is none other than the operative principle of tonal harmony, the very gift that allows us to make music. How the ear decodes and interprets complex harmonies compounded from simple ones is almost a complete mystery to us, although there has been some fascinating speculation (discussed in the afterword). My way of softening the mystery is to remind myself that the ear and sound are not unrelated things, in the same way that a glove and a hand are not unrelated. The ear was made to hear sound. That it responds to the elemental wave forms locked inside complex harmonies does not seem unnatural. Even though we can't describe it yet, we sense that the anatomy of hearing is similar to the anatomy of harmony. When you study one you study both. The study of music is the study of one's own ear. That's why it is not enough to simply listen to a harmony (such as a major

*Quoted in Levarie and Levy, *Tone: A Study in Musical Acoustics*.

second) and say, "I hear it." You have to go so deeply into your experience that you hear yourself hearing it.

Although we will not continue on with the tripling process at the moment, as many new notes as we can use are thus generated by the powers of three. Indeed, Pythagoras, who lived in Greece around the same time that Lao-Tzu lived in China, thought that tripling was the only acceptable harmonic principle; consequently, the harmonic system generated by compounding fifths and reducing octaves is called Pythagorean.

## Singing a Compound Tone: *Re*

You could use a piano to generate two fifths, because the piano's equal-tempered fifths are not too badly mistuned. But a more certain path is to tune two guitar strings as well as you can by ear, as shown in example 6.3a. To check your tuning, match the third partial of C (the appropriate node is over the seventh fret) with the second partial of G (the node is over the twelfth fret).

G string:

D string tuned
down a step:

*Example 6.3a*

When your tuning is pure, proceed by sounding the fourth partial of the C (the appropriate node is over the fifth fret) together with the third partial of G (seventh fret), as shown in example 6.3b. If you get the tuning right, with the overtones robust and well sustained, the hollow spaciousness of the "dissonance"—for such is how we conventionally term the "interval" of the major second—is illuminating.

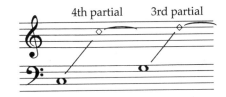

*Example 6.3b*

Now it is time to experience through singing exactly how simple sounds create complex sounds. Listen to the elements of the major second as demonstrated in example 6.4.

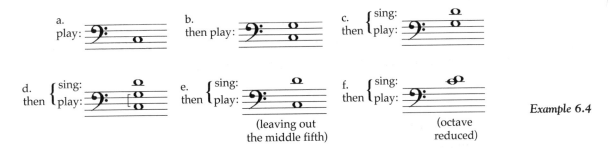

*Example 6.4*

Practice these steps in sequence until you can hear the fifth-y quality of the major second. Sing the syllable *re*, using the retroflexive *r*.*

*The retroflexive *r* can be approximated by pronouncing, in a British accent, "very, very rich" and noticing how the tongue curls up and backward slightly to expose the underside of the tip to the back of the front teeth. The retroflexive *r* is something like a softened *d*, and totally avoids the pursing of the lips, thereby leaving the vowel open from the onset of the tone.

Remember that listening to overtones and pure harmonies can serve as a guide only; let the proof of what you are seeking be in your singing. That proof is not here on the page. It is (bless the fact) in your own body.

While you are singing, remember to appreciate that, in harmonic terms, C and D are not neighbors but live two houses away. One might ask the riddle, "Harmonically speaking, what lies between C and D?" (If you say "C♯" or "D♭" the author will have to immolate himself immediately.) Awareness of the reality in which G lives between C and D—whether or not it is being heard as a note in the air—is the goal. It is a light that goes on inside.

With appropriate octave reduction, we now have an attractive four-tone scale, shown in example 6.5. Against a C and G drone, very slowly improvise melodies in this scale,

*Example 6.5*

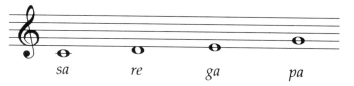

singing in tune, feeling the qualities, and knowing that you know the harmonic derivations as you go. The enormously subtle change of flavor between *re* and *ga* is especially recommended. A hungry musician type could spend very long moments savoring that one.

## A Map Emerges

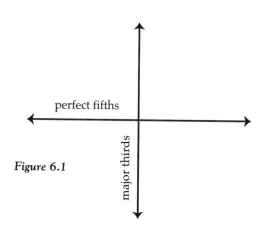

*Figure 6.1*

At this point, we could profit from a new notation. Since there are two harmonically functional elements (perfect fifths and major thirds) and two dimensions on a sheet of paper (horizontal and vertical), we can array the fifths along a horizontal axis and the thirds along a vertical axis. A picture of harmonic space will begin to emerge, as seen in figure 6.1.

The notion that perfect fifths can be drawn along a strictly horizontal east–west axis and major thirds along a strictly vertical north–south axis has been usefully employed in the study of acoustics since the late nineteenth century. We'll call such a depiction *compass orientation* and employ it frequently later on in the book.

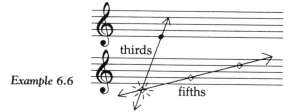

*Example 6.6*

Now, if the picture is combined with staff notation (this is the new part), we can read it in the same way we read music. To do this, we have to skew the axes somewhat, as shown in example 6.6. The generating tone (C) is indicated by small radiating lines.

Notice that the horizontal axis is tilted somewhat counterclockwise, now lying more in the southwest-to-northeast direction, while the vertical axis is tilted slightly clockwise, leaning to the northeast. Although our "directions" are now less easily named, there is a great advantage in using the musical staff as a reference. We'll call this kind of scheme *staff orientation* and use it exclusively throughout part 1.

Let's call the line of fifths a "spine." We'll continue to generate new notes by adding, one by one, major thirds above the spine of fifths.

## The Major Seventh

The next note to examine is the major seventh, B. Just as E is the third above C, B is the third above G. Example 6.7 shows the entire harmonic map so far. Notice that solid lines indicate the connection of the fifths to one another and the connection of the major thirds above each fifth.

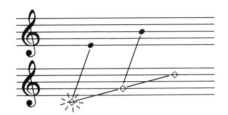

*Example 6.7*

To experience the major seventh in its harmonic fullness, follow the procedure shown in example 6.8.

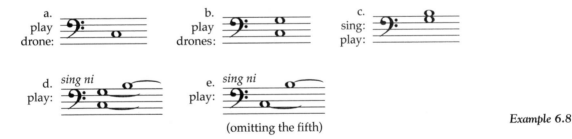

(omitting the fifth)

*Example 6.8*

It is amazing to realize how the major seventh has, hidden inside it, the consonances of both the major third and the perfect fifth. Discovering this is a little like looking through a microscope and finding the abundance of cells in one drop of blood difficult to believe even though you are seeing them with your own eyes. If you go over the procedure for playing and singing given above, however, the incredible seems at least more familiar and comfortable. Most of the music you have ever heard or will hear is essentially perfect fifths and major thirds, similarly compounded, and the wonder of that never goes away.

Since the major seventh is compounded from a fifth and a third, would it be reasonable to expect that its quality reflects, somehow, the sum of the qualities of its constituent elements? Maybe so, maybe not. Many have said much on this subject, but it is your work to realize your own sensibilities. You have to keep checking the B with the G and the G with the C and the B with the C and not giving up.

## The Harmonic Path

The specific steps in compounding a perfect fifth and a major third to produce a major seventh can be shown simply by drawing arrows indicating the procedure, as shown in example 6.9.

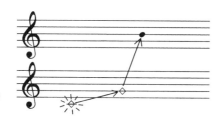

*Example 6.9*

Furthermore, we can say that the arrows show the *harmonic path* of the major seventh, and we can then extrapolate the harmonic path from the staff notation, to indicate that this type of major seventh is "a fifth up and a third up," as shown by figure 6.2. (The term *harmonic path* is more fully explained in chapter 10.)

*Figure 6.2*

Here's a general note about harmonic mapping: If you first build a major third up from C—to E—and then add the fifth, you will end up on the same pitch as if you had gone up a fifth and then a third. This is simply a result of the commutative law of multiplication, which says that $ab = ba$, or $\frac{3}{2} \times \frac{5}{4} = \frac{5}{4} \times \frac{3}{2}$ ( $= \frac{15}{8}$, that is, 15:8, the ratio of the major seventh). But I usually find it more useful, when building from the tonic, to take the fifths first, then add the thirds, although there will be exceptions to this later on.

## Scale Practice with Five Notes: The Flying Swan

We now have a gorgeous five-tone scale, up and down, as shown in example 6.10.

*Example 6.10*

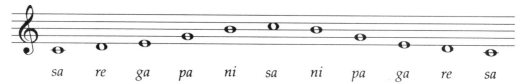

These five notes are the basis of a North Indian *raga* called *The Flying Swan*. The tones seem spontaneously to generate melodies on their own. Example 6.11 is an example of such a melody.

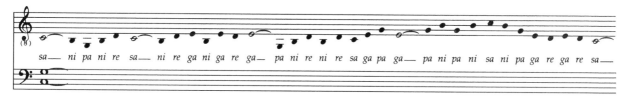

*Example 6.11*

Now make up one of your own. When you are improvising on this scale, be sure to keep the drone sounding in the air as well as in your ear. Try to appreciate your melody not so much as an up-and-down ride, or even as a series of intervals, but rather as a succession of related harmonic states, a succession of moods. The secret of melody is that it is a thread of feeling-states such as these.

You can spend a long time on these five notes, delving into the various relationships among the qualities, heightening the mood. Give them a chance to do their work on you—that is a musician's deepest work.

## The Augmented Fourth

The next note to examine is F♯, the augmented fourth. Before reading on, try to figure out for yourself how this tone would be derived from perfect fifths and major thirds.

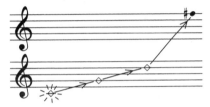

*Example 6.12*

The F♯ we are looking for is a major third above D; or, figuring from C: two fifths up, then a third up. Example 6.12 shows the harmonic map. Figure 6.3 shows the harmonic path.

To learn to sing it well, try tuning a third string, this one a fifth above G, and follow the steps shown in example 6.13. Sing the syllable *ma* open and relaxed. Keep checking the F♯ with the D, the D with the G, and the G with the C, until you are absolutely certain of the chain of consonances. When sung in tune, the augmented fourth, F♯, will take on an extraordinary luster. To leaven its complexity, alternate it with the G a semitone higher. Keep checking with the D a third lower.

*Figure 6.3*

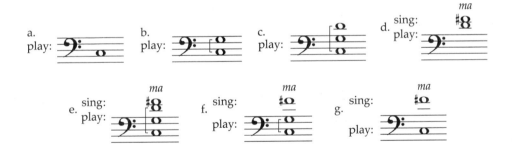

*Example 6.13*

## Scale Practice with Six Notes

As the harmonies we study become more complex, our responses seem comparably richer. Whatever quality is in a major seventh, that quality seems heightened in the augmented fourth. People refer to a longing quality, the force of being pulled from a great distance. Notice that both the major seventh and the augmented fourth can move upward by a semitone to a note of relative simplicity, giving a feeling of great harmonic release as a result of a small melodic step. Taken all together, our collection of harmonies can make a rich and buoyant scale, up and down, as seen in example 6.14. (Remember that the indications for sharp (*tivra*) and flat (*komal*) are not intoned while using the sargam syllables for singing.)

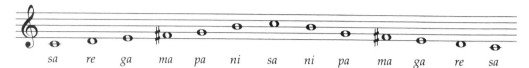

*Example 6.14*

sa   re   ga   ma   pa   ni   sa   ni   pa   ma   ga   re   sa

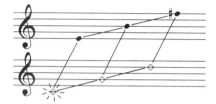

*Example 6.15*

The full harmonic map so far is shown in example 6.15. Notice how the added thirds now form their own spine of fifths, E–B–F♯, located precisely a major third above the original spine, and shown with its appropriate connecting lines. This begins to show the organizing principle of a tone lattice: spines of fifths stacked a third apart.

It is a useful and challenging practice, at least at this point, to try to keep in mind the harmonic derivation of the tones, even while you are singing. I like to use *pa* and *ga* as generic mental abbreviations for "perfect fifths (3:2)" and "major thirds (5:4)." The harmonic derivation of D, then, is "the *pa* of *pa*" (or grand-*pa*: ha ha). The major seventh then becomes "the *ga* above *pa*," and the augmented fourth becomes "the *ga* above the *pa* of *pa*"

(the third above the fifth above the fifth). The harmonic map is thus labeled in example 6.16.

Practice improvising melodies in our new six-tone mode. There are some especially beautiful combinations. Example 6.17 shows some of the possibilities. Go slow. It takes a lifetime to hear everything.

*Example 6.16*

ga        ga of pa        ga of pa of pa

sa        pa        pa of pa

ni   ma   ga____   ni   ma   pa____   ni   re   ga   ma   ni   pa____   ni   sa   ni   ma   ga____   re   ma   re   ga   ni   re   sa____

*Example 6.17*

# Where Does This Stuff Come From?

Here is a remarkable truth that is emerging from the work we are doing: We know that the overtones of a single fundamental are not entirely obvious to the ear, and that the overtones of the overtones are less obvious still. They are soft at best and disappear rapidly into inaudibility. So when we sing tones compounded from the first five partials, we are making audible and sensible a real but inaudible world locked inside the fundamental tone. For instance, you will not encounter the overtone corresponding to the F♯ we have just been singing until you climb to the *forty-fifth* partial (its ratio is 45:32), and that is an overtone entirely inaudible from any string. But you can learn the resonance of that F♯ with such certainty that you can put it in your pocket. We don't hear harmony simply by matching overtones—it happens another way, a more ecological way. The overtones and our voices are relating not so much to each other as to a higher principle. Something prior organizes both. The overtones are our siblings, not our parents. The forces that govern the production of overtones govern our ears also, and our ears' responses, and our hunger for musical harmony, and our pleasure in it. It is true that we can represent these parental forces as a schema of low prime numbers, but the forces themselves confound our minds. That is why we so love to experience them as music: It is a way of honoring our minds' source. The hidden universe inside a string we thus make explicit and resounding by our singing. And what are we singing? We are singing what is already there. Our tones render the subliminal sensible. They represent a once angelic, refined world now made coarse, a heaven brought down to earth—spirit incarnate, *condensed*.

## What Are We Doing?

We are mapping harmonic territory in the form of a two-dimensional lattice structure, pure fifths in one dimension, pure thirds in the other. The map extends infinitely outward from every point, but we are going to make our first objective a lattice of twelve tones with C in the center. We have discovered so far exactly half of this central area of twelve notes (the upper half). It would be wise to tarry here before going on to the other half. Be patient and practice your singing against the drone. Let your melodies be driven and drawn by harmonic states. Gain enough certainty in this overtonal world to claim familiarity with the neighborhood. Gain the trust of the notes, and their friendship. Give them something. These are the kinds of friends that can save lives.

# THE PERFECT FIFTH BELOW: HELLO, MOTHER

OUR OPERATIONAL PREMISE IS THIS: Harmony consists of perfect fifths, major thirds, their compounds, *and their reciprocals*. That is different from saying that all the notes in music are overtones—such a claim could not be made. The truth is that the overtone series *encodes* the secret of all tonal harmony. By examining directly the first few overtones and their compounds we have done the easier part. The deep part is next.

## Reciprocal Tones

Let me begin with a statement that may seem odd: The note we recognize as the fourth degree of a major scale does not appear in the overtone series. If the generating tone is C, then the F above it, the "perfect fourth," never appears, not even if you ascend to the millionth overtone. It's not there. Yet that note has been discovered in virtually every culture; all human ears want it and find it. Humans who sing, sing it. It sounds and feels close to home, safe, and totally right. So if it isn't an overtone, what is it?

To answer this question, let's pose another, not-so-innocent question: What exactly is the overtone series of this famous F we've been talking about? When you see it and hear it, the answer to the riddle of the perfect fourth is not far off. Look for a moment at example 7.1.

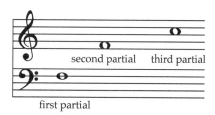

*Example 7.1*

The third partial of F is that very tone—C—which in its role as the fundamental, or generating tone, has given meaning to all the other tones we have studied so far.

To bring this more into your own experience, play C in a higher octave and sing F in low range (for women) and midrange (for men) as in example 7.2. The exercise is to tune the F in your voice until it sounds as if C is your third partial, or perfect twelfth.

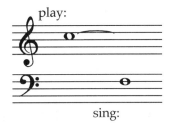

*Example 7.2*

This may be musically obvious or it may not be. In any case, let's adopt a rigorously patient attitude here. Of all the mysterious events in music, we have come to perhaps the most mysterious of all—mysterious because of how the tables have turned: Instead of resonating with a note that has already been placed into the musical space by a generating tone, we have invented—*created*—a note that contains the generating tone in its harmony. It is one thing to produce a vibration that is already given, that is "already there." It is quite another to become that vibration which produces, as one of its children, the very tone you started with.

Within the boundaries of music, the generating tone does behave somewhat like a creation principle. It is the god of its tonal world. C is the god of the realm of all C modes, of all the music "in C." But when you sing F you *create* C. How can you create the creative principle? How does one go about giving birth to a musical god? That is the work of the Musical Mother. Hello, Mother. You who dare to sing F in the C world become the embodiment of the creative and the sacred.

This is only a way of talking, of course, but it is an old and useful way. The nonverbal truth dawns at the very moment you position yourself to become the generator of the generating tone, when you set about to tune the sung F. Practicing this is a kind of uncovering. During the most intense moment of listening to the C, that split second between inhaling and actually singing the F, ask yourself what is happening in the muscles of your throat, in your inner hearing, in the seeking part of your nature, in your feeling. Scrutinize the entire range of feeling at the moment of first vibration, as an exercise in the fleeting present. Whatever that feeling is, it is a crucial kernel of musicality. When you can catch a glimpse of it, the meaning of the term *reciprocal* clarifies.*

## Dominant and Subdominant Compared

Now is the time to compare the forming of the fifth above the tonic with the forming of the fifth below. With this practice, the full breadth and beauty of the harmonic landscape begins to come into view, and we can begin to imagine the other side of the world.

When a string sounds C and you sing a G above, you the singer are inside the string: You are climbing or leaping up inside it, magnifying it and using it. It is like riding a horse: The horse and the saddle are there—you just jump up and take a ride. You are an overtone cowboy.

---

*Reciprocal tones have been termed by some theorists "undertonal" or, by Harry Partch, "U-tonal." It seems to me, however, that "under" is a less complete idea than reciprocal, and also slightly misleading, since the tones are not actually produced audibly below the generating tone in the same way that overtones are produced above it. A more likely choice is *inversional*, which I used for a while, but it is a term too easily confused with the inversions of chords. *Reciprocal* wins.

When a string sounds C and you sing an F below, you become the generating tone of the C. The string now resides inside the singer. *It is in you.* You become its creator, the mother of it, the overtone mother. Sing some more G's and some more F's. To distinguish between their affects, use the new information about harmonic reciprocity, but don't forget the microscope of intuition.

The nature of the reciprocity between these two tones is found not only in their feelings and in their sounds; it is also reflected in their numbers and names. In the European nomenclature, the fifth above the tonic is called the dominant; the fifth below is called the subdominant. The name "subdominant" has been persistently misunderstood by generations of theory students: Most musicians, even well educated ones, think that the subdominant is so named because it is the fourth degree of its scale, just one degree below the dominant, which is the fifth degree. It is true (alas) that the supertonic—the second degree of the scale—is so named because it is one degree above the tonic. It is also true that the subtonic—the seventh degree—is one degree below the tonic. But the nomenclature is, as usual, inconsistent.

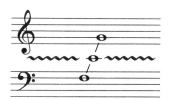

*Example 7.3*

The "sub" of subdominant actually refers not to its scalar position but to its harmonic reciprocity. (Later in this book, we sometimes refer to the note a fifth below a given note as the "*pa* below" that note, indicating a sort of "reciprocal dominant" relationship.) In example 7.3, imagine the G is a tree on the shore of a pond, the C is the water line, and the tree's reflection in the pond is the F.

Example 7.4 shows how this image is preserved on the harmonic map. Notice the strategically placed bass clef. Example 7.5 shows how the entire harmonic map looks so far. Over history and around the globe, the fifth above has been recognized as having yang properties. It is the honcho among the overtone cowboys, which are, generically, expressive, radiant like the sun, and of course, masculine.

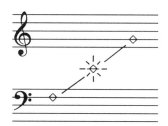

*Example 7.4*

The fifth below is usually recognized as having yin properties. It is the Superior among overtone mothers, which are responsive, receptive and luminous like the moon, and of course, feminine.

One might also note that in Indian *sargam*, the fourth degree of the scale is called *ma*, thus rendering the name of the female principle *ma* and the male principle *pa*. Very funny.

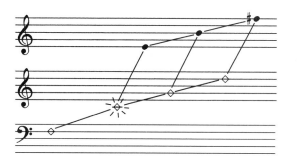

*Example 7.5*

It might be timely to point out that in our culture's music, the chordal progressions based on the triads of the dominant and the tonic—called "authentic cadences" or "perfect cadences"—are forthright, final, and defining. Progressions based on the triads of the subdominant—called "plagal cadences" (derived from a Greek word for "oblique")—are the substance of blues and gospel music as well as the European "Amen"; they seem to lead upward and out into the open. The dance between these upward-leading and downward-tending energies is the basic two-step of our musical heritage. Much more will be said about this subject later, beginning in chapter 20.

## Singing Practice with Ma

All these names are concepts our minds have invented to describe unnameable musical qualities. It is important to remember that the qualities are not mutually exclusive but are constantly exchanging and overlapping aspects of themselves, tumbling and mating in uncountable dimensions. What is needed is not a precise description but the experience of your own voice, singing fifths above and fifths below, so that whatever these qualities are, they become conscious in you.

What is truly tantalizing is what happens in the psyche when the F is lifted from below, where it functions most clearly harmonically, up through the octaves until it sounds a fourth above the tonic, where it lives in the major scale. It still sounds hollow and sonorous, similar in that regard to the sound of a perfect fifth; the perfectness of a "perfect fourth" is easy to hear. But in some sense it is upside down, since it lies above its own overtone. It feels unstable and is considerably more difficult to find and hold—to tune—than a perfect fifth. Is it like a triangle balanced on a point instead of resting on a base? In the world of sixteenth-century counterpoint it is recognized as a perfect consonance, yes, but treated as if it were dissonant, undoubtedly because of its inherent instability and the consequent difficulty for the singer.

The best way to practice *ma* is in small collections of scalar neighbors. Example 7.6 shows a few possibilities.

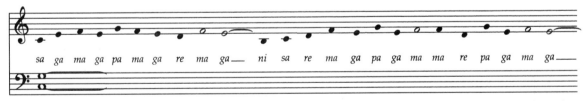

*sa  ga  ma  ga  pa  ma  ga  re  ma  ga___  ni  sa  re  ma  ga  pa  ga  ma  ma  re  pa  ga  ma  ga___*

*Example 7.6*

Don't be too surprised if your certainty of *ma* comes and goes; she is a wise crone and a capricious maid at the same time. If you aren't quite sure of the resonance, remember to keep checking your sung note against a tonic sounding a fifth (or a twelfth) above your voice. Example 7.7 gives a few more adventurous melodic shapes.

*re  ga  ni  ma  pa___  re  ni  pa  sa  ma  pa  ni  pa  ma___  re  ni  sa  ma  ni  ga  ni  ma  ga  ni  re  sa___*

*Example 7.7*

We have now placed on the harmonic map both an F and an F♯. They live quite far from one another—at opposite ends of the known world, in fact. Although we will study the subject of "chromatic pairs" in detail as we proceed (especially in chapter 15), at this stage it is clear that these two notes, though near each other in the scale, are far apart harmonically. They are not versions of one another. We will wait until later to mix their energies in a single phrase of music.

## Internalizing *Ma*

It takes even advanced musicians a while to master *ma*. I currently have a composition student who is one of the creative and developed jazz musicians in my part of the world, an in-tune trumpet player. Recently during a composition lesson, although genuinely surprised to discover the true nature of the subdominant, he seemed sufficiently clear to go on to the next thing. He shrugged and nodded and said, "OK, OK," much as someone who, suddenly coming upon the immense panorama of an alluvial valley, might say, "Fine, let's push on."

Now it is the following week, and my friend arrives at his lesson perplexed and untalkative. He lurches onto the piano bench, leans on the keyboard, looks up, and says, "Tell me again about *ma*."

The best wisdom you don't get all at once. *Ma* wisdom works on you from the inside and radiates slowly. My student was upset when he recognized that he hadn't really seen the valley he had been shown. I assured him that entire populations had passed that way without ever once looking up, or coming back. I love these moments in teaching, when musical realization is suddenly widened and deepened almost, it seems, from within the intentions of the Muse herself.

My teacher Pandit Pran Nath used to say that singing *ma* is like stopping time. He told me to color the vowel by putting a slight pressure on my glottis, moving the open *ah* toward the darker *uh*. That way, he said, you can hear the color of the sky at midnight.

Sing fifths above a tonic and fifths below. Compare. Don't expect the earth to move or the sky to crack open. Just listen, and enter what you hear.

8

# THE MAJOR THIRD BELOW

HERE IS A REPHRASING OF OUR OPERATIVE PRINCIPLE: There are two harmonic elements, fifths and thirds, subject to two procedures, above and below. We have found the fifth above, the fifth below, and the third above; now only the third below—the last quark—remains.

## Singing Reciprocal Thirds

I think it is fair to point out the progressive difficulty in these adventures. Fifths above are more obvious than thirds above. Thirds above are more obvious than fifths below. Thirds below are not as obvious as any of these. In order to develop your ability to hear reciprocal thirds, here is a game. Sing "Three Blind Mice," just the first three notes. (Be careful, now: If this were as simple as it seems I wouldn't get to have any fun.) You know the tune, do you? Now, with the aid of a piano or a guitar, pick out a single, random pitch in your singing range. Matching that fresh pitch, sing, "Three." Now, without playing any more notes on the instrument, sing the two remaining notes of the phrase so that you will have sung "Three Blind Mice" by ear, using the new note as the highest pitch. Now leave out the middle note, and sing, "Three Mice," as shown in example 8.1.

Now choose another pitch at random and do the same thing, until you can respond to any pitch by singing the major third below it. Maybe you can already do this with-

*Example 8.1*

out effort. Most musicians, however, do a double take here. The two usual errors are shown in example 8.2. Check it out, making sure your choices for new starting pitches are randomly

and

*Example 8.2*

play:

sing:

*Example 8.3*

chosen. You know you have it when your response is virtually instantaneous. (The practice of singing a given interval from a randomly chosen pitch is good for every interval.)

Now let's rephrase the problem in harmonic terms. We are in C. We ask the question, "What is C the fifth partial *of?*" (Answering this question, and others like it that will arise, requires familiarity with the overtone series throughout the chromatic scale—see chapter 1). The answer is A♭. Play the C above middle C on the piano or guitar, but don't play the A♭ on the keyboard or the fretboard. Find it in your voice (it is a well-tuned "Mice") and tune it so that it sounds both correct in pitch and harmonically resonant, as shown in example 8.3. Use whatever octave transposition or reduction that makes you most comfortable. Sing the syllable *dha* with a clean, open vowel. (As mentioned in chapter 7, even though the full *sargam* name is *komal dha*, the *komal* is omitted in singing practice.)

The C drone, now above you, is your fifth partial as well as the pure third of a major scale starting on A♭. Remember that in order to generate A♭, we momentarily pretended that it was the tonic, even though our larger context is C. We are not really *in* A♭. That is precisely the trick of perception implicit in reciprocal harmony: A♭ generates the harmony, but C is still home—that is, A♭ becomes the harmonic *root*, but C remains the *tonic*. Keep practicing this exercise until you are convinced that C is your fifth partial—that is, until you have found the reciprocal version of pentamerous resonance.

Remember how the singer of *ma* placed himself or herself in the position of creating the entire known universe (i.e., the generating tone) as his or her third partial? Similarly, as the singer of *komal dha* you produce the universe as your fifth partial. This is a sophisticated, deeply musical skill that most musicians in the world do quite intuitively (although this tone is not as universal as *pa*, *ma*, *ga*, or *re*). I am asking you to render this complex human magic as a conscious action in the present, to both *hear* the fifth-partial relation between your A♭ and the C above you and to *know* that you are hearing it as the fifth partial. Just as E is the *ga* above C, A♭ can be experienced as the *ga* below C, the reciprocal mirror image of E.

sing:
play:

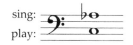

*Example 8.4*

The next step is to bring the C drone back into the bass, so that the A♭ is a minor sixth above it rather than a major third below it, as shown in example 8.4. It might help, in finding the sweet spot of this harmony, to imagine the higher C above your voice even if it is not sounding explicitly. Maybe that imagining is actually part of the process of singing the note in tune. In any case, the harmonic resonance of the minor sixth is intensely moving. When it is in tune it flies—it seems actually to leap like fire and be upward tending, as if it were looking toward the high drone for a mate. Meanwhile, that very drone is your overtone.

On the harmonic map, the reciprocal third appears on a new spine positioned below the central spine as shown in example 8.5. Notice the square, solid note head I use for the new spine now emerging. Notice also the new bass clef. The full harmonic map up to this point is given in example 8.6. A cautionary reminder: Equal-tempered major thirds are a little sharp. Another way of saying this is that they are too *wide*; conversely, just major thirds may seem too low—or too *narrow*—for ears conditioned to equal temperament. Now, when you turn an equal-tempered third upside down, it is still too wide; conversely, a just third may at first seem too high—that is, the interval between it and the tonic above it may seem too narrow for equal-tempered ears. So when you sing a minor sixth, your piano ears may guide you into singing a little flat. Don't sing flat. Hold out for the resonance. When you find it, it will indeed be slightly sharp to the piano A♭; the same amount sharp, in fact, that you find the just major third is flat to the piano E.

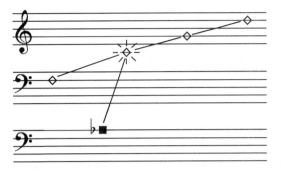

*Example 8.5*

## Scale Practice with *Komal Dha*

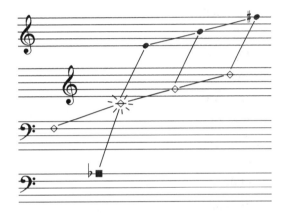

*Example 8.6*

The four tones of example 8.7 make an extremely useful scale practice, up and down. These notes are nothing less than the two harmonic elements (a fifth and a third) plus their reciprocals, all bunched together by octave reduction. Example 8.8 is a map that clarifies the symmetry.

Improvise over a C drone using only these four tones while pointing to the notes you are singing as they appear on the harmonic map. Example 8.9 shows some of the melodic possibilities.

Notice especially how the alternation between *ga* and *ma*, which is a small melodic interval, carries you over into opposing harmonic territories: *Ga* is an overtonal third, while *ma* is a reciprocal fifth. The alternation between *komal dha* and *pa*, on the other hand, presents the mirror inversion of the above case: *Komal dha* is a reciprocal third, while *pa* is an overtonal fifth. If you are watching the map as you sing these pairs, you will be following the symmetry visually while at the same time feeling the tight weave of melody and harmony. Learn to

*ga    ma    pa    dha    pa    ma    ga*

*Example 8.7*

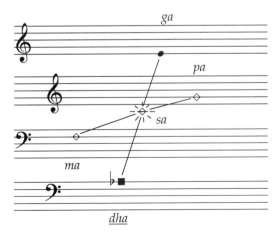

*Example 8.8*

ga ma pa ma pa dha pa ma ga ma pa dha ma pa ga ma— ga pa dha pa ma ga pa— dha pa ga ma dha pa—

*Example 8.9*

appreciate the linear closeness and the harmonic complementarity simultaneously.

There is one combination of tones that is almost bizarre in its affect: the alternation between *ga* and *komal dha,* the overtonal and reciprocal thirds. Traveling vertically on the harmonic map is considerably more difficult than traveling horizontally. The ear moves more easily by fifths than by thirds. We are reminded of the alternation between *ma* and *pa* (in chapter 7) and how one can flip between overtonal and reciprocal fifths by moving between adjacent scale steps. In contrast, sing example 8.10 and notice what happens to you.

*Example 8.10*

ga   dha   ga   dha   pa   ma   dha   ga

One reason it may be more difficult to navigate between the E and the A♭ is that there are four scale steps involved, not two. (The interval is a diminished fourth.) But the real difficulty is that thirds are more complex than fifths, so flipping their polarity feels more complex. Fifths are used structurally in music; they are less evocative, more of a resolution than a plot. But thirds have drama in them, a kind of grain or current—almost as if you could detect the 5:4 working itself out in the fluids and membranes of the ear. When you flip that energy you are flipping your inner life.

## A Map of Affects

If *ma* and *pa* are the Mamas and the Papas, who are *ga* and *komal dha?* In Indian music, *ga* has been associated with the quality of compassion. One of the *mudras* (hand positions) used to realize compassion calls for both palms down, parallel with the earth, fingers outstretched. *Komal dha* has been associated with fire (passion fire, if you ask me), and a *mudra* for fire calls for palms up to the sky, fingers outstretched.

Figure 8.1 is a kind of map to experiment with as you sing. Maybe this is just somebody's idea; maybe not. It is what some people have thought, but people think a lot of things, and you shouldn't believe any of it until it becomes, through experience, true for you. Whatever experience is true for you, however, you must admit that, all things considered, music is one of the better ways of passing time.

COMPASSION
ga

SUN
pa

ma
MOON

sa

*dha*
PASSION

*Figure 8.1*

## *Komal Dha* in a Seven-Tone Scale

The next step is to incorporate komal dha into a seven-tone scale. I suggest the one given in example 8.11 (over a C drone).

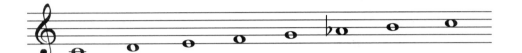

*Example 8.11*

This is, of course, our familiar major mode but with a minor sixth. It is full of surprising possibilities. Why not compose a melody in this mode and learn to sing it beautifully in *sargam*? Or improvise in *sargam*, deliberately feeling the woofs and warps of melody and harmony weaving your feelings and ideas together.

# 9

# THE CENTRAL SECTION OF THE MAP COMPLETED

IF IT WERE TRUE THAT TO KNOW THE NATURE OF ATOMS is to know the nature of being, then we would know music by now, since we have learned its atoms. But it is not enough to know atomic physics alone—there is chemistry, architecture, gardening, angelology . . . .

In this chapter we investigate the harmonic qualities of four new compound tones.

## The Major Sixth: *Dha*, 5:3

The major sixth, A, is the first of many tones we will study that is the result of moving in opposing dimensions on the harmonic map. *Opposing* means both up and down: up fifths and down thirds, or down fifths and up thirds. In the case of the major sixth, we will begin with the upward third, and then proceed downward by a fifth, as shown in example 9.1.

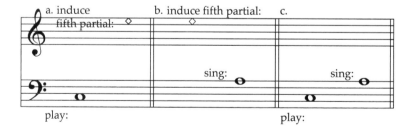

*Example 9.1*

You are now singing the reciprocal fifth of the overtonal third. You are the *pa* below the *ga* above; you are subdominant to the major third.* The harmonic path is given in example

---

*One could argue for "*ma of ga*" as a more accurate name, but it will soon become clear that *pa* is a better term for describing all 3:2 relationships, both overtonal and reciprocal.

9.2. Notice the position of the bass clef: It locates the pitch of the A.

*Example 9.2*

Though the procedure for finding this harmony may seem a bit abstruse, the harmony itself tunes easily and naturally. To me it has a softness and a gentility, combining the qualities of *ga* (the third above) and *ma* (the fifth below): Its ratio is 5:3 (see page 95). Compassionate moon? Even though I want you to feel everything I feel, I must let the resonances speak for themselves. Listen to *dha* over many days. Hear internally the perfect fifth your voice makes with the E above it. Let the vowel of *dha* be open and clear; hear the breath in it, as if the vowel were the continuation of the *h*. Example 9.3 gives some melodic shapes; it also demonstrates the Lydian mode, of which much more will be said in the next chapter. (Notice that for convenience we are now using the initial consonant of the *sargam* syllable to stand for the whole syllable.)

*Example 9.3*

Example 9.4 gives the full harmonic map up to this point. The map shows that there is another way of arriving at this same ratio of 5:3. You could first go down a fifth to F, and then go up a third to A. Now the ear will hear the tone as the *ga* of *pa* below (instead of the other way around). Although the tone has the same frequency and ratio as before, the context has changed. And as the context changes—even the conceptual context—so changes our experience of the note. The harmonic path will now be as shown in example 9.5.

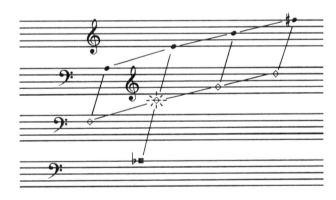

*Example 9.4*

Perhaps the most reliable way of experiencing this quality involves tuning the low E string of a guitar up a semitone to F so that it makes a perfect fifth below the C

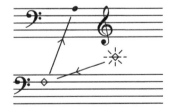

*Example 9.5*

string (which is actually the old D string tuned down a whole tone). The way to proceed is shown in example 9.6. Notice that the first five steps simply insure that the two strings are indeed a perfect fifth apart.

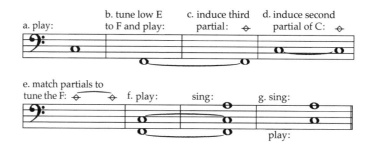

*Example 9.6*

Example 9.7, to be sung over a C drone, gives some phrases that emphasize the generation of *dha* by *ma*.

g  p  m  g  m  d——  p——d  m  d  p    d  n  s  m  d  m  p    d m  d  p———  d  p  m  s  r  m  g  d  m  p—

*Example 9.7*

This is the familiar Major mode, of course, which it may be useful to reexamine in terms of our newly acquired harmonic language of *pa* and *ga* (using our primary definition of *ga*). Example 9.8 indicates the compounding process for the tones of C Major.

*Example 9.8*

sa        pa of pa      ga        ma        pa      pa below ga    ga of pa      sa

Try singing a simple melodic sequence such as the one shown in example 9.9 extremely slowly, tracking the harmonic derivations as you sing by pointing to the tones on the harmonic lattice of example 9.4.

*Example 9.9*

s  r  g      r  g  m      g  m  p      etc...      s  n  d      n  d  p

After singing such a sequence at least once with your brain thus occupied, sing it many more times for the simple pleasure of it. Then, finally, improvise freely (but mostly stepwise) in the mode of C Major, moving intuitively from resonance to resonance. You may find an old friend newly interesting.

## The Minor Third: *Komal Ga*, 6:5

The next tone we'll examine is the minor third, E♭; it is perhaps the most surprising of all. E♭, like the major sixth, A, requires two opposing moves for its generation; it is a fifth up and a major third down, the reciprocal third of the overtonal fifth. Example 9.10 shows how to find the just minor third using the two drone tones, C and G. Example 9.11 shows the harmonic path.

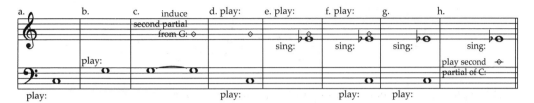

*Example 9.10*

Since this minor third—whose ratio is 6:5—seems like such a basic fact of musical life, it is strange to realize that it is not an element but a mixture of two more elemental things. We are so used to hearing this interval as a minor third *up* from the tonic that it seems roundabout to refer *down* from the dominant for its identity. This becomes familiar with practice, however.

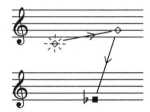

*Example 9.11*

Just as A♭ is the *ga* below *sa*, E♭ is the *ga* below *pa*. Dwell on the reciprocal third (example 9.12).

Play the G and sing the E♭ until you are certain you are the "mice" of "Three Blind Mice." Then, holding on for dear life, add a lower C to the mix: You will be the minor third of a pure minor triad.

*Example 9.12*

When I first found my own voice inside a just minor triad, I couldn't believe it was so—well, so (arggh! I can scarcely say the dreaded word, but here goes)—so . . . *happy*. There. We are told from the beginning that minor is sad, the designated mode for angst and funerals. Well, to be honest, the equal-tempered version of the minor triad *is* rather sad. The equal-tempered major third down from G to E♭ is too *wide*, making the minor third between C and E♭ too *narrow*, or flat. So piano minor is flat and sounds dull—the fire is out of it. But minor thirds in just intonation, and the minor triads they support, are swift and burning. They have the gypsy left in them, and do some leaping kind of dance.

Is a fifth up and a major third down sun/passion?

In scale practice, while singing the E♭, look for the G internally. Be sure to keep looking for that upward major third, even though the manifest sound is the downward minor third. This is characteristic of reciprocal harmonies.

The full harmonic map so far is shown in example 9.13. The map shows that—as we saw in the case of the major sixth—there is another way to generate the minor third: You could go down a major third and up a fifth, as the arrows of example 9.14 indicate. Although this path results in the identical pitch as the way shown in example 9.11, it is less useful to us

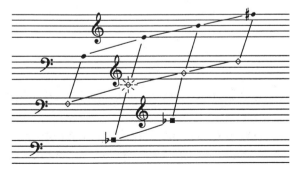

*Example 9.13*

musically at this point. If you are interested, though, try the experiment suggested by the map.

Although many modal combinations have now become possible within our growing harmonic territory, let's for the moment limit our scale practice to notes and phrases most compatible with the minor third. I suggest the mode called the *Harmonic Minor*, shown in example 9.15.

Example 9.16 (to be sung over a C-and-G drone) shows some melodic shapes you may find useful in learning to improvise in this mode.

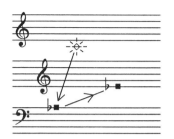

*Example 9.14*

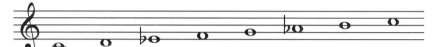

*Example 9.15*

s  r  p  m   g    r  m   g  d  p–   n  p  d   g  m  r  m  d  p–   n  p   g  r–   n  d  s  n   d  p  m   g  r   s—

*Example 9.16*

# The Real Secret of the Minor Third

induce:

play:

*Example 9.17*

Every time you sing a minor third against the tonic, an astonishing event takes place just beneath the surface of the sound. To expose what happens, play C on an open guitar string (not a piano string for this) and induce the fifth partial over the fourth fret, as shown in example 9.17.

Now play the open G string and sing E♭, the reciprocal third. For men, proceed as in example 9.18a. For women, induce the second partial of the open G string, and sing down a third, as shown in example 9.18b.

*Example 9.18*

Now—and this is tricky at best—play C and G, then induce the fifth partial, E, while singing the E♭. For men, proceed as in example 9.19a; for women, as in example 9.19b.

And now, for the finale, allow the fifth partial to continue, damp out the C and the G, and hang on to the E♭ without flinching. What remains is example 9.20a for men and 9.20b for women.

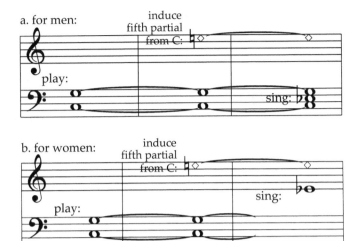

*Example 9.19*

Cripes! The interval (in the form of example 9.20b) is called an augmented octave. It is so screechingly dissonant that it hardly ever occurs naked anywhere in traditional non-Western music and was virtually banned from Western music until its wanton use in the twentieth century. Yet there it sits, quietly bright, beckoning beneath the surface of every minor third. I think this is the very quality that makes minor minor. Once you become conscious of the floating major third produced by the fifth partial of the tonic, its mixture into the harmony of the minor third an octave or more below becomes familiar, then expected, then ravishingly gorgeous. So addicted have I (among others) become to the beauty of this particular ratio (the E♮ to the E♭, octave-reduced, is 25:24) that in my own music I am continually coaxing it out of the closet onto the stage, where it flourishes. Perhaps it takes some time to love it; lucky for us, time is all we have.

*Example 9.20*

## The Minor Seventh: *Komal Ni, 9:5*

The next note to study is the minor seventh, B♭, the third below D (which is two fifths up). The harmonic path is shown in example 9.21. To sing it, you need first to produce the three tones shown in example 9.22. Make sure your fifths are true, either by tuning a third string accurately or by inducing the third partial of a low G string. To do this, tune the guitar A string a whole tone down, so it is an octave below the G string. Then induce the third partial of that low G string, as shown in example 9.23.

Now play and sing example 9.24a,

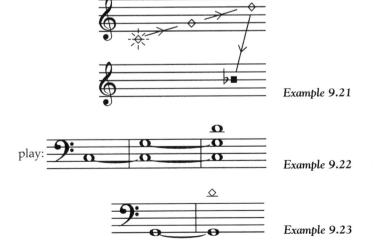

*Example 9.21*

*Example 9.22*

*Example 9.23*

making sure that the B♭ is true "mice." Then add the lower fifths, and finally damp out everything except the C and the B♭, as shown in example 9.24b–c.

*Example 9.24*

This B♭ is possibly sharper than you expect; indeed, of the four (yes) minor sevenths we will eventually consider, this one is the highest in pitch. But let the resonance of the reciprocal third from D be your guide—when that is right, the pitch is right. The harmonic map up to this point is shown in example 9.25.

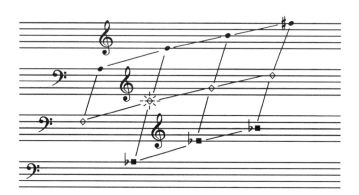

*Example 9.25*

Since we have derived our new tone by going up two fifths (the sun of a sun?) and down a third, could we possibly describe it as star/passion? Is this an ancient prophecy realized in the modern mind, or is this New Age psychoacoustic babble? Or is it simply the ratio 9:5—no less, no more? The nonsinging reader will never know for sure. But the singer who sings it in tune gets to choose a name that is true for him or her. You sing it. You call it.

For scale practice, I suggest singing in your lower octave, concentrating first on the tones of example 9.26. Gradually including higher tones, melodies can be improvised like those in example 9.27.

*Example 9.26*

*Example 9.27*

A next good step would be to substitute for the major third and major sixth, the minor third and minor sixth, as shown in example 9.28.

*Example 9.28*

## The Minor Second: *Komal Re*, 16:15

The tone that completes the center of the harmonic map is the minor second, D♭. It is the reciprocal third of the reciprocal fifth, or, more simply, down a fifth, then down a third, as shown in example 9.29. This tone is possibly the most difficult to learn; it is certainly the least familiar to Western ears. If a Hollywood movie wants to evoke an exotic locale, it shows a guy in a turban and on the soundtrack some reedy instrument plays something like example 9.30.

*Example 9.29*

*Example 9.30*

But making friends with a stranger can result in an intimacy not possible with the old friends back home. Finding the resonance of this new harmony opens up an area of feeling that some of us never knew was in us all along.

The singing practice requires retuning the G string (the higher one, that is) to F. That means matching the third partial of that string (seventh fret) to the fourth partial of the C string (fifth fret), as shown in example 9.31. If the two overtones match, the F will be a just perfect fourth above C.

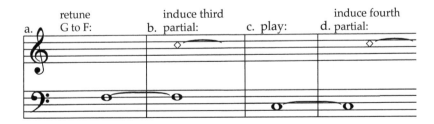

*Example 9.31*

Now men will sing the major third, D♭, below the F, as in example 9.32a. Women will induce the second partial above the F and then sing the major third below that, as in example 9.32b.

*Example 9.32*

Finally, when you are sure of your resonances, add the C drone, for men as in 9.33a, and for women as in 9.33b.

*Examples 9.33*

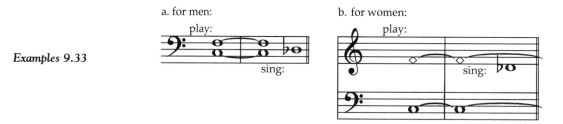

The process will be made more musical if you then resolve your sung D♭ gently to C, in agreement with the drone. Do this many times, creating a tension and resolution that brings more life to the harmony.

When you find the resonance of this D♭, you are singing the *ga* below *pa* below. "Moon passion?" we ask in passing.

For melodic practice, retain the F in the drone, at least for now. But you have to keep reminding your ear to hear C as the tonic, the home note. If you are not careful, you might begin to perceive the tonic as F, which is not unmusical, but also not the point. Try the combinations suggested in example 9.34 over a C-and-F drone.

*Example 9.34*

The mode I am suggesting, written as a scale, looks like example 9.35.

*Example 9.35*

This is called the Phrygian mode and contains all of the reciprocal thirds we have studied so far. The wisdom of these reciprocal thirds reveals itself over the many hours of many days of practice. When the mode begins to feel familiar, replace the F in the drone with G, if you like. The resulting harmonies will be more complex and commensurately more evocative. To ensure the integrity of the tuning, concentrate on the notes F, D♭, and C in your vocal line. The more certain you are of the resonances, the more compelling will be the melodies drawn out of you.

## Reciprocal Mystery

At some point during the examination of the minor second, an inquisitive mind might ask, "How can my brain make sense out of this D♭ that is a reciprocal of the note F even when the F is not sounding?" I think the missing F of example 9.36a is no different from the missing G of example 9.36b (or, for that matter, the missing G of example 9.36c) except that it's simply upside down.

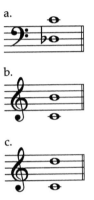

"But isn't music made from the ground up?" Yes and no. It's easier from the ground up, but it happens the other way too. Music is made, rather, from the center *out*, more like the concentric forces of an atom, or—to fairly include gravity into the metaphor—like the limbs and roots of a tree. What we can know from our own center is that there is some fearful symmetry inside the musical ear, and that the way to dissect it and analyze its subterranean procedures is by singing from our own inside out, tone by tone, resonance by resonance, over the slanting hours until the cows come home.

*Example 9.36*

## The Center Is Complete

Meanwhile, we have accomplished our immediate task. The central area of the harmonic map of the tone C is now complete, as shown in example 9.37. We'll refer to it from time to time as the five-limit lattice of twelve notes.

Why not take a long quiet moment, after all this dutiful practice and before going on, to scrutinize the map, with its rich field of possibilities and complementarities, just to see what can be seen.

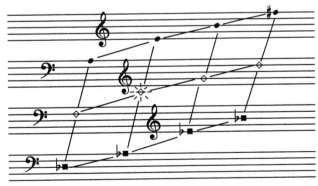

*Example 9.37*

# THE FIVE-LIMIT LATTICE
# OF TWELVE NOTES

## Drawing the Map

Let's retreat from singing and the sounds of things for a while and try to sharpen the visual image of the harmonic map. The best way to learn it is to draw it from memory. First notice the unconventional arrangement of clefs; special care must be taken with their placement. The treble clefs must form a column down the middle of the page tilted toward the lower

*Figure 10.1*

right-hand corner. The column of bass clefs, closer to the left-hand margin, must tilt slightly downward toward the lower left, as in figure 10.1.

The central tone of the map, the tonic, I designate by an open diamond with radiating lines. Any tone could be chosen as the tonic, but our discussion has been in the key of C so far, so C belongs in the center: Place it just at the foot of the second treble clef from the top and just behind the coif of the third clef from the top, positioned midway between staves, as shown in example 10.1.

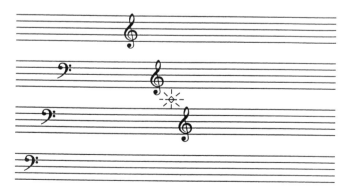

*Example 10.1*

Now from memory and in pencil (always and forever in pencil) draw that much of the map on a clean piece of manuscript paper. Choose manuscript paper that has the smallest possible distance between staves.

The next step is to draw the line of fifths ascending and descending from C, which is called the central spine of fifths and is notated with open, diamond-shaped noteheads. The trick lies in placing the notes along an imaginary line that is as straight as possible, and as close to horizontal as possible. It can't be entirely straight because of the space between staves; it can't be horizontal, of course, because the pitches need to be shown at various degrees above and below the generating tone. When you have drawn the central spine of fifths, lightly draw the connecting line, with small breaks to accommodate the noteheads. Example 10.2a shows good form. Example 10.2b shows bad form: The notes are too close and the unbroken line too steep.

a. 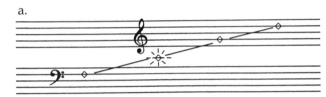 b.

*Example 10.2*

Now begin fresh and draw that much of the map from memory. Expensive as it is, don't try to save manuscript paper; use clean paper and use enough. You'll waste less in the long run by being generous to yourself.

The next move is to add the thirds above. If you place the first one correctly you'll get all of them right. Note that a major third always needs to go on a separate staff above its generating tone. Place E in the top staff closer to the C than to the G; then connect E and C with a line, as in example 10.3.

*Example 10.3*

Now add B in the top staff closer to the G than to the D, and connect the G and the B with a line. Be sure to place the B so the line connecting G and B and the line connecting C and E will be parallel, as in example 10.4.

Now add F♯ above and to the right of D; add its connecting line parallel to the others. For reference, you can consult the lattice as it appears in example 9.37 (p. 61).

Now add A closer to the F than to the C, on the second staff from the top, to the right of the bass clef and just to the left of the treble clef. Don't be confused by the strange-looking portion of the map shown in example 10.5.

Now draw the connecting lines along the spine of

*Example 10.4*

*Example 10.5*

overtonal thirds (A–E–B–F♯). At this point, your map should look like example 10.6.

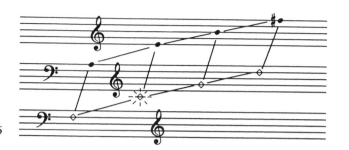

*Example 10.6*

To be certain you have the right image of these eight notes, draw this much of the map from memory. Added to the blessings you are already deriving from your (sharpened No. 2) pencil should be those flowing from a good soft rubber eraser.

To learn the spine of reciprocal thirds, first draw A♭ below C in the bottom staff (not the one adjacent to middle C) so that a line drawn upward from A♭ to C to E will be straight, as in example 10.7.

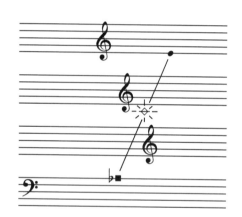

*Example 10.7*

Now do the same for E♭–G–B. Notice that E♭ belongs in the third staff from the top, to the right of the treble clef. Now draw in the B♭ a fifth higher, so that B♭–D–F♯ is a straight line.

Next draw the D♭ in the bottom staff so that D♭–F–A is a straight line. Finally, draw the connecting lines along the lower spine, D♭–A♭–E♭–B♭, and compare your result to the complete lattice of twelve notes shown in example 9.37. Now at last, on a fresh sheet of manuscript paper, draw your own lattice of twelve notes from memory.

To be sure you have it, draw another one transposed up a whole tone so that D is the central tone. (It will contain three sharps and two flats.)

## Review and Clarification of Terminology

To further clarify our work, here are some definitions adapted from David Doty's *The Just Intonation Primer* (see the list of sources at the back of the book).

*Just intonation* is any system of tuning in which all the intervals can be represented by whole-number frequency ratios, with a strongly implied preference for the simplest ratios.

*A prime number* is a positive whole number that has as factors only itself and one. There is an infinite array of prime numbers, but only the first few (1, 2, 3, 5, 7, 11) have obvious musical significance. The primes that we have considered in this book so far are limited to 1, 2, 3, and 5, by which is meant unisons, doublings (i.e., octaves), triplings (perfect fifths), and quintuplings (major thirds). A tuning system limited to these primes is called *five-limit just intonation*.

Two intersecting sets of parallel lines form a *lattice*. Spines of fifths and spines of thirds form a *five-limit lattice* in just intonation. A page has two dimensions: horizontal and vertical. The prime number three—the triplings that become a spine of perfect fifths by octave reduction—occupy the horizontal dimension. The prime number five—the quintuplings that become a spine of major thirds by octave reduction—occupy the vertical dimension. (In this study, we have so far skewed our axes into *staff orientation* so that the horizontal now has a *pronounced* southwest-to-northeast tilt, and the vertical has a *slight* southwest-to-northeast tilt.) The prime number two does not appear functionally on the lattice because we have reduced away the octaves; in other words, each position on the lattice stands for a note and all its octaves. Later we extend the lattice outward in both dimensions, but so far we have confined our discussion to a specific field of twelve notes. Hence "a five-limit lattice of twelve notes."

# Harmonic Paths

Once you are able to draw the lattice from memory, the boon of its maplike qualities becomes more apparent. This means that when you understand the harmonic relationship of any tone with C, that same harmonic relationship from any other tone becomes graphically clear. For example, the path of B, the major seventh from C, proceeds up a fifth and up a third, as shown in example 10.8. The path without the staff looks like figure 10.2.

*Example 10.8*

If you start on any other tone and follow the same path, you will derive the same harmony with the same quality but from that new tone. Thus, for instance, from F to E, which makes the same harmony, appears as in example 10.9. The same path can be drawn from D♭ to C, as well as for three other major sevenths on the map. (What are they?)

*Figure 10.2*

By way of contrast, B♭ to A appears on the lattice as shown in example 10.10. Figure 10.3 shows the generic harmonic path for this more complex type of major seventh.

The harmonic path is down two fifths, up two thirds, and then down another fifth, or a total of down three fifths and up two thirds (plus an octave in these cases in order to make a major seventh as opposed to a minor second). This is obviously a less direct and more distant harmony than the other type of major seventh.

*Example 10.9*

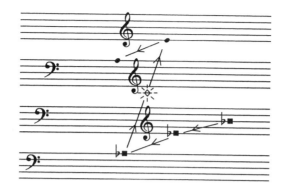

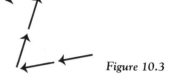

*Example 10.10*

*Figure 10.3*

Let's look at major seconds. The kind we have already examined carefully results from two fifths up, shown specifically in example 10.11 and generically in figure 10.4.

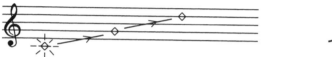

*Example 10.11*

*Figure 10.4*

There are a total of six of this type of major second on the lattice of twelve notes. But how do you get from D to E? The path is quite different, not as direct, as can be seen from example 10.12 and figure 10.5.

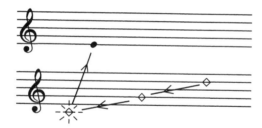

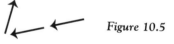

*Example 10.12*

*Figure 10.5*

This type of major second, intervalically smaller than the other, has a darker quality; it is a different breed, since it contains pentamerous harmony. There are four of these on the lattice of twelve notes. Can you find them? The larger major second, two fifths up, is called the *major whole tone*. The smaller major second, two fifths down and a third up, is called the *minor whole tone*. These are useful names, and will become more so as we progress.

There are also two types of minor third: three fifths down (figure 10.6) and a fifth up and a third down (figure 10.7). How many of each?*

*Figure 10.6*

*Figure 10.7*

*Three of the first and six of the second.

# Lattice Practice

For further mastery of the lattice, try spelling a chromatic scale (C, D♭, D, etc.) while pointing to the notes on the map as you name them quickly as possible.

Also try singing familiar diatonic or modal tunes against the C–G drone, pointing to the notes as you sing. As you sing the melody you will be pointing out your course through the harmonic territory.

At this point these activities are merely exercises meant to provide insight. But with more practice and more music making, the five-limit lattice will become quite personalized, a picture of your own harmonic experience.

Although three-limit and five-limit tuning systems have been both employed and quantified for well over two thousand years, the first formulation of a five-limit lattice in just intonation was made, I believe, by Alexander Ellis, in the appendix to his 1885 English translation of *On the Sensations of Tone* by Hermann Helmholtz. His purpose was quite different from ours, however. Ellis, among many of his generation, was chafing against the musical compromises imposed by twelve-tone equal temperament; he wanted desperately to believe that music of the common practice period (roughly the eighteenth and nineteenth centuries), although conceived in equal temperament, could be realized more beautifully and powerfully with an elaborately extended five-limit lattice. The impossibility of that has already been elegantly demonstrated by Easley Blackwood in *The Structure of Recognizable Diatonic Tunings* (see the list of sources). I wish to acknowledge, however, that Ellis intuited over a hundred years ago the practical value of the lattice design, which has now become standard in contemporary thinking about just intonation. The addition of musical staff notation increases even further the practicality of the lattice, allowing its meaning to evolve in real time for each musician as his or her music evolves.

# AVAILABLE MODES: LYDIAN THROUGH PHRYGIAN

Within the five-limit lattice of twelve notes there is available a great variety of seven-tone modes. We will assume for now that a seven-tone mode contains seven discrete scale degrees designated by the letters A, B, C, D, E, F, and G.

We'll first consider a group of modes ordinarily taught with natural letter names as "the church modes"—the white notes on the piano beginning on C, then D, then E, and so on. We show these "in C," however, with each mode beginning and ending on C, thus making use of the black keys as well. By this method, all twelve notes from the lattice will make their appearance. Study example 11.1.

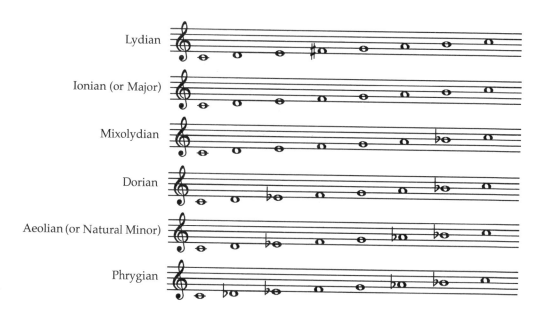

*Example 11.1*

The names of these modes are derived from place-names in ancient Greece. The connection of the actual musical sounds to the actual places, however, has been fuzzed, reversed, or (most likely) obliterated over time and temperament. Yet the names persist in common usage, their false histories rolling sweetly off the tongue. Furthermore, each of these modes has a large number of alternative tunings worldwide. What we are studying here are the least complex modes that are available from the five-limit lattice of twelve notes.

Notice first, as you go down the page from Lydian to Phrygian, that the C and the G do not change; they are fixed. The other five scale degrees have alternate forms. Example 11.2 combines all twelve of the notes into a reference scale that demonstrates this.

*Example 11.2*

Let's track the degrees as follows:

The fourth degree, F, is augmented (sharped in this case) in Lydian, but perfect (natural in this case) in all the others.

The seventh degree, B, is major in two modes and minor in four.

The third degree, E, is major in three modes and minor in three.

The sixth degree, A, is major in four modes and minor in two.

The second degree, D, is major in five modes and minor in one only, Phrygian.

Notice also that in example 11.1 the modes are arranged on the page so that all five of the degrees that have alternate forms are in their high form at the top of the list and in their low form at the bottom of the list.

By virtue of their intervalic makeup, these six scales form a group. Not only are the intervals confined to half steps and whole steps only, but the *clustering* of whole steps is the same for each mode. There is a cluster of two whole steps and a cluster of three whole steps; the clusters are separated by half steps. The situation is most clear and familiar in the Ionian mode, as seen in example 11.3. The brackets beneath the notes show the clustering of whole tones.

*Example 11.3*

Example 11.4 shows that in Lydian the clusters are reversed.

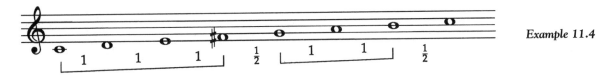

*Example 11.4*

Phrygian starts with a half step, as shown in example 11.5.

*Example 11.5*

In the other modes, even though the tonic is located in the middle of a cluster, the pattern of clustering is maintained. Hence the pattern in Mixolydian is as shown in example 11.6.

*Example 11.6*

One might say, as a general rule, that it helps to know where the half steps are.

Although these six modes are in the same intervalic family, the family contains an enormous range of moods. *Mood* and *mode* are both from the Latin *modus*, which refers to the measure of something, its limit. *Mode* refers to a limit that regulates the way in which a thing is done. *Mood* has come to mean the temper or condition of the mind or the heart. Our progression of modes is also a progression of moods. To understand this better, let's take a look at the harmonic map of each mode in turn, tracking the gradual transformation from Lydian to Phrygian.

## The Lydian Mode

Example 11.7 shows the Lydian mode and its harmonic map.

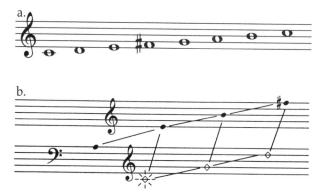

*Example 11.7*

Over the spine of three fifths we see a spine of four overtonal thirds. The only hint of reciprocal energy is in the A, which is a mixture of overtonal and reciprocal energy (up a third and down a fifth). Otherwise the mode is purely overtonal. If overtones are sunny, then, within the confines of our lattice, this is as sunny as any seven-tone mode gets.

For singing in these modes, use the seven syllables of Indian *sargam: sa, re, ga, ma, pa, dha,* and *ni,* regardless of accidentals. When you sing in Lydian, you may notice that the four overtonal thirds of the upper spine (A, E, B, and F♯) have a somewhat similar quality. They are all *ga*-blooded, of course, whereas the notes of the central spine are all Pythagorean.

*Ga*-blooded?

## Digression on Terminology

As we have already discussed, a system of tuning containing only octaves and perfect fifths (or doublings and triplings: a three-limit system) is called Pythagorean, based on the philosophical principle that in order to reflect the ideal of perfection music must be limited to the purest—that is, the lowest—generating prime. When we speak of Pythagorean intervals, or ratios, or harmonies, we mean music generated by a single spine of perfect fifths. Systems generated in part or entirely by 5:4-type major thirds do not have such a convenient term; "pentamerous" and "tertiary" are both OK, and I use them both from time to time. But I would like the reader's permission to borrow from *sargam* and use the term *ga-blooded* for tones that mix the energies of perfect fifths and major thirds. The only purebred *ga*'s in our lattice (computing from C) are E and its reciprocal, A♭—the third above and the third below. All the other notes on the other spines are mixed with perfect fifths, hence *ga*-blooded. Pure thirds and the tones that contain their energies sound juicy, *ga* is a great syllable to sing juicy tones with, and blood is the primal juice. Is this going too far?

Back to singing over a drone. *Ga*-blooded notes sing beautifully together, especially when they are harmonic neighbors, such as A and B, or E and F♯. Example 11.8 demonstrates this.

g   m d n___   d m g   r   g r p___

*Example 11.8*

Notice how the *ga*-blooded notes contrast with the Pythagorean G and D. Notice also how the half step between the dissonant F♯ and the consonant G and likewise the half step between the dissonant B and the consonant C constitute a built-in system of tension and release. In North Indian music this mode is called *Yaman*, and musicians often achieve a wondrous, floating effect by avoiding the resolution notes of G and C for long passages. Within such a passage you can hang on to the major seventh for what seems like a week. You may also notice how, since the mode is made mostly of overtones, it takes on a tingling kind of relaxation, a brilliant ease.

## The Ionian Mode

Example 11.9 shows the scale and the map of the Ionian mode, which is identical with the Major scale. The most overtonal note, F♯, is gone. In its place is F, the reciprocal fifth, the subdominant. In terms of the lattice of twelve notes, the generating spine is now complete: The four Pythagorean tones are F–C–G–D. Notice that the tones generating thirds

*Example 11.9*

(F–C–G) are *centered* on C, the tonic, thus giving this mode a particularly stable, grounded quality. Because of its harmonic stability, Ionian has become the favored mode of the West; we will say more about this in part 2.

For now, try observing the effect of singing only the Pythagorean tones of the mode, as in example 11.10.

*Example 11.10*

Then gradually fold *ga* and *ga*-blood into the mix.

The half steps are between B and C (as in Lydian) and also between E and F, which is fascinating because these are so complimentary: E is the third above and F is the fifth below, representing both qualities and both directions. Of the two, F is more consonant but less stable; E is thicker, but more of a release—it simply sits there like the overtone it is. A singer can thereby travel a small melodic distance while covering a wide harmonic sweep. Such felicitously paired neighbors often inspire expressive usage, including trills and ornaments of every description.

It is curious to note that in India, where this mode is the standard reference for singing and teaching, it is not much used in actual music. When Indian kids are first learning their *sa-re-ga* they sound not unlike American kids learning their *do-re-mi*. But the mode rarely shows up in *raga*. Too stable, I think, for everyday dronal fare.

Yet in our culture we are surrounded by the Ionian mode and the harmonies it generates from cradle to grave, and it is easy to take it for granted: plain old Major. But you can never be too alert—the very thing you need most has a way of turning up under your nose.

## The Mixolydian Mode

Example 11.11 shows the scale and the harmonic map of the Mixolydian mode.

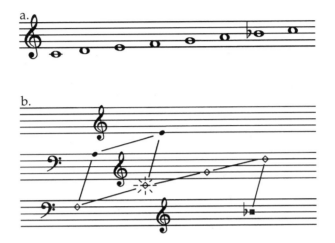

*Example 11.11*

In this mode one more overtonal note, B, is replaced by a reciprocal third, B♭. All four kinds of five-limit harmony are included here: overtonal fifths, overtonal thirds, a reciprocal fifth, and a reciprocal third. Mixolydian, which can be a relaxed and easy mode, is a favorite of improvisors from jazz musicians to Indian musicians to "folk" musicians around the world. Notice how there is no half step adjacent to either the tonic or the dominant, thus perhaps damping the urgencies of tension and release. But both half steps can be melodically evocative; especially notice the unique blend of qualities between A and B♭, both *ga*-blooded. (This semitone is unique among diatonic semitones in this lattice—see chapter 10, example 10.10.) If improvisation has seemed a bit risky for you, this is a good mode for spreading your wings.

## The Dorian Mode

Example 11.12 shows the scale and the harmonic map of the Dorian mode.

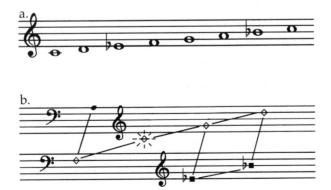

*Example 11.12*

The Dorian mode, curiously balanced among its harmonic qualities, has been historically pivotal in the development of Western music and is one of the most-used modes in the world. The central spine is complete. There is one overtonal third and two reciprocal thirds. The entire mode is shaded slightly toward the reciprocal or reflective side of the map, just as Mixolydian (with the difference of one note) is shaded slightly toward the overtonal or active side. The new note, E♭, leads by a half step to and from the adjacent Pythagorean D. The E♭ also makes an augmented fourth with A, which may feel unfamiliar in this position.

Traditionally in the West, modes whose third degrees are major are called "Major" and modes whose third degrees are minor are called "Minor." The first three modes on our list can therefore be thought of as Major; Dorian is the first of the three Minor modes we will consider. It is true, at least to our ears, that the change in energy from overtonal E to reciprocal, *ga*-blooded E♭ is some kind of threshold: Something crucial in us turns around or flips over.

During medieval times in Europe, before the era of keyboards, triadic harmony, or the musical forms derived from fifth-driven cadences, the Major mode—with its major triad on the dominant—was not the cultural standard of reference. The Dorian mode, with its delicate balance between overtonal and reciprocal energy, occupied the center of the harmonic aesthetic. D Dorian, to be precise. The note D had become, roughly, the central reference pitch. This is still true: D, not C. The strings of our modern orchestra are still tuned as shown in example 11.13.

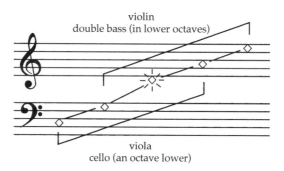

*Example 11.13*

Thanks to our Western harmonic hungers, we are biased toward the overtonal side of harmonic space, at least in our conceptual thought. But the Major mode itself is not central to harmonic space; Dorian is. And D Dorian is central, both to early music and to modern nomenclature. The Dorian mode in D is all "naturals," all white notes on the modern keyboard, which happens also to be topographically symmetrical around that note (check out the arrangement of white and black keys with D in the center.) It is easy to see how D is the center of our nomenclature: Go up four fifths and you meet the first sharp (F♯); go down four fifths and you meet the first flat (B♭). Same with a third up and a third down.

In the 1960s, when jazz had become extremely sophisticated harmonically, John Coltrane, Miles Davis, and others began to simplify its chains of modulating keys and improvise for long stretches in a single, embellished mode. Interestingly, their improvisational mode of choice was Dorian. Dorian is also a worldwide mode of prayer.

I am saying so much about Dorian, which sits in the middle of our list, because I want you to be able to hear it in a new way, with ears that are not entirely defined by history and culture. I think the secret power of music is in its bare sounds—that is why, with a couple of tunable strings at your disposal, and a voice, and some time to spend, you can discover so much of the true nature of music for yourself. My hunch is that the central position of the Dorian mode in music making is reflected by its central position in our psyche. But that hunch belongs to me. If you get a different impression, it is just as valid. And each person's valid impression may in fact be different. One truth common to everyone, though, is that the validity of a listening experience is a function of the quality of the listening.

## The Aeolian Mode

The scale and harmonic map of the Aeolian mode are shown in example 11.14.

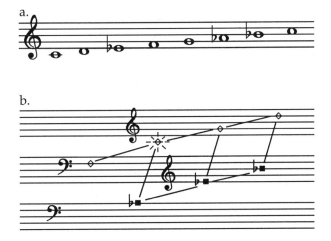

*Example 11.14*

The Aeolian mode is our usual reference for Minor. It contains a central spine of fifths and three reciprocal thirds. There are no overtonal *ga*'s, and the mode seems to have a kind of stability in the Minor realm that Ionian does in the Major realm. It is very familiar to our ears, and indeed, seems almost universal around the world. Notice the strong leading of the half step from A♭ to G, a force so ingrained in our ears that it is difficult for some of us to learn the Dorian mode, which differs from the Aeolian only in that its sixth is major.

Another characteristic sound is the mixing of the energies of A♭ and B♭, expressive reciprocal thirds that are whole-step neighbors melodically sandwiched between the dominant and the tonic. Like Mixolydian, this mode is a natural for improvisation; it seems intrinsically to encourage the shy. The reciprocal thirds are upward tending; they draw us up and out.

## The Phrygian Mode

The scale and harmonic map of the Phrygian mode are shown in example 11.15.

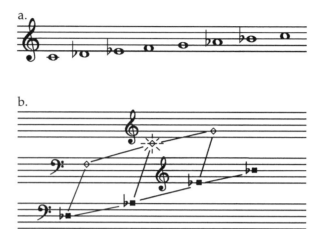

*Example 11.15*

This is perhaps the mode least familiar to our ears. The most overtonal note in the central spine, D, is now gone; it has been replaced by D♭, which completes the spine of reciprocal thirds. In Phrygian there is no overtonal *ga* blood, and only one pure overtonal fifth, G. Harmonically the subdominant is prominent, so this is about as reciprocal as music gets, a musical extreme (although, like most extremes, this one can be pushed farther—see chapter 26).

Notice how the four lower tones of the scale (C, D♭, E♭, F) have the same intervalic progression as the four upper tones (G, A♭, B♭, C): half, whole, whole. Both the tonic and the dominant are approached by half steps from above.

Although it takes people in our culture a while to feel comfortable with the Phrygian mode, it is well used and much adored in others, especially in Islamic and Hindu music. Our best strategy is to treat it like the exotic stranger it is, and build trust as we go along.

## Is This a Rainbow?

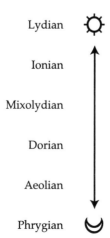

*Figure 11.1*

In singing over a drone from Lydian to Phrygian, one moves gradually from overtonal to reciprocal, from northeast to southwest, as well as—one might say—from sunny to moony. Figure 11.1 may be helpful.

Consider the central spine of all of these modes. By glancing through their harmonic maps it is clear that the central tones of the central spine—C and G—are always present. Only in the extremely overtonal Lydian is the reciprocal end of the spine, F, missing. Only in the extremely reciprocal Phrygian is the overtonal end of the spine, D, missing. Notice that as you progress down the list of modes, the tones in the overtonal spine of thirds disappear in order one by one, and the spine of reciprocal thirds gradually grows, until it has replaced the overtonal one. Notice especially how, in the middle four modes—framed on top by Ionian (Major) and on the bottom by Aeolian (Minor)—the central spine does not change. *What changes is the directionality of the thirds.* This is a crucial redefinition of Major and Minor, which we will take up again in chapter 13 and beyond.*

For now, the main thought is that the directionality of the thirds determines the mood. As you work your way down example 11.1 from Lydian to Phrygian, mode by mode, mood by mood, and then back up again from Phrygian to Lydian, you can sense yourself going through a spectrum of sensations, much as if you were riding back and forth through a rainbow. One might consider it a dream journey through the psyche that the singer/dreamer both responds to and controls. You choose and shape the mode, and the mood takes you. You strike a deal with the muse: Sing in tune and she will show you your own heart.

This is the time to get comfortable, set up your tonic-and-dominant drone as musically as possible, and improvise your way gradually from one modal extreme to the other and back again. Take all the time in the world. It is OK to spend an hour on one pass. Or, as you become more certain in your singing, you can make the full compass in a few eventful minutes. I like it both ways.

What about beginning with Phrygian, working your way up to Lydian, and then back down? Fine, but at your own risk—best to watch your feet as you walk away. Anything is fine. It doesn't matter how you learn these sounds and the relationships among them as long as you are singing, singing in tune, in tune and awake with the intention of knowing.

This is a perfect moment *not* to say, "Don't go on until you learn this." Any one mode is more than a life's work, so this is the work of more than six lives. Work until you gain some musical experience you can bring forward into the next pile of work. I hope you will be revisiting this place many times, and that singing in these modes will gradually become part of the narrative of your life.

---

*Although Alain Daniélou hinted at this new definition in 1943 in *Introduction to the Study of Musical Scales* (now known as *Music and the Power of Sound*—see list of sources), I think it was first spelled out in print in a 1962 report titled *Organization in Auditory Perception* by Boomsliter and Creel. Reading the report in 1972 was a thrilling moment of corroboration for me: I had come to the same conclusion entirely as a musician, and here before me was the scientific quantification. It was a good demonstration of how concepts are realized as they are needed not by an individual but as a collective tendency.

# 12

# Mixed Modes

THERE ARE THIRTY-TWO SEVEN-TONE MODES available from the lattice we have constructed. Of these, we have already considered six; before looking at the rest of them we need to adopt a flexible naming system.

## Naming the Tetrachords

The word *tetrachord*, from Greek, means literally "four strings," but in its broadest usage it refers to any four consecutive scale degrees. Thus the *lower tetrachord* of a scale refers to degrees one through four of the scale; the *upper tetrachord* refers to degrees five through eight. It is easier to divide a mode in half and name each half than it is to name every possible mode. We conventionally name our very own selves the same way for the same reason: We have both a given name and a surname.

When singing scales, and also when talking about them, we ordinarily begin at the bottom and proceed upward, of course. But when *naming* scales we say the upper tetrachord first and speak of it as being *over* the lower tetrachord. MA/MI is spoken "Major over Minor" and means "the top four notes of a Major scale over the bottom four notes of a Minor scale." If we were to demonstrate this scale, we would begin by ascending from the lower tonic, as shown in example 12.1. It's too bad about the confusion between directions but, fellow traveler, we sing up and we read down. The same problem was encountered in naming ratios.

*Example 12.1*

Notice that the brackets indicating the tetrachords are above the notes, whereas the brackets we have been using to indicate whole-tone groupings are below the notes. The tetrachord system of naming will clarify and become more complete as we go through the process of examining the modes one by one.

## Modes with Four Consecutive Whole Steps

Like the Lydian-through-Phrygian group of modes, the next group of modes contains only whole steps and half steps. In this group, however, four of the whole steps cluster together and one stands alone. Remember, we are looking at intervals—distances between pitches—not the pitches themselves. Consider the intervals of the mode in example 12.2.

*Example 12.2*

This mode appears in the conventional nomenclature as "the ascending Melodic Minor," so named even though the scale is liberally taken in both directions. In North Indian music as well as in contemporary Western uses it is not necessarily direction oriented. Jazz musicians in the 1990s call it "Jazz Minor." There are four modes with a similar whole-tone clustering within our lattice, listed in example 12.3.

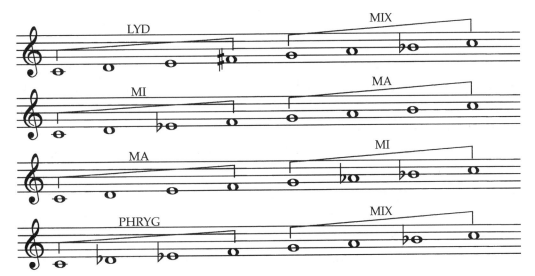

*Example 12.3*

We now consider them individually.

### Mixolydian over Lydian (MIX/LYD)

The MIX/LYD scale and its harmonic map are shown in example 12.4. The map reveals a new phenomenon: The upper spine has a gap in it. One of the vertebrae has migrated to the

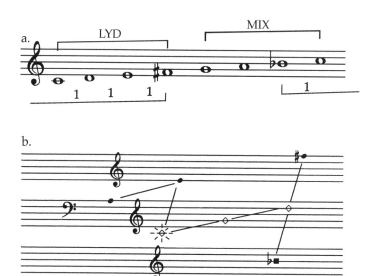

*Example 12.4*

lower spine. This new way of mixing overtonal and reciprocal thirds is characteristic of this group of modes. Notice that the tone D has a major third both above and below it. Notice also the diminished fourth from F♯ up to B♭.

This mode does not appear frequently in the world's music, the notable exception being in jazz, where, thanks to its amenable harmonic nature, it is extremely useful in modulation. Jazz musicians call it the "Lydian-dominant" mode because it is a cross between Lydian and the "dominant seventh" mode, which is a nickname for Mixolydian. More practically, it is called "sharp-four flat-seven" (or "aug-four minor-seven" more recently and more correctly). Phrases such as example 12.5 are typical in bebop.

*Example 12.5*

Indeed, jazz players usually cut their teeth by learning to improvise fluently in this mode in all twelve keys—a high-literacy stunt few jazz musicians have ever regretted.

## MAJOR OVER MINOR (MA/MIN)

Example 12.6 shows the MA/MIN scale and its harmonic map. In this mode the central spine is complete, but the third degree, now minor, has migrated to the lower spine. Even though we hear the mode as basically Minor (as we have mentioned), there is nonetheless a balanced mix of overtonal and reciprocal energy that gives its music a kind of rounded feeling. Notice that it is now the note G that has major thirds sprouting up as well as hanging

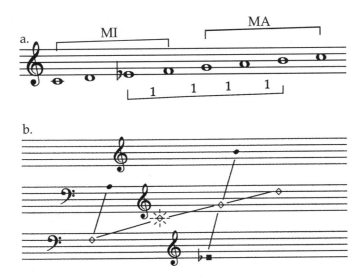

*Example 12.6*

down from it. The diminished fourth is from B up to E♭, giving fascinating melodic possibilities within this compass, shown in example 12.7.

The cluster of four whole tones spans from E♭ up to B, allowing the melodic sequence of major thirds shown in example 12.8. I don't like to play favorites, but I will report that this mode has been a deep source of music in my life. It generates gorgeous compositions in North Indian music, but is, apart from region or history or style, intrinsically generous. European classical music uses it only fleetingly, so when

*Example 12.7*

*Example 12.8*

you stay inside it for a long while the music seems familiar yet new. Every now and then I get to give a really hot tip, and now is one of those times: Check out this mode. It is a clear window into the pure resonances music is made from.

## MINOR OVER MAJOR (MIN/MA)

The MIN/MA scale and its harmonic map are shown in example 12.9. The central spine is complete. E, which has resumed its place on the upper spine, is now the lone overtonal third, and the gap appears in the lower spine. The mode sounds essentially Major to us, but with a strong mixture of Minor. Notice that it is C, the tonic itself, that supports a major third both above and below. Also notice how the tonic sits exactly in the middle of the cluster of four whole tones, with two above and two below; this probably tends to smooth out melodic tension. The diminished fourth is now from E up to A♭, and very juicy in that position. When you sing it, be sure, as usual, to keep the major third mellow and the minor sixth bright: Don't let the E creep high and the A♭ creep low, that is, melodically toward each other.

Although this mode also occurs fleetingly in classical music, it does not seem to be much

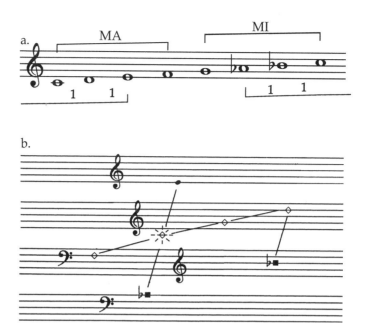

**Example 12.9**

used worldwide. Yet I find it a great comfort to the singer, compositionally friendly, and an accessible mixture of the homey and the exotic.

## MIXOLYDIAN OVER PHRYGIAN (MIX/PHRYG)

Example 12.10 shows the MIX/PHRYG scale and its harmonic map.

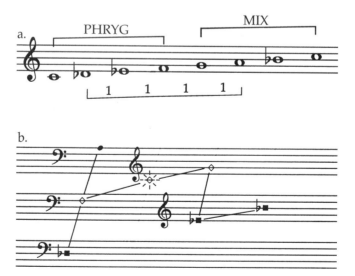

**Example 12.10**

I call the last of this group of modes Dark Horse because even though it is strange to the point of seeming alien, it contains winning possibilities when you learn to handle it. Dark Horse has only one pure overtone: the dominant, G; the tone that supports a major third both above and below is the subdominant, F. It is identical to Phrygian but for the major sixth, which makes it doubly difficult for us to hear. Although you will most probably find the tonal combinations unfamiliar, it is still part of our five-limit lattice of twelve notes, and well within the experiences of resonance we have undergone so far. I've rarely heard Dark Horse performed in this tuning—which doesn't mean it isn't alive and thriving somewhere. You can save it for a rainy day, or let it graze on you occasionally if it gets hungry. The nature of a dark horse is to appear unexpectedly.

## Modes with Five Consecutive Whole Steps

There remains an additional group of modes consisting of only half steps and whole steps. In this group all five whole steps cluster together. If we continue to keep the tonic and the dominant fixed—as we must inside our lattice of twelve notes—there are only two modes that arise within this definition.

The first is *Minor over Lydian*, written MIN/LYD. The scale and its harmonic map are shown in example 12.11.

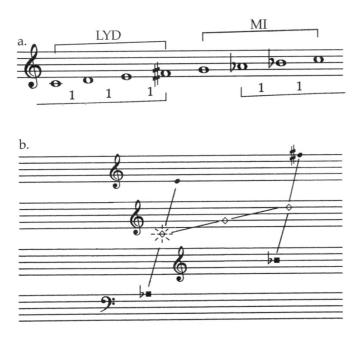

*Example 12.11*

The harmonic symmetry of the map (around G) is amazing. Both upper and lower spines have gaps. Now both C *and* D have major thirds above and below. But melodically, aside from the two half steps, which cling to G, everywhere you sing is whole steps, and that seems to place an uncanny constraint upon the ear. One way of approaching the problem is to sing within only one tetrachord at a time, folding each tetrachord into the other cautiously, note by note.

The other mode of this group is *Major over Phrygian*, written MA/PHRYG. The scale and its harmonic map are shown in example 12.12.

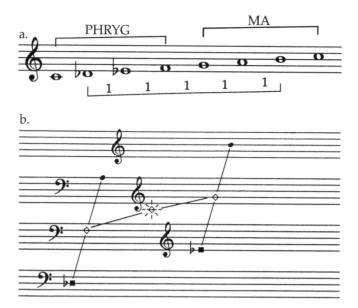

*Example 12.12*

In this case the harmonic symmetry is positioned around C itself. Also, the half steps surround C. Now the whole steps span from the second degree, D♭, all the way up to the seventh degree, B, giving the singer a most bizarre task. Yet once again the problem can be ameliorated by proceeding one tetrachord at a time while seeking serendipitous introductions across borders. I've never heard either of these two modes performed in dronal music, although they both have benign harmonic results (especially in equal temperament, discussed in chapter 24). At this point you could consider them instructive oddities. On the other hand, one never knows for certain where one might find a friend.

## Modes Containing Augmented Seconds

Within our lattice there are no more modes consisting of only half steps and whole steps—we have "exhausted the possibilities," to use Arnold Schoenberg's oft-quoted phrase. There are, however, twenty (!) more modes available in the lattice, each containing at least one augmented second. Some of these modes are extremely useful musically, others quite marginally so—or at least, they are seldom used. Although we will not examine each one of them in detail, I would like to present a practical framework within which these modes, as well as all seven-tone modes in general, can be considered. First, however, let's look at the augmented seconds available in our lattice and familiarize ourselves with the properties of this new interval. The three possibilities are shown in example 12.13. Example 12.14 shows their harmonic maps.

*Example 12.13*

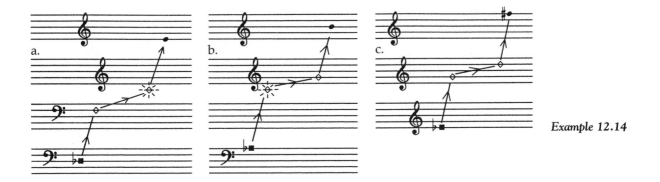

*Example 12.14*

The harmonic path for each augmented second, shown in figure 12.1, is a third up plus a fifth up plus another third up, or a total of one fifth up plus two thirds up. Augmented seconds have a tainted reputation in the Western mind. The usual reason given for their ban in pre-nineteenth-century polyphony is that the extra distance between scale degrees interrupts the melodic flow or in some other way unduly calls attention to itself. But it may also be, since the augmented second was—and is—an extremely evocative interval typical of non-European (specifically Middle Eastern and Asian) music and does not appear in the lexicon of church modes, that the ban may have functioned as an unspoken social and racial boundary, a code for identifying us and them. In the nineteenth century, when association with ethnic roots came to be viewed in a more positive light, augmented seconds began to creep into the music of Chopin, Smetana, and other Eastern European composers. But they still sound foreign to most of us unless we grew up in the Bulgarian countryside, or in Cairo, or Calcutta, or attended a shul in Brooklyn.

*Figure 12.1*

Augmented seconds are not to be avoided. They present, in the form of adjacent scale steps, a harmonic path between reciprocal and overtonal thirds, which means they are emotionally juicy and can be musically nourishing.

Here are some modes with augmented seconds in them.

## HARMONIC MINOR

Harmonic minor is taught in classical European theory not as a scale to be ordinarily used in its own right, but as the scalar residue of the harmonic cadence most characteristic of the Minor mode (example 12.15). The tones in that cadence, arranged in scalar order, are shown in example 12.16.

*Example 12.15*

*Example 12.16*

Apart from the circumstances of its common name, however, the melodic use of this mode over a drone can be exceedingly powerful.

## HARMONIC MINOR OVER MINOR LYDIAN (HAR.MIN/MIN.LYD)

This mode, sometimes called "Gypsy Minor," has two augmented seconds, as shown in example 12.17.

*Example 12.17*

Notice the diminished third from F♯ up to A♭. The mode has many surprising uses and I have found it to be pleasingly addictive.

## MINOR OVER PHRYGIAN MAJOR (MI/PHRYG.MA)

The MIN/PHRYG.MA mode, common in Spanish music and essential to Flamenco music, is shown in example 12.18. It probably found its way to Europe from the Middle East and Asia.

*Example 12.18*

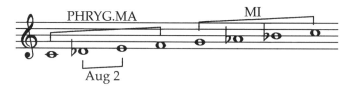

## HARMONIC MINOR OVER PHRYGIAN MAJOR (HAR.MI/PHRYG.MA)

The HAR.MI/PHRYG.MA mode, which also contains two augmented seconds, is shown in example 12.19.

*Example 12.19*

In India it is called *Bairov* and is widely used to express profound feeling. Notice that the upper tetrachord (HAR.MI) and the lower tetrachord (PHRYG.MA) have the same intervalic content, but differ in their function, that is, where they occur in the scale.

## HARMONIC MINOR OVER PHRYGIAN LYDIAN (HAR.MI/PHRYG.LYD)

The HAR.MI/PHRYG.LYD mode is shown in example 12.20.

*Example 12.20*

This mode looks a bit crazy to us, but in Indian music, where it is called *Todi* (and has various subtle tunings), it is a specialty, a kind of connoisseur's mode made all the more incomprehensible by the virtual omission, in practice, of the fifth degree, G, especially in ascending phrases. I once complained to my teacher, Pandit Pran Nath, that I was having trouble singing even the scale in tune, much less the music that comes from it. "It is difficult in India," he said, which made me feel, actually, much better.

## The Remaining Possibilities

It is possible to list methodically all thirty-two modes available in our lattice of twelve notes, but instead, let me demonstrate an organization that allows them all to be seen at a glance.

Since C and G are fixed, there are only four possible upper tetrachords, as shown in example 12.21.

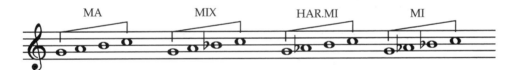

*Example 12.21*

As for the lower tetrachord, let's pretend for the moment that F also is fixed—F♯ does not exist for now. In that case, the lower tetrachord also has only four possibilities, as shown in example 12.22.

*Example 12.22*

Now substituting F♯ for F, we will run those four possibilities again, as shown in example 12.23.

*Example 12.23\**

*Was there ever a tetrachord begging for a better name?

By means of the arrangement of tetrachords shown in example 12.24, the full range of combinations can be seen.

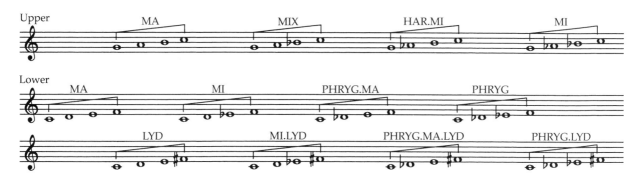

*Example 12.24*

Here is how to use the arrangement: Choose any lower tetrachord, then combine it in turn with each of the four upper tetrachords. For instance, beginning with the MA lower tetrachord, we get MA/MA (which is simply Major, of course); MIX/MA (which is Mixolydian); HAR.MI/MA; and MI/MA. Then go through the same process for the MI lower tetrachord, and so on until you have gone through all eight lower tetrachords.

Why do this? To satisfy curiosity is one good reason. The possibility of uncovering a sleeper mode is another good reason. But for me the reason is that it gives a good general model for the construction of most seven-tone modes and, as we proceed onward to equal temperament, it becomes a powerful model indeed—an excellent way to keep your bearings when modes begin to modulate. (Chapter 40 is devoted to the mechanics of modal modulation in equal temperament.)

Meanwhile, having looked at every mode generated by the five-limit lattice of twelve notes, we have, so to speak, covered that field. There is such a wealth of potential music in this material that we need to pause from constructing maps and charts and mental models. It's time to gather up this information and carry it inside the house to our private room and sit quietly with the sound of it all for a while without being too distracted by the gossip of the intellect.

# 13

# INTERNALIZING THE LATTICE

## Tell Me Again Why I Should Do All This Singing

It is unlikely that—at least up to now—you have dedicated your life to singing over a drone. We are not a culture of North Indian singers. (Neither is North India anymore—the up-and-coming young bloods want to write film scores.) It is true that our jazz and country and pop singers often sing quite beautifully in tune above and beyond, so to speak, their equal-tempered accompaniments. With my own ears I have, from time to time, heard American opera and art song vocalists sing in tune. Generally speaking, however, we are not a population of singers who want to know, systematically and intellectually, what we are doing. So when I ask you to be calm and sing in tune and know precisely where you are both melodically and harmonically, I am asking you to go against culture.

Does this mean that there could be something lost or forgotten in the culture that we can help to replace? Yes, it does. Singing in tune is the central experience that fully realizes tonality in us, and since the dawn of the age of the fretboard and the keyboard that realization has lost its edge. I think Europe in the fourteenth century was very much in tune, as in tune as the tribal Africa of today or the classical India that still survives, and careful readings and excellent contemporary performances of the works of Machaut and Landini and Ciconia corroborate this. But in America especially that sensibility has, over the centuries, drained away. The music of the folk, by which I mean us bebop heads and country music lovers, tends to react against this trend: Good singers and players of every style strive to be in tune, of course. But the battle against prevailing standards is uphill. If the inherently pure harmony that is lost to us—that lost causality, one might say—is ever to be reclaimed, each one of us has to claim it individually for herself or himself. It would not be the first time that musicians have led culture.

I'm not saying that other cultures historically have learned to sing in tune by singing consciously over a drone. Some have, some haven't. What I'm saying is that with a couple of tunable strings and some time to burn you can teach yourself what the culture does not know how to teach you. This is the work that must be done to fully comprehend (as opposed to simply use) the tools of modern music making. It is what I am asking you to consider, and it is a consideration not only for yourself. By singing a tone in tune, you tune your room and your family and your neighborhood. It is not otherworldly that this is so. You place the energy of your sound into *this* world, and this world's energy does not die; instead, it transforms. And whatever it transforms into carries with it forever the history of your good intentions.

Here are some practical considerations that may help you with the process of singing in tune.

## Vibrato

One can sing with or without vibrato. In cultures where in-tune singing is primary, the singing voice is essentially straight, with vibrato used deliberately for ornamental and evocative purposes. The situation in the West is quite different. By the nineteenth century cities had swollen, concert halls had grown proportionately, and the operatic voice that could rise above the orchestra to the farthest seat of the highest balcony had become the aesthetic paradigm. Singing became equated with aural and emotional power, gut driven and gut minded. From the powerful muscles of the diaphragm can arise a vibrato so wide—often a whole tone or more—that the center of pitch easily becomes unfocused. The resulting sound is often glorious, but refinement of pitch is rare.

Some singers raised on the Western operatic model fear that they will lose power—not just volume, but emotional and psychic power—if they lessen their vibrato. Yet all you have to do is listen to the truly powerful singers of Africa and India and Bulgaria to see how provincial that view is. You need not lose your power by singing without vibrato. The same process that gives a singer an open sound also gives sovereignty over vibrato. Once you know you are in tune, once you feel that, then you can use vibrato intentionally as a beautiful, conscious refinement. Vibrato used in such a manner typically looks like figure 13.1.*

*Figure 13.1*

## Double Think

This is a reminder about the separate yet interpenetrating realms of melody and harmony. The fact that harmonic and melodic sensibilities are both disjunct and conjoined is hard to learn and easy to forget. You do not need to be intellectually aware of this with every note you sing, of course; that would take you too far from the action. But as an occasional, delib-

*A few great singers who use vibrato exquisitely: Billie Holliday, Emma Kirkby, Dietrich Fischer-Dieskau.

erate reminder of the interpenetration of realms, it is good, with a lattice map before you, to sing simply in *sargam* while your eye travels from note to note within the harmonic grid (as introduced in chapter 10).

## Between the Notes

People who read music, especially keyboard players, are conditioned to suppose that music consists of a series of points in space, and that to make a melody we proceed directly from point to point. This model has something in common with the kid's comic-page game of Connect the Dots: You connect numbered dots with straight lines to produce an image. The straight lines themselves have no shape; only what they connect has shape. In the sounds produced by keyboards, keyed woodwinds, fretboards, and valved brass, the fixed-pitch model engendered by our notation is carried forward into a culture of Connect-the-Dots music.

Most of the rest of the world's music neither proceeds from nor is communicated by notation—at least not a notation as sophisticated as ours. Rather, it passes aurally from musician to musician, parent to child, mouth to mouth, heart to heart. The tones of such music are not so much dots as they are shapes in and of themselves, impatiently alive and wriggling. They are drawn with a wide palette of curves and angles and textures in thin and bold strokes, and the meaning of the music is given at least as much by these shapes as by the dots they connect.

Furthermore, if we perceive the tones of a melody as their harmonic essences, as states of resonance, then the shapings of the notes become journeys from one feeling state to another. The ride becomes as important as the destination. Since, in just intonation, the destination is a discrete absolute, the singer can continuously contrast the fleeting adventures of the journey with the certainty of the outcome. This lends even "simple" melodies a dramatic, emotionally redolent context that becomes the through line of the music, the plot of the story. As Pandit Pran Nath used to say, "The music is between the notes."

In Western classical singing, the art of connecting notes is called *portamento*; it is used both evocatively and decoratively. In North Indian music it is called *meend* and is cultivated not only to deepen the sensibilities of the singer but also to strengthen and refine the voice. Let me suggest a basic *portamento*, or *meend*, practice that can raise the singing of lattice melodies to a new plateau of musical possibility.

The basic trick is to use the name of a note while moving it around. For example, sing the pitch *ga* using the syllable "ga" in the usual straightforward manner; then slide slowly up through the half step to *ma*; then, a moment after you arrive at the perfect fourth, articulate "ma," as shown in figure 13.2.

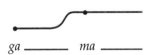

*ga* _____ *ma* _____    *Figure 13.2*

A melodic sequence can be made of this. An ascending version can be seen in figure

13.3, and example 13.1, which shows both graphic and staff notation.

*Figure 13.3*

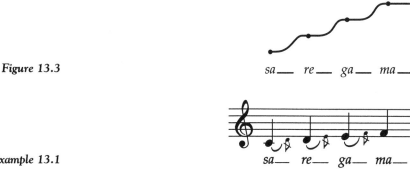

*Example 13.1*

Figure 13.4 and example 13.2 show the descending version.

*Figure 13.4*

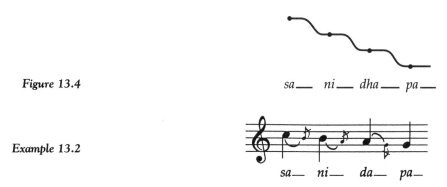

*Example 13.2*

The various dimensions of the *meend* are yours to shape: the slope of the line, the amount of time spent on the old note before leaving it; the amount of time spent on the new note before naming it, the dynamics, the vowel shapes, and so on.

Some hints:

- Be sure the resting places are really in tune.
- Smooth the slope. Imagining a smooth curve helps.
- Try various speeds, but be sure you understand slow-motion *meend*. The more time you hang out between notes, the more you will learn.

There are four basic kinds of *meend,* shown in figure 13.5 and example 13.3. All four are beautiful and have appropriate uses. Experiment with one at a time slowly, as if each were a new friend whom you will get to know gradually over the years.

We have examined *meend* using only steps, but thirds, fourths, and even larger leaps, including octaves, are common. These will most naturally come into your singing once the stepwise versions are familiar.

*Meend* vivifies melodies, making them sanguine and glossy and velvety by turns, saturating them with feeling. Even a small dose of this practice can significantly change the way you listen to music, especially sung music, by opening up the deep world that lies underneath the surface. The compelling melodic subtext that was always there—perhaps even in your own music—will seem lit from the inside.

Figure 13.5                                                              *Example 13.3*

## The Territory

Our work so far has been confined to twelve specifically tuned tones sounded against a drone, and we have tried to articulate, in various ways, the harmonic experiences that result. We have described the hearts of triple and pentamerous nature and traced how our responses are the architects of a coherent system of modes. To locate the coordinates of our responses, we have made a map for the eye and explored its many roads, using the vocabulary of map reading: north, south, east, and west. To maximize the connection to real music in real time we have employed musical notation and observed the appearance of sharps (one so far) and flats (four). For the sake of certainty, we have quantified our experiences with numbers, pinning down the tones by means of their ratios like so many chloroformed butterflies. To further describe an ordered spectrum of responses we have used such archetypical symbols as sun and moon, or such archetypical characters as mothers and cowboys, and an array of sensual metaphors like bright and easy and velvety. Finally, we have hinted at the notion that harmony is some kind of inner real estate, a landscape through which, perhaps like oxen, perhaps like mermaids, or even like falcons, we draw and navigate and fly our music.

As you spend time improvising dronal music, I hope that your curiosity about this last subject will emerge. What is harmonic territory the territory *of?* Is it the territory of the inner ear? Or the mind, or the brain? Or the heart, or the psyche? Or somehow all of these?

The answer is, of course, that even if it proves impossible to describe, it is nevertheless *your* territory and is eminently possible to explore. A true musician knows the inner ground.

Singing is the royal road to this inner land. Once inside, you become the mapmaker. You name the canyons and ranges, the hidden valleys, the underground rivers, the unnameable. The most amazing thing is that your map seems to be more or less identical to mine. That's why music connects individuals, communities, cultures, maybe someday a global population: We are more the same than different. And yet, *vive la différence*. Without it, music, like evolution, would be long gone.

In any case, sing, sing, sing. Let the lattice be your guide until, like a good guide, it becomes invisible against the scenery.

## Singing Practice

You can't learn everything right away, but you can expect to form good habits, which means, basically, practicing regularly and staying awake. However long your practice sessions, I suggest you spend most of the time using *sargam* and the rest of the time using open vowels—*ah* mostly—or any syllables that bear repetition or accrue power through repetition. It is good to have favorite modes that you learn well; you don't have to learn more than a few to cover most of the ground. For instance, Lydian and Phrygian between them take in all twelve notes. Try composing melodies in your favorite modes, learning them with appropriate *meend*, and then using these as departure points for improvisation.

The results of singing practice come on quickly. You can expect your ear to improve, with better pitch and greater certainty. You gain musical authority. And you learn, too, about your own musical behavior, including both the denial and acceptance of your innate gifts. And last but not least, you set the stage for what is to come: an understanding of the entire range of harmonic experience in twelve-tone equal temperament.

# 14

# NUMBERS AND MYSTERIES

## Ratios of the Twelve Lattice Tones to Tonic

Just as familiarity with skeletal structure can help an athlete, so familiarity with ratios can help a musician. Ratios Xray the skeleton of music, revealing the structure behind its motions. Let's take some time to clarify what has already been said about ratios and then proceed a little farther. First we will revisit "octave reduction."

A ratio (3:2) operates enough like a fraction ($\frac{3}{2}$) that we may substitute one form for the other when talking about music. We have already seen that the point of octave reduction is to place all relationships within the compass of an octave, that is, between a given tonic, which we call 1, and its octave, 2:1. Since 2:1 as a fraction equals $\frac{2}{1}$, or simply 2, we can now redefine the purpose of octave reduction as follows: We want the numbers to be greater than 1 and less than 2. In other words, the value of all our ratios expressed as fractions must lie between 1 and 2. To accomplish this we simply double either the numerator or the denominator a sufficient number of times, as our examples will soon demonstrate.

A simple process for finding the ratio that corresponds to the harmonic relationship of a scale tone to its tonic is as follows: Let a given tonic (C, for the time being) be known as 1. Track the harmonic path of the scale tone on the lattice. Each time you go up by a fifth, multiply times 3—that is, place 3 in the numerator. Each time you go up a third, multiply times 5—that is, place 5 in the numerator. Each time you go down a fifth, divide by 3—that is, place 3 in the denominator. Each time you go down by a third, divide by 5, placing 5 in the denominator. The resulting fraction indicates the harmonic relationship of the two tones. If the fraction is greater than 1 but less than 2, the second tone lies within the compass of an octave above the tonic. But if the fraction is less than 1 or greater than 2, we need to octave-reduce by halving or doubling the numerator or the denominator a sufficient number of times until the fraction lies between 1 and 2. That new number is the ratio of the two tones within an octave, with the tonic represented by the denominator and the scale tone by the numerator. It is musically helpful to realize that the ratio is not an abstraction floating in the mind. It quantifies actual physical stuff: how many times the upper tone is vibrating (in a given period) in respect to the lower tone. (Remember "$x$ of these per $y$ of those" in chapter 2?)

For example, here are the twelve tones of the lattice, each expressed as a ratio with C. Let's begin with the central spine.

C with itself is 1:1.

G is up a fifth, or $\frac{3}{1}$, octave-reduced to $\frac{3}{2}$, or 3:2. We say "G is 3:2" meaning "G is to C (a fifth down) as 3 is to 2."

D is up two fifths, or $\frac{3\times3}{1}$, or $\frac{9}{1}$, octave-reduced to $\frac{9}{2}$ to $\frac{9}{4}$ to $\frac{9}{8}$, or 9:8. D is to C (a major second down) as 9 is to 8, or 9:8.

F is down a fifth, or $\frac{1}{3}$, octave-reduced—or perhaps here we ought to say octave-*expanded*, since the fraction is being brought up from less than 1 to more than 1—from $\frac{1}{3}$ to $\frac{2}{3}$ to $\frac{4}{3}$—thus bringing the F up to a perfect fourth above C, or 4:3. F down to C is 4:3.

Now for the spine of overtonal thirds.

E is up a third, or $\frac{5}{1}$, octave-reduced to $\frac{5}{2}$ to $\frac{5}{4}$, or 5:4. E down to C is 5:4.

A is up a third and down a fifth, or $\frac{5}{3}$, or 5:3. A down to C is 5:3.

B is up a fifth and up a third, or $\frac{3\times5}{1}$, or $\frac{15}{1}$, octave-reduced to $\frac{15}{2}$ to $\frac{15}{4}$ to $\frac{15}{8}$, or 15:8. B down to C is 15:8.

F♯ is two fifths up and a third up, or $\frac{3\times3\times5}{1}$, or $\frac{45}{1}$, octave-reduced to $\frac{45}{2}$ to $\frac{45}{4}$ to $\frac{45}{8}$ to $\frac{45}{16}$ to $\frac{45}{32}$, or 45:32. F♯ down to C is 45:32.

And finally, the spine of reciprocal thirds.

A♭ is down a third, or $\frac{1}{5}$, octave-expanded to $\frac{2}{5}$ to $\frac{4}{5}$ to $\frac{8}{5}$, or 8:5. A♭ down to C is 8:5.

D♭ is down a fifth and down a third, or $\frac{1}{3\times5}$, or $\frac{1}{15}$, octave-expanded to $\frac{2}{15}$ to $\frac{4}{15}$ to $\frac{8}{15}$ to $\frac{16}{15}$, or 16:15. D♭ down to C is 16:15.

E♭ is up a fifth and down a third, or $\frac{3}{5}$, octave-expanded to $\frac{6}{5}$ or 6:5. E♭ down to C is 6:5.

B♭ is up two fifths and down a third, or $\frac{3\times3}{5}$ or $\frac{9}{5}$, or 9:5. B♭ down to C is 9:5.

Example 14.1 shows the ratios in respect to C of each of the tones of the lattice, arranged in descending order.

2 : 1    15 : 8    9 : 5    5 : 3    8 : 5    3 : 2    45 : 32    4 : 3    5 : 4    6 : 5    9 : 8    16 : 15    1 : 1

*Example 14.1*

## Ratios of the Tones to One Another

So far, we have been discussing the ratios of various tones with C, the generating tone of our lattice. But once that procedure has been learned, the ratio between any two tones on the lattice can be easily perceived. In chapter 8 we noticed variations among sizes of certain intervals: two kinds of whole tone, for instance. The major whole tone comprises any two tones distant by two fifths (and octave-reduced). The path will always look like figure 14.1 and the ratio will always be 9:8.

The minor whole tone comprises any two tones distant from one another by two fifths down and a third up; the harmonic path will always look like figure 14.2 and the ratio will always be 10:9. Any pure minor third will be a fifth up and a third down, will look like figure 14.3, and will be 6:5.

Likewise, any Pythagorean minor third will be three fifths down, will look like figure 14.4, and will be $\frac{1}{3 \times 3 \times 3}$, octave-expanded to $\frac{32}{27}$, or 32:27. Any two tones a major third apart will look like figure 14.5 and be 5:4, of course.

But there is another kind of major third that is not yet on the lattice. It is derived from four perfect fifths up, will look like figure 14.6, and be $\frac{3 \times 3 \times 3 \times 3}{1}$, octave-reduced to 81:64. This is called the Pythagorean major third and will soon become important to our work.

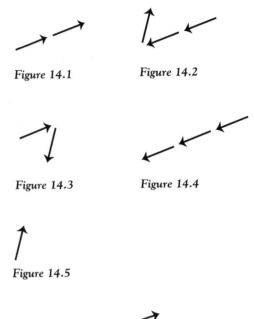

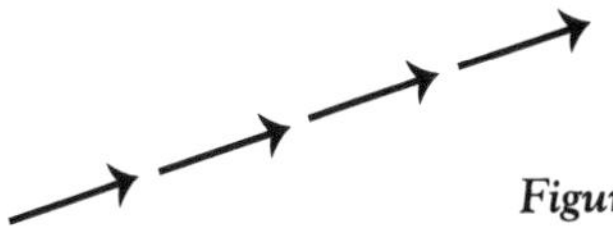

*Figure 14.1*   *Figure 14.2*

*Figure 14.3*   *Figure 14.4*

*Figure 14.5*

*Figure 14.6*

## Why Are There Seven Tones in a Scale?

I have been harping on the musical benefits that accrue to those fluent in ratio-speak. I would like to amplify this by raising what may seem at first to be a tangential question: Why are there seven tones in our scales?

Two ready answers are: (1) even though many theories have been put forth, no one actually knows; and (2) there aren't necessarily seven. I often put the question to other musicians, especially composers, in order to sound out their thinking. This morning I asked my student Marie, a gifted pianist and a promising composer, why there are seven tones in our scales. "Because there are seven planets," she said.

"I thought there were nine," I replied.

"Those two don't count."

"OK, let's include seven heavens and seven days of the week. Maybe seven is just an inherently attractive number, and the same quality that makes it attractive to an astrologer or a philosopher also makes it useful to a musician. But that doesn't answer my *why*: Why are there seven tones?"

"When we've both died and we're *on* the seventh planet, then you'll get it."

I laughed. She's right, of course. But that doesn't help me now.

The most usual musical explanation is the Pythagorean one, which states that seven tones come naturally from the spine of fifths. If you begin with the tone F and go up by fifths you will get F–C–G–D–A–E–B. Octave-reduced and beginning on C, these make a seven-tone scale with amazing properties. There are, for instance, only two kinds of scale steps: 9:8 whole steps and 256:243 half steps. (Remember, this way of deriving the scale is different from what we've been practicing so far in this book.) Also, the upper tetrachord is an exact transposition of the lower. This scale (and other three-limit scales derived by octave-reduced triplings only) have been theoretical favorites ever since the dawn of music theory, possibly because of the conceptually attractive procedure of deriving an entire musical language from the lowest, hence purest, generative prime. But the objection to the theory that the three-limit, Pythagorean system generates seven tones is that, when you allow five-limit or seven-limit systems into the mix, the resulting seven-tone scales are just as convincing. So even though the problem has a specific and elegant Pythagorean elaboration, it doesn't have a general Pythagorean solution. We still need an answer that covers all cases, including our own extra-Pythagorean music.

The present discussion has been framed by a question about "our" music of seven tones, but it may be timely to point out that much of the music of the present world, and most of the music of the historical world, is pentatonic—that is, made up of five-tone scales. Even at this late date, five-tone music probably covers just as much surface area of the globe as seven-tone music. Many Western trained musicians, with a kind of musical colonialism, think that five-tone scales are just seven-tone scales with two tones missing—a primitive version of their own more highly evolved modes. But when you listen openly to true pentatonic music, each mode creates a complete universe. Some of the most intricate and challenging of the North Indian *ragas*, for instance, are pentatonic. The complex rhythmic structures of African music are supported by pentatonic scales. The Balinese have invented unique pentatonic tunings that permanently alter the mind. Love songs to man and god are driven to the limits of the psyche in five tones over half the world. We haven't said much in this book about pentatonic scales because our central question involves the behavior of tonal harmony in twelve-tone equal temperament, a harmony that is essentially heptatonic and triadic. But the subject is ancient, vast, and fascinating.

And what about six-tone scales? And eight- and nine-tone scales? They all exist. These considerations all combine to reinforce the mystery of why seven-tone scales sound so right to us. Now let's ask an even tougher question.

## What Is a Degree?

The issue may be further focused by asking, What is a degree? A rung of a ladder is easy to find: It is where your full body weight is supported, where your foot comes to rest, where it stops falling, where it belongs. There are a given number of rungs in a ladder. Are there a given number of places where your voice stops?

As a young child I was slow at developing pitch sense. I remember being in nursery school (age four) and having a hard time keeping up with the singing of the class—sometimes the sounds simply didn't make sense. One day when I was absent, the teacher taught the class "Eensy Weensy Spider" (replete with the finger dance), which, lest ye forget, goes like example 14.2.

*Example 14.2*

The next day, the whole class knew "Eensy Weensy Spider" and I did not. "You just listen," said the teacher, and I did, apprehensively. Later, during recess, I found myself at the drinking fountain alone and unwatched, and I performed the finger dance of "Eensy Weensy Spider" on the real fountain spout while singing the tune, which, to my surprise, I remembered. The instant is acrylic in my memory: I am standing at the little kids' fountain; its worn brass spout is glistening in the sun. I am transfixed by the clarity of the melody I have just heard myself singing. Without moving my eyes from the dazzle of the sun on the spout, I hear wordlessly in my mind's ear:

*Example 14.3*

The tones in my mind are blazing horizontal lines, perfectly positioned. "There are three *places*," I think, and hear the melody again. "Three places for my voice to go," and the whole playground is lit gold with my happiness. That was the moment I discovered degree, and over the years I have accepted seven as the magic number of them, along with the rest of us. After fifty years of singing scales, however, including twenty-five of *raga*, the magic number has begun to wobble. The Indian construct is, like ours, seven tones, but there are circumstances in *raga* where the seven-tone condition evaporates. In many *ragas* the augmented prime—C♯ to C (specifically, 25:24)—is a scale tone called *re*; that is, it is treated as though it were the second scale degree. But correctly named according to its harmonic nature, that tone is truly C♯, a "chromatic" version of the tonic. Likewise the augmented fifth, G♯ (25:16). (These tones are discussed in detail in chapter 16.) Since C and G themselves never go away, we now have seven degrees according to the *sargam* but, according to the harmony, only five different letter names plus two chromatic pairs. The technical reason for this is that the letter names are generated by a three-limit system, and their utility becomes compromised in the pentamerous dimension, which, of course, we use often and liberally. So the concept of seven tones appears to spring leaks, especially beyond the confines of the Pythagorean system. If you can't trust the seven-degree construct, you can't trust any of the nomenclatures that are derived from it. So, back to square one: What is the principle behind seven tones?

All we can say, I believe, is that most of Earth's music is in either five or seven tones, that heptatonicism seems to be a most useful convention even if it leaks, and that there doesn't seem to be a general theory (not even mine) to account for our responses.

## Terminology Check

In light of our present knowledge and ignorance, then, let's review the names we use to identify our place in musical space.

1. *Letter names* (A, B, C) specify notes but imprison you in the seven construct; when you run out of letters you have to begin again using sharps or flats.

2. *Degree names* (tonic, supertonic, etc.) ascribe diatonic function—that is, the character of the work done, or the niche occupied—to a degree (e.g. "dominant"). But, as we have already mentioned (chapter 7), these names are inconsistent and, of course, limited to the seven construct they describe.

3. *Intervalic names* (unison, second, third, etc.) measure the number of scale degrees between two tones, but their usefulness ends there. They are limited by the seven construct, and they do not take into account the harmonic generation of tones. The problem isn't their limitation but their overuse. When you measure musical meaning by linear names, the greater, harmonic dimension becomes obscured. Overuse of intervalic names is a direct result of the loss of harmonic understanding in our music making and teaching.

4. *Interval modifiers* (perfect, major, minor, augmented, and diminished) are adjectives that modify interval names. *Perfect* hints at harmonic derivation (perfect intervals are three-limit only: primes, octaves, fifths, and fourths); otherwise *major* and *augmented* simply mean "the large (or larger) kind" and *minor* and *diminished* mean "the small (or smaller) kind" of scale distance.

5. *Ratios* are the only absolute and precise names for relationships between tones. They ascribe no diatonic function; in fact, they avoid any scale construct whatsoever. Furthermore, they code for the generating tone: Factoring reveals the harmonic path from the source. But sometimes they have too much detail and become rapidly unwieldy when tracking the relationship of melodic tones to one another (rather than to the tonic). Also, the farther away from the tonic you get, the larger and less decipherable the numbers become. Finally, although all the above names break down sooner or later in equal temperament, ratios, thanks to their precision, break down soonest (as we shall see).

6. *Solfege* and *sargam* syllables, although based on the seven construct, are geared
   toward making that construct automatic while concentrating on pure sound,
   and thus are welcome to the singer. One could, however, devise a system of syllables based on ratio alone. 10:9 could be *ri*, 9:8 could be *ray*, and 8:7 could be
   *ru*.*

## Treating Names as If They Were True

There are many ways of making ladders—not too many rungs, not too few, with the rungs
not too close together and not too far apart. There are likewise many ways of making scales;
the seven-tone model, although obviously not the only one, is nevertheless extremely useful. For now it is to our advantage to treat the naming systems that arise from the seven-tone
scale as if they were true. But we must remember that they are not quite true. It is crucial to
understand the limitations of the names we use. The half truth of a construct in the mind
can actually close our ears to the truth of a sound in the air. Incomplete or false constructs
may lead us away from the subtlety we seek. Eventually, thanks to our enhanced harmonic
experiences and our nimbleness with ratios, we will indeed witness the borders of the heptatonic system becoming permeable, but from now on we will have been forewarned, and
prepared for imminent wobbles and collapses. We will understand and adjust. Meanwhile,
we will opportunistically make some practical musical distinctions based on the seven-tone
model. These distinctions are the focus of the next chapter.

*I would not be startled to learn that, unbeknownst to me, such a scheme has already been devised.

# 15

# CHROMATIC PAIRS

## Diatonic versus Chromatic Half Steps

There are two kinds of half steps in our twelve-note lattice. One kind has adjacent letter names, for instance, E to F, F♯ to G, G to A♭. These are called, in a broad use of the term, *diatonic*, meaning that they proceed from one scale degree to the next. The other kind of half step is spelled with same-letter names, for instance E♭ to E♮, A♭ to A♮, F♮ to F♯. These are generally called *chromatic*, meaning that the scale degree does not change even though its position is adjusted. The ladder-and-rung model of chapter 14 will be useful again here. Let seven rungs of a ladder correspond to the seven diatonic degrees of a scale. Rungs one and five are fixed in position, but the other five rungs each have a high notch and a low notch. There are thirty-two possible rung arrangements (corresponding to the thirty-two available modes) with this type of ladder, as we have seen. But there is another way you can use this ladder: You can adjust the height of a rung *at the same time that you are standing on it*. This presents a huge increase in the number of strategies for moving up and down the ladder.

In musical terms, the moving rung is a chromatic half step, and it allows our modes—or moods—to be enriched with a deeply felt harmonic motion. How can one distinguish musically between stepping to the next rung (a diatonic half step) and moving the rung itself (a chromatic half step)? Is it a real distinction, or merely a result of the ephemeral seven-tone construct? Who rungs these ladders, anyway, and who drills their notches? We can frame such questions and suggest ways of working them out, but the real answers, the musical answers, can come only from each person's experience. Personally I find the formal distinction between diatonic and chromatic half steps real enough to be extremely useful in learning modal music, and even more so in applying the experiences of just intonation to the understanding of equal-tempered harmony.

# Major and Minor Thirds

In the course of our modal study, we have already discussed all seven of the diatonic half steps available in the lattice of twelve notes. Let's now examine the five available chromatic half steps and explore their qualities. The most familiar chromatic half step is from the minor third degree of a scale to the major third degree—$E^\flat$ to $E^\natural$ in the key of C. It is familiar because we conventionally divide all our scales into two types, Major and Minor, depending on the state of the third. Consequently we train early to distinguish between major and minor thirds. Thinking melodically, the difference between the two thirds depends on their distance up from the tonic. Thinking harmonically, however, the difference is a question of the directionality of the generating major third: To derive "major" you go *up* a major third from the tonic; to derive "minor" you go *down* a major third from the dominant. The "interval of the minor third" between C and $E^\flat$ is what is left over after deriving $E^\flat$ from G; it is a secondary result, not a primary harmony. Although, as we have just discussed, it is not intellectually obvious why we hear both $E^\natural$ and $E^\flat$ as being the third degree of the scale, we typically do, so the assignation of same-letter names and the designation "chromatic" are both appropriate.

Observe that the harmonic path from $E^\flat$ to $E^\natural$ is (starting from $E^\flat$) up a third to G, down a fifth to C, and up a third to E, or a total of up two thirds and down a fifth, as in figure 15.1.

The fraction for "up two thirds and down a fifth" is $\frac{5\times5}{3}$, or $\frac{25}{3}$, octave-reduced to $\frac{25}{6}$ to $\frac{25}{12}$ to $\frac{25}{24}$, or 25:24. $E^\natural$ is vibrating twenty-five times for every twenty-four times $E^\flat$ is vibrating. This ratio quantifies all major/minor pairs thus derived, of course, and the sound it represents is a musical gold mine. You may notice that the half step is very small indeed. The usual diatonic half step, E to F, for instance, is down a third and down a fifth. The harmonic path looks like figure 15.2. Its fraction is $\frac{1}{3\times5}$ or $\frac{1}{15}$, octave-reduced to $\frac{16}{15}$, or 16:15. Would you rather receive a $\frac{16}{15}$ return on your money or $\frac{25}{24}$? (Choose the big bucks.)

Example 15.1 is a convenient way to experience the 25:24 half step of a major/minor chromatic pair. Although a just-tuned instrument is preferable, a tempered instrument (like the piano) is OK for the played pitches. Men may sing and play an octave down, although the falsetto voice may give more control. Be sure to tune the major third up from C and the minor third down from G.

*Figure 15.1*

*Figure 15.2*

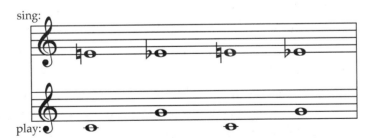

*Example 15.1*

Now try example 15.2. Over the C-and-G drone, you can feel the different qualities and sizes of half step in your voice.

Example 15.2

Notice that the interval *size* is not the crucial affective factor. What is crucial is that in the major/minor pair, the third energy is flipped between reciprocal and overtonal, whereas in the diatonic pair the harmonic path is less extreme. Specifically, the major/minor pair involves, as part of its nature, the stacking of two major thirds, that is, the compounding of two *ga*'s—hence the number twenty-five in the ratio—and is thus (please accept the language) *ga-ga* in both name and feeling. As thirds stack up, the mind tilts.

Non-Western musicians the world over love major/minor pairs and use them freely for heightened intensity of feeling. But when Western music began to temper its scale, the affective difference between diatonic half steps and chromatic half steps became so diluted that it was all but lost. To make matters worse, as the use of equal temperament became more common, major/minor pairs began to be misspelled. Incorrectly spelled notes (e.g., a written D♯ when an E♭ is intended) are rare or nonexistent in pre-Bach music, and in all of Bach's enormous output of written works I do not know of one spelling error. The man tuned his own instruments. He knew what key he was *in* and what degree he was *on*, and in cases of ambiguity he chose judiciously. But in the following generation, guess what happened. By 1780, misspellings were common, and Herr Mozart was as sloppy (gasp!) as anyone. Example 15.3 is a typical Mozartean misspelling. It is from the Sonata in B♭, K. 570, bars 14–16, which I've transposed to C for consistency with this discussion. Properly spelled, the passage would read as in example 15.4.

Yes, I can see how the great new market of bourgeois music buyers, and the publishers

Example 15.3

Example 15.4

who serviced them, did not want to see rows of accidentals on the page; diatonic steps were thought easier than chromatic steps to read. But we can pinpoint right here the loss of precious musical subtlety, which was to continue over the ensuing centuries. Consider the phrase in example 15.5, in Mozart's original spelling, from Sonata in F, K. 332 (bars 49–51).

*Example 15.5*

Now consider the phrase with its spelling indicating the generating harmony (example 15.6).

*Example 15.6*

A beautiful new dimension is restored, one that I would wager was in Mozart's ear all along, temperament and spelling be damned. Consider not only the affective beauty of the E♮ and the E♭ sounding simultaneously as a diminished octave, as well as the play of reciprocal energy brought about by their rapid succession, but also the sweet contrast between the chromatic half step against the tonic harmony (in the first bar) followed by the diatonic half step against the dominant harmony (in the second bar)—and all this within the swirling effect of the three-against-two rhythm. I don't want to characterize what your responses ought to be. I want you to investigate the phrase for yourself in just intonation with two perfectly tuned drone strings, as shown in example 15.7. (You may use the piano for your drone, if need be.)

*Example 15.7*

Incidentally, the passage obviously does not imply the key of E Minor, so the D♯ in Mozart's spelling is not its diatonic major seventh (whose ratio to C would be 75:64). Nor is the D♯ in the key of C. Or is it? Can you (honestly) hear a D♯ over a C drone—that is, truly in the key of C—as a raised second without it either becoming a minor third in your head (in which case it is E♭), or modulating to E Minor? I think the D♯ in this harmonic context is simply a wrongness, albeit a convenient kind of wrongness, a kind that appears increasingly as equal temperament becomes the European norm. Such misspellings intersect with other problems of nomenclature, rendering tonal harmony a difficult subject to learn and teach—one feels one has to machete one's way through a twisted thicket of wrong names. Nonetheless, we have opportunistically caught the culprit in the act: an early example of a great master who, at the very moment of composing a deathless phrase, strips away from its nomenclature the reciprocity of its major/minor play. Zooming out now with a wide-angle shot, we view an entire continent, preoccupied with modulation and its pleasures, looking on with passive consent.

Let's not carry the plot too far too soon, however. The task at hand is to gain clear interior knowledge of the quality of E♭ and E♮ as they musically combine in just intonation. The rest will come.

Once again I suggest, in order to learn the tones well, that you confine your singing practice at the beginning to the compass of tetrachords. Try using only the notes of example 15.8.

The bracketed notation means, essentially, "the choice is yours." Use either E♭ or E♮ or both together in every combination imaginable. Stay in tune. Observe the mood that enters your music.

*Example 15.8*

## Major and Minor Sevenths

In our lattice of twelve notes there are two other major/minor pairs that behave more or less the same way the third-degree pair does. The seventh-degree pair, B♭ and B♮, lies between the fifth G to D; the sixth degree pair, A♭ and A♮, lies between the fifth F to C. Both are likewise (reckoning from the lower tone of the chromatic pair) up a third, down a fifth, up a third; their harmonic path again looks like figure 15.1. B♮ down to B♭ is 25:24; likewise, A♮ down to A♭ is 25:24. All three major/minor pairs flip pentamerous energy the same way, with commensurate *ga-ga* results. The difference is simply where each pair lives in respect to the tonic.

B♮ and B♭ are both relatively dissonant against the tonic. The B♮ leads nicely—but definitely not necessarily—upward to C. B♭ leads nicely down to either A♮ or A♭, but not necessarily to either. Great beauty lies in the juxtaposition of the two sevenths. Example 15.9 is a typical use.

*Example 15.9*

p  s  n____  p  s  d  n_____  d  n___  d  p

North Indian vocalists can develop a *meend* between B♮ and B♭ (as well as between E♮ and E♭) so subtle and swift that the notes sound actually mixed together, as though the overtonal and reciprocal sprites were caught mating in real time. They are not actually sounding simultaneously, mind you, but rapidly sliding and oscillating back and forth in such a way as to evoke both qualities at once. It seems, during such moments, that complementary states of the psyche are indeed conjoined. In Western music it has become common practice to sound the two forms simultaneously (within certain restrictions). Example 15.10 is a generic phrase of late Baroque.

*Example 15.10*

Indeed, the minor scale with a fixed minor sixth and both sevenths, as shown in example 15.11, is so ubiquitously useful in Western classical, jazz and popular music that it merits the special name *Utility Minor,* which Dr. Overtone hereby confers upon it.

*Example 15.11*

## Major and Minor Sixths

The sixth-degree major/minor pair, A♮ and A♭, is much less used; the combination seems difficult for us to hear; does it have a kind of smoky quality? Example 15.12 suggests a few phrases to try.

*Example 15.12*

A pedagogically constructed scale, Melodic Minor, has different ascending and descending forms (example 15.13).

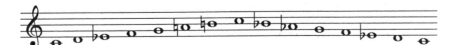

*Example 15.13*

The rationale for the name is that the raised sixth and seventh are supposed to be used in melodically ascending passages and the lowered sixth and seventh in descending ones; but in practice this proves to be the case only sometimes, and this explanation gives the erroneous impression that the chromatic forms are direction limited instead of direction oriented. I prefer the name *Full Minor*, which has the written form of example 15.14 and allows the musician the freedom to discover how each possibility can be musical.

*Example 15.14*

## Learning Major/Minor Pairs

How can we be both creative and methodical in our approach to learning major/minor pairs? I suggest improvising, over many weeks or months, in the sequence of modes given in example 15.15.

*Example 15.15*

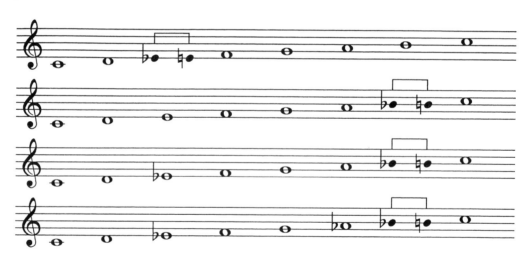

The big prize is being able to improvise in Full Minor. To approach this goal, adopt example 15.16 as your mantra. It is the upper tetrachord of the Melodic Minor. Sing this continuously one million times or until you are certain you hear it perfectly, whichever comes first. Then one day practice singing using only the tetrachord shown in example 15.17a.

*Example 15.16*

Next use example 15.17b. Then try the upper tetrachord of Full Minor (example 15.17c). Find every permutation, every combination. This is a real musical test and may take a while to pass,

*Example 15.17a*

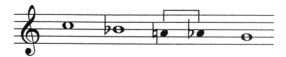

but it is one of the best seed practices for musical growth.

*Example 15.17b*

Eventually try improvising in C Full Minor—all nine tones. Then, for the added reward of greater range, try adding a vacillating major/minor third degree, so that you are now using ten tones, making musical choices, and singing dead in tune. This is big work.

*Example 15.17c*

## Perfect and Augmented Fourths

There are two more chromatic half steps in the lattice, but they have a different quality from the major/minor pairs. F♮ to F♯ is up three fifths and up a third; the harmonic path looks like figure 15.3.

The ratio of F♯ down to F♮ is $\frac{3 \times 3 \times 3 \times 5}{1}$, octave-reduced to 135:128. It flips simple subdominant *galess* energy with an overtonal *pa-ga* mix. It defines the boundary between Major and Lydian, which is a good context to practice it in. Example 15.18 suggests the beginning of such a practice.

*Figure 15.3*

s  g  m  d     m  g  m  g     s  g  m  d     m  p  n  p     m  g  m  d     m  p——

*Example 15.18*

Although the F♯ clearly leads upward to G and the F♮ leads downward to E, investigate all cases. The two fourth degrees seem to resist mixing, but that may simply be a cue to continue the investigation.

## Major and Minor Seconds

The remaining chromatic pair, D♭ to D♮, has the same harmonic path as F♮ to F♯, that is, three fifths up plus a third up. But due possibly to its more reciprocal address in relation to C, the two tones are especially difficult to juxtapose, and they seem resistant to mixing. The best way to practice them is at the cusp between Phrygian and Aeolian, as shown in example 15.19.

s   g   r   m     d  p  m  r     s  n  g   r     m   r   s——

*Example 15.19*

If you try mixing the two forms of the second degree, take extra care singing the pitches in tune. It is all too easy to stray over to the couple of different C♯s loitering nearby, at which point the distinction between chromatic and diatonic half steps will become more obscure than it already is in this case. (The agenda so far has been to confine our practice to the five-limit lattice of twelve notes. The next chapter extends the five-limit lattice indefinitely.)

## Using All Twelve Tones

Given our new tool of chromatic mixing, there are now, instead of the thirty-two heptatonic modes we have already considered, hundreds of possible modes that one might devise containing eight, nine, ten, eleven, or even all twelve tones. Indeed, if seen from an appropriate distance, these possibilities taken together begin to look like One Big Mode.

Example 15.20 shows all five chromatic pairs in a single comprehensive mode. Example 15.21 shows the same material, but the notehead shapes indicate also the exact location of each note on the five-limit lattice. Such notation is called *tone lattice notation*.

*Example 15.20*

*Example 15.21*

Lattice notation can reveal harmonic relationships at a glance. Notice in this case how the chromatic pairs for *ga, dha,* and *ni* all have the same type of harmonic relationship (they are major/minor pairs), whereas the pairs for *re* and *ma* are distinct from the others, and similar but not identical to each other. Lattice notation will take on more importance as we proceed, culminating in a method of looking at actual music, called *positional analysis*, in chapter 43.

Example 15.22 is an exercise (suggested by Pandit Pran Nath) that places all twelve notes in a melodic sequence with no mixing—that is, without moving directly from one form of a scale degree to its alternate form.

r   s   g   r m   g   p   m   d   p   n d s   n   r s n   s d   n p   d   m   p g   m r   g   s   r   n   s

*Example 15.22*

Exercises for mixing, other than those already given, are yours to invent. You learn eventually to feel quite comfortable with these twelve friends who all have agreed, after so much musical persuasion, to attend at the same hour your private little party. It is up to you to make them happy. You will need the sympathies of an expert hostess: impeccable timing and the knack of orchestrating moods. During the course of an evening there may be only a single moment when everything clicks just right, but that is the moment everyone remembers.

# 16

# BEYOND TWELVE NOTES: THE EXTENDED FIVE-LIMIT LATTICE

OUR FIELD OF MUSICAL POSSIBILITIES is about to expand again, but I don't want you to feel overwhelmed by a barrage of new tones. Rather, let this chapter serve as an exploratory survey and as a reference for the future. The material on just intonation is supplemented by the "Glossary of Singable Tones" in the back of the book and by the discussions of equal temperament in parts 2, 3, and 4. The work of learning the various harmonic qualities will occur naturally over time, the way tumbling stones make each other smooth.

## Cents

To cope with the widening range of tones, we need a precise system of measurement—one with a very small unit of measure. To follow the conventional scientific method, we begin with the twelve-tone equal-tempered scale, which by definition divides the octave into twelve equal semitones. Each semitone is then further divided into one hundred equal parts, each of which is called a *cent*. There are thus one hundred cents in an equal-tempered semitone and twelve hundred cents in a full octave. A cent is a very small unit indeed—a pitch variation of one cent is virtually undetectable by human ears. A variation of two cents, however, can be heard as a change of pitch and can be felt harmonically. Since the end of the nineteenth century the cent has been the standard measurement of musical interval used by acousticians, and in recent times it has been generally adopted by musicians as well.

Although the use of cents as a measurement is useful and benign, it is important to understand the fundamental differences between cents and the low-prime ratios we have been using. A critical difference is that equal-tempered tuning is cyclic and just intonation is not. Cyclic intervals stack up to an octave. If you stack up twelve equal-tempered semitones, they will, by definition, add up to an octave—that is what they were invented to do. In a sense, there *is* only one interval in equal-tempered tuning, and that is the semitone.

Everything else is stacked semitones. An equal-tempered whole step is two stacked semitones, and six of them make an octave. Four stacked minor thirds (each made of three semitones) make an octave; three stacked major thirds (each made of four semitones) make an octave; twelve stacked fourths (five semitones) make five octaves, which reduce to an octave; two tritones (six semitones) make an octave; twelve stacked fifths (seven semitones) make seven octaves, which reduce to an octave; and so on. On the other hand, apart from the octave itself, *no* just interval stacked *any* number of times will *ever* make an octave. How can this be?

A little mathematical common sense will help to understand this. Since an octave is a doubling of the frequency, "making" or "coming back to" an octave means you have multiplied your original frequency times two, or by some power of two. When you generate tones by pure perfect fifths you triple the frequency (and then octave-reduce, which we will omit for now). Three is a prime number, of course, which means it is not divisible by any other whole number. It means also that when you multiply three times itself any number of times, the resulting number is not divisible by any other whole number except some other three-generated number. For instance, no power of three is ever divisible by two. (Is 9 divisible by 2? Is 27? Is 81? 243? 729? Try some more.) That means you can stack pure perfect fifths until the end of time and never come back to any octave of your starting place. The same is true in respect to pure major thirds, which are quintuplings (in reduced form). No power of five is divisible by two. No number of stacked pure thirds (5:4) will ever make any octave of the generating tone. Same with septuplings. Same with any prime-generated tone. Prime-generated tones are not cyclic; they don't come 'round. Just intonation doesn't make circles; it radiates outward from its center until the ear gives up. It's not closed like a dome; it's open like a prairie.

The prime-number ratios we have been using so far represent the pure harmonies of just intonation, our responses to which, to some degree, define our humanity. Cents, on the other hand, were thought up as an arbitrary unit of measure. They were devised so that 1200 of them will stack up to make an octave, which means that if you multiply a cent's ratio times itself 1200 times you will get a doubling, or 2:1, or simply 2. Now, what number multiplied times itself 1200 times gives 2? The answer is this: a very small irrational number. Irrational numbers cannot be expressed in terms of whole numbers. The ratio of one cent to the number 1 is $\sqrt[1200]{2}:1$, or "the 1200th root of 2 to 1"; its approximate ratio to 1 in decimal numbers is 1.0005777895:1. Remember, this is an inaudibly small interval.

Now let's consider audible intervals. The ratio of the equal-tempered D♭ to C is the irrational $\sqrt[12]{2}:1$, but the interval measurement in cents is 100 even. Conversely, the ratio of the just D♭ to C is the rational 16:15, but that interval expressed in cents is the irrational 111.731 . . . cents. Because they are grounded in irrational numbers, cents as a measure of prime-number ratios will always be approximate; nonetheless, they are a convenient means of comparing the various distances between tones. Even though, up to now, intervalic distance has not been our focus, as we proceed with the investigation of equal temperament, symmetrical scales, and eventually atonal music, the deep forces of pure harmony loosen and weaken, and the surface measurement of distance becomes increasingly needed, and cents sufficeth.

# Extending the Central Spine of Fifths

We are now prepared to extend the lattice beyond its present twelve-note limit. We'll begin with the central spine of fifths.

### THE PYTHAGOREAN MAJOR SIXTH

The next fifth above D is A, sometimes called the Pythagorean major sixth. Its map is shown

*Example 16.1*

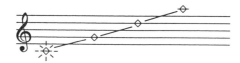

in example 16.1. Its harmonic path is three fifths up and looks like figure 16.1. Its ratio is $\frac{3 \times 3 \times 3}{1}$, octave-reduced to 27:16. To learn to sing this in tune, it is best to have a third string so you can tune C–G–D in fifths

*Figure 16.1*

(with only two strings you could induce the D from the G) and then sing the A as the next fifth. Then sound your new A with C. In respect to the old familiar 5:3 A, the Pythagorean A is indeed new. It is about twenty-two cents higher, for one thing, (that is, 22 percent of an equal-tempered half step); more crucially, it has quite a different harmonic quality. But that quality is an extension of something that is *not* new to us: If you sing 1:1 *sa*, then 3:2 *pa*, then 9:8 *re*, and then the 27:16 *dha*, you can hear how the tones generated by pure fifths are a family. Obviously they increase in complexity as they advance along the spine, but there is a binding qualitative thread. In the context of the upper tetrachord shown in example 16.2, the 27:16 A sounds quite natural and is in fact an exact intervalic transposition of the extremely familiar lower tetrachord we have been singing all our lives.

The 27:16 A, though not as common worldwide as 5:3, is definitely the

*Example 16.2*

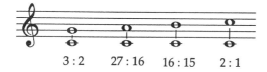

3:2    27:16    16:15    2:1

tone that many people (in China and Japan, for instance) hear as the major sixth degree of the scale. Even though it may sound sharp to some of us, it isn't sharp, it's what it is.

Example 16.3 shows how both tetrachords are the same. Notice the numbers. The lower tetrachord is the familiar version of the Major mode: C to D is a major whole tone, and D to E is a minor whole tone. In the upper tetrachord, G to A is likewise a major whole tone, and A to B is a minor whole tone. A to C is 27:16, the Pythagorean major sixth.

In unfolding the lattice of pure harmony, the discovery of 27:16 marks a new day. We now have in our language two distinct tones that are very close in pitch and that share the same diatonic function, the same letter name, and the same solfege syllable. They are *stepsiblings*. Stepsiblings share the same domicile but have different combinations of parents.

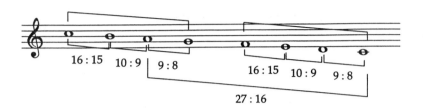

*Example 16.3*

The 5:3 A is *ga*-blooded, that is, a union of both (reciprocal) *pa* and *ga*; the 27:16 A is of pure overtonal *pa* lineage. The two A's both live in the sixth degree, but have different harmonic generation.

It is crucial, when learning a new tone very close in pitch to another tone you already know, not to give in to the temptation of comparing their pitches directly—at least not too early in the process. It would be like comparing a new friend to an old friend too soon. You might perceive that the new one is a quarter-inch taller, but beyond that you must give the new friend's personality a chance to become known. Once you have internalized the harmonic qualities of both tones, you may find it useful, or at least interesting, to ascertain the difference in pitch. But it is not the relative height of tones that is musically nourishing. What's vital are the harmonic paths, the resonances they produce, and the way those resonances live in the body.

Harmony is the way things are together. When a tone is harmonically related to a tonic (whether or not that tonic is sounding in the air), we vibrate sympathetically with that harmony. As the sympathy is internalized, the crucial difference between near tones is recognized primarily as a difference in mood, a change in the light, of the sun/moon energy; that is what grabs us and holds us and keeps us coming back for more—not small differences in pitch. We distinguish the 5:3 major sixth from the 27:16 major sixth the same way we recognize two friends—one may be gentle and generous, the other nervous and edgy. So seek to learn the friends' individual natures first; then their relative intents and purposes will clarify from the inside out—from the harmony—not superficially by the measurement of their intervals.

## THE PYTHAGOREAN MAJOR THIRD

The next note along the central spine is the Pythagorean E. Its harmonic map is shown in example 16.4. Its harmonic path is four fifths up and looks like figure 16.2.

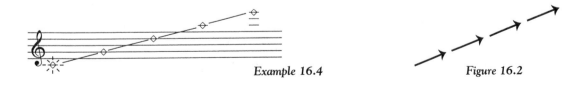

*Example 16.4*        *Figure 16.2*

Its ratio is $\frac{3\times3\times3\times3}{1}$, octave-reduced to 81:64. One could call the Pythagorean E the *re* of *re*, or two stacked major whole tones. I practice hearing it by inducing the third partial,

D, from the G string, isolating it, then pretending that D is the tonic. Once I am convinced that D is the tonic I sing *re* (9:8) above that. Then, gingerly, I add in the low C string and voila! the Pythagorean E. It is fair to say that this note, not used much in the West, is hard for us to hear. The 5:4 third is overwhelmingly the third of choice, of course, so if you don't take special care the 81:64 third will simply sound like a sharp third. It is indeed about twenty-two cents higher than its stepsibling. But it has its own independent Pythagorean quality, which you will find with patience.

## THE PYTHAGOREAN MAJOR SEVENTH

The most overtonal member of the Pythagorean family we will study is the major seventh B. Its harmonic map is shown in example 16.5. The harmonic path is five fifths up and looks like figure 16.3.

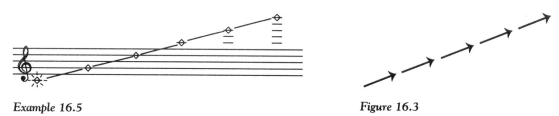

Example 16.5                                               Figure 16.3

The ratio is $\frac{3\times3\times3\times3\times3}{1}$, octave-reduced to 243:128. It is about twenty-two cents (yes, the very same) sharper than its stepsibling 15:8, and ten cents sharper than the equal-tempered major seventh, which makes it the highest major seventh used conventionally by anyone anywhere. To learn to sing this one in tune you need at least three, and preferably four strings, tuned by perfect fifths. Some string players use it (or think they are using it) because it seems to lean upward with the urgency of resolution to the tonic above it. But as a standing tone it has its own edgy, complex tartness, like a very dry white wine.

## THE PYTHAGOREAN MINOR SEVENTH

We will now continue to extend the Pythagorean spine in the downward, reciprocal direction. A fifth below F is the Pythagorean B♭, the subdominant of the subdominant. Its harmonic map is shown in example 16.6. The harmonic path is two fifths down and looks like figure 16.4.

Example 16.6                        Figure 16.4

It is thus grand-*pa* below. Its ratio is $\frac{1}{3\times3}$, octave-expanded to 16:9. It is about twenty-two cents lower than its *ga*-blooded 9:5 stepsibling—the B♭ we have already studied. The best way to learn it is to tune the G string to F, induce the fourth-partial F (fifth fret), then sing the B♭ a fifth lower, and finally mix in the C drone. It makes a major whole tone with the C above it, and is the reciprocal version of the overtonal 9:8 *re*. Perhaps you will notice its Pythagorean family likeness—*ga*-bloodless and crystal pure.

The minor seventh is a very mutable area of the scale, so it is easy to get lost here, but do resist, at least at first, comparing the pitches of the two B♭'s. Again, learn the new tone by virtue of its harmonic essence and place that in your body as best you can. Musical sense will follow.

## THE PYTHAGOREAN MINOR THIRD

The Pythagorean E♭ is three fifths down. Its harmonic map is shown in example 16.7. The harmonic path looks like figure 16.5. Its ratio is $\frac{1}{3 \times 3 \times 3}$, octave-expanded to 32:27. This E♭ is the reciprocal of the 27:16 major sixth; it is about twenty-two cents lower than its much more sim-

*Example 16.7*

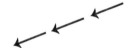

*Figure 16.5*

ple and familiar stepsibling the 6:5 E♭. To be certain in your singing, tune three strings C–F–B♭. If you find it difficult to track the Pythagorean quality of this one (partly because, for all the world, it sounds like a too-flat minor third), it is OK to come back to it later.

## THE EXTENDED CENTRAL SPINE OF FIFTHS

The entire central spine as we have discussed it so far looks like example 16.8.

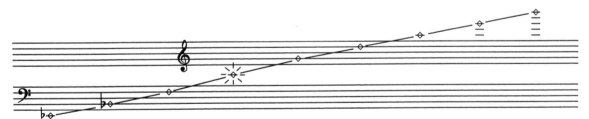

*Example 16.8*

The spine is infinite in both directions. As it ascends, it uses up the seven letters over and over again, adding sharps, then double sharps, and so on. As it descends it adds flats, then double flats, and so on. Where does it end for our present practical purposes? It ends where the ear can no longer discriminate distinct harmonies in respect to the tonic drone. The classic Pythagorean system of twelve tones gives the following series of ascending fifths:

D♭–A♭–E♭–B♭–F–C–G–D–A–E–B–F♯

The more extreme extensions (D♭, A♭, F♯) can be considered theoretical for now. But what is presently theory will become practice in later sections of the book.

# Extending the *Ga* Spine of Fifths

We will now move our attention to the spine of fifths that is a major third above the central spine, which we call the *ga* spine of fifths. Let's consider two new tones, one an extension in the reciprocal direction, the other an extension in the overtonal direction.

## THE 10:9 *RE*

Let's look at the reciprocal tone first: It is D, a fifth below the 5:3 *dha*. It is a third up and two fifths down. The harmonic map is shown in example 16.9. The harmonic path looks like figure 16.6. The ratio is $\frac{5}{3 \times 3}$, octave-expanded to 10:9.

*Example 16.9*

The 10:9 *re* is about twenty-two cents lower than its stepsibling the 9:8 *re*. It is *dha* above F, which is probably the best way to learn it: Tune the G string to F, sing the tone that makes a 5:3 *dha* with it, then check that tone back against C. You will hear an extremely intriguing harmony: *ga*-blooded like its upper spine-neighbor, the 5:3 *dha*, and sweet, and maybe a little shy. If the 9:8 *re* is the dazzling older brother who is always whizzing about, then the 10:9 *re* is the dark younger sister who seldom goes out. But the dark sister is not at all uncommon in the world's music. She appears, for instance, in *Kafi* (the North Indian version of Dorian), and in good Western singing whenever reciprocal harmonies (subdominant or submediant) are in play.

*Figure 16.6*

## ALTERNATING 9:8 AND 10:9—A PENTATONIC EXAMPLE

One pentatonic use of the 10:9 *re* is so striking and revealing that it is worth analysis here. The two most popular pentatonic scales in the world are given in example 16.10. These are conventionally considered to be identical except for the placement of the tonic.

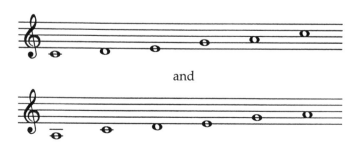

and

*Example 16.10*

In common use, however (at least, in African and African-derived music), a beautiful tuning difference further differentiates the two modes. When C is the tonic (which can be supported by emphasis on the C–G relationship) the scale follows the map shown in example 16.11.

Notice that D to C is the major whole tone, 9:8; D is on the central spine and relates directly to G. A typical phrase might be as given in example 16.12.

*Example 16.11*

*Example 16.12*

But when A is the tonic (which is supported by emphasis on the A–E relationship) the harmonic map is as given in example 16.13. Notice that D to C is now the minor whole tone, 10:9, and that it is

*Example 16.13*

subdominant to A. The D is darker, *ga*-blooded and reciprocal: It belongs to the *ga* spine of fifths, not the central spine, and no longer relates directly to G. A typical phrase might be as given in example 16.14.

*Example 16.14*

Comparison of the phrases reveals how modulation is inseparable from the harmonic generation of the tones. Notice that we have not compared the two D's directly, nor measured their pitches, but have given each tone an appropriate musical setting and appreciated the respective results. Forgive me if this example takes us a little ahead of our game, but it provides a practical improvisatory method for exploring the differences between two tones whose harmonies are disparate but whose pitches are close together. The exercise also gives us a glimpse of the nature of modulation, which will soon enough (parts 3 and 4) be our preoccupation.

## THE 135:128 C♯

If we extend the *ga* spine of fifths one note beyond its present overtonal limit we generate C♯. It is three fifths up and a third up. The harmonic map is shown in example 16.15. The harmonic path looks like figure 16.7 and the ratio is $\frac{3 \times 3 \times 3 \times 5}{1}$, octave-reduced to 135:128, a far-out ratio by any standard.

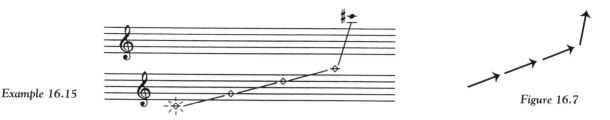

*Example 16.15*

*Figure 16.7*

It is not to be thought of (I think) as a tone to be sung directly against C; it will show up in our chordal studies later on (chapter 16) against G, as the Lydian note of the dominant. My advice: Don't deal with it now, just know that it is there, a sort of trust fund that you can spend after you've read a certain number of pages. The *ga* spine of fifths now looks like example 16.16.

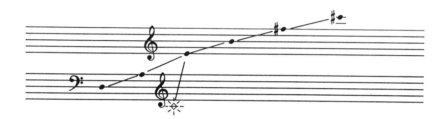

*Example 16.16*

# The *Ga-Ga* Spine of Fifths

*Example 16.17*

A few other tones I would like to mention require brand-new spines and new notational symbols. Just as the perfect-fifth dimension of the lattice goes on forever, so likewise does the major-third dimension. The major third above C is E; it is the first overtonal note on the central spine of thirds that defines the vertical axis, the pentamerous dimension of the lattice; it is also the central tone in the *ga* spine of fifths that stretches out to the right of it (B, F♯, etc.) and to the left of it (A, D, etc.). The major third above E is G♯; it is the next overtonal note on the vertical spine of thirds; it will also serve as the central tone for a new spine of fifths—the *ga-ga* spine of fifths, which stretches out to the right and left of it. Let the symbol for the *ga-ga* spine of fifths be an upward pointing, filled-in triangle, as shown in example 16.17, the harmonic map of our new note, G♯.

## THE 25:16 G♯

*Figure 16.8*

The 25:16 G♯ is two major thirds up from the tonic; the harmonic path looks like figure 16.8. In pitch it is about forty-one cents lower (almost a quarter tone) than its comma sibling, the 8:5 A♭, which appears on the lattice three major thirds below on the central spine of thirds. (A *comma* is the distance between two tones very near in pitch. When stepsiblings do not share the same letter name we will call them *comma siblings*.) The best method for learning *it:* Induce the fifth partial (E) from the C string; isolate it; sing *its ga,* G♯, against it; then add in the C drone. Not only is the harmony of this tone musically moving in its own right, but it also functions as a chisel that eventually cracks open the seven-stone scale model; so it will become doubly useful. For now, however it is sufficient to let our eyeballs roll ever so slightly as we sing it. The *ga-ga* feeling is demonstratively addictive; we will be visiting back this way many times.

## THE 25:24 C♯

There is a tone closely related to G♯ that is also worth tasting now: the C♯ a fifth below it on the *ga-ga* spine of fifths. From C it is a third up and a fifth down and a third up (or any permutation of these). Its harmonic maps are given in example 16.18. The corresponding harmonic paths look like figure 16.9 and the ratio is $\frac{5 \times 5}{3}$, octave-reduced to 25:24.

This should remind you of something we have seen already: the ratio between major/minor chromatic pairs. Indeed, if you were standing on the 5:3 A (known as the tonic of the "relative minor" of C) this very C♯ would be your pure major third. It thus represents the parallel Major of the relative Minor (A Major related to C Major through A Minor) and effects a kind of modulation when you sing it in tune, further weakening the seven-tone construct. To sing it, induce the fifth partial from C and isolate that by damping out the fundamental completely. Then sing down a fifth to A; then while hearing the A clearly in your mind, sing up a third. (If that is too iffy, tune a string to the A, then sing the C♯ to it.) Then add in the C drone and hang on. This tone is about forty-one cents lower than the 16:15 D♭ and thirty cents below the tempered semitone. In North Indian *raga* it is sung at dawn when the sun is just showing itself above the sea. It evokes distance and rising energy, a wake-up call of sorts—some say temple bells—though at first it might sound merely weird.

The *ga-ga* C♯ and its neighbor the *ga-ga* G♯ will serve, for now, as two sentries stationed at the remote outpost of the *ga-ga* spine, one peering northeast, the other southwest.

*Example 16.18*

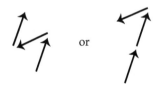

*Figure 16.9*

## The *Ga-Ga-Below* Spine of Fifths: F♭

An even more remote outpost is headquartered two thirds below C. Down one third from C is A♭; down two thirds is F♭. I do not suggest you learn to sing the F♭ now, since it requires

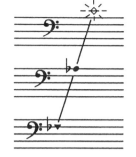

*Example 16.19*

too much modulation to learn properly; that will come later. I am introducing it here to visually balance the lattice by adding the central tone of a new spine of fifths located two thirds below the central spine. Let this be called the *ga-ga-below* spine of fifths, and let the symbol on this spine be a filled-in downward-pointing triangle. The harmonic map for F♭ is shown in example 16.19.

## The Extended Five-Limit Lattice

To summarize the names of the spines of the lattice: We now have a total of five spines of fifths arrayed above and below the central spine, each distant from the next by a major third, as shown in figure 16.10.

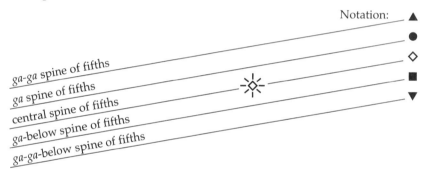

*Figure 16.10*

We can now clearly discern spines of the vertical dimension. Radiating overtonally upward and reciprocally downward from C is the *central spine of thirds*. To the left and to the right of the central spine are additional spines of thirds, each distant from the next by a perfect fifth, as shown in figure 16.11.

Example 16.20 shows the five-limit lattice as it has unfolded so far. Although we have grown spectacularly from a lattice of twelve notes to a lattice of twenty-two notes, it is clear that the five-limit lattice could be extended infinitely in both directions of both dimensions, and that an infinite number of notes would thereby be generated. Already we have the possibility for more modes than there are people alive to sing them. Doesn't a useful musical system need only a few tones that work well? The truth is that perfect fifths and major thirds acting together do generate a large number of usable tones (we have covered most of them), but only a few—five, seven, maybe nine—are typically used *at once* in a single musical context. Our dilemma is a typically modern one: We are interested in a lot of different contexts, and we like our contexts rangy and mutable. And since we

*Figure 16.11*

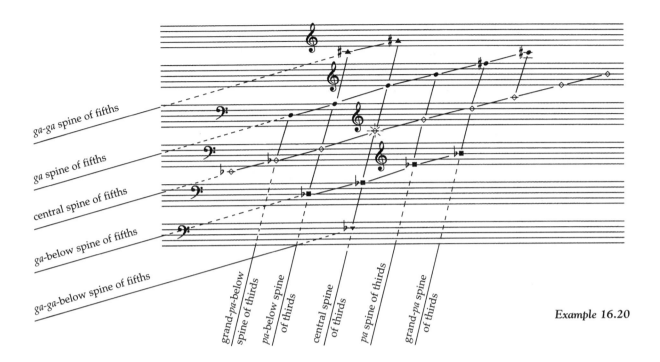

*ga-ga* spine of fifths

*ga* spine of fifths

central spine of fifths

*ga-below* spine of fifths

*ga-ga-below* spine of fifths

*grand-pa-below* spine of thirds

*pa-below* spine of thirds

central spine of thirds

*pa* spine of thirds

*grand-pa* spine of thirds

*Example 16.20*

have only recently learned to appreciate the music of all humanity, it is only natural to feel like we've just arrived at a big party where we hardly know anybody. Gradually, however, as the evening unfolds, we begin to recognize these tones as the authentic elders of our own native village, and then the party begins to feel more like home. The rediscovery of singing in tune against a drone is the tool that opens the possibility of listening with world ears.

The present chapter has been a kind of survey, as promised, and the practical hands-on value of all these milling strangers will increase as we proceed. Chapter 18 includes more complete suggestions for how to use all of these harmonic behaviors in just intonation, as well as a discussion of what expectations we might have about understanding their uses and abuses in twelve-tone equal temperament.

But there is still a little more lattice work to do. Remember how I fudged on statements like, "*Most* of the music you have ever heard is perfect fifths and major thirds"? The next chapter deals with what is left over after "most": A spanking new dimension wearing the number seven (days of the week? planets? heavens?) will come into play.

# 17

# THE SEVENTH PARTIAL AND BEYOND

## Each Prime Its Own Realm

Each prime number generates its own musical universe. The number one generates the world of oneness, of unity. Its music has one note: itself. The number two generates octaves only—an infinite but musically empty space. Perhaps one could imagine beings from another galaxy who limit their music to doublings only: two-limit music. They dance ecstatically as the full thirty-octave range of their audio capacity is stimulated by blasts from their sound-producing antennae. But for us earthlings, two-limit produces no music, no dance.

The number three generates an infinitely long line of perfect twelfths. To make these musically useful they must be octave-reduced, that is, mixed in with the number two, making a three-limit system. The resulting spine of fifths gives a replete system with as many notes as we can musically use; the four central notes are used by almost everyone.

The prime number five alone generates only a few tones that the ear understands. Even when these are octave-reduced (making a system that is a mix of the primes two and five), the ear gives up after two moves either up or down. Except as a theoretical measure, the B♯ three major thirds above C simply isn't there for our ears, nor is the D♭♭ three major thirds below C. That leaves at best a five-tone scale bizarre to the extreme, as example 17.1 shows.

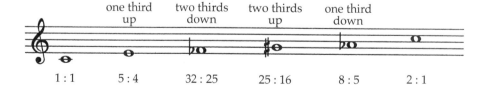

*Example 17.1*

Now our familiar nomenclature lets us down: Since the seven-tone scale model is alien in this context, letter names, accidentals, and staff notation are confusing misnomers. But when this system is mixed in with the prime number three, the entire five-limit lattice arises, as we have chronicled over these pages.

## The Seven Realm

What about the next prime number, seven? To learn the unique quality of the seventh partial, simply induce it from the C string (one-seventh of the string length away from the nut, or between the second and third frets) and listen. Try not to compare it with anything; just hear it, then sing it. What is this new energy? It is obviously overtonal, but is it yang? Is it restful or moving? You don't need to come up with qualifying adjectives, since like any another musical element, this one simply is what it is; but I do want you to hear and sing what it is.

Since there is no dedicated solfege syllable for the seventh partial, Dr. Overtone, for reasons that will soon become clear, hereby christens it *blu*—not so much for singing as for theoretical identification—and suggests that all compound tones with which it shares energy henceforth be known as *blu*-blooded.

As the primes ascend farther from unity, they become less functional as musical elements, less able to generate their musical worlds. The prime two generates an infinite number of overtonal and reciprocal tones with no loss of harmonic identity; the prime three generates at least a dozen; the prime five generates four tones, maybe five, before we can no longer track the harmony. How many can the prime seven generate? Is there a *blu* spine?

If so, it is short indeed. *Blu* of *blu*, yes. *Blu* below, probably. Both my ear and conventional use stop there. But I am not a seventh-partial specialist. The composers La Monte Young and Ben Johnston, among others, have long been fascinated by the possibilities of higher primes, and have trained themselves and others to sing more complex tones, some of which are listed in the "Glossary of Singable Tones in Just Intonation." The present task is to learn the essential quality of the seventh partial and a few of its compounds.

You can try singing the seventh partial as part of the "scale of harmonics" as shown in example 17.2.

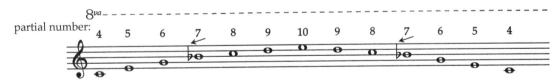

*Example 17.2*

These are the overtones of the C string, of course, as well as the harmonic series of an open C trumpet. A musical phrase might take shape like example 17.3.

*Example 17.3*

The seventh partial from C is a B♭ thirty-one cents lower than the equal-tempered B♭ and forty-nine cents below the 9:5 B♭, which is a lot of cents—about a quarter tone's worth. Yet both tones seem indeed to function in heptatonic modes as versions of the minor seventh degree.

You may find that you recognize the resonance of the seventh partial very well, but this might not have been the case in any Western country a hundred years ago. Seventh-partial harmony has long been thought by European theorists to be in fact inharmonic, or worse, demonic, and incompatible with five-limit tuning, and it was consequently banished from the European aesthetic. But the seventh partial is clearly present in the music of many cultures. Toward the end of the nineteenth century something strange and wondrous began happening to American music—the musical legacy of the African-American freed slaves began to mix with its entrenched European harmonies. By the 1920s Americans were hearing jazz and blues redolent with seventh-partial harmonies. By the 1940s the new harmony had become sufficiently ingrained in the American ear for millions of us in living rooms full of families and friends to find it amusing to round out our renditions of "Happy Birthday" as shown in example 17.4. (The ratios are with C.)

*Example 17.4*

Hap - py  Birth - day    to      you,      and  ma - ny    more

3:2  5:3  3:2        7:4

The tag is a send-up of blues harmony, and the subtext is, "We are sincere and truth-telling, just like real blues singers," but the heavy vibrato is exaggerated and the vital energy satirized. Such is the ease with which we appropriate power while simultaneously (and often unconsciously) denigrating its source. The actual power of the seventh partial fuels the harmonic quality of a music that helped transmute the humiliations of slavery into the hard joys of survival.

To more fully experience the pure tuning of a blues scale, tune a string to F, induce its seventh partial, and sing it with the F sounding. Then mix in the C string. This note is E♭, the *blu* of *ma*; it makes 7:6 with C. Learn to sing it in the lower tetrachord, as suggested in example 17.5.

*Example 17.5*

1:1   7:6        4:3   7:6

The seventh partials of C and F, mixing with the heart of the Pythagorean spine—F, C, and G—form a pentatonic scale that has woven its *blu* threads into the design of the West, and on into the ears of the planet, as shown in example 17.6. (The ratios are with C.)

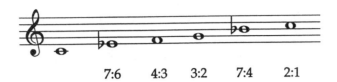

*Example 17.6*

Also part of the blues harmonic language is the seventh partial of G, the *blu* of *pa*, an F that sounds beautiful when dominant harmony is in play. Against C it makes 21:16, and resolves gorgeously downward a small semitone (21:20) to the 5:4 third, a musical move found among in-tune singers in styles as diverse as medieval sacred sequences and African love songs. As a standing harmony, 21:16 may be hard for us to hear, but the note is definitely there, twenty-seven cents lower than the 4:3 *ma*. We will call it *blu ma*.

We now have a spine of *blu*-blooded notes—a genuine *blu* spine of fifths. For purposes of lattice notation, let the symbol for a seventh partial be the same shape as the tone that immediately generates it, but with a slash drawn downward from left to right. Hence a seventh partial generated by a tone in the central spine of fifths is indicated by a slashed open diamond.

Since each prime is its own realm, we also need a new dimension. We have used up horizontal and vertical; now we must go above and below the flat plane of the page, a three-dimensional effect that can be achieved with proper perspective. In example 17.7, the seventh partials are thought to be located above and to the right of their generating tones.

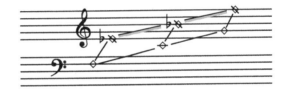

*Example 17.7*

Fascinating musical structures can be created by using third partials and seventh partials while omitting fifth partials. (La Monte Young has honed this principle.) Conventionally, however, a very limited field of seventh-partial tones are added into the five-limit lattice, as is the case with blues and the jazz that came from it.

For a clear shot of essential blues harmony, try tuning three strings by perfect fifths to F, C, and G; then play and sing example 17.8.

*Example 17.8*

We will have more to say about blues harmony later, especially in chapter 33.

# Prime Numbers beyond Seven

We have nearly run out of conventionally useful primes. The overtone series up to the sixteenth partial is given in example 17.9.

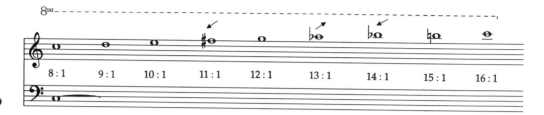

*Example 17.9*

The next prime after seven is eleven. Its ratio with C is 11:8, and its pitch is almost dead center between the equal tempered F and F♯, a tad sharp of the center between the 4:3 F and the 45:32 F♯.

The eleventh partial shows up naturally in any music using the scale of harmonics, that is, the uncompounded overtones of a single drone, most spectacularly in the Tuva music of Mongolia, where it appears as a colorful passing tone. To discover its harmonic quality, induce the overtone and try singing it for yourself. You may find it elusive. The question of whether the eleventh partial generates a usable spine of its own, and the extent of its ability to compound with lower primes, is beyond our scope for the moment.

If the eleventh partial is rare, the thirteenth partial is almost nonexistent. At 841 cents it sits only seven cents below the quarter tone that splits the major and minor sixth. Some people say they hear it *in situ* in Arabic music. In any case it is at or beyond the frontier of just tones suitable for our present purposes.

This completes our primary survey of just tones that make up the harmonic template on which twelve-tone equal temperament rests. Before entering with you into the Babylon of equal temperament, I would like to suggest some ways that your work in just intonation can be more useful in music and beyond it.

# 18

# THE PRACTICE OF PURE HARMONY

WE GAZE AT THE CAT; gazing back at us we see our mammalian nature long before it was painted over by civilization. Through our pets we see our ancient selves, the animal as template of the citizen. For the contemporary Western musician, the pure harmonies of just intonation are like animal guides, preexisting patterns of intelligence that shape the sophistications and bifurcations of the modern soul. Singing in just intonation opens up the guide part of yourself, the template of your own hearing. It is an integrative practice that goes beyond music into the nature of vibration itself. When you sing in tune you can go as deeply into existence as you want.

Aside from the interior dimension, there is a historical dimension to singing in tune: You can realize the European legacy through it. It's like being alive in the fourteenth century in a cathedral or a castle's great hall. There is also the global dimension. It is powerful, upon hearing the music of strangers from Iceland, Bhutan, Pakistan, Ghana, Egypt, and New Guinea, to recognize the common threads that connect the harmonic resonances of various peoples. This is not personal authority but the collective power of being human. Whether or not you were musically trained, you would sense the power of the harmonic resonances. But when you yourself can make such sounds, you realize the way in which you *are* this power.

Here are some practice suggestions, iterated and reiterated:

1. Make sure your drone instrument is operative and handy and, if you are using the fifths of a piano, as well tuned as a piano can be. Equal-tempered perfect fifths are not optimal, but they are usable. (Equal-tempered thirds will bite you.) Care for your drone.
2. The singing of standing tones—sustained tones of unvarying pitch—is good practice if only to constantly reexamine the pure harmonies. This is not an endurance contest. Remember to follow the wisdom of your breath.

3. The alternation of two standing tones with one another, *ni/sa* or *ni/dha* or *dha/pa*, for instance, safeguards against being mesmerized by one tone. Sometimes contrast with another color brings out both colors.

4. Practicing within tetrachords, or any small field of adjacent tones, is probably the most efficient way to learn musical space. Sometimes you can spend a half hour on one tetrachord without breaking your concentration.

5. One way to heighten your concentration is to construct a mode that is most appropriate to a given moment of practice. To do this, first sing *sa* (against a drone, of course). Then ask, "What kind of *re* do I want right now?" You choose, for instance, the 9:8 *re*. "Which *ga* is perfect for this moment?" You choose the 6:5 *komal ga*. Then, say, no question about the 45:32 *tivra ma*. Then *pa*. You sing what you have chosen so far (*sa, re, komal ga, tivra ma, pa*) and ask which sixth fits your mood. You choose the 5:3 *dha*. And the exactly right seventh seems to be the 9:5 *komal ni*. Your mode of the day—or *mode du jour*—turns out to be MIX/GYPSY MI. *Mode du jour* is an example of making your feelings conscious and then illuminating them with intelligence and discipline.

6. You can increase your musical certainty by improvising within a simple metric structure—two-bar or four-bar phrases. Start simply: Improvise in C Major for two bars of $\frac{4}{4}$ time. A phrase might be as shown in example 18.1a or 18.1b.

*Example 18.1*

Keep track of the beats on your fingers, or however you can. By graduating to longer phrases, less familiar modes, and triple or compound time, you can incrementally develop your musical language. It is a good idea to compose a series of related four-bar phrases that you notate only in *sargam* letters and then learn to sing rapidly and perfectly. (These are called *tans* in North Indian music.)

Figure 18.1 is a composition in Dorian. Notice that a dot above a letter means the octave above, a dot below means the octave below, and the underlined letter means komal. Example 18.2 shows the same composition in staff notation, for reference.

I would like to add a word about keyboards tuned in just intonation. Pianos can sound fantastic in just tunings, but only an extremely specialized tuner can accomplish this, and such tuners are rare. Perhaps, with a little help from a knowledgeable professional, you can

S  R  M  G̲  |  M  P  N̲  D  |  N̲  Ṙ  Ṡ  N̲  |  D  M  P  —  |

R  R  N̲  D  |  P  M  N̲  Ṙ  |  Ṡ  N̲  D  P  |  M  R  G̲  —  |

R  R  N̲  Ḍ  |  G̲  G̲  R  M  |  P  N̲  D  Ṡ  |  N̲  Ṙ  Ġ̲  Ṙ  |

Ġ̲  Ġ̲  Ṙ  N̲  |  Ṡ  D  N̲  P  |  D  M  P  G̲  |  M  R  S  —  |

*Figure 18.1*

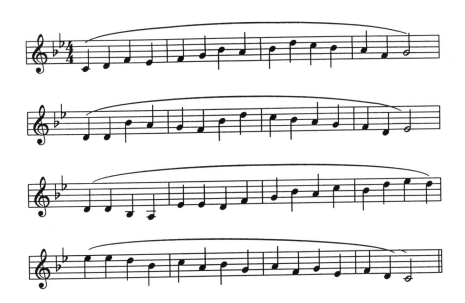

*Example 18.2*

train yourself. Various electronic keyboards have programs for just intonation, and these also can be instructive, especially in regard to some of the material in parts 2 and 3. But for now I urge you to consider how keyboards place the responsibility for the tuning away from the musician and onto the tuner or the programmer. My advice is to be the actual source of the sound, not merely the operator of an ingenious machine. At least in the present phase of your music learning, you need a decent drone and your voice and a pleasant room with a window and a door that locks from the inside so that the pure tones can learn to be alive inside your body.

# PART TWO

# THE SELECTIVE USE OF EQUAL TEMPERAMENT

# 19

# LEAPING FROM PARADISE

## One Foot in Eden

In part 1 we have been singing in the lattice of just intonation, moving from pure tone to pure tone, threading melodies through a honeycomb of resonances. Why would anyone ever choose to leave this Eden? Many musicians who are native to places not yet paved over by Western influence have never left their tonal paradise. For the Pygmies of Central Africa, the Uighurs of Central Asia, the Azerbaijanis of the Caucuses—to name only a few among many indigenous peoples—the primal resonances that connect singer and soul are still alive within their vital musical traditions. Even in certain populations that have been partially Westernized, such as India and China and most of the Middle East, the central culture remains coherent and the musical tunings are still pure.

By the late Middle Ages, Western European culture had not yet emerged from tonal paradise. Fourteenth-century composers and performers had learned to produce music that was at once entirely in tune, highly melodic, rigorously polyphonic, and harmonically broad in scope. By broad in scope I mean that when mapped out on the lattice, the music, correctly sung and played, would routinely make harmonic journeys outward from the central tone, cover a wide swath of territory, return to the central tone, then range out to another area and return, over and over again, allowing the music to accumulate an unprecedented dramatic range. In doing so the singers typically encountered, over the course of one piece, many more than seven—often more than twelve—different tones in various harmonious combinations. Each tone, however, remained a true low-prime ratio to the tonic, its resonance and quality intact. The composer's artistry was defined, to some extent, by the capacity to cover a wide harmonic range while unambiguously using an expanded language of tones (chapter 41 looks at a fourteenth-century piece that does just this). Even though some of these tones were very close to one another in pitch—the distance separating a pure major third from a Pythagorean third, for instance—they were nevertheless harmonically disparate, each occupying unique and precise harmonic coordinates. Composers such as Machaut, Landini, and Ciconia were masterful in constructing labyrinthine journeys through the lattice of just intonation. Their elegant style produced a golden age of singing—subsequently lost but recently in revival—that contained an affective magic like none other.

But by the fifteenth century something had happened. Adam had gotten hungry. His mind had contracted a fearsome restlessness, and his ear, so long content to range near home, had begun to roam beyond the old borders.

## The Need for Simplification

As harmonic range increased, the number of notes necessary to express it increased also. As long as musicians and composers agreed to preserve the accuracy of the pitches and hence their affective quality, the new harmonic territory could be vibrated into being. Remember that there was no unifying, viable musical theory at the time—certainly no practical one—that clarified procedures. (There still isn't, unless this is it.) Essentially people relied on their ears and feelings; that is the way agreements are reached in paradise, and in this case it produced marvelous results. But as harmonic hungers became keener, the singers' difficulties increased: Yet more pairs of tones separated by small pitch differences appeared, as well as more chromatic pairs. Harmonic leaps became bold and easy to misinterpret, the harmonic labyrinths easier to get lost in. The musical agreements began to be threatened. Three forces eventually toppled the balance: the simultaneous sounding of multiple pitches, an interest in modulation, and the increasing use of fixed-pitch instruments.

### SIMULTANEITY

So far, our working definition of harmony has been limited to the ratios that various tones form when combined with the tonic. A larger definition involves how tones combine not only with the tonic but with each other. How those combinations have developed in the West is the essence of its musical history. By the tenth century, tones had begun to combine in *parallel organum*, Gregorian chant that had been thickened with fifths or fourths and octaves. By the thirteenth century, the three-part harmonies we call triads were commonly sung as shown in example 19.1.

*Example 19.1*

The typical way of combining tones in late Medieval times was through polyphony, a practice that retains the rhythmic and melodic integrity of the individual voices while producing overall harmonic agreement. (Most of us first encounter polyphony by singing rounds, such as "Frère Jacques.") Since each melody has its own harmonic territory, their combined territories can become extremely wide. But remember that the farther away tones are from one another on the harmonic lattice, the more remote is their harmony. The greater the territory, the less the agreement among the far-flung provinces. Something had to give. Compromise was in the wind.

## MODULATION

Modulation is a change of tonic. Dronality is left behind, and the original key becomes a memory of home in the ear of the listener, a kind of longing that is typically satisfied by a return to the original tonic. If the music modulates to a near place on the lattice (a fifth away is typical), only a few new tones will come into play. But if the music modulates to a more distant place, for instance a half step away (not unusual by the nineteenth century), the total number of tones can double or more. Nonetheless, polyphonic, modulating music that stays within certain harmonic limits can be sung in tune by excellent singers, as many modern performances of fourteenth-century music incontrovertibly attest. When the composer exceeds those extremely subtle limits, though, the agreements begin to falter.

## FIXED-PITCH INSTRUMENTS

Instruments of *variable pitch* can be precisely tuned in the act of playing: In addition to the voice, they include stringed instruments with no frets, such as the violin, and brass instruments with slides, such as the trombone. Instruments with *fixed pitch*—harps, keyboard instruments, fretted instruments—cannot be tuned in the act of playing. The pitches of certain wind instruments with holes (most woodwinds) or valves (most brass) can be somewhat modified during playing, but where the holes are drilled, and how long the valve tubing is, determine for the player the basic tuning. Likewise, the pitches of fretted instruments—guitar, lute, gamba—can be somewhat altered by pushing or pulling on the strings. But generally, fixed-pitch instruments all present the same basic problem: To what selection of pitches should they be tuned? Where to drill the holes? How long to make the tubes (or pipes)? Where to place the frets? And how to design and build the keyboard?

Although a singer can sing an infinite number of notes within the octave, many fixed-pitch instruments have only five or seven. Modern harps have twelve, as do modern keyboards. Frets have to be far enough apart for the fingers to fit between them; there is a limit to the number of strings that can fit on a harp frame. Given our ten fingers, as well as our other human dimensions, twelve notes to the octave has become the consensus over the centuries. The first keyboards with seven notes forward and five raised notes in back originated in the mid-fourteenth century, and although many experimental keyboards have been designed and many tuning schemes put forth, that particular arrangement of twelve notes to the octave is what eventually has been accepted and learned.

## The Two Possibilities within Fixed Pitch

There are two ways to proceed with a fixed-pitch instrument. The first seems rather obvious: Get the limited number of pitches in tune, then make music that stays within the harmonic possibilities of those pitches. This is often done, of course, and to fine effect. But historically, this choice did not satisfy the desire of the Western ear for an ever-increasing harmonic territory. Another choice, less obvious, depends on the tiny differences in pitch between many of the newly desired resonances. Why not tune one string between two tones of near pitch, and let that string *stand for* either one? Let it be a single approximate (i.e., slightly out-of-tune) pitch that substitutes for both of the precise ones. Is this a ridiculous idea? Considering the enormous delight we take in the harmonic resonances of precisely tuned low-prime ratios, this plan would not, on the face of it, seem to be desirable. But by the fifteenth century, the counter-delights of wide harmonic range, richly woven polyphony, tonal modulation, and fixed-pitch instruments had been long a-borning. The steep price of these new pleasures: the obfuscation of resonance.

It has taken about five hundred years for our modern system of approximation—twelve-tone equal temperament—to be accepted to the extent it has. Many musicians have fought it heart and soul along the way. It has been railed against, despised, and excoriated in many languages, right up to the present time. And no wonder. In twelve-tone equal temperament, only the octaves are in tune, nothing else. The perfect fifths are two cents flat from 3:2, and the major thirds are fourteen cents sharp from 5:4. As far as tonality is concerned, nothing is actually anything. *Everything* is wrong. Except for unisons and octaves, every event *stands for* some other event that we are somehow reminded of, but does not actually transpire. How could an entire mega-culture come to have accepted this?

The reason twelve-tone equal temperament has been so generally accepted is simple: It makes Bach and Beethoven and Mozart sing. It renders Ravel and Bill Evans soaring and translucent. It lets Stravinsky and Bartók open us as we have never been opened. At some very useful level, it works.

Before we begin playing the twelve-tone equal-tempered keyboard that is such a triumph of our history, however, let's consider more closely how we have allowed ourselves to be so amenably deceived.

## Approximation versus the Real Thing

The primary concern of this book is the behavior of twelve-tone equal temperament, and we raise a question central to it: Physiologically and psychologically, how can we accept a musical approximation for the real thing? Any answer to this question, at least at the present state of our knowledge, must be subjective, evanescent, and nonquantifiable. Even the terms of the question cannot be rigorously defined. Scientific method cannot save us. We do, however, have ourselves, not only individually but also collectively. By examining deeply our own responses to musical phenomena, we can shed light on our musical behavior. And by examining the music that people leave in their wake we can understand human response on the scale of human populations.

To better explain what I mean by "the real thing," let's step outside the musical frame of reference for a moment and use, as an example, the sense we have of what is "vertical" or "perpendicular" or "a ninety-degree angle with the horizon" or "straight up and down." We all have an inborn sense of the plumb line of gravity; it is part of the nature that made us. This inborn sense functions as an internal norm from which we can discern more or less deviation: We know how to "zero in" on a center we can feel. The internal norm is further formed and nurtured by experience: We learn to walk; to balance our way across logs; we practice ballet; we study geometry; we build houses, internalizing what is "vertical" from the hard world outside. We might call this sense of center that is both given by nature and internalized by experience an *inner/internalized norm*. Both inborn and amplified by learning, it is an active interface between the inside and the outside world.

What is fascinating, and relevant to our musical study, is how things can appear slightly off the vertical yet be accepted by us as if they were vertical anyway: Telephone poles and streetlamp standards are good examples. Even skyscrapers—those perfect symbols of straight-upwardness—lean a little. On the other hand, consider our response when the norm is stretched beyond our tolerance: Aunt Edith's painting that never seems to hang quite straight, or the ever-defiant Leaning Tower of Pisa. Things that are approximately vertical still refer to the vertical norm up to a certain point, but where is that point? The same goes for things that are approximately horizontal. How tilted does your bed have to be before you can't sleep? How flat *is* Kansas? Given the intrinsic quantum lumpiness of atomic energy, how flat is anything? Do you know what I mean when I say "flat" on account of a norm that neither one of us has ever actually experienced? Is there such a thing as a straight line? If not, how crooked can it get and still be straight? Can a field be square? Can a cookie be round?

These are the kinds of questions that will become crucial to our study as we step back inside the musical frame of reference.

## Low-Prime Harmony as Norms

The pure unisons, octaves, fifths, and major thirds we have been learning to sing function musically as inner/internalized harmonic norms. They are an aspect of our nature, yet we nurture them by study and practice. In order to understand harmony in its fullness, we need to study not only the musical realization of these norms but also the divergences from them that are typical in music.

## UNISONS

Perhaps the most perfect unison we can hear in everyday life lies in the midrange of an excellently tuned piano. The three strings that, sounding together, produce the C above middle C (for instance), are about as close to a unison as music ever gets. It is interesting to damp out two of the strings with your fingers, leaving only one to sound, and then to compare that with the sound of all three together. Not quite the same—partly because of minute idiosyncratic differences between the strings. If three excellent violinists play that same C, we also perceive a unison, but the difference between a single bowed violin string and three bowed strings is now quite noticeable because the human agency in the bowing and touching of the strings introduces innumerable small deviations in pitch and tone. A unison produced by three excellent sopranos, even if sung with "no vibrato" and sounding almost like one voice, would have even more characteristic deviations of pitch and tone. What about three not-so-excellent singers? What about the women in the congregation singing the same hymn, but not exactly together? Now, what about a kindergarten class singing "The Star-Spangled Banner" with many stragglers? Perhaps the children are pushing the musical envelope, but the proud parents are enjoying the national anthem with no recognition problem. These examples, which run the gamut from the nearly perfect unison to the extremely rough approximation, all refer to the same norm, that is, 1:1.

I think the reason the piano and the accomplished violinists and sopranos sound so pleasant to us is that it takes so little effort for the ear to recognize the unison. Our sense of rightness is stimulated directly. A keen pleasure I have as a teacher is to witness a student at the very moment his or her musical experience first comes into line with that interior—but previously unrealized—knowledge. I like to teach people who think they are "tone-deaf" for this very reason. During the first moment a tone-deafer is aware of singing a true unison with another person, a longtime hunger is suddenly satisfied by a resonance that floods the senses. There is a tremendous upwelling of connectedness as outer and inner finally and seamlessly interlock.

On the other hand, it may take considerable effort for the ear to refer the kids' raggle-taggle singing to the 1:1 norm; indeed, to a Ba-Benjelle Pygmy it might sound like an amusing sort of polyphony. But our hearing contains a cultural recognition that allows our brain to do the work of sorting it all out and putting it back together as a single melody.

## OCTAVES, FIFTHS, AND THIRDS

The more complex the harmony, the more the ear tolerates deviation from the norm. Octaves, 2:1, are slightly more complex than unisons and so subject to a slightly larger range of deviation. As all singers know, it is considerably more difficult to tune octaves precisely than unisons because they don't lock in nearly so easily. However, groups of men and women singing together in octaves can go considerably astray from 2:1 without breaking off relations entirely. It is even the practice of some piano tuners to "stretch" octaves, that is, to tune them slightly too wide, believing that this procedure increases the sonority of the piano; in this case the typical ear forgives the deliberate de-tuning.

Perfect fifths, 3:2, are yet more complex, and the ear will tolerate more deviation in them than it would in a unison. Equal-tempered fifths are two cents flat, which is barely detectable and not entirely irksome; the same deviation in unisons could not be seriously entertained for long. Historically, the most generally accepted temperament before equal temperament was called *meantone* tuning; it required the fifths to be 5.4 cents too small, which is definitely discernable but was standard practice for generations before Bach.

Major thirds, 5:4, are of course considerably more complex than perfect fifths, and predictably can take more abuse. The equal-tempered third, as we shall study in detail in chapter 20, is still functional at fourteen cents too wide, but it can also be mistaken for the Pythagorean major third (81:64) under certain circumstances. That very ambiguity is a primary focus of part 3.

## Where Does the Ear Draw the Line?

As we go on with our study of tonal harmony in twelve-tone equal temperament, part of our work will be to notice exactly how much approximation we can stand in the more complex harmonies before our recognition of the inner/internalized norm snaps. The point at which we say, "That's not an *almost* something, that's a *different* something," will be at the center of our inquiry.

Meanwhile, it can be astonishing to notice how forgiving, under certain circumstances, the ear can be. The out-of-tune pianos in restaurants and nightclubs are good examples. In fact, the sound of a honky-tonk piano with its built-in wailing dissonance has come to represent a kind of uplifting defiance: We can't afford a piano tuner but we can damn well play good music. I once happened upon a piano that had been abandoned in the damp woods for a year, yet had somehow defied its own disintegration. It was wonderful to play on because, although music was hideously and hilariously distorted, it was still recognizable. For me, that experience was a cartoon representing the truth that nothing manifest is free from distortion. Existence is a piano in the woods.

When you get down close enough, everything is wildly gyrating energy fields anyway. The Sufi teacher Hazrat Inayat Khan is quoted as having said, "If two strings were ever actually in tune they would break," by which I think he meant that since no two things in Creation are exactly the same, such exactness cannot exist in this universe. Yet even though we live in this world of near misses and second guesses, we hunger all the while for the hidden center that does not move. It is a tough paradox that the unmoving center cannot be experienced in the exterior world as pure, static form. So we need a balanced communication, a resonance, between inner knowledge and outer experience. That is why as a musician you have to know your inner life, which means intimacy with the norms of rhythm and harmony. If you lose the inner sound, the slippery, slidey, hit-and-miss music of our world loses its reference, and the meaning is diminished, and the beauty and the fun go out of it. That is why singing in tune makes the equal-tempered keyboard more palatable: When the inside is clear, the outside becomes navigable.

## The Hunger for the Center

I think that one must learn to value the hunger of the psyche for touching the internal norms. The intelligence and cunning with which that hunger drives us to derive meaning from the approximations and illusions of modern life is otherwise hard to imagine. Civilization itself is nothing if not a panorama of sophisticated illusions: Zoos are wilderness, chemicals are food, reality is virtual, and twelve-tone equal temperament is tonal harmony. The good news is that as the century turns there is an awakening to what we have lost, and to our acculturated denial of loss. Wilderness is becoming precious, not expendable; tribal values and rituals honored, not denigrated; and the resonances of pure harmony sought after and taken to heart. In *My Name is Chellis and I'm Recovering from Western Civilization*, Chellis Glendinning points out the relationship between the individual psyche and the planetary environment: We can't heal the earth unless we heal ourselves. She puts it on a survival basis and, as far as pure harmony goes, so do I. Using the approximations of twelve-tone equal temperament intelligently and beautifully while at the same time staying connected to the low-prime resonances of its source is a kind of musical survival strategy, an insurance that the hungers of the ear remain consciously nourished and beneficially used, not denied and thus perversely distorted.

## Our Plan

Our keyboard study can be considered an examination of the way in which our norms of harmony are referred to, played with, tempted, seduced, betrayed, violated, and finally transcended in twelve-tone equal temperament. Don't worry that you will ruin your hearing by listening deeply to the approximate harmonies of the keyboard. No matter how loudly your culture is shrieking at you, you cannot forget your beginnings: Pure harmony is hard-wired. If you are balanced and open-minded in your practice, you can integrate all functional musical systems into your hearing; you yourself can become more integrated through that work.

    All of part 2 takes place in the key of C and demonstrates the entire gamut of equal-tempered harmonic possibilities from one tonic. We'll begin keyboard practice with musical structures where no harmonic ambiguity is presented to the ear, that is, situations that could be defined by pointing to a spot on the harmonic lattice and saying, with 100 percent certainty, "I am here." There are three ways the ear gains certainty as to its whereabouts: pitch, degree, and tonic. In chapters 20 and 21 we'll discuss equal-tempered situations in which there is zero ambiguity of pitch, degree, or tonic. The practices in chapter 23 introduce ambiguity of pitch. Ambiguity of degree enters in at chapter 26 and is developed intensively (along with ambiguity of the tonic) in parts 3 and 4. Thus we will move methodically through situations where the uncertainty and ambiguity are increased until there is 100 percent harmonic uncertainty, that is, situations in which you could be anywhere, there is no map, and the tones have equal tonal meaning: atonality.

This might be a good moment to peruse again the table of contents and introduction to become reacquainted with the overall scheme of the book.

Then it's time to leap into keyboard practice.

# 20

# Six Unambiguous Chords

## A First Glimpse at Equal Temperament: The Overtone Chord

For this beginning work with twelve-tone equal temperament you will need a guitar or harp string tuned to the C an octave below middle C, as well as a conventionally—and recently—tuned piano (for which an electronic keyboard makes a less desirable but serviceable substitute). Review the section "Numbering" in chapter 1 before you begin.

First, tune the guitar or harp string as precisely as possible to the C on the piano. Then vigorously pluck the string and review the tones in the overtone series in your mind and in your ear until you can severally or collectively hear the six distinct partials of example 20.1.

Reacquaint yourself with the totality of this chord, its simplicity, complexity, and rightness. Then, at the piano keyboard, strike that same C with considerable force, softly adding the five remaining tones onto the chord in a slow, upward arpeggio. Take about five seconds to articulate the entire chord, delicately folding the higher tones into the gradual decay of the fundamental tone, as shown in example 20.2.

*Example 20.1*

Listen for the ways in which the two differently produced chords are the same and the ways in which they are not. Both chords shimmer, but they shimmer differently. Every instrument has its own idiosyncratic resonances and damping characteristics: Tones fade in and out in com-

*Example 20.2*

plex, unpredictable ways. Also, all strings (particularly metal ones, and especially metal ones under extreme tension, like piano strings) have intrinsic inharmonicity, which means that the overtones are increasingly sharp as they climb the ladder.* Moreover, the piano strings are *deliberately* de-tuned: The G's are tuned two cents flat and the E is tuned fourteen cents sharp. After making sure that the C of the guitar and the C of the piano agree as much as possible, check this out for yourself. The induced fifth partial of the guitar string, to which the *very* quietly played E of the piano is added, is especially dramatic.

Indeed, the more deeply and closely you listen, the more differences you will hear between the two chords. But if you listen another way, from a certain perceptual distance one might say, there can be no question that the two chords have the same basic functional meaning—the piano chord is a little rough, that's all. There is, among certain performing musicians who have to come to terms with the impossibilities of tuning their instruments, a tired but tenacious expression: "Oh well, it's good enough for jazz," or "good enough for folk music," or perhaps more recently, "good enough for classical music," to which I might add, "Oh well, its good enough for Western civilization." I don't mean to be cynical—only to point out that historically we have learned to accept the piano chord as the real thing. All of us who have ever enjoyed a Mozart symphony or a hit song have accepted it. The ear knows how to hear the piano chord as the overtone series as surely as the eye knows how to see the lines of print on this page as straight.

By striking the fundamental C of the piano chord loudly and then softening the upper tones, we have been minimizing the discordances inherent in the instrument. If you play only the top three tones and play them all with equal force or bring them down an octave, as in example 20.3, the impurities are even more prevalent.

*Example 20.3*

These chords do not abide so easily in the ear; indeed, it takes a while for a pianist to learn to make a piano sing. But even at their most brash, such triads are accepted as the heart of the overtone series. Even though we package them and build our music out of them, it is good not to take them for granted. In its natural state—as a chord consisting of the fourth, fifth, and sixth partials of a plucked harp string, for instance—the major triad is scarcely audible; it twinkles like a star, and could almost be perceived as an aural gate to heaven itself, some ephemera between flesh and spirit. But to tumble the triad down to the lower octaves, to render it in earth colors and de-tune it in the service of our hungers, is to make a servant out of an angel and cloud its face with the hint of a scowl. Historically, the Western ear has indeed made the leap downward from the 6:5:4 combination of pure harmonics to the equal-tempered triad, and used that triad as the basic building block of its harmonic system. As you do the practices in this book

---

*Remember from chapter 1 that a theoretically perfect string would not only vibrate along its entire length but also divide into halves, thirds, quarters, and so on, each division making its own sine wave and producing its own partial. In reality, stiffness at the bridge and nut inhibits the ends of the string from vibrating freely and throws off the precision of the divisions. The greater the string tension, the greater the inharmonicity of the overtones. On most stringed instruments the tension is so low as to make the deviation negligible; on the piano, however, the sharpness of the overtones is quite apparent. Piano tuners use various tricks, including "stretching" octaves, to compensate for the string's innate out-of-tuneness.

you will find yourself reliving this historical leap from just template to equal-tempered approximation within many different contexts.

## Drawing the Major Triad

On the lattice of perfect fifths and major thirds, the three tones of a C-major triad look like example 20.4. To schematically identify the triad, a third line can be drawn; it is a broken line to indicate that it is not one of the two generating axes of the lattice and hence not an elemental harmony. Major triads form an upward-pointing triangle. In the center can be placed the capitalized letter name, as shown in example 20.5.

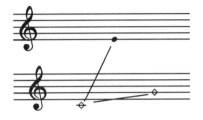

*Example 20.4*

Of course, as soon as we have invented one major triad we have invented as many as we can use. Example 20.6 shows the same configuration of tones from F and from G.

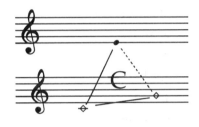

*Example 20.5*

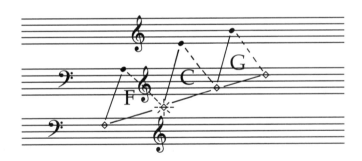

*Example 20.6*

The harmonic qualities that exist between two *tones* that are distant by a fifth also exist to some extent between two *triads* whose roots are distant by a fifth. We are about to invent music consisting of three triads whose roots relate by perfect fifths.

## Three-Chord Music: The Ping-Pong Cadence

Given that a major triad is a condensation of the overtone chord and that the strongest harmonic connection is by fifths, consider the construction shown in example 20.7: the overtones of C and its nearest harmonic neighbors, G above and F below.

Awkward as it may be to play, begin with the C chord, then play the F chord, then the C chord again: then the G chord, then the C chord again: left, center, right, center, much like a ping-pong or tennis game (C is the net).

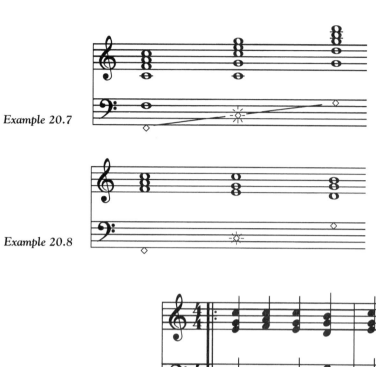

*Example 20.7*

*Example 20.8*

Now let's turn the construction into piano music by octave reduction, and by thinning the chords to four tones each, as in example 20.8.

The exercise can now be written as shown in example 20.9. Play this until it is smooth. It can be made considerably smoother by tying the common tones, as shown in example 20.10.

*Example 20.9*

*Example 20.10*

The totality of the sound will be better understood, and better played, if you hold over the common tones and listen for four independent voices blending perfectly together, as in example 20.11.

r.h.

l.h.

*Example 20.11*

Learn to play this sweetly and seamlessly, as though it were a sort of musical mantra, because, basically, that's what it is. The energies that govern this back-and-forth musical flow seem soothing and right. It contains a power central to our musical legacy. It is OK to listen to it over and over again.

To appreciate the back-and-forth flow of energy even more, try to hear the notes as if they were being sung, and consider the part of each singer in turn. Consider the harmony of the soprano and the bass in example 20.12.

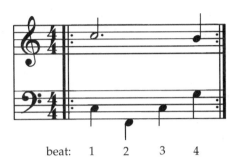

*Example 20.12*

In the first beat the soprano is singing the fourth partial of C; she holds that note through the second beat, where it becomes (magically for her) the sixth partial of F. In the third beat it returns to the fourth partial of C. In the fourth beat, by lowering her pitch a half step she sings the fifth partial (octave-reduced) of G. Play the bass on the piano and sing the soprano part in tune (an octave lower for males). Enjoy at each beat your position in the overtone chord.

Now follow the alto, shown in example 20.13.

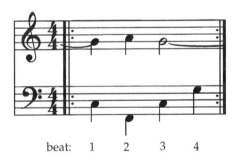

*Example 20.13*

In the first beat the alto sings the third partial of C, then moves a minor whole tone up to sing the fifth partial of F, then back to the third partial of C, which she holds as it becomes (more magic) the second partial of G, which she holds as it becomes the third partial of C again. Sing this for yourself as you play the bass, again savoring the way in which you are sampling the bass-generated overtone chords in such a way as to move your voice the minimal melodic distance.

Figure out the tenor part in this same way, singing it while playing the bass. The bass part itself makes the best harmony, of course, but the worst melody: all leaps and no steps. For the moment, however, it will be sufficient to rely on the patience of bass singers everywhere.

Now play again the ping-pong mantric cadence (example 20.11) at the keyboard as though you were all four singers in perfectly blended harmony.

To bring our ping-pong metaphor even more into the physical realm, think of a rubber band stretched vertically between two points. Beginning at the center, stretch the rubber band to the left, then relax it back to the center, then stretch it to the right, then relax it back to the center. Now instead of the rubber band between two fixed points, imagine a musical string vibrating in slow motion. The string sets up complementary energies on both sides of a central point of rest. This ping-pong harmony we are studying behaves much like the periodic motion of a string. The chordal sequence of its harmony is, in actuality, the result of the combination of many strings sounding together in close agreement, but behaving collectively with the same oscillating dynamic as a single string: back and forth motion through a center. This may all seem a little obvious, but it can't be too entirely obvious, since it took humankind about a million years to discover it through experience and another few hundred to figure it out and describe it.

This is a good time to ask again, "What exactly *is* this territory we seem to be moving through?" The subject is a mystery, of course—no one knows objectively what goes on in the brain or the psyche when we hear harmony. But what you can know indelibly is how it sounds to you as a musician: literally, how it moves you. Let your insides move with these chords. Resist "been there, done that" because this harmony is trying to tell you something that no one has ever heard all of.

## The Whole Cadence

Consider how a drunkard reaches for his bottle: first, too far to the left; then, catching his mistake, too far to the right; then—squinting—just a *little* too far to the left; finally, success, and a toast. When we are sober, the margin of error is perhaps less, but our perceptions operate on the same principle: We zero in on what we want, not unlike a vibrating string that comes to rest at its center of motion. Harmonic progressions likewise resolve at the center after motion toward either side. A perfect example of this is example 20.14a, an extrapolation from the mantric cadence. It is usually written as in example 20.14b

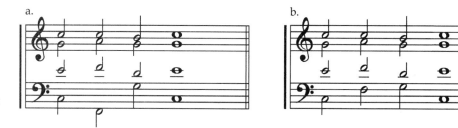

*Example 20.14*

The F chord is "too far to the left," the G chord is "too far to the right," and the C chord is the motionless center. Called a *perfect cadence* or *full cadence* or *whole cadence*, this harmonic formula or some variation of it typically indicates the end of a phrase, a set of phrases, or an entire piece. The word *cadence* is from the Latin *cadere*, "to fall," which is akin to the Sanskrit root *cad-* and the Greek *kad-*, with the same meaning. It has here the same usage as the "fall" of the voice at the end of a sentence. More recently *cadence* has come to mean "rise and fall" as in "the cadence of her speech," and that is the actual case in a musical perfect cadence: The reciprocal fifth (the subdominant F) rises to the overtonal fifth (the dominant G), which falls to the generating tone C; or *ma* to *pa* to *sa*; or moon to sun to earth; or yin to yang to balance. You call it.

The salient point here is that F and G, either as tones (as discussed in chapter 6) or as triads, are not harmonically adjacent. In a typical whole cadence (as in example 20.14b), the middle term, the C chord, is at first deliberately omitted, forming, between the F chord and the G chord, a musical ellipsis (that is, something left out). The final C chord then becomes satisfying as the event that, central to the others, reconciles both. You leave out something, then you give it back. Thus the whole cadence can be thought of as a filled-in ellipsis.

There is no chance of overemphasizing how important the whole cadence has become to our cultural ear. For over three centuries it has been sculpting the flow of our music, yet its basic wavelike reciprocity has not been well articulated in our teaching. It is up to you to listen for its true meaning and to come to terms with how to use it—and, if you teach, how to open the secret for others. To bring yourself closer to the sound, review chapter 4 (on *pa*) and chapter 7 (on *ma*). Then, as you play both the mantric cadence (example 20.11) and the perfect cadence (example 20.14) on the keyboard, try to follow the triangles on the lattice in example 20.6 with your eyes. Imagine that each triangle glows when you play its chord. I think that actually is what happens—according to its many dimensions—to the lattice in the brain.

## Three-Chord Music

To best experience the balance of harmonic energy around the tonic, write some music using only the major triads of C, F, and G. In the left hand play only the roots at the pitches given in the ping-pong cadence (example 20.11). In the right hand, play only the three notes of the triad, but you may position them so that any chordal tone appears on top. Start and end on C.

Example 20.15 gives the idea.

*Example 20.15*

After writing such a piece, learn to improvise within the same framework. Next, compose another exercise using the same rules, but with this difference: The bass may be in any octave. With the sensitive use of rhythm, this piece can be somewhat elaborate. The point is to discover this elaboration *as a function of the harmonic balance*. In other words, when you find a harmonic flow whose balance pleases you, the melodic and rhythmic elements tend to discover themselves. Example 20.16, a short composition of three-chord music, offers a glimpse at one of the most astonishing aspects of Western tonal music: *harmony as form*.

*Example 20.16*

Before you write your own, consider example 20.17, which shows how a Major scale can be harmonized using only the triads of the tonic, dominant, and subdominant.

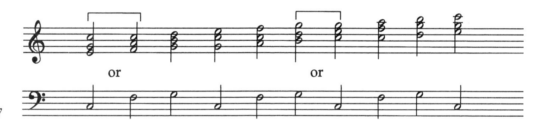

*Example 20.17*

It is not surprising that the Major scale sounds so well matched to the primary major triads, since the Major scale itself can be seen as a stepwise arrangement of the very tones in these triads, that is, the overtones of C and its nearest harmonic neighbors, F and G. The secret to the stability of the Major scale is precisely, in fact, that it is made from the overtones of a central tone and its nearest harmonic neighbors.

After you compose your best piece, try improvising within the confines of this language. Transpose the exercise to other keys, at sight if you can. Be sure not to sell three-chord music short. A person who is tired of these combinations is tired of music. The mystery in them is as deep as breath. The three-chord matrix of blues, gospel, and country music—even ultra-manufactured pop and rock music—nourishes hundreds of millions of souls, and it is important, especially if your own sophistications have extended your tastes far beyond this central harmony, to stay empathetically tuned to what is most simple and powerful in the musical language.

## Drawing the Minor Triad

On the lattice of perfect fifths and major thirds, the three tones of a minor triad appear as

shown in example 20.18. (This is a good time to review the section on the minor third in chapter 9.) Remember that the primary functions are the perfect fifth between C and G and the major third between G and E♭; hence the line drawn from C to E♭ is broken, indicating that it is not elemental harmony. "C mi" is written in the center of the downward-pointing triangle.

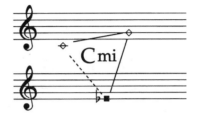

*Example 20.18*

C minor is called the *parallel minor* of C major. C major is called the *parallel major* of C minor. Examine the image of the parallel major/minor pair shown in example 20.19. Notice how the third up from C (on one hand) and the third down from G (on the other hand) seem to give two versions of the same construction.

As I mentioned in chapter 9, singing the 6:5 minor third in tune against a C-and-G drone (thus producing a minor triad) was one of the revelatory moments of my musical education—it was like experiencing real musical fire for the first time. Of

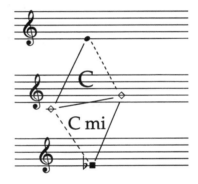

*Example 20.19*

course I use the equal-tempered minor triad continuously as a composer and performer and suppose it to be, on the whole, a blessing to humanity. But it must be said that the minor triad of equal temperament is not a very satisfactory representation of "the real thing"— much less fulfilling (to me, anyhow) than the equal-tempered major triad, even though the fourteen-cent disparity of the third (too large in major, too small in minor) is virtually identical. Nonetheless, it has clearly come into common and, for the most part, unquestioned usage. Your job is to sing an in-tune 6:5 E♭ against a C and G drone, and then listen to what you get on your equal-tempered keyboard, and then come to your own conclusions. The bottom line for the equal-tempered version of the chord is the same as the bottom line for equal temperament as a whole—it works. But in this case especially, it pays not to forget what you are missing. Forgive, but don't forget.

## Cadences in Minor

The parallel minors of our three major triads are shown in example 20.20.

The ping-pong cadence, using all minor triads instead of all major triads, sounds like example 20.21.

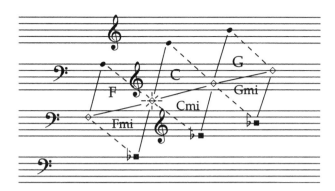

*Example 20.20*

*Example 20.21*

Since the minor triad itself is more complex and consequently less stable than the major triad, it doesn't function harmonically quite as well as a chord of resolution. (The ratios of the minor triad are 15:12:10; the ratios of the major triad are 6:5:4). The all-minor ping-pong cadence seems pastel and floaty; the C-minor triad seems less commanding as a center. For this reason, the cadential function of these chords is usually enhanced by retaining the major version for one or two of them. The most usual convention is shown in example 20.22.

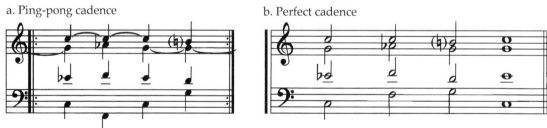

*Example 20.22*

This is perhaps the strongest possible minor cadential harmony; example 20.23 shows that its notes, reduced to a scale, produce the Harmonic Minor mode (see chapter 12).

*Example 20.23*

Another strong possibility is shown in example 20.24, which produces the MA/MI mode of example 20.25.

a. Ping-pong cadence          b. Perfect cadence

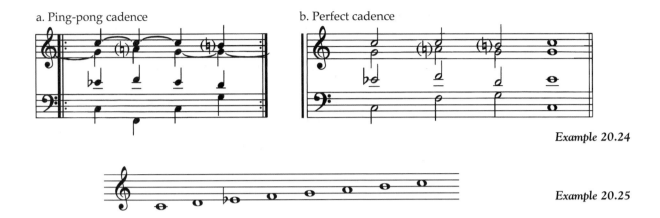

*Example 20.24*

*Example 20.25*

Further possibilities of great beauty use the major tonic chord (thus characterizing these modes as essentially Major); these cadences are shown in examples 20.26 and 20.27.

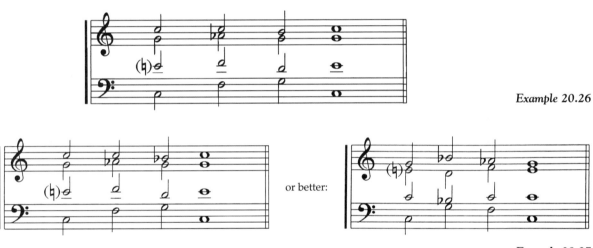

*Example 20.26*

or better:

*Example 20.27*

The remaining possible combinations of mixed-mode cadences are Mixolydian (example 20.28), and Dorian (example 20.29).

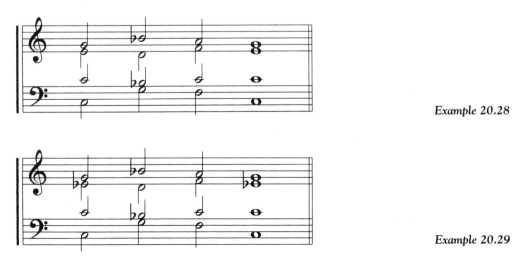

*Example 20.28*

*Example 20.29*

# Harmonic Rhythm

Although every one of these eight versions of the ping-pong cadence produces the same yin-yang rocking harmonic motion, each has its own characteristic modal flavor. You will find it truly useful to compose or improvise (or both) three-chord pieces in each version. Never lose sight of C as the tonic. The point is to be harmonically and rhythmically cogent while deriving a soprano part that is as melodious as possible. Notice how your sense of harmonic balance around C shapes the composition. Notice also that it is not only *where* you are but also *how long* you remain there that is musically telling. This combination of where and how long is called *harmonic rhythm*, and of all the treasures of the Western musical heritage, it is the most sophisticated and elaborate. The harmonic rhythm of a piece is its blueprint through time. When you confine your music making to only three root options (tonic, subdominant, and dominant) plus the modal complexity that comes from mixing overtonal and reciprocal thirds (major and minor triads)—as we are doing here—then the generative power of harmonic rhythm can be experienced in a pure state. By composing with only these six chords, you are exposing to scrutiny one of the deepest musical mysteries.

# 21

# TWELVE UNAMBIGUOUS CHORDS: TONAL HARMONY WITHIN THE LATTICE OF TWELVE NOTES

HARMONIC MOTION BY PERFECT FIFTHS, which has been our concern in chapter 20, is only half the story. Now we need to mix in the energy of movement by thirds.

## The Relative Minor

On the lattice of perfect fifths and major thirds, the three tones of an A-minor triad appear as shown in example 21.1. As in the C-minor triad, the broken line indicates that the harmony of the minor third (C to A in this case) is not elemental, as is the harmony of the perfect fifth (A to E) or the major third (C to E). Like all minor triads on the lattice, the triangle points downward.

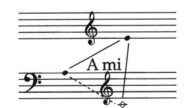

*Example 21.1*

Now examine the image of the relative major/minor pair, shown in example 21.2. The tones C and E are common to both triads; notice the symmetry around the line that connects them. In the C-major triad, the fifth is upward from C; in the A-minor triad, the fifth is downward from E. Consider, then, the pivotal function of E: It is the overtonal third of C, *and* A is its reciprocal fifth. The word *relative* probably derives from the fact that the modes of C Major and A Aeolian both contain the same tones—at least, on the equal-tempered keyboard.*

*Example 21.2*

*As has been discussed in chapter 16, the D to C in C Major is 9:8; in A Aeolian it is 10:9, one of the subtle distinctions disguised by equal temperament.

The harmonic motion from C major to A minor is so smooth that it is easy to miss. It seems obvious and beckoning at the same time. The popular music of Thailand (among other Westernized Asian countries) often slides seamlessly and endlessly between relative major/minor pairs. Try playing the two triads alternately at the keyboard, maybe singing the common E as you play, to increase your awareness of the subtle nature of this harmony.

## Parallel versus Relative

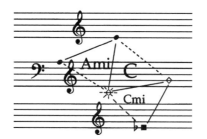

*Example 21.3*

We have now examined two minor chords that both relate to C major but in different ways. All three triads together look like example 21.3. To better hear the relationship among these triads, let's look at the reciprocity between the note E♭ and the note A. In relation to the tone C:

E♭ is a fifth up and a third down; A is a third up and a fifth down.

Their harmonic paths are the same, but their directions are opposite. (Figure 21.1 shows the harmonic path of E♭, and figure 21.2 shows the path of A.)

Their ratios are reciprocal.

E♭ is 6:5; A is 5:6, octave-extended to 10:6, or 5:3.

*Figure 21.1*

The *parallel* relationship of C major to C minor represents overtonal-fifth energy plus reciprocity between the thirds: The fifth stays the same while the polarity of the third flips.

The *relative* relationship of C major to A minor is the opposite. It represents overtonal-third energy plus reciprocity between the fifths: The third stays the same while the polarity of the fifth flips. Only the tone C is common to all three triads.

*Figure 21.2*

These polar flips affect us in the *ga* dimension in much the same way the ping-pong cadence affects us in the *pa* dimension. Ping-pong in Ga-land would look like example 21.4.

*Example 21.4*

We don't ordinarily associate this progression with a harmonic cadence, but nonetheless I want you to recognize the particular rise and fall of energies it contains. That recognition prepares the way for a new proclamation:

> The dominant/subdominant reciprocity in the *pa* dimension combines with the rel-
> ative/parallel reciprocity in the *ga* dimension to produce all the tonal harmony that
> exists.

This is a broader formulation of our original premise—that harmony consists of perfect fifths, major thirds, their reciprocals, and their compounds. Both statements are subject to codicils, but our new decree is nonetheless a powerful conceptual tool for making music.

Advice: Reread this section now or come back to it soon. It is a crucial—and almost entirely overlooked—piece of the harmonic puzzle and may take some getting used to.

## The Twelve Triads in the Lattice of Twelve Notes

The lattice of twelve notes we so patiently sang into existence in part 1 contains the lowest possible five-limit ratios; it is the "real thing" that we will now represent by approximation on the equal-tempered keyboard. If we move carefully, the approximations of equal temperament will not confuse us, our position on the lattice at any moment will be unambiguous, and we will be able to appreciate the affect that comes with the territory. Let's begin by studying example 21.5, which shows the major and minor triads available in the lattice of twelve notes.

Since we are dealing with triads as units, it is useful to have a diagram with the triadic names only. In figure 21.3 the staff lines have disappeared, but the skewed axes of lattice nota-tion remain (that is, the figure is in "staff orientation," intro-duced in chapter 6). This new configuration we will call a *chord lattice*.

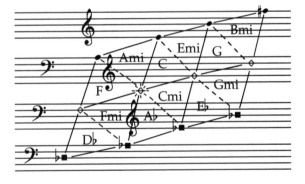

*Example 21.5*

Notice how, in figure 21.3, solid lines connect all the major and minor triads a fifth apart, as well as each relative pair and each parallel pair. Since the connection of a major triad to its mediant (C major to E minor; A♭ major to C minor, etc.) is very close but not primary, those connection lines are broken; the same is true, of course, for any minor chord and its submediant (E minor to C major).

*Figure 21.3*

# Matchstick Harmony

Figure 21.3 reminds me of the matchstick puzzles and games we played as kids. As grown-ups, our puzzle will be to create cogent harmony that the approximations of equal temperament do not obscure. Our harmonies must remain so closely connected that their meaning remains clear even though everything is slightly out of tune. Therefore you may move from one chord to another in the chord lattice of figure 21.3 only if the two chords are connected by a line (or a dotted line). There is one rule and one exception, in addition to several guidelines.

*Rule:* You can move to any chord connected by any line.

*Exception:* Occasionally you can leap the distance of two perfect fifths if you immediately fill in the chord you leapt over. For example, from F major you could move to G major, providing that C major (or C minor) were the next chord; or from A minor to B minor to E minor. Of all such possibilities, the best ones by far are those that look like perfect cadences, that is, the roots leap two fifths up to a major triad, then fall one fifth down. Leaping *down* and then filling (G major to F minor to C major, for instance) is OK but not as strong. Certain moves in this leap-and-fill category sound remarkably weak: G minor to F major to C minor; use these infrequently and with discretion. Notice also that from G major to A minor is *not* two perfect fifths on this lattice.

A basic characteristic of melodic motion—*steps are easy, leaps are hard*—is likewise true for the motion of triadic harmony. The above rule and exception simply assure that you proceed harmonically stepwise, that is, by matchsticks.

Here are some further guidelines:

- Start and end on C major.
- All chords will be of the same duration (two beats, for instance).
- Play chords in close position with the root in the bass at all times.
- Pythagorean harmony (root motion by fifths) is easier to hear than pentamerous harmony (root motion by thirds). Use more descending thirds than ascending thirds; the latter should be rare. (I'll expain why at the end of the chapter.)
- Parallel chords (C major to C minor, for instance) are a form of pentamerous harmony and should be used sparingly.

Example 21.6 is a brief, unambiguous chord progression.

*Example 21.6*

C    Ami    Emi    Bmi    Emi    Ami    F    G    C

Notice how the harmony takes us to the relative minor, canvasses the overtonal third territory by climbing up fifths, then falls by fifths along that spine of minor triads, then cadences. It contains root motions of a total of two falling thirds, three falling fifths, two rising fifths, and an upward leap of two fifths.

Practice this example until it is rapid and legato and you can truly hear the harmonic movement in it without thinking about your fingers. Then try improvising some other progressions within the same constraints using only these six chords.

A contrasting passage is given in example 21.7.

*Example 21.7*

Notice how this harmony swings down through the territory of reciprocal thirds, sweeps upward by fifths through the parallel minors, and finally cadences with a minor subdominant. Its root motions include four falling thirds; the remainder is Pythagorean. Again, learn to play this so smoothly that your fingers go away and the shape of the harmony becomes vivid. You might also try improvising (within the rules) using only these eight chords—the six reciprocal-third triads plus G major and C major.

Now for an even longer excursion, let's combine these two progressions. Example 21.8 shows the result. As you play this through, be aware of the progressions by fifths, and of the overall surge from overtonal to reciprocal territory. Ask yourself a thousand times: *What is the sound of this?*

*Example 21.8*

# Adding a Melody

Once the harmony is heard and understood, the next step is to compose a melody above the harmony using these guidelines:

- Do not leap to or from nonchordal tones.
- Use unsurprising passing tones and neighboring tones.

- Be sparse. Try to compose in three or four parts, with as transparent a sound as possible.
- 4–3 suspensions are occasionally OK.
- Go for beauty, not weirdness. Be far in, not far out.

Example 21.9 consists of a melody added to the harmonic progression of example 21.8.

*Example 21.9*

Now it is your work to compose a similar exercise (or two, or several) following the rules and guidelines.

# What Are We Doing?
# The Reason behind Unambiguous Harmony

If you could hear the music we have been composing played in just intonation, it would sound exactly the way it does on your equal-tempered keyboard except a little more sonorous. That is, the harmonic meaning of both versions, their sense of harmonic motion and place, would be, thanks to the precautions we have taken, identical. Our procedures have assured a tonal context so unmistakable that every time we press down a piano key it produces a tone whose unique harmonic coordinates we instantly recognize. Because we have weeded out all pairs of tones separated by a comma (i.e., stepsiblings and comma siblings, such as G♯ and A♭), there is no chance of ambiguity, even though the tuning only approximates the just template. The strongest, simplest ratios in their clearest contexts have been chosen. These special lattice exercises produce *no-comma music*, as close to pure harmony as equal temperament allows: *Nonmodulating music with zero ambiguity of pitch, degree, or tonic.*

But why do this? The reason it is critical to become familiar with progressions that are not functionally altered by equal temperament is that so many progressions in actual music *are* functionally altered by equal temperament. A full, precise description of how such progressions deform the just-intonation template is the central purpose of our work, and we are now nibbling at the edge of the issue. But first we must methodically produce from equal temperament everything that is *not* unique to it. These harmonies we are now playing sound the way they do not because of but in spite of their being in equal temperament. The only difference just intonation would make is a little more color in the cheeks.

The full understanding of equal-tempered harmony depends in part on the fullness of your experience in just intonation. Events that were single tones when we were singing against a drone are now combined into triads whose harmonic qualities are distributed over a wider range (triangular areas, in this case), and whose ratios are slightly disturbed. So keep referring back to the basic act of singing in tune. That way there is hope of wringing some meaning out of our increasingly complex keyboard universe.

In fact, if you have access to an electronic keyboard that allows you to play in five-limit just intonation, or if you know a tuner who can tune your piano that way (the list is short), or if you can do it yourself, then by all means, tune up and take off. If you are actually playing in just intonation, the lattice position of a chord is defined not only by musical context but also by the tuning itself; so you can become more adventurous and experiment with harmonic leaps, for instance: C to Ami to Bmi to Gmi to E♭ to D♭ to C, or C to Fmi to Ami to Emi to C to Gmi to A♭ to G to Bmi to C, and so on. But, experimentation and beauty aside, our present concern is not how to make music in just intonation. At issue here is how twelve-tone equal temperament behaves—specifically, its relationship to the inner/internalized norms of just intonation.

Meanwhile, back at the equal-tempered keyboard, my advice is to spend enough time with these twelve chords that you can hear them reliably in your head away from the instrument. (I think the ideal distance "away from the instrument" is about six feet: close enough to check what you hear and far enough away to have to get up to do so.) Such inner certainty does come with practice.

Before asking you to plunge ahead with further exercises, I would like to amplify some of the guidelines already given. First, you'll notice that if you play all the chords with the upper three parts in close position, and always move to the nearest voicing of the next chord (that is, make use of all common tones and move your fingers the least possible distance), then you will always end up in the same position in which you began. Make certain that, when leaping two fifths, you take the upper parts (that is, the right hand) in contrary motion to the bass; this will give the same result as if the elided fifth had been inserted. The examples demonstrate this.

Second, you may have noticed one harmonic move that is excluded from our current practice: In these exercises there can be no stepwise motion in the roots, with the exception of the two-fifths-filled-in-immediately rule. For instance, you can't go from G to Ami (it's not two fifths on the lattice) or E♭ to F (same reason), or G to A♭, or F to Emi. This preserves zero ambiguity. Stepwise root motion, certainly typical of tonal harmony, will appear in due time.

Third, a note about root motion by thirds. Notice carefully the difference between descending thirds and ascending thirds. Progressions like G to Emi to C to Ami to F, or E♭ to Cmi to A♭ to Fmi to D♭, sound totally familiar and right to us. After all, the most-used progression of American popular music is C to Ami to F to G to C. In these cases, any two descending thirds always add up to one descending fifth: C to Ami to F gets you from C down to F; Gmi to E♭ to Cmi gets you from Gmi down to Cmi. Now try all these examples backward: ascending thirds. They are no less functional ascending than descending, but definitely they are less strong, less used, even downright unfamiliar. Any two will add up to an ascending fifth, and ascending fifths are less used than descending fifths. But they do have their powers. I don't know why ascending thirds have been so typically eschewed, but I appreciate that our ancestors left us a little something untrammeled. It must be said again, however, that root motion by fifths is easier to hear and structurally more sensible than root motion by thirds, or than parallel relationships, which is another way of saying that Pythagorean is simpler than pentamerous, or, to be precise, that the prime three is lower than the prime five. Pentamerous moves can be beautiful, but they are like sudden changes in the weather, and the ear needs time to become acclimated to them.

Fourth, it is important when doing these exercises to keep your ear in the key of C, so that C is the be-all and end-all, exactly as it was in our dronal studies. In fact, these *are* dronal studies, using triads instead of tones and equal temperament as an approximation of just intonation. But there is no sounding drone; your ear's *memory* of the tonic functions as the drone.

One more thing. These exercises you are writing are not supposed to be immortal masterpieces; they are for learning and then burning. By all means be rigorous, take time, and be as musical as possible, but don't be too original. For the time being, dedicate yourself to learning this particular musical language, not to making great art. Believe it or not, that's the sneaky way great art has of getting made.

Here's one final example of a piece of quasi-music with zero ambiguity of pitch, degree, or tonic. Example 21.10 shows the chords.

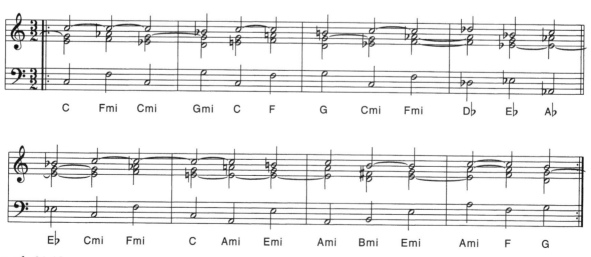

*Example 21.10*

Example 21.11 shows the added melody, along with a few (heretofore forbidden) inversions of chords, and passing tones in the bass.

*Example 21.11*

# 22

# Unambiguous Triadic Harmony in the Extended Lattice

THE PRACTICES IN THIS CHAPTER, like those in chapter 21, produce equal-tempered music with zero ambiguity of pitch, degree, or tonic; that is, at all times you can be certain of your coordinates on the lattice of perfect fifths and major thirds. As in chapter 21, these progressions would sound substantially the same in just intonation as they will in equal temperament, only sweeter and richer. The difference is that the music of this chapter takes place within an extended lattice. Theoretically, a lattice extends forever in both dimensions from a given central tone (our central tone is still C). Later in the book we will ask how far out from the center the ear is able to hear without losing its memory of the tonic. For the present we will impose territorial boundaries and precise procedures that insure zero ambiguity. Within these limits, our progressions will have a special luminosity and, even in equal temperament, result in a pristine kind of harmonic experience.

Example 22.1 presents the newly extended lattice of notes centered on C, with its triads named.

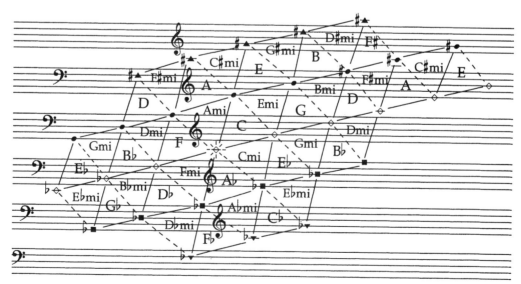

*Example 22.1*

If we supply only the chord symbols and their lines of connection, we are left with the chord lattice shown in figure 22.1. Remember that even though the staff lines are invisible, the figure remains in staff orientation.

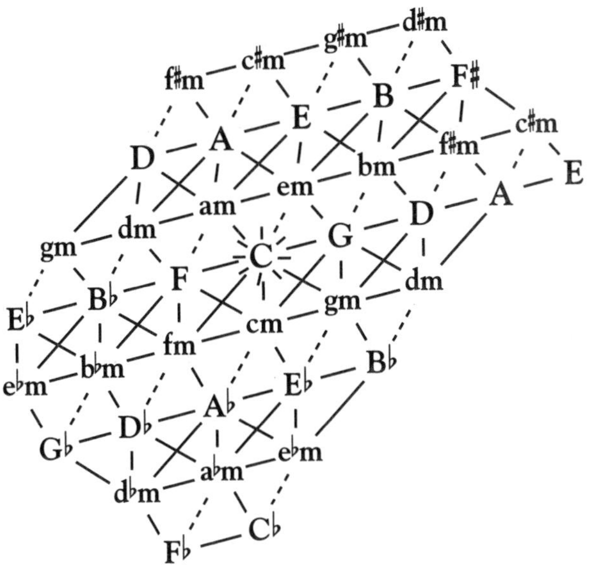

*Figure 22.1*

Our new harmonic galaxy involves a total of thirty-one unique tones and forty unique triads. Further examination of the extended lattice reveals that, unlike the lattice of twelve notes, there are now various pairs of pitches with identical names—twelve such, to be exact. Of the white piano keys, only C has no stepsibling; each of the black piano keys has to represent *three* discrete pitches; indeed, the black note between F and G represents four (two F#'s and two Gb's). This generosity of pitches is reflected in the triads. About half of the twenty-four triads (major and minor) playable on the keyboard have at least two possible positions on the lattice; a few have three. (Find them.) Tell me again how only twelve keyboard pitches can do the work of so rich and varied a harmonic field?

In just intonation, harmonic meaning is derived from both resonance and context. In equal temperament, meaning is derived primarily from context. If the context is clear, the meaning is clear. In these exercises, the context is given by a continuous harmonic path, a progression of connected chords that lead, like consecutive footprints, away from home and back again. The path may meander, double back, or make wide loops, but if every step is present, the path will still make sense. If there is a break in the path, especially if you are far from home, you are likely to get lost. In real music we *want* to get lost, at least sometimes and in some ways; that lostness is much like the deliberate confusions of a mystery story, where clarity is saved for the denouement. But for our present musical purposes we always want to know exactly where we are, and so we need to insure harmonic continuity. That means no harmonic leaps, no breaks in the path, no missing footprints: matchstick music.

# Harmonic Journeys

You are about to take a series of journeys through the extended lattice. To guarantee that you always know your harmonic coordinates, follow the rules and guidelines given in chapter 21 for the lattice of twelve notes, with these special reminders:

- Be sure to begin and end on a C-major triad, and to have C as the tonic clearly in your ear. Return often enough to a C triad so that C never loses the feeling of home.
- Be especially wary of leaping by two fifths, even when the leap is properly "filled in." If you do leap, remember that leaping up two fifths to a major triad and then falling back a fifth is best.
- Use parallel modality (C major to C minor, or vice versa) sparingly.

Example 22.2 is an unambiguous harmonic journey through the extended lattice.

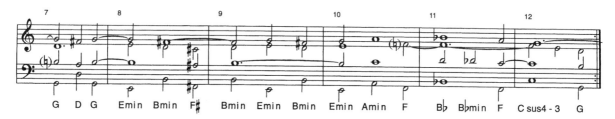

*Example 22.2*

Learn to play this example until you can listen to it without thinking about your fingers. Additionally, it may help to make a tape of it (or a sequenced version) and listen back over it many times in a kind of focused trance. As you listen, you will know you are moving—going somewhere—but where? Some gentle but persistent force leads you around; a harmonic wind blows you about from place to place. Here I am over here; now I'm up in the corner; how did I get down here? and now I'm home again (at the first beat of bar 1).

A simplistic but perhaps useful concept is to divide the lattice up into geographical quadrants: northeast, southeast, southwest, northwest. Northeast is then pure Sharpland—overtonal fifths and overtonal thirds combined. The F♯-major triad is Maine; the Pythagorean E major is Long Island. Southeast then becomes overtonal fifths and reciprocal thirds combined: B♭ major (the dominant of the relative major of the parallel minor) is South Carolina; C♭ major is Florida.

Southwest is pure Flatland—reciprocal fifths and reciprocal thirds combined. F♭ major is Texas; Southern California is G♭ major and E♭ minor. Northwest is reciprocal fifths and overtonal thirds combined: Northern California is the Pythagorean E♭ major and its mediant, G minor; D major (the subdominant of the relative minor) is Washington State; and F♯ minor (its mediant) is the Canadian Rockies. The central tone C is an open field somewhere in the middle of Kansas—corn as far as the eye can see.

This is crudely approximated, hopelessly Americanized, and terminally silly, of course, but it can be a useful intermediate concept. Now, instead of hard real estate, try to come to terms with psychological states, your own states of feeling. Are there qualities of feeling that characterize the quadrants? To answer this, go back to the simplest acts of singing, to the perfect fifths and major thirds of just intonation and the responses they evoke in their various combinations. Your work is to make that connection in your person, a connection that is, at this stage of our inquiry, still unambiguously knowable. In part 1 we used concepts such as yin and yang, responsive and expressive, moon and sun, and even mothers and cowboys to describe the harmonic states of single tones in reference to the tonic. In the case of triads, we are experiencing the combined effect of three tones sounding at once, and of their relationship to other triads as well as to the tonic. So it is not surprising that these responses are more difficult to pinpoint, with or without words or graphic metaphors. But in composing these journeys through the lattice, that is precisely what I am asking you to do. As you play your way through these progressions you should notice your responses in the same way you might observe your responses to changing colors if you were magically walking around inside a rainbow.

Try playing the progression through again, this time imagining that each triangle on the extended lattice glows (or *winks*?—no, that is going too far) as it is sounded. Or simply trace the route with your finger. It is not surprising that in Europe the development of tonal harmony and opera developed and peaked simultaneously, since the dramatic potential of tonal harmony greatly enhances the psychological and emotional storytelling of opera. By the nineteenth century, as tonal harmony was being rapidly and thoroughly explored, even the pure forms of concert music had become much more than mere evocations of mood. Many listeners have described the experience of a classical symphony as a kind of odyssey where the listener is Ulysses, braving forth from home on a spiritual quest and encountering changes of fortune. Our goal as listener-Ulysses is also to return, and during the course of a single piece we do return many times. Each time we are relieved but unfulfilled; thus we venture out again and again until finally, older and spiritually enriched, we return home for good.

Another, perhaps less noble, metaphor is the prairie dog. He pokes his head up from his safe burrow, ventures out cautiously, and then, after an exploratory foray, scurries back home. In each successive excursion he travels longer and farther before he runs back to his haven. In this way he eventually covers his range and will find the prairie grass he needs in order to return home, well fed, to sleep.

Now let's look more closely at example 22.2, using the lattice in example 22.1 as a map. The first two bars swing north to overtonal thirds (relative minors) clear up to B major (invoking the tone D♯). The G of bar 3 falls back to the Pythagorean spine one move east of the tonic (the dominant, of course) but then dips below the Mason-Dixon Line (so to speak) to the parallel minors, then to G again in bar 4, which dips again to G minor. We then take the Pythagorean Express down to the D♭ major of bar 5; then back through old territory all the way past G to D major, a fifth higher in that realm than we've yet been; then back again through old territory to the F♯ major in bar 8, a fifth higher in *that* realm then we've yet been (invoking the outré tone A♯). Now we cautiously come back to the A minor of bar 10, again where we've been before, but then immediately we explore new reciprocal space: due west to the B♭ major of bar 11, then south to B♭ minor. We then revisit F major, hurry home briefly, on to the dominant and then home to stay (on the first beat of bar 1).

Notice how many of the moves are by fifths (about three out of four), some of them using the centering aspect of cadential energy (the C minor of bar 4, the G major of bar 7, the B minor of bar 9, the final C major). There are no leaps of two fifths, so our progression is, harmonically speaking, entirely stepwise. Notice also the several returns to the tonic triad (C minor as well as C major, in this case).

Now compose several such exercises for yourself—at least three separate progressions. Take your time to complete, learn, analyze, and internalize each exercise. Be patient—several hours on one exercise is not unusual. It is OK to spend several weeks on this chapter. Remember that the deepest musical perceptions can be brought forward by knowing internally *how* you are feeling and at the same time knowing *what* you are hearing as you traverse the quadrants of unambiguous harmonic progressions. Be the conscious hero or heroine of your own harmonic odyssey. That is how to learn the subject.

Here are some more examples for study purposes. Example 22.3 doesn't travel as far as example 22.2, but it uses more relative/parallel energy. Centering-by-fifths energy is used twice only, the first time involving the cadential leap of two fifths up followed by one down:

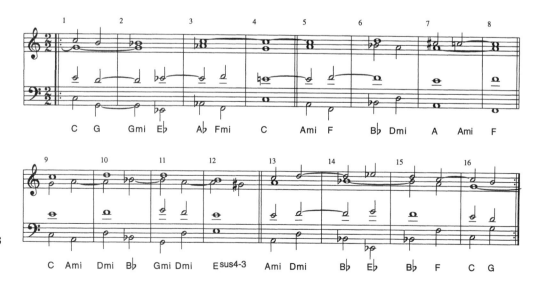

*Example 22.3*

Dmi to E to Ami in bars 11–13; the second time is at the end: F to C to G to C (on the repeat). After an initial swing south, this progression is almost completely northwestern. Notice also that I have allowed longer rhythmic values at phrase endings.

Example 22.4 presents the southern view.

Cmi  G    Fmi  Cmi    E♭  B♭    A♭mi  E♭mi    C♭  A♭mi    D♭mi    A♭    D♭  B♭mi    Fmi    G

*Example 22.4*

Example 22.4 begins on a C-minor triad, which is already pointing south, and then stays almost entirely southern (except for G major), extending all the way to the (current) reciprocal-third boundary of D♭ minor. Unlike example 22.3, it travels a long distance in a short time, but—also in contrast to example 22.3—it has very strong fifth-centering energy: around C minor and also E♭ minor.

We have already pointed out that, generally speaking, motion along the *pa* spines is much more fluid than motion involving the *ga* spines. As an experiment to bear this out, compare

$$\text{B♭ to F to C to G to D to G to C}$$

with

$$\text{A♭ to Cmi to C to Emi to E to Emi to C}$$

Obviously, the energy of perfect fifths is easier to hear and understand than the energy of major thirds. East-west travel is relatively unrestricted, so to speak, but one can never be too cautious in traveling north-south.

You may also have noticed that these examples have an even number of bars, which makes it easier to balance the harmonic rhythm.

# Harmonic Balance

These progressions could be considered little essays in harmonic balance. What we are balancing is the energy of perfect fifths and major thirds, packaged up in triads, and set in motion around a given central tone. The harmonies seem to have an intellectual clarity as well as a psychological effect. What underlies both is the hunger for home.

The hunger for the center is the composer's open secret. Like the fear of death and the love of life, it is what everyone feels most deeply yet talks about most indirectly. We have tried to characterize this vitality and to further distinguish between its various flavors: the feelings of the different quadrants. It is interesting to note that the northeast quadrant, which generates the most sharps, and the southwest quadrant, which generates the most flats, are the most-used harmonic areas. They seem to directly complement and encourage one another. The other two quadrants, northwest and southeast, seem generally more bland and difficult to distinguish, and indeed they are used less in actual music. But bland is neither good nor bad in this game. Only balance is good.*

There seems to be a historical fluctuation in the popularity of the quadrants. In Baroque times music was tilted northeast, toward the dominant and relative-minor side of the harmonic landscape. In the nineteenth century the reciprocal/parallel world of flats became increasingly enticing, until flats began to accumulate in the collective ear up to high levels. A predilection for the yin, responsive, nourishing grottos of Flatland continues to this day.†Your work is to thoroughly and consciously explore the harmonic territory of the extended lattice, and to compose harmonic journeys that are true for you.

## Adding Melodies with Passing Tones

Once you feel certain that a harmonic progression is clear and balanced, you may add a melody to it, thickening or thinning the four-part texture as you find appropriate. (I like to keep things in three or four parts.) In a way these melodies write themselves. If a harmonic progression is balanced, the melodies inside it are eager to be awakened. As in the previous chapter, be sure to use unsurprising nonchordal tones, that is, passing tones connected to a triadic tone above or below, or stepwise neighboring tones that are harmonically unadventurous. Examples 22.5–7 are melodies to the previous three progressions. Examples 22.8–10 are three more complete progressions for good measure.

## Where Are We?

We have been investigating the limits of nonambiguity in equal temperament. We have confined ourselves to the stability of major and minor triads and the certainty that results from stepwise harmonic motion through the lattice. Our harmonic coordinates at any given moment have been precise and unequivocal. Yet the harmonic range of our explorations has been astonishingly wide. If the harmonic range of actual music never went beyond the boundaries of our extended lattice, we could now declare the subject of harmony thoroughly understood and fully explained. And indeed, much harmony does indeed behave in the way

---

*The subject of harmonic balance is developed variously throughout the book; see especially chapter 38.

†Twelve-step programs have developed nationally to support composers who want to wean themselves from overdependency on reciprocal energy. There is probably a Flats Anonymous nearby in your city or town. A countermovement has also arisen, however, and its most recent publication, *Nurturing the Double Flat Within*, is available upon request.

*Example 22.5*

*Example 22.6*

Example 22.7

Example 22.8

*Example 22.9*

we have described. But we have most carefully avoided a crucial aspect: the ambiguities that arise in twelve-tone equal temperament the moment our rules are transgressed.

As we proceed, harmonic ambiguity will begin to seep into our music like ground fog; the paths will cloud; they will fork and loop; we will head east and find ourselves west; we will swear we have passed a landmark only to see it emerging around the next bend. In the throes of your work in later chapters you will probably hearken back to the crisp clarity of these unambiguous journeys through the quadrants and maybe even return for a visit. Meanwhile, you should keep working in this chapter, composing more progressions and learning the ones you have written, at least until you have gained some new experience of

*Example 22.10*

the nature of the quadrants and gained some new insight into the harmonic power of low prime numbers.

Beginning with chapter 23 and continuing until the end of part 2, the conditions for harmonic exploration will change. In one way we will go back to an earlier regimen: Our music will be essentially dronal, which means that the drone will always be present (or very close by) so that the identity of the tone in the center of the lattice will never come into question. But thanks to equal temperament, new elements will come into question. Harmonic ambiguities will arise, and as they do we will examine closely our responses to them. Eventually we will discover in those responses the crucial organizing principle of equal-tempered tonal harmony.

# 23

# DRONALITY IN EQUAL TEMPERAMENT: LYDIAN THROUGH PHRYGIAN

HERE IN PART 2 WE HAVE BEEN CONCERNED PRIMARILY with achieving and maintaining harmonic certainty in twelve-tone equal temperament. We have employed two powerful tools to accomplish this: the stability of major and minor triads, and the continuity of progressions that proceed harmonically stepwise. These strategies have given us the ability to take unambiguous journeys on equal-tempered keyboards through the extended lattice of perfect fifths and major thirds.

Now we'll change our game and revive an ancient tool to achieve harmonic certainty: the drone. From here until the end of part 2 our aim will be to explore the qualities and the boundaries of dronality in equal temperament. Then, having combined our experience of unambiguous harmonic journeys (chapters 19–22) with our new understanding of the limits of dronality (chapters 23–26), we'll enter—properly initiated and fully armed—the vast, ambiguous thicket of tonal harmony (part 3).

We'll use C as our drone and include the G above it; these will pin us to the center of a specifically bounded lattice. Although the central C and G will remain unambiguous, other ambiguities will be allowed, for the first time in our study, to enter in. The drone will serve as a king so powerful that confusions and contradictions will be able to exist safely within the kingdom.

## The Overtone Chord versus the Chord of Fifths

Let's begin by comparing a new chord with a familiar chord. First, at the equal-tempered keyboard, play the chord in example 23.1, which is simply a stack of perfect fifths. The harmonic map of the chord is shown in example 23.2. Notice how any two tones a fifth apart sound like any other two tones a fifth apart; by definition, all equal-tempered fifths sound the same. Notice also the effect of the accumulation of fifths. Whatever else they may sound

*Example 23.1*

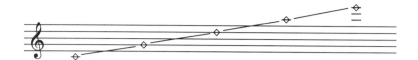

*Example 23.2*

*Example 23.3*

like, they never seem to stop sounding like fifths. Now compare this to the overtonal chord shown in example 23.3, previously identified (in chapter 1) as the source of the just major triad. Its map appears in example 23.4.

Now play the two chords back and forth, as shown in example 23.5. Next concentrate for a moment on the sound of the E. As the fifth partial of the overtone series we hear it as 5:4, the third of a just triad. As the top fifth in a stack of four perfect fifths, we hear it as

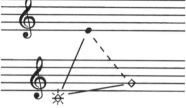

*Example 23.4*

*Example 23.5*

81:64, the Pythagorean major third. We can actually hear, or imagine we can hear, both harmonic functions. But in just intonation, which is the template of our hearing, the latter is sharper than the former by about twenty-two cents (see chapter 16). How can the E on the piano fulfill both roles at once? What are we hearing?

The situation is even more confounding when we listen with jazz ears. Example 23.6 is a stylistic example of the chord of stacked fifths functioning *as if* it were the tonic major triad.

*Example 23.6*

The harmonic map of the coexisting possibilities of the tonic chord looks like example 23.7. Notice the curved line that connects the two E's, the "stepsiblings" who share the same letter name and the same scale degree, but whose pitches, in just intonation, are different.

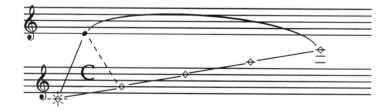

*Example 23.7*

The Pythagorean third has already been introduced in chapter 16, where we also discussed the twenty-two-cent difference between Pythagorean tones and their stepsiblings. A minute interval separating two tones is called a *comma*. The stepsiblings we have been studying are separated by an interval called the *Didymic comma*, named after Didymus, a musician-philosopher of the first century. The pairs of tones we have been calling stepsiblings we now have the option of calling *Didymic pairs of tones*. In part 3 we will quantify the Didymic comma in more detail, trace its function in modulating harmony, and compare it with other kinds of commas. For now we will accept the map of the E's in example 23.7 as a model for Didymic pairs of tones. Generally it can be said that the Didymic comma is the difference in pitch between four pure perfect fifths up and a pure major third up.

When we use a single tone on the equal-tempered keyboard to represent both siblings, do we become confused about pitch? Do we hear the pitch sliding around in some way? If we confine this question to fixed-pitch instruments, I think probably the answer is no. After all, a struck string is a struck string; it has the pitch it has. Then how could we accept both versions of the harmonic function as true? Could it possibly be that a single approximate event could stand for two separate "real things"? Could it be that the resulting confusion is a *positive* event, an active ingredient in musical behavior? Could it be that equal temperament, the ugly little villain of our tuning history, is showing us some especially amusing magic?

Let's proceed by taking our stacked-fifths-versus-triad method, applying it to the Lydian-through-Phrygian set of modes that we have already examined in just intonation (in chapter 11), and letting confusion be our guide.

## The Lydian Mode in Equal Temperament

There are two ways of representing the tones of the Lydian mode in equal temperament. The first is as a stack of fifths from C, as shown in example 23.8.

*Example 23.8*

Play example 23.8, appreciating the perfect-fifth-like quality of each new tone as you pile it onto the stack, and the accumulated energy of all seven tones.

The second way, shown in example 23.9, uses the *ga* spine and generates the major and minor triads—three of each.

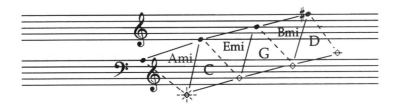

*Example 23.9*

Play these triads in ascending order starting with A minor and ending at D major, and then the reverse, over the drone, as shown in example 23.10.

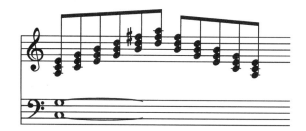

*Example 23.10*

Example 23.11 shows all the tones combined; it maps the harmonic territory of the Lydian mode in equal temperament.

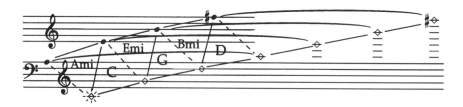

*Example 23.11*

Notice the curved lines that connect the four Didymic pairs of tones: two each of A, E, B, and F♯. Lydian is a seven-tone mode, and it is played on the equal-tempered keyboard with seven pitches. But there are eleven possibilities on the map. Clearly, I can make the keyboard sound Pythagorean by playing a stack of fifths. Clearly, I also can elicit *ga*-blooded triads. In actual practice, I can make music using both triadic and Pythagorean qualities that merge with and separate from one another like transparent light forms. When does the ear hear what? In order to sort things out, let's consider first the strongest triadic harmonies.

## TRIADIC LYDIAN HARMONY

It is a property of equal-tempered seven-tone modes that the available triads within a given mode sound OK in any order: The triads form a permutable set. But within that OK-ness, some progressions are stronger and more certain, others are weaker and more ambiguous. Remember that *strong, weak, certain,* and *ambiguous* are not the qualities that determine the beauty of a harmonic progression any more than *primary* or *pastel* are the qualities that determine the beauty of a painting's colors. These qualities are simply the tools that artists use. Our present purpose is to discover the inherent qualities of equal-tempered tools.

In the Lydian mode the strongest progression is C to D to G to C. A Lydian melody harmonized using this progression, or some variation of it, might look like example 23.12.

Remember, these are studies in dronality, which means you have to keep your ear absolutely rooted to C as the tonic, which means you probably have to keep the drone sounding. Otherwise you may all too easily modulate to the key of G Major, which may be delightful but defeats the purpose of the exercise.

*Example 23.12*

Example 23.13 gives some perhaps less obvious progressions in Lydian. Since the triads of Lydian result from the interaction between only two spines of the lattice (the central spine and the *ga* spine), you can observe how these Lydian triadic progressions seem to move up and down the lattice along the southwest–northeast slope of those spines. One instance, however, is an ominous harbinger of the triadic ambiguities to come: When you move directly from A minor to D major (or the reverse), the temperament allows us to believe that the root motion is a perfect fifth, but our lattice map insists that such a move is a harmonic leap, not the harmonic step of a perfect fifth. It

C  Bmi  Emi  Ami  G    C

C   Ami  Emi  Bmi  C

*Example 23.13*

tells us that the A-minor triad is clearly the relative minor of C (with the drone itself as a common tone) and that the D major triad could be none other than the dominant of G. So what do you hear when you hear example 23.14?

C  Ami  D  G     C  Ami  D  Ami     D  G  C

*Example 23.14*

This question, and many similar questions that are soon to arise, must be considered thoughtfully; however, the answers, crucial to an overall understanding of equal temperament, are almost vanishingly subtle, and there may well be different answers for different ears. Furthermore, example 23.14 is a particularly subtle case—all the more reason to keep both ear and mind open.

The music we are now making is not playable on a twelve-note keyboard in just intonation. In just intonation, the A that forms part of the A-minor triad is not the same pitch as the A in the D-major triad. It is the equal-tempered A's ability to *stand for* both pitches that makes example 23.14 playable on an equal-tempered instrument.

This is new. The resonances of just intonation are nothing if not specific; you can't make puns in the language of low-prime ratios. So we have definitely made some sort of leap from the Eden of just intonation—but where have we leapt to? The truth is, you don't have to come to any grand conclusions about what you are hearing right now. Virtually every example of equal-tempered harmony we study from this point onward will contain some degree of ambiguity, or, one might say, deliberate confusion. But don't let a little thing like confusion confuse you. One develops harmonic discernment only gradually. All that is really needed now are open ears and an open mind.

## THE LYDIAN MODE WITHOUT TRIADS

Since triads supply a context that clarifies the position of the ear on the lattice, one can *increase* ambiguity by abandoning triads. What do we hear when we simply play the Lydian scale over the drone, as in example 23.15?

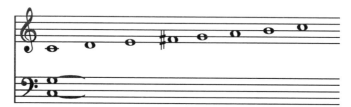

*Example 23.15*

Let's question the tones one by one. C is given; G and D are clearly Pythagorean. E, B, and F♯ could be Pythagorean if properly fifth-stacked, but suspended individually over the drone without any other context they tend to be heard as the *ga*-blooded siblings. The sixth degree, A, however, seems to be caught between its two identities. If it associates with C and E, as in example 23.16, it can easily sound like the *ga*-blooded 5:3 major sixth. If it associ-

*Example 23.16*

ates with D and F♯, however, as in example 23.17, it can be none other than the Pythagorean 27:16 major sixth. But simply as a step in the Lydian scale, what is heard?*

*Example 23.17*

Notice that there is no ambiguity of *degree:* We hear both siblings as the sixth degree. But we have the option of hearing either of the harmonic qualities that the stepsiblings would generate were they precisely tuned. The equal-tempered pitch itself falls in between: It is sixteen cents sharp of the simpler 5:3 *dha* and six cents flat of the more complex 27:16 *dha*. Doesn't the Pythagorean 27:16 *dha* win, since it is closest? Maybe, maybe not. The simpler ratio is compelling. What is this strange sensation that is *both* and *neither?*

---

*The question of how we hear equal-tempered seven-tone modes without a drone is addressed in part 3.

## POSITIVE CONFUSION

This sense of being caught between qualities is a special state, and that state is the primary subject of our search. If, up to now, we had had no conscious bodily experience of just intonation, we might not even realize our confusion, or at best, it would not seem particularly remarkable. But given our experiences not only of the resonances of just intonation but also of the unambiguous harmonic uses of equal temperament, we can begin to hear, in the music we are making now, a special state of ambiguity, perhaps pleasant or disturbing, that is inherent in our modern tuning system and thus quite possibly a defining quality of our culture's music. Our purpose is not to get rid of the ambiguity but to understand it. We may be perfectly willing to be confused, but we want to be able to label and categorize our confusions.

Consider an analogy with psychology. Historically, the sciences of the psyche have been devoted to characterizing the confusions arising between conflicting desires. The aim is to understand the terms and vectors of the mind. We know today that the mental conflicts of childhood do not simply disappear once we have brought them forward into consciousness; rather, we use our understanding of them as a lever to balance our lives. Conscious and exposed, conflicts thus become less like obstacles and more like operative mechanisms. Likewise, the inherent harmonic tensions of our tuning system, which nest in our cultural ear, can be brought into the light of conscious hearing, where we can use them to our fullest advantage. That is why the dynamics of harmonic ambiguity have become our main focus.

## IMPROVISING IN EQUAL-TEMPERED LYDIAN

It is time to improvise freely at the equal-tempered keyboard in the Lydian mode. Probably the best way to proceed is to begin by improvising vocally in just intonation against a drone (singing against your piano drone is OK). You might also check out some of the Pythagorean degrees, especially the 27:16 sixth and the 81:64 third. The next step is to review at the piano the equal-tempered Lydian progressions in this chapter. Then, finally, forget about the theoretical problems, listen to the sound of your piano, and respond musically to what you hear. Play lots of single-note melodies and some chords also. Remember to keep the drone sounding in the left hand, but don't use the drone to beat time—that gets old fast. Rearticulate the notes of the drone only when you need to hear them. I know that such a limited use of the left hand reduces the pianism of what you play, but this is a limited exercise with limited objectives; there is still a lot of music to discover inside it. Try using your left thumb as a kind of countermelody; or bring the entire left hand into a higher octave to help out, providing that the drone business has been taken care of. You can sometimes drop the drone an octave for a change of texture. Example 23.18 is an example of what is possible.

The Lydian mode belongs to the intervalic family wherein the whole steps cluster in twos and threes, as we discussed in chapter 11. We will now guide our keyboard music through the rainbow of these modes (exactly as we did in just intonation, as singers) observing how our changing position on the lattice correlates with the changing qualities of the

*Example 23.18*

modes. This time, however, we will be tracking the positions of the Didymic pairs of tones on the lattice and listening for how these pairs influence the quality of the equal-tempered modes. We will show how the primary colors of our lattice rainbow become mixed and mottled by the ambiguities of equal temperament.

# The Major (Ionian) Mode in Equal Temperament

The Major mode can be represented on the equal-tempered keyboard as a stack of perfect fifths from F, as shown in example 23.19. As in the Lydian stack of fifths, appreciate the perfect-fifth-ness of each new tone, and the oddly beautiful and convincing full chord.

*Example 23.19*

To map the available triads we need three spines, as shown in example 23.20.

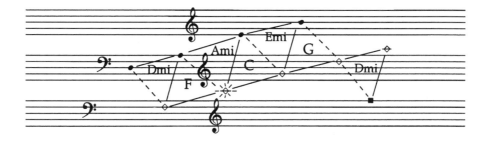

*Example 23.20*

Notice that there are two possible D-minor triads, which we will call a *Didymic pair of triads*. Play all the triads of the mode (over the drone) in ascending order from the lower D minor (on the left) up through G major to the upper D minor, and then back again. Ask yourself if you notice any difference in harmonic function between the two D-minor triads. That is, is there any noticeable difference in affect between D minor in a subdominant context and D minor in a dominant context?

Example 23.21 shows all the tones combined; it maps the harmonic territory of the equal-tempered Major mode.

*Example 23.21*

The curved lines represent five Didymic pairs of tones (the pair of D-minor triads we have just considered comprises three of these pairs of tones). The *seven* white notes of C Major on the piano thus stand for *twelve* different tones on the lattice. We are assuming that neither of the drone tones, by definition, are heard ambiguously. With this definition, it may be said generally that a seven-tone mode can generate a maximum of five Didymic pairs of tones. (Ambiguity of the tonic and dominant will show up in part 3 when we leave the drone behind.)

To sort out the various possibilities, let's look first at the strongest triadic progressions.

## TRIADIC HARMONY IN THE MAJOR MODE

The strongest triadic progression in Major, of course, is C to F to G to C, the cadential mantra we know and love, discussed at length in chapter 20. Weaker progressions using the minor triads are both beautiful and extremely familiar in popular music, for example, C to Emi to Ami to F to G to C. That progression contains no D-minor triad, and as long as D minor is avoided, there will be no harmonic ambiguity in the Major mode. But the function of the D-minor triad is often ambiguous. There are, after all, two locations for "D minor" on the lattice: One is the relative minor of the subdominant, F; the other is the minor dominant of the dominant, G. Each has its own affect. Can an equal-tempered progression clarify which affect is intended? Yes, I think so. If the D-minor chord is in a subdominant context, for example:

**C to Ami to F to Dmi to F to Ami to C**

then it reflects its reciprocal environment. If the D-minor triad is in a dominant context, for example:

**C to Emi to G to Dmi to G to C**

then it reflects the overtonal environment. In each case, we leave home on a harmonic journey and return by retracing our route.

Example 23.22 combines the above progressions in a shortened version that allows you to directly compare the two situations.

*Example 23.22*

On the piano, the two D-minor chords are obviously the same in pitch, but in function they are not the same.* Sung correctly in just intonation, the more overtonal, dominant-associated D-minor triad would be twenty-two cents sharper than the more reciprocal one. But in equal temperament, meaning is derived from context. The question you must eventually address is, Do the two different D-minor triads affect you differently? In unambiguous cases like the above, the affect, though truly subtle, is nonetheless real and pervasive, a kind of refined magnetism, a hidden polarity. As singers in just intonation, we know this polarity intimately; it is what moves us, drawing the psyche through the regions of its own nature. As pianists, this inner motion is well disguised; it is like recognizing a face that has been covered with gauze.

But what about truly ambiguous cases? What happens when the function of the D-minor triad changes *at the moment it is sounding?* We have come, gentle listener, to the nub of the problem.

Possibly the most common progression in the Western world is C to Ami to F to Dmi to G to C, as in the '50's cliché shown in example 23.23.

*Example 23.23*

*To intensify the harmonic functions in example 23.22, as well as in similar triads-over-drone examples in this chapter, it may be quite helpful to temporarily abandon the drone in the left hand and play the chord roots instead.

In this case, we are led by unambiguous harmonic steps to the subdominant function of the D-minor triad, but then, in mid-use, its function flips, becoming the dominant of the dominant. We leave our house by the southwestern route and return from the northeast. When we approach the D-minor triad we are in subdominant yin territory, and when we leave it we are in dominant yang territory. We go in subdominant and come out dominant. Does our perception flip? At what point? And how on earth could singers ever tune their pitches?

The backward version of this harmony arises in the following way: C to G to Dmi to F to C. Such progressions are less common but equally perplexing. The general problem can be summarized in this question: How do we respond to ambiguous equal-tempered events?

In this case, the "event" is the harmonic function of an entire triad, and the specific question is, What is the reality of the second-degree triad in the Major mode? Theory teachers call it "the problem of ii" and usually conclude, along with their relieved students, that it sounds the way it sounds. The same conclusion will eventually be ours as well, of course. But rather than sweep the specialness of this problem under the rug, our aim is to extract from it a crucial secret about ourselves and the way we hear our music.

But not so fast. By framing the problem this way we have accomplished enough for the present. In part 3 the drone disappears and we will meet the source deities of equal-tempered ambiguity head-on, quantifying and categorizing as we go. We might even be issued clipboards and get to wear white smocks. Meanwhile, I will point out not only the Didymic pairs of tones but also the Didymic pairs of triads as they occur throughout dronality. We'll try to discern the amazing patterns they create in the lattice, and we'll search for their musical meanings. A good strategy for now is simply to listen to the various dronal possibilities as they come out of the instrument, and never stop asking, "What is this?"

## THE MAJOR MODE WITHOUT TRIADS

Without the clarifying context that triads provide, a simple C Major scale played over the drone yields, probably, two Didymic pairs of tones. The sixth degree, especially, seems caught between its two selves. It can easily be the Pythagorean sixth 27:16 thanks to G and D, but as soon as it associates with F or E it will want to be the 5:3 *dha*. In Western dronal music it is almost always sung in its lower form, 5:3. But once when I was teaching a just intonation class, one of the students, a beautifully in-tune singer who had recently arrived from her native Japan to live in the United States, kept singing *dha* sharp, or so I thought. I would correct her, she would bravely sing 5:3 and then wrinkle her nose. The next time she sang the scale, there was *dha,* sharp again. Only after a few passes did I realize that she was singing 27:16 most wonderfully in tune—a shining example of the Pythagorean major sixth. "*Duh,*" I said to myself, and assured her that her *dha* was perfect.

The D in C Major also yields, although marginally perhaps, a Didymic pair of tones. To evoke the 10:9 *re,* however, the G of the drone should not be sounded, and F should be in the air or close by.

For these Didymic pairs of tones, as for all of the issues raised in this chapter, dipping back into the direct experience of just intonation is the most—perhaps the only—clarifying action.

## The Mixolydian Mode in Equal Temperament

The equal-tempered Mixolydian mode can be drawn as a stack of fifths from B♭, as shown in example 23.24. Notice how the spine is becoming more balanced around C. Example 23.25 is a map of the available Mixolydian triads.

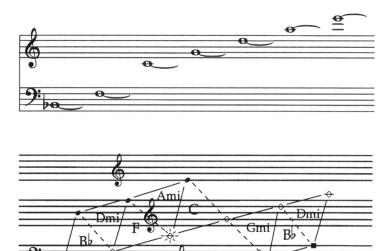

*Example 23.24*

*Example 23.25*

To the pair of D-minor triads that appeared in the Major mode is now added another Didymic triadic pair: two B♭-major triads. The lower set of B♭-major and D-minor triads is constructed from *reciprocal* fifths and *overtonal* thirds; the upper set uses *overtonal* fifths and *reciprocal* thirds. Play the unambiguous progression given in example 23.26. How do you perceive the harmonic continuum? (Don't forget to try roots instead of the drone in the left hand.)

C   Ami   F   Dmi   B♭   F   C   Gmi   B♭   Dmi   B♭   Gmi   C

*Example 23.26*

Example 23.27 shows all of the tones combined; it maps the harmonic territory of the equal-tempered Mixolydian mode, again revealing five Didymic pairs of tones.

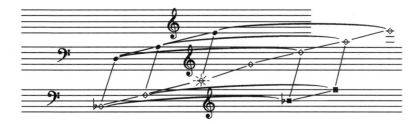

*Example 23.27*

## TRIADIC HARMONY IN MIXOLYDIAN

Once more we find that the strongest cadence involves the major triads: B♭ to F to C. This progression of rising fifths, which we could call the Mixolydian cadence, was not uncommon in European music around the sixteenth century, but from early Baroque times until quite recently it fell from common usage. It is a kind of reciprocal version of the cadence of falling fifths—D to G to C—which for three hundred years has been a standard Western cadential formula. In the early 1960s the Mixolydian cadence began to show up, surprisingly and pleasantly, in British and American popular music, and thus has found new life in modern times.*

There are many more bland but very smooth progressions using the minor triads. Experiment. You may find that ambiguity comes easily in Mixolydian. Play C to Gmi to B♭ to F to C (over the drone), following with your eyes your position on the lattice. How do you reconcile where you are with what you hear? As we approach the B♭ triad it is the relative major of the minor dominant, but as we leave it, it is the subdominant of the subdominant. Where does the polarity flip? Now try an opposite version: C to F to Dmi to B♭ to Gmi to C. (Try the root version of the left hand also.) As we approach the B♭ triad it is subdominant to us, but as we leave it we step directly onto the dominant. Could the B♭ triad, like a homonym, hold two meanings at once?

## THE MIXOLYDIAN MODE WITHOUT TRIADS

Without the use of triads, a Mixolydian scale played over a drone gives rise to perhaps three Didymic pairs. The sixth degree, A, and the second degree, D, behave much like they do in the Major mode, although each leans somewhat more convincingly toward its *ga*-blooded version. Additionally we have a new Didymic pair of tones: the minor seventh degree, B♭. The tempered tone is only four cents sharper than the purely reciprocal 16:9, and is a full eighteen cents below the overtonal/reciprocal mix of 9:5. Nevertheless, because of their peculiarly balanced harmonic relation to the tonic, this one seems like a toss-up: The equal-tempered tone seems to be suspended between two worlds. Notice that the Didymic pair on the minor seventh degree is the exact mirror inversion of the Didymic pair on the major

*I find it remarkable—heartwarming, actually—to notice that this reversal of cadential energy, this flip of polarity from yang to yin, was synchronous with a time of renewed social conscience and spiritual reawakening. It has often been claimed that the musicians of a culture signal the quality of its approaching era, and the sudden emergence of the Mixolydian cadence at a time when a new bright star of Western receptivity was beginning to rise lends credence to that claim.

second degree. But since reciprocal harmony is generally more difficult to hear, the ambiguity seems greater between the two minor sevenths than between the two major seconds.

What kind of minor seventh do singers sing? This is a mysterious subject, made even more mysterious by the tempting possibility offered by the seventh partial. There are thus three perfectly beautiful resonances occupying the niche of the minor seventh, two of them reciprocal and the other *blu*. What a choice! Usually, good singers do make a clean and musically convincing decision. But the minor seventh seems to be a particularly watery place in the scale, a fine opportunity for expressive ornaments and vibrato. That leaves the ambiguity of the tempered note very ambiguous indeed.

So if you want to know what you are hearing, sing the just resonances in appropriate contexts, then review the harmonic possibilities in equal temperament while eyeballing the lattice, and then improvise the night into oblivion. An amusing (and gorgeous) trick, incidentally, is to use all three of the Didymic pairs discussed above in the left-hand voicing shown in example 23.28 while improvising melodically in the right hand. It seems as if the entire available harmonic territory is lit up at once.

*Example 23.28*

## The Dorian Mode in Equal Temperament

The Dorian mode can be heard as a stack of fifths from E♭, as shown in example 23.29. Notice that C is now in the center of the stack. Example 23.30 shows the harmonic map the Dorian triads.

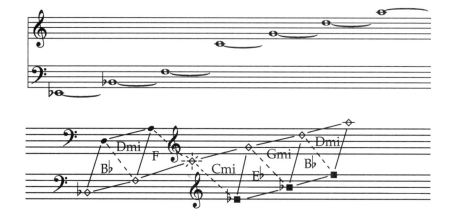

*Example 23.29*

*Example 23.30*

The Didymic pairs of triads are the same as for Mixolydian: two D-minor triads and two B♭-major triads. Example 23.31 shows one way of traversing the harmonic continuum. (Try roots in the bass as well.)

*Example 23.31*

Cmi  E♭   B♭  Dmi  Gmi  E♭   Cmi  F   Dmi      B♭   F   Cmi

Example 23.32 shows all the tones combined; it maps the harmonic territory of the Dorian mode in equal temperament.

*Example 23.32*

## TRIADIC HARMONY IN DORIAN

Perhaps because of the way the overtonal and reciprocal forces are balanced in this mode, Dorian seems to have an especially pastel quality. There are no truly emphatic Dorian equal-tempered progressions, although Cmi to F to B♭ to F to Cmi is fairly strong. Another quasi-cadential progression is Cm to Gmi to F to Cmi. Try it in the voicing shown in example 23.33. (Don't forget the roots-in-the-bass option.)

Cmi  Gmi  F  Cmi

*Example 23.33*

Example 23.34 shows a way of comparing the harmonic feeling between the two D-minor triads.

Cmi  Gmi  Dmi  Gmi    Cmi  F  Dmi  F

*Example 23.34*

Now try comparing the quality of the two B♭ triads as shown in example 23.35.

Cmi  E♭  B♭  E♭    Cmi  F  B♭  F

*Example 23.35*

Although a primary tactic we have employed in this study of dronality is to allow no ambiguity in either of the drone tones, C or G, a special exception might nevertheless be made in Dorian in order to enjoy the reciprocal Pythagorean E♭ triad. (We will omit the G from the drone, thereby invoking the spirit of "wretched *pa*": see the "Glossary of Singable Tones.") This produces an elongated version of the Dorian cadence: E♭ to B♭ to F to Cmi. One is then able to compare the two E♭ feelings by means of the progression shown in example 23.36. Roots in the bass will especially intensify this harmony.

*Example 23.36*

Cmi    E♭  Gmi  E♭  Cmi    F   B♭   E♭  B♭   F

Our next task is to approach the ambiguous harmonies of the Dorian mode. To get the D-minor triad to flip, play Cmi to F to Dmi to Gmi to Cmi. You went in with subdominant energy and came out with dominant energy, although given the position of the minor triads and the general quality of the mode, the entire harmonic dynamic seems muted (and quite lovely in that).

To feel the polarity flip around the B♭ chord, try example 23.37.

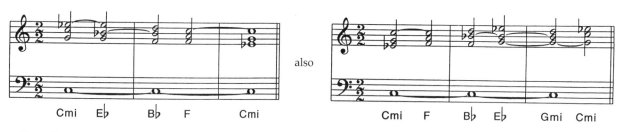

also

Cmi    E♭       B♭    F       Cmi            Cmi    F       B♭   E♭      Gmi  Cmi

*Example 23.37*

As you play these progressions, track them with your eyes on the harmonic map.

## THE DORIAN MODE WITHOUT TRIADS

Without the stabilizing benefit of triads, a Dorian scale over the drone generates two, possibly three, Didymic pairs of tones, much like Mixolydian. In the North Indian scale most closely associated with Dorian—called *Kafi*—the lower, darker 10:9 *re* is used about as frequently as its brighter stepsibling, 9:8. As is also true with both the Major and Mixolydian equal-tempered modes, you have to suppress the G and bring forward the F (or F together with A) to evoke the 10:9 *re*. Singing Dorian in just intonation will clarify what you hear in equal temperament.

A characteristic feature of Dorian is the tritone between E♭ and A. As a singer, you may have noticed that is not an obvious leap. Be sure, when you are playing in equal-tempered Dorian, to pay that leap its due. Generally it may be said that if it takes extra time or effort to sing something well, you should take the extra time also when you play it, because even if your fingers don't need the time, your ears do, and your ears should be leading your fingers.

# The Aeolian Mode in Equal Temperament

The Aeolian mode can be heard as a stack of fifths from A♭, as shown in example 23.38. Notice that there are more reciprocal tones than overtonal tones. The Aeolian triads are shown in example 23.39.

*Example 23.38*

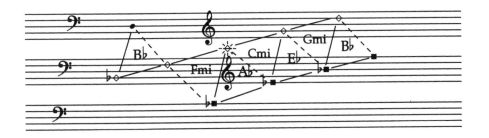

*Example 23.39*

The two B♭ triads constitute the single Didymic pair.

Example 23.40 shows all the tones combined; it maps the harmonic territory of the equal-tempered Aeolian mode.

*Example 23.40*

### TRIADIC HARMONY IN AEOLIAN

The tonic, subdominant, and dominant triads are all minor. The major triads, A♭, E♭, and B♭, balance around E♭, so one may have to resist, while improvising, the tendency of the tonality to drift to E♭ major—even with the drone prevalent. Remember that our present intentions are strictly dronal and nonmodulatory. Example 23.41 shows two strong, unambiguous progressions in equal-tempered Aeolian.

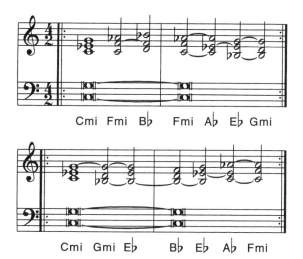

*Example 23.41*

To elicit the ambiguity of the Didymic pair of B♭ triads, try example 23.42. As we approach the B♭ triad it seems dominant to us, but as we leave it, it seems subdominant.

*Example 23.42*

Example 23.43 shows another case. This time, as we approach B♭ it seems subdominant, but as we leave it, it seems dominant.

*Example 23.43*

The confusion arising in going from Fmi to B♭ reminds us of a similar confusion: going from Dmi to G in key of C Major: indeed, it can have the effect of the "ii to V" problem, but modulated into E♭ Major. Modulation is still waiting in the wings, however, and can't come onstage until its cue in part 3. In any case, Aeolian is another mode where the ambiguity is especially subtle, and again it is OK to enjoy the qualities of the mode without dwelling overly long on their causes.

## THE AEOLIAN MODE WITHOUT TRIADS

When you play an Aeolian scale over a drone, there is ambiguity in the D and the B♭ (the same as in Dorian). As usual, a reciprocal context will induce the meaning of the lower sibling of each Didymic pair, and an overtonal context will induce the meaning of the higher sibling.

# The Phrygian Mode in Equal Temperament

The Phrygian mode can be heard as a stack of fifths from D♭, as shown in example 23.44.*

*Example 23.44*

Example 23.45 is the harmonic map of the Phrygian triads.

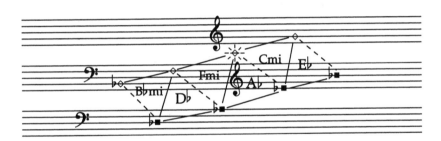

*Example 23.45*

In Phrygian there are no Didymic pairs of triads.† The stack of fifths and the triads combine as shown in example 23.46.

*Example 23.46*

---

*It's possible, from the purely Pythagorean standpoint, and focusing on the key signatures alone, to draw a parallel between the progression of modes from Lydian to Phrygian and the progression of Major keys around the circle of fifths from G Major to A♭ Major. This may be a highly practical mental construct, since in European music our prominent reference is the Major mode. But to think of the rich variety of these modes simply as a kind of transposed Major mode is, as I hope we have seen, a limited construct indeed.

†I could make a weak case for the existence of B♭ minor as the minor dominant of the relative major (v/III), but I won't.

We see that, as in the case of the Lydian mode, there are only four Didymic pairs of tones.

All the triads of Phrygian are reciprocal or have strong reciprocal components. They all lead unambiguously toward the tonic triad. Example 23.47 shows a typically strong progression.

*Example 23.47*

Notice how the final thirdless chord sounds nearly like a major triad, since the fifth partial of C becomes prominent. Here we are allowing the strong suggestion of a major third—and hence the chromatic pair E♮/E♭—into the mix. This is a usual Phrygian practice, and we will let it stand as a harbinger of the chromatic pairs coming up in chapter 25.

Phrygian is a good mode to experiment freely in. The triadic harmony is stable, clear, and for many, unfamiliar, which makes fertile ground.

The equal-tempered Phrygian scale over a drone generates only one Didymic pair of tones: B♭, the minor seventh. Do you notice any difference in quality between the two different B♭'s in example 23.48? To investigate further, try locating all the tones on the lattice as you play them.

*Example 23.48*

The Phrygian mode is a great harmonic tool for the equal-tempered musician. Try improvising softly, and going wherever the mode takes you.

# Lydian to Phrygian and
# Back Again in Equal Temperament

This is a good time to review chapter 11, especially examples 11.1 and 11.2 at the beginning of the chapter, and "Is This a Rainbow?" at the end. Against a drone, sing Lydian to Phrygian and back again in just intonation. Then, against a drone in equal temperament, play Lydian to Phrygian and back again. This presents a splendid comparison between the qualities of the two tuning systems. Within the just-intonation rainbow, you can track in a very pure way the interactive dynamics of overtonal and reciprocal energies. Within the equal-tempered rainbow you can track those same energies, but they are not so pure. Mixed in are the ambiguities of equal-tempered dronality: Didymic pairs of tones and triads obscure the modes in a fine mist, making them shimmer as they progress.

After you have become familiar with the available triads at the keyboard, other combinations will occur naturally: four-tone and five-tone chords in various inversions and distributions, chords based on fourths or fifths, clusters of tones, or simple *collections* of tones. While improvising it is sometimes permissible to allow the drone to disappear momentarily, but only if you are absolutely certain that the tonal center has not changed. In other words, the drone must never leave your ear. But it is *your* ear. Since you are the judge of the tonal certainty of your music, the game of dronality is played between you the improvisor and you the listener.

Your modal excursions can take one minute or ten minutes or longer. You can take your time and investigate the mood of each mode, or you can make a convincing allusion and pass on. If you have enough brain left over to remember some of the ideas you played as you worked your way from Lydian to Phrygian, you can refer to them again when you are going back the other way.

There are two paths of wisdom inside this way of learning. The wisdom of one path is telling you to keep your mental construct of the lattice intact and to track the commas as you play your music. The wisdom of the other is saying: You don't need all this mind to practice dronal improvisation—just do it. The truth is, we are now on both paths at once; combined, they make a single path that will lead us directly through the territory ahead.

Example 23.49 is an example of an equal-tempered piece, a kind of written-out improvisation, that moves from Lydian to Phrygian and back again. Play it; then make one thousand of your own.

*Example 23.49 (page 1)*

*Example 23.49 (page 2)*

*Example 23.49 (page 3)*

# 24

# DRONALITY IN EQUAL TEMPERAMENT: MIXED MODES

## Gaps in Stacks

The modes we have studied in chapter 23, the so-called church modes, account for only six of the many seven-tone modes (about three dozen) that hold their own in equal-tempered dronality. None of the others, however, can be displayed as a continuous stack of fifths, as the church modes can. This is important, because if the central Pythagorean spine is shortened or broken (contains gaps), then the ambiguities that arise from the Didymic comma tend to disappear, thereby affecting the quality of the mode.

Why should harmonic ambiguity be less when the central spine of fifths is shortened or contains gaps? Remember that it is the property of the temperament to allow a single tone to stand for two separate tones, each of which occupies a discrete position on the lattice of just intonation. In the church modes, where *all* the tones can be heard as Pythagorean, any tone that can *also* be heard along an adjacent spine (in other words, as a *ga*-blooded tone) automatically suggests a Didymic pair of tones. In the other seven-tone modes, generally speaking, the shorter the Pythagorean spine, or the more the spine's context-generating power is weakened by being discontinuous, the fewer the opportunities for the Didymic comma to be a factor in our response. Let's examine this in more detail.

## Modes with Four Consecutive Whole Steps

Modes containing four consecutive whole steps were introduced in just intonation in chapter 12. Since this chapter parallels that one, a review would be timely. Example 24.1 shows the maps of all four equal-tempered modes of this type.

When we were singing these modes in just intonation, we confined ourselves to a lattice of twelve tones only. Our lattice has now become "extended" and will soon include all the

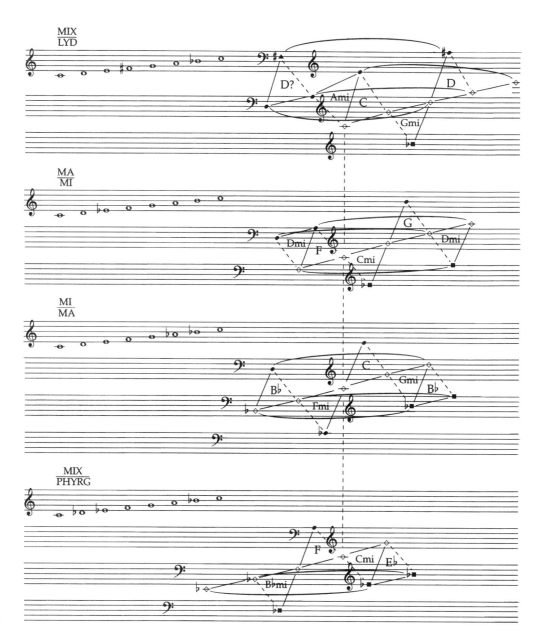

*Example 24.1*

tones that equal temperament is able to evoke under any dronal circumstance. Notice how the harmonic maps above are exactly like the ones in chapter 12, but with various additions to certain spines. The essential fact is that equal temperament does not allow the ear to extend the *central* spine in this type of mode.* Each of the central spines contains only five tones, exactly as in just intonation. Contrast this with the modes of the Lydian-to-Phrygian set (in the previous chapter), whose central spines are extended in equal temperament to a continuous stack of seven tones. The outcome: These modes are harmonically less ambiguous than those. We are more certain of where we are.

*In equal temperament, the ear will not allow the central spine of fifths to extend unless it is continuous—no gaps. A gap will snap the Pythagorean spine. Tones that might have appeared beyond a gap are readily appropriated for *ga*-blooded purposes. This is further discussed at the end of this chapter.

Also in contrast to the church modes, there now are four (not six) available stable triads: two majors and two minors. This smaller pool of available stable triads probably means that the weaker, less stable triads—two diminished and one augmented—as well as four- and five-tone chords and other collections of tones, will play a larger role in the harmony of these modes. Play the triads from each scale degree, making sure you stay true to the mode you are in. Then, for some amazing and useful surprises, try all the seventh chords and all the ninth chords as they arise, degree by degree.

Both a review of chapter 12 and conscious singing practice will remind your body of the collection of resonances that characterize each of these four modes in just intonation. Then, to put their equal-tempered equivalents in your ear, spend some time improvising dronally at the piano in each of them—they are rich and may take some getting used to. Find the two diminished triads and the one augmented triad in each mode. Notice especially how the augmented triad is a result of two stacked major thirds, and that its *ga-ga* nature is at the heart of the sound of each mode.

Now, back to the maps. Look at the central spines of fifths. Notice how the modes have been arranged so the central spine notches a fifth lower for each mode as you move down the page (as in the Lydian-to-Phrygian set in chapter 23).

Now notice how the *ga* spines of fifths and the *ga*-below spines of fifths all have gaps, or develop gaps. Why is that?* Now compare the *ga* spine of fifths in MIX/LYD with the *ga* spine of fifths in MA/MI: It also has moved down a fifth, gap and all. Observe how the progression continues down the page, and also how the *ga*-below spine of fifths changes from mode to mode.

There are four Didymic pairs of tones in MIX/LYD, and only two in MIX/PHRYG; the other two modes have three pairs each. Each mode has only one Didymic pair of triads except for MIX/PHYRG, which contains zero triadic ambiguity. All in all there is considerably less ambiguity in this set than in the Lydian-to-Phrygian set: That's what you get with shorter stacks of fifths, and hence a lower potential for Pythagorean energy. Here are some specific comments about each mode.

## MIXOLYDIAN/LYDIAN

I am not at all certain that an authentic pair of Didymic triads is formed by the two D-major triads. I suspect the lower one may not be heard in equal temperament. In other words, my dronal ear prefers the harmonic path shown in figure 24.1, which contains a leap but centers on the tonic, to the path shown in figure 24.2, which is direct, but leads you farther from home (even unto the *ga-ga* F♯).

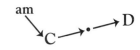

*Figure 24.1*

That leaves four unambiguous triads, two Didymic pairs of tones (E and A), and pentamerous reciprocity centered on D (F♯ and B♭).

Example 24.2 shows all the available seventh chords—that is, four-tone stacks of thirds.

*Figure 24.2*

*Because the overtonal and reciprocal pentamerous energies are mixed: See chapter 12.

*Example 24.2*

The inversions of these chords offer beautiful and often unexpected results. Example 24.3 features various seventh chords in third inversion (not counting the drone).

*Example 24.3*

## MAJOR/MINOR

This mode is as generous in its equal-tempered ways to pianists as it is to singers in just intonation. Aside from the more obviously strong cadential type of progressions involving i, IV, and V, there are beautiful four-tone (and five- and six- and seven-tone) chords. Learn to improvise, for instance, using nothing but third-inversion seventh chords, as demonstrated in example 24.4.

*Example 24.4*

In this mode, as in the other three of its type, you can always find an effective melodic use for the short stack of thirds that constitutes the augmented chord—E♭, G, and B in this case. Example 24.5 shows such a phrase.

*Example 24.5*

## MINOR/MAJOR

The diminished fourth from E up to A♭ is almost as juicy in equal temperament as it is in just intonation (see chapter 12). Example 24.6 gives a typical use.

*Example 24.6*

## MIXOLYDIAN/PHRYGIAN (DARK HORSE)

As in just intonation, this mode is both unfamiliar (the diminished fourth from A up to D♭ is downright weird) and clear (there are no Didymic pairs of triads). I like the slightly off-putting mystery of this mode. It keeps you looking at it out of the corner of your eye for years, then one day—bam!—it pays off.

It takes many hours of many years to learn the resonances of these modes as a singer of pure harmony, and to make use of their full musical energies at the equal-tempered keyboard. Let the organization and the maps and the comparisons presented here be a useful reference for those hours spent.

## Modes with Five Consecutive Whole Steps

The equal-tempered maps of the two available modes in this set are precisely the same as they are in just intonation. Example 24.7 presents them, for reference.

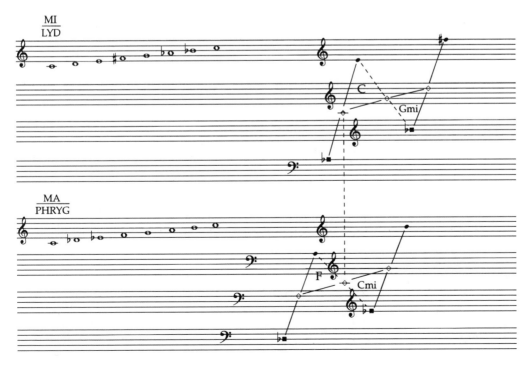

*Example 24.7*

No Didymic pairs of triads or tones! No commas! Why? Because the central spine contains only three tones; the other four are produced in gapped *ga* spines. That gives a very low level of ambiguity, but also only two stable triads. Both modes yield fascinating collections of tones as well as difficult-to-hear yet beguiling melodies. It does not detract from their potential to point out that these modes are rarely used.

## IS AMBIGUITY GOOD OR BAD?

The relative rarity of the two modes above gives us a clue—namely, that zero ambiguity in equal temperament is not necessarily, by itself, a musical advantage. On the contrary, without the added options brought about by ambiguity, temperament doesn't seem to add anything to this mode, it merely subtracts resonance. And indeed, we have seen that certain equal-tempered modes containing the highest levels of ambiguity, like Dorian and Mixolydian, have been found the most useful. Could it be that ambiguity is desirable in equal temperament? Do the wider harmonic choices work in our favor? Does the fuzziness induced in our template-memory act as compensation for existential out-of-tuneness? Or at least act as a buffer against it?

# Modes Containing Augmented Seconds

Among the modes containing augmented seconds, the first to consider is the familiar Harmonic Minor. If we consider also its transpositions both up a fifth and down a fifth over a constant drone, we will have a set of three modes whose intervalic content is identical. Example 24.8 shows their scales and their harmonic maps.

Notice how, when you read the maps down the page, all the spines notch down by a fifth. There are no commas, no gaps in the spines, zero ambiguity. And there are four strong triads in each mode.

Although they all would sound fuller in just intonation, of course, these modes are nevertheless quite tantalizing to play in equal temperament. Pure melodic invention over the drone is suggested, but the triadic harmonies are particularly compelling. The progression in example 24.9 uses the triads of each mode in turn.

There are stunning four-tone chords and other collections of tones are available for the asking. Example 24.10 also moves through each mode in turn.

Many other modes contain augmented seconds, including some that evoke ambiguity of a new kind. A few of these will be discussed in chapter 26. If you are curious about the harmonic properties of a mode that is not discussed in this chapter, I urge you to draw your own harmonic map. In order to do so you will have to make conscious what your ear is actually hearing when you play the mode in equal temperament over a drone and then describe that in terms of the just-intonation lattice in your brain. It is easy to become confused. The subject is confusing. Indeed, the subject is confusion itself. But there are a few clear guidelines.

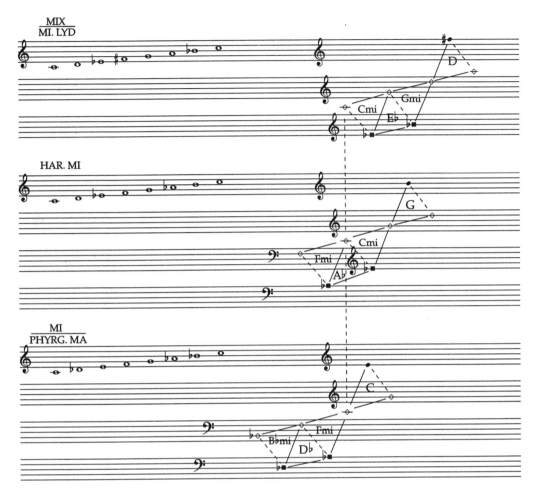

*Example 24.8*

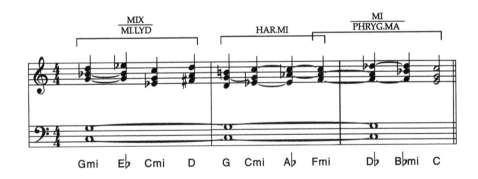

*Example 24.9*

*Example 24.10*

First, everything is something. Aside from some *blu*-ish notes in *blu*-ish modes, everything authentically heard as dronal in twelve-tone equal temperament refers to one or more tones on the five-limit lattice depending on musical context. Everything is *pa* or *ga* above or below, or some combination thereof. At least, that is our primary operating principle.

The secret lies in harmonic continuity, because—just as in coherent speech—continuity is what generates context. If tones are generated by an unbroken line of fifths, they can be heard as fifths. But if the line of fifths is broken, that meaning disappears. A whole step—between B♭ and C, for instance—is not automatically 9:8 (two fifths distant). In the case of MIX/LYD there is no F in the mode to connect B♭ by fifths to C, so the B♭ will likely associate with the D as its reciprocal third. The D is the available context that gives the B♭ meaning; this particular B♭ has no Pythagorean context to resolve its meaning, only a pentamerous one, so it is heard as 10:9 with the upper tonic. In MA/MI, for another example, there can be no Pythagorean B because there is no E in the mode to connect B by fifths to A; therefore, the B will most likely associate with the G as its overtonal third and be heard as the 15:8 major seventh. But you do have to remember that since equal-tempered major thirds are fourteen cents too wide, any context for *ga* identity has to be convincing.

Again, my advice is first to experience the possibilities of the mode by singing against a drone in just intonation. Then listen to the equal-tempered version with no prejudgment and let your ears tell you what they are hearing. Then improvise. Then compose.

# CHROMATIC PAIRS
# AND THE MAGIC MODE

WE HAVE INVESTIGATED THE SEVEN-TONE MODES available in equal-tempered dronality. Our goal now is to explore equal-tempered dronality in its most extensive expression, using its fullest resources. This chapter, which parallels somewhat the just-intonation investigations of chapter 15, deals with the five most-available chromatic pairs.

The pianist's equal-tempered dronal world is different from the singer's dronal world. The singer seeks maximum harmonic resonance by producing tones that are site-specific on the lattice. For the pianist there is less resonance from pure harmonies, less harmonic truth in the body, and more territorial fuzziness due to the approximations of equal temperament. But the pianist has ten fingers and can sweep through expanses of territory with swift mobility. As one gains harmonic facility, those sweeps widen and quicken until the tonal center itself begins to tremble for its life. Our aim is to pull and push and test and retest the power of the tonal center. Ultimately we want to learn the language of modulating tonal harmony, which is the movement in equal temperament through various key centers. To learn that, we need to know how far the influence of a single tonal center extends, how it attenuates, and where it ends.

Our present plan is to fold the five most-available chromatic pairs methodically into our seven-tone modes, noticing, in each case how the harmonic palette increases. Since certain chromatic pairs engender more problematic contexts than others, let's begin with the clearest cases.

## Major and Minor Sevenths Combined

The most commonly used chromatic pair is formed by a major and a minor seventh, which we will examine in the context shown in example 25.1. This eight-tone scale contains all of the possibilities of the Major mode and the Mixolydian mode combined.

Example 25.1

This part of your work can be enormously rewarding musically. For the fullest benefit, first remind yourself of the sound and feeling of this mode when you sing it improvisationally against a drone. Make musically intuitive choices as to which seventh you use and how you mix them. Then improvise melodically at the keyboard over a C-and-G drone, making choices and listening to the results. Then start using major and minor triads. This mode's triad map, shown in figure 25.1, combines the maps of Major and Mixolydian. (Notice that figure 25.1 is in staff orientation; that is, the triads appear positioned as they would on a lattice in staff notation, except that the staff and its noteheads have disappeared.)

Figure 25.1

If the drone is intact and care is taken with the voice leading, the ear has no difficulty in tracking harmonic leaps like B♭ to G, or Gmi to Emi, or even Emi all the way to B♭, as shown, for instance, in example 25.2. (Also try the roots-in-the-bass version.)

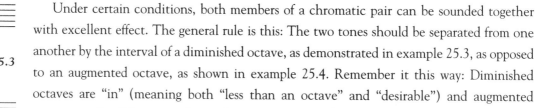

Example 25.2

There is something new in these leaps. Remember that chromatic pairs are melodically close but harmonically distant. When they occur consecutively in such triads, the harmonic territory, thanks to the centering effect of the drone, seems suddenly and dramatically to expand, and the music takes on a kind of complexity we have not met with before. What we have is more than simply two modes combined; we have a new mode with a larger compass. This realization will eventually allow us to make the conceptual leap from combinations of modes to a single all-encompassing mode.

Under certain conditions, both members of a chromatic pair can be sounded together with excellent effect. The general rule is this: The two tones should be separated from one another by the interval of a diminished octave, as demonstrated in example 25.3, as opposed to an augmented octave, as shown in example 25.4. Remember it this way: Diminished octaves are "in" (meaning both "less than an octave" and "desirable") and augmented octaves are "out" (meaning "more than an octave" and "far out").

Although diminished octaves involving the seventh degree are quite common (as I mentioned in chapter 15), augmented octaves are rare for two reasons: They are extremely dis-

Example 25.3

Example 25.4

sonant, and they easily revert in equal temperament to their much more common enharmonic version, the minor ninth. But true augmented octaves can be beautiful and musically appropriate. In a certain sense, my own harmonic development can be defined in terms of my understanding and increasingly frequent use of them. They grow on you. I will point out various uses of diminished and augmented octaves as we proceed.

We have examined the triads resulting from two forms of the seventh degree. Now, by examining the Pythagorean aspect—that is, the fully extended central spine of fifths—we have an opportunity for a new look at the mechanics of equal temperament. The extended lattice of our new eight-tone mode is shown in example 25.5.

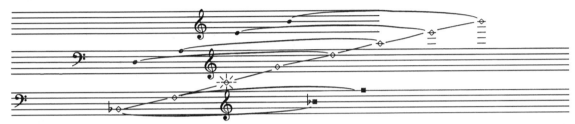

*Example 25.5*

This diagram shows us an inevitable truth (as discussed in chapter 24): When the central spine is extended, Didymic commas proliferate. In this case we have six Didymic pairs of tones, which means that the eight notes of our mode as played on the keyboard stand for a total of fourteen different locations on the lattice. Although it is true that certain combinations of possibilities are much more likely than others, the entirety of this new harmonic compass is nonetheless intriguing. Consider simply the central spine of eight notes. Play these on the piano in a sustained upward arpeggio and listen to the augmented octave thus produced between the low B♭ and the high B♮. Example 25.6 is a phrase evoking that augmented octave.

*Example 25.6*

Notice how this augmented octave, which is separated by seven perfect fifths, and which we will call a *Pythagorean augmented octave*, compares with the augmented octave shown in example 25.7.

*Example 25.7*

*Figure 25.2*

In example 25.7 the two sevenths are constructed as a minor/major pair. The path between B♭ and B♮ is shown in figure 25.2. Can you hear the difference between the pure *pa* dissonance of the Pythagorean pair and the *ga*-blooded dissonance of the major/minor pair? This is a fine point, it is true, yet authentic harmonic knowledge rests on fine points such as these.

Let's turn the Pythagorean tables. Here is a musical context evoking the Pythagorean *diminished* octave: In example 25.8 there are seven perfect fourths between B♮ and B♭.

*Example 25.8*

The much more common diminished octave generated by the major/minor pair of sevenths sounds like example 25.9. The harmonic path from B♮ to B♭ is given in figure 25.3.

*Example 25.9*

*Figure 25.3*

Now compare these two versions of the diminished octave. What do you hear?

Probably the most common context for the simultaneous use of both seventh degrees is that shown in example 25.10.

*Example 25.10*

We have already named this mode the Utility Minor (chapter 15). Its major and minor triads are shown in figure 25.4.

There are eight triads in figure 25.4, including one Didymic pair. The triads yield progressions such as the one shown in example 25.11. To the stable triads may be added the unstable but evocative E♭ augmented triad, which is actually a stack of two major thirds up from E♭.

This mode is an excellent teacher. Of all the eight-tone modes, this one seems most to be able to demonstrate the musical potential of a chromatic pair in an otherwise seven-tone mode.

*Figure 25.4*

G    Cmi    Ab    Bb    Eb    G    Cmi

*Example 25.11*

The Pythagorean properties of the Utility Minor are less extensive than those of the Major-Mixolydian mode described above. Why? Because the eight tones cannot be expressed continuously as a stack of fifths; specifically, E and A are missing from the central spine, as example 25.12 demonstrates.

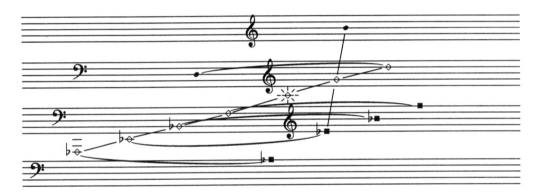

*Example 25.12*

The shorter central spine means fewer Didymic pairs of tones (five), less harmonic range, and more harmonic certainty. It also means that there are no strictly Pythagorean augmented or diminished octaves. Consequently, in this mode the major/minor quality of the pair is brought forward; this is especially so in jazzy-sounding harmonies such as the one given in example 25.13. (I am omitting the drone here, since the harmony is entirely unambiguous without it.)

*Example 25.13*

Jazz delights in allowing the minor/major pair of sevenths to sound in juxtaposition at the interval of the augmented prime (as well as the diminished octave), as shown in example 25.14.

*Example 25.14*

The rare and difficult-to-induce *ga*-blooded augmented octave (between the Pythagorean B♭, 16:9 and the *ga*-blooded B♮, 15:8) sounds as shown in example 25.15.

*Example 25.15*

There is no better musical practice than to learn the properties of the Utility Minor experientially and experimentally at the keyboard—it is a crucial step in the harmonic unfolding. If you can hear the effects of this chromatic pair in the contexts given above, the affects of less congenial pairs in less familiar contexts will open more easily for you. Example 25.16 offers some suggestions for additional modal contexts in which to practice using both the major and minor sevenths.

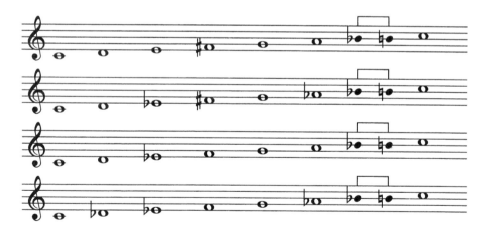

*Example 25.16*

After choosing a mode, remember to improvise first, then analyze, then improvise some more.

## Major and Minor Thirds Combined

A good mode for investigating the properties of the major and minor thirds together is Mixolydian-Dorian, shown in example 25.17. The major and minor triads are given in figure 25.5.

*Example 25.17*

There are ten triads in example 25.5 including two Didymic pairs. It is a good idea, before experimenting with a new mode, to play all of the available triads (including diminished and augmented triads) as well as all the available four-tone seventh chords. This can be accomplished by simply walking your hand up the keyboard. Example 25.18 shows that in this case, for instance, the mode yields eleven possible seventh chords.

*Figure 25.5*

*Example 25.18*

Example 25.19 is a musical phrase using some of the seventh chords.

*Example 25.19*

After a certain period of time spent at the keyboard investigating a mode, such combinations will arise spontaneously. The mode itself teaches them to you. Your work is to notice them, and to remember and label what pleases you. When you hear a good sound, ask yourself "What is this?" Then name it and file it, either in your head or in your sketchbook, preferably both.

Example 25.20 is an example of a diminished octave, followed by an even more dissonant augmented octave, produced by the major/minor pair of thirds.

*Example 25.20*

The Pythagorean possibilities are suggested by the map shown in example 25.21.

*Example 25.21*

Example 25.22 suggests modes for further investigation of the major/minor third.

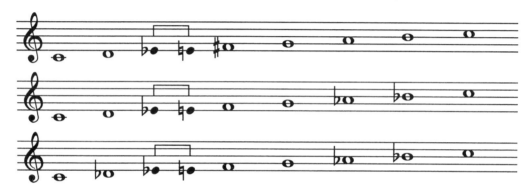

*Example 25.22*

# Major and Minor Sixths Combined

To investigate the properties of the two sixth degrees, try using the Dorian-Aeolian mode, as shown in example 25.23.

*Example 25.23*

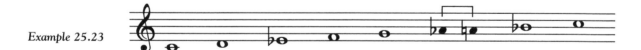

Methodically find all the triads and all the four-tone seventh chords. Improvise. Check out the Pythagorean possibilities. Improvise some more. Remember what is good.

Example 25.24 suggests other good contexts for the major/minor sixth.

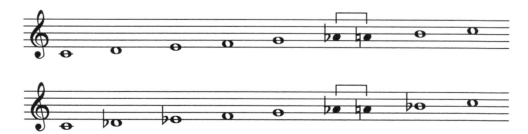

*Example 25.24*

## Perfect and Augmented Fourths Combined

To investigate the properties of the two fourth degrees, use the Lydian-Major mode, as shown in example 25.25.

*Example 25.25*

F♮ and F♯ as a major/minor pair is evoked in this progression of triads: C to G to Dmin to D to G to C. F♮ and F♯ as separated by three fifths and a major third can be brought out this way: C to Amin to F to D to G to C. Is there a difference in effect?

Other good modes in which to peruse the qualities of the two fourths are given in example 25.26.

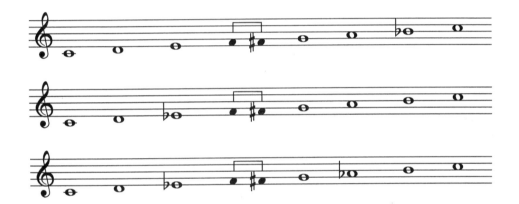

*Example 25.26*

## Major and Minor Seconds Combined

Example 25.27 gives a mode wherein the two seconds can easily be heard as a major/minor pair.

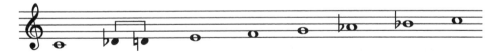

*Example 25.27*

A sample phrase is given in example 25.28.

*Example 25.28*

But the mode in example 25.29 includes major triads on both G and D♭, allowing a different kind of harmony between the D♮ and the D♭ than those we have encountered so far.

*Example 25.29*

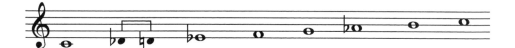

Example 25.30 is a passage in this mode reminiscent of nineteenth-century style.

*Example 25.30*

In this case, the ear hears the two seconds as being separated by three fifths and a third. (This typical Phrygian harmony remains unambiguous without the drone.) Does your ear discern differences in the chromatic harmonies represented by this example and example 25.28?

With C as the tonic, it is also possible to generate cases in which the ear perceives the black note between C and D on the equal-tempered keyboard to be a C♯ (or, for that matter, the black note between G and A to be G♯). These will be discussed in chapter 26.

Learning to use the chromatic forms of the various degrees in a variety of modal contexts opens the door to advanced musical practice. Our plan now is to hear the fluctuating chromatic forms of *two* different degrees simultaneously in the same mode; then three different degrees; then finally all five at once. Don't be alarmed by the amount of study needed to hear these combinations. Every new harmony adds a hundred years to your life.

## Two Simultaneous Chromatic Pairs

Since the Melodic Minor mode is so common in our musical language, let's use that model as a starting place for studying two simultaneously occurring chromatic pairs. In chapter 15 I introduced the term *Full Minor* to better describe this nine-tone mode, reviewed in example 25.31.

*Example 25.31*

Notice that our harmonic maps now become even more extensive. Figure 25.6 shows the major and minor triads.

There are five differently named major triads and four differently named minor triads in Full Minor and two Didymic pairs. Of the less stable triads, there are three diminished and one augmented. There are many flavors of diminished and augmented octaves. The full tonal range, with all of the commas, is shown in example 25.32.

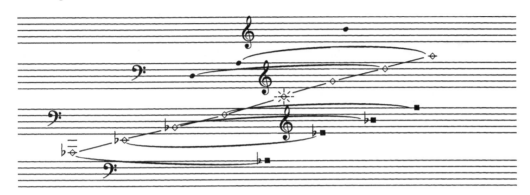

*Figure 25.6*

*Example 25.32*

The object is to make coherent modal music from your nine keyboard tones, while at the same time feeling intimacy with the various combinations of major and minor degrees. Just as an accomplished painter mixes color by truly seeing the paint, you mix these harmonies by truly hearing the sound you play. What continues to be amazing is the increase in musical beauty that can arise from the increasing palette of harmonic choices.

Example 25.33 shows a familiar harmonic progression using Full Minor. Notice that the bass follows the model of the Melodic Minor scale, that is, the sixth and seventh are minor as they descend and major as they ascend. Notice also that the passage uses only tonic, dominant, and subdominant triads (albeit with the help of the first inversion) and in this respect is a more developed version of the mixed-mode cadences of chapter 20 (see examples 20.24–20.31).

*Example 25.33*

Learn to improvise freely using this bass line and these triads in any configuration. (Be aware, however, that when the bass voice is the third of a triad, that tone should not be emphasized in the soprano.) Example 25.34 is an unfinished passage demonstrating some of the available harmony in Full Minor.

In addition to Full Minor, there is a huge variety of modes with two chromatic pairs waiting for you to explore them. Some suggestions are given in example 25.35.

The idea is not to exhaust the list, but to use it to help internalize some of the effects of two chromatic pairs per mode (still over a drone, of course). This may be the time in your

*Example 25.34*

*Example 25.35*

progress for a greater emphasis on composition. As the doorway of equal temperament gets wider, on-the-fly spontaneity and slowed-down deliberation need to balance one another. Pick a few modes from the list above and write a short piece for each one. Then play them consecutively as a suite.

## Three and Four Simultaneous Chromatic Pairs

Before going on to the inevitable five pairs, you should have at least some experience investigating three, and maybe four, simultaneous chromatic pairs. Example 25.36 is a good starting place. The triads are shown in figure 25.7.

There are six differently named major, six minor, four diminished, and two augmented

*Example 25.36*

triads. How many four-tone seventh chords are there? Twenty-four! Plus uncountable collections of various tones. All this adds up to the possibility of a lot of half-heard nonsense unless you are careful. Don't lose the source, which is the resonance of the pure harmonies of low-prime ratios. Keep checking in with your deepest hearing. At this point, ten

*Figure 25.7*

notes on the keyboard stand for eighteen locations on the extended lattice (ten different spellings plus eight Didymic pairs), as shown in example 25.37.

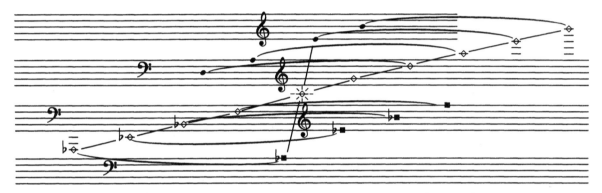

*Example 25.37*

Other suggested ten-tone modes are given in example 25.38.

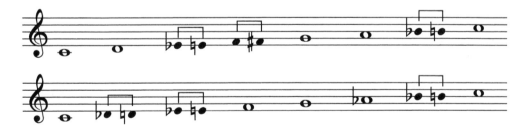

*Example 25.38*

With *four* simultaneous chromatic pairs the question becomes: Which of the five degrees that *can* have a chromatic pair will *not* have one? Unless your curiosity leads you into it, it is OK to leave out this step. The Big Reward is coming right up.

# Five Simultaneous Chromatic Pairs: The Magic Mode

All five chromatic pairs existing simultaneously are written as a scale with the notation shown in example 25.39.

**Example 25.39**

On the page, example 25.39 looks exactly like example 11.2 (p. 69), but there is an essential difference. The twelve notes in the earlier example represent the five-limit lattice of twelve notes. Now, however, we are working in equal temperament, and the twelve notes of our present example represent many more than twelve notes and cover a wide harmonic territory that is shot through with ambiguity. The entire range is shown in example 25.40.

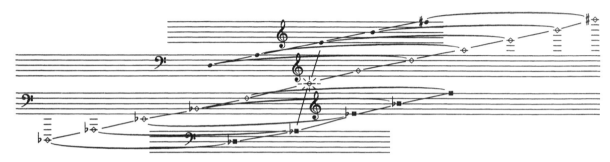

**Example 25.40**

Notice that the Pythagorean spine alone extends through twelve notes, and that all the notes, with the exception of the tonic (C) and the dominant (G), form Didymic pairs. Those ten pairs equal twenty (10 × 2) discrete notes, which with C and G add up to *twenty-two* lattice locations. So there are twelve notes within the equal-tempered octave whose pitches potentially stand for twenty-two locations on the lattice. The Big Reward of equal temperament comes when you can evoke, from these twelve equal-tempered tones, any of those twenty-two locations by means of the musical contexts you construct, and your music contains the blessings from all of those resonances even if only through the veil of temperament.

There are sixteen differently named stable triads and only two Didymic pairs (two B♭ majors and two D minors). The entire sweep of this harmonic territory taken at a glance can be perceived as a single mode with five chromatic pairs whose center is C. I call this full palette of dronal (hence nonmodulating) modality in twelve-tone equal temperament the "Magic Mode,"* a conceit for which I beg the forgiveness of the reader, who has shown every forbearance up to now. My defense is only that there is a quality within equal temperament, some illusion hidden inside its shell games and its substitutions, that does seem to have a kind of magic in it. I know it's a trick my own ear plays on me, these approximations so brazenly *standing for* real things, but it takes me in anyway, at least sometimes. It is also true that when one has been raised in a culture centered on the limits set by the Major and Minor modes only, the extraordinary range of modality that can radiate from one tonal center using only twelve equal-tempered tones definitely has its charms.

So this is where we are: In twelve-tone equal-tempered dronality, there is only one mode, one gigantic ocean of a mode, the Magic Mode. Intimacy with it, and freedom within it, is modal mastery. Modal mastery is what precedes mastery of modulating tonal harmony.

---

*An optional name is the "Omnimode."

Modulation involves moving the tonal center of a mode to a new tonic, a new key. But you can't artfully move something you don't fathom the nature of. So it is crucial to gain modal mastery at some point—sooner rather than later—in your musical development.

How does one proceed to learn this magic? We have been incrementally leading up to it ever since singing our first unison with a drone. The best way to proceed now, I think, is through some careful composition. Write a Magic Mode piece, not a long one. Better yet, write a series of Magic Mode pieces that are between one and two minutes long. Take full advantage of what you have already composed. Go slowly. Review the previous material generously. Sing.

Soon enough—in the very next chapter—we will test and extend these limits. But let's pause here long enough to reap benefit from the language we have labored to learn.

Example 25.41 is a Magic Mode piece in C.

*Example 25.41*

# 26

# PUSHING THE MAGIC MODE ENVELOPE

IN THIS CHAPTER WE WILL BE LIKE SMALL CHILDREN who discover the nature of toys by bending and twisting them until they become something else. Before we play, however, it would be clarifying to review and put forward certain rules and assumptions:

1. The ear perceives frequencies related by low-prime ratios to be harmonious. Singing in just intonation centers such harmony in the body, where music lives.

2. Tonality is sensible in equal temperament because the approximations of the tuning sufficiently (although selectively) awaken our responses to low-prime frequency ratios.

3. Besides the drone (*sa*), all of the tones in our tonal system are either *pa* or *ga*, or compounds of these overtonally or reciprocally, up to the limit of the comprehension of the ear.

4. The study of tonality is by definition the study of the harmonic center. We need to pin the center down, to focus it sharply, in order to examine it thoroughly. In nonmodulating modality the tonal center is assumed to be immutable. To insure this, we have been working within the somewhat more constrained *dronality*, where the drone is virtually always in the air. We want to avoid any perceived change in the *sa*, which would constitute a change in the center; the same is true, to a slightly lesser extent, for the dominant, *pa*. *Sa* and *pa* are thus rendered unique; they occur only in the center of our harmonic maps, and the spines above and below the central spine are truncated before the appearance of a Didymic sibling of either *sa* or *pa*. (Note the exceptions in examples 23.36 and 23.37. Note also that we have allowed the subdominant, *ma*, to have a Didymic sibling.)

5. In equal-tempered dronality we have so far allowed no tones on the *ga-ga* spine of fifths, nor on the *ga-ga*-below spine of fifths, nor have we allowed any seventh-partial tones.

6. According to the above ground rules, the twelve tones within an equal-tempered octave generate twenty-two tones on the lattice of perfect fifths and major thirds.

## Testing the Rules

Throughout our study, all the items above need to be questioned and tested many times. Let's proceed by questioning the last item: Can there be more than twenty-two locations on the lattice to which the ear refers? The question leads us to investigate certain highly specific—and very fertile—conditions under which harmonies even more remote on the lattice than those we have studied can be evoked in equal temperament. But these tricks have to be performed in most acutely particular ways or there will be no magic. Isn't it true that the more subtle a thing is, the more refined has to be your energy to bring it out?

Specifically, Dr. Overtone claims that there are three tones on the *ga-ga* spine of fifths (see chapter 16) that can be brought forward in equal-tempered dronality: C♯, G♯, and D♯. Altering the sequence of our original discussion of these tones, let's consider the C♯ first.

## The Augmented Tonic

Consider the unfamiliar but attractive mode shown in example 26.1.

*Example 26.1*

Now play example 26.2 and continue improvising. Take some care to associate the D♭ with both the F and the B♭, emphasizing thereby its reciprocal source.

*Example 26.2*

Next play example 26.3 repeatedly, legato, softly, and seamlessly.

*Example 26.3*

In the case of example 26.3, the tone A has been made so prevalent in the tenor that it creates a special context for the black note between C and D: We hear it as a C♯. Is this cheating—that is, modulating away from our agreed-upon center? Not if you keep your ear in C, which the drone does indeed allow you to do. But at the same time, we have brought forward the parallel major triad (A major) of A minor: A minor is itself the relative minor of C. Once you identify the A-minor sound on the lattice in your brain, the C♯ appears to make a major/minor pair with the tone C, and in that context is harmonically much closer to C than is D♭. Example 26.4 is a map of the combined aspects of the mode, showing the harmonic derivation of both C♯ and D♭.

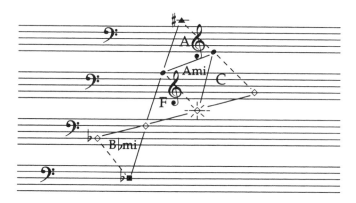

**Example 26.4**

The more the tone F is prevalent in the musical context, the greater the potential for the ear to identify the black note above C as D♭ (a major third below F). The more the tone A is prevalent, the greater the potential for the appearance of the C♯ (a major third above A).

The problem is, by evoking the C♯ we have produced the augmented tonic, something that a *raga* singer would not allow, or even comprehend, as a meaningful concept. *Tivra sa*— the sharped tonic—would obviate the immutable nature of the generating tone, the source of music and a metaphor for the source of being. But, as we have already mentioned in chapter 16 (see p. 121), this particular resonance, 25:24, is an especially evocative one, a harmonic constituent of many of the most beautiful North Indian compositions. The Indian musician invariably calls this tone *komal re*; its full name is *ati ati komal re*, which means very, very flat (actually, "tender") *re*. *Ati* indeed. It is forty-one cents lower than the 16:15 D♭.

Calling that note by the name of C♯ under these special circumstances might not greatly disturb our Western-trained minds, but something else might. When we use C♯ instead of D♭, the scale of the mode looks like example 26.5.

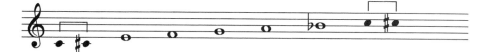

**Example 26.5**

We now have *a scale of only six degrees*, with two forms of the tonic, a special sort of six-tone mode. Once we allow tones from the *ga-ga* spine of fifths out of hiding and into our consciousness, they tend to weaken the seven-degree paradigm. But you may recall from chapter 14 that although the seven-degree scale is an extremely practical concept, it is not a sacrosanct one. In chapter 16 we promised to threaten its integrity with a chisel, and now we have the chisel in hand.

Let's compare the alternative interpretations further by melodic means. Example 26.6 is a passage emphasizing the C♯.

*Example 26.6*

First sing the passage in tune over the drone. Then play it in equal temperament. Can you still hear C and C♯ as a major/minor pair? If so, you are playing a (weird) six-tone mode.

Next, to restore the seven-tone model, consider again example 26.2. Sing it first, taking care with the 16:15 *komal re,* and listen for the seven degrees to click back into their familiar positions. Then play the passage in equal temperament.

The central issue of this book is the behavior of twelve-tone equal-tempered tonality. We have addressed it already by tracing the ambiguity caused by Didymic pairs of tones and Didymic pairs of triads. Now we are asking if we can construct a phrase on the keyboard so that the ear leaps harmonically between C♯ and D♭. The answer is yes; furthermore, it is a leap that releases a jolt of harmonic energy that is deeply affective, and that we respond to characteristically.

## The Great Diesis in Equal-Tempered Dronality

Looking again at example 26.4, observe that the harmonic distance from C♯ to D♭ is three major thirds. On the piano keyboard, a stack of three major thirds results in an octave. But each major third tuned purely 5:4 is narrower than an equal-tempered third by about 14 cents; a stack of three such thirds is narrower than an octave by $3 \times 13.6$ cents, or about forty-one cents. This means that if you begin with D♭ and go up one pure third to F, up another to A, and up another to C♯, you will not only have climbed up through three harmonic layers, which is a fearsome harmonic distance, but also you will be shy of the octave of your original D♭ by forty-one cents. Forty-one cents is the difference—the *comma*—between three major thirds and one octave. This is the second important comma of our study and is generally called the Great Diesis (dee-*ay*-sis or die-*ay*-sis). This wonderful name, possibly derived from a Greek word meaning separation, was used by Alexander Ellis (the translator of Helmholtz) among others. But the same comma has also been referred to as the *enharmonic diesis,* and even the *lesser diesis.*

The confusion over names reflects the nonlinear evolution of music theory over the centuries. What some acoustic texts call the "Great Diesis" can be observed in our text in example 26.40 as the distance between the *ga-ga* F♯ and the Pythagorean F♯ (two thirds down and eight fifths up, or the distance of two Didymic commas). That interval computes to about forty-three cents (hence, "great") and is almost entirely a theoretical interval—that is, it is never evoked and rarely encompassed in actual music. The comma we are now introducing—the interval by which an octave exceeds three major thirds—is over forty-one cents (hence "lesser"), but because its employment is so central to European music, it has come to be known as the Great Diesis, or simply, the diesis (by which we will also identify it once it has become more familiar). Meanwhile, let's coin the name megadiesis for the forty-three-cent comma and keep Great Diesis for the more functional and greatly appreciated (if smaller) comma. The name does have a devotional ring to it, does it not?

> *O Great Diesis! Jolt us with your leaping energy.*
> *Assuage our upturned ears with your vast difference.*
> *Our humanity adores your harmony, O Tertiary One,*
> *Affect us! Affect us!*

We will say a great deal more about the Great Diesis in part 3, qualifying and quantifying it until it has become a familiar concept as well as a hands-on practical tool for making music. Meanwhile, we can say that the leap of three major thirds—in this case between D♭ and C♯ (in either direction)—can occur functionally in equal-tempered dronality and that such leaps serve as communication between the far-flung territories of the north and south and are part of the palpable magic of the Magic Mode. Try the passage shown in example 26.7.

*Example 26.7*

There is a Great Diesis between the C♯ in the A minor/major context and the D♭ in the context of the B♭-minor triad. As you play the passage repeatedly, your ear leaps back and forth between a location on the northern *ga-ga* spine of fifths and a location on the southern *ga*-below spine of fifths, a triple-*ga* journey that is harmonically resolved at the central point, C. Such is the power of the Great Diesis.

Again let me point out that there is a certain feeling of motion, a *leaning* toward the A as the tonal center, when C♯ is induced. This motion is not modulation, exactly, but in part 3, when we break the bonds of dronality, that leaning will become an actual stepping away from the tonal center: modulation—in this case, a particular type of major-third-driven modulation. Meanwhile, we will continue our search for more tones on the *ga-ga* spine of fifths, and hence more invocations of the Great Diesis within dronality.

## PURYA: ANOTHER C♯/D♭ DIESIS

One of the most beautiful modes in the world (called *Purya* in India) looks like Lydian with a minor second, as shown in example 26.8.

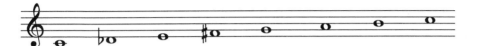

*Example 26.8*

But if the C♯ spelling is used, the scale appears as in example 26.9, and we have an almost entirely overtonal scale of six degrees with two forms of tonic.

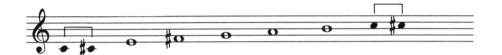

*Example 26.9*

This definitely qualifies as a weird mode—but then again, the future of music lies in weird modes. The map of both versions of the scale combined is shown in example 26.10.

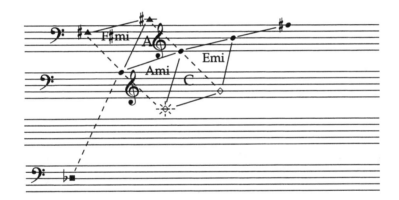

*Example 26.10*

The D♭ will come out in stepwise passages such as example 26.11.

*Example 26.11*

But strong association with F♯ and A will elicit the C♯, as shown in example 26.12.

*Example 26.12*

An even simpler way of bringing out the C♯ is through a kind of floating A Major pentatonic scale, which will stabilize back to C by the interpolation of either the tonic or the dominant of C into the melody, as shown in example 26.13.

*Example 26.13*

Is this bimodal? Yes and no. I can hear it in two keys at once if I want to, but more easily I hear it as a weird C mode with a chromatic pair on its tonic degree—that way seems to have more charge.

## G♯ AND A♭ IN EQUAL-TEMPERED DRONALITY

Two useful modes demonstrate the Great Diesis between the 25:16 G♯ and the 8:5 A♭. The first of these, in its most familiar form, is Harmonic Minor over Major, shown in example 26.14.

*Example 26.14*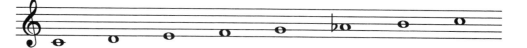

The G♯ can be brought forward in the alternative version shown in example 26.15.

*Example 26.15*

The map of both versions combined is given in example 26.16.

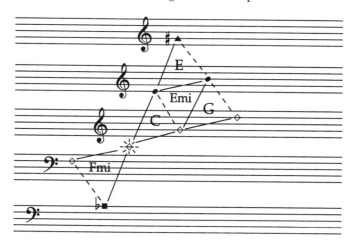

*Example 26.16*

Notice how this stack of thirds includes the tonic, C, which is a fifth higher than the previous example (which included the subdominant, F, and produced the C#/D♭ Diesis).

Example 26.17 is a passage evoking first the A♭, then the G#.

*Example 26.17*

As you play this passage over and over you can hear more and more clearly how the change of function from overtonal G# to reciprocal A♭ brings forward the harmonic ground that lies between them, and how the harmony centers on the triad that lies in the middle position. Experiment on your own with this version of the triple-*ga* journey.

A related mode, given in example 26.18, whose seven-tone version could be called Harmonic Minor over Phrygian Major, is analogous to *Bairov*, an extremely common mode in North Indian *raga*. Notice the two augmented seconds.

*Example 26.18*

In its alternative version, the same notes on the keyboard produce an astonishing pentatonic mode with chromatic forms of both the tonic and the dominant degrees, as shown in example 26.19.

*Example 26.19*

The combined maps are given in example 26.20.

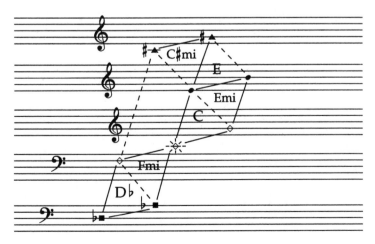

*Example 26.20*

Notice that the central spine has only three tones. Notice also that the stack of thirds from D♭ is missing a tone (A). But notice especially that there are *two* Great Dieses in this mode. Here we are truly pushing the envelope of our Magic Mode model, but, gentle composer, give a listen to example 26.21.

*Example 26.21*

Do the D♭ and A♭ of bar 2 alternate harmonic function with the C♯ and G♯ of bar 5? Hint: Learn the passage so well that you can play it repeatedly and flawlessly without effort; only then ask your ears what they are hearing. Two simultaneous *ga* journeys? Wholesale *ga* flippage? The territory of equal-tempered dronality is wide and mysterious.

## D♯ AND E♭ IN EQUAL-TEMPERED DRONALITY

I would like to include here, with the hope of arousing your curiosity, two more modes lying at or beyond the boundary of the Magic Mode. Each invokes—or tries to invoke—the D♯ that is a fifth higher along the *ga-ga* spine of fifths than the G♯ we have just considered. The first of these could be called Major over Gypsy Minor. Example 26.22 gives the seven-tone scale.

*Example 26.22*

The six-tone scale, shown in example 26.23, has a chromatic pair at the second degree.

*Example 26.23*

The map of both scales combined is shown in example 26.24.

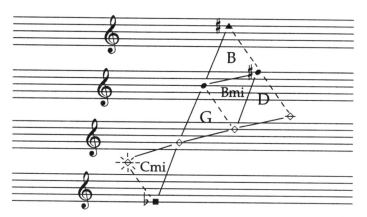

*Example 26.24*

The other mode of this type is often called, in its conventional seven-tone form, Gypsy Minor, and has two augmented seconds, as you can see from example 26.25.

*Example 26.25*

But it could also be heard, possibly, as shown in example 26.26.

*Example 26.26*

The combined map is shown in example 26.27.

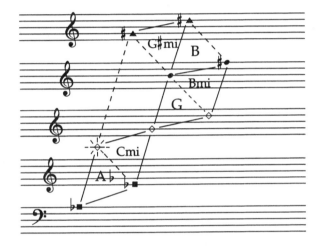

*Example 26.27*

Notice the three-tone central spine, the missing note (E) in the stack of thirds from A♭, and the two Great Dieses.

For purposes of comparison, example 26.28 (on p. 232) gives the maps of the six modes we have just discussed in the order we have discussed them. As they progress down the page they become generally more overtonal. Compare all the dieses, how the spines differ from mode to mode, and of course, the qualities of the various keyboard harmonies you derive from them.

## ONE BRIDGE TOO FAR?

The last mode to consider in this entire discussion of the Great Diesis in dronality is probably beyond the fringe, but fascinating nevertheless. It is none other than the infamous *Todi* (refer back to example 12.20), a favorite of Western composers who borrow source material from *raga*. Compare example 26.29 with the version given in chapter 12.

*Example 26.29*

*Example 26.28*

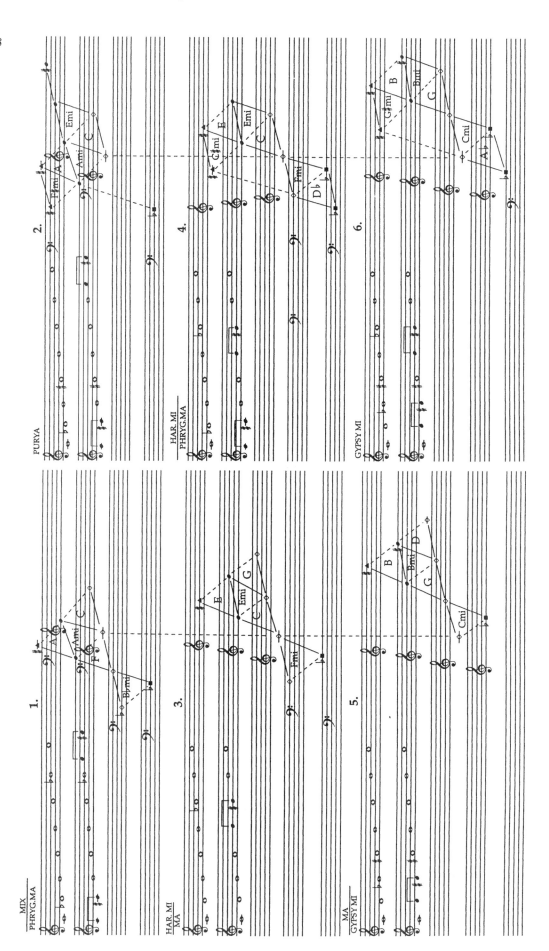

However weak this mode may be in triads or other contextual clues, its B Major pentatonic aspect seems to assert itself, if only bimodally. Example 26.30 gives the five-degree model, the hidden pentatonic scale is exposed in example 26.31, and the entire harmonic scope of the mode, in all its aspects, is shown in example 26.32.

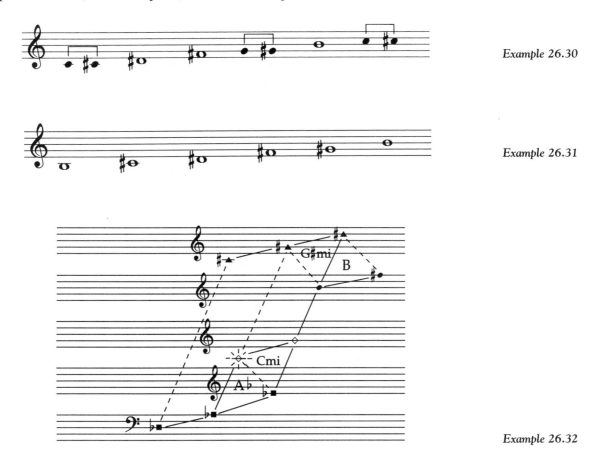

*Example 26.30*

*Example 26.31*

*Example 26.32*

# Supra-Lydian and Sub-Phrygian

The modes involving Great Diesis pairs bring us almost, but not quite, to the farthest reaches of the lattice. There yet remain two more tones on the five-limit lattice of just intonation that can be brought forward in equal temperament. One is more Lydian than Lydian, the other is more Phrygian than Phrygian.

The Lydian mode is generally characterized by the F♯ 45:32. A perfect fifth above this tone is the C♯ 135:128, a harmony ordinarily too remote to evoke in dronality. But if the tonal center is skewed toward the dominant side—not a modulation, exactly, but a tilt or tendency toward the dominant—then the C♯, which characterizes the dominant's Lydian, becomes sensible. Example 26.33 shows the map of the tone's location and an example of its use.

*Example 26.33*

When a strong V or V⁷ harmony is in effect (and only under that condition, I think), the ear can induce the harmonic function of this particular C♯ quite clearly. Notice that the F♯ need not be present to evoke the C♯. The resulting scale is shown in example 26.34. Jazz musicians call this scale the "Lydian Dominant" (often regardless of context or function—more will be said about this in part 4).

*Example 26.34*

At the reciprocal terminus of the Magic Mode lies the tone G♭, which is a perfect fifth below the D♭ characteristic of Phrygian. It usually shows up in what is known as the Locrian mode, which is like Phrygian, but with the fifth diminished—that is (in the key of C), with G♭ in the place of G. The harmonic map for the G♭ is given in example 26.35. It makes, with C, the ratio 64:45.

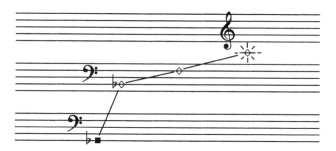

*Example 26.35*

In my book—and this is my book—the Locrian mode is suspect in that it exists as a latter-day theoretical construct generated to complete the compass of the church modes. You may have noticed that you can generate a white-note mode from all of the white notes on the piano except B; so, for the sake of tidiness, why not designate B as a generating tone also, and call its mode "B Locrian"? My skepticism arises from the sense that a mode needs a perfect fifth to sound stable; if the fifth is diminished the mode will tilt irrevocably toward the subdominant. B Locrian, in other words, is heard as E Phrygian; C Locrian is heard as F Phrygian. But, one might ask, what if the drone is so assertive that it successfully establishes itself as the tonal center? My answer is that if a drone is sufficiently assertive—that is, loud—you can put anything above it, including a chain saw, and it will prevail as the tonic of your invented *x*-mode. But don't listen to me, listen to Locrian. Maybe it truly is on the cusp between modality and modulation.

Another case of the diminished fifth as a scale degree occurs in blues or blues-flavored jazz, where it is mixed in with the perfect fifth, as shown in example 26.36.

*Example 26.36*

Notice that the quality of the descending semitone (G♭ to F in the second bar) is nicely offset by that of the ascending semitone (F♯ to G in the first bar). But I wonder about any Phrygian analysis. I have heard the blues G♭ inflected many ways, including a lot of ornamental bending. Blues singers seem to sing it lower than the G♭ 64:45, and lower, even, than the F♯ 45:32. Also, Phrygian and blues are different things: Phrygian is reciprocal *ga* music; blues is overtonal seventh-partial music. That note could conceivably be the seventh-partial of A♭, but it is more likely the *eleventh* partial of C, which makes the very small ratio 33:32 with F. Another possibility is the *ati komal re* of F, which is the F♯ that makes 25:24 with F. Or it could simply be the semitone between F and G. Or all or none of these. (Do I hear blues musicians chuckling?) In any case, the blues-style diminished fifth sounds most true in the context of subdominant harmony, and whatever it is, it can retain its stylistic blues sound in equal temperament.

## Seventh-Partial Tones

To complete our survey of the Magic Mode we must include the special case of the three tones that comprise the *blu* spine of fifths, which appear in chapter 17, and are reproduced in example 26.37 in a slightly different form.

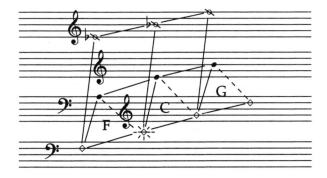

*Example 26.37*

The characteristic seventh-partial harmony is immediately recognizable in the blues as it is sung and played on variable-pitch instruments. But on the equal-tempered keyboard the seventh-partial tones added onto the I, IV, and V triads cannot be distinguished from their five-limit stepsiblings unless the context is clarified stylistically, which is a culturally learned response, not an acoustic one. Acoustic help can be given, however. The seventh partial is about thirty-one cents lower than its keyboard equivalent, so in order to give the illusion of lowering the pitch, blues piano players typically adjoin the semitone below, as shown in example 26.38.

*Example 26.38*

Similarly, blues-influenced voicings of jazz chords often occur in forms similar to those shown in example 26.39.

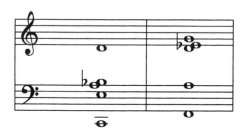

*Example 26.39*

Blues-flavored seventh chords and the cadential dominant seventh chords of European music are compared and discussed further in chapters 32 and 33.

## Things Not Considered

Before presenting the total content of the Magic Mode as we have defined it, perhaps it would be clarifying to mention what we have left out. There are no tones from the *ga-ga-below* spine of fifths—I do not think they can be induced without a definite change of tonal center. Also conspicuously absent are any Didymic pairings with the drone tones: There is only one C and there is only one G. (Well . . . to be honest, the G of the *ga* spine of fifths— wretched *pa*—was admitted for a brief moment of ascending Pythagorean harmony in Dorian, p. 189). Otherwise, however, as mentioned in rule 4 at the beginning of this chapter, we have been steadfast in refusing entry to the C on the *ga*-below spine of fifths (which might be called "pathetic *sa*"). Drawing the territorial line this way is a simple matter of definition. The purpose of the Magic Mode model we have constructed is to conceptualize the shape of the five-limit lattice that the *nonmodulating* scale stands for in equal-tempered music. The displacement of the drones by a comma does entail a kind of modulation, a leap away from the center. The ear's tremendous desire for the integrity of the center results in a precious benefit: an enormous modal territory to make music in, even when that territory is subject to the hocus-pocus of equal temperament. It is true that, eventually, equal temperament will dissemble the ear's longing for home and, in atonality, be the very instrument of its suppression, but we have a long way to go before then. For now, let there be no commas at the center.

## The Harmonic Map of the Magic Mode

Example 26.40 shows the map of the Magic Mode. (The *blu* tones are not shown.) There is a total of twenty-eight tones, twenty-nine triads, twelve Didymic commas between various spines, and four Great Dieses.

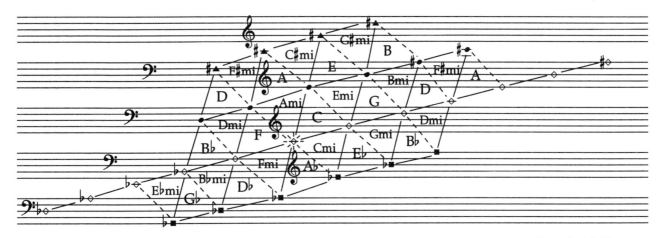

*Example 26.40*

For reference, example 26.41 shows all of the tones (including the *blu* tones) written out as a scale—the Magic scale—with the harmonic locations of each tone indicated by its appropriate symbol. These are the thirty-one tones in the key of C that the twelve tones of the equal-tempered scale can, depending on musical context, evoke.

*Example 26.41*

## Boundary Weather

Boundaries are places where disparate forces can creatively merge. Between the Magic Mode and modulation lies bimodal and bitonal territory—unstable, moveable ground. Several of the modes given here, especially ones involving the *ga-ga* spine of fifths, can be played at this cusp, and it is a good place to play. Between dronality and modulation there is a searching kind of energy through which the internal behavior of our aural responses reveals itself. When you can freely cross and recross—and even straddle—this boundary with your intellect awake, you are experiencing tonal harmony in a wonderful way. The boundary territory is self-revelatory, but you must know what you are hearing inside the nonmodulating Magic Mode to master its wisdom.

## How to Proceed

The problem with music theory is that it tends to make the simple and direct seem complex and remote. Instead of simply playing music over a C drone, we now seem to have a pile of off-putting problems. Don't let that be. Play. Music theory won't get interesting until you have a musical sensibility, and music theory won't give you that sensibility, it can only refine it. You have to acquire it by making music. So play—play freely, and then compose. Spend many dozens of full hours discovering your version of Magic Mode music. Remember, the key of C is only one of twelve.

Here are some ideas to keep in mind about dronality in equal temperament:

Everything sounds OK.
Some things sound better than others.
A few things sound really good.
Something sounds perfect.

It is true that dronality in equal temperament has a kind of grayness about it, but that is partly offset by subtle, darting flashes into the far-flung territories.

## Magic Mode Compositions

Example 26.42 is a Magic Mode composition that uses twenty tones. What are they? In composing Magic Mode pieces, be sure to proceed slowly and carefully enough that you are absolutely certain of where you are on the lattice. Then learn to play your piece well enough to project its harmonic effect.

Example 26.43 is a Magic Mode piece in E by the composer Kirk Whipple. Notice that in E, Lydian has five sharps and Phrygian has no accidentals. To make a thorough analysis, it may help to draw a harmonic map with E at the center. (He uses all twenty-eight tones.)

Compose your own Magic Mode piece in E. Then try composing a Magic Mode piece in F, where Lydian has no accidentals and Phrygian has five flats. Indeed, would it not be a fine project to compose a series of twelve Magic Mode pieces, each with its own key center? A kind of *Magic Clavier?*

Example 26.42 (page 1)

*Example 26.42 (page 2)*

*Example 26.43 (page 1)*

*Example 26.43 (page 2)*

*Example 26.43 (page 3)*

PART THREE

# THE FUNCTIONAL COMMAS OF EQUAL-TEMPERED TONAL HARMONY

# 27

# COMMA PHENOMENA

TO OPEN COMPLETELY THE SUBJECT OF modulating tonal harmony in equal temperament, we must examine the central issue of commas more closely. This chapter is the long-promised chat on commas, including their mathematical quantification, as well as a brief general discussion of modulation.

## What Is a Comma?

The word *comma* comes from the Greek root *komma,* meaning "to cut off," or "set apart." In our written language it is, of course, a mark indicating a pause or a separation. In the mathematics of musical acoustics, large numbers are often generated by multiplying low-prime numbers together—usually some combination of 2, 3, 5, and 7—and a comma is the result of the very small difference that will sometimes occur between two such large numbers. The numbers represent the frequencies of musical tones. Ratios such as 81:80 stand for the relationship between the frequencies of two tones, and the "very small difference" between them will be heard as a minute, yet specific, change in pitch, that is, a very small musical interval. This interval is called a comma.

We have already introduced the two most musically active commas: the comma of Didymus and the Great Diesis. Before going into greater detail about these, however, it may be useful to discuss the Pythagorean comma. It is the first comma to reveal itself historically, and even though the practical musician will not make hands-on use of it, it is nonetheless theoretically and conceptually prior to the others.

## The Pythagorean Comma

Pythagoras of Samos lived twenty-five hundred years ago. According to the philosophers of his time, music was not so much an expressive art as a kind of audible mirror of an ideal world. By means of musical relationships one could grasp the harmonies of the entire universe, including those laws governing the concentric crystal spheres thought to surround the world in a vast harmony of the spheres. Much of what we know about Pythagoras and his work we know by legend (a fine way of knowing, to be sure), and according to legend, he invented the monochord, a musical string stretched over a ruler used for measuring the various divisions of the string. Because the discovery and quantification of the overtone series is credited to him, we may think of him as the Original Dr. Overtone, the Ur-Doctor of Overtones.

Equating simplicity with goodness, Pythagoras taught that music should properly consist only of tones that combine in ratios compounded of the lowest primes, namely, two and three. Thus, in the Pythagorean system, all admissable musical harmonies have duple or triple nature only, which means—besides unisons—octaves (2:1) and twelfths (3:1), along with their octave expansions and reductions and their overtonal and reciprocal compounds. In other words, Pythagorean harmony is a strict universe of perfect fifths. No pentamerous energy, no seventh partials, no anything else. If it is not 3:2 or a compound up or down, it does not belong.

Such a music system is called Pythagorean, and Pythagorean tunings are not uncommon today. We have adopted Pythagorean terms in this book: The central spine of fifths, for instance, is sometimes called "the Pythagorean spine."

One particular result from the process of stacking fifths still amazes contemporary musicians as much as it undoubtedly amazed Pythagoras: A stack of twelve perfect fifths adds up to only slightly more than seven octaves. The small amount by which twelve fifths exceed seven octaves was first described by Pythagoras and bears his name: the Pythagorean comma.

Let's use the full piano keyboard to visualize the phenomenon. Our object is to compare a stack of seven perfect octaves with a stack of twelve perfect fifths. The keyboard procedure for comparing seven octaves with twelve fifths can be represented on staff notation as shown in example 27.1.

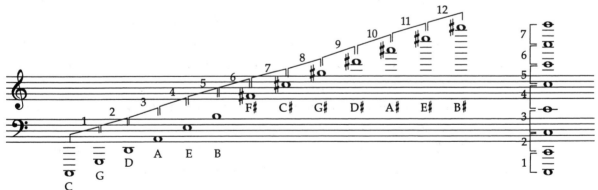

Example 27.1. Twelve perfect fifths (3:2) compared with seven perfect octaves (2:1)

Imagine for the moment that the frequency of the lowest C on the piano has a value of 1. The first octave above it doubles the frequency, so let that value be 2. The second octave will then be 4, then 8, 16, 32, and 64. Finally, the highest C on the piano, the seventh octave above the starting point, will be 128, or two times itself seven times, or two to the seventh power ($2^7$).

Next, return to the original lowest C, to which we will again ascribe the value 1. This time, however, we will ascend by fifths. Furthermore, we will imagine these fifths to be tuned perfectly in a ratio of 3:2, or, to use the fractional notation, $\frac{3}{2}$. So the first fifth will be G and its value will be $\frac{3}{2}$, which can also be written 1.5. The second fifth in the stack will be D, and its value will be $\frac{3}{2} \times \frac{3}{2}$, which is the same as $1.5 \times 1.5$, or 2.25. For each additional fifth in the stack, multiply (on your calculator) by 1.5, progressing in turn through A, E, B, F♯, C♯, G♯, D♯, A♯, E♯ and, finally, to the twelfth fifth, B♯. The value is 129.74632. The value of the frequency of the B♯ exceeds the value of the frequency of the highest C by $\frac{129.74632}{128}$. Another way of writing it: B♯ exceeds C as $\left(\frac{3}{2}\right)^{12}$ exceeds $2^7$.

Example 27.2 is another way of visualizing the Pythagorean comma that is perhaps more musically palatable: Build downward from middle C by six fifths, and build upward by six fifths also, making a total spread of twelve perfect fifths built outward from a central tone.

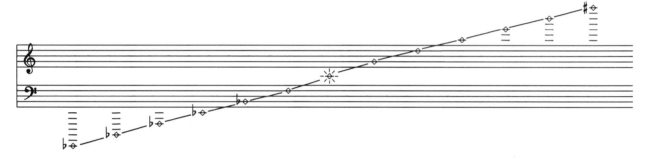

*Example 27.2*

All of these tones are at least within hailing distance of the Magic Mode of C. The reciprocal Pythagorean G♭ (we might call it distressed *komal pa*) is distant from the overtonal Pythagorean F♯ (exacerbated *tivra ma*) by twelve perfect fifths, which in just intonation will exceed the compass of seven octaves by the Pythagorean comma.

A mathematically more pure way of perceiving this comma—and the way in which Pythagoras himself undoubtedly perceived it—does not employ the 3:2 octave reduction that allows its musical compass to fit on a modern keyboard. For this computation, simply multiply 3 (which stands for the triple nature of the third partial) times itself twelve times; then multiply 2 (which represents the duple nature of the second partial) times itself nineteen times and compare those numbers. The answer is $\frac{3^{12}}{2^{19}}$, or $\frac{531441}{524288}$. This is the exact value for the Pythagorean comma. The number says that if you stack twelve third partials you will arrive at a tone that is this specific amount sharper than a stack of nineteen second partials. The computation of this large ratio is possible today in a trice with an inexpensive calculator, but it may give you some historical perspective to imagine the staggering intellectual feat it must have been twenty-five hundred years ago. Although Pythagoras did seem to sense the philosophical significance of his effort, he did not anticipate its application to our modern tuning system or its implications for our music.

Since modern Western musicians are so used to "the circle of fifths" as a theoretical concept as well as a practical learning tool, it may be surprising to some that twelve perfectly tuned fifths stacked up from C do *not* equal some distant octave of C, and that there is hence no circle of perfect fifths. But do consider the reason: A perfect fifth is the harmonic embodiment of triple nature, and an octave is the embodiment of duple nature; and these worlds are as pristinely distinct as is the prime two from the prime three. Appeal to your intuition: How many times would you have to multiply three times itself to achieve an even number, that is, a number divisible by two? Think about it. The answer is, No power of three is ever even, that is, divisible by two. Conversely, how many times would you have to multiply two times itself to get an odd number? It can't happen. Which means that when you stack fifths you will never come to any octave of your starting tone. If you enjoy pondering, the truly absorbing issue is the deep quirk of providence by which twelve perfect fifths contrive to come so close to seven octaves that they nearly but don't quite touch.

The salient point is that *so close* is also *so far*. Think of instances in real life where entirely different worlds are separated by the smallest boundary. Two strangers sleeping in adjacent motel rooms separated by a few inches of wall. Oncoming traffic separated by a yellow line. The inside of your body separated from the rest of the world by your skin. Musical commas are these narrow but real boundaries that separate, or cut off, one harmonic realm from another at a particular point where melodically (i.e., intervalically) they almost touch. The melody is close but the harmony is far.

The interval of the Pythagorean comma is about twenty-four cents. The twelfth fifth up, B♯, is twenty-four cents *too wide*, that is, sharp, from the octave-generated C. What would happen if *each* fifth in our stack were narrowed by exactly one-twelfth of the comma, or about two cents? In that case, the twelve narrow fifths would indeed add up to exactly seven octaves, and the stack of these newfangled fifths, now called equal-tempered fifths, could be drawn in a circle to indicate their cyclic nature. When we play these same twelve tones chromatically within an octave we generate "the twelve-tone equal-tempered" scale, or the scale of the modern piano.

So each equal-tempered fifth is about two cents flat. How flat is two cents? About one-fiftieth of a semitone, which means barely audible. If you train to listen for the flatness of an equal-tempered fifth you can hear it. When piano tuners tune an equal-tempered circle of fifths they are actually *de-tuning:* They are flattening each pitch by two cents. But they are not using their pitch discrimination to do this. They are instead listening for the interference beats that indicate a certain amount of out-of-tuneness. In other words, they are not so much tuning as *counting* the desired number of *wah-wah-wahs* per second needed to de-tune that particular fifth. Shocking, perhaps, but true. We have a great system of music but our fifths are flat. Welcome to the West.

The first inkling of the musical utility of twelve-tone equal temperament probably took the form of a theoretical speculation by the Chinese prince Chu Tsai-yii in 1596. But the concept did not become a useful musical option until the eighteenth century in Europe, and then was accepted only gradually and often reluctantly. Although the Pythagorean comma lies at the heart of the standard modern tuning system, it does not function actively in real-time music like the other commas we will study in more detail. The limited musical possibilities of the Pythagorean comma are discussed in chapters 33 and 41.

## The Didymic Comma

In previous discussion about the Didymic comma (especially in chapters 16 and 23) we have talked in terms of stepsiblings, Didymic pairs of tones, and Didymic pairs of triads. It is now time to describe the comma in more detail and to demystify its math as much as possible.

Didymus was an academic philosopher of first-century Greece who allowed pentamerous energy into the Pythagorean system. The Didymic comma is the amount by which a stack of four perfect fifths exceeds the fifth partial. As in the case of the Pythagorean comma, we will again use the piano keyboard, but our method of computation will be slightly different, the better to visualize the ratios involved. First, examine example 27.3.

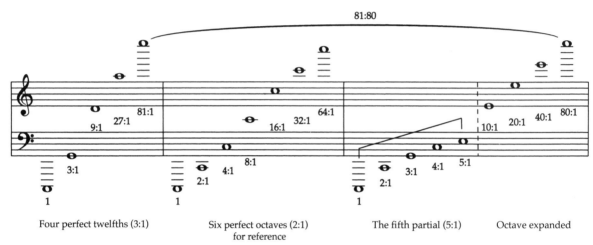

Four perfect twelfths (3:1)          Six perfect octaves (2:1)          The fifth partial (5:1)          Octave expanded
                                          for reference

*Example 27.3*

If you start on C, a stack of four third partials (3:1) results in the Pythagorean E, whose ratio is $\frac{3}{1} \times \frac{3}{1} \times \frac{3}{1} \times \frac{3}{1}$, or $\frac{3 \times 3 \times 3 \times 3}{1}$, or $\frac{81}{1}$, or, as a ratio with the generating tone C, 81:1. Skipping over the middle bar of the diagram for the moment, notice that the fifth partial produces an E whose ratio is 5:1 with the generating tone. We'll now proceed to raise this E by four octaves (you'll soon see the method in this madness). When you raise 5:1 by four octaves it becomes successively 10:1, then 20:1, then 40:1, and finally 80:1. We now have the Pythagorean E (81:1) and the octave-expanded fifth partial (80:1) right next to each other in the same octave. Comparing them we see that they stand to each other as the number 81 stands to 80, or 81:80. This ratio represents the amount by which the Pythagorean E exceeds the pure major third. The middle bar of the diagram shows the intervening octaves.

Example 27.4 is another way of arriving at the same answer: Simply stack four perfect fifths and compare that with the fifth partial.

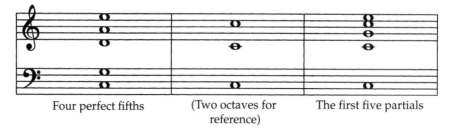

Four perfect fifths          (Two octaves for          The first five partials
                                  reference)

*Example 27.4*

Here is the math: Four perfect fifths is $\frac{3}{2}$ times itself four times, or $\frac{3\times3\times3\times3}{2\times2\times2\times2}$, or $\left(\frac{3}{2}\right)^4$, or $\frac{81}{16}$. Now, the fraction representing the fifth partial is $\frac{5}{1}$, which can also be written as $\frac{80}{16}$ (check it). Now that our two fractions have the same common denominator, we can compare them and see that $\frac{81}{16}$ stands to $\frac{80}{16}$ as 81 stands to 80, or 81:80.

Here is yet another way to see it, a most practical way. First, octave-reduce both kinds of third. The Pythagorean E in its most expanded form is $\frac{81}{1}$, as we have seen. Reduced successively it becomes $\frac{81}{2}$, then $\frac{81}{4}$, then $\frac{81}{16}$, and finally $\frac{81}{64}$, the fraction representing the Pythagorean major third. (You can see this by comparing the top notes of the first two bars of example 27.3.) The fifth partial we already recognize in its reduced form: $\frac{5}{4}$. Now, if you multiply $\frac{5}{4}$ by 16, a nice thing happens: It becomes $\frac{80}{64}$. We can now compare $\frac{81}{64}$ with $\frac{80}{64}$ and see again how the two tones stand in relation to one another as 81 stands to 80, or 81:80.

Here is one more method for good measure. We know already "two fifths up," if octave reduced, is 9:8. This ratio stands for the "major whole tone," which is the most usual *re*. Two of these stacked *re*'s can be expressed as $\frac{9}{8}\times\frac{9}{8}$, or $\frac{81}{64}$. We can now compare that fraction with the pure third $\frac{5}{4}$, which we will write in the form $\frac{80}{64}$, and $\frac{81}{64}$ stands to $\frac{80}{64}$ as the ratio 81:80.

But to me the clearest representation of all is simply a factoring of the fraction $\frac{81}{80}$, which is $\frac{3\times3\times3\times3}{5\times2\times2\times2\times2}$, or $\frac{3^4}{5\times2^4}$. The expression $\frac{3^4}{5\times2^4}=\frac{81}{80}$ seems to be a most elegant way of saying that pure triple nature is not the same thing as duple nature and quintuple nature combined, even though under this particular condition they amount to *almost* the same thing (which would be $\frac{1}{1}$). If you read the numbers this way they tell you that, from a unique point of observation, you can witness separate orders of infinity coming together in a near miss.

We have already mentioned that the Didymic comma is an interval of about twenty-two cents, oddly near to the value of the twenty-four cents of the Pythagorean comma, even though it is derived quite differently. Unlike the Pythagorean comma, the Didymic comma has an ongoing, real-time, active, pitch-sensitive musical function for musicians who sing or play variable-pitch instruments, and its effects remain sensible in equal temperament. In other words, although the performing musician will virtually never have to deal with the difference between twelve fifths and an octave (the Pythagorean comma), the difference between four fifths and a pure third comes up in even relatively simple harmonic situations. This subject has already been discussed in chapter 23 and is the primary subject matter of chapters 28 and 29.

## The Great Diesis

The Great Diesis is the least hidden of all the commas, and the most sensible in equal temperament. (A review of chapter 26 might be timely.) It consists of the difference between a stack of three 5:4 major thirds and one octave. The math in this case is easy. A stack of three thirds is $\frac{5}{4}\times\frac{5}{4}\times\frac{5}{4}$, or $\frac{125}{64}$. An octave is $\frac{2}{1}$, also expressible as $\frac{128}{64}$. The Great Diesis is the difference between an octave $\frac{128}{64}$ and a stack of three thirds $\frac{125}{64}$. The two fractions stand to one another as 128 stands to 125, or 128:125. Example 27.5 shows the notation.

*Example 27.5*

The upper C is wider than the B♯ by 128:125. The musical interval of this comma, about forty-one cents, or almost a quarter tone, is huge compared to the other commas. The difference in just intonation is easily audible, and the effect in equal temperament is enormous, as we shall soon chronicle.

In equal temperament there are "circles of thirds" just as there is a "circle of fifths." We just mentioned that in order to get pure perfect fifths to be cyclic, each is shaved by two cents, which is scarcely audible. To get pure major thirds to be cyclic, however, each is expanded by almost fourteen cents, and fourteen cents sharp is quite audible. The roughness of the equal-tempered major third seriously compromises the pentamerous beauty of our culture's musical language. But with the loss of one kind of beauty another emerges: the wondrously affective operations of the Great Diesis in modulating tonal harmony, a subject discussed in detail in chapters 30 and 31.

## The Diaschisma

The third functional comma in music is subtle and less common but can be most artfully employed. It is the amount by which a stack of three octaves exceeds a stack of four perfect fifths and two major thirds. It will arise only in certain specialized situations, the most common of which symmetrically straddles the tonic, as shown in example 27.6.

For the math, let's use this practical computational short cut:

Up *pa* means multiply by 3

Up *ga* means multiply by 5

Down *pa* means divide by 3

Down *ga* means divide by 5

Octave-reduce or -expand as necessary

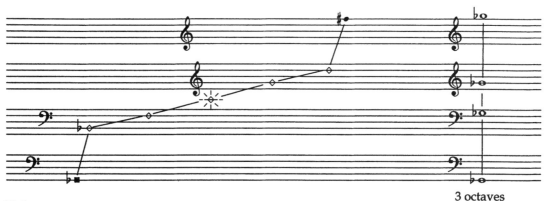

3 octaves

*Example 27.6*

In the case of the diaschisma, the question is, "By what amount do three octaves exceed four perfect fifths and two major thirds?" Proceeding upward from the G♭ in the example we have one *ga*, four *pa*'s, and one more *ga*, or $5 \times 3 \times 3 \times 3 \times 3 \times 5 = 25 \times 81 = 2025$. It is now necessary to octave-expand the generating tone to the nearest duple number, in this case $2^{11}$, or 2048. Three octaves exceeds four perfect fifths and two major thirds by $\frac{2048}{2025}$. This amounts to an interval of about twenty cents. Even though 2025 is an awfully high number to be sensible in just intonation, much less to be traceable in equal temperament, under various conditions it nevertheless does come into play. The diaschisma is discussed in detail in chapter 32.

## The Four Commas Compared

Each comma reminds us in its own way that prime numbers generate mutually exclusive mathematical worlds. The commas are points at which these worlds come into view of one another, never touching or merging.

The Pythagorean comma tells us that 2 is not 3
(octaves are distinct from fifths)
The Didymic comma says that 3 is not 5
(fifths are distinct from thirds)
The Great Diesis says that 5 is not 2
(thirds are distinct from octaves)
The diaschisma says that $3 \times 5$ is not 2
(fifths plus thirds are distinct from octaves)

If you are math shy—many musicians are—Dr. Overtone means to assure you that this math is no more difficult than making change and definitely easier than figuring your taxes. If you want to skip ahead a little, take a glance at example 34.2. But if your eyes are getting glassy, skip this part and go on over to the keyboard where the better stuff is. You may be back, though, to nail down the numbers. They truly amount to little more than multiplying and dividing by two, three, and five.

## Modulation

Modulation is a shift from one tonal center to another, a "change of key." Although some of the chord progressions we have used in part 2 have allowed a considerable expansion of the tonal center, or even a kind of circumnavigation of it, until this point we have eschewed actual modulation, which requires the clear establishment of a new tonal center. As we study the functions of the commas in equal temperament, modulation will become increasingly important, so a general discussion of the subject is now in order.

Modulation is the jewel of the West, a territory that Western culture has pioneered and plowed. Westerners tend to think in a proprietary way about it, as though it had a Western patent, but it is useful to recognize that modulation is an extension of modality, not a break from it. It is not a shedding of the old but an evolutionary response: Expanded language is developed to express expanded experience. As the intellectual and geographical explorers of Europe moved outward from their ideas and their towns, the tonal language of their music had also to increase its range.

Remember that the simplest pentatonic scale can modulate by simply changing its emphasis. Consider once again the basic pentatonic examples 16.10 through 16.14. We will assume that an unaccompanied singer is moving smoothly back and forth between the two modes. As the tonal center alternates between C and A, each of the tones acquires alternative functions. When the center moves from C to A, for instance, the E that used to be the third is now the fifth; the old fifth, G, is the new seventh, and so on, only to revert back to the original functions when the music moves back to C. This effect assumes that the two tonal centers are closely related harmonically, which means that they are geographically close on the lattice and therefore share substantial territory, much like two neighboring towns whose fields are held in common.

Perhaps the most beguiling modulatory aspect of all is when two related keys split up the ownership of a pair of tones related by a comma. In just intonation, the two tones of such a pair will differ considerably in function as well as slightly in pitch. In equal temperament, the difference of pitch disappears, but the modulatory effect of the comma is still present.

To illustrate, example 27.7 is another look at the territories of "C Major pentatonic" (C, D, E, G, and A) and "A Minor pentatonic" (A, C, D, E, and G), as discussed in chapter 16.

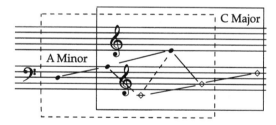

*Example 27.7*

The solid line encloses the C Major pentatonic scale. The broken line contains the A Minor pentatonic scale. As the center rocks back and forth from C to A, four tones (C, E, G, and A) are held in common (i.e., they appear in both boxes), and their functions change synchronously with the change in tonal gravity. But the case of D is different because there are actually two of them: the two D's of a Didymic pair of tones. They are *noncommon* tones: One belongs to C Major, the other belongs to A Minor. In just intonation, the 9:8 D of C Major is Pythagorean; the 10:9 D of A Minor is *ga*-blooded. They are set apart by the Didymic comma in both pitch and harmonic function: We hear a small change in pitch as we hear a large change in function. In equal temperament the pitch difference is gone, yet the harmonic effect, washed out as it may be, is not washed away.

The many-faceted pleasure of this rocking, back-and-forth motion probably dates from ancient times, counted in millennia, and certainly predates triadic European modulation. But the ancient modal modulations and the complex modulations of modern tonal harmony are based on the same principle: Harmonic continuity allows modulation to be sensible. Harmonic continuity means geographical proximity on the lattice—clear connection by *pa* and *ga*. In part 1 we have described the relationships among *tones* in terms of the harmonic continuity between them. In part 2 we have described the journeys of *triads* in terms of the harmonic continuity between their roots. Now, in part 3 (and in part 4 also), we will describe the relationship between *keys* by the harmonic continuity of their tonics. Just as any two tones are heard as closely related if they are distant by (for example) a fifth, and just as any two triads will be heard as closely related if their roots are distant by a fifth, so will any two keys be heard as closely related if the tonics are distant by a fifth.

But to understand fully the mechanics of modulation, it is not enough to look only at the tonics; we must consider as well all of the other tones involved. In the modulation from C Major to G Major, for instance, the tonics are distant by a fifth, and the keys share most of their tones (five or six, depending on the tuning) in common. In the modulation from C Lydian to F Phrygian, whose tonics are again distant by a fifth, the keys contain only one tone in common (C). Both modulations work well because of the fifth between the tonics, but the difference in the amount of territory held in common produces a great difference in effect. So to understand modulation, which involves the quality of harmonic continuity (or discontinuity) between keys, both the relationship between the tonics and the mutuality of the territory need to be perceived.

## Where Are We?

We have, as singers, experienced the various resonances of just intonation; as both singers and players we have tracked through the common and not-so-common modes of the Magic Mode; we have drawn triads the length and breadth of the lattice, and done our math homework. Now it is time to stride into the forest of commas. We will first examine the effects of the Didymic comma in equal temperament, even though these are more muted and subtle than the effects of the Great Diesis. Why not examine the Great Diesis first, since it is easier to feel and understand and is generally more convincing? A good answer is that the Didymic comma, though more difficult to grasp, operates closer to the tonal center, is conceptually prior, and arose earlier in history. But the real answer is that this is a book, and books tend to be coherent, orderly, linear, and rational, everything that music learning is not. So once more let me offer this advice: Don't get stuck. One learns music in dozens of passes over the same theoretical ground, and hundreds, even thousands of repetitions of corroborative harmonic experience. Get what you can, move on, and come back later. Learning is a game, especially learning from books, and one must be sure never to let a book, especially a book about music, get the upper hand.

# 28

# DIDYMIC PAIRS OF TONES

## The Didymic Saga So Far

We first encountered the Didymic comma in chapter 16, where we identified the two forms of the major sixth degree (5:3 and 27:16) as a Didymic pair of tones we called stepsiblings. We noticed that the stepsiblings share the same letter name and solfege syllable and, though near in pitch (only twenty-two cents apart), are quite different in their harmonic origins. We tracked their disparate harmonic paths. We also made a point of *not* singing the two tones consecutively because, at the time, the large harmonic discrepancy between them was more germane to our purpose than the small melodic interval between them.

In chapter 23 we began to put Didymic stepsiblings side by side, first by juxtaposing a stack of fifths from C to E with an overtone chord that had an E on top. By the end of the chapter we had met a Didymic pair of triads, had framed "the problem of ii," and were able to track other Didymic pairs of triads throughout the modal system. It had become clear that in equal-tempered dronality, the more familiar modes contain certain triads that are able to serve as harmonic pivots, flipping dominant and subdominant energy within the mode.

In chapter 25 we tracked the various Didymic pairs of tones and pairs of triads in the Magic Mode. We described how the harmonic palette expands, through their agency, from twelve to twenty-two tones and finally, in chapter 26, through the agency of the Great Diesis (as well as some seventh partials) to thirty-one tones in the Extended Magic Mode. Our purpose now is to meet the Didymic comma "head on" as promised, and to go even farther: to connect the quality of the comma in just intonation with its quality in equal temperament.

Let's take up the thread of inquiry by going back to the experience we specifically avoided in part 1. How does it feel to sing Didymic stepsiblings side by side, and what could be the musical value of such an experience? In answering this question we will step inside the Didymic comma and walk directly through the small number that separates two large numbers. We will enter the unknown place that lies between known places.

# The Didymic Comma of the Major Sixth Degree

## SINGING THROUGH THE COMMA IN JUST INTONATION

We need a Pythagorean spine of four tones—F, C, G, and D—comprising three pure perfect fifths, as shown in example 28.1.

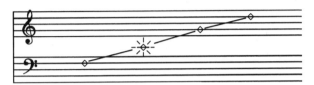

*Example 28.1*

There needs to be some octave juggling. The best procedure is to tune four guitar or harp strings as shown in example 28.2.

(concert pitch)

| E string (VI) | A string (V) | D string (IV) | G string (III) |
|---|---|---|---|
| up to F | down to G | down to C | down to D |

*Example 28.2*

Be painstaking in this work and check your tuning frequently. Alternatively, you could use a synthesizer with a Pythagorean tuning program. But if neither of these options is possible or practical, an equal-tempered piano will do. This may seem surprising, but consider: An equal-tempered fifth is two cents flat, which is a scarcely sensible difference. A stack of two tempered fifths is flat by 2 + 2 = 4 cents: F to G, for instance, is a major ninth (or major second) flat by four cents, which is not terribly noticeable. A stack of three tempered fifths results in a Pythagorean major sixth (F to D, octave-reduced) that is six cents flat, and the true nature of the harmony is indeed somewhat compromised. A stack of four tempered fifths produces a Pythagorean third (F to A) flat by eight cents, which is clearly not the "real thing" of 81:64. However, the comma we are trying to navigate is twenty-two cents wide; since the equal-tempered keyboard slashes off eight cents, that still leaves sixteen cents to listen to, and our experiment, though perhaps not as convincing as it would be with a perfectly tuned Pythagorean spine, will still demonstrate the phenomenon.

So, using the best tuning available for the Pythagorean bass, realize example 28.3 by playing the bass and singing the melody (an octave lower for men).

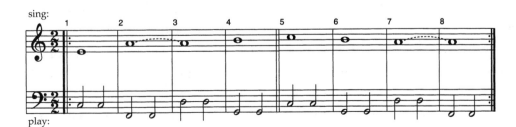

*Example 28.3*

The eight notes needed to sing and play the example above are positioned on the lattice as in example 28.4.

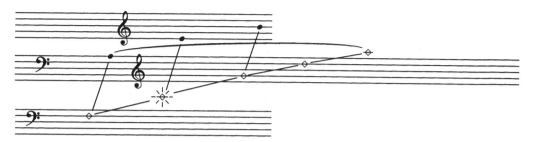

*Example 28.4*

We will discuss all of the tones bar by bar.

*Bar 1.* The E is the pure major third above C.

*Bar 2.* The A is the pure major third above F.

*Bar 3.* Something strange happens when you strike the bass D. That A you were singing in such sweet agreement with the bass F is not the same A needed for harmonic agreement with the bass D, that is, its pure perfect fifth. You must sharpen your pitch by twenty-two cents (sixteen cents if you are playing the bass on an equal-tempered instrument) to stay in tune. This change of tuning is the heart of the matter. If you are listening receptively to the bass, it is natural to respond to the most active harmonic resonances of each tone. The A of bar 2 is the fifth partial of the bass F, and it almost sings itself; its sharper stepsibling in bar 3 is the third partial of the bass D and arises almost of its own accord. For centuries singers have been adjusting their pitches in such passages without giving the theoretical aspects a thought. For the singer, the most resonant tunings simply *happen*, because acoustically they are already happening as the bass notes sound.

Notice exactly what happens to you at the downbeat of bar 3, at the very moment the natural resonance of the bass D encourages the pitch to rise. Examine your internal energy as you sing your way across the space of the comma. Take all the time you need, and do it many times. The focus is on a very small moment that has a very large meaning.

Now, continuing the passage:

*Bar 4.* The B is the major third above G.

*Bar 5.* The upper C is the octave of the bass.

*Bar 6.* As in bar 4, B is the pure major third above G.

*Bar 7.* As in bar 3, the A is a pure perfect fifth above the bass D. Your voice will find the Pythagorean A, the upper stepsibling that stands 3:2 to D and 27:16 to the tonic.

*Bar 8.* If you are being sensitive to the harmony implicit in the bass string, at the downbeat of bar 8 you will feel the harmonic energy of your note change and its pitch will descend. The note that was the perfect fifth of D becomes the major third of F. The 27:16 *dha* gently lowers itself to the 5:3 *dha*. Again, let me advise you to take your time in practicing this. The way you feel when you navigate this comma is the dot in the center of our circle of interest. Is it pleasant? Unsettling? Can you sense how what happens between bars 7 and 8 is the reverse of what happens between bars 2 and 3?

There is obviously another solution to the tuning of this passage, namely, that all the A's be sung 27:16 with C. In that case the thirds above F are Pythagorean, 81:64. In fact, E and B could be Pythagorean also. This would wipe out the comma, but it would also negate the purpose of the exercise. The idea is to sensitize yourself to the most available resonances of just intonation in order to discover the anomalies that occur when triple nature and pentamerous nature mix. These are the necessities that mothered temperament in the first place, and under which twelve-tone equal-tempered tonal harmony arose.

The short definition of tonal harmony is being someplace on the lattice of fifths and thirds in respect to a central tone. The above example generates at all times an unambiguous harmonic context, a discrete position in the tonal fabric, so that the Didymic comma arises naturally as a consequence of harmonic resonance. Sing the entire passage many times, tracking where you are on the lattice and appreciating the reversal of harmonic polarity as it occurs. Insist on vocal accuracy and maximum harmonic resonance. These resonances open music like the sun opens growing things.

## MELODIC VERSUS HARMONIC CHARACTERISTICS

From the point of view of mere pitch, moving through the comma is simply a slight rise or fall, less than a quarter of a semitone. From the singer's point of view, the vocal chords tighten or loosen by a tiny increment. But harmonically, moving through the Didymic comma is a complex event. If there is any sensibility at all in the metaphor of harmony as a physical place (as in the lattice), then we will perceive ourselves, when singing through the comma, as being shifted from one spot to another, perhaps rapidly, perhaps gently, perhaps even instantaneously, but physically nonetheless. In this case we are shifted by a distance of four fifths and a major third—the Didymic shift, so to speak. Some musicians describe this feeling as if they were passive and the comma did the work: "we are shifted" or "flown" or "conveyed"; "it is a chariot"; "we are in a new landscape"; "a new slide comes onto the screen"; "the light and shadow is different"; or "it is a different time of day." Others describe it more actively: "we leap" or "break through." The singer in this case not only leaps across the harmonic terrain but also "contains it" or "takes it in" or "ropes it in" or "lassos it" or "captures it" or "entraps it." There is generally a sense of bringing forward, or making real, the harmonic space that the comma surrounds. In the process of melodically navigating the comma, we evoke, or induce, or activate, the harmonic territory between two fixed positions.

Remember that it is not just the large harmonic leap that comes into play here, but the combination of large harmonic leap and small melodic interval. The singer takes a leap in one dimension by means of a very small step in another. Our fascination with the large result from the small action is related to the early philosophers' keen interest in commas as minute distances that somehow arbitrate large, disparate things.

We do not have to resort to commas to discover musical uses of the contrast between a small melodic interval and a harmonic leap. Consider for instance the commonly used

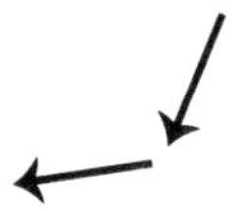

*Figure 28.1*

"leading tone" relationship: B to C in the key of C. The melodic interval is a half step, the harmonic ratio (C to B) is 16:15, and the harmonic compass is a fifth and a third, shown by the path in figure 28.1.

Next consider a more extreme case, a major/minor chromatic pair (see chapter 15). In the case of E♮ and E♭, for instance, the melodic distance is again a half step, but a smaller one (the ratio is 25:24), and the harmonic territory between the tones is greater—a fifth and two thirds, shown by the path in figure 28.2.

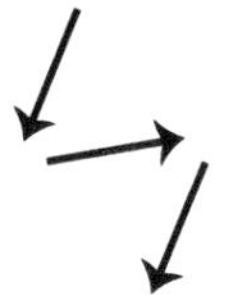

*Figure 28.2*

Now compare those cases with the Didymic comma we have been singing: The melodic interval is much smaller at 81:80, and there is no functional difference of scale degree, since both stepsiblings serve as the major sixth. But the harmonic territory between the two tones is now much larger—four fifths and a third, shown by the path in figure 28.3.

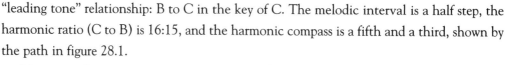

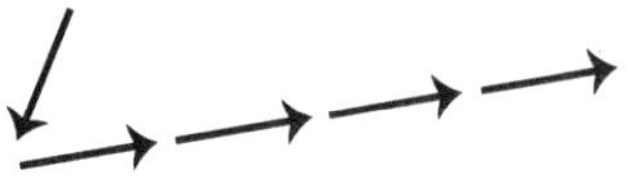

*Figure 28.3*

So the Didymic comma is a sort of rarefied leading tone, doing maximum harmonic work with minimum melodic motion. Let this seeming paradox never lose its allure. It is the hidden power of tonal harmony and, as we shall see, one of the drivers of equal temperament.

## HARMONIC REVERSAL

The essential experience in singing through the comma is the sudden sense of reversal in harmonic polarity. In the example above, as the resonance of bar 2 changes to the resonance of bar 3, you move in a blink from reciprocal, subdominant, yin, moon energy to overtonal, dominant, yang, sun energy. The immediacy of the reversal functions like a musical change of intention, a discontinuity of mood, a jump splice in the feeling. But we don't avoid it; indeed, we've learned to love it, to seek and savor it. If a jazz singer were singing the passage, an expressive ornament would typically appear between the two A's: a scoop or a bend or a change in the speed or depth of the vibrato, or some other motion to express the emotional change in the harmony. Same with a country singer, or one in any ornamented style: The commas drive the ornamentation. It is as if the singer has to wriggle the tone because she is wriggling inside.

In light of the emotional charge at the moment of the comma, it is illuminating to compare the movement between bars 2 and 3 with the movement between bars 7 and 8. As you sing the full passage through, compare your own singing impulses and how they affect the quality of your voice at those two points. Although we can map the harmonic territory, there is no real map through your responses except the one you draw for yourself. Once you are in tune with your own responses, the fascination with what others do deepens.

Remember that the core math is truly simple: 81:80 represents pure triple nature close to but not quite touching pure quintuple nature. If your universe actually were *ruled* by the numbers governing these resonances, wouldn't it change rather fundamentally if its pure triple self were suddenly infused with Pentamerous Alien Ones? Or, conversely, what if you and your kin were *ga*-blooded from the beginning of time, and suddenly your world became infused with Dry Seed Cavity Beings and their bloodlessly pure *pa* nature? The truth is, when you are in tune, your universe *is* ruled by numbers, or their musical equivalent, resonance.

## THE DIDYMIC COMMA IN DRONALITY

The musical example we have been singing constructs its harmonic context essentially from triads in root position. The ear is given a total of eight pitches, most of them connected by continuous harmonic bonds, to get its bearings. What about a strictly dronal case where the context is established only by a tonic and a Didymic pair of tones? When we sing through the comma, does the intervening harmonic territory still become activated? Does the polarity flip? Does the chariot appear?

It is true that the effect of the comma in just intonation, subtle in triadic harmony, is even more veiled in dronality, yet in my experience, the answer to all the questions above is an unequivocal yes. Time and again my *raga* teacher Pandit Pran Nath lassoed harmonic territory by singing perfectly through a comma, vanquishing my heart yet once more. True, his school of singing (Karana style) specializes in this type of interplay between melody, harmony, and expressive ornamentation, but I believe that if you are motivated to hear these things, given your own voice, a couple of drone strings, and some practice time, you can discover them for yourself. The more times you return to such practice, the clearer the process becomes. You may find it extremely helpful to record yourself and listen back—a little modern technology to learn the old ways. It is odd, isn't it, that this ancient way of hearing seems to us planet-hopping Westerners the cutting edge of harmonic research?

## PLAYING THE COMMA IN EQUAL TEMPERAMENT

When the experience of singing through the Didymic comma of the sixth degree in just intonation becomes even a little bit familiar, it is time to return to the keyboard. Is the effect of the comma sensible in equal temperament? If so, is the effect altered in some way?

Our musical example will now be fleshed out, with more notes helping to clarify the harmonic context. Play example 28.5 at the equal-tempered keyboard.

*Example 28.5*

Notice that the bass is arranged to give the clearest representation of the Pythagorean spine. The full lattice is shown in example 28.6. The two stepsiblings of the sixth degree now have the same pitch, of course, and their harmonic context ranges from the subdominant to the dominant of the dominant. It is entirely clear that there is a harmonic leap, or

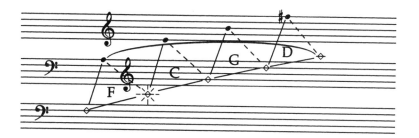

Example 28.6

discontinuity, between the F triad and the D triad, and that even though the pitch of the A remains the same, what it *stands for* on the lattice—its just-intonation reference—is different for the two triads. The ear fully accepts the function of both triads and therefore fully accepts the harmonic leap. The affect of the harmonic leap in equal temperament may differ from its affect in just intonation because, melodically speaking, in equal temperament the chariot is impeccably at rest; that is, the intervalic distance of the comma has been reduced to zero. We are thus entirely stationary as the world shifts around us.

Whatever forces are at work here, it is important to remember that we are dealing not only with the acoustical properties of vibrating things but with our own perceptual processes as well. The general question involves how the brain mirrors and models reality. But more specifically, questions arise involving, on the one hand, how the brain comprehends the inherent structure of the just lattice and, on the other hand, the ear's threshold for deviation under various circumstances. How are we allowed instantaneous travel with no change in pitch? By what throw of the dice is the equal-tempered major sixth acceptably flat (by six cents) of 27:16 and acceptably—though barely—sharp (by sixteen cents) of 5:3? By what serendipity could $9(\sqrt[12]{2}):1$ (the ratio of the equal-tempered major sixth) fulfill this function? What kind of luck is this, to have a switch of polarity, a guaranteed androgyny, hard-wired into our tuning system? Is this the luck of the West?

The crucial experience that vitalizes and illuminates these questions is the frequent comparison of singing through the comma in just intonation and playing through it in equal temperament. Don't be too hungry to come to any conclusions, or even to form strong opinions about what you are hearing; just listen and remember.

# The Didymic Comma of the Second Degree

## SINGING THROUGH THE COMMA IN JUST INTONATION

Wherever you stand on the just lattice, if you count four fifths up and a third down, or if you count four fifths down and a third up, you will find your Didymic stepsibling. All of these various possible sibling pairs relate to each other the same way; what is different about them is their position in respect to the tonic (which is C for now). As you no doubt have noticed from studying harmonic maps, the most frequently occurring Didymic pairs have one tone on the central spine of fifths and its same-lettered stepsibling on either the *ga*-above or the *ga*-below spine of fifths. Such will be the case for the fifteen pairs we will eventually study. The following examples, then, will begin to show how the various Didymic pairs relate to the tonic. Note that where C is located in relation to the arc drawn between the siblings is a fair visual image of the tonal effect of the comma.

Observe in example 28.7 how the stepsiblings of D, the major second degree, are more centered around the tonic C than those in example 28.6, the stepsiblings of A, the major sixth degree.

*Example 28.7*

Many useful harmonic pathways arise from the implicit balance of this arrangement. Track the following paths with your eyes, remembering that what the eye can track on the central lattice, the ear can hear.

If you start on the lower D (on the left), the path to the higher D can be either up four fifths to F♯, then down a third (figure 28.4), or inversely, down a third to B♭ and up four fifths (figure 28.5).

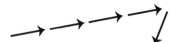

*Figure 28.4*

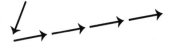

*Figure 28.5*

Computing from C, however, the harmonic balance comes into focus. In this case, the lower D is either: a third up and two fifths down (figure 28.6) or two fifths down and a third up (figure 28.7), while the upper D is two fifths up (figure 28.8).

*Figure 28.6*

*Figure 28.7*

*Figure 28.8*

So, from C, the entire harmonic compass of that Didymic pair of tones looks like figure 28.9.

Example 28.8 is a singing practice that brings forward the quality of the Didymic comma between the two D's in just intonation. It's best to use guitar or harp for the bass.

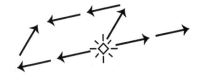

*Figure 28.9*

In bar 3, take care to sing the D as the fifth partial of B♭; then in bar 4 the D will rise through the Didymic comma to become the third partial of G. As in the previous example, you move from reciprocal, subdominant, yin, moon energy to overtonal, dominant, yang,

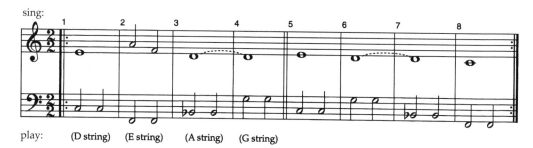

*Example 28.8*

sun energy, although in this instance the exquisite balance of forces is especially remarkable.

Conversely, at bar 6 sing the D as the third partial of G, taking care to lower it fully through the comma so it becomes the fifth partial of B♭. The reversal of harmonic polarity will now flow in the other direction: pure dominant to *ga*-blooded subdominant.

Practice singing and playing this passage as you would any challenging passage of music: Respect it and take command over it at the same time. Remember that the focus of the inquiry is the logic and feeling of your own response, so sing in tune and stay inside.

## PLAYING THE COMMA IN EQUAL TEMPERAMENT

Fleshing out the example above at the equal-tempered keyboard yields example 28.9. Again, the bass is arranged so that line of fifths is clear to the ear.

While playing the exercise, observe the effect of the temperament as the D is tied and

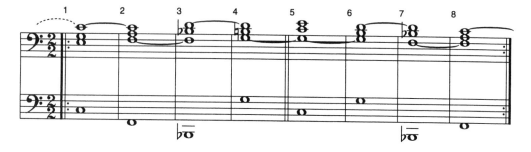

*Example 28.9*

the harmony leaps. Can you feel the harmony balance around C? What happens to you at the moment the harmony leaps and the D changes its meaning? To further investigate your response, try improvising melodically in your right hand while you play the chords in your left, reacting to the harmony and playing the music it tells you to play. Compare your experience in equal temperament with your experience in just intonation. Resist finding words for these ephemera—there aren't any anyway, as I am so elegantly proving. Better to simply immerse yourself in the music and identify with what you feel.

# The Didymic Comma of the Seventh Degree

## SINGING THROUGH THE COMMA IN JUST INTONATION

Example 28.10 is the harmonic map of the Didymic pair of B♭'s.

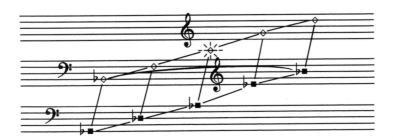

*Example 28.10*

If you start on the higher B♭ (on the right), the path to the lower B♭ can be either down four fifths to G♭ and up a third (figure 28.10) or, inversely, up a third to D and down four fifths (figure 28.11).

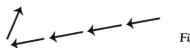

*Figure 28.10*

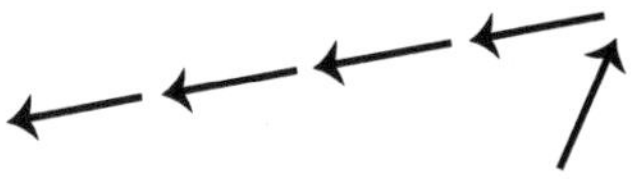

Computing from C, however, the harmonic compass between the pair of B♭'s becomes clear. The higher B♭ is now either a third down and two fifths up (figure 28.12) or two fifths up and a third down (figure 28.13), while the lower B♭ is two fifths down (figure 28.14).

*Figure 28.11*

*Figure 28.12*

*Figure 28.13*

*Figure 28.14*

So, from C, the harmonic compass of the two B♭'s looks like figure 28.15. There is a beautiful symmetry between the Didymic pair of D's and the Didymic pair of B♭'s as they center around C.

Describe to yourself the symmetry between figures 28.15 and 28.9 (reproduced here for direct comparison).

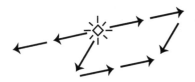

*Figure 28.15*

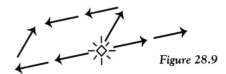

*Figure 28.9*

Example 28.11 is a singing practice to evoke the Didymic pair of the seventh degree, using the tones of the central spine of fifths. It is not convenient to use a guitar for this practice, so if no other just system is available, the piano will do.

*Example 28.11*

Play the bottom two parts on the piano and sing the top. In passing from bar 3 to bar 4, if you are very sensitive to your tuning of the B♭ in bar 3, you will notice that the note you are singing is sharp to the piano bass in bar 4. You are experiencing the fact that 9:5, the major third below the dominant of the dominant, is not the same as the subdominant of the subdominant 16:9. The dominant harmony suddenly becomes subdominant harmony. The entire process is reversed between bars 9 and 10: You'll have to raise the pitch to make an in-tune G-minor triad; at that moment, the subdominant harmony becomes dominant harmony.

## PLAYING THE COMMA IN EQUAL TEMPERAMENT

Instead of singing the top part of the above example, play all the parts at once and listen to the harmonic leaps and the effect of the comma across the tied B♭'s. Try playing bar 3 loud and bar 4 quite soft; also try playing bar 9 loud and bar 10 soft. Be sure to tie the B♭'s. The change in dynamics emphasizes the harmonic discontinuity and brings forward the effect of the comma in equal temperament.

## MORE ABOUT THE SYMMETRY BETWEEN D AND B♭

Overtonal harmony is easier to hear and understand than reciprocal harmony, and I have found that, when listening to actual music, I can recognize the effects of overtonal pairs more readily than reciprocal pairs. The Didymic pair of D's is overtonal; the Didymic pair of B♭'s is reciprocal. The perfect symmetry that exists between them is lovely to experience and contemplate in its own right, but beyond that, the D's can teach you what to listen for in the B♭'s. We have already looked at the symmetry of their harmonic maps and harmonic paths. Table 28.1 makes some more comparisons.

**TABLE 28.1**

|  | THE PAIR OF D'S | THE PAIR OF B♭'S |
|---|---|---|
| Easy | **The *higher* tone is:**<br>9:8 (Pythagorean)<br>Two fifths up<br>Dominant energy | **The *lower* tone is:**<br>16:9 (Pythagorean)<br>Two fifths down<br>Subdominant energy |
| Not so easy | **The *lower* tone is:**<br>10:9 (*ga*-blooded)<br>1 *ga* up, 2 *pa*'s down<br>On the *ga*-above spine<br>Relative-minor energy | **The *higher* tone is:**<br>9:5 (*ga*-blooded)<br>2 *pa*'s up, 1 *ga* down<br>On the *ga*-below spine<br>Parallel-minor energy |
|  | 2 *pa*'s down, 1 *ga* up<br>Subdominant-major energy | 1 *ga* down, 2 *pa*'s up<br>Dominant-minor energy |

The salient point is that the Pythagorean tones mirror each other in the cadential and structural world of perfect fifths, and the *ga*-blooded tones mirror each other in the expressive, pentamerous world. In the next chapter, as triadic harmony comes into play, we see how these symmetries and reciprocities are the very design of tonal harmony.

# 29

# DIDYMIC PAIRS OF TRIADS

HAVING EXAMINED THE BEHAVIOR of Didymic pairs of tones in equal temperament, we are ready to examine Didymic pairs of triads. The change of meaning made possible through a single tone is considerably more pronounced by means of an entire triad because a triad covers more territory and provides more of a harmonic context. Remembering that meaning depends on context, consider a tone as if it were an atom. A triad would then be a molecule, and a molecule provides a richer context than an atom. Harmonic meaning tends to come into focus as triads progress because so much meaning is already inherent in them.

Now we are free finally to examine the harmonic meaning of triads in equal-tempered tonality.

## The Usual Preliminary Advice

The material in this chapter presents a kind of overview of the function of the Didymic comma in equal temperament and culminates in a sort of aerial map, a table of Didymic triads. It is a map that has never been drawn before (as far as I know), and for its mapmaker there is a tremendous excitement in seeing it for the first time. But it is also true that there is more information here than an intermediate or even advanced musician might care to ingest at one sitting. Nor do I need to point out that seven centuries of ravishing tonal music has been composed in a variety of temperaments involving Didymic phenomena without the benefit of this map. Wonderful as it may be to have a new analytical guide, be sure not to let the conceptual models presented here be an albatross to your real-time music making. This is a book about music, but it is not music. Especially, it is not *your* music, and you need to balance this book and your music according to your best impulses. If that means taking a glance and pushing on, glance well. If that means poring over musical phrases and prose paragraphs, hang on and let's go.

# Staff Orientation and Compass Orientation

The terms *staff orientation* and *compass orientation* were introduced in chapter 6 (p. 36). Until now, all of our chord lattices have been constructed in staff orientation; that is, the triad names appear in the same configuration as they do on a lattice of tones. The only difference between a chord lattice and a tone lattice is that in a chord lattice the lines of the staff, as well as the noteheads themselves, have disappeared. Since we will now rely more and more heavily on chord lattices (as well as their extensions, *key lattices*), it will become increasingly useful to "unskew" our axes, that is, to return them to the strictly perpendicular orientation of a typical *x/y* graph. This enables us to visualize triads whose roots ascend by fifths as moving due east, and roots descending by fifths as moving due west, as shown in figure 29.1. Triads whose roots ascend by major thirds will now move due north; roots descending by major thirds move due south, as shown in figure 29.2.

$$\text{G}\sharp$$
$$|$$
$$\text{E}$$
$$|$$
$$\text{-C-}$$
$$|$$
$$\text{A}\flat$$
$$|$$
$$\text{F}\flat$$

**Figure 29.2**

$$\text{E}\flat - \text{B}\flat - \text{F} - \text{-C-} - \text{G} - \text{D} - \text{A}$$   *Figure 29.1*

In compass orientation, parallel major/minor relationships are no longer north-south, but northwest-southeast, as shown in figure 29.3. (This is the tricky one.) Relative major/minor relationships are still basically northwest-southeast, as shown in figure 29.4.

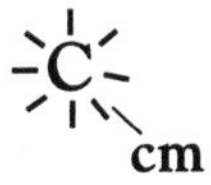

-C-
cm   *Figure 29.3*

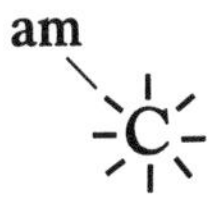

am
-C-   *Figure 29.4*

For purposes of comparison, figure 29.5 shows the twelve triads of the central lattice in both staff orientation and compass orientation.

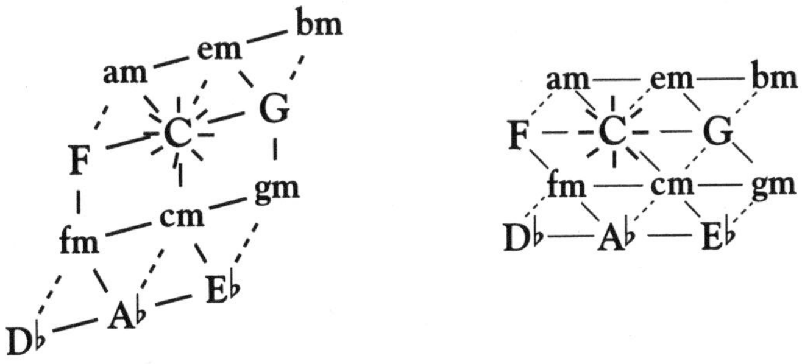

**Staff orientation**          **Compass orientation**          *Figure 29.5*

The obvious advantage of staff orientation is that the positions of the triads relate directly to the positions of the tones on the staff, thereby linking the ear's capacity to compound pure fifths and pure thirds with our ability to read music. The advantage of compass orientation is that it refers the elemental harmonies (perfect fifths, major thirds) directly to the cardinal directions (east-west, north-south). This in turn allows us to "box the compass," a most useful construct in classifying and comparing all of the harmonic motions available in equal temperament. We lose the musical staff, but we gain a powerful conceptual aid. This will become more clear as we progress, but if you are curious to see the results of such analysis, glance ahead to chapter 41, especially to its cumulative schematic, figure 41.37, on page 472. Further discussion can be found in chapter 43.

Which orientation should be used when? Basically, staff orientation is a microscope: Through it you can see the music at the level of its atoms (notes) and atomic bonds (fifths and thirds). Chord lattices, however, give the perspective of standing back from the music; key lattices even take you on a helicopter ride above it. Each perspective has its appropriate analytical use, as we shall see.

## The Didymic Comma of the ii Triad

Let's resume our discussion of the Didymic comma in equal temperament by reviewing some of the material in part 2, deepening and expanding as we go. In the key of C Major, consider the arrangement of the triads shown (in compass orientation) in figure 29.6. This can be seen as a map of the harmonic territory bracketed by the two D-minor triads. A continuous, step-by-step visit through this territory can be accomplished with the progression in example 29.1, which is essentially the one given in example 23.22, but this time there is no drone.

*Figure 29.6*

$$dm \text{—} am$$
$$F \text{—} C \text{—} G$$
$$dm$$

*Example 29.1*

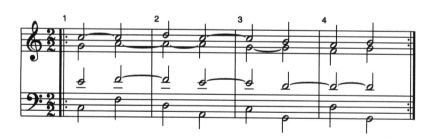

The first ii chord (bar 2) has a subdominant context; the second one (bar 4) has a dominant context. In just intonation, all of the tones in the second D-minor triad would be a Didymic comma higher than those in the first one. Play the progression rapidly at the equal-tempered keyboard until the two meanings of the D-minor chord clarify.

Next, play the common progression shown in example 29.2. It employs the ii chord in a pivotal position. (This is given in popular music form in example 23.23.)

It's useful to know that this passage is unsingable in just intonation without pitch adjustments. Specifically, the soprano will have to sing the lower D in bar 2 to agree with the alto A, but will then have to raise the pitch at bar 3 to agree with the G's (which of course must agree with the C's in bar 4). Meanwhile, what is the bass to do? If he sings the low D, the

*Example 29.2*

interval between it and the oncoming G will be a too-small fifth, which would be OK, but he must also agree with the soprano—did she move up early to avoid the change of pitch at the downbeat? If so, did she take the poor alto with her? Who changes when? These are the kinds of questions that sensitive singers must answer intuitively in the act of singing in order to stay in tune.

But the two meanings of the D-minor triad are collapsed in equal temperament. The listener simply deals with both functions simultaneously, or at least within the same small moment of hearing. At some point we remember where we've been while recognizing where we are going. Example 29.3 is a slightly clearer case.

*Example 29.3*

This example tonicizes F by means of the C⁷ in bar 1 and tonicizes G by means of the D⁷ in bar 3. Its lattice of chords is shown in figure 29.7. (All of the chord and key lattices will now be in compass orientation.)

*Figure 29.7*

Consider what the ear hears at the downbeat of bar 3. The D of the first inversion is not *necessarily* the V of V. The progression could easily have gone as shown in example 29.4.

*Example 29.4*

In such a case its lattice of chords (and harmonic path) would have been as shown in figure 29.8, which is to say, an entirely unambiguous progression with only one D-minor triad and no comma.

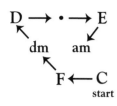

*Figure 29.8*

The point is, the ear is not automatically jerked to dominant territory at the downbeat of bar 3 in the original example; it figures out, after a chord or two, where it must be. This assumes, of course, that the ear recognizes the C chord at the end as the same C chord at the beginning. "Of course it does," we say, but let's investigate the alternative.

Let's pretend that the ear hears the first version of the above example as progressing as shown in figure 29.9. In this scenario, we end up a Didymic comma, that is, twenty-two cents, flat from where we began, and each time we repeat the passage, we'll be that much flatter. After four repetitions we'll be almost a semitone flat; after nine repetitions we'd be a whole tone flat. That can't be right. What *is* happening?

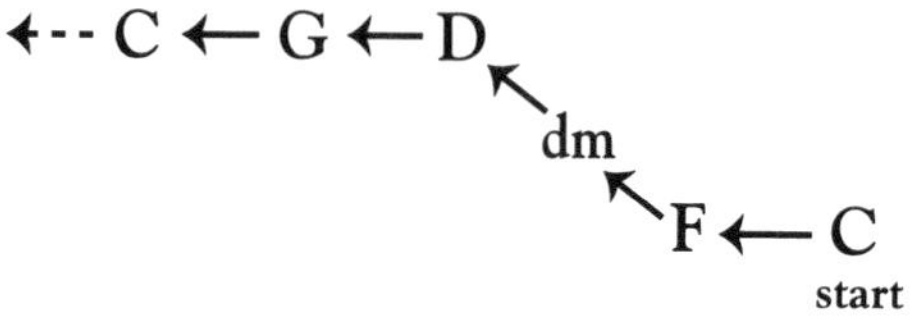

*Figure 29.9*

We have in fact been operating under the basic premise of tonality: that the ear loves the posited tone, the tonic, and holds that tone in the center of its harmonic world. If the center does not hold, the meaning and the delight go out of its universe. Now, gradually, we are coming to realize that if maintaining the center means adjusting reality, then the ear finds its own way of adjusting reality.

## Pathfinder versus Homebody

The desire for the center may be the basic operative principle of tonality, but it is not the only one. There is a logic to harmony, a great beauty in the continuity of its motion, and a concomitant drama in its leaping discontinuities. These are the mechanisms that allow for meaningful journeys through harmonic territory. I like to think of the ear's ability to track harmonic motion along the paths of the lattice as the Pathfinder capacity in us. It is our capacity for logic, for map making and map following, our love of sweet reason and tidiness of plot, our abiding adherence to the sanity of linear order. It has a yang feeling, this part of us, a masculine, no-nonsense, this-is-the-way-things-are clarity.

The love of the center is our other side. It is our capacity for integration, for holistic thought; it our sense that the world holds together not through reason but through mutual attraction, and that, ultimately, everything fits. This homebody part of us feels yin; it has the feminine quality of encompassing unity and the certainty of the hearth.

These two sides of our nature are not mutually exclusive; they may even be versions of one another. But when we listen to tonal music in equal temperament, we can feel their separateness. Play through example 29.3 a few more times. Then follow along with this scenario.

As we begin bar 1, Homebody is stirring the hearth coals while Pathfinder, eager and alert, is sitting on the edge of the easy chair. At the sound of the B♭ in bar 1, Pathfinder's ears go forward and his nostrils flare; by the end of the bar he has sprung forward and is halfway out the west door; Homebody takes down the kettle. By bar 2, Pathfinder is in Full

Track Mode, and at the end of bar 2 communicates telepathically with Homebody, who is pouring rainwater into the kettle, "Position check: relative minor of the subdominant and tracking." Homebody, smiling inside, hangs the kettle from the hearth arm and swings it out over the fire. A moment later, at the D chord at the downbeat of bar 3, a crackling message comes over the telepath: "Potentially confused. Could be in for a long journey—do you read me?"

Homebody puts the tea ball into the teapot and sends the message, "Would you like some lemon?"

At the second beat of bar 3 (the C), there is a quivering kind of flash in the hearth room, and Homebody's chest, already warm, suddenly feels bigger than the house. Meanwhile, Pathfinder is being overcome by a pervasive electric tingling and a momentary loss of gravity. Over the telepath, amid much crackling static, there are two simultaneous voices. "Uncertain conditions . . . lightheaded . . . cannot account for direction," cries Pathfinder, while, as in a duet, Homebody's voice sings out, "Your tea . . . is . . . steeping . . . " Scarcely a moment later, at the G in the bass of bar 4, Homebody receives a clear message: "Blue skies, gliding in from the east." Now Homebody pours the tea. At the B of bar 4, Pathfinder's message is heard as a strong presence just outside the east door: "Lemon, please." At bar 5, Homebody hands Pathfinder a steaming cup of fresh tea, pungent with lemon, in a porcelain cup with rosebuds. "Your tea is the best tea," says Pathfinder.


It might be interesting to play this passage several times, first imagining the scenario from Pathfinder's point of view, then from Homebody's, and finally from the single point of view of you the listener. You will probably find that the critical moment in each case is the C of bar 3. That is the moment when Pathfinder has the electric experience culminating in the recognition that the only return to Homebody is through the east door. At that very moment, Homebody's central feeling extraordinarily expands. Each character gets zapped, by which I mean that each has an experience that transcends normal capacity. The solution to "the problem of ii" arises from a transcendental interaction: Something happens to the two characters that could not have happened normally to either alone.

From the single perspective of the listener, both zaps are one zap, the zap of the Didymic comma. In the tiny proscenium of the ear, and within a few seconds, the hunger for reason and the love of unity have interrelated dramatically, resulting in a transformed capacity for both. The journey through darkness and void to light and grace has thus transformed the traveler.

Equal temperament, the potential villain of our tuning history, is, heroically, the enabling mechanism here, but the genius of our own response should get half the credit. The crucial mechanism by which we respond to equal temperament is the built-in adaptability that allows us to accept approximation for the "real thing." Did Pathfinder *really* come home? We think so. Maybe the transcendental zappage of the comma in equal temperament is the brain's confrontation with its own processes. To the extent that this surmise is true, it confirms that, for the study of music, the method is the self.

## Each Comma Works in Both Directions

In the example we have been studying (29.3), Pathfinder leaves by the west door and arrives by the east door. Specifically, the ii chord, first apprehended as the vi of IV, is subsequently remembered as the v of V. Example 29.5 reverses that order. The lattice of chords for this passage is shown in figure 29.10.

*Example 29.5*

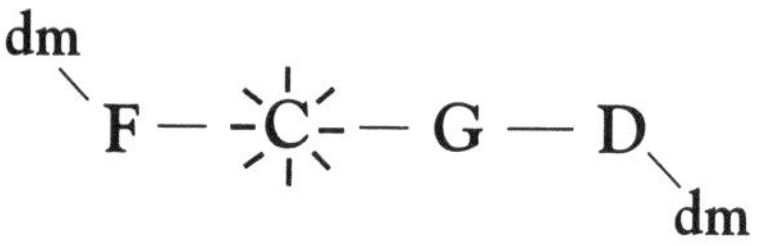

*Figure 29.10*

In this case, the D triad at bar 2 is clearly the V of V, and the minor-ing of the triad simply allows us to hear it as the v of V—the minor dominant of the dominant. A moment later, however, the subdominant appears with the tonic in the soprano, and the ii chord we have just heard is remembered as the vi of IV—the relative minor of the subdominant. We then coast into a perfect cadence, tethered by the original C. By heading straight out the east (dominant) door, we come to western territory (the subdominant of bar 3).

This example, as well as the dozens of others coming soon, resembles passages from European classical music in that they are all driven by perfect cadences, ending with IV (or ii)–V–I, or at least V–I, and hence all of them are biased toward the dominant in the final approach to the tonic. But these harmonic models do take care to assure that if a triad is intended to have a reciprocal identity before arriving at the inevitable penultimate dominant chord, it does so as convincingly as possible. In the present case, it does so by means of the F chord in bar 3—or, at least, such is the unequivocal tonal memory once the tonic is reached.

The pivotal nature of the ii chord is especially clear in this example. To clarify this graphically, figure 29.11 shows the lattice of triads with the names of only the tonic triad and the Didymic pair of ii chords visible.

It is extremely useful to alternate between the two ii-chord examples we have just examined (examples 29.3 and 29.5). Their juxtaposition brings the reversal of the zap, that is, the polarity of the comma, forward. Example 29.6 brings them together in a repeated phrase; play it many times, until you are no longer thinking chords or functions or fingers, but simply bobbing along in the harmonic energy, whatever it is.

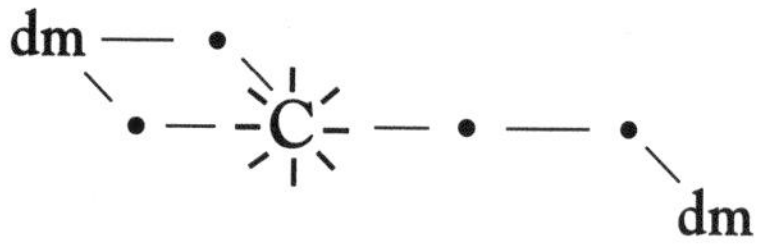

*Figure 29.11*

Realize that the two D-minor triads we have been discussing represent a unique har-

*Example 29.6*

monic discontinuity within the tonal gravitational field of C. There are at least fourteen other pairs of Didymic triads within C's sphere, and we will soon look at the organization of the entire group. But let's first examine in detail a few more specific cases, eliciting in each case the reversal of polarity that so clarifies the effect of the Didymic comma.

## The Didymic Comma of the ♭VII Triad

Consider the triads shown in figure 29.12, which gives one possible representation of the harmonic territory bracketed by the pair of ♭VII triads.

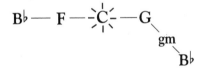

*Figure 29.12*

Now play example 29.7.

*Example 29.7*

At bar 2 we are at the subdominant, and then the subdominant of the subdominant, deep in the heart of western reciprocity. (The faster the tempo, the clearer becomes the rhythmic effect resulting from the ties between bars 2 and 3.) The G-minor triad at the second pulse of bar 3 does not by itself indicate a flip to the dominant; but the change to G major in bar 4 is unlikely to be heard any other way (although it *could* progress to A[7] to Dmi to Ami to F to C.) At the downbeat of the last bar, one definitely gets one's hot tea with lemon.

Where did Pathfinder's sense of direction get zapped? Somewhere between the end of bar 3 and the downbeat of bar 5. Perhaps the zap was gradual, that is, distributed over several beats; this conjecture will come up frequently as we proceed. In any case, the B♭ triad that at first seemed like the IV of IV turned out to function as the III of v, and west became southeast.

To better realize the comma, imagine you are singing the tenor part. In bar 2 you will want to sing a pure third above the Pythagorean B♭; but in bar 3, as you sense both the bass and the alto reaching for the Pythagorean G (the dominant), you realize your pitch will be too low for the perfect intervals to sound between the parts. Thus either you will drag them down by a comma, along with the soprano in bar 4 and everybody in bar 5, which would not be nice, or else they will force you up through the interval of a comma, which would be slightly odd, perhaps, but nicer. In equal temperament, of course, these adjustments are internal to the listener.

Since each comma works in both directions, let's look at the polarity reversed, as shown in example 29.8.

*Example 29.8*

The second beat of bar 2 (G minor) is heard as the minor dominant; the downbeat of bar 3 (B♭ major) as its relative major. So the B♭ chord is first perceived as the III of v. But it follows a strict Pythagorean path back to C, so that by the time you get to bar 4, the B♭ is remembered as the IV of IV. We leave by the east door (dominant) and return from the west, even though the passage is finalized by a IV–V–I perfect cadence. (Despite the ellipsis of the cadence (IV–V), the continuity in the Pythagorean spine is assured by the C tied over from bar 3 to bar 4.)

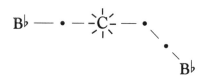

*Figure 29.13*

To clarify graphically the pivotal nature of the B♭ triad in both examples, figure 29.13 names only the Didymic pair of triads and the tonic, C. Now repeatedly play the two examples side by side as shown in example 29.9 until you are not even hearing chords anymore, just feeling the harmonic wind.

*Example 29.9*

Be so sensitive to this wind that you can let it vaporize you and then blow you back together again time after time. Become that wind. Let this happen to you just the way it happens (or used to happen) when you hear (or heard) the music you most love (or loved—remember?). That is the only way to learn this crazy language.

## The Didymic Comma of the II Triad

The triads of figure 29.14 are a representation of the harmonic territory bracketed by the Didymic pair of D-major triads.

Now play example 29.10. The D-major triad in bar 2 is clearly Pythagorean—you are on the dominant of the dominant and have left home by the east door. But by bar 3, the key of A Minor has been toni-

Figure 29.14

cized by means of a full cadence (D to E to Ami), ending with the tone C (the original tonic) in the soprano—could we still be in dominant territory? By the second pulse of that bar we know we have been zapped: we are on the subdominant triad; it then proceeds to a perfect cadence in C.

Example 29.11, which reverses the polarity, is a bit more elaborate.

Example 29.11

The first pulse of bar 2 is the iv of A Minor, and we hear the two chords of that bar as the iv–V of a full cadence in A Minor. The downbeat of bar 3 is a trick, however. It is easily heard at first as the major subdominant of a IV–V–i cadence in A Minor, since that has been set up by the context, but that is not what happens. At the second pulse of bar 3, the soprano renders the D into D⁷, the expectation for a Pythagorean descent to the hearth is aroused, and sure enough, within moments, hot tea once more.

The two D triads bracket the tonic as shown in figure 29.15. This picture contrasts reciprocally with the picture of the two B♭ triads in figure 29.13.

Now play both examples continuously, as given in example 29.12. Don't forget about harmonic wind.

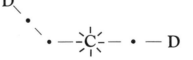

Figure 29.15

Example 29.12

## The Didymic Comma of the ♭vii Triad

This harmony, less commonly found, makes an unusually clear example. Consider the triads of figure 29.16.

*Figure 29.16*

Now play example 29.13. The B♭-minor triad in bar 2 is clearly Pythagorean, the iv of iv; in fact, the continuous line of reciprocal fifths reaches all the way to A♭. At bar 4, the iv–V–i cadence allows you to remember these chords (perhaps from the E♭ triad) as connected through the relative major, that is, E♭. Perhaps the comma is distributed from the B♭⁷ in bar 2 to the G of bar 4. What is convincing is the western territory of the B♭-minor triad, and the southeastern outcome.

*Example 29.13*

The reverse case, given in example 29.14, is quite beautiful.

*Example 29.14*

The second pulse of bar 2 is a passing E♭ triad (III of i), followed in bar 3 by its dominant and then its minor dominant: the v of III, unequivocally southeastern. The journey home is pure ascending fifths, however (B♭ to Fmi to Cmi), ending with a perfect cadence. The zap seems more focused on the B♭-minor triad here.

The two B♭-minor triads bracket the tonic as shown in figure 29.17. The overall comma phenom-

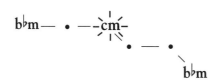

*Figure 29.17*

*Example 29.15*

ena of this Didymic pair seem particularly sensible. Practice as shown in example 29.15.

## The Fifteen Pairs of Didymic Triads

We have discussed four Didymic pairs of triads: D minor, D major, B♭ major, and B♭ minor. There are at least fifteen such pairs sensible from any given tonic (for now, as usual, we are staying in C). Each of the pairs we have studied is actually a representative from an entire family of such pairs; there are a total of four such families, each of which has its own harmonic flavor, or color.

Let's begin with the family that contains the D-major pair of triads. As we have already seen (in figure 29.15), the two D-major triads straddle C as shown again in Figure 29.18.

*Figure 29.18*

Actually, each of the D-major triads is only one in a row of four major triads linked by perfect fifths. Both rows are shown in figure 29.19.

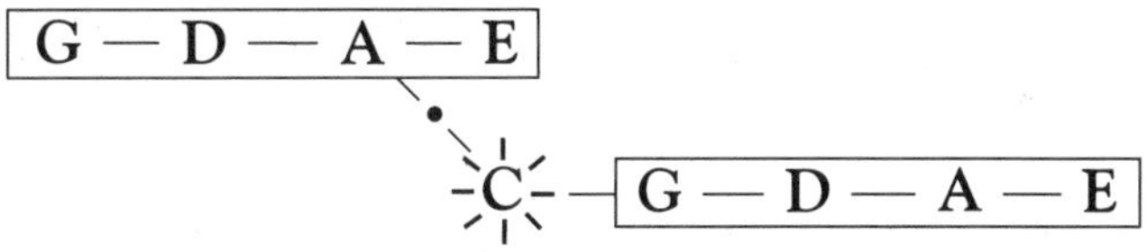

*Figure 29.19*

The four triads that appear in the upper row of this lattice can be called *ga*-major triads; that is, their roots are in the *ga* spine of fifths and their mode is major. The four triads in the lower row can be called *pa*-major triads; their roots are in the (central) *pa* spine and their mode is major. That makes a total of eight triads in this family: an upper row of four triads, each of which is paired with a sibling in a lower row of four triads. We'll arbitrarily call this family of eight the Red Family. Notice that the borders around these two rows are straight-edged.

Next, let's consider the D-minor pair. As we have already seen (in figure 29.11), the two D-minor triads straddle C as shown again in figure 29.20.

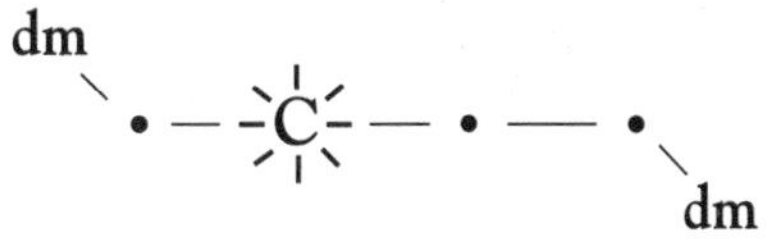

*Figure 29.20*

Actually, each of the D-minor triads belongs to a row of four minor triads linked by perfect fifths. Both rows are shown in figure 29.21.

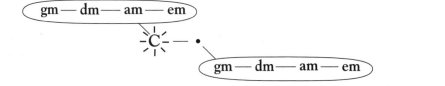

*Figure 29.21*

The four triads in the upper row can be called *ga*-minor because their roots are in the *ga* spine and their mode is minor. The four triads in the lower row can be called *pa*-minor; their roots are in the *pa* spine and their mode is minor. We'll call this family of eight the Orange

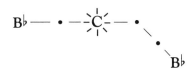

*Figure 29.22*

Family. Notice that the borders around these two rows are oval.

Now let's look at the pair of B♭-major triads. They straddle the tonic as in figure 29.22. Figure 29.23 shows the complete rows. The four triads in

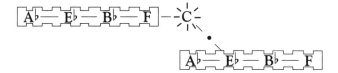

*Figure 29.23*

the upper row we will call *pa-below*-major because their roots are reciprocal fifths of the central spine and their mode is major. Let the four triads in the lower row be *ga-below*-major; their roots are in the *ga*-below spine and they are major. We'll call this family the Green Family. Notice that the Green Family's borders are saw-toothed.

Finally, let's look at the B♭-minor pair, which straddles the tonic as in figure 29.24. This pair's family portrait appears in figure 29.25.

*Figure 29.24*

*Figure 29.25*

There seem to be only three sensible pairs in this group, which we'll call the Blue Family. Notice the curvy borders. Let the upper row be called *pa-below*-minor, since their roots are on the *pa*-below spine, and the lower row be called *ga-below*-minor, since their roots are on the *ga*-below spine.

Now, at last, figure 29.26 shows all fifteen pairs of Didymic triads posed together in their respective families. It will help enormously to understand this subject—and ultimately to apply it as a practical musician—if you color in by hand the respective colors of the families. While you're at it, try yellow for the two tonic triads, C major and C minor. Then stare at it for a while.

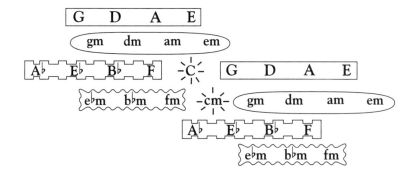

*Figure 29.26.
The whole family
portrait of the Didymic
pairs of triads in the
key of C*

What we have found is a discrete pattern of triads within the five-limit lattice. To turn the picture into music, read on.

# The Table of Didymic Triads

What follows is, first, a table of, and later a kind of map through, the territory of Didymic harmony. The table and the map show, as much as possible, exactly where in the harmonic fabric each of thirty triads that surround C turns into its Didymic sibling, and how this can be accomplished in four-part equal-tempered keyboard harmony. We'll discuss the table, shown in example 29.16, first.

We have already seen the fifteen pertinent pairs of triads that surround C. We have also practiced playing model progressions for four of these pairs. For each pair there is a harmonic progression that travels essentially from northwest to southeast, and another that reverses the polarity, traveling from southeast to northwest. Since each pair needs two harmonic models to demonstrate its nature, fifteen pairs require thirty models, which are duly presented here.

These models are not easy to compose (although I encourage you to try your hand at it) because Didymic comma phenomena in equal temperament are by nature ambiguous and slippery. Specifically, the zap effect of the comma is often spread out over several chords, blurring distinctions and clouding the ear's discrimination. Perhaps that is why this particular map is being drawn more than three hundred years after the settlement of the territory. The territory is conducive to exploration, but its shape is difficult to imagine. Moreover, we are mapping not only a particular thing but our response to that thing as well, so to that extent we are mapping ourselves.

Some of the differences from example to example seem tiny. In some, the comma is surprisingly difficult to sense; in others it leaps out. From one model to the next, chords may be inverted, rhythms displaced, hidden dimensions turned inside out. But each model presents the same basic phenomenon—a specific type of shift in harmonic position—from a different angle and hence in a different light. Ultimately, then, the table of Didymic triads is a multiple exposure of a single thing.

I use two diacritical marks. Didymic pairs of triads are separated not only by certain distances along the Pythagorean spines but also by a single pentamerous move up or down a *ga* spine. Usually that amounts to a change of a triad's mode from major to minor or vice versa. This change is indicated with an *m*. Also, in each progression I try to pinpoint the pivot chord, if there is one, with an arrow. If there is no actual pivot chord, the arrow points to the center of the zap, as near as my ear can hear.

## THE USES OF THE DIDYMIC TABLE

The organization of the models in the table is not the only possible one. Their arrangement, for instance, is not the same as the arrangement of the triads in the whole family portrait

*Example 29.16.*
*The table of*
*Didymic triads in C*

(figure 29.26), which the models are supposed to elucidate. That is because in the table I want the fifteen pairs of polarity reversals to be immediately accessible to the player.

Here are various practice suggestions.

1. Whatever you play, track your journey at least once in the whole family portrait. Know where you are on the lattice and the direction of the flow.

2. Learn each four-bar passage until it is comfortable to play and you have a musical sense of it. Then proceed either down the page or across the page. There is no wrong way of doing this, although some juxtapositions seem more enlightening than others. As mentioned above, it is especially important to be able to hear the polarities immediately reversed, but there are many possible procedures.

3. One of the best routines is to play eight-bar phrases repeatedly until they are clear to you; then move down the page. That is, start with the G-major pair and practice bars 1–8; the next set is the G-minor pair, then D major, then D minor, and so on. This preserves the polarity reversal for each triad, as well as giving a sense of the comma energy moving gradually east (or west), like an intricate weather pattern traveling slowly across the sky.

4. Another way to compare the models is to practice straight across the page, sixteen bars to the line, and then work your way down the page—as one would normally read music, in fact. This allows you to track the energy of the Didymic comma as its Pythagorean bond with the tonic becomes increasingly remote. That *is* subtle. Another way to track the same thing, but with mode reversals, is:

> G major, F minor, G minor, F major;
> D major, B♭ minor, D minor, B♭ major;
> A major, E♭ minor, A minor, E♭ major;
> E major, E minor, A♭ major.

## THE TABLE BECOMES A MAP

Perhaps the most conceptually clarifying practice is to place the four-bar models in precisely the same physical configuration as the whole family portrait—that is, as their source triads appear on the lattice. This is demonstrated in example 29.17. Such an arrangement looks like a highly elaborated form of the lattice itself.

The model in example 29.17 no longer displays the reversal of polarity between the Didymic pairs; instead, the five-limit lattice organization comes into line for both eye and ear. Starting at the upper left, you can play all of the *ga*-major Red Family (G, D, A, E) and hear them transform themselves into their southern siblings. Then, all of the *ga*-minor

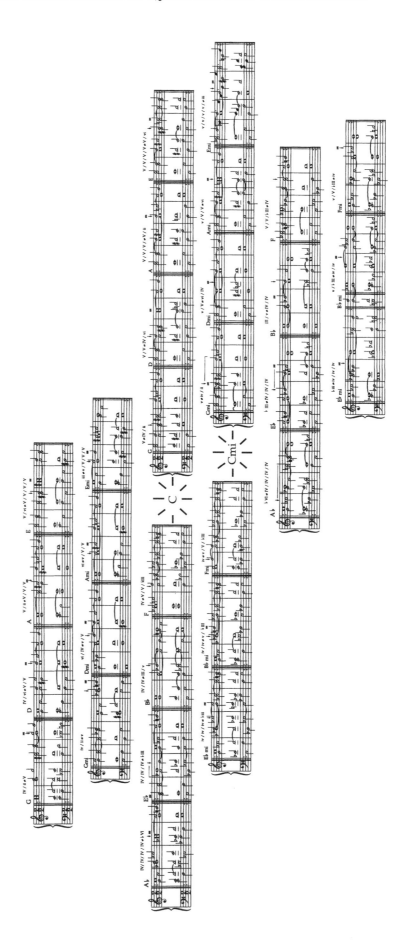

*Example 29.17.*
*The table of Didymic*
*triads in lattice*
*configuration*

Orange Family (Gmi, Dmi, Ami, Emi) transforming themselves into *their* southern siblings. Then likewise the *pa-below*-major Green Family (A♭, E♭, B♭, F). Then likewise the *pa-below*-minor Blue Family (E♭mi, B♭mi, Fmi).

Then you can play all of the *pa*-major Red Family as they transform into their northern siblings. And then, the *pa*-minor Orange Family, followed by the *Ga-below*-major Green Family, and finally the *Ga-below*-minor Blue Family. Or you could reverse the order of the last four rows.

## More about Practice

Should you memorize these models? I don't think so. Should you learn to improvise on them? Yes, definitely. Should you compose your own versions of the models? Absolutely. (I would be most interested in seeing them.) Should you transpose everything to the eleven other tonal centers? Eventually, of course.

What will have been gained from all of this? This work with the Didymic comma expands musicality in the usual manner of technical practice, by which I mean that the point is not to learn models, or even to recognize commas (although you can learn to do that as certainly as you can learn to recognize chord progressions); the point is to feel more familiar with the territory of tonal harmony. When the terrain is sufficiently familiar and friendly it gives vitality to your own musical creativity. You don't ultimately navigate by place-names but by ear, by associative memory, by the milestones of experience—in short, by feel. These exercises give you the feel of the Didymic comma in its many manifestations.

There are other ways besides these triadic, cadence-driven models to demonstrate the Didymic comma. Some of these will be demonstrated in part 4, some you will find yourself, perhaps some have not been found. If these exercises crease your brain and fry your ear, go on to something else, with my blessings and commiserations—we all have our comma quota. Meanwhile, here are the Didymic comma phenomena in toto. Work them into your musical life gracefully.

The next chapter goes through another entire cycle of commas, but the cycle is shorter, is more obvious to the ear and eye, and produces music of great harmonic range and heightened expression. When you have had your fill of the Didymic comma, at least for now, it is onward to the Great Diesis.

# 30

# THE GREAT DIESIS: THE BEAUTY OF THE BEAST

IN PART 1 WE EXAMINED the fifth partial and the pentamerous domain. Among other things, we came to realize the difficulty with which the ear compounds two major thirds (to make an augmented fifth), and we sang not only the enticingly strange *ga-ga* G♯ but also the wondrously bizarre *ga-ga* C♯.

At the end of part 2, while pushing the limits of the Magic Mode (chapter 26), we first encountered the Great Diesis between that G♯ and A♭, although we pointedly did not attempt to sing or play through that interval; that is, we did not cause A♭ to become G♯ while sounding. In this chapter we will make that attempt, after first revisiting some oddities of pentamerous harmony.

Earlier, in part 2, while composing balanced harmonic progressions, we noticed (in chapter 22) that the most structurally solid and acoustically sensible root motions are Pythagorean—by fifths up or down—and that movement along the *ga* spines (north-south in the lattice) is typically harder to sense and definitely more difficult to sustain. To corroborate this, let's try an exercise that will both review and further intensify pentamerous harmonic experience: we'll make harmonically continuous music and deliberately delete all fifth motion in the roots.

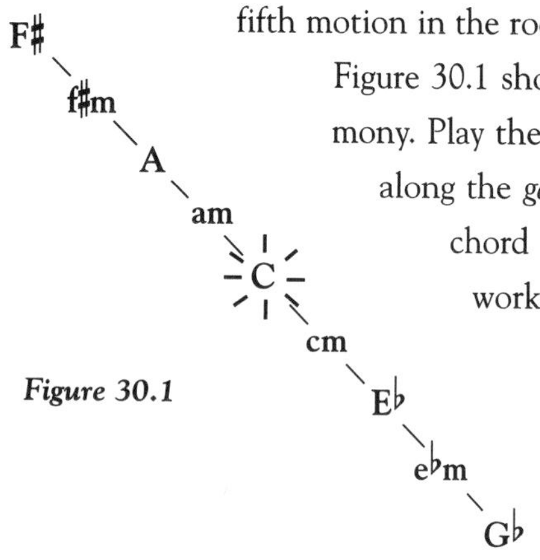

Figure 30.1 shows a series of triads related alternately by parallel and relative harmony. Play these triads, beginning at C. Since there can be no leaping whatsoever along the *ga* spine in continuous harmony, work your way northward chord by chord to F♯, then come back the same way all the way down to G♭, then work your way back to C, as shown in example 30.1.

This is not commonly heard harmony—perhaps it is too much of a good thing to be musical—but hearing fifthless root motion over such a wide range gives insight into the rapid and radical change of scenery implicit in pentamerous harmony. To flesh out the music, try to improvise or compose believable music based strictly

F♯
   f♯m
     A
      am
       C
        cm
         E♭
          e♭m
           G♭

*Figure 30.1*

*Example 30.1*

on this harmonic progression. It isn't easy. Example 30.2 is my attempt.

*Example 30.2*

# The Minor Sixth and the Augmented Fifth Compared

After this taste of pentamerous harmony, we are now prepared to traverse the entire compass of harmony that sweeps from the resonance of pure major thirds in just intonation to the effect of the Great Diesis in equal temperament. We'll begin the journey by comparing the minor sixth and the augmented fifth in just intonation. First, sustain middle C on the piano, sing the just major third below, and then, while still singing, add in the lower octave of C, as shown in example 30.3. (Review chapter 8 if this is not really clear.)

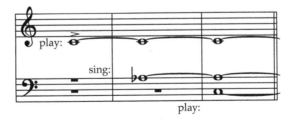

*Example 30.3*

The next thing is to hear for yourself an equal-tempered context that refers convincingly to that experience. The cadences in chapter 20 and the progressions in chapter 21 supply many examples; example 30.4 is a model for our present purposes. Example 30.5 is a more extended use.

*Example 30.4*

*Example 30.5*

What you are trying to find is the effect of the reciprocal major third, the *ga* below, at the equal-tempered keyboard. The work is to ascertain how successfully these contexts allow the equal-tempered A♭ to stand for the 8:5 minor sixth.

The next step is to sing the 25:16 G♯. We fleetingly sang this tone at the end of chapter 16 (pp. 120–121); now we should spend more time with it. The best strategy is to tune the guitar's D string to C, then, using its fifth partial to be sure, tune the G string down to the 5:4 E. When you are certain of the purity of the third, damp the C, pluck the E, and sing *its* 5:4 major third, that is, G♯. Then, when you are sure of the resonance, add in the C. Finally, damp out the E, as shown in example 30.6.

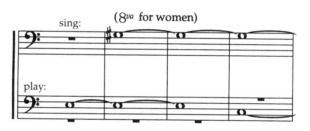

*Example 30.6*

To more fully appreciate the *ga-ga* nature of the harmony, bring your sung G♯ up a semitone to the 5:3 A, whose leading tone it is. You can check this on the lattice of tones: The harmonic path between G♯ and A is as shown in figure 30.2. Try leaving the E sounding as you do this, as shown in example 30.7.

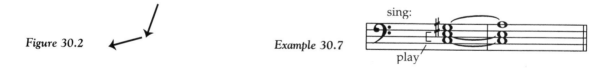

*Figure 30.2*                                   *Example 30.7*

What you have produced is, of course, the harmonic motion characteristic of modulation to A Minor. The G♯ will, in fact, be more secure in a context made from the tones of A Minor, given in example 30.8.

*Example 30.8*

Does this amount to singing in A Minor with its mediant in the bass? To find out, try singing in conventional C Major (with a 3:2 G and a 9:8 D). Now, if you sing back and forth between the just A-minor triad and the just C-major triad over a C drone, you are on the boundary between mode and modulation, a very musical place to be.

*Example 30.9*

The next step is to convince yourself of the equal-tempered referent. You could simply play example 30.9 on the keyboard. Example 30.10 is a more convincing cadential construction.

*Example 30.10*

Example 30.11 is a more elaborate passage.

*Example 30.11*

The work is to make whatever connection you can between the feeling of the 25:16 G♯ and the equal-tempered G♯. What strikes me about this harmony is how far out the 25:16 G♯ is, but how familiar and tame the equal-tempered modulation to vi has become through constant use. It is an aural leap to make that black note between G and A into a 25:16 G♯—a forgiveness of twenty-eight cents, to be exact, but by now it fits like an old shoe. When temperament was new, that shoe was new. One learns to hear with ancient ears.

The next step in our A♭/G♯ comparison is to compare the harmonic effects each produces. We have already done this in equal-tempered dronality (refer back to example 26.17); now we are using more modulatory material. First, play example 30.5, then example 30.11, alternating between them many times. The passage containing A♭ we associate with the reciprocal thirds of C Minor, the *parallel* minor of C Major; the passage containing G♯ we associate with the overtonal thirds of A Minor, the *relative* Minor of C Major. As seen from the vantage point of C Major, then, these two passages represent an alternation between parallel and relative territory. We first were introduced to this concept in chapter 20 but did not dwell on the contrast in feeling between the two realms. Now, with our harmonic language expanding, we can more clearly hear how evocative is the complimentarity in mood between the reciprocal thirds of the parallel Minor and the overtonal thirds of the relative Minor.

One way you can practice appreciating this is to learn each of the two previous chordal examples well enough to improvise on them. Example 30.12 is a written-out improvisation on each.

*Example 30.12*

Everyone touched by Western culture is familiar with the complimentarity, in the Pythagorean dimension, between dominant and subdominant harmonies. At the outset of our training, both as listeners and as musicians, we learn to recognize and form the cadential energies of I, IV, and V triads. What is also part of the culture, but in a less pronounced way, is the pentamerous version of the cadential dance, the parallel/relative flux that balances the ear at the tonal center in the pentamerous dimension. The point of your work now is to juxtapose parallel and relative harmony in such a way as to develop an intuitive affinity with reciprocity in the *ga* dimension just as you already have in the *pa* dimension. (This crucial step is omitted in conventional theory and its pedagogy.) Sensitivity to the directionality of energy flow in the *ga* dimension will open your sensitivity to the effect of the Great Diesis, which is a kind of short-circuit in that flow.

Try to improvise freely using the following key scheme: C Major to A Minor to C Major to C Minor (repeat this many times). Be sure to use the tone G♯ in A Minor and the tone A♭ in C Minor. Try to bring each realm into being with an economy of means, as suggested in example 30.13.

*Example 30.13*

Example 30.14 shows a jazz version.

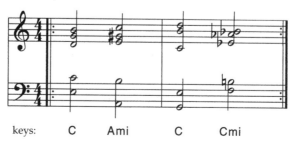

*Example 30.14*

An even more abbreviated, but dangerous, that is, potentially ambiguous, use is shown in example 30.15. (There will be more discussion about diminished seventh chords as we proceed.)

*Example 30.15*

Although the idea is to manipulate the musical context so as to convince yourself that the black note between G and A is either the A♭ of C Minor or the G♯ of A minor, try not to meld the two meanings. We will soon enough do that deliberately, and in quite specific ways. For now, try to rock convincingly between the two functions until you can hear the music in your head without touching the keyboard.

## Singing through the A♭/G♯ Diesis in Just Intonation

It is time, finally, to sing through the Great Diesis in just intonation. To accomplish this you need to tune two guitar strings to C and E, as you did for example 30.6, then tune the B string up to C (or tune the high E down to C). As always, be perfect in tuning.

We'll proceed at first by singing only from A♭ to G♯, not the other way. Pluck the C; find the in-tune A♭ with your voice; then, being certain to damp out the C, immediately pluck the E, letting your voice relax down into the G♯, as shown in example 30.16.

And relax it will: forty-one cents worth of relaxation. This comma is definitely perceptible as a change in pitch—by almost a quarter tone. (The ratio of the A♭ to the G♯ is 128:125; see chapter 26.) Notice that as the pitch lowers, the harmonic energy rushes

*Example 30.16*

from the reciprocal *ga*-below region to the extremely overtonal *ga-ga*, a northward harmonic surge of three major thirds. So as the pitch goes down, the harmony goes up, unlike the pitch and harmony of the Didymic comma, which have a more subtle relation. (Check that out in both staff orientation and compass orientation.)

Practice singing through the comma several times, double-checking the tuning of your strings as you go. Try to identify, and identify *with*, the responses evoked by navigation through the Great Diesis.

In the previous chapter, we spoke of the "zap" of the Didymic comma. That zap is intensified in the case of the Great Diesis for three reasons: The pitch difference is greater (almost double); the harmonic distance is greater (the two extra *ga*'s more than make up for the four fewer *pa*'s); and the direction of the pitch moves entirely contrary to the direction of the harmony. One author (Easley Blackwood) quotes a Greek source meaning of *diesis* as "a discharge," and it does seem to be true that a buzz of energy is unleashed in the brain at the moment of the diesis.

The zap of the Great Diesis is unique and pronounced; but what is its quality? Perhaps it is more than merely musing to observe that Pathfinder, the protagonist we met during our Didymic adventures, seems not so stressed or confused in the diesis context. The experience is more like an elaborate, instantaneous acrobatic flip than a disintegration and reintegration, possibly because the harmonic path, though far, is direct: a straight shot in the *ga* dimension. Discovering your deep response to the Great Diesis is surely one of the ten thousand greatest things you can do, and definitely at the heart of this study. Yes, you have to learn it over time. It is also true that once you become aware of it you never forget it.

Example 30.17 demonstrates a very practical way that the Great Diesis, in a somewhat compromised version, can be evoked at the equal-tempered keyboard with the help of your voice. The temperament shaves off about a third of the comma (about fourteen cents), but you will still be able to feel your way by seeking the pure tunings for the thirds you sing.

*Example 30.17*

In North Indian *raga*, singing through the Great Diesis is a sublime though unusual expressive device. But in most other music meant to be sung with pure harmony, the sounding of the Great Diesis is even more rare. Why so uncommon? Because such music—late Medieval European music, for instance—ordinarily does not gobble up in a single moment an amount of territory large enough to require singing through the Great Diesis. It takes a large palette of harmonic possibility to structure and define a tonal swath wide enough to require an A♭/G♯ dovetail, and a large palette of available triadic harmony is precisely what temperaments produced. The musical use of the Great Diesis arose more or less synchronously with the rise of temperaments, especially twelve-tone equal temperament, wherein it becomes an extremely useful harmonic pivot, as we shall see. Our aim is to follow the thread of experience that shows how the sensibility of such harmony in equal temperament is grounded upon its reference to the resonances of pure pentamerous harmonies.

## PLAYING THROUGH THE A♭/G♯ DIESIS IN EQUAL TEMPERAMENT

Consider the music in example 30.18.

*Example 30.18*

Bar 1 is in C Major but "borrows" the A♭ from the parallel Minor. Bar 2 begins unambiguously on an F-minor triad, and at the third beat the music could easily return to C; the G of the soprano, for instance, is heard as the major seventh above A♭; likewise, the D is heard as Pythagorean. But all of the tones of bar 2 could have another meaning as well, and by beat 4 that possibility is foremost, thanks to the E-major triad, which immediately is identified as the V of A Minor. The soprano G, as it turns out, was a diminished octave above the bass G♯, the interval created by a chromatic major/minor pair of sevenths: G♯/G♮ in A Minor; likewise, the Pythagorean D becomes its darker Didymic sibling, the subdominant of A. The A-Minor triad of bar 3 is perceived only momentarily as a tonic chord; it quickly functions as part of a vi–IV–V cadence in C Major. The note on which the diesis occurs here is the G♯ in the bass in bar 2; it supports the upper voices as the harmony flees northward. What happens in your ear during the last half of that bar?

Example 30.19 places the diesis tone in the soprano and offers a more definite modulation to A Minor.

*Example 30.19*

Notice how the diesis tone is central to the expression. In bar 3 the ear wants to dally on the semitone that the alto's entrance makes with the soprano, at least for a moment; but when the E strikes at bar 4 it is as if we cannot linger long enough to absorb the new feeling. The soprano's upward leap of a diminished seventh keeps us lingering even longer, but as it resolves the harmony clarifies, the tempo resumes, the big moment is history, and everyone goes back to the beginning to do it again.

As always, examine your response at the moment of the diesis. Remember, at some level the ear is forgiving forty-one cents. What exactly replaces that change of pitch? What is the feel of this upward pentamerous harmony? What *happens?*

Example 30.20 is a clear and efficient version that does nothing to suffuse, or even soften the edges of, the effect of the comma. To tell ourselves what happens, we can use the language that we developed in the study of the Didymic comma and say that we leave home (C) by the southern door (the parallel realm) and arrive from the northwest (the relative realm). We can say we were zapped over a distance of

*Example 30.20*

three thirds in the overtonal direction. We can examine the lattice of tones note for note, tracking our position at every moment. Indeed, all of the descriptive and metaphorical language we have developed for one comma we can use for the others. What is different from comma to comma is the character, the quality, of the musical experience, and each musician has to sense, remember, and categorize for himself or herself the qualities of the commas. Your music will soak up these qualities in a unique and personal way. It is all a private matter, and the deeper your hearing the more private it becomes. The miraculous aspect is that once your music is made, the private room nobody could enter except yourself turns out to be the very room that everyone longs to share in common, and does. The common room of this deep harmonic experience is the reason that music is our first and best hope for a universal language.

## SINGING THROUGH THE G♯/A♭ DIESIS IN JUST INTONATION

We'll now go back to singing this comma, but in the other direction. The big difference is this: By any measure, A♭ is within the tonal field of C; G♯ is only marginally so. Moving from A♭ to G♯, as we have just done, moves you from C to the edge of its tonal boundary. Beginning with G♯ and moving to A♭ takes you from the fringe and moves you closer to the center. Also, the pitch of the diesis tone rises as the harmony falls.

We will use our same two guitar strings, having meticulously checked their tuning. Play and sing as shown in example 30.21.

*Example 30.21*

Play C first, to establish the tonic in your ear, then play E and damp C. Now sing the pure third above E and hang on until you are sure of the resonance. Still hanging on, play C while damping E, and try to find C's reciprocal pure third. You'll glide upward, but that's OK—practice to make the forty-one-cent hop (it will feel like a small leap) as clean as possible. That will conceptually clarify the comma, even though the experience may not feel terribly musical. Singers and players, when forced by harmonic circumstances to negotiate the comma, glide rather than hop through it. Indeed, it can be downright disconcerting to take the comma all at once, much more so in just intonation than in equal temperament, where only the context changes, not the pitch. Try hopping, then gliding, and compare the two.

Example 30.22 is the keyboard-assisted version, which is fourteen cents narrower but easier to navigate—the ready-made fifths do help.

*Example 30.22*

How does the G♯/A♭ comma compare with the A♭/G♯ comma? What is the effect of the reversal of polarity—a southward as opposed to a northward zap? How is relative-to-parallel different from parallel-to-relative? Although I am asking you to sing one and then the other and compare the effect, I am not recommending that you sing back and forth many times between them, which would yo-yo you recklessly up and down the *ga* spine. One must protect oneself from pentamerous overindulgence.

## PLAYING THROUGH THE G♯/A♭ DIESIS IN EQUAL TEMPERAMENT

Play example 30.23.

*Example 30.23*

The diesis tone is exposed in the alto over the bar line. The augmented triad on the last eighth note of bar 1 is slightly ambiguous, softening slightly the effect of the diesis, but at the downbeat of bar 2 the harmony has almost certainly reversed, and the entrance of the E♭ in bar 2 clinches it.

It is, in fact, most usual to buffer the moment of the diesis with ambiguous material such as the augmented triad at the end of bar 1. This ambiguity, which arises from the temperament itself, distributes the function of the comma over a longer period, thereby attenuating its effect. We can think of this ambiguous material as the equal-tempered version of a singer in just intonation who glides, rather than hops, through the comma.

Example 30.24 is an extremely direct and unambiguous version, more of a leap than a hop.

*Example 30.24*

The harmony moves unambiguously from E⁷ at the end of bar 1 to F minor at the downbeat of bar 2. In this direction of harmonic flow—from the G♯ of the relative Minor to the A♭ of the parallel Minor—the diesis harmony seems particularly compelling, and in conventional music it is the preferred direction. I can think of two reasons for this. First, it is the same type of direct falling harmony (from overtonal to reciprocal) that produces, in the *pa* dimension, the yang decisiveness of the perfect cadence. Falling fifths are certainly the engine of European tonal harmony; the harmony we are studying now involves instantaneously falling thirds, so it can be considered as the pentamerous, comma-induced version of the West's main move. Second, the voice leading is particularly serendipitous. Three tones from the *ga* spine that appear in A Minor, namely A, E, and B, appear a semitone lower in C Minor as A♭, E♭, and B♭, providing many opportunities for a sighing trio of downward-leading major/minor chromatic pairs to enhance the descending harmony. In fact, the only rising aspect of this harmony is the forty-one-cent rise in the pitch of the diesis, which is, of course, absorbed by the temperament.

Besides ambiguous material, another means of smoothing the effect of the comma is through dissonance. Consider the jazz version in example 30.25.

*Example 30.25*

The stacked-third dissonances characteristic of jazz replace the purity of triads and establish modal contexts instantaneously. The downbeat of bar 2, for instance, contains five tones from A Utility Minor (including the diminished octave from G♯ to G♮); the second beat contains five tones from C Utility Minor (rendering the old diminished octave G♯ to G♮ into a major seventh A♭ to G, and adding a *new* diminished octave, B♮ to B♭).

Contrast the lush jazz version with the austere triadic passage in example 30.26.

*Example 30.26*

or the extremely stark, abrupt version in example 30.27.

*Example 30.27*

# Comparing the Rising and Falling Harmony of the Great Diesis in Equal Temperament

Here are several passages that have been adapted from previous examples to present the Great Diesis in both directions. Play example 30.28.

*Example 30.28*

In example 30.28 the soprano G♯ becomes A♭ at bar 2, and the harmonic energy falls; at bar 4, the bass A♭ becomes G♯ and the harmonic energy rises. Now play example 30.29, where the soprano A♭ becomes G♯ at bar 4 and the harmonic energy rises; at bar 11 the alto G♯ becomes A♭ and the energy falls.

*Example 30.29*

Next are two circular examples that compare the stark purity of triads and the smoky dissonances of third-stacked harmonies. The triadic loop is given in two versions in example 30.30.

*Example 30.30*

Example 30.31 is the jazz version.

*Example 30.31*

In bar 2 the G♯ of the bass becomes A♭, and in bar 4 the tenor A♭ becomes G♯.

Example 30.32 shows one more loop: the special case of diminished seventh chords. The

*Example 30.32*

diminished seventh chord of bar 1 is ambiguous: Without additional context we would expect it to be Bdim⁷, containing an A♭, since A♭ is closer to a C-major triad than G♯. But when we hear the A-minor triad, the ear recognizes the continuity of the G♯ and remembers the chord as the vii/vi, or G♯ dim⁷. In bar 2 the G♯ is at first believed, since we have now tilted toward A Minor. But as soon as we hear the C triad, the ear recognizes the continuity of the A♭ and remembers the chord as the vii/I, or Bdim⁷, with the A♭ borrowed from Minor. Since the two diminished seventh chords contain identical pitches in equal temperament, the ear is confronted with ambiguity in a repeated, condensed form.

Unlike major or minor triads, which strongly suggest context, an isolated diminished seventh chord presents so many potential harmonic contexts that it signifies virtually none. The ear therefore tends to hear it for what it is: a division of the octave into four equal parts, a quadrisection of an octave. Such equal divisions give rise to symmetrical harmony, of which there is an abundance in equal temperament. The ear recognizes symmetrical harmony as a middle ground between tonality and atonality. Every diminished seventh chord contains the potential for various commas, and they are a favorite diesis-generating device. They can generate commas in cycles that spin away from the tonal center, flirting with symmetry and eventually atonality. These circumstances will be discussed much more fully in part 4.

All of the musical passages quoted above exemplify, in their various ways, a triple *ga* leap between the *ga-ga* spine of fifths and the *ga*-below spine of fifths, with the Great Diesis, induced by proper context, providing instant transport. What I have advised you *against* doing in just intonation I strongly recommend in equal temperament: reiterated practice of the Great Diesis, bringing it forward until it is your friend. The secret is, I think, to enter willingly into the moment of the unknown and to be filled with it. There is no question that we unconsciously seek similar little swoons in art and in daily life. We "go out" on experience whenever we can, smelling a rose, taking in the stars, enjoying the first sip after a long abstinence—little everyday commas that purposefully overwhelm the mind. I am asking you to do this consciously in the highly structured circumstances of diesis practice. Enter the smoky moment of the comma with your lights on. There is a fierce wisdom in the way music creates new harmony by confounding the logic of the old.

> *O Great Diesis, Liberator of our mind!*
> *We cherish your passing strangeness that frees us*
>     *from the bondage of certainty and smug knowing.*
> *Shape our inner ear with your short-circuitry!*
> *Let your fiery discharge blast what it must*
>     *so our souls wear the face of your beauty.*

# 31

# THE TONAL ARRAY
# OF THE GREAT DIESIS

NOW THAT WE'VE EXAMINED the Great Diesis between A♭ and G♯ from the vantage point of the tonic C, a new question emerges: How many Great Dieses are functional within a given tonal center, and how are they organized? Remember (how could you forget?) that in chapter 29 we found fifteen pairs of Didymic triads and drew a map depicting their relationships. But the situation with the Great Diesis is not quite analogous. For one thing, although a pair of diesis *tones* can exist—marginally—within a tonal center, the harmonic disparity between a pair of diesis *triads*, A♭ major and G♯ major, for instance, is too great to be contained by one tonal center. There is, however, an orderly array of diesis pairs of *tones* within a single tonal center. Each pair behaves more or less like the A♭/G♯ pair we have studied, yet each generates a harmonic color all its own. We'll now consider them one by one.

## The Overtonal Diesis Family

There are three major thirds within the compass of the A♭/G♯ diesis; *two* lie above C and *one*

lies below. Since such an arrangement favors the overtonal direction, let A♭/G♯ be called an *overtonal diesis* in C. Consider, then, the similarly configured dieses shown in example 31.1.

All of these dieses might be considered as emanating from the *ga-*below spine of fifths: D♭–A♭–E♭–B♭. I've drawn arrows from each tone in the *ga-*below spine of fifths to its

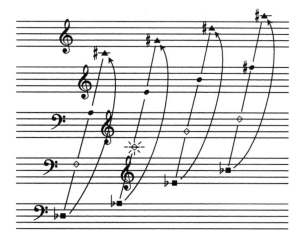

*Example 31.1*

diesis mate in the *ga-ga*-above spine of fifths, indicating that the pentamerous harmonic energy flows away from the center in the overtonal direction. (It might help to color the arrows, from left to right, blue, yellow, orange, and red.) The only difference among these diesis pairs is their placement in the Pythagorean dimension; the work all of them do in the pentamerous dimension is identical. We will call these four pairs, then, the overtonal diesis family.

Does the harmonic energy flow back the other way—is there a reversal of polarity within overtonal family pairs? In the case of the A♭/G♯ pair, we have seen that it does. But in equal temperament A♭ is much more securely a part of the tonality of C than is G♯; a harmonic context inducing G♯ requires either a modulation to A Minor or a nascent sense of one. As we go along, we will likewise not only consider the reversal of harmonic polarity within each pair but also describe its modulatory behavior.

# The Minor Second/Augmented Prime Diesis

## SINGING THROUGH THE DIESIS IN JUST INTONATION

We have already sung both the 16:15 D♭ and the 25:24 C♯. They are both highly evocative in dronal just intonation, partly because of the dissonance they create with the drone, and partly because of their innate harmonic qualities. What we have not done is sing through the Great Diesis that separates them. Alas, our usual method, using the guitar, is a bit cumbersome: We need, besides the C string, a pure 4:3 F and a pure 8:5 A. Try tuning the high E string to F (carefully, so as not to break it). Then tune the B string to A. (Alternatively, the entire experiment could be lowered a semitone.) When you are certain of your tunings, try the sequence of events shown in example 31.2.

*Example 31.2*

You might find this experience both strange (because of the *ga* compounding combined with the dissonance) and illuminating (because of the especially juicy Phrygian/*Purya* mix; see chapter 26). The same effect, with somewhat reduced intensity, can be achieved at the equal-tempered keyboard as shown in example 31.3.

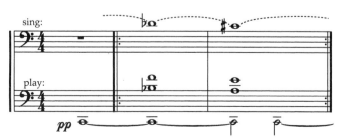

*Example 31.3*

Ensure that the third between the piano F and your sung D♭ is pure; likewise between the piano A and your sung C♯. You might practice first without the drone C, adding it in only intermittently and barely audibly. The exercise is difficult at best, but diesis wisdom is well worth the effort.

## PLAYING THROUGH THE DIESIS IN EQUAL TEMPERAMENT

Play the music of example 31.4.

*Example 31.4*

The first two bars establish the Phrygian Major mode. At bar 3 the music could still be in Phrygian Major, despite my spelling of C♯; but by the resolution of bar 4, the force of the comma has been "discharged" and we are in D Minor. So the ambiguities of the diminished harmonies in bar 3 distribute the effect of the comma over the bar. At the end of the third beat of bar 6 there is a momentary V$^7$ chord, reminding us of I (although inducing a Didymic pair of D-minor triads to do so). In bars 7 and 8 D Minor is reestablished. At the downbeat of bar 9 there is the momentary ambiguity of the D♭ augmented chord, but by the E♭ of the third beat we are in B♭ Minor, which cadences, in Phrygian style, back to C. So the force of the comma is distributed over several beats in the C♯–D♭ direction also.

Example 31.5 is less elaborated and more direct.

*Example 31.5*

The second beat of bar 1 is heard in C Phrygian Major, but the third beat is an ambiguous chord, first heard as the Edim$^7$ of C Phrygian Major, but at the downbeat of bar 2 we are tossed upstairs, so to speak, into D Minor, and the previous chord turns out to have been the C♯dim$^7$ of that key. By bar 3 we have returned to C (by means of a ii–V Didymic comma), then we immediately leave it (by the downbeat of bar 4), using the D Minor material that has just sounded. The second beat of bar 4 could be in D Minor but turns out to have been the $V^7$ (in second inversion) of C Phrygian.

Example 31.6 shows an even more direct, purely triadic approach (and omits all trace of the ii–V Didymic energy central to the previous two examples).

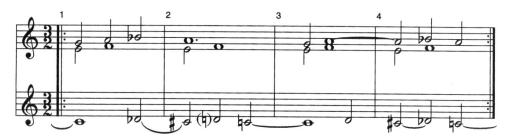

Example 31.6

For an even starker version, try the bass an octave higher, as shown in example 31.7. The diesis energy is particularly well exposed but not necessarily more beautiful than when it is covered in a lower voice or distributed over more time.

Example 31.7

These examples all show various degrees of dissonance and consonance; contrast them with the standing dissonances of jazz, which mellow the comma energy, as demonstrated in example 31.8.

Example 31.8

Example 31.8 shows the reversal of polarity: The C♯–D♭ direction appears first, then the D♭–C♯ direction. Also, it is more clearly modulatory than preceding ones. To help understand this example, notice that the dissonant collection of tones shown in example 31.9 is common to both D Utility Minor and F Aeolian (or C Phrygian).

D Minor version          F Minor version

*Example 31.9*

The change in spelling represents the diesis. Notice in example 31.8 how a simple difference in passing tones (the E♮ of bar 4 has become E♭ in bar 5; in bar 6, A♮ becomes A♭) changes the context from D Minor (with a C♯) to F Minor (with a D♭). The process is reversed in the second half of the passage: The E♭ and A♭ of bars 11 and 12 become E♮ and A♮ in bars 13 and 14, effectively changing the context from F Minor to D Minor.

Notice also that although these keys are tonicized, they are still clearly heard as iv and ii from the vantage point of C. The C♯/D♭ diesis is thus heard as bracketing, or encompassing, the territory between the two. The entire construction lies, in fact, a fifth below the A♭/G♯ diesis and is a subdominant version of it. In both cases the energy shifts between material associated with the parallel Minor (C Minor, F Minor) and the relative Minor (A Minor, D Minor). We will continue to look at this particular parallel/relative way of straddling the tonal center; it is the distinguishing characteristic of the overtonal diesis family. In working with the D♭/C♯ examples and comparing these with the A♭/G♯ examples, try to discern the musical differences between them. Go past the notes into the harmonic quality, where the source of the musical power lies.

Before going on, let's look at the diminished and augmented triads associated with the D♭/C♯ diesis. Play example 31.10.

Edim⁷        C♯ dim⁷              D♭ aug        F aug

*Example 31.10*

The D♭/C♯ diesis tells you that Edim⁷ is not C♯dim⁷, and also that a D♭ augmented triad is not an F augmented triad.

# The Minor Third/Augmented Second Diesis

Play example 31.11.

*Example 31.11*

Bars 1 and 2 are in C Minor. The second beat of bar 3 could be heard as an F#dim[7] moving to G Major, but by the third beat the alto is unambiguously D#, so the comma is distributed over only one beat. In bar 4 the F in the bass signals C Minor, and the following E♭ is clearly the third of a C-minor triad. The passage tonicizes E Minor from C Minor using the E♭/D# diesis and is another example of how the Great Diesis facilitates reciprocity between parallel Minor and relative Minor domains (at the mediant, in this case).

Example 31.12 is a stark statement of the same motion.

*Example 31.12*

The two augmented triads serve as conduits: In bar 1 the E♭aug of the second beat (E♭–G–B) is remembered as Gaug (G–B–D#); the situation is reversed in bar 2.

In example 31.13, the chord E♭/D#–A–D is common to both keys, changing spelling as it changes meaning.

*Example 31.13*

Since this diesis proceeds from E♭, it is part of the C Minor mode (as opposed to C Major). This allows the direct comparison of two Minor keys separated by the distance of a major third: C Minor and E Minor. These were hinted at in the A♭/G# diesis (F Minor and A Minor) and in the D♭/C# diesis (B♭ Minor and D Minor), but in this case one of the keys is the tonic itself, so we can enjoy the ride with no intermediary.

Consider the common material between two specific modes: C MA/MIN and E U-MI, as shown in example 31.14.

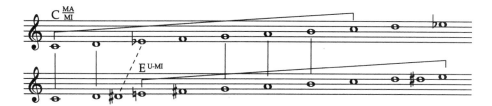

*Example 31.14*

Beginning with C, the common tones between the two modes (indicated by unbroken vertical lines) are C, D, G, A, and B. E♭ and D# are diesis mates (indicated by a dotted line). The half step D–E♭ is a diatonic semitone in C Minor; in E Minor the half step D♮–D# is a chromatic pair. (Visually, looking at the keyboard, it seems as if, when the F of C Minor goes away, the E and F♯ of E Minor appear to replace it. Can you trace what actually happens, degree by degree?) In this arrangement of modes (two Minor keys separated by a major third) lies a rich vein of music.

All of the above examples move from C Minor to E Minor and back again, demonstrating the oscillation between parallel minor and relative minor territory. None *begins* with E Minor, since D♯ (unlike either G♯ or C♯) is scarcely available to us in the equal-tempered domain of C. There is no way the ear will hear the music of these examples as simple events in C; it is neither dronal nor modal—we have left those worlds for now. This music clearly moves us away from C; it modulates. It is an example of what is conventionally termed "modulating tonal harmony," or sometimes simply "tonal harmony."

Example 31.15 is a passage that begins in C Major, tonicizes E Minor (by means of its ii$^7$–V$^7$), then, at the moment of diesis, borrows from C Minor—a complex and beautiful harmonic path, as opposed to simply a "chromatic" one.

*Example 31.15*

Although they have already shown up in the above examples, I'll list here the augmented and diminished triads appropriate to the E♭/D♯ Diesis: Moving south to north, E♭aug is distinct from Gaug, and F♯dim$^7$ (the vii$^7$ of V) is distinct from D♯dim$^7$ (the vii$^7$ of iii).

# The Minor Seventh/Augmented Sixth Diesis

A♯ is unquestionably beyond the domain of equal-tempered modality in C. We need to begin in a C mode that contains the 9:5 B♭ and then somehow find A♯. Example 31.16 makes the attempt.

*Example 31.16*

Notice how the B♭ augmented triad in bar 2 (B♭–D–F♯) is distinct from the D augmented triad (D–F♯–A♯) implied in bar 3. Example 31.17 is more direct.

*Example 31.17*

This is fairly remote harmony, since the C mode (MIX/LYD) is none too stable, and the B mode is relatively distant from C. Still, I hear it as a modulatory event leading out from and back to C, and the diesis mates do straddle the 9:8 D, as example 31.1 has indicated. I cannot convince myself, however, that the F/E♯ diesis, which would be the next fifth higher on the lattice, is part of C, so my list stops here. Nor, incidentally, can I convince myself that the G♭/F♯ diesis, which would be the next fifth lower than the most subdominant harmony in the overtonal diesis family (D♭/C♯), is part of the tonality of C. The tonal function seems to drop off steeply at both the east and west ends of the series, like continental slopes, leaving us high and dry with four functional diesis pairs in the overtonal diesis family. Reexamine example 31.1, and at the keyboard compare the models exemplifying the various pairs. In each instance ask yourself:

- Where am I on the lattice?
- In which direction is the energy flowing?
- What is the feeling of the moment of the diesis?
- How strong is the connection to the tonal center of C?

Also, try to track the parallel Minor/relative Minor reciprocity in every case.

When you feel some familiarity with these dieses, try improvising or composing your own examples. Don't be shy about imitating the models presented here—your own original versions will surely emerge. The blessing of the Great Diesis is that it both goads and guides us toward our own perception of it.

## The Reciprocal Diesis Family

Reciprocal Great Dieses behave exactly as their overtonal cousins do; the only difference is their north-south placement in respect to the tonal center. Instead of two of the three major thirds lying above the central Pythagorean spine and one lying below, only *one* major third lies above the central spine and *two* are below, as shown in example 31.18.

The reciprocal diesis family, then, stretches southward all the way to the *ga-ga-below*

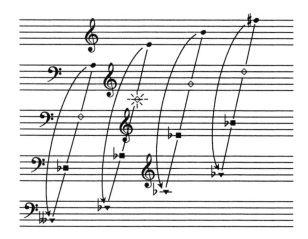

*Example 31.18*

spine of fifths. It can be thought of as originating from the overtonal *ga* spine A–E–B–F♯; the pentamerous harmonic energy flows downward through the center toward deeply recip‑ rocal territory. Each arrow follows the energy from a tone on the *ga* spine of fifths to its rec‑ iprocal diesis tone-mate on the *ga-ga* below spine of fifths. It might help to color the arrows left to right, blue, yellow, orange, red. As before, the difference from pair to pair is only a matter of east–west positioning along the Pythagorean spine.

All of the dieses of the reciprocal family involve modulation away from C. But notice how very satisfying are the round-trip journeys in this particular kind of vehicle.

## The Major Sixth/Diminished Seventh Diesis

We'll begin with the most subdominant of the diesis pairs and move to the right on the lat‑ tice—up by fifths.

Study example 31.19, which straddles F.

*Example 31.19*

The 5:3 A occurs in bar 1 as part of a C MA/MIN scale. The mode turns Phrygian at the D♭ triad of bar 2, but then tonicizes D♭ Major (while at the same time borrowing from D♭ Minor) with the Cdim[7] chord on the third beat of bar 2. The energy of the A/B♭♭ diesis has thus been distributed over five beats. The Cdim[7] is reiterated at the downbeat of bar 3, but turns into an F triad (V of vi in D♭; IV in C Minor) on the second beat, and by the third beat, C Minor is the context again, so the moment of the diesis as it returns is just one beat. Try emphasizing the bass in bars 2 and 3 to maximize the effect.

This diesis pair is the most far-flung of all those we will consider, but it is still sensible.

*Figure 31.1*

It has to make the II chord of C Phrygian (D♭) a tonal center, and then, from its own parallel Minor, borrow the minor sixth degree (B♭♭). That may seem like stretching it, and it is. But the situation *seems* less extreme if you transpose everything down a semitone to the key of B Minor, which will render the diesis pair, instead of A/B♭♭, the conceptually more benign G♯/A♭. I'll leave you on your own with only the map in figure 31.1 as a clue.

## The Major Third/Diminished Fourth Diesis

Still remote from C but far more sensible is the diesis pair E/F♭. Play example 31.20, whose thirds straddle C.

*Example 31.20*

The 5:4 E of the opening chord becomes, perhaps ambiguously, the 32:25 F♭ in the *ga-ga*-below spine of fifths on the very next chord. But by the second beat of bar 1, that tone is remembered as F♭, and by the third beat we remember it as the minor sixth of A♭. By the end of bar 2, with the E of C⁷, the harmonic energy has returned to the *ga* spine of fifths. From the vantage point of C, A♭ is sufficiently functional to borrow the F♭ from its parallel minor, while remaining within C's domain. The effect of this diesis is, to be frankly subjective, smoky to the max, by which I mean that it is a deeply reciprocal pentamerous zap, fully appreciable from the vantage point of the tonal center.

In respect to the associated diminished-seventh harmony, the E/F♭ diesis pair tells us that Edim⁷ (vii of F) is not Gdim⁷ (vii of A♭).

## The Major Seventh/Diminished Octave Diesis

These models are climbing by fifths; the B/C♭ diesis straddles G and, though modulatory, is clearly sensible from C. Play example 31.21.

*Example 31.21*

The 15:8 B in bar 1 is remembered as the 48:25 C♭ by the third beat of bar 2. This raises the question of how we perceive the "moment" of the diesis. Can the moment be in the remembering of it, as opposed to the sounding of it? Perhaps the meaning of anything temporal depends partly on memory. But notice how, in bar 3, the C♭ in beat 1 is *suddenly* the unequivocal B♮ of beat 2, a zap in real time. It is fascinating to compare the diesis energy as it is distributed over two or more beats with diesis energy that is instantaneous. The drawing out of the diesis energy over time attenuates its force but does not necessarily produce a less musical result. On the contrary, a gradual release is often more meaningful than a sudden discharge, a conclusion we may extrapolate from various life experiences.

In terms of diminished-seventh harmonies, this diesis tells us that B dim[7] (vii of C) is not Ddim[7] (vii of E♭).

## The Augmented Fourth/Diminished Fifth Diesis

By far the most effective reciprocal diesis in C is the one straddling C itself (E/F♭); only slightly less affective is the one straddling G, the dominant (B/C♭). As we saw in the first reciprocal example, the diesis energy straddling F, the subdominant, (A/B♭♭) is remote, but still sensible from C. The present example, F♯/G♭, which straddles D (two fifths up from C), is almost beyond the fringe. Example 31.22 may or may not convince you.

*Example 31.22*

The 45:32 F♯ in bar 2 becomes (suddenly) the 36:25 G♭ of bar 3, and returns (just as suddenly) at bar 5. It is a clear round-trip journey, but off center: east coastal, so to speak. Figure 31.2 may help to visualize the harmonic path. The diminished seventh chords associated with this diesis are F♯dim[7] (vii of G) as distinct from Adim[7] (vii of B♭).

I believe we have now exhausted the possibilities for Great Dieses that can be heard from the vantage point of C—in other words, without having to modulate away from C both northward *and* southward in order to evoke each of the two tones of a diesis pair. So we can now take a look at the whole array of available pentamerous harmony, the whole family portrait of Great Dieses in C.

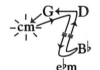

*Figure 31.2*

## Pentamerous Harmony

The term *pentamerous harmony* refers to harmony that employs the 5:4 major third in its primary function. In conventional analysis the term *tertiary harmony* refers simply to harmony that moves by thirds. But some thirds are major, some are minor, some are *ga*-blooded and some are Pythagorean. In the progression of major triads C–F–D–G–C, for instance, the motion from F to D is an overtonal leap of three perfect fifths, which produces a Pythagorean minor third, whose quality is Pythagorean, not pentamerous. So we need a new name to help us make this crucial distinction between the harmony of perfect fifths and the harmony of pure major thirds. Failure to do this accounts for the confusions and disappointments of conventional theory.

Specifically, pentamerous harmony moves north and south along four spines of thirds, namely, the *pa*-below spine of thirds, the central spine of thirds, the *pa* spine of thirds, and the grand-*pa* spine of thirds. (See the discussion preceding example 16.20 for a review of lattice nomenclature.) Pentamerous harmony has its own special character, which contrasts with Pythagorean harmony in the most musically useful ways. A primary purpose of this study is to bring forward that contrast and render it practical for every musician.

Example 31.23, then, is the lattice of Great Dieses, a combination of the overtonal and the reciprocal diesis families, a compilation of the eight dieses we have studied originating from the tonal field surrounding C. (Again, it is best to color the arrows a pair each of blue, yellow, orange, and red.)

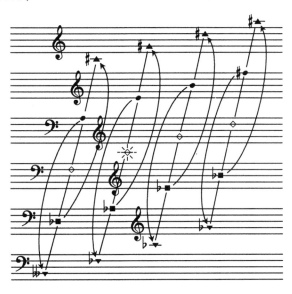

*Example 31.23. The lattice of Great Dieses in C*

For a Great Diesis to function within the domain of C, two conditions have to be met: (1) One tone of the diesis pair must originate clearly in C, and (2) the two tones in the diesis pair must straddle one of the four central Pythagorean tones (F, C, G, or D). Those conditions yield the eight pairs depicted above in example 31.23. Notice also that the twelve central notes of this lattice—the three central spines of fifths—are the same as "the central area of the harmonic map" shown in example 9.37. This area is "central" because it comprises the tones with the lowest ratios in respect to C.

Moving the diesis one fifth further to the right or one fifth further to the left takes us beyond the corona of C: The pull of tonal gravity will no longer be centered. Moving the diesis a third further up or a third further down requires too great a modulation from C and the tonal thread will be broken. *Nevertheless*, if a reader with a keen ear and a pentamerous flair can compose an example of a diesis that functions within the framework of C beyond those discussed here, I will send, by return mail, a personalized drone ring (include initials and ring size please) or its equivalent. Meanwhile, it is at least pragmatic to say that, to be tonally stable, one tone of the diesis pair must be in the twelve-note lattice of the tonal center, and the territory of the diesis must straddle the central spine.

# Triadic Harmony Associated with the Great Diesis

Three kinds of triadic harmony are associated with the Great Diesis—augmented triads, diminished seventh chords, and dominant seventh chords, each with its own orderly array. We'll discuss these in turn, culminating with a comprehensive chart in example 31.31.

## AUGMENTED CHORDS

Within the twelve-note lattice there exist four augmented triads, each balanced evenly around the Pythagorean spine. Their roots are D♭, E♭, A♭, and B♭. Each triad may be considered a stack of two major thirds, for instance, A♭–C and C–E. Looking at the lattice, we see that we could stack one more third on top of this chord, producing A♭–C–E–G♯, which results in the A♭/G♯ diesis (see example 31.24a); or we may add one more third to the bottom of the original chord, producing F♭–A♭–C–E, which results in the E/F♭ diesis (see example 31.24b).

*Example 31.24*

Since the diesis facilitates such harmonies in profusion, it can be useful to picture the entire diesis lattice as four augmented triads placed pivotally in the center of the harmonic territory, and then tipped either overtonally or reciprocally according to the needs of the music. (The typical resolutions are given in example 31.31.)

## DIMINISHED SEVENTH CHORDS

Because neither augmented triads nor diminished triads enclose harmonic territory as do major and minor triads, (which we picture on the lattice as triangles), they cannot be considered as proper triads, although they can be musically oriented to function momentarily as such. They are, rather, much looser collections of tones whose harmonic territories are open-ended and spread out over a larger area, and they thus play an important role in the dynamic ambiguities of equal temperament. As we have seen above, an augmented triad looks like a straight line—part of a *ga* spine—on the lattice. A typical diminished triad looks like example 31.25.

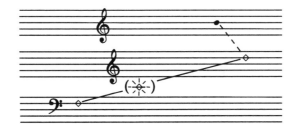

*Example 31.25*

But the same three notes on the equal-tempered keyboard could also, in a more *ga*-oriented context, imply the harmonic territory of example 31.26.

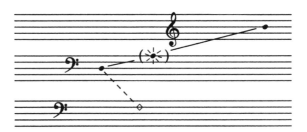

*Example 31.26*

Now, if you add A♭ to the B diminished triad of example 31.25, the chord becomes a "B diminished seventh," which resolves most convincingly to either a C-major or a C-minor triad. In example 31.27, notice the beautiful symmetry of the Bdim[7] chord around the point midway between the tonic and dominant (C and G). The resolution of the chord is nothing less than the collapse of the perimeters of the territory into the center.

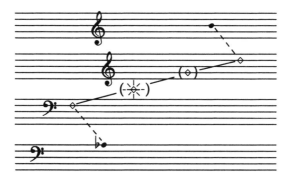

*Example 31.27*

If, however, you add G♯ to the B diminished triad of example 31.26, it becomes G♯dim[7] and encompasses the territory shown in example 31.28, collapsing inward toward either an A-major or an A-minor triad.

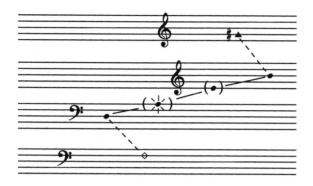

*Example 31.28*

Thanks to the A♭/G♯ diesis, then, the harmony of example 31.29 is readily available in equal temperament, within which it seems both smooth and (to us) obvious.

*Example 31.29*

Such resolutions for all the diminished seventh chords associated with our eight diesis pairs are shown in example 31.31, along with their typical resolutions.

## DOMINANT SEVENTH CHORDS

A diminished seventh chord is conventionally treated as a dominant seventh chord with an added minor ninth and a missing root. For instance, $G^{7(♭9)}$

*Example 31.30*

without the root becomes Bdim$^7$, as shown in example 31.30. Although the two chords are definitely not identical (there are indeed substantial differences in their use), their primary functions of resolution (to C in this case) so serendipitously overlap that they are considered pals, if not twins. Example 31.31 affords the opportunity to compare the elements of these related harmonies in respect to their positions on the lattice. The dominant seventh chords are shown in diesis-driven resolutions.

On the bottom brace of staves in example 31.31 is a condensed form of the diesis lattice: Each tone of the central spine of fifths, F–C–G–D, serves as central tone of a *ga* spine; that is, each tone is straddled by two major thirds above and two major thirds below. Directly above this construction are to be found the chords typically generated by these tones, listed (reading down the page) in the order we have discussed them: augmented triads, diminished seventh chords, and dominant seventh chords.

It is useful to simply play this collection of harmony straight through, reading either across (like actual music) or down (in columns). Do observe your relation to the "condensed lattice" as you play. It also may be interesting to review, in light of this overall pentamerous schema, the musical examples of chapters 30 and 31. More will become clear about the uses of pentamerous harmony as we proceed.

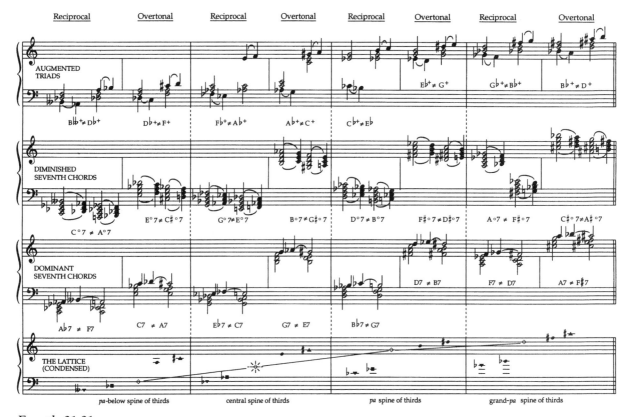

Example 31.31.
Augmented triads,
diminished seventh
chords, and dominant
seventh chords
associated with the
diesis lattice

# The Modal Truth of the Great Diesis

A further illustration of the modal dynamics between the overtonal diesis and the reciprocal diesis might help clarify the most mysterious—and perhaps most compelling—aspect of pentamerous harmony. To accomplish this, we will select and compare two dieses available from C: an overtonal diesis as seen from C Major and a reciprocal diesis as seen from C Minor.

First, imagine we are standing in C Major invoking the overtonal diesis A♭/G♯. To involve A♭, we borrow it from the *ga*-below spine of fifths, which lives in the territory of our *parallel* Minor, C Minor. The A♭/G♯ diesis then flips us to our *relative* Minor, A Minor. We have borrowed the G♯ from the *ga-ga* spine of fifths, which lives in the territory of A Major (which is in turn the parallel Major of A Minor). The salient point: *We have gone from C Major mixed with Minor to A Minor mixed with Major.* From the vantage point of C Major, it looks like figure 31.3. Even though the keys of C Major and A Minor are the central keys in the A♭/G♯ diesis, the Diesis pair itself is taken from spines adjacent to those central keys: the *ga* spines below (for A♭) and above (for G♯).

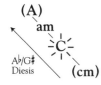

Figure 31.3

Now follow me patiently through the reciprocal language of the above situation. Imagine that we are standing in C Minor and invoking the reciprocal diesis B/C♭. To involve B, we borrow it from the *ga* spine of fifths, which lives in the territory of our *parallel* Major, C Major.

The B/C♭ diesis flips us to our *relative* Major, E♭ Major. We have borrowed the C♭ from the *ga-ga*-below spine of fifths, which lives in the territory of E♭ Minor (which in turn is the parallel Minor of E♭ Major.) The salient point: *We have gone from C Minor mixed with Major to E♭ Major mixed with Minor.* From the vantage point of C Minor, it looks like figure 31.4. Even though the keys of C Minor and E♭ Major are the central keys in the B/C♭ diesis, the diesis pair itself is taken from spines adjacent to those central keys: the *ga* spines above (for B) and below (for C♭).

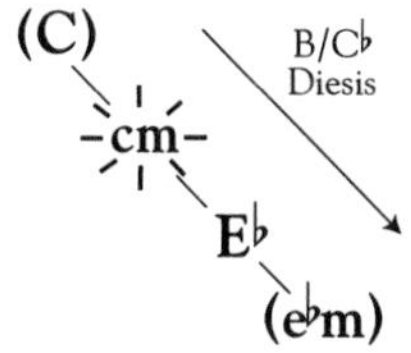

Figure 31.5 presents both situations for visual comparison. It shows the pentamerous horizon northwest and southeast while standing on the tone C. The arrows show each comma flowing round trip—outward from the tonic and then back toward it.

Even though this pentamerous reciprocity is woven with the greatest imaginable subtlety into the diesis lattice, its effects are nonetheless clearly present and entirely sensible in

*Figure 31.4*

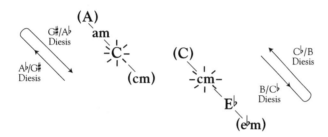

*Figure 31.5*

actual music as it is sounding. I hope this demonstration helps clarify the pentamerous harmony for the mind's eye as well as the ear. (Diesis practices at the keyboard are given in chapter 39.)

# The Uses of the Lattice

The goal is to learn to recognize the various effects of the Great Diesis and weave them with facility and confidence through your own music. My suggestion is to experiment with the diesis tones one pair at a time, beginning with A♭/G♯, until you have a repertoire of combinations involving that pair. Then try the same with D♭/C♯; next, from the reciprocal family, B/C♭, all from the vantage point of C, of course. Then E♭/D♯; then experiment with the others. Whether you practice hearing reverses of polarity or moving the diesis pairs by fifths, any direction you turn on the lattice will be a useful one.

But too much concentration on any of the commas can make you woozy—this one especially. Practicing the Great Diesis is like working in an incense factory. I recommend intense concentration over mercifully brief periods of time. Revisit and hone your compositions. Learn the other eleven keys. (Remember, it takes a decade to learn a key, so if you are assiduous you will live long.) Never lose touch with the pentamerous source. Keep a special niche in your altar for the pure major third.

Taken as a group, the Great Dieses of equal temperament have provided a mechanism for the beauty of Classical and Romantic concert music to arise out of the very temperament many feared would be the death of harmony. It is true that, given the rough approximations and maddening inflexibility of equal temperament, something did die. We lost the deep resonances, and in the process became sadly distanced from some primal part of ourselves. But in that same process, an astonishingly affective musical language was born.

Pentamerous harmony has been not only the glory of equal temperament but also, more recently, its undoing. The role that the equal-tempered major third has played historically in the development, transformation, and eventual unraveling of tonal harmony will be discussed later, especially (in part 4) in respect to cyclic and symmetrical harmony.

# 32

# THE DIASCHISMA

THE THIRD (AND LAST) OF THE COMMAS functional in twelve-tone equal temperament is the diaschisma, the amount by which three octaves exceeds four perfect fifths and two major thirds (see chapter 27). Our study of the diaschisma will differ somewhat from our study of the Didymic comma and the Great Diesis primarily because the harmonic territory that the diaschismic pairs of tones encompass is so vast. The immediate result of the harmonic shift occurring over so wide an area is that the affective zap is attenuated: The longer the distance the weaker the signal. Furthermore, the tonal ambiguity is heightened; contexts in which the diaschisma occurs can easily jeopardize the stability of the tonal center or even set it spinning. Although these events are difficult to produce and rarely heard in just intonation, equal temperament is well suited to convey their harmonic meanings, and nineteenth-century European harmony thrives on them.

## Singing through the D♭/C♯ Diaschisma in Just Intonation

So large is the harmonic compass of the diaschisma, in fact, that with narrow exceptions, pairs of diaschismic tones do not exist within the same tonal center, at least not in dronality. But there is a single case where singing through the comma in dronal just intonation is very useful. Sing and play at the keyboard example 32.1.

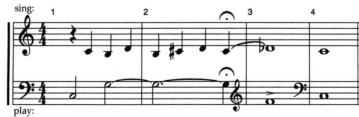

*Example 32.1*

Sing the D of bar 1 as the 9:8 *re*. In bar 2, the C♯ has to make 45:32 with the G; that is, it needs to be the *tivra ma*, or augmented fourth, of the G Lydian mode. The other tones in the melody will help to evoke the Lydian quality. When you come to the downbeat of bar 3, transform the note you are singing into the D♭ a pure major third below F, which is to say, the *komal re*, or minor second, of the C Phrygian mode. If the played pitches were tuned in just intonation, your voice would rise about twenty cents in singing through the comma from C♯ to D♭. But if you use the equal-tempered keyboard, the tuning adds about four cents to the comma, actually making it a little more sensible for the singer; it's nice, for a change, to get an equal-tempered break in our favor. In any case, if we call the C♯ "super-Lydian" (a fifth higher than the Lydian F♯), then we might say that the comma spans a *Super-Lydian/Phrygian* compass, as demonstrated in example 32.2.

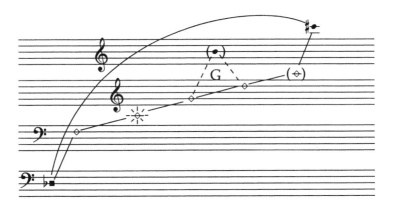

*Example 32.2*

This Super-Lydian/Phrygian type of diaschismic function takes place (if marginally) within a *modal* context; in this case, for instance, both the C♯ and the D♭ are heard in reference to C. But there is another, more familiar diaschismic function that is typically a *modulatory* device; it is used expressly to catapult the ear away from the tonal center. Historically, from the late eighteenth century on, as the affective possibilities of equal temperament were discovered by European composers and unveiled in their music, this modulatory usage became more and more frequent. To understand it fully we must briefly examine, and perhaps redefine, certain common harmonic practices.

## The Dominant Seventh Chord

We all know that the dominant seventh chord has the power to "resolve" to the tonic chord, thus heightening the sense of the tonic as the tonal center, but there is not much general agreement as to why it does so. One camp says that in a $G^7$ the F is naturally heard as the seventh partial of G (21:16 with C; *blu ma* to us) because that tone results in a pure, beatless tuning. Another camp says that F is actually the subdominant of C (4:3 with C), which not only generates less consonance, but also causes a harmonic discontinuity to appear. Notice that, on the harmonic map of $G^7$, the subdominant tone F is thus a kind of spur of the dominant triad, as example 32.3 shows.

Some theorists recognize that both explanations are useful, but in differing musical contexts. As we have already discussed (in chapters 17 and 26), the seventh-partial version is preferred in blues and blues-flavored jazz not

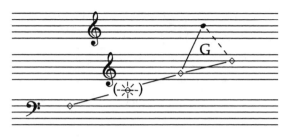

*Example 32.3*

only on the G triad but also on the C and F triads (the septimal B♭ and E♭, respectively). The F⁷ is specifically *not* a "dominant seventh" chord in that the function of its root is not to fall by a fifth. It rises inevitably to the tonic: It is a *sub*dominant seventh. When one realizes that the C⁷, although it has the *option* of falling a fifth, often does not but in fact stands tall as a perfectly correct final chord, one realizes the truth: The seventh partial is a *blu*-blooded native ancestor who resides in the overtone series and doesn't have to "resolve" anywhere.

What is less understood is why the 4:3 *ma*, added to the dominant chord, has such a fine resolving power to C. My answer is that the "resolution" required to power the perfect cadence is not so much a matter of consonance or dissonance as one of harmonic opposition; cadential energy thrives best when its harmonic material straddles the tonic along the Pythagorean spine in such a way that it *collapses* toward the center. In the previous chapter we mentioned "collapsing" diminished seventh chords; dominant seventh chords provide an even more basic example. A dominant triad will fall toward the center in any case; but when the subdominant tone is added to the mix, the total force becomes not just a fall but a contraction, not unlike the force felt when a rubber band is slipped over one's thumb and index finger and held apart.

Tonality doesn't depend on rubber bands, it depends on tonal gravity. A collapse toward the center is another way of speaking of gravitational attraction—in this case, the tonal gravity of the tonic. The sine qua non of tonality in music is the tonal gravity of the tonic, just as certainly as the sine qua non of earthly life is the gravity of the Earth. Could musical tonality be a psychoacoustic metaphor for planetary gravity? Is that why it seems so completely to nurture us?

Let us accept as a working hypothesis, at least, that the 4:3 tuning for *ma* shown in example 32.3 vivifies the force that drives cadences and cadential modulation.

## Augmented Sixth Chords

We'll now examine the doppelgänger of the dominant seventh chord: its diaschismic partner, the "augmented sixth" chord. Over the centuries, classical music theory has developed a wide variety of misleading concepts, but in no area has its collective wisdom more widely missed the mark (or caused more flunking out of theory class) than in the subject of so-called augmented sixth chords. The harmony we wish to reexamine sounds typically like example 32.4.

*Example 32.4*

The F♯ was originally heard, toward the end of the seventeenth century, as a euphonious, melodic passing tone between F and G. Since it also contains palpable harmonic value, it soon achieved its own harmonic identity. It came eventually to be theoretically understood as a "chromatic variation" of the minor subdominant triad in first inversion, that is to say, an F-minor "six three" chord, or simply "sixth chord" with a "chromatic alteration" of the root, F.

In example 32.5, for instance, the first chord becomes the second chord.

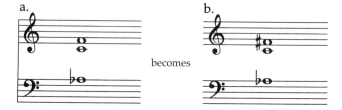

*Example 32.5*

When a type of harmony is baffling or utterly mysterious, it is often referred to, by convention, as a "chromatic variation," or better yet, as "altered." Dr. Overtone eschews such terminology. To him, the harmonic map of an augmented sixth chord behaves as shown in example 32.6.

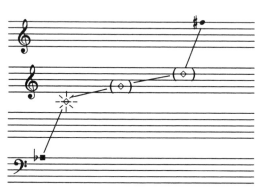

*Example 32.6*

Here we have a clear case of harmonic forces straddling the center. The F♯ does not relate primarily to A♭ but to C, just as surely as the A♭ relates to C. The F♯ pushes downward as the A♭ pulls upward; or one might say that C attracts both tones inward toward itself. The damage is done (and this explains the Doctor's pique) by a misleading name: To define the F♯ in terms of A♭ as a root is at best misleading. Harmony students weep with confusion, and rightly so, because the interval of the augmented sixth, which does indeed occur between the A♭ and the F♯, is not what structures the sound. What structures the sound is the mixture of overtonal and reciprocal energy within the same (not necessarily triadic) collection of tones. Furthermore, since the chord has come to be conceived as a triad based on A♭, that is, the ♭VI triad of C, it looks like this on paper: ♭VI#6—and when people say it, they tend to refer to the "flat six sharp six chord," not making a verbal distinction between Roman and Arabic numerals and further confusing those they wish to enlighten. File this in the dossier of cases where harmonic events are identified by means of melodic, that is, intervalic, names.

If Dr. Overtone were to rename the chord he would look for something like "Lydian-minor," but he is not going to try. Would he then have to rename dominant seventh chords "dominant-subdominant"? The Doctor realistically, if sadly, realizes that pragmatic names for collections of tones, triadic or not, cannot convey the entirety of their harmonic significance. We will let "augmented sixth chord" stand as an unfortunate fact of language, like someone's infelicitous surname that never goes away: Harold Snide, as fine a valedictorian as ever graduated from Analy High. We will also, regretfully, use the conventional "♭VI" to stand for harmony rooted on the minor sixth degree, regardless of the spelling of its actual notes.

There are three commonly recognized versions of the augmented sixth chord, called (with no authentic historical or geographical basis) Italian, German, and French; example 32.7 gives all three in the key of C.

*Example 32.7*

Example 32.8 is the map of all the tones in these three versions combined. The German version makes clear how well the overtonal F# can mix with the reciprocal pentamerous harmony of the parallel minor of C. To Dr. Overtone's nearly continuous consternation, the E♭ is not only often misspelled as D# by composers but also analyzed by teachers as if the D# had tonal function in C. (Basic misunderstandings like this remind us why resonance needs to be revived.) All of the sev-

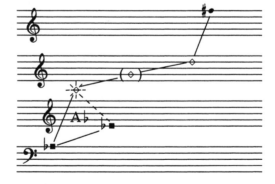

*Example 32.8*

enth chords and augmented sixth chords we have been discussing in this chapter are easy to tune and sing. When you experience the true harmony for yourself, the analysis is clear and the misspelling is obvious.

The French version is especially intriguing because of its clear symmetry around the dominant, as seen in example 32.9. By looking at the map, you can almost feel with your eyes the mutual tug of the tones toward the dominant (to which the chord characteristically

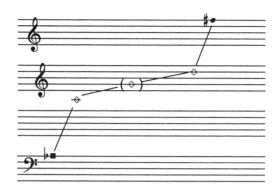

*Example 32.9*

resolves). The French sixth is actually as much a D chord as it is an A♭ chord, and the lustrous beauty of its tension in just intonation simply cannot be described. It retains much of its allure in equal temperament, and it stands as an elegant model of complementary harmonic tension (as opposed to triadically conceived consonance and dissonance) as the engine of cadential energy.

But why are we dealing with these particular engines at this particular time?

# The Ambiguity of Function between Dominant Seventh Chords and Augmented Sixth Chords

It is clear by playing a "German sixth" chord at the keyboard that, out of context, it appears to be something much more prosaic, namely an A♭7, or the V7 of D♭. And indeed, the ♭VI function of an augmented-sixth type chord and the V function of a dominant-seventh type chord can, in equal temperament, be magically melded into one event. When that happens, the diaschisma is invoked. This is the "more familiar" type of diaschismic function I referred to above; we can call it the augmented-sixth/dominant-seventh function, or the aug6/7 function. (This will sometimes occur with the terms reversed, i.e., "the 7/aug6 function.")

We are now prepared to examine the array of diaschismas centered around C. A diaschisma contains within its compass two major thirds. There are two families of diaschismic harmony. As we saw in the case of the Great Diesis, which also has two families, what distinguishes one diaschismic family from the other is the position of the major thirds in relation to the tonal center.

In the case of a diaschisma, when one major third lies above the central spine of fifths and the other lies below, the resulting harmony belongs to the *ga*-balanced diaschisma family. The *ga*-balanced family contains examples of both types of diaschismic function we have defined above ("Super-Lydian/Phrygian" and "aug6/7").

When *both* major thirds lie above the central spine of fifths, the resulting harmony belongs to the *ga-ga* diaschisma family. This family contains only type: the aug6/7 function.

I know this is a barrage of information, but the sound of the music itself will lead us eventually to a clear perception of diaschismic harmony.

# The *Ga*-Balanced Family of Diaschismas

## THE DIASCHISMA OF THE AUGMENTED FOURTH/
## DIMINISHED FIFTH: F♯/G♭

Play example 32.10.

*Example 32.10*

In bar 1, the F on the third beat is the 4:3 *ma*. It passes, on the next beat, to the 45:32 *tivra ma*, which sounds simultaneously with the 8:5 A♭, the reciprocal third of C. The mixture of overtonal and reciprocal energy is what to listen for. For a guaranteed thrill, sing up to the downbeat of bar 3 (but no further for now) with two other in-tune friends, and experience the dramatic tension of the A♭ and the F♯ releasing, by half steps in contrary motion, to the octave G. It is this dramatic quality, this exquisite pull of opposites in both melodic and harmonic realms, that characterizes the "augmented sixth" function. In bar 2, the third pulse completes a deceptive cadence, V–♭VI; the harmony of bar 1 is reestablished and then, in bar 3, reiterated once again in an abbreviated and redistributed form. The bass of the fourth beat of bar 3 is heard as F♯ at first, since that is the context that has been set up, but by the downbeat of bar 4 the ear remembers the previous chord not as the ♭VI♯$^6$ in C but as the V$^7$ of D♭, which uses, as its seventh, the 64:45 G♭. This is immediately confirmed in the next two beats: We are momentarily perched on D♭. This kind of harmonic function is the aug6/7 type of diaschisma. Example 32.11 is a map of the diaschisma that occurs between the F♯ and the G♭, along with the other tones and triads in example 32.10.

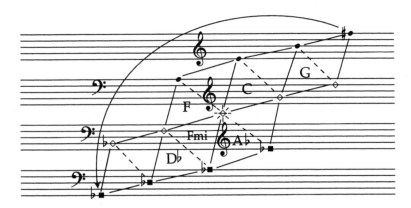

*Example 32.11*

Notice how the effect of the diaschisma is distributed over the bar line between bars 3 and 4. In equal temperament, the clearly overtonal augmented fourth becomes the deeply reciprocal diminished fifth with no change of pitch. In this study we have so far generally excluded G♭ from the tonal palette of C because it is almost impossible to recognize without moving the tonal center in the reciprocal direction; indeed, in the passage we are considering, D♭ must be convincingly tonicized for the G♭ to be evoked and the diaschisma to appear. The diaschisma in this example, and generally in this type of function in this family, helps to propel us reciprocally away from C.

Notice also how, at the final beat of bar 4, the alto plays B, the leading tone of C. The note is obviously not C♭, and the chord containing it is thus correctly named D♭ aug6 * and not D♭7, a distinction that is made in classical analysis as a matter of course, but never in the nomenclature of jazz, contributing both to its pragmatic simplicity and its theoretical opacity.

Play this example enough times to clarify the comma; also play the parts individually. This type of diaschisma is definitely in the category of tricky harmony, the kind that the European ear came to love (and overlove) in the nineteenth century. To understand that culture's music, and the music it influenced throughout the world, you need to understand the trick. The *best* trick, however, is to be able to distinguish and identify the characteristic zap of the diaschisma so that it becomes a hands-on tool in equal temperament.

We have been emphasizing that there are two types of diaschismic function within the *ga*-balanced overtonal family. Indeed, both types can occur through the agency of the F♯/G♭ diaschisma. We have just seen an example of the aug6/7 type; example 32.12 shows the Super-Lydian/Phrygian type.

*Example 32.12*

As in the previous example, the F♯ (in bar 1) is the 45:32 augmented fourth, and the G♭ (in bar 2) becomes the 64:45 diminished fifth. But the triads involved in this harmonic function are different from those of the aug6/7 type of function, and the feeling seems to be as modal as it is modulatory. (Does it leave C?) Example 32.13 is a harmonic map of the tones used in example 32.12. Compare it with example 32.11: same diaschismic pair of tones, different harmonic context.

Since the G♭ is the tone used in the Phrygian of the subdominant, let's call this function the Lydian/Sub-Phrygian function, to keep it consistent with the name Super-Lydian/ Phrygian of example 32.2 (which is the same type of harmony but lies a fifth higher: two peas in a pod). Notice that the chord on the last pulse of bar 2, which in root position would be spelled G♭–B♭–D♭–E, is an augmented sixth chord based on the ♭II of F, that is, a Phrygian cadence to the subdominant.

---

*Even though I have relented in the case of "♭VI," I cannot bring myself to use the conventional "♯6" sign when there is no actual sharp in the spelling.

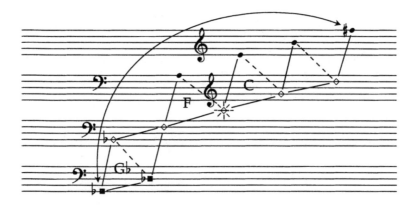

*Example 32.13*

In its simplest form, the extremely symmetrical diaschismic pair of example 32.14 could be what we are hearing in the jazz context. This subject came up before, in chapter 26 (p. 235). What do you think this time around?

*Example 32.14*

Now let's move our entire diaschismic picnic up a fifth.

## THE DIASCHISMA OF THE AUGMENTED TONIC/ MINOR SECOND: C♯/D♭

Example 32.15 is an example of the augmented-sixth chord harmony for the C♯/D♭ pair.

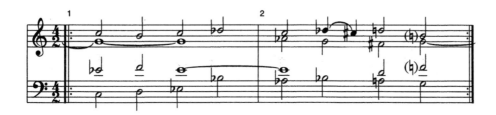

*Example 32.15*

In bar 2 the D♭ on the second beat is the 16:15 *komal re*; it is also the subdominant of the 8:5 A♭. It is immediately remembered, however, as the Super-Lydian C♯ (135:128) resolving to the 9:8 D, whose leading tone it is. Example 32.16 is a more direct use. Note that in both of the above examples the dominant-seventh type chord precedes the augmented sixth, so they are called 7/aug6 functions.

*Example 32.16*

Example 32.17 is the harmonic map of the tones and triads in examples 32.15 and 32.16. The effect of this augmented-sixth harmony is sweet and bright. It is in progressions such

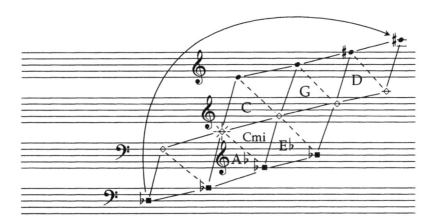

**Example 32.17**

as these that the quality of equal temperament becomes wholly endearing, as if the monstrous, gnarly thing we were forced to adopt in order to play our keyboards and effect our modulations was beginning to show, by means of these agreeable sonorities, the true generosity of its nature.

I must mention an early use of this diaschisma; it occurs in a gorgeous and economical way in the B Minor Fugue that concludes Book 1 of Bach's *Well-Tempered Clavier*. For purposes of comparison with other examples in this book, and with my apologies to the composer, example 32.18 gives the opening subject transposed to C Minor.

**Example 32.18**

The D♭ of F Minor (which is tonicized in bar 2) becomes C♯, the leading tone to the dominant of G Minor (which is tonicized in bar 3), and all this in a single voice. Bach loved the harmonic possibilities that exist between two Minor keys separated by two fifths (e.g., F Minor and G Minor). As far as we know, he favored temperaments that were not equal but weighted toward certain tonal centers (theorists call these "well temperaments"; hence the name of Bach's collection). Throughout his music he negotiated all the commas without compromising the spelling. He knew precisely what he was hearing. The man tuned his own keyboards; harmonic resonance was still alive and well in Bach's brain. A generation after his death in 1750, equal-tempered tuning was becoming the rule rather than the exception. Diaschismas were flying about all over Europe, and spelling errors were rife in published music. What a blessing and curse is twelve-tone equal temperament!

The C♯/D♭ diaschismic pair, like the F♯/G♭ pair we have just studied, also manifests a Super-Lydian/Phrygian type of function in equal temperament. We have already touched on this while learning to sing the diaschisma in just intonation. Example 32.19 is the equal-tempered version.

The map of all the tones and triads in example 32.19 is shown in example 32.20. Compare it with the map of the G♭/F♯ pair (example 32.13).

*Example 32.19*

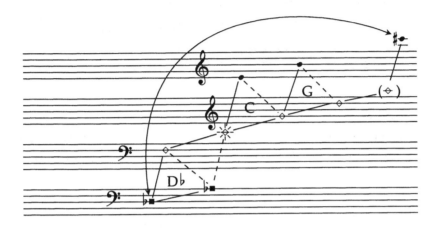

*Example 32.20*

Notice that in example 32.19 the C♯ appears first and the D♭ subsequently, so that the energy flows downward. Example 32.21 is an example showing how the polarity can reverse in this pair.

*Example 32.21*

In this diaschismic pair, the modal aspect of the Super-Lydian/Phrygian type of function is especially clear, because C♯ and D♭ are both clearly within the tonal domain of C. The D♭ 16:15 is, of course, part of the twelve-note lattice. The C♯ is one fifth beyond the overtonal boundary of the lattice, but is convincingly invoked when it is closely wedded to the dominant G. The energy of the comma seems to flow easily in both directions entirely within the domain of C. Example 32.22 is a jazz version that even contrives to use both tones simultaneously.

*Example 32.22*

## THE DIASCHISMA OF THE MINOR SIXTH/
## AUGMENTED FIFTH: A♭/G♯

The diaschismic pair A♭/G♯ can generate the 7/aug6 type of harmony in one special case: if the augmented sixth chord is based on the ♭VI of the V of V. Study example 32.23.

*Example 32.23*

The first two bars of example 32.23 set up the MI/MA mode of C, which includes the 8:5 A♭. In bar 3 the A♭ is remembered as G♯, the leading tone of the Pythagorean A, which proceeds downward by fifths: A[7]–D[7]–G[7]–C.*

The G♯/A♭ diaschismic pair also manifests a Super-Lydian/Phrygian type of function. Just as D is a fifth higher than G, example 32.24 is a fifth higher than example 32.19, and we could hence call G♯/A♭ the Supra-Super-Lydian/Minor pair. Its energy can flow both ways.

*Example 32.24*

Example 32.25 is the harmonic map of the tones in example 32.24. (Compare it with example 32.20).

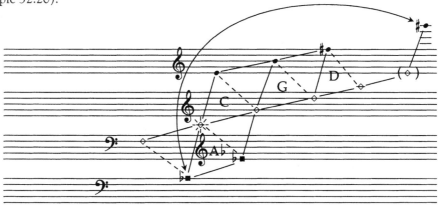

*Example 32.25*

*Ordinarily the augmented sixth chord built from the ♭VII—B♭♯[6] in the key of C—proceeds via A[7] to D *minor,* which functions, at least when first heard, as the relative minor of the subdominant. That would occur if the F♯ in the soprano of bar 4 were F♮ for the entire bar; if this were the case, the comma between A♭ and G♯ would be the Great Diesis, not the diaschisma. Notice that the two target D's in question (the V/V, 9:8, as opposed to the vi/IV, 10:9) are positioned a Didymic comma from one another. Does this mean that the difference between the diaschisma, which is evoked in the first case, and the Great Diesis which is evoked in the second case, is a Didymic comma? The answer—both conceptually delightful and musically obscure—is yes.

## THE DIASCHISMA OF THE MAJOR SEVENTH/
## DIMINISHED OCTAVE: B/C♭

The portrait of the *ga*-balanced family of diaschismas is completed by the most subdominant of the group, B/C♭, which catapults the energy reciprocally away from C. Study example 32.26.

*Example 32.26*

Bar 1 sets us up to expect the last eighth note of bar 2 to be B♮, but it is instead its diaschismic partner, C♭, modulating us decisively away from C into G♭. In bar 3 the energy comes back the other way. Example 32.27 is the harmonic map.

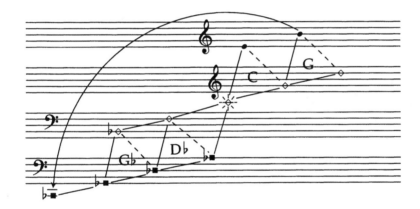

*Example 32.27*

Playing this example over and over gives a kind of yo-yo effect, casting the energy down and away but still attached to us by the strong, thin diaschismic string, then snapping it back to where we can grasp it. Since the harmony is subdominant in essence, we could call this the Yo-Yo *Ma* Effect—but nah, we won't.

## THE FAMILY PORTRAIT OF GA-BALANCED DIASCHISMAS

Example 32.28, a compilation of the maps that have been presented so far in this chapter, shows the entire array of the four *ga*-balanced diaschismic pairs within the domain of C.

Notice that each diaschismic pair contains one reciprocal tone in the *ga*-below spine of fifths and its overtonal partner in the *ga* spine of fifths: C♭/B, G♭/F♯, D♭/C♯, and A♭/G♯. Arrows showing the direction of the harmonic energy connect the partners. The only difference between the pairs is their position in relation to the tonal center, C. Notice how, as usual, the available harmony is somewhat skewed toward the overtonal side: We hear overtones more easily than reciprocal tones.

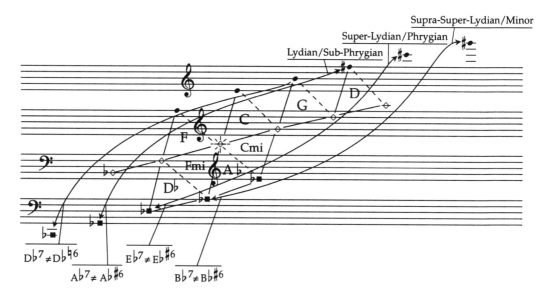

*Example 32.28*

The *ga*-balanced family yields four cases of the modulatory, augmented-sixth/dominant-seventh type of ambiguity: $D^{\flat 7} \neq D^{\flat \text{aug}6}$; $A^{\flat 7} \neq A^{\flat \text{aug}6}$; $E^{\flat 7} \neq E^{\flat \text{aug}6}$; and $B^{\flat 7} \neq B^{\flat \text{aug}6}$. These terms are shown at the bottom of the map, connected to the diaschismic pair responsible for their function.

The *ga*-balanced family also yields three cases of the modal, Super-Lydian/Phrygian type of ambiguity: Lydian/Sub-Phrygian (which involves both C-major and $G^{\flat}$-major triads); Super-Lydian/Phrygian (which involves G-major and $D^{\flat}$-major triads); and Supra-Super-Lydian/Minor (which involves D-major and $A^{\flat}$-major triads). These terms are shown at the top of the map, appropriately connected to their diaschismic agents.

This may seem like a lot of harmony to learn, and I guess it is; but remember that there are only two different types in this family, a modal type and a modulatory type; even if you recognize only one example of each, you still have the essence. What remains is largely a matter of repositioning by fifths, which changes the flavor but not the essential quality of the harmony. Your best strategy is immersion in the music itself. As usual, learn to play the models, then elaborate them improvisationally, then experiment on your own. If you are unclear about where you are in your travels, check the map.

## The *Ga-Ga* Family of Diaschismas in C

Each diaschismic pair in the second family of diaschismas, the *ga-ga* family, contains a stack of two thirds above the central spine of fifths. All of the harmony generated by this family catapults the harmonic energy overtonally away from C. It is all clearly modulatory; there are no modal examples. Consequently, there is only one type of diaschismic function, namely, the 7/aug6 ambiguity. There are three cases only; we will begin with the most overtonal case and work our way down by fifths.

## THE DOMINANT SEVENTH AND THE F/E♯ DIASCHISMA

Consider the progression in example 32.29.

*Example 32.29*

In bar 1, the second chord is obviously V⁷. When it appears again on the fourth beat it is again heard as V⁷, but then, in memory, as the ♭VIᵃᵘᵍ⁶ of B Minor. The diaschisma has hurled the energy overtonally away from C. The map of that moment is shown in example 32.30.

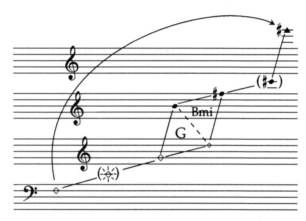

*Example 32.30*

Notice that the symmetry of the diaschismic pair lies precisely around the tone B. Realize also that F, that is, the subdominant of C, which has been added to the dominant triad G major for cadential efficacy, is allowed by the equal-tempered diaschisma to be heard as E♯, the leading tone of the dominant of B (one might say the Lydian note of B). It is that very tone, B, that stands exactly halfway between the wildly divergent diaschismic partners, F/E♯. Furthermore, the entire zap is smooth as silk. No muss, no fuss; you thought you were in C, but now you are in B Minor, which is, of course, so close to G that you can modulate back home through the entirely convincing D⁷–G⁷–C cadence. Thus does equal temperament allow E♯, an impossibly distant *ga-ga* harmony entirely outside the domain of dronal just intonation, to connect with and flow effortlessly from F, four perfect fifths and two major thirds below. Equal temperament is amazing.

## THE V⁷/IV AND THE B♭/A♯ DIASCHISMA

Consider the progression in example 32.31. In bar 1, the chord at the fourth beat is heard as C⁷, the V⁷/IV, but then is immediately remembered as Cᵃᵘᵍ⁶, the ♭VI/iii. The diaschisma lobs the harmonic energy overtonally away from C (example 32.32).

*Example 32.31*

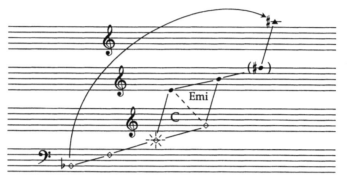

*Example 32.32*

The symmetry of the diaschismic pair is now balanced around the tone E; the entire event is positioned a fifth lower than the previous case (examples 32.30 and 32.31).

## THE V⁷/IV/IV AND THE E♭/D♯ DIASCHISMA

Next in order of descending fifths is the E♭/D♯ diaschisma. This case is slightly different: Whereas G⁷ and C⁷ are dominant-seventh functions that normally resolve to primary triads in C, F⁷ does not (except in blues, where it is not a falling dominant seventh but a rising septimal seventh). The harmony in example 32.33 is unusual but sensible.

*Example 32.33*

The comma occurs on the second beat of bar 3; the map of that moment is shown in example 32.34.

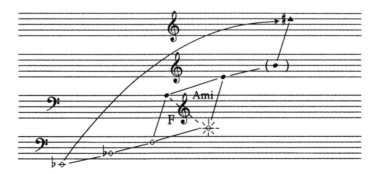

*Example 32.34*

As in the B♭/A♯ diaschisma of the previous case, the energy moves overtonally, although this time the symmetry is centered around the 5:3 A, and both diaschismic partners are about equally far from home.

Incidentally, the occurrence of ♭VI^aug6/vi harmony—that is, augmented-sixth harmony based on the minor sixth degree of the relative minor—is not unusual when it involves not the diaschisma but the Great Diesis, an example of which is given, for purposes of comparison, in 32.35.

*Example 32.35*

This harmony is akin to (and a fifth higher than) the harmony mentioned on page 328 (example 32.23).

## THE GA-GA DIASCHISMA FAMILY PORTRAIT

Example 32.36 combines the trio of *ga-ga* diaschismic pairs into a *Ga-Ga* Family Portrait.

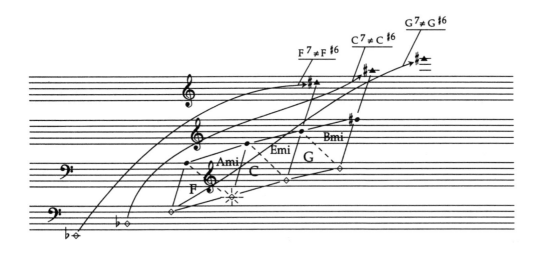

*Example 32.36*

The *ga-ga* family yields three cases of the modulatory, dominant-seventh/augmented-sixth type of ambiguity: $G^7 \neq G^{aug6}$; $C^7 \neq C^{aug6}$; and $F^7 \neq F^{aug6}$. These terms are shown at the top of the map, connected to the diaschismic pair responsible for their function. It will help, in understanding this harmony, to review the musical examples of this family not only in the order of descending fifths (starting with $G^7$, as given in example 32.29) but also by ascending fifths (starting with $F^7$, as given in example 32.33).

## The Array of Diaschismic Pairs in C

We have now exhausted the possibilities of diaschismic harmony in the domain of C.* The two harmonic families—the *ga*-balanced family and the *ga-ga* family—are combined in example 32.37, showing only the diaschismic pairs themselves (plus C), so that you can see at a glance the range and symmetry of this comma.

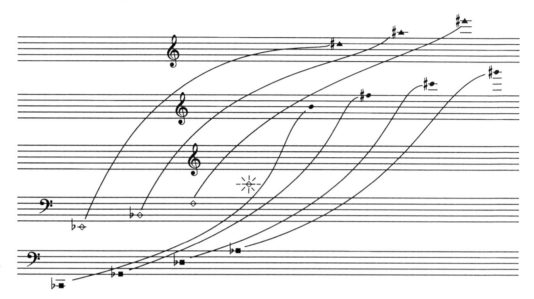

*Example 32.37*

The four pairs of the *ga*-balanced family (lower and to the right) propel the harmony reciprocally away from C by means of aug6/7 (or 7/aug6) ambiguity. In addition, all but the most subdominant pair (B/C♭) belonging to this family have a modal function that allows reversals of polarity within an expanded C domain.

The three pairs of the *ga-ga* family (higher and to the left) propel the harmony overtonally away from C by means of 7/aug6 ambiguity.

## The Power of the Diaschisma

In its affective power, the harmony of the diaschisma lies somewhere between that of the Didymic comma and the Great Diesis. It is much more robust and obstreperous than the Didymic comma, which contains only one pure third instead of two, yet it is not so compellingly expressive as the Great Diesis, which contains three pure thirds.

Although one learns all comma phenomena slowly over the years, it is not unusual to learn diaschisma harmony especially slowly. This is undoubtedly due not only to its wide range but also to the particulars of its use in actual music. The modulatory dominant-seventh/augmented-sixth type of ambiguity that was so characteristic of nineteenth century

---

*The unique case of a cadential *ga-ga*-below diaschismic pair of *triads* (E♭♭/D) will be demonstrated in chapter 38.

music and the popular forms that sprang from it (including popular music appropriated by early jazz musicians) is out of fashion today, and when you hear it in contemporary music, it's often perceived as a historical allusion. The modal type of usage is more current, however, and remains in the practical lexicon of harmonic moves. Of course, harmonic fashions are as predictable as wind. Historical allusion itself, for instance, has become fashionable as the twentieth century recedes into the past. But don't be guided by fashion. Learn diaschismic harmony not because it is current but because it is part of the geography of the mind.

The good news is that, except for a few nooks and crannies, we have explored the entire array of harmonic possibilities in equal-tempered tonality. We won't celebrate, however. Not just yet.

# 33

## QUASI-FUNCTIONAL AND NONFUNCTIONAL COMMAS

DOES THE LIST OF FUNCTIONAL COMMAS that allow twelve equal-tempered tones to stand for many more end abruptly at three? Almost, but not quite.

## Is There a Septimal Comma?

Septimal harmony arises from harmonic ratios that contain the prime seven. It has caught the ear of many contemporary composers who use just intonation; they are quick to point out its undiscovered pleasures and as yet untrammeled byways. But septimal harmony, even in its most basic manifestations, can scarcely be made to appear in equal temperament. The seventh partial of C is thirty-one cents flat from the equal-tempered B♭, more of a divergence from its equal-tempered stand-in than any tone we have met on the five-limit lattice—the 25:24 C♯ is a close runner-up at thirty cents, and you remember what a tough time we had bringing *it* forward in equal temperament. (How the septimal B♭ can be invoked on the keyboard is discussed in chapter 26.) The question is, given these very narrow limits, can there ever be a septimal comma in equal temperament? The answer is: In jazz, yes, there are three types of septimal comma, and each type has its own niche in the style.

## The Septimal Seventh/ Dominant Seventh Comma, 64:63

The first type of septimal comma occurs when a $C^7$ is set up as a septimal tonic seventh but is subsequently treated as a $V^7/IV$, as shown in example 33.1. The harmonies of the first three

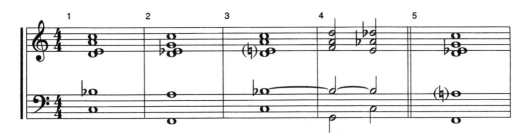

*Example 33.1*

bars suggest septimal sevenths for each chord, which means that the tuning for the B♭ in bar 3 is 7:4.* But the ear soon remembers that tone as the subdominant of F, that is, the 16:9 B♭, because of the clear tonicization of F (including some borrowing from F Minor) that has occurred by bar 5. Example 33.2 is a map of the comma. Remember that septimal harmony, generated by the new prime seven, must have a lattice dimension of its own. Septimal tones should be visualized as hovering above the page, their plane vertically intersecting the five-limit lattice.

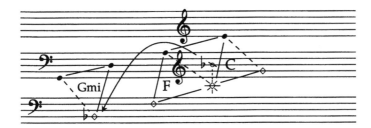

*Example 33.2*

In just intonation, this comma is the amount by which two perfect fifths down (octave-juggled into two fourths up) exceeds 7:4, or $(\frac{4}{3} \times \frac{4}{3}) \div \frac{7}{4} = \frac{64}{63} = 64{:}63$. It is generally known as the septimal comma, and has its primary uses in just intonation, but it does show up at the equal-tempered jazz keyboard when a septimal seventh turns into a dominant seventh.

The example above lets you hear the ease with which septimally inflected blues harmony, or *blu* harmony, intertwines with five-limit harmony, and how well equipped equal temperament is, within the context of the jazz aesthetic, to stand for the mixed functions of *pa*, *ga*, and *blu*. Additionally, singers as well as players of variable pitch instruments make the tuning adjustments necessary to bring out the true tuning of *blu* harmony, often moving accurately and evocatively through the comma, leaning into the notes with the seemingly effortless strokes of a long-distance swimmer. From the septimal (7:4) B♭ to the dominant-seventh (16:9) B♭ is a rise in pitch of twenty-seven cents. I first heard its buoyant, brightening effect played by Lester Young (1909–59), a.k.a. "Prez" (because he was the President of the Tenor Saxophone), so for me, this is Prez's comma.

Incidentally, the *blu* F⁷ is not treated the same way. A *blu* F⁷, in order to have been *blu*, must return to C, and will not become the V⁷ of B♭. Nor does the *blu* G⁷, which is typically allowed to resolve directly to the 5:4 pure third of the tonic chord, seem to be a part of this

*I say "suggest" because we associate these voicings with the jazz style; would the same harmonies heard by Bach in 1730 have suggested septimal harmony to him? Unlikely. What *would* equal-tempered keyboard jazz have sounded like to Bach? Lukewarm, I think, though I'll bet he would have been deeply drawn to the tonal nuances of the singers and players of variable pitch instruments.

comma phenomena. In equal temperament, the distinction between the *blu* G[7] and the dominant G[7] doesn't seem to come across.

# The *Blu*/Minor Comma, 36:35

The second type of septimal comma occurs between *blu* tones and their comma partners in the *ga*-below spine of fifths. There are two such cases, one based on the tonic triad and the other on the subdominant triad.

### THE TONIC SEPTIMAL SEVENTH/GA-BELOW MINOR SEVENTH: B♭

This harmony occurs when the *blu* B♭ (7:4) becomes the minor seventh B♭ of the C Minor scale (9:5). The ratio is $\frac{9}{5} \div \frac{7}{4} = \frac{36}{35} = 36:35$, which we will call the *blu*/minor comma. The pitch difference is almost exactly a quarter tone: forty-nine cents, larger even than that of the Great Diesis, and indeed *blu*/minor translates into the most beautiful equal-tempered harmony, as shown in example 33.3.

*Example 33.3*

The first chord is heard as the *blu* C[7]; the second is V[7] with reciprocal *ga* harmony borrowed from the parallel minor (C Minor). Notice how the two B♭'s are in different registers here.

Example 33.4 is the map of all the tones, showing their elegant symmetry around C and G.

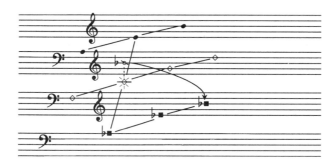

*Example 33.4*

### THE SUBDOMINANT SEPTIMAL SEVENTH/MINOR THIRD: E♭

The same *blu*/minor harmony a fifth down on the lattice occurs in the progression shown in

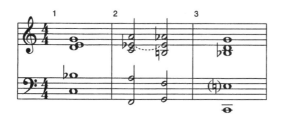

*Example 33.5*

example 33.5. Unlike example 33.3, the comma appears here in the same register: The 7:6 *blu* E♭ becomes the 6:5 E♭ (from the parallel Minor of C) on the second chord of bar 2, G7[(♭9)(♭13)].

You can hear an astonishingly clear version of this deeply moving *blu*/minor mix in just intonation by singing in tune and playing on the piano as shown in example 33.6.

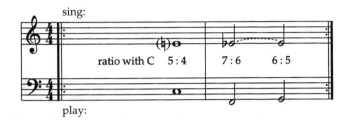

*Example 33.6*

At the moment of the comma in bar 2, the voice will lead upward by forty-nine cents from the 7:6 E♭ to the 6:5 E♭, and from there it is only seventy more cents to the E♮ 5:4. Example 33.7 is a map of these tones.

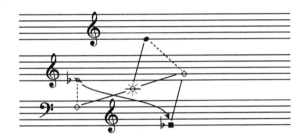

*Example 33.7*

Example 33.8 is one more instance of the *blu*/minor comma on E♭, a use characteristic of 1930s jazz.

*Example 33.8*

# The *Blu/Ga-Ga* Comma, 225:224

There is one more jazz comma involving the 7:6 E♭, which, though remote, is surprisingly evocative in equal temperament. Play example 33.9.

*Example 33.9*

In bar 2, the *blu* function of the septimal E♭ is transformed by context into D♯, the leading tone of the V of vi; that is, F *blu* becomes F^aug6. E♭ 7:6 thus becomes D♯ 75:64, a move that is only seven cents upward in just intonation, but is harmonically a shift involving a septimal seventh, two fifths and two major thirds, and the extremely small ratio of 225:224. Example 33.10 is the map.

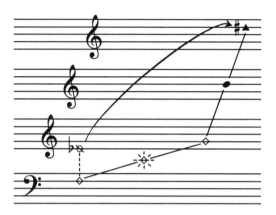

*Example 33.10*

I realize I have just stated that in order for subdominant *blu* harmony to have been truly *blu* it must rise a fifth back to the tonic and not fall. This special case rises, but not a fifth; it rises a third to vi, and may be considered, perhaps, a *blu* deceptive cadence.

## Other Commas

We have discussed the Pythagorean comma in chapter 21 and chronicled its conceptual importance for music theory and its pragmatic importance for tuning. But does it have an artful use in sounding music? I think not. To bring the Pythagorean comma forward, you would have to get my ear around the circle of fifths in a musical manner quickly enough that tonal memory of the starting point remains alive, and although it is easy enough to do this as an exercise (see chapter 41), as a useful musical option it doesn't occur. Even jazz musicians, who often obsessively practice chords and scales around the circle of fifths, never use it in actual performance or composition except as a stunt.

Are there other functional commas we have not considered? I don't think so. All the useful combinations of two, three, five, and seven have been considered, and primes past seven cannot be wrung from equal temperament. But, patient reader, you may find one, and if you do, write to Dr. Overtone because the Doctor needs to know.

Of course, on an infinite lattice, an infinite number of commas can be drawn connecting an infinite number of tones, replicating outward from the center until the last trumpet blows. Some of these are fascinating as well as musically useful in just intonation. We are concerned here only with the tonal possibilities of equal temperament. As equal-tempered harmony becomes more and more remote from the tonal center and the forces of tonality loosen, the symmetrical and atonal qualities inherent in equal temperament begin to assert themselves. At present we will be satisfied to go only up to the point where the inherent equality of the temperament begins to swallow up the subtlety of the harmony, and we have reached that point. The cusp between symmetrical harmony and tonal harmony has preoccupied many composers since the late nineteenth century, and it shall preoccupy us as well in the following chapter and in part 4.

But for now we are fresh out of commas and can take a moment to reflect on the long road we have traveled. Our original purpose was to describe the available tonal possibilities of twelve-tone equal temperament, and we have experienced at least one musical application for each of them. The next thing to do is to draw back and take a look at the overall shape of tonality.

# 34

# THE SHAPE OF
# TONALITY

FROM THE PHYSICAL WORLD OF THREE DIMENSIONS we have drawn a variety of metaphors for tonal harmony as it sounds in the ear. How literally should we take these descriptions? As literally as is useful. The physical location of music in the brain, and its temporal dynamic there, are neuro-acoustic questions, and at this writing, the answers from an objective view are largely speculative. (This subject reemerges in the afterword.) Although it will someday be illuminating to discover what actually happens in the brain when we hear harmony, what we musicians need now is a reliable visual metaphor, a multi-dimensional picture that helps us master the tonal language in real time. Three key concepts have helped us build up that picture:

*Distinguishing three from five.* Our first and most important task in this study has been to distinguish Pythagorean harmonies (generated by the prime three) from pentamerous harmonies (generated by the prime five) at every level of musical structure—from overtones and dronal dyads all the way to the most complex modulations of equal temperament. Everything depends on this discernment between three-generated and five-generated tones. Most of the inaccuracies, confusions, and disappointments of classical analysis can be traced to the undervaluation of this distinction. We have approached the matter not as a more or less attractive intellectual construct but as sensual experience: We feel the numbers and the numbers feel good. As direct descendants of the first musicians to draw notes from hollow reeds, we remain true to the sensual pragmatism of our nature. As we follow this path of number feeling through the music of the world, we realize that human ears are amazingly more the same than different. Most of us love low-prime harmonies and use them in our music without surcease to nurture ourselves and our children.

*The two-dimensional lattice.* A huge conceptual leap is made from the sensual qualities of low-prime harmonies to the construction of a two-dimensional five-limit lattice. Once you have drawn a lattice you have a shape in space. The ephemeral becomes substantial; patterns of waves become a thing on paper, a thing with a function. If there were no other components to the tonal architecture than *pa* and *ga* (plus their compounds and reciprocals), then our functional picture would be complete. The entire harmonic universe would be as flat as the page: a five-limit lattice in a two-dimensional plane, extending indefinitely.

*Tonal gravity.* To this basic picture we can add an additional quality, "the love of the center," the reflection of our desire to return to home: tonal gravity. From the moment a piece of tonal music begins, a center establishes itself, from which emanates a field of attraction. In this, the tonic is not unlike the nucleus of an atom or the sun of a solar system. Substituting magnetism for gravity, one might imagine the force field of the lattice as the iron filings that pattern themselves around a pair of magnets. It is a joy to witness a child's first play with two magnets: She holds the objects apart from one another experiencing for herself the mysterious invisibility of the forces between them. She invests the space between the objects with physical characteristics: color, dynamic lines, magic beings. Likewise, we can observe our own wonder as we gradually become aware of the pull of the tonal center— from the first perception of leading-tone-to-tonic, to our first comprehension of perfect and full cadences, and finally to the elaborate tonal schemes of classical literature. We are just like kids playing with magnets, and the wonder of it is the essence of our work.

The staff notation we have developed to demonstrate the lattice is a practical hands-on tool, but it is misleading in at least one particular: This magnetic pull is not proportionately represented. As tones compound, the attractive force of the center upon them decreases exponentially (as is approximated by the increasing distances between planets as one moves away from the sun), not arithmetically (as the even spacing of staff notation implies). What would happen, for instance, if we drew a spine of fifths whose tones were placed proportionately according to the ratios (that is, where G were three units from C, D were nine units, A were twenty-seven units, etc.) and a spine of thirds where E were five units from C, G♯ were twenty-five units, and so on? It would look something like example 34.1.

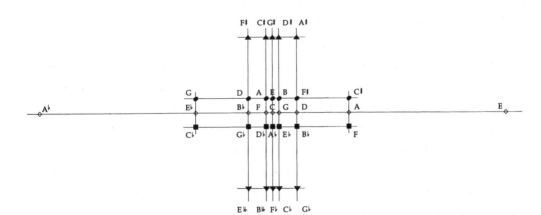

*Example 34.1*

This representation is still inaccurate in at least two ways: *Pa* compounds more easily than *ga* (27:16 is much more common than 25:16), and the ear hears overtones more easily than it hears reciprocal tones. Yet even without any proportional modifications, the essential graphic metaphor of a two-dimensional lattice, ruled by tonal gravity, remains viable.

## The Folding Plane

Music in just intonation that moves through a comma does not alter this essential picture. Singing through a Didymic comma, for instance, transports the singer by a large harmonic distance of four perfect fifths up plus one major third down by means of a small change in pitch, and the movement through the territory is entirely trackable on the lattice. So if there were no such thing as temperament, our picture of five-limit harmony would be functionally complete: It is a flat plane through which the ear travels in a variety of ways.

Temperament, however, alters the essential nature of the picture. To better understand how, let's choose the example of the Great Diesis partners G♯ and A♭. In equal temperament they are the same pitch. To represent this identity, let us investigate what the lattice would look like if G♯ and A♭ would momentarily *touch*. The plane would have to fold up like a book, or a pancake. Imagine that the point at which C is located is immobile, and that the locations of G♯ (north) and A♭ (south) rise up, fold toward one another, and their energies touch; then the pancake unfolds and lies flat again. Remember that music takes place through time, and that commas dispense their energies as musical contexts change. In just intonation, the singer simply moves from point A to point B on a two-dimensional lattice. But in equal temperament a single pitch functions for both tones, and the entire plane folds and unfolds as the musical context—and hence the function of the fixed pitches—changes. Our new picture is a 3-D movie of a folding and unfolding plane.*

As long as equal-tempered music is 100 percent nonambiguous (the way we practiced it in the first four chapters of part 2), the lattice remains flat. When equal-tempered ambiguity appears, the various commas also appear, and each kind of comma folds the lattice in its own characteristic way so that its pairs of tones can touch and zap. As the significance of the zap clarifies, the plane becomes flat again. That is the secret of how Pathfinder gets home: A new dimension comes into the story, transforming the capabilities of the original dimensions.

## The View from the Center

It may be helpful to imagine that you are Homebody standing at your hearth right on C, in the middle of a lattice that is a vast plain, a prairie stretching on all sides as far as the eye can see. (We will do our imagining in staff orientation.) When a pair of tones is about to participate in a zap they get a little excited and rise up out of the plain a bit, like small volcanoes. You can see them both at once. In the case of the G♯/A♭ diesis, you see the G♯ volcano way off to your north (and slightly east) and the A♭ volcano to your south (and slightly west), not nearly so far. You know that Pathfinder is off to the north, approaching the G♯

---

*Readers familiar with Madeleine L'Engle's novel A *Wrinkle in Time* may recognize this as a *tesseract:* the phenomenon of getting from point A to point B instantaneously by curving space so the two points touch. *Ed.*

volcano. First you see a puff of smoke, then sparks, then suddenly the ground curves upward in both directions, up over your head. You look straight up—amazing sight!—blazing volcanoes from the north and the south approach each other, their fires blend in a flash, and then, abruptly, the sky looks normal again and the prairie is just a prairie. "No wonder he loses it every time," you think, as Pathfinder, slightly punchy, gallops up from the south.

Still standing in Homebody's position by the hearth on the prairie, imagine the same scenario but with a different kind of folding: the Didymic kind. Say the two tones are the Didymic pair of D's, 10:9 and 9:8. Instead of thrusting up from the distant north and the near south, the ground curves up from the middle-near northwest (10:9) and the middle-near northeast (9:8). The motion is gentle, less disturbing, more light than fire. What if the Didymic pair of ii *triads* were involved—whole counties would gently rise up to touch and exchange energy.

Next, consider the diaschismic kind of folding. The diaschismic pair C#/D♭ would have the distant northeast and the middle-far southwest arching up and meeting. I'll leave the qualitative adjectives up to you. Let your imagination be guided by the affective quality of the diaschisma.

## A Picture of Three Commas

As music becomes harmonically more complex, various commas can pile one on top of another, or even dovetail, or conceivably nest inside one another. It becomes increasingly difficult, even for the topologically inclined, to imagine any folding of the lattice corresponding to such comma activity. Therefore it may be useful to have a clear perception of all three functional commas simultaneously in two-dimensional, static space. Example 34.2 is a diagram of a Didymic comma (between the 9:8 D and the 10:9 D), a Great Diesis (between the 25:16 G# and the 8:5 A♭), and a diaschisma (between the 135:128 C# and the 16:15 D♭), all seen simultaneously.

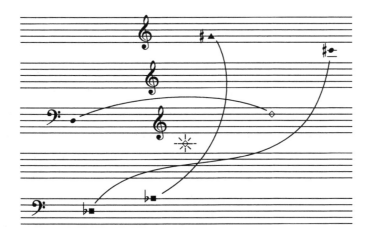

*Example 34.2*

The purpose of this diagram is to get you to consider, in your mind's eye, the simultaneous potential of these three commas. They don't all happen at once; I just want you to see them all at once. Later on (in chapter 41) certain specific combinations will be demonstrated. In addition, the Pythagorean comma, which I have omitted here, will be included in the discussion. (I realize that within the construct of this spatial model, envisioning the septimal comma is problematic, since we have already assigned the third dimension to the property of folding.)

As the harmonic ambiguities of equal-tempered tonal music are worked out through time, the harmonic territory becomes flat and variously folded by turns. This working out is both apocalyptic and effortless at the same time—that's how life is on the prairie. Perhaps this way of imagining such events—by literally standing under them—is one way of understanding them.

## Position and Expressivity

There is one more distinguishing characteristic of tonal harmony that we have observed but barely discussed: the relation between position and expressivity. It is hardly possible to define, much less to quantify, the psychological and emotional responses that various tones evoke. It is even likely that responses vary considerably from culture to culture and from individual to individual within a given culture. As was pointed out in the introduction, this is the problem with a theory of affects: Its logical consequence is a standard of response and the subsequent deployment of the Affect Police. Nevertheless, it seems to be generally true that as tones are positioned closer to the center they seem stronger, more stable and more structural; and as they move farther away they become weaker and less stable and more expressive. The more distant a tone is from the center, the more potential it has for the deep evocation of complex feeling. The *least* expressive tone is *sa*; *pa* is a close runner up. These tones do not channel emotional energy so much as disperse it; they release tension and return composure to the body. It is the far-out tones in the outlying provinces, like the 25:24 C♯ from *Ga-Ga* Land, or the extreme Pythagorean 243:128 leading tone B, or even the Dark Sister 10:9 D, that throw us to our extremes, make us long for resolution, and induce trill-like flutterings and tremblings in our bodies.

But there is also this to consider: The greater the distance, the weaker the signal. As the evocative qualities become more intense and complex, their force gradually attenuates, until finally, as the distance passes beyond the domain of the tonic, the harmonic thread breaks and the emotional complexity becomes merely incomprehensible, a kind of noise, an out-of-tuneness. The dialectical force between the complex, fence-sitting responses from far-out tones and the simple, certain pleasures from close-in tones is one of music's greatest sophistications. This oppositional balance is a special aspect of the tonal gravity that exists within the dynamically folding lattice.

# The Dark Side

The ear is deep; it is difficult to overestimate the collective profundity of the ear. And the depth of the ear's musical response is cumulatively enhanced and nurtured by culture, passed on from one person to the next, from generation to generation. I am alive in the first generation of ears that can listen to the greatest master musicians of virtually every culture and subculture. For a few dollars I can buy recordings of the best musicians in the world, some of whom are long gone from us. The more I listen the more I can hear the wit, pathos, and intellectual complexity that connects the Australian aborigine's didjeridoo and the European conductor's baton, and the more I realize that there is only one pair of ears.

What continually amazes me is the fierce love of harmonic resonance that is evident everywhere. Not all music has the complex tonal system or the counterpoint of the European legacy, or the modal variety of India, or the rhythmic complexity of Ghana, but everywhere one listens one hears the same passionate intelligence. The most subtle conceivable nuances of intonation are shared worldwide. It becomes apparent that our one pair of ears recognizes how wide harmonic territories can be traversed by small melodic intervals. Even in music that does not require commas, micro-intervals that radically affect the harmonic flow show up again and again. This is true for the best musicians regardless of culture or style—the hip pop singer in the recording booth no less than the muezzin in the tower or the cellist in the concert hall. Worldwide listening reveals that master musicians sing and play the gamut running from the dead-in-tuneness of low-prime norms, through harmonic complexities of every sort, all the way to momentary, deliberate out-of-tuneness. Playing with simple, pure harmonies is like playing with light, and the fascination with that cusp between complexity and out-of-tuneness is like playing on the dark side. The flirtation between the light and the dark is a kind of confrontation with destiny itself, a reenactment of the battle between survival and annihilation, harmony and noise. We cherish this in our music. As long as we are singing about life and death we know we are still alive. The various commas, whether they are used as expressive shading or as a functional way of zapping through harmonic territory, far from being the pesky problems that many theorists have assumed them to be, are in fact windows to the affective dark side of the psyche, and they enable music to fill up to the brim with the full range of human feeling.

Even the commas implicit in twelve-tone equal temperament imbue equal-tempered music with a tremendous range of human response. We need to elevate the status of the equal-tempered comma from that of a pun, where a single thing stands for two incidentally related things, to that of matchmaker, where complementary energies are conjoined and synthesized into a higher meaning.

# Ambiguity at the Center

Tonality is predicated on the immutability of the central tone. Up to this point, we have held to the premise that whatever else happens, the center does not move. But what would happen if there were ambiguity at the center?

There are two kinds of tonic ambiguity: contiguous and noncontiguous. Contiguous ambiguity means that the tonic can move about within a neighborhood of tones that are harmonically bonded on the lattice. For instance, within the neighborhood of C Major the tonal center might move from C to G, or from C to A. In the neighborhood of C Minor, the tonal center might move from C to E♭, or C to B♭. Although this implies that there are many common tones within such shifts, not all the tones involved need to be in common. We have already discussed the oscillation between C Major pentatonic and A Minor pentatonic that includes four (not five) common tones. C Major and F Lydian, for another example, also share the same neighborhood, but with only five (not seven) common tones (or perhaps six common tones, depending on the tuning of the D). In some music, especially Medieval European music, the tonic is more like an area, a neighborhood of interrelated tones, affording various combinations of initial and final tonics. It is as if you ask the music where it lives, and instead of giving a street address, it says, "Around here." This practice attenuates the force of tonality and, within a restricted area, allows it to float. Floating tonality both expands and softens the tonal experience but does not essentially challenge its premise.

Noncontiguous ambiguity is another story. Here is a typical scenario: You begin in C Minor and wander on a continuous journey that comes to an end in, say, B Major—the musical equivalent, for the protagonist, of exile. It doesn't feel bad, necessarily, it just doesn't feel right. Not surprisingly, such journeys are rarely made in music, although a scurrilous exception is the show tune practice of raising the final chorus by a half step, a superficial boost in energy. Scenarios like the following, however, are common in equal temperament: Pathfinder starts out from C Minor and wends pentamerously southward, say, to A♭ Major, then to A♭ Minor, then to F♭ Major (follow this!), then to F♭ Minor, and finally, by way of A♭♭ Major, to D♭♭ Minor. That's it—the piece is over. Pathfinder makes his usual reentrance and discovers Homebody at the hearth pouring tea, smiling as usual. But there is something strange about her smile. And what's this? *It's not real lemon*—it's from frozen concentrate. He squints at Homebody. "Are you sure you're you?" he asks timidly. "And what about yourself?" she replies sweetly. Then, as Pathfinder sinks down into his trusted armchair, *it* feels strange, and he realizes that although he is home, he is not home. "Ah, well," he muses, "it's been a great trip."

Of course, Pathfinder has *not* found his way back to the home he started from; he has arrived at the home of his comma sibling, in this case, the D♭♭ a Great Diesis distant. The equal-tempered pitch is identical, but the harmony is disparate; the ambiguity is noncontiguous, that is, not in the immediate neighborhood of the initial tonic. Pathfinder is satisfied with his surrogate home in a way; it is not unpleasant, and he is indeed oddly—very oddly—stimulated to be so near and yet so far. But he is simultaneously annoyed. Something is missing: It's the clarity. Where is that reassuring, level gaze of recognition? Where is the Homebody he left behind? "Ah, well," he sighs again, ruminating over his travels, which damn near tore him apart, "it's good to be virtually home."

# Virtual Return

As soon as equal temperament appears, so does the phenomenon of *virtual return*. What a development this is in our history! Both feet have left Eden; our innocence is finished. By the early 1800s it had become commonplace for instrumental music to begin in one key and end many commas distant, the displacement often marked by an "enharmonic change," that is, an addition or subtraction of twelve accidentals to the key signature (the six sharps of F♯ Major become the six flats of G♭ Major). The first movement of Beethoven's "Appassionata" Sonata, Op. 57, for instance, begins in F Minor and ends, after adding twenty-four flats, in A♭♭♭♭ Minor (A-quadruple-flat Minor)—pure fodder for those who nurture their inner double flat. Even though the pitch of A♭♭♭♭ and F are the same, I think the effect of such virtual returns on the listeners of two hundred years ago was probably revolutionary, extraordinary, stimulating, and disturbing. Even today, if you compare two pieces of modulatory keyboard music, one with an actual return (like the models given at the end of chapter 27) and one with a virtual return, the difference in affect is clear. I think that, historically, virtual return was an artistic and psychological epiphany and the harbinger of modern music. It stated that the center does not always hold, that for the sake of the journey we will sacrifice the integrity of the hearth, in the name of progress we will compromise purity of heart. This is not to rail against progress (I do love my Beethoven, and my Bartók, too) but to describe, in harmonic terms, what actually happened.

In our time we have learned that, to cope with progress, ancient values and inner traditions need to be continually reaffirmed. At the turn of the twenty-first century, the pleasures of "virtual reality" are coming under scrutiny; they are suspected of being the inferior substitutes characteristic of ersatz reality—not an essential abstraction so much as a dangerously incomplete imitation. People are wary. Likewise, there is a strong trend among some musicians against harmonic virtual return. It's OK to leave Eden, but not to forget the way back; we want to hold open the option of claiming the Homebody we left behind. And so resonance revives, and dronality and harmonically contiguous tonality become once again common practice. These were never lost, of course, not even in Western concert music, just dozing beneath the crust of the times.

# The Value of Ambiguity

It is in any case fascinating and fulfilling to experience and understand ambiguity of the tonic as a dramatic—even dark—force in music. The mutability of the tonic shakes up the harmonic ground, which in turn shakes up the psyche. The commas of equal temperament can spin that ground in circles of thirds or fifths, extruding the psyche by centrifugal force, exposing what was hidden. It is no wonder that spinning tonality and symmetrical modes developed in Europe alongside conceptual models of the unconscious mind. There are places in Beethoven where you can sense the composer's almost physical grasp of his own unconscious; his music exteriorizes and embraces the inner dark with the same passionate focus that Freud displays in his quest for a functional science of it. In this sense, the weakening and eventual loss (in twentieth-century atonality) of the tonal center can be seen as a kind of survival tool, a highly specialized way of gaining sufficient self-knowledge to stave off self-destruction. Just as psychotherapy is a tool for living, so can the harmonic ambiguities that lead to symmetrical and atonal harmony be a tool for inner sight. Whatever your aesthetic inclinations, it is valuable to broaden your harmonic study past tonal harmony into symmetrical harmony and atonality in order to find your bearings in the whole of the culture's legacy, and in the whole of yourself.

## The Best Strategy

Perhaps now that the picture of tonal harmony is fleshed out with folded planes, temporal dynamism, and psychoemotional force fields, the best strategy is to close your eyes, listen to a favorite piece of music, forget everything we've said, and simply observe what happens to you. These pictures we have called forth are meant only as aides to get you closer to the essence of music, including your own music, and must not be mistaken for it. Music is ultimately itself. Even after fifty years of musical training, sometimes I haven't the foggiest idea what I'm listening to, and I like it that way. These moments of pure listening are when I learn the most, I think. But there comes a day when you need a picture, and we have drawn it and animated it.

## A Time Line

Figure 34.1 is a time line (nonproportional) that may help to place tonal harmony and the consequences of equal temperament into the overall historical scheme of things.

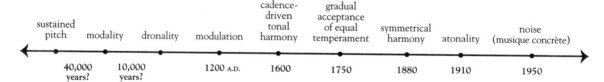

*Figure 34.1*

Many of the procedures of symmetrical harmony are outlined in part 4; the techniques of atonality are beyond the scope of this book. Our purpose so far has been to develop a comprehensive, functional model of equal temperament that serves as a practical tool for making music. We can also claim that by working through the musical practices outlined here we are staging our own revival of resonance. The essential agreements of harmonic resonance are our inner teachers, and we need for them to survive and thrive.

# PART FOUR

# Harmonic Practice, Analysis, and Review of the Theory

# 35

# PRACTICAL MATTERS

OUR AIM IS TO WEAVE THE HARMONIC MATERIAL we have been studying into hands-on, real-time daily musical life. Intellectual comprehension is not enough to attain this, nor are peak harmonic experiences. Fluency is crucial.

Chapter 35 deals with certain general problems of harmonic practice, especially the relation between name and sound. Following this are seven chapters dealing with harmonic practice, progressing from diatonic sequences (chapter 36) through cadential practices (chapters 37 and 38), modulatory practices (chapters 39 and 40), cyclic sequences (chapter 41), and finally, practices in symmetrical harmony (chapter 42). Chapter 43 demonstrates certain new analytical procedures using examples from various musical periods. Chapter 44 is a summary of the theory. So now is the time to attend to some practical matters.

## The Coexistence of Just Intonation and Equal Temperament

It is natural to wonder if your sensitivity to the affective lacework of just intonation will be compromised—or ruined—by the rough edges of equal temperament. Or, more grievously, whether a lifetime of acculturation to equal temperament has inured you to its imprecision. The larger question is, Are the two systems mutually exclusive, or is there a productive area of mutual existence?

Historically, many have approached the two systems as if they were natural antagonists, as opposed to one another as rational and irrational numbers. There is no dearth of theorists (Easley Blackwood, for instance) eager to demonstrate the futility of trying to retune, according to just ratios, music originally intended for equal temperament. Others (Alain Daniélou, for instance) simply dismiss equal temperament as a spoiler of the natural ear, a kind of pollution rising up from the skyline of modern music.

Each of these points of view is only too true. Anyone who has tried will soon realize the impossibility of rendering Beethoven, or even Schütz, in just intonation. Aside from the pitch problems that arise in exposing the commas, it is the very quality of the temperament itself, as we have begun to see in this study, that imbues such music with much of its character. And as for equal temperament ruining ancient sensibilities, the presence of equal-tempered harmoniums has seriously compromised North Indian raga; equal-tempered electronic keyboards have deeply bled the celebratory and the sacred from African music. To hear this for yourself, all you have to do is compare modern versions with early recordings or with extant versions of traditional music. Inside the rough-beating intervals of equal temperament you can hear bulldozers leveling villages to make room for shopping malls: The shamans want to be paid in Levis. The curious thing is how many of the young musicians not only don't seem to mind but even enjoy the newfangled way of doing business. Meanwhile, in the dim corners of longhouses, elders are longing to hear what they will never hear again.

If you draw back far enough, however, another perspective comes into view. In situations where just intonation and equal temperament have had many generations to accommodate to one another, extremely productive alliances have been made. This is in part the result of a serendipitous psycho-acoustic phenomenon. In most music, a discrimination is made between foreground and background. The ear focuses on the foreground, examines it closely, wants it to be in tune, and doesn't forgive much. But the ear is considerably more tolerant of the background. Specifically, it forgives tuning differences between the foreground and the background. That means that a truly in-tune soprano can sing a Mozart aria in front of an orchestra and perfectly peg every last heart-wrenching, pentamerously affective tone even if the orchestra accompanies her in something much closer to equal temperament. Will there be differences between the soloist's just thirds and the orchestra's wide thirds? Yes. Will the ear forgive the differences and respond to the true ratios? Yes. What if the loudness of the foreground and the background were equal, the ear hearing the soprano no more prominently than, say, the violas? The performance would then sound out of tune.

This phenomenon is easy to ascertain in the present era of multitrack recording, where the mixer has independent control over foreground and background. There exists, in fact, a particular balance between foreground and background that optimizes the tuning, and this balance is the musical ideal.

The alliance between just intonation and equal temperament has had well over a hundred years to mature in the African/European mixture that has become jazz. The wailing seventh partials of the old blues belters and the equal-tempered seventh chords of the pianists were out of tune with each other, but the ear is drawn by the longing of the blues resonances at the same time it is led by the harmonic logic of the equal-tempered accompaniment. Throughout the history of jazz, players of equal-tempered instruments and players of variable pitch instruments (including singers) have learned to find the *optimal tuning* for the circumstances.

Optimal tuning uses the best of both worlds: the modulations of equal temperament and the affective resonances of just intonation, adjusting moment by moment according to the musical conditions. Are there ever direct confrontations that have no solution? Indeed. One such circumstance can occur when a jazz acoustic (or fretless) bassist is close-miked (or direct-miked) and accompanying a piano soloist, doubling the pianist's bass notes. The bassist will either play in equal temperament (some may be unable and few would be willing to do so) or accept being out of tune with the pianist's bass line. (The solution: They should share fewer pitches.) There are worse cases: Sarod and piano is not a great bet except in cases of heroic restraint. But generally speaking, optimal tuning is common practice for sensitive musicians in every style (including especially pop music) whenever equal-tempered and variable-pitch instruments are combined.

Tuning problems can arise even within just intonation, of course. In contemporary performances of Medieval music (and most likely in Medieval performances as well) the lutes and harps typically tune in a modified Pythagorean tuning—a long spine of fifths with a note or two fudged toward the *ga* side—while the singers and vielle players tend toward pure thirds. You can hear the pitch differences between singers (loud) and harp (soft) if you are listening that way, but the music implores you to appreciate the pentamerous feeling as well as the Pythagorean structure. The performers' responsibility is to maintain an acoustic balance that enhances both aspects. It is done intuitively: One seeks the best sound.

Each individual needs to find the solution to the tuning problems that are generated by his or her music. My own case: Piano is my primary instrument, but I am renewed and inspired by singing in just intonation against a drone. When I need the truth of just resonances in my music, one method is to select tones on the keyboard that are mostly within the central Pythagorean spine of whatever key I am in, thereby giving my voice leeway to sing overtonal and reciprocal *ga*'s without conflict. That way I can modulate anywhere and sing whatever I want wherever I land. Another method that minimizes tuning discrepancies is to play soft, close-spaced clusters as a vocal accompaniment. But these are the tricks of one musician. My advice: Don't sweat the tuning problem. When you are making music in just intonation, enjoy it. When you are playing in equal temperament, use the temperament well and enjoy it also. If you are conversant with both systems, you will find ways of integrating them; your optimal tuning will appear. Meanwhile, mutual respect avoids conflict. As long as your ears are alive to the resonances of just intonation and aware of the spells and potions of equal temperament, one system need not be counterproductive in relation to the other. In fact, there are undoubtedly beautiful, useful ways of combining prime-number tunings with various temperaments that have yet to be explored. (This subject will surface again in the afterword.)

## Key, Degree, and Path: Positional Analysis

According to conventional wisdom, if you know what key you are *in* and what degree you are *on*, you know your whereabouts in the harmony. What our experience has shown, however, is that key and degree are not enough: You have to know your position on the lattice as well, that is, your coordinates by perfect fifths and major thirds. For harmonic analysis to be real, the discrimination between Pythagorean and pentamerous derivation is crucial. We will call the method outlined in this book *positional analysis*; to the degree that music is tonal, such an analysis can always be made.

# Nomenclature

Adam's job in the Garden of Eden was naming all the plants and animals. Likewise, for most musicians, tending our gardens is not enough; we need to name the things we find growing there. (Since you've stayed with me this far, I assume you feel this need, too.) Following are some observations on the tricky practice of naming things in music.

## GRABBERS

As harmonic complexity deepens, the issue first raised in the introduction is brought front and center once more: "Why name it?" This time around we will approach the main question with a related one: "Why name it falsely?" I am referring to the kind of name that musicians sometimes call "grabbers."

A grabber is a name that may be extrinsic to the thing named (like a mnemonic), or is incomplete, misleading, or even false, but that nonetheless immediately tags a musical event and allows the musician to grab it in real time. For keyboard players especially, the payoff of wrapping your fingers around the necessary notes, regardless of method, is compelling. The black-and-white topography of the keyboard is itself a grabber: We memorize in part by the pattern of keys as we see them with our eyes and move among their hillocks and canyons with our fingers. Even fingerings are a way of remembering music. Chord symbols of all types are functional filing systems for the musical brain in action. The names of scales and modes serve likewise—we ourselves have contrived some bizarre ones (see chapter 12). To the question "Should we tolerate grabber names—or any names—that are a barrier to analytical insight?" we must answer, "Yes and no." Yes, if the name takes you closer to that point of clarity where all names are transcended; everything is fair if you win that game. No, if the name gets you stuck so that you cannot conceptualize—or hear—beyond the name.

An example of yes: Jazz musicians call a certain scale the "altered" scale (see chapter 37). The name is wrong in that it suggests an alteration from a norm that doesn't exist (altered from what?), but it does as little harm as a nickname (Bucky), or those persistent family names (Bobums) that arise from a younger sibling's inability to pronounce a proper name. An example of no: Jazz musicians also call the middle chord in example 35.1 "G⁷⁽♯⁹⁾," which implies that the top note is A♯.

*Example 35.1*

A$\sharp$ is what that note is not; it is the seventh degree (B$\flat$) of the approaching tonic (C). The correct name is G$^{7(\flat 10)}$— no more difficult to say, write, or think than the incorrect one. Dr. Overtone and his cohorts must defend this correct name, since it leads to the constructive harmonic analysis that its evil twin obfuscates forever.

The truth is that all names lie; even pictures lie. But names and images are the kinds of lies that can lead you closer to the ideal; in this case the ideal is for music to arise from all modes of perception. On the way to the ideal, names, including grabbers, can play a crucial role. Every musician must decide when the convenience of a false name so undermines its utility that it must be abandoned or changed.

## "HARMONIC" VERSUS "MELODIC"

Throughout this book we have been trying to bend the meanings of *harmonic* and *melodic* apart from one another. *Harmonic* is used in its sense of "agreement" between two or more tones, a relationship that can be described in proportionate ratios. *Melodic* is used to refer to the mere up-and-down-ness of a line of tones, a linear proximity that can be measured intervalically by counting steps. The aesthetics of up-and-down-ness can easily be seen in the outlines of distant mountains, just as it can be heard in the songs of wolves. All up-and-down-ness is not equally pleasing: Certain mountain views are more "scenic" than others. Perhaps breath and other metabolic functions are internal norms of reference that guide us in this response. In any case, the difference between a wolf song and an art song is essentially the agreement, in the latter, of the tones with one another: They have harmony. The musical quality that people ordinarily identify as "melodic," as in "what a gorgeous melody," is, according to our definition, actually an artistic combination of both melodic and harmonic components. It is the function of analysis to sort out what the ear naturally conjoins.

One of the most fundamental musical rules is, "Steps are easy, leaps are hard." In *melodic* space, this means that the ear hears tones as connected when they are distant by a half step or a whole step; unrelenting leaps of fourths, fifths, and larger intervals are hard to hear, hard to sing, and generally less melodic. In *harmonic* space, "steps easy, leaps hard" means that matchstick relationships, especially Pythagorean ones, are heard as connected, and that the farther away on the lattice two chord roots are, the more leapy and hard to comprehend is the harmony. In music generally, when something is difficult in one dimension, the other dimensions are made easy; the rule is, "Don't do two difficult things at once." This means that a melodic leap is most easily heard in the context of a harmonic step (or when the harmony stands still), and a harmonic leap is best understood when the melody is stepwise (or stands still). That is why arpeggios can so easily occur against standing harmony, and why, when the chord does change, especially radically, the melody typically moves by a step.

An enormous conceptual barrier is raised when a harmonic leap is misidentified as a melodic step, and it happens all the time. For instance, many would say that in the progression Cmi to G$^7$ to A$\flat$, the harmony "works" because "it is just a half step" between G and A$\flat$. The half step helps the harmony seem close, but we are responding as well, if not primarily, to the purely harmonic aspects: We have fallen suddenly into reciprocal, pentamerous territory, and the $G^7$ and the $A^\flat$ want to harmonically collapse toward the tonic.

A similarly egregious misconception results when music such as example 35.2 is said to make "smooth" harmony.

*Example 35.2*

Actually, it makes jagged harmony, as a check on the lattice will show. What it does make is creamy smooth, thick melody. In fact, it sacrifices harmonic organization for the simplicity of mere up-and-down-ness, which can be quite pleasing. Such parallel harmony is common in music, from Gregorian chant to fauxbourdon to big-band jazz (where it is called a "thickened line").

In order to understand harmony most fully, one must separate the purely harmonic from the purely melodic. Then the mutual influence of harmony and melody on one another clarifies.

## "TONAL" VERSUS "CHROMATIC"

A related confusion exists between the terms *chromatic*, which refers basically to the smallest incremental up-and-down-ness of melodic space, and *tonal*. Often people will explain a passage by saying "it's simply chromatic," as if there were no further analyzable *tonal* context. Very little that is simply chromatic occurs in tonal music. Play example 35.3.

*Example 35.3*

*That* is "simply chromatic." Now play example 35.4.

*Example 35.4*

Although example 35.4 contains chromatic semitones, these have *tonal* function. The passage is fully *tonal*, and it also happens to be chromatic, but it is the combination of tonal function and the many semitones that give the passage its character, not simply the semitones. Chords or tones may appear to be chromatic on the page, but they are not "simply chromatic" unless the tonal context has disappeared, which of course does happen in twentieth-century music. But whenever there is even the slightest hint of tonal context, it should be accounted for harmonically and spelled accordingly.

There are legitimate uses of the term *chromatic*. Any two tones a semitone apart that share the same letter name, such as F and F♯, are chromatic pairs. But be wary in thinking that tonal territory can be usefully described by calling it chromatic. Be especially wary of the term "chromatic alteration," or "chromatically altered chords." This is like calling a complex person a deviant: The term suggests what the person is not, with no reference to what he is. (Chapter 42 deals in some detail with the tonal function of chromatic and other symmetrical scales.)

## SPELLING AND MISSPELLING

We have already railed (especially in chapter 15) about misspellings. They occur for two reasons: ignorance and convenience. The former is both forgivable and reparable. But when clarity of harmonic function is intentionally sacrificed for a cleaner page or a superficially easier reading, Dr. Overtone places his foot squarely down. Composers and performers alike should demand spelling that indicates lattice position as correctly as possible; much more is gained in true understanding of the harmonic environment than is gained in the name of convenience.

There is, it is true, a limit to the number of double flats and double sharps one can recognize, and enharmonic change is sometimes needed. There are some keys—B, F♯, G♭, and D♭ especially—wherein even moderately rangey harmony incurs a plethora of double accidentals; for these keys there is often no completely satisfactory solution. Also, in cases of tonal ambiguity there is often no best option. But as a rule, insistence upon the spelling that most easily facilitates positional analysis will result in deeper musical insight, which ultimately means better composition and better performance.

## KEY AND MODE

A particularly foggy patch of nomenclature lies between *key* and *mode*. *Key*, in its narrowest (and clearest) definition, refers to the tonic of an unspecified scale. "The key of C" means that the tone C is the center of tonal gravity, but it offers no information about the other scale degrees. (*Keynote* and *tonic* mean the same thing.) A *mode* is best thought of as a collection, or set, of tones that clusters about, or associates with, the tonic. The modal maps in chapters 11 and 12 give a clear representation of this; the Magic Mode is an expansion of the concept. (A *scale* refers to the tones of a mode arranged in alphabetical order). Unfortunately, the common usage of *key* has been extended beyond its primary meaning to include mode as well: "The key of C," for instance, conventionally means the white notes, with C as the tonic. The full name would be "key of C, Major mode," just as we would more naturally say, "key of C,

Phrygian mode." The shortened terms "C Major" and "C Phrygian" are of course more convenient, but the distinction between key and mode must be kept clear in one's thinking.

## TONIC, ROOT, AND BASS

There are three types of reference points used for musical naming: *tonic* (what key you are in), *root* (the letter name or Roman numeral name of the chord you are on), and *bass* (the lowest sounding tone). These locations are nested one inside the next. We are familiar with nested locations: You live in a country, in a state, in a town, on a street, in a house; you are in a room, sitting on a chair. It is natural for us to say, "I am in the northern part of the country, in the southern part of the state, on the west side of town, watching the sunrise from the east bedroom." In music, likewise, we are in the key of C Minor, on the chord of G major (also called the V chord), whose third (B) is in the bass. We are singing the tone D, and understand our musical address as follows: Our D is a major second above the tonic, C, a perfect fifth above the root, G, and a minor third above the bass, B.

In becoming conscious of one's harmonic whereabouts, one must take care not to overemphasize the value of the root, especially at the expense of the tonic. Since you are *on* a root and *in* a key, the superficial immediacy of the *on* can overshadow the deeper (albeit more subtle) gravitational effect of the *in*. Jazz theory in particular has seriously crippled itself with what could be called root abuse: Conventionally, each new root is thought to generate a new scale, whereas in actuality modal variations generated by a single tonic are used over long harmonic periods. (This subject is discussed in detail in chapter 37.)

With practice, the gestalt of your harmonic position is just as immediately sensible to you as your location in your room on your street in your town. At any moment, the nested hierarchy of relationships to bass, root, and tonic becomes equally as intuitive—and just as intellectually retrievable—as your address. In fact, the ease with which we comprehend the nested geography of music indicates that the harmonic lattice is not merely a metaphor for musical behavior but corresponds to a spatial geography in the brain. (This subject is discussed in the afterword.)

## TRIADS AS SPECIAL COLLECTIONS

Any combination of two or more tones can be called a collection. There are myriad collections of tones that are useful and beautiful, some more so than others. Certain collections are extremely stable: the major triad, for instance, and, less so, the minor triad. Diminished and augmented triads are unstable; because they serve as tonally functional triads only as weak links in chains of primarily major and minor triads, we might call them quasi-triads (as we shall discuss in the next chapter). It is valuable to understand triads in the same way one understands all collections, "triadic" or not—that is, by the lattice positions of their constituents in respect to the tonal center. To the extent that harmony is tonal, it can be revealed by one principle only: its agreements by fifths and thirds (begging the question of the seventh partial for the moment). Triads do not represent a separate magic, only a more potent version of the only magic in town. The fact that major and minor triads enclose a triangle on the lattice is an indication of the stability that the proximity of their fifths and thirds gives them. Augmented triads, however, are sections of a spine of thirds, that is, a straight line whose end points are not proximate. Diminished triads come in three different configurations, as shown in example 35.5.

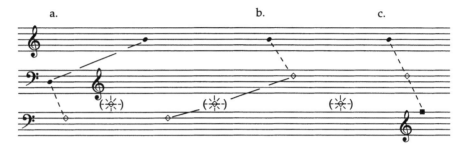

*Example 35.5.*
*The three diminished*
*triads in the key*
*of C Major*

In addition to sorting out the harmonic qualities of the various conventional triads, positional analysis allows a precise perception of and comparison among the various suspended, inverted, incomplete, or "altered" triads, as well as every other conceivable collection. We can see that a seamless continuum of tonal value spans from fundamental resonances to the nether regions of tonal perception, and that triads do not necessarily determine or broker it. To be blunt: Harmonic analysis by triads and their supposed deformations, along with the scalar triadic functions that are ascribed to them (in other words, traditional harmonic analysis), is extremely limited. The triadic concept has tyrannized music theory long enough. We will reinterpret triads by defining them as particularly stable collections within a very large array of possible collections, all of which are subject to positional analysis.

## When to Analyze and When Not

Before leaping into an ocean of analytical models and a lifetime of practice internalizing them, let's reaffirm that analysis is a tool—a means, not an end. It helps you when you are lost; it allows your mind to expand; it hones your ear; it can point the way. It can also *get* you lost and obscure what is real in music. My advice: Analyze only if you also don't analyze. Make yourself think things through; but also learn to let yourself hear things without naming them. There comes a day when these two modes merge. Remember how long it took you to coo, then babble, then talk baby talk, then say whole sentences, then diagram sentences, then write essays and debate your friends, all leading toward that moment when, entirely focused and without any thought to language, you declared yourself to be the person you are. Musical language is the same: half thought out, half blurted out, clever mind and blind heart lurching and tumbling toward their eventual union. In certain ways, it happens by itself. But it helps to intentionally separate analytical pursuit from nameless listening, to teach yourself to enter either or both at will, to balance each against the other, so you can guide them toward their marriage.

# 36

# A SMALL SYLLABUS OF DIATONIC SEQUENCES

THE TWO MOST BASIC KINDS OF HARMONIC PRACTICE are sequences and cadences. A harmonic sequence is a series of chords, usually triads or triad-based, whose roots progress in an intervalic pattern. A harmonic cadence is a progression of chords that centers unequivocally in one key. Sequences and cadences are traditionally learned by means of models that have been abstracted especially for pedagogical purposes.

Harmonic models are generally singable by four singers, soprano, alto, tenor, and bass; but they are also intended for keyboard practice and fit easily under the hands. They are configured to optimize (1) coherent melodic motion within each individual part, (2) contrapuntal relationships among the parts, and (3) clarity in the overall harmonic progression. Coherent melody moves essentially by steps; the occasional leap is usually followed by stepwise motion in the opposite direction. Transparent counterpoint requires a maximum of contrary motion, no parallel octaves or fifths between any two parts, and the fewest possible leaps to or from dissonance. Clarity in the harmony is usually enhanced by placing the most compelling melodic part in the soprano.

The sequences and cadences presented in part 4 are like organic molecules that combine in elaborate ways to bring tonal harmony to life. The purpose in learning them is to have automatically at your disposal every harmonic move in every key. The entire compass of available triadic harmony in twelve-tone equal temperament can be accounted for by a surprisingly small number of basic models—three dozen, plus or minus a dozen, depending on your level of detail. Although the basic moves are few, it does take a while to internalize each model's highly concentrated stream of information into the muscles of your hands, and into your ear and brain. After a certain period of time, the information is simply there, exactly like a fluent language, instantly available for retrieval, elaboration, and taking apart and putting back together. Over time, the ardors and agonies of learning fall away and are forgotten; even the necessity of a keyboard falls away. Then harmony belongs to you.

Does anybody ever actually do this?

Yes, with decreasing frequency. One hundred years ago, educated musicians in Europe were expected to have these skills, or some version of them, and to demonstrate them improvisationally at the keyboard. But as that era of concert music recedes from view, so do its ideals and its pedagogy. In the United States, as one travels west (away from Europe) one encounters fewer and fewer people who know tonal harmony well. However, whenever and wherever you live, if you want to learn tonal harmony in all of its manifestations, fluency in sequential and cadential models is probably the fastest and most comprehensive route.

Chapters 36 (diatonic sequences), 38 (cadences), and 41 (cyclic sequences) contain virtually all the fundamental harmonic models needed for mastery of the subject. Our study in this chapter will begin as simply as possible, using only the triads of the Major mode. Then seventh chords will be considered, as well as other modes.

Harmonic sequences can be classified according to the intervalic motion of their roots. Three categories (and their inversions) account for all the intervals: thirds (or sixths), fifths (or fourths), and seconds (or sevenths). Each classification has its characteristic part motion, as we shall see.

## Descending Root Motion by Thirds

Example 36.1 shows a series of chords in root position; the roots descend diatonically by thirds. Notice that the soprano (stems up) and the alto (stems down) are written in the upper staff, and the tenor (stems up) and the bass (stems down) are in the lower staff—a convention we will observe whenever practical. In this example, play the upper three parts with the right hand.

*Example 36.1*

Notice that in the upper three parts, only one part moves at a time: first the alto (G to A), then the tenor (E to F), then the soprano (C to D), then the alto again, and so on. Each part ascends stepwise in contrary motion to the bass, and each tone of each part lasts three beats, once the pattern gets going. Notice also that if you were singing soprano, on the first beat you would be singing the root, on the next beat the third, and on the next the fifth, continuing successively root, third, fifth, and so on. Sequences with such a threefold pattern can be called *tricyclic*. To demonstrate the tricyclic nature of this sequence even more clearly, play example 36.2; notice that at every third chord the bass leaps up a sixth (instead of down a third). Compared with the preceding example, this sequence can be continued for many more bars (try it) before running out of keyboard.

*Example 36.2*

An interesting and useful musical effect results from arranging the bass so the upward leap of a sixth occurs after every four chords instead of after every three, which gives a duple cast to the threefold nature, as in example 36.3.

*Example 36.3*

The challenge is to continue the sequence after the written music stops. If you have trouble doing so, play the parts individually; the sequential order of each melody reveals itself instantly; you will then hear better how to proceed in four simultaneous parts. The models should be practiced until they are legato and effortless, that is, until their harmonic quality can be clearly sensed.

## Distribution of the Comma

If example 36.1 were in just intonation and each chord were harmonically continuous to the next (in proper "matchstick" fashion), then each reiteration of the tonic triad would be a Didymic comma lower than the preceding one, and, traveling ever westward on the harmonic lattice, one would eventually end up in subsonic territory. To picture how the progression would begin, follow the arrows of the chord lattice in figure 36.1 (which is in staff orientation).

*Figure 36.1*

At the diminished chord, the most continuous solution would look like example 36.4.*

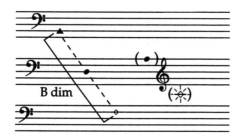

*Example 36.4*

*Positional analysis of diminished triads began in chapter 31 on page 310; see also example 35.5.

The progression would then continue as shown by the arrows in figure 36.2, arriving at the next tonic, pitched a Didymic comma lower. But a cappella singers would not let that

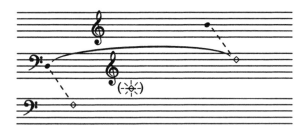

occur; they most likely would adjust their tuning at the diminished chord, intuitively singing the 15:8 B and raising the D substantially—probably more than half the comma—enabling them to tune the succeeding G chord by raising it the rest of the way. Example 36.5 is what the singers' B diminished chord looks like on the lattice of tones. (It is a combination of *a* and *b* in example 35.5.)

*Figure 36.2*

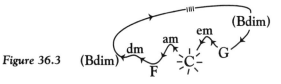

*Example 36.5*

Since the G triad is the last chance to tune, it is safe to say that the comma would be distributed over at least those two chords, probably not much earlier and definitely not later. The singers' overall map would look like figure 36.3.

What happens in equal temperament? My sense is that the temperament does not alter the essential quality of the sequence. In equal temperament, the D-minor chord is first heard as the subdominant-oriented version based on the

*Figure 36.3*

10:9 *re*. Again the diminished chord provides an escape hatch: When it sounds, the D becomes ambiguous; at the sounding of the G chord, the ear recognizes the D as the 9:8 *re*, and the return to the real tonic is assured. Pathfinder has had a nice ride, and Homebody serves the usual tea.

So in equal temperament the comma is still distributed over two chords, perhaps with a slightly different feeling of twist or pull than in just intonation, but with the same overall effect, that is, of traveling continuously southwest and repeatedly rematerializing in the northeast. The melodic continuity in the upper parts, the tricyclic pattern of the voicing, and the reciprocally flowing harmony, all combine to smooth out the inevitable discontinuity between ii and V; so much so, in fact, that the entire stream of chords seems almost seamless. Almost, but not quite. There's still something peculiar about that diminished chord beyond its innate sound. I think it is the very fact that it is not a full-fledged triad but a quasi-triadic, motley collection of tones that allows it to carry the tuning adjustment in just intonation, as well as the change in our sense of location in equal temperament. It is the less stable, more flexible construction that absorbs the comma—a fascinating example of a chain's weakest link evolving into a crucial function. The diminished chord is a weak triad but a talented carrier of ambiguity.

## Ascending Root Motion by Thirds

Each of the basic root motions (thirds, fifths, and seconds) has two directions, up and down. As we mentioned in chapter 21, root motion by ascending thirds is less common and usually associates immediately with one of the other motions. A sequence of ascending thirds is extremely rare. But to experiment for yourself, play example 36.1 backward. The less-common harmony is by no means less pleasant. Try the upper three parts without the bass.

## Descending Root Motion by Fifths

Example 36.6 is the most fundamental model for diatonic triads whose roots descend by fifths. Notice that we are beginning on V, not I. The bass will need to leap up every so often, so as not to fall off the end of the keyboard; we will take the leap after every third note, to bring out the tricyclic nature of the upper parts.

*Example 36.6*

The sequence of descending fifths is similar to that of descending thirds in that it is tricyclic, and also in that the upper parts rise by steps contrary to the bass. The difference is seen in the uneven rhythm of the individual parts: Once the pattern is underway, each part sings a half note followed by a whole note. Also, on every beat, two parts move in parallel motion (at the interval of either a third or a sixth) and one part holds. For example, from the G chord in bar 1 to the C chord, the soprano and tenor ascend stepwise in parallel sixths, while the alto holds. In the next move, the alto and tenor ascend stepwise in parallel thirds while the soprano holds, and so on.

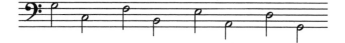

*Example 36.7*

A much smoother version of the bass would leap after every other note, producing the bicyclic arrangement shown in example 36.7.

Now, if the upper parts are also arranged in a bicyclic pattern, the configuration becomes as shown in example 36.8.

*Example 36.8*

This version is the conventional reference for diatonically descending fifths and the one to practice. Indeed, it sounds so familiar to our ears that it is easy to overlook the enormous trick inside it.

The trick is that a melodic discontinuity has been built into the part motion. From the first chord to the second is melodically continuous, as before, but from the second chord to the third, both the soprano and the tenor leap. In the continuous version (example 36.6) the F chord is a position higher, and indeed, all the parts thereafter continue to ascend. But in example 36.8 the F chord has lost elevation; it is a position lower, and the stepwise bonding has been infiltrated with small leaps. But an extraordinary new potential has come into play thanks to this manipulation, as we shall see (beginning with example 36.17).

What about the distribution of the Didymic comma in this sequence? I think that the F chord progresses directly to the version of the B diminished chord shown in example 35.5b—that is, with the 9:8 *re*—so the comma does *not* come into play at that point. The comma does occur between ii and V, the classic case described in chapter 21. So there is only one comma event every seven-chord cycle, but there are *two* downward sweeps: The trout leaps upstream from F to B diminished without incurring a comma, and from D minor to G by means of the comma. (Compare this with what happens when the roots descend by thirds: There is a single upward leap of recovery, as shown in figure 36.3.) Notice that even though the intervalic and melodic aspects of the sequence can be described in terms of an unbroken pattern of intervals, harmonically the pattern is rich and various, each cycle of seven chords containing two different kinds of upward-leaping discontinuities and two

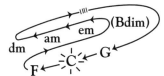

*Figure 36.4*

downward sweeps. Figure 36.4 attempts to show this graphically. The interrupted line shows the involvement of the Didymic comma.

Figure 36.5 shows the path without the chord names. This is a good time to point out that by virtue of its bicyclic configuration, the sequence of example 36.8, although it contains seven different chords, takes fifteen chords to come around to its starting position. Notice how, at the eighth chord, you are on the chord where you

*Figure 36.5*

began, but not in the distribution in which you began. By the fifteenth chord you are back to the same chord *and* the same distribution.

This sequence of diatonic descending fifths is probably the most-used and useful one in tonal harmony. Before examining its many elaborations, let's pause to consider various ways of practicing sequences in general.

# Internalizing the Wisdom of Harmonic Sequences

It is one thing to recognize the wealth of information stored up in a sequence and quite another to be able to use that wealth as your own. The following practice regimen transforms harmonic models in general from rigid exercises into living language.

1. *Learn the model.* When you first look at a harmonic model, play each part individually through at least one complete cycle, starting with the bass, then the soprano, then the tenor, then the alto. Then listen to the relationships between every pair: bass and soprano (outer parts), bass and tenor (lower parts), tenor and alto (inner parts), and alto and soprano (upper parts). It is also good practice to sing each part while playing one or two or three others.

Next, play all four parts at once, articulating each chord separately, that is, with no tied notes. Then, as soon as you are clear about the notes, tie all common tones, as notated in the models given here. This generates the greatest possible rhythmic diversity between the parts and clarifies the harmony. Since it is difficult to keep track of the motion of three parts played in one hand, whenever possible play two parts in the right hand and two in the left. This provides a balanced stereo effect in the body and brain, and it allows the part motion to be better felt as well as better heard. The models so far presented require three parts to be played in the right hand because of the great separation between bass and tenor. Example 36.8, however, benefits from its own special hand distribution, shown in example 36.9.

*Example 36.9*

The tenor part thus alternates between the two thumbs. This may seem like a tidy bit of trouble to go to, but remember that the point of these models is to appreciate the linear/harmonic mix that drives European tonal harmony. It is difficult at best—next to impossible is more like it—to hear four simultaneous melodies as clearly as if you were singing them, so any advantage that helps track the linear aspect is worth the effort.

Use any fingering that increases the legato; once the optimal fingering is smooth as possible, add pedal where needed. The effect should be just as if the chords appeared in an actual passage of graceful, transparent music.

It helps enormously to hear the models actually sung in tune by four singers. Another option is to sing two parts with a friend and play the other two parts. Each part will then naturally achieve its proper rhythm and legato, and the extraordinary power that results when melody and harmony are optimally balanced leaps forward. Your work is to find and keep that balance at the keyboard.

2. *Arpeggiate the model.* The next step is to arpeggiate the model, first upward from bass to soprano, as shown in example 36.10.

*Example 36.10*

Then continue, using any other patterns you devise, as, for instance, in example 36.11.

*Example 36.11*

3. *Ornament the model.* The next step is to ornament the model part by part with uncomplicated melodic and rhythmic figures. Example 36.12 shows the sequence with only the soprano ornamented.

*Example 36.12*

Example 36.13 gives ornamentation in the bass and tenor.

*Example 36.13*

In example 36.14 all the parts are ornamented at once.

*Example 36.14*

4. *Expand the model.* The next step moves the notes out from directly under the hands into the full orchestral range. This is a crucial abstraction, since the model, instead of being a tether, is now a reference. The idea is to learn the model so well that it is harmonically, melodically, visually, and conceptually available to you even in the act of transforming it. Example 36.15 is a modest expansion.

*Example 36.15*

5. *Improvise on the model.* There will come a point when you can further extend your techniques of elaboration and improvise freely on the model, using whatever you need to make music any way you hear it. This is the true use of harmonic models: They serve as both the touchstone and the departure point for your own musical explorations. They will also, incidentally, render transparent to you the music of classical composers and their progeny.

6. *Transpose.* It is my duty to keep reminding you that there are twelve keys, and that developing equal—or even decent—facility in all of them is the most time-consuming part of learning tonal harmony. But this is exactly what makes the models so valuable: They are the most efficient way of gaining fluency in keys. If you are comfortable improvising on a model in C, and you learn the model really well in D♭, you are on your way to comfort in D♭. So the time you spend learning harmonic models is saved many times over during the life-long working out of your musical values.

Now back to more sequences.

# Root Motion by Fifths Ascending

Example 36.16 is a backward version of example 36.6.

*Example 36.16*

Although rising fifths are heard consecutively in actual music two or perhaps three at a time, this complete sequence is rarely heard in its diatonic form. In its cyclic form it is also less common but extremely useful nonetheless, and that is how we will study it later (in example 41.9).

# Extended Use of Descending Fifths: Inversions and Seventh Chords

The sequence in example 36.17 is like example 36.8, but the nonmelodic leaps in the bass have been replaced by steps and thirds through the convention of making every other chord a first-inversion chord. The symbol for a chord in first inversion is $\frac{6}{3}$; 3 alone indicates a chord in root position.

*Example 36.17*

The only difference from example 36.8 is the *arrangement* of tones. Notice that the old alto of example 36.8 is the new tenor of example 36.17; the old soprano is the new bass; the old bass is distributed alternately between the new soprano and the new alto; and the old tenor likewise between the new alto and the new soprano. The seamless melodicism of this arrangement is almost dangerous: Everything is so smooth that one tends to forget that the real power still lies in the Pythagorean bonding of the roots. It is a harmonic sequence with a felicitous melodic aspect, not the other way around. This is a crucial point. It is still the "agreement" among the tones that is calling the shots in this game; their intervalic proximity simply smooths out the harmonic path. (If you don't believe me, play the left hand as written while playing the right hand a half-step higher than written.)

The harmony demonstrated in example 36.17 is ubiquitous in the culture, yet we never tire of it. Many profitable hours can be spent learning to improvise on it in all twelve keys. But it can be extended further. Play example 36.18.

*Example 36.18*

In this case, every other chord is a seventh chord in first inversion (the symbol is $\frac{6}{5}$). To fully appreciate this harmony you must make sure to understand the available seventh chords in the major mode. Example 36.19 labels them in both Roman numeral and letter name notation.

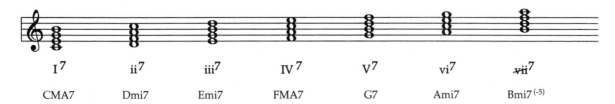

| I⁷ | ii⁷ | iii⁷ | IV⁷ | V⁷ | vi⁷ | ~~vii~~⁷ |
|---|---|---|---|---|---|---|
| CMA7 | Dmi7 | Emi7 | FMA7 | G7 | Ami7 | Bmi7⁽⁻⁵⁾ |

*Example 36.19*

Before discussing the harmonic qualities of these chords, however, we need to take a moment to discuss their nomenclature.

# The Nomenclature of Seventh Chords

First let me point out that cardinal numbers (like ⁷) mean one thing in Roman numeral notation and another in letter name notation. Roman numeral notation is diatonic; that is, it is based on the prevailing key signature. Thus the ⁷ in I⁷ means, "Add the seventh degree above the tonic, whatever note that happens to be according to the key signature." The Roman numeral system is used primarily to show *function*; the numeral I means, "This chord functions as the tonic chord." To actually play the chord you have to know what key and what mode you are in. Letter name notation, however, is note-specific. C⁷ refers to the notes C–E–G–B♭, regardless of context, but it does not tell you the function of the chord.

The difficulty with letter name notation is its inconsistency. There is a kind of subterranean method in its madness, however, which we will try to fathom. Let's begin with the letters themselves.

An uppercase letter standing alone (C) indicates a *major* triad; it says, "The interval of the third above this root is major." In other words, *the major-ness of the third is understood.*

If you want the third to be minor, however, you have to say so: Cm or Cmi or Cmin are the accepted symbols. It is best to avoid C⁻ because the dash is conventionally reserved for diminished intervals. The lowercase cmi can be graphically useful sometimes, as on the lattice maps. A lowercase letter standing alone (c) invites confusion into an already confused realm; it should never be used. The publishing convention is to use uppercase letters only.

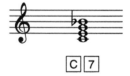

*Example 36.20*

Now for the numbers: ⁷ standing without a modifier means, "The interval of the seventh above the root is *minor*." In other words, *the minor-ness of the seventh is understood*; hence, example 36.20. The point: An unmodified letter, a naked C, indicates a *major* third, but a naked ⁷ refers to a *minor* seventh.

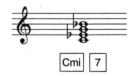

*Example 36.21*

Now what about Cmi⁷? Remembering that the modifier *mi* is reserved for the third and that the minor-ness of the seventh is understood, picture the symbol Cmi⁷ as in example 36.21.

If you want the seventh to be *major* you have to say so: CM⁷ or CMA⁷ or CMAJ⁷ are the accepted symbols. Remembering that the modifier MAJ is reserved for the seventh and that the major-ness of the third is understood, picture the symbol CMA⁷ as in example 36.22.

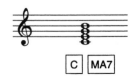

*Example 36.22*

Example 36.23 shows all four possibilities. It is prudent, especially in speech, to make a

*Example 36.23*

CMA7        C7        Cmi7        CmiMA7

clear verbal distinction between the names of intervals and the names of chords. "The interval of the minor seventh above C" means the note B♭; "the chord C minor seven" means C–E♭–G–B♭. "Add the seventh to C" and "play the minor seventh of C" are both unclear.

We need to discuss one more type of seventh chord. It is the last one shown in example 36.19. It is a B diminished triad with the interval of a minor seventh (A) added above the root. This type of chord has many names, some of them conflicting. The time to deal fully with the nomenclature of seventh chords based on diminished triads has finally—as promised in chapter 31—arrived.

First, for reference, example 36.24 gives the names for the various intervals of the seventh above the tone B.

*Example 36.24*

major seventh        minor seventh        diminished seventh

The symbol for a diminished triad is *dim*, or sometimes ° or, in Roman numeral notation, a slash through the numeral. Since, as we have seen, the naked ⁷ means, "Add the interval of the minor seventh above the root," Bdim⁷ must mean B–D–F–A, right? Wrong. It *should* mean that, but the logic of the shorthand gets short-circuited at this point.

Somewhere in its history, the chord of example 36.25 confusingly became known as "B diminished seventh," although clearly it should be called "B diminished diminished seventh" or "B double diminished seventh" or some such. But the collective mind that invents language, especially shorthand language, balked, and "Bdim⁷" now indelibly refers to that stack of minor thirds. The name for our chord in question, that is, example 36.26, most correctly should be Bdim^(mi 7), which means, "a B diminished triad with the addition of a minor seventh above the root," but the common name has become Bmi7^(-5), which means, "a triad whose third is minor, seventh is minor, and fifth is diminished," or less accurately but more popularly, Bmi^7(♭5), "B minor seven flat five."

*Example 36.25*

*Example 36.26*

Even this has proved too unwieldy, so we have collectively invented the name "B half-diminished seventh," along with the symbol Bᴼ̸, which wins the icon contest but loses the cogency grant. My preference, in the name of accuracy, is either of the longer symbols: Bmi7^(-5) or Bmi^7(♭5). Also, since the chord so frequently occurs on the leading tone of the Major mode, it is often called a "leading-tone seventh chord." But if you discover these same intervals built up from some other degree (it is the supertonic seventh of Aeolian, for instance), it is better to use the term *leading-tone-seventh-type* chord.

Now back to the array of seventh chords diatonic to the major mode.

# The Harmonic Qualities of Seventh Chords

Each kind of seventh chord has its own characteristic quality just as surely as does each kind of triad. The musical work is to learn to recognize the particular mixture of resonances that each kind of seventh chord offers. Then sequences of such chords become even more alive to the ear.

There are four kinds of seventh chords in the major mode, as can be observed by reviewing example 36.19.

1. The I⁷ and IV⁷ are both major seventh chords: major triads with the addition of the interval of the major seventh above the root. Consulting the lattice, one sees that the tones of each chord enclose two triangles representing a major triad (on the left) and a minor triad (on the right), as shown in figure 36.6.

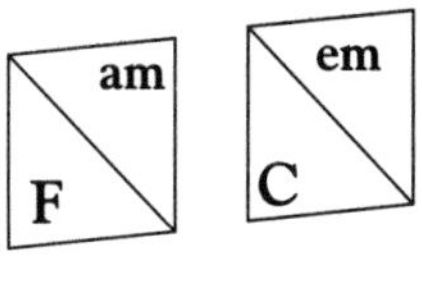

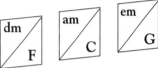

*Figure 36.6*

2. The ii⁷, iii⁷, and vi⁷ are all minor seventh chords: minor triads with the addition of the interval of the minor seventh above the root. On the lattice, the Ami⁷ and the Emi⁷ enclose two triangles representing a minor triad (on the left) and a major triad (on the right); the more reciprocal version of the Dmi⁷ has the same configuration, as shown in figure 36.7. There are other configurations of the ii chord, depending on how the comma is heard.

*Figure 36.7*

3. The V⁷ is the dominant seventh chord: a major triad with the addition of the interval of the minor seventh above the root. We have discussed the harmonic properties of this chord in chapter 32 and shown its map: a triad with a subdominant spur. It is the "dominant" seventh, of course, because its root is the fifth degree of the scale, but people often use "dominant seventh" to refer to any chord built up from these intervals regardless of its function. This particular type of confusion (which we have already encountered in the case of the leading-tone seventh) arises in two ways. First, a chord with the same intervalic construction as the "dominant seventh chord" can occur on degrees other than the dominant (G–B–D–F, for instance, is the subdominant seventh of D Dorian, or the supertonic seventh of F Lydian). Second, in modes other than major, the actual dominant seventh chord—the one based on the fifth degree—is more often than not some other kind of chord (in D Dorian, for instance, it is A–C–E–G, an Ami⁷.) To stave off dementia, the best term for major triads with the added interval of the minor seventh that do *not* have a dominant function is *dominant-seventh-type* chord.

4. The vii⁷ is a minor seventh with a diminished fifth. An examination of the lattice shows a large number of possible configurations for this chord; since it often functions as a shunt for the Didymic comma, all of the possibilities might come into play at one time or another. As example 36.27 shows, each tone has a Didymic stepsibling on the other side of C.

Now, after having considered the harmonic properties of these complex and intriguing chords, play example 36.18 again. At first, linger on each chord, delving into its nature. Notice especially how the seventh of each seventh chord leads down a step to the third of

*Example 36.27*

the following triad, and track that motion through each flavor of seventh chord through each degree. Then draw back a little and glide through example 36.18 effortlessly. How could all that complication add up to such a felicitous little slice of musical life? Could it be that *we* are a little bit complicated?

## The Ultimate Sequence of Descending Fifths

Play example 36.28.

*Example 36.28*

In this sequence, all the chords are seventh chords, alternating between first inversion and third inversion (for which the figure is $^4_2$). This sequence is remarkable in that each part is now descending by steps. We have traced, one by one, the transformations that have culminated in this result, but it is amazing nonetheless to realize that (with no change in the root pattern) what began as upward stepwise motion in the top three parts (example 36.6) is now downward stepwise motion in all the parts. Notice also, as you play through the sequence, that the inversions swap after the first cycle of seven chords and come around again after fourteen chords.

An even more familiar version can be seen if we reconfigure the parts to alternate between second inversion and root position and close up the voicing. We'll start on ii[7] and follow the sequence through seventeen chords, as shown in example 36.29 ($^6_3$ stands for a seventh chord in second inversion.)

This sequence sounds good in any imaginable distribution. Notice which parts move together (the C and the A move first). Try continuing the sequence from each of the initial chords shown in example 36.30.

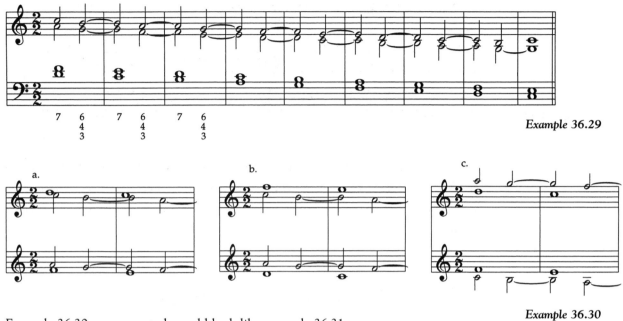

*Example 36.29*

*Example 36.30*

Example 36.30c, ornamented, would look like example 36.31.

*Example 36.31*

# Modes Other Than Major

Most of the sequences given in this chapter are best practiced in the Major mode. All of the modes of the same intervalic type as Major (i.e., Lydian through Phrygian—see chapter 23) will devolve into sounding like Major, owing to its unique harmonic stability. Also, modes containing augmented seconds do not sequence very smoothly. But some other modes are fruitful. We have already mentioned the rich variety of seventh chords that can arise from certain modes (see chapter 24). Follow the seventh chords of MA/MI, for instance, as they spiral through a sequence of descending fifths, as in example 36.32. The $^\flat\mathrm{III}^{7(\mathrm{aug}5)}$ (at the downbeat of the third bar and at the upbeat of the sixth bar) is especially interesting.

*Example 36.32*

By all means, experiment with sequences in a variety of modes, especially if you are curious about less conventional possibilities.

## A Practice Involving Modulation

Example 36.33 is a good template for improvisation that involves tonicization of the relative minor.

*Example 36.33*

Practice this in all twelve keys, get plenty of rest, and call me in the morning.

## Root Motion by Seconds

Root motion by seconds occurs typically only in combination with root motion by fifths (or fourths, of course) or thirds, or both. Follow the bicyclic sequence of example 36.34 through fifteen chords.

*Example 36.34*

Notice what happens in bar 1 as the G chord moves to Ami: The three upper parts all move in the same direction (down), which is contrary to the bass (which moves up). This requires a melodic discontinuity in the tenor. The version with the *least* melodic motion would be example 36.35.

*Example 36.35*

Within the contrapuntal aesthetic, however, such motion, which involves parallel octaves and parallel fifths, is always avoided; the four independent voices collapse into one thick melody. Small melodic leaps in motion contrary to the bass (such as in example 36.34) are not difficult to hear; with their aid, maximum transparency between the parts is assured.

You may recognize the first few chords of this sequence as the harmonic substrate for much music, including the Pachelbel Canon in D, wherein the basic progression is as shown in example 36.36.

*Example 36.36*

This particular progression of eight chords, common to a variety of styles, is remarkable in that it is harmonically unambiguous: no-comma music. Check it out on the lattice. Also notice the felicitous effect of alternating 9 to 8 and 4 to 3 suspensions, as shown in example 36.37.

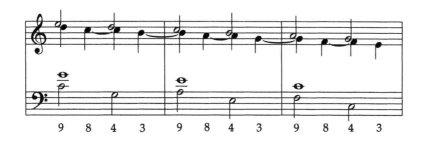

*Example 36.37*

Now (without the suspensions) play the sequence in its ascending form, shown in example 36.38.

*Example 36.38*

Example 36.39 is one more root-position diatonic sequence; it features descending fifths (in the form of ascending fourths) and descending thirds.

*Example 36.39*

## Summary of Root Motion and Voice Leading

It is useful to summarize the connection between root motion and voice leading in root-position diatonic sequences, since such sequences fundamentally model all voice leading in triadic harmony.

There are three types of root motion, each generating its own characteristic part motion.

1. Root motion by a third:

   two parts are common; one part moves contrary to the bass.

2. Root motion by a fifth (or fourth):

   one part is common; two parts move by parallel thirds or sixths.

3. Root motion by a second:

   all parts move contrary to the bass (two parts step, one leaps by a third).

A clear understanding of the above is a powerful analytical tool.

## Additional First-Inversion Sequences

Example 36.40 shows three additional progressions relying on first-inversion triads to give them an almost seamless melodic flow without invoking parallel octaves or fifths. Notice that the voice leading is quite different from root-position models.

*Example 36.40*

# One More Sequence

Example 36.41, an especially rich mixture of harmonic and melodic forces, uses first-inversion and second-inversion triads as well as chords in open root position (the last of each bar). Be sure to identify the root of each chord.

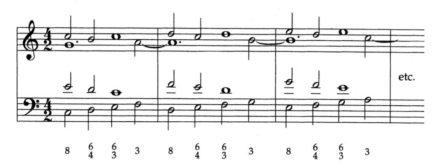

*Example 36.41*

# Practicing in Keys

The sequences shown in this chapter are a fair representation of the possible combinations of diatonic triads in C. The idea isn't to memorize every possible move, but to use representative models to train your ears and fingers to hear naturally the special mix of polyphony and harmony that is the European legacy. The hardest part of the subject is the transposition into the eleven other keys. It is next to impossible (unless you are musically innocent through and through) to have equal facility in all keys—or at least, I've never met anyone who has. Even Mozart and Bach had better and worse keys. Why? Because we are trapped by the notation, by the keyboard, and by our history. D is the center of the notation (see chapter 11), and as long as our ears are skewed toward the major mode, C remains the fundamental reference of the keyboard. Yet it is also true that the more you practice in keys, the more overall harmonic facility you gain, and these harmonic models, apart from their innate beauty and fascination, are a most efficient means to that end.

# 37

# CADENTIAL PRACTICES: PARALLEL BORROWING

THE HARMONIC CADENCE is a centering device. It focuses the ear on a specific tone on the lattice and says, "This is your home (for now)." Although cadences have important melodic and rhythmic dimensions, our primary concern here is with harmony. In chapter 20 we presented the ping-pong cadence and the whole cadence as types of wave energy that oscillate in the *pa* dimension (east-west on the lattice) centered on C. "Polar flips in the *ga* dimension" were shown to be the pentamerous analogue of the "whole" cadence. We went on to compose long, looping triadic journeys based on these two dimensions of motion oscillating around C. The particular mechanisms by which harmonic cadences concentrate and center their energy will be the subject of chapters 37 and 38.

Our chief concentration in chapter 37 will be the modal strategies that contribute to cadential power: in other words, the dynamics of pentamerous cadential energy. We will confine ourselves to relatively simple cadences, that is, forms of the whole cadence (IV–V–I), and will focus primarily on the scales that arise from various modal combinations.

## Scales against Cadential Chords

Consider the passage in example 37.1.

*Example 37.1*

In this deliberately simple passage, the pertinent question is, What is the tonality of the scales in bar 2? The answer is that the passage not only centers on C Major but also sounds as though it is in C Major all the way through. The scales in bar 2 are C Major scales repositioned in the ear onto other degrees. Specifically, the F chord is not heard as a change of tonal center, nor is the G chord. Those chords are perched respectively on the fourth and fifth degrees of C, and the C Major scale, first heard in the treble of bar 1 as ascending an octave starting from C, in bar 2 is heard again, this time ascending an octave starting from F, then again descending an octave from G, and finally, in bar 3, descending from C.

The reason for going on at length about such an obvious example is that common wisdom—especially the common wisdom of jazz theory, a primary reference for most improvisors—states the case differently. According to the prevailing teaching, a new scale is generated from the root of each new chord. Accordingly, the scale against the C chord is C Major; the scale against the F chord is F Lydian; and the scale against the G chord is G Mixolydian. The notes are the same according to either naming system, of course, but the false names, seemingly harmless in this simple case, will quickly lead us into the familiar quicksand of a failed nomenclature.

To be true, a name needs to reflect true feelings. The distinction here is whether, at the F chord in bar 2, we feel *on* or *in* F. The reason *on* wins over *in* is context. The context in this case is a harmonically balanced cadence; we feel the ping-pong of Pythagorean energy. If the same progression were stretched out over ten minutes—five *seconds* for the first chord, five *minutes* for the F chord, five *minutes* for the G chord—the Pythagorean energy would be marginalized and we would develop a sense of modal modulation. But in the cadential context given here, there is no Lydian or Mixolydian feeling. We zip through aspects of C Major, *on* the roots, but not *in* their keys. Check this out for yourself as you play the passage. Do you stay in the key of C or do you move to other keys and modes? (You may want to review chapter 11 for the nature of Lydian and Mixolydian modes in dronality.) The remarkable thing is how, among musicians, there never seems to be disagreement about the feeling—all who hear it agree that the passage never leaves the key of C. It is the concept that is problematic—the conceptual distinction between *on* and *in*—and it is a crucial one for understanding harmony.

Rule: *Name scales from the tonic, not the root.* Name tonal events from the tonal center—what you are *in*. Tonics generate the prevailing feeling and meaning of the music. Do not name scales from the triadic roots—what you are *on*. Roots are colorful and useful, but their organizational function is not as strong as tonics. Chords generally cluster together in groups organized by one tonic, especially at cadences, although also, as we have seen, in sequences and in less-patterned progressions. Tonics change much less frequently than roots. Their pull is stronger, their organization higher, and their requirements not only more compelling but more generous. Roots are sprites. Tonics are gods.

If we name from the roots in example 37.1, we will have three keys generating three modes. If we name from the tonic, we have one key and one mode viewed from three positions. The ear repositions tonal material easily and immediately; it changes tonics much less readily. As our examples increase in complexity, the wisdom of naming from the tonic, and the conceptual purgatory resulting from naming from the root, will emerge. Avoid root abuse.

Here is the full rule: *Name tonal material from the tonic you are in, as perceived from the root you are on.* The first scale of bar 2 is then "a C Major scale perceived from F"; the second is "a C Major scale perceived from—or *standing on*—G." "Standing on" is a good convention. It is like seeing the same house from different rooms.

Next, let's change the cadential model slightly. The F-major triad will now be its neighbor, a first-inversion D-minor triad, as shown in example 37.2.

*Example 37.2*

The first scale in bar 2 is a C Major scale as perceived from D—standing on D. You are not *in* D, and it is not a D Dorian scale, OK?

Now let's make another change, a change of mode: Example 37.3 is similar music in C Harmonic Minor.

*Example 37.3*

Now the tonal center is even more clearly C. The question is, How is the tonal material over the D diminished triad (in the first half of bar 2) to be named? If it were some sort of D mode, it would look like example 37.4 and we would name it "D Locrian-Mixolydian over Phrygian," or "D Locrian major 6."

But the key is actually C and the mode is Harmonic Minor and we are hearing it from D (which is the *root*, even though the *bass* is F). Notice that Harmonic Minor is a mixed mode in the sense that

*Example 37.4*

E♭ and A♭ are reciprocal thirds (contained in C Minor) and B♮ is an overtonal third (contained in C Major). In such cases of modal mixing, the ability of the ear to perceive the entire cadential passage in terms of the tonic is especially clear.

## Borrowing from Minor

Once it is understood that the ear recognizes tonal content in respect to the tonal center, it becomes possible to track modal changes that occur within a cadential phrase. Example 37.5

is in the key of C, but the mode undergoes change.

*Example 37.5*

The first two and a half beats spin out the notes of C Major, but the reciprocal A♭ and E♭ (from C Minor) appear during the V harmony. Major is then restored in bar 2. The use of such reciprocal material in an otherwise major cadence is called *borrowing from Minor*.

Musical cadences can be considered miniature dramatic stories replete with a thickening of the plot (the chords preceding the dominant chord), a climax (the dominant chord) and a denouement (the resolution to the tonic). It is the release of resolution that we all want, the return to the hearth, the satisfaction of the Homebody instinct after the adventures of Pathfinder have spun themselves out. Precisely as in literal storytelling, the moment of return in music is the moment of emotional catharsis, the promise of which has led us forward. The gradual infusion of reciprocal *ga* material serves as a thickening of the plot; typically this continues until the moment of the final tonic major chord, which suddenly flips us back to the release of overtonal stability. Borrowing from Minor—the reversal of polarity in the *ga* dimension—can thus be understood as a heightening of the dramatic tension.

Often the borrowing is even more extreme, that is, more reciprocal. Example 37.6 uses the minor second degree of C, D♭, in a construction common in classical music, the so-called Neapolitan sixth.

$♭II^6_3$

*Example 37.6*

In this case, the climax in reciprocity is on the $♭II^6_3$ chord; the D♮ returns before the final close. This might be called *borrowing from Phrygian*. An elaboration of the above is shown in example 37.7.

*Example 37.7*

Sometimes, especially in jazz, the borrowing from Phrygian is withheld until the most dramatic moment, that is, the chord before the final close. A typical jazz use is shown is example 37.8.

*Example 37.8*

Dmi9          Db aug6          CMA6

Especially in jazz, the reversal of *ga* polarity that occurs at the moment of release is increased a notch by returning not to Major but to Lydian. A typical jazz cadence—typical to the point of being a cliché—is shown in example 37.9.

*Example 37.9*

Notice how the first chord simply stacks up, by thirds, the tones of C Phrygian (starting from Db), whereas the second chord stacks by thirds the tones of C Lydian (from C). The translation to the visual metaphor of the five-limit lattice of twelve notes is particularly revealing here. The "dramatic moment" uses all four reciprocal thirds; the "catharsis" uses all four overtonal thirds. We are flipped from yin to yang, neat as a pin. And look what happens when you combine all of the tones of the jazz cadence into one scale: It is none other than the Magic Scale of chapter 25, shown again in example 37.10.

*Example 37.10*

The end of the first Magic Mode piece (example 25.41, bars 16–18) is another example of the Phrygian-to-Lydian flip (see also the end of example 26.43). Try composing or improvising your own examples of such cadences in C, and in other keys as well.

Now, for a moment, glance again at example 37.1. When you hear cadential material in a form that is melodically scalar and harmonically stable, the changing of roots in the chord progression does not obscure the clarity of the tonal center; all of the material is an obviously single mode of a single key. But when the mode begins to move through its various overtonal and reciprocal forms, it takes some discernment to recognize that modal borrowing does not constitute a change of tonic, that even though the roots move and the mode changes, the tonal center holds. This is more than a fine point; it is at the heart of cadential harmony and our response to it.

Consider how, in dronal music, one's entire emotional cast can swing around at a single pentamerous reversal. In tonal harmony (equal-tempered or not) cadential passages are just as key-centered, just as fixed on the tonic, as in dronality, except that the drone is not sounding. In place of the drone is the rich context afforded by triads and other, more dense collections of tones. The rainbow of feeling, the height and breadth provided by the ancient modal system, is never so clearly present in modern music as it is in cadences that explore the modal palette of the target key. Such cadences provide the same ride from sunny to moony and back again that we dronal singers experienced in chapter 11, and the mechanism that determines the mood is the same: the polarity of the thirds.

## Borrowing from Major

Does the polarity of the borrowing ever work the other way; that is, in a Minor cadence is there borrowing from Major? Yes, but much less frequently. Example 37.11 is such a passage.

*Example 37.11*

The so-called Melodic Minor itself is a mixture of overtonal and reciprocal thirds, and its ubiquitous use from the eighteenth century to the present demonstrates how reversals of pentamerous polarity have become part of the common tonal language. (More extensive and methodical schematics of the mutual reciprocity of cadential harmony are presented in chapter 38.)

## The "Altered Scale"

Jazz musicians use the term "altered scale" to describe the scale shown in example 37.12.

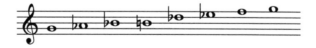

*Example 37.12.*
*G "altered scale"*

Example 37.13 shows a typical use.

*Example 37.13*

The scale is thought to be intervalically attractive (about which more in a moment) as well as tonally rich. Its strange name persists because its true derivation has not been understood. In our view, tonal material should be identified in terms of the target tonic. Accordingly, the tones of the altered scale are described as follows: A♭, E♭, B♭, and D♭ are borrowed from C Phrygian; B remains from C Major. The note C, although it *could* be included in the scale, is typically omitted for the same reason that the tonic is usually absent from any dominant-functioning harmony: One avoids the punch line during the setup of a joke. The tonic is the punch line, and it is best reserved for the end. The altered scale is then redefined as a C Phrygian scale, perceived from G, with two forms of seventh (B♭ and B♮) and the tonic unspoken. In other words, it is an especially sonorous form of borrowing from Phrygian.

The same scale, perceived from D♭, is sometimes misidentified as a D♭ "Lydian Dominant" scale. Example 37.14, referred to in jazz as "the ♭II substitution," is in fact the very same borrowing from Phrygian—one might say the "Phrygianization"—of C.

*Example 37.14*

Now, about the allure of the intervals. The so-called altered scale is intervalically attractive because it contains the whole tone–half tone pattern of a "diminished scale," as well as five out of the six possible tones of a whole-tone scale (shown in example 37.15).

*Example 37.15*

Both of these patterns invoke the symmetry inherent in twelve-tone equal temperament, a quality that arises as tonal bonds weaken. (The operation of symmetric harmony and its relation to tonal harmony is discussed in detail in chapter 42.)

## What Can Be Added to a Dominant Seventh Chord?

We have described the cadential formula as a kind of drama involving modal swings and coming to a climax at the dominant seventh chord. The question arises, What can be added to a V⁷ chord to heighten its dramatic effect? Example 37.16 shows the possibilities (*in* C, *on* G).

*Example 37.16*

G is the root; it makes 3:2 with C.

A♭ is the minor ninth from G (G$^{7(♭9)}$); 8:5 with C.

A is the major ninth from G (G$^9$); either 5:3 or 27:16 with C, depending on context.

B♭ is the minor tenth from G (G$^{7(♭10)}$); 9:5 with C.

B is the major third of the G triad; 15:8 with C.

C, the tonic, is a perfect fourth from G and cannot be added to a G-major triad without obscuring its function, but it can temporarily replace the B to become a suspension (G$^{7(sus4)}$).

C♯ is the augmented fourth (or eleventh) from G (G$^{7(♯11)}$) and can be added especially in cases where it resolves upward to D; it is the super-Lydian tone and makes 135:128 with C.

D♭ is the diminished fifth from G (G$^{7(-5)}$); it usually replaces D and characterizes C Phrygian; 16:15 with C.

D is the perfect fifth of the G triad; 9:8 with C.

E♭ is the minor thirteenth from G (G$^{7(♭13)}$); 6:5 with C. D is usually omitted from the harmony when E♭ is present.

E is the major thirteenth from G (G$^{13}$); 5:4 with C.

F is the minor seventh from G (G$^7$); it is 4:3 with C.

Certain functions can sound simultaneously in beautiful ways; some of these are discussed in chapter 38 as *standing dissonances*.

Notice that D♯ has been omitted from the list above, as well as the symbols G$^{7+}$, G$^{+7}$ and G$^{aug}$, which are the often-invoked false names for what is actually the addition of an E♭ to the tones G, B, and F. Notice also that we have not included F♯, the function of which contradicts the pull of the dominant seventh (although it can be used as a stunning passing dissonance).

Example 37.17 is a passage that includes everything.

*Example 37.17*

This introductory look at cadential material defines cadences as having a fixed tonic with moving roots and changing modes. In the next chapter we will broaden the cadential field, and take an overview of the entire subject of cadential energy.

# 38

# THE LONG CADENCE: A COMPREHENSIVE VIEW OF CADENTIAL ENERGY

EXAMPLE 38.1 IS PROBABLY THE MOST frequently recurring cadential model from the common practice period.

**Example 38.1**

PPU      sus.PU      PU            U

For the moment, we will let this model stand for all cadences in general and use it to help us define some important terms. We will use the term *ultimate chord* (U) to define the closing tonic chord of a cadence. The chord immediately preceding the ultimate chord can then be called the *penultimate chord* (PU); it is almost always based on the dominant triad, although there are some exceptions. The chord directly preceding the penultimate chord in example 38.1 we will consider a kind of deformation of it, a double suspension (which will be discussed in detail momentarily); we will call it the *suspended penultimate chord* (sus.PU). The chord before *that* we will call the *pre-penultimate* chord (PPU).

By definition, the chords in cadences are arranged to have greater and greater specificity for the tonic, by which I mean that the closer the chord is to the tonic, the more the tonic attracts it, much like metal objects around a magnet, or like meteorites as they approach Earth. By the time the cadence has reached the penultimate chord, the pull of the tonic is so great that there is only one possible outcome, and the cadence resolves. Although there are an indefinitely large number of variations of the basic cadential model, there is only one basic dynamic, which can be seen on the lattice as an inevitable contraction toward a central tone. Example 38.2 presents an overview of that dynamic using conventional notation.

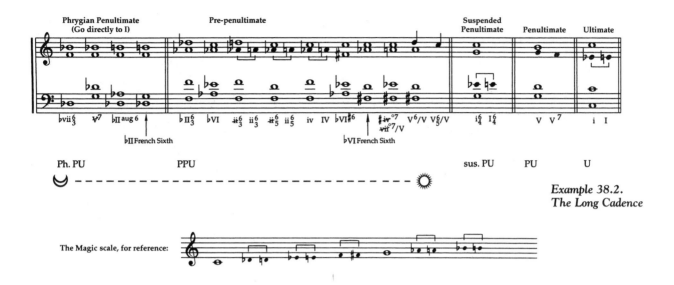

Example 38.2.
*The Long Cadence*

## The Long Cadence: General Characteristics

Example 38.2, which we will call the Long Cadence, categorizes and presents in temporal order most of the triadic functions in the variously configured cadences of tonal harmony. Before discussing these chords individually, here are some general remarks about the Long Cadence.

*The Phrygian penultimate.* Notice first that the Phrygian-based chords (in the first bar) are understood to resolve directly to the tonic chord, which, in the Phrygian cadence, is usually either major or the "open" dyad C–G. These chords can be called *Phrygian penultimate chords* (Ph.PU); they are discussed later in this chapter.

*General motion.* The Long Cadence can be read, generally, left to right. No PPU chords, or one PPU chord only, or several PPU chords may be used; if more than one, they typically appear left to right. Notice how the overall progression of PPU chords is roughly from moony to sunny, that is, reciprocal to overtonal, although cadences are pliable constructions and there are many specific exceptions (including borrowing; see chapter 37). The sus.PU is optional; its use is most characteristic of the century between 1750 to 1850 and evokes identification with that period.

*The Cadence as a special case of the Magic Mode.* If all the equal-tempered tones in the Long Cadence were placed within an octave, they would constitute (once again) none other than the twelve-note Magic scale, with its five chromatic pairs and fixed tonic and dominant. We have seen this same scale in just intonation (examples 11.2 and 15.22), in equal-tempered dronality (example 25.39), and as a scalar reduction of the jazz cadence (chapter 37). Now it is appearing in example 38.2 as the scalar template of tonal cadences.

*The Long Cadence on the lattice.* The notes of the equal-tempered Long Cadence (like the notes of the Magic Mode), when represented on the five-limit lattice, are seen to form a large harmonic field surrounding the tonic. ("Large" because the field contains several

Didymic pairs and is thus not limited to twelve lattice positions.) The purpose of a cadence is to center the ear on one tone, and every motion that occurs within a cadence can be felt as a dramatic event that either hastens or delays the inevitable climax and resolution. Harmonically speaking, a cadence is like a special kind of board game. The board is the lattice, the players are the voices, and every player's objective is to land gracefully and convincingly in the center of the chosen area of play, which is the tonic. Each player approaches or retreats according to his or her particular position and logic while keeping in harmony with the others. The final moment of absolute convergence is also the moment of total agreement, and every player wins.

*Melodic versus harmonic components of cadences.* Although this is a book about harmony, we need to bear in mind the vital linear aspect of cadential motion. For instance, in example 38.1, as the bass is cuing the harmonic motion by surrounding the tonic by a fifth below (that is, the subdominant) and a fifth above (the dominant), the soprano is melodically surrounding the tonic by steps, as shown in example 38.3.

*Example 38.3*

In respect to Medieval music especially, cadences have traditionally been perceived in melodic terms. One can hear melodic forces unadorned by polyphony or triadic harmony in the swooping tropes of plainchant, as well as the homophonic modal melodies of the world. But there needs to be a harmonic scheme even in monody, an agreement among the tones. One need only to seriously de-tune such melodies to hear their melodic forces reduced to the songs of wolves and coyotes. The cadences of human speech—the rise and fall of it—is inherent to its meaning, but its tones are not in whole-number ratios. Harmony is the larger context within which melodic forces can be musically effective. No harmony, no human music.

On the other hand, it is entirely possible to have cadences—huge thundering orchestral cadences—with virtually zero melody. As a thought experiment, imagine hearing a giant orchestra with a frequency range that stretches seamlessly from subsonic to ultrasonic—just a smooth sheet of sound—playing the major triads C–F–G–C. There is no tune that stands out anywhere—it is a melodic Rorschach—but the tonal effect of centering occurs just the same, because the lattice, which knows no octaves, operates *even without melodic bonding.* Good melodies make good harmony better, and vice versa. But good harmony can exist with *no* melody. The most useful classical models—the ones I have tried to choose for this general overview of cadential energy—represent the strongest melodic bonding within the greatest harmonic compass.

## The Long Cadence Chord by Chord

We'll discuss the material in the Long Cadence from right to left, that is, from greatest to least specificity for the tonic. This will have somewhat the effect of analyzing a mystery story starting from the resolution of the plot and working backward through its mysterious complications.

## THE ULTIMATE CHORD: THE TONIC, I/i

The tonic chord can be either major or minor. Quite often, cadences with a high reciprocal content will end in major, as we have seen in examples of borrowing. There is, of course, a more "ultimate" harmony than a triad, namely, an octave, or even a unison. Indeed, many classical pieces, especially ones with drawn-out, convoluted final cadences, are not over until the sounding of the final tonic octave or unison.

## THE PENULTIMATE CHORD: THE DOMINANT, V

We have discussed the added interval of the minor seventh above the root of the dominant triad—the F of a G[7]—in chapter 32: It is 4:3 with C and tends harmonically to center the V onto the I, as well as melodically to fall stepwise to the third of the tonic chord. Although it increases the drama, the seventh is not a necessary addition to the V chord. Without it, the cadence sounds more pure, more innocent somehow, and no less compelling in its transparency. (See the cadential examples in chapter 20.)

For all we have experienced in this study, and for all we and others have said about the resolving power of the dominant triad, when I hear it without thinking about it, and respond to it simply, there remains mystery at the heart of it. I get it and I don't get it. Maybe this mystery is the actual definition of tonality: the mystery of the center. Let's leave it at that for now. More kinds of people have to get interested in the problem, more kinds of inquiries have to be made. Someday a nice young neuro-acoustician will call me and say, "Hello, is this Dr. Overtone? . . . "

## THE SUSPENDED PENULTIMATE CHORD: I$^6_4$

The suspended penultimate chord both is and is not a tonic triad. Yes, it contains the same notes as the tonic triad, but these come at the wrong time (too soon) and in the wrong position (the dominant is in the bass) to *function* as a tonic triad. The chord is best thought of as a double suspension of V. The familiar 4-3 suspension of a G triad is shown in example 38.4, along with the less familiar 6-5 suspension and both suspensions taken together.

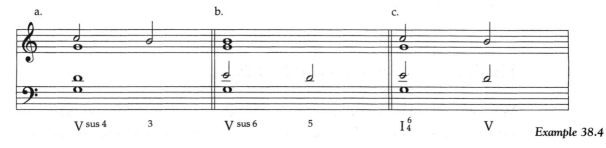

*Example 38.4*

Each suspension by itself is an effective means of delaying the force of the V–I resolution; taken together, the delay is sufficiently dramatic to have developed, in the classical concerto, into a signal for the cadenza: an opportunity, toward the end of a movement, for extended improvisation on the part of the soloist.

There is another fascinating aspect to the meaning of the chord, however. Generally, the I$^6_4$ chord is placed directly between reciprocal harmony (such as IV, iv, ii, or ii°) and the overtonal V. Its position and configuration is such that harmonic energy can proceed from reciprocal territory and cross through the tonic territory without claiming it (that is, settling in it) on its way to overtonal territory. The I$^6_4$ therefore operates as a kind of centered bridge under which harmonic energy swarms and swirls as it changes sides. It is dramatic—if not theatrical—to stand on this bridge poised between the contemplative remembrance (of what has been heard) and the eager anticipation (of the resolution soon to come), and such is indeed the function of the I$^6_4$ cadenza.

## THE PRE-PENULTIMATE CHORDS

*The V$^6_5$/V chord* (D$^7$ in first inversion) is the dominant of the dominant; hence the D and the A both are Pythagorean by definition. The effect greatly enhances the overtonal feeling, almost like dropping down onto the tonic from two stories up instead of just one. The chord can occur in root position with less melodic flow in the bass; in the form given here, the F♯ to G in the bass melodically sets up the following B to C in the soprano.

The *vii*°$^7$/V (F♯ dim$^7$) is the diminished seventh chord associated with the V$^7$/V (D$^7$). The difference between the two chords lies not only in the E♭, which is the *ga*-blooded 6:5 with C, but also in the A, which is at this moment probably the *ga*-blooded 5:3 with C (as opposed to the 27:16 Pythagorean A). So in example 38.5, between the last chord of bar 1 and the first chord of bar 2, the E♭ moves to D and the A becomes its Didymic sibling.

*Example 38.5*

Notice how the F♯dim$^7$ seems to mix effortlessly the overtonal quality of the F♯ with the reciprocal quality of the E♭; it is a perfect case of collapse toward the center (see chapters 31 and 32).

*The "French sixth"* (A♭–C–D–F♯), because it is at best a quasi-triad and is truly a collec-

*Example 38.6*

tion, does not have a proper triadic name, but if it did, I would prefer to think of the root as D, making it D$^{7(♭5)}$. In the first inversion, as given in the Long Cadence, it elides smoothly with the chord immediately following, but it is more often seen in the second inversion, as shown in example 38.6.

Regardless of its distribution, it is harmonically balanced around the dominant in a beautiful way (see example 32.9).

The *"German Sixth,"* $^\flat VI^{aug6}$ ($A^{\flat\sharp 6}$) is discussed in detail in chapter 32.

The *IV or iv chord* (F or Fmin) can be major or minor, not usually both, but if both, then something like example 38.7.

*Example 38.7*

The *ii$^6_5$ or ⊘ii$^6_5$ chord* (Dmi$^7$ or Dmi$^{7(-5)}$ in first inversion). The ii$^6_5$ is almost as much an F chord as a D-minor chord; in any case, both the D and the A tend to be the lower of their Didymic siblings. The ⊘ii$^6_5$ is even more reciprocal, of course, and the A$^\flat$ is entirely unambiguous.

The *ii$^6$ or ⊘ii$^6$ chord* (D minor or D diminished in first inversion) expressively fulfills the reciprocal function in whole cadences. The diminished form, even though it can function in a variety of ways, seems particularly effective in telegraphing the onset of a cadential phrase, and as such can be a kind of dramatic pointer.

The *"Neapolitan sixth,"* $^\flat II^6$ (D$^\flat$ in first inversion) is entirely reciprocal, but it is also a major triad, relatively stable, and is not in so much of a hurry to move on as is the unstable ⊘ii$^6$. We identify it as the Phrygian aspect of the harmonic territory, the "Phrygianization" of C. The F in the bass allows the reciprocal *ga*-blooded derivation of the tone D$^\flat$ (a major third below F and 16:15 with C) to stay in the ear. The D$^\flat$ in the soprano is the strong upper leading tone to C. In example 38.8, notice how the soprano surrounds the tonic with both upper and lower leading tones, and also how effectively the i$^6_4$ serves as a bridge between the entirely reciprocal $^\flat II^6$ and the entirely overtonal V.

*Example 38.8*

Composers typically reserve this harmony for especially dramatic moments. It is a high card and needs to be played judiciously (see chapter 37).

## COMBINATIONS OF CADENTIAL CHORDS

Since an indefinitely large number of cadential progressions can be derived from the chords in the Long Cadence, how do you learn which to use, and how many, and in what order? What should be their relative durations? How do you know when to go backward (right to left)? When do you exercise the $I_4^6$ option? There are basically two answers: Study the literature of the eighteenth and nineteenth centuries, and experiment. The particular manner in which the energy of cadential resolution is heightened and obscured, promised and withheld, and finally delivered to the listener defines in large measure a classical composer's style. With a little historical empathy and the familiarity that comes with practice, the Long Cadence will begin to appear like a full spectrum of colors laid out on a palette, waiting for the painter.

Example 38.9 is a brief and somewhat arbitrary compendium of commonly used cadences. Chords enclosed in brackets are optional; try the cadence both with and without them.

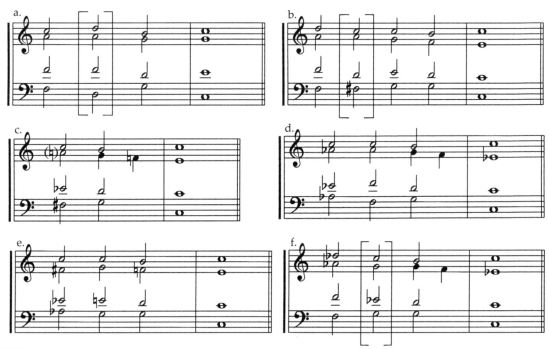

*Example 38.9*

## THE PHRYGIAN PENULTIMATE CHORDS

Phrygian penultimate chords generally proceed directly to the tonic major.

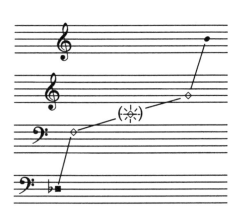

*Example 38.10*

The *French-sixth-type,* $\flat II^{aug6}$ (D$\flat$–F–G–B) is harmonically balanced around the tonic in perfect symmetry, as shown in example 38.10. This chord, like the French sixth positioned a fifth higher, is best thought of as a collection of tones, or perhaps as a quasi-triad, in which case the root is G, making it $G^{7(\flat 5)}$ in second inversion. In the position shown on the Long Cadence it elides perfectly with the major tonic. Notice how both the upper and the lower leading tones of C sound simultaneously, and then resolve in contrary motion, as shown in example 38.11.

The *German-sixth-type*, ♭II^aug6 (D♭–F–A♭–B) is more reciprocal in quality than the French-sixth-type ♭II (A♭ has now replaced G), but both chords retain the use of the overtonal leading tone B and can be used in place of (or in addition to) the penultimate V^7. The popular misspelling of D♭^aug6

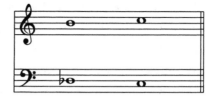

*Example 38.11*

as "D♭^7" is ubiquitous. Many are taught that "D♭^7 is a substitute for G^7." More helpful, I believe, would be the idea that D♭^aug6 is the Phrygianization of the dominant function. Example 38.12 is extremely common in jazz harmony. (Further consideration will be given this harmony later in this chapter.)

The ⚹^7 *chord* (G–B♭–D♭–F) is the first of the penultimate chords we have discussed that does not make use of the half step between B and C. This chord is the dominant

*Example 38.12*

seventh of the Phrygian mode, and ⚹^7 to the major tonic in its various configurations is the principle harmonic engine for the Flamenco style. Example 38.13 shows all four positions.

*Example 38.13*

The ♭*vii*^6 (D♭–F–B♭) is entirely reciprocal, in this sense akin to plagal cadences.

## Plagal Cadences

Cadences that move directly from subdominant harmony to the tonic are called plagal cadences. Example 38.14 gives the possibilities, shown in what we might call the Long Plagal Cadence. IV–I is sometimes called the Amen cadence because of its use at the end of hymns. The progression ♭VII–IV–I is known as the Mixolydian cadence (see chapter 23). Generally, subdominant cadences might

*Example 38.14*

be thought of as rising, instead of falling, to the tonic, and their more gentle yin quality is beguiling in that the tonic seems less fixed and the musical meaning more open and mutable. Such rising cadences are one of the open secrets of twentieth-century harmony (retold by Paul Hindemith, among many others).

## Extending the Territory: Locrian Lives

It is possible to construct a cadence that legitimizes the presence of G♭ as a part of the key of C, rendering G♭/G♮ a chromatic pair with the same harmonic relationship as D♭/D♮ but a fifth lower. Example 38.15 is my version.

*Example 38.15*

## The Double Leading-Tone Penultimate

This compendium of cadential chords cannot be concluded without mentioning a striking cadence from late Medieval times that actually belongs near the front of the list, a kind of ur-penultimate chord. It is the double leading-tone cadence, which typically progresses as shown in example 38.16.

*Example 38.16*

The upward melodic leading to both the tonic and the dominant is compelling, but it is also the heightened overtonal harmonic aspect that attracted the Medieval ear, and ours as well. The two chords (B minor and C) are not contiguous on the lattice, but the bright overtonal flash is well grounded by melodic bonding. Another version, sometimes called the Landini cadence, in use from Machaut to Monteverdi, as shown in example 38.17.

*Example 38.17*

## Deceptive Cadences

Deceptive cadences typically progress from the penultimate V to either vi or ♭VI. The musical intention is to divert the harmonic flow, and after the "deception" occurs, there follows another cadential progression, which succeeds in completing itself. Speaking generally, any noncompletion of the penultimate-to-ultimate sequence can be considered a deception, including those in example 38.18.

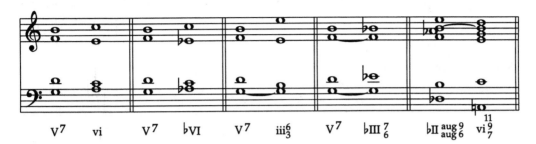

$$\text{V}^7 \quad \text{vi} \qquad \text{V}^7 \quad \flat\text{VI} \qquad \text{V}^7 \quad \text{iii}^6_3 \qquad \text{V}^7 \quad \flat\text{III}\,^7_6 \qquad \flat\text{II}\,^{\text{aug}\,9}_{\text{aug}\,6} \quad \text{vi}\,^9_7{}^{11}$$

*Example 38.18*

It would be most instructive to draw a chord lattice for each of these cadences to appreciate graphically the particular way each one avoids the tonic.

## Half Cadences

Cadences that pause on the dominant are called half cadences (sometimes imperfect cadences). The phrase that ends on V is intended to be the "question" part of a question-and-answer phrase; the answering phrase concludes with a perfect cadence. Both deceptive cadences and half cadences can be thought of as specialized (and extremely common) uses of the cadential energy. A deceptive cadence interrupts the flow, a half cadence extends it; but neither are intrinsic to the basic model of cadential energy.

## Commas in Cadences

In looking over the harmonic material of the Long Cadence and envisioning that material as it appears on the lattice, it is interesting to note the possibilities for the various commas. A simple schema of the cadential territory around C could be portrayed (in compass orientation) as shown in figure 38.1.

**Overtonal Field**

am   em   bm
-C-  G   D  (←A ← E)
-cm- (←gm ←dm)

**Reciprocal Field**

(A♭ —→ E♭ —→) B♭   F   -C-
( . . . e♭m →) b♭m  fm  -cm-
(G♭→)  D♭  A♭  E♭  (←B♭)

*Figure 38.1*

The chords in parentheses have not been included in our discussion in this chapter (some do occur in parts 2 and 3) but could be used as part of Pythagorean chains that settle or rise by fifths to the tonic, providing they are played only in Pythagorean order (according to the arrows).

Even without the parenthesized chords, however, you can see that this field has more Pythagorean spines (five) than pentamerous spines (three)—it is longer than it is tall. Consequently we may well encounter Didymic pairs, which involve four perfect fifths but only one major third. (They are primarily on the pitches D and A, and perhaps B♭; see chapters 28 and 29.) Diaschismas, which involve two major thirds, are rare (see chapter 32). Great Dieses, which involve three major thirds, do not occur. Cadences arise in music as the territory of the tonic is being enclosed, narrowed down, and finally centered onto a single tone; under these conditions the farther-flung commas will be out of bounds. Within the field, however, there is a tremendous fluidity, including reversals of right-left direction (flips in the *pa* realm), borrowing (flips in the *ga* realm), and various other kinds of harmonic discontinuity, all held together by the pull of the tonic and the intention of the music to close in upon it.

## Overtonal/Reciprocal Balance

Although the perfect cadence (V–I) is entirely overtonal, and the minor plagal cadence (iv–i) is almost entirely reciprocal, some sort of balance between overtonal and reciprocal forces is normally an inherent factor in cadential passages. Certain chords (the French-sixth-type ♭II, for instance) array themselves symmetrically around the tonic, but most instances of cadential collapse toward the center are not symmetrically balanced. One reason for this is that most music, especially Western cadential music, is skewed toward the overtonal side. It is therefore quite illuminating to construct a special kind of cadence that matches overtonal and reciprocal energies tone for tone. This not only gives you a pure experience of a core harmonic force but also suggests a useful tool for further exploration.

To construct such a cadence, first examine example 38.19.

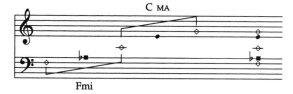

*Example 38.19*

Notice that the note-for-note reciprocal of a C-major triad is an F-minor triad. Notice also that the diagonal line of notes compresses three spines into one; the *ga* spine of fifths, the central spine of fifths, and the *ga*-below spine of fifths are all aligned along the central diagonal. To the right of that line, the notes are further compressed into a vertical column.

Likewise, the E-minor triad pairs with the D♭-major triad, as shown in example 38.20.

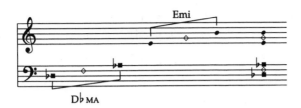

*Example 38.20*

F major pairs with C minor, and D minor (the relative minor of F) pairs with E♭ major (the relative major of C minor), as shown in example 38.21.

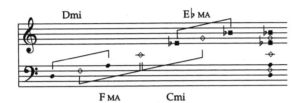

*Example 38.21*

Let's now consider more carefully the chord on the right. In an actual lattice, these notes are not vertically aligned. To generate the alignment, we have compressed a staff-oriented chord lattice as shown in figure 38.2.

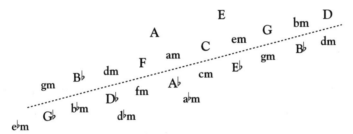

*Figure 38.2*

Now imagine that with a scissors you cut along the dotted line, then you take the lower half of the lattice and turn it over, as if turning a page. The letter names will be seen backward through the page, so you have to rewrite them frontward. Then you line up the lattice halves as shown in figure 38.3.

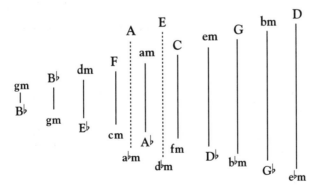

*Figure 38.3*

What has been gained from this? The left-right symmetry has vanished from the *ga* spines, and only their vertical symmetry remains. In other words, instead of two dimensions of pentamerous symmetry (north-south and east-west), we now have only one (north-south). This renders a graphic image of a compelling type of harmony.

Example 38.22 is a lattice reconfigured according to the twenty-four triads of figure 38.3 wherein pentamerous reciprocity is seen vertically. The upper half of the chart shows ten triads using the *ga* spine and two triads using the *ga-ga* spine. The lower half of the chart shows ten triads using the *ga*-below spine and two triads using the *ga-ga*-below spine.

*Example 38.22*

Notice that the C major triad is labeled "0." The triads using the *ga* spine in combination with the central *pa* spine are then numbered to the right consecutively (1, 2, 3, 4) and to the left (-1, -2, -3, -4, -5). Their reciprocal pairs (using the *ga*-below spine) are numbered to the right (R1, R2, R3, R4) and to the left (R-1, R-2, R-3, R-4, R-5). Additionally, there are two triads involving the *ga-ga* spine and two more involving the *ga-ga*-below spine.

The numbering system of example 38.22 is carried forward to the cadential models of example 38.23 below to help you track the lattice position as you play. Once the symmetry of the cadential loops is clear, however, learn to play these models effortlessly and, if possible, mindlessly, so their effect can be absorbed at the most fundamental level of vibration. Then experiment on your own with this cadential symmetry.

*Example 38.23*

*Example 38.23 (continued)*

## Standing Dissonances

Standing dissonances are those that do not necessarily resolve to consonance. The jazz cadence given in example 37.8, an archetype of standing dissonance that covers a wide swath of harmonic territory surrounding the tonic, is only one of many commonly used standing dissonances in jazz and other contemporary music. Usually these complex chords are thought of as being built upward from a triadic foundation, as shown in example 38.24. (In jazz notation, [6] means "add the interval of the major sixth above the root.")

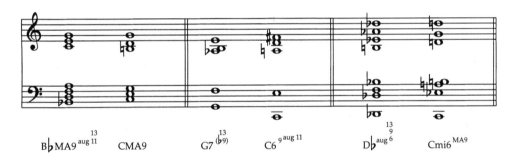

*Example 38.24*

Often it is best to consider such complex chords as collections of tones, each with its own blend of flavors. Locate on the lattice each of the tones shown in example 38.25.

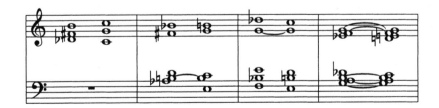

*Example 38.25*

In a certain sense, *any* collection of tones, including extremely dissonant ones, will serve as a penultimate chord, as the following experiment shows. Play example 38.26, and at the X, strike downward on the keyboard with both palms open.

*Example 38.26*

This is ridiculous, but it is *some* kind of cadence nonetheless. The point here—and the one that has eventually to be made in respect to dissonance—is that musical context, harmonic rhythm, and the mere contrast between consonance and dissonance are all components of the cadential effect.

## Tonicization versus Modulation

It is too simple to suppose that music is always in one key or another. There are many shades of certainty and uncertainty between two tonics, especially at moments of transition between them. A cleanly accomplished change of tonic is called a *modulation;* it usually involves an elaborated full cadence, and often indicates that the music is about to either say old things in a new way or say entirely new things. A less declamatory, more tentative move is called a *tonicization*. It implies a milder form of commitment than does modulation, a passing through rather than a digging in, a momentary continuation of an old idea in a fresh new key rather than a new statement or a restatement. Some tonicizations are quite fleeting— only a nod in the direction of the new key as opposed to a formal greeting. Indeed, since the nod may be almost imperceptible, there exists a cusp between tonicization and extended modality that is nebulous and subjective (though no less musical in that).

The F♯dim⁷ chord in the Long Cadence is a perfect example. Are we in a mode that mixes F♯ and E♭, or have we tonicized G (borrowing from its minor), or both?

Consider example 38.27.

*Example 38.27*

The C⁷ clearly moves to F, but the drone holds the ear to C. One foot is in the key of F, the other in C.

Certain passing tones over cadential chords do tend to tonicize their roots. Play example 38.28.

*Example 38.28*

The D-minor harmony is first heard as the subdominant variety; the C♯ is heard as the leading tone of the 10:9 *re*, giving that *re* fleeting credibility as a tonic. Incidentally, the C♯ makes 25:24 with C; is it also heard that way? Maybe. In any case, the C♯ has brought forward the meaning of the 10:9 *re* as a reference if only for a sixteenth note or so: A momentary tonicization. Such ephemera are the fine needlepoint of cadential elaboration. The delicacy lies in not obstructing too much the primary cadential flow while at the same time vivifying certain selected tones that surround the eventual tonic.

Example 38.29 is a more reciprocal example.

*Example 38.29*

The G♭ makes the D♭ into a tonic until the second beat of bar 2. Or does it? Try the passage replacing the G♭ with G♮. What do you hear?

# Dr. Overtone Keeps His Word

This is a fine time to fulfill a promise made in chapter 32, namely, to show a cadential diaschismic pair of triads, E♭♭aug6/D[7], with the tuning of the tonic C remaining fixed while its secondary function changes from the augmented sixth (of E♭♭) to the minor seventh (from D). Play example 38.30.

*Example 38.30*

The C^{dim7} chord in bar 2, replete with the note B♭♭, does fairly tonicize D♭. The second chord of bar 3, then, is first heard as Phrygian harmony in the new key, that is, the ♭II of ♭II, or E♭♭aug6 (in first inversion); but then the ear immediately remembers it as the V[7]/V. So the triad changes but the added tone in both cases is the tonic 1:1, and it stands still. I will leave it to you to draw this rare but informative diaschismic pair of triads on the lattice.

# How to Practice Cadential Energy

Since tonal music involves cadential energy about half the time, the practice of cadential models is a highly efficient means of gaining both fluency at the keyboard and insight into the structure of tonal harmony. Two things make cadential practice seem daunting, however: (1) There are countless combinations of chords, especially pre-penultimate chords, and (2) there are twelve keys. The best strategy is to develop a few cadential models that cover many typical cases, and then subject each to the same routine outlined for sequences in chapter 36, namely:

1. Play the parts separately, then learn all four parts super-legato, two parts in each hand (whenever possible).
2. Arpeggiate the model.
3. Ornament the model.
4. Expand the model.
5. Improvise freely on the model.
6. Transpose everything.

For reference (as well as practice), example 38.31 shows a kind of catch-all cadential model featuring various standard moves. Example 38.32 is an elaboration.

*Example 38.31*

*Example 38.32*

Finally, example 38.33 shows a jazz model. The basic model is given in brace C. The jazz voicing is shown in brace B. Scale practice is given on staff A, and a typical passage is shown in brace D.

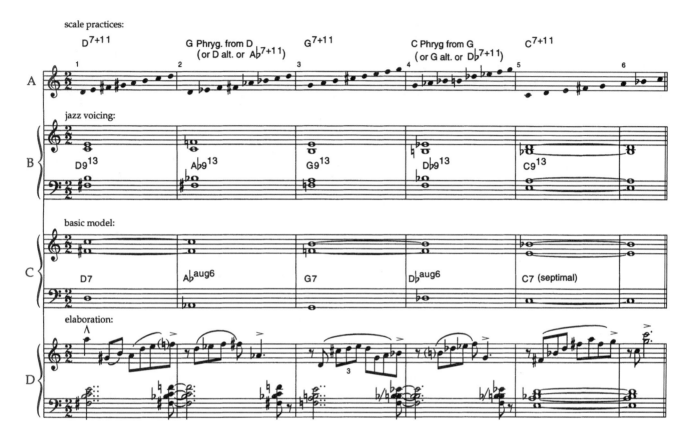

*Example 38.33*

# 39

# TONICIZATION AND MODULATION

THIS CHAPTER IS A GENERAL SURVEY of the basic mechanisms of modulation (and its milder form, tonicization) from the viewpoint of positional analysis; it includes a wide range of practices designed for maximum versatility among the twelve keys of twelve-tone equal-tempered harmony. It would be timely, before plunging ahead, to review the material on modulation that has already been presented. A general definition of modulation is given in chapter 27. The "relative" bond between pairs of triads such as C major and A minor is discussed in chapter 21. In chapter 16, in the midst of a presentation of Didymic pairs of tones, there is a relevant discussion of the Didymic comma on D that occurs when modulating from C Major pentatonic to A Minor pentatonic.

Although modulation can be accomplished by means of a sudden, unprepared, and even ambiguous leap into distant territory, what interests us here, at least initially, is the far more usual circumstance of what could be called *common-ground modulation*, that is, a change from one tonal center to another by means of passage through territory held mutually by both. Common territory can be a single tone, or a triad, or any other chord, or any collection, including an entire set of seven or more tones. Both tonal centers are sensible from the common ground; indeed, the listener often feels the tug of war that springs from rival allegiances.

Let's continue our exploration of modulation with a more detailed look at a basic monophonic practice: modulation for the unaccompanied singer.

## Common-Tone Modulation: The Pivot Tone

Modulations typically include many tones in common, but there is often one particular tone on which the motion between two tonal centers seems best to pivot. We will examine several cases of such pivot tones.

First, let's take a closer look at E as the pivot tone between the keys of C Major and A

Minor. Sing example 39.1 and hear the E as being the third above the tonic C.

Now sing example 39.2 and hear the E as the fifth above the tonic A. The musical context helps to establish the tonic, but there is also an internal adjustment that you, the singer, have to make. Try sustaining the E and hearing it in your head as the third above the tonic C, without sounding out the C Major example. Next, sustain the E again,

*Example 39.1*

*Example 39.2*

but hear it as the fifth of A without sounding out the A Minor example. Now suppose a friend is listening to you, and sing the two E's again. The two E's that your friend hears are the same in each case, and for you (the singer) they are the same also, at least as far as pitch is concerned. But for you there is a significant difference: The context has changed in your mind, and consequently so has the function and feeling of the note. Practice sustaining the E for a full breath, while changing the meaning in your ear from the third of C Major to the fifth of A Minor, back and forth. Remember, there is no change in pitch. Become aware not only of when the gravity shifts but also of the quality of feeling that goes along with the shift. This is very subtle, inside work.

Here are some more practices to quicken your sense of pivot tone modulation. First sing each example as written. Next, sustain the pivot tone while imagining the change of tonic. Example 39.3 shows F as the pivot tone between C Major and F Major.

Example 39.4 shows C as the pivot tone between C Minor and A♭ Major.

Example 39.5 shows D as the pivot tone between C Major and D Minor.

Example 39.6 shows C as the pivot tone between C Major and G Major.

Now go through the list again, but this time improvise your own examples that accomplish the same objective, both externally and internally. The more active you are in creating modulating monophonic music—by improvising it out loud or by hearing it in your head—the more familiar you will become with that deep place where the change of feeling occurs.

*Example 39.3*

*Example 39.4*

*Example 39.5*

*Example 39.6*

# Common-Chord Modulation: The Pivot Chord

Back to the keyboard. Play these chords: C–Ami–F–G–C.

Now play C–Ami and complete the above progression in your head, without touching the keyboard. At this point you are hearing Ami as the vi in the key of C Major, right?

Now play Ami to $E^7$ to Ami.

Now play Ami and complete that progression your head. You are hearing Ami as i in the key of A Minor.

Now play C–Ami–F–G–C–Ami–$E^7$–Ami. The second A-minor chord has two functions: It is both the vi triad in C Major and the i triad of a perfect cadence in A Minor. The second meaning comes on as the phrase completes itself.

Now for the really internal part. Play C–Ami–F–G–C–Ami and complete the above progression internally, by hearing $E^7$–Ami in your head. Repeat that experience until you are absolutely convinced you are hearing the dual function of the second Ami chord without having to have the new context sounded out.

The second A-minor chord is the pivot chord, of course, and if you are doing the exercise correctly, when you stop playing after sounding the pivot chord, you have created another case where the player hears one thing and the objective listener hears another. The last chord the listener hears wants to resolve back to the key of C Major; for you, a new context is given to that chord even as it is struck, because you are hearing ahead. This internal hearing ahead is what allows an improvisor to construct cogent harmonic journeys. As an aspect of musical craft, this may seem a bit mysterious, but it is quite familiar in spoken language. Consider how, when improvising a bedtime story for a child, you plot sufficiently ahead to make the story both logical and surprising. The same holds true for the syntactical constructions of everyday speech—one thinks sufficiently ahead to turn phrases into sentences and sentences into paragraphs. For the improvisor (or the composer) this means sensing the target key before the listener does. You have to be ahead of the listener in the same way a mystery writer has to be ahead of the reader, or, more obviously, the way a driver's vision is ahead of the wheels.

On with more pivot chords.

Play Cmi–A♭–Fmi–$G^7$–Cmi–A♭–$B^{♭7}$–E♭.

Now play it again but stop at the second A♭ and hear the cadence to E♭ internally. A♭ functions as the pivot chord: It is both VI in C Minor and IV in E♭ Major.

Play C–Ami–F–G–C–Ami–$B^7$–Emi.

Now play it again, stopping at the second Ami: It is both vi in C and iv in E Minor.

Play C–F–G–C–G–$A^7$–Dmi.

Now play it again, stopping at the second G: It is both V of C and IV of D Minor.

Play C–F–G–C–C–$D^7$–G.

Now play it again, stopping at the third C: It is both I in C Major and IV in G Major.

Play example 39.7.

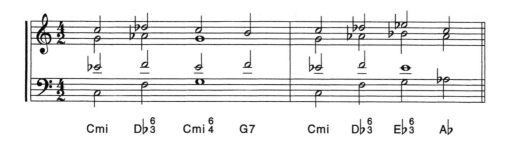

*Example 39.7*

Now play it again, stopping at the D♭♭₃⁶ chord of bar 2: It is both ♭II of C Minor and IV of A♭.

Now make up your own examples. Hint: There is a cache of pivot chords in the table of Didymic triads (example 29.16).

## Secondary Dominants and the Diatonic Family of Keys

All of our chord progressions so far have used perfect cadences to target their tonics. The dominant seventh chord is the strongest driver of modulation, so much so that the mere sounding of the dominant-seventh-type chord usually implies that the tonic lies a fifth below. (Proof: Walk up to a piano in any bar, play a B♭⁷ arpeggio, and twenty-five people will start to sing "Over the Rainbow" in E♭.)

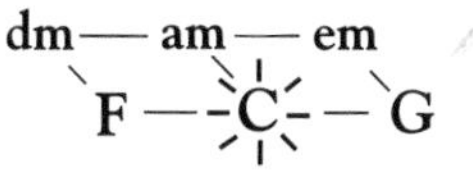

To examine this phenomenon further, consider the set of triads shown in figure 39.1. (All chord lattices and key lattices in this chapter will be in compass orientation unless otherwise stated.) These are, of course, none other than the three major and three minor triads that arise from the key of C Major, namely, the tonic, dominant, and subdominant triads, plus their relative minors. Consider how, in the early phase of our study (part 1), the object was to become conversant with each individual tone in the key of C as a unique state of resonance with a scalar function, and how in the next phase (part 2), each tone generated a triad with a unique function in respect to the tonic. What used to be tones (C, D, E, etc.) became triads (C major, D minor, E minor, etc.). Now a new conceptual leap is made: What used to be triads are about to become keys (the key of C Major, the key of D Minor, the key of E Minor, etc.). Just as the set of *tones* in a major scale are a closely knit harmonic family, so is the set of *triads* generated by that scale, and likewise so is the set of *keys* whose tonics are the roots of those triads.

In figure 39.1, the chord symbols can stand also for entire keys. To clearly evoke these keys, we can precede each chord by its own dominant seventh, as shown in figure 39.2. One way to play these pairs of chords is as follows: G⁷–C; A⁷–Dmi; B⁷–Emi; C⁷–F; D⁷–G; E⁷–Ami.

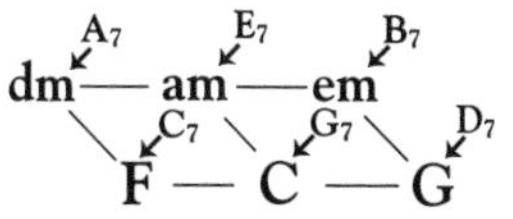

The dominant of C is G, of course, and G⁷ is called "the dominant seventh of C." But as long as the larger context remains the key of C Major, all of these other dominant seventh chords are called *secondary*

*Figure 39.1*

dm —— am —— em
  F —⫶C⫶— G

*Figure 39.2*

          A₇    E₇    B₇
dm —— am ——em
       C₇ \  G₇ \  D₇
    F — C —— G

*dominants* of the key. So A⁷, B⁷, C⁷, D⁷, and E⁷ are secondary dominants in the key of C Major. Example 39.8 is a compact keyboard model for learning the family of keys most closely associated with the key of C Major. Notice that in this particular model all of the dominant sevenths are in first inversion, and that the keys are arranged first in ascending and then in descending scalar order.

*Example 39.8*

Each of the secondary keys is said to be tonicized by its secondary dominant; that is, the new tonics are evoked, but they are not established as firmly as they would be by using a whole cadence. This scheme of twelve chords and six keys nested within a parent key accounts for a large fraction of what happens in tonal harmony, and considerable mobility within the tonal system can be gained by mastering this model. The scalar arrangement of keys shown here is convenient, but there are more musical arrangements of the same material. Example 39.9 presents the same family of keys, but arranged as a sequence of descending thirds, starting in G Major, ending in D Minor, and cadencing finally in the parent key of C Major.

*Example 39.9*

As with all harmonic models, the next step after learning the model itself is improvising an elaboration of it. Example 39.10 is an elaboration of example 39.9.

All chromatic options should be available for each Minor key (both major and minor sixths, both major and minor sevenths), which is to say that the best Minor is Full Minor.

*Example 39.10*

This exercise, incidentally, presents an ideal opportunity to practice conceptualizing the scale of the approaching tonic as perceived from the root of the dominant. For instance, in the case of B[7]–Emi, one perceives the material in E Full Minor first from the vantage point of the root B, then from the root E, as shown in example 39.11.

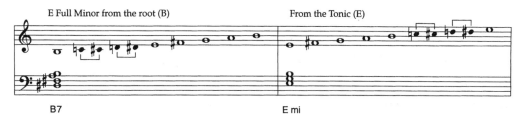

*Example 39.11*

This mental rearrangement should be well understood—well *seen*—at the keyboard and well heard in every tonicization that arises. Conceptualizing tonal material in terms of the approaching tonic is a crucial part of learning your way around tonal territory, and these sequences, with their tight clusters of secondary keys, offer an efficient practice for learning that skill.

The family of keys that centers on C Major also centers on A Minor. Our schema can also be drawn as shown in figure 39.3. The only difference is a matter of emphasis. The efficacy of A Minor as the center can be heard simply by substituting an A Minor cadence at the end of example 39.9, as is shown in example 39.12.

dm — —am — —em
F — C — G          *Figure 39.3*

*Example 39.12*

For reference and further practice, example 39.13 gives another version of the descending scalar arrangement found in the descending part of example 39.8.

*Example 39.13*

Example 39.14 is the same material arranged so the tonics ascend by fifths.

*Example 39.14*

# Borrowing from Minor

It is very sweet, when tonicizing Major keys, to borrow from their parallel Minors (as outlined in chapter 37). Example 39.15 is an elaboration of example 39.12 that demonstrates borrowing from Minor.

*Example 39.15*

The next step is to add a pre-penultimate chord of the secondary key (as the above example already begins to do). Example 39.16 is a sequence presenting the family of keys around C Major, each tonicized by a whole cadence using $ii^7$ as the pre-penultimate chord (borrowed from the parallel Minor, in the case of each Major key).

*Example 39.16*

# The Extended Family of Keys

The six keys we have been studying are the ones most likely to be heard as a family group,

as their compact position on the lattice implies. But the domain of the parent key is not necessarily bounded by these six. Any triad contiguous to one of the basic six has the potential to generate a key on the fringe of the core family. Building out from the basic six keys thus yields the extended family shown in figure 39.4.

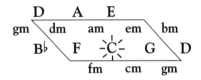

*Figure 39.4*

In addition, the parallel Minor keys (such as C Minor) generate *their* parallel Majors (such as E♭ Major). Adding those keys (plus a few more) to the extended family yields the extra-extended family of keys around C Major shown in figure 39.5.

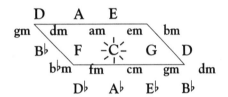

*Figure 39.5*

The modern ear has learned to feel right at home within this large family. Example 39.17, for instance, efficiently and beautifully traverses eight keys centered on C Major.

Figure 39.6 shows the harmonic journey through the keys of example 39.17 in *key lattice notation* (see chapter 43; corresponding bar numbers occur along the path of the arrow). See if you can track and name the four comma events that involve enharmonic changes in spelling.

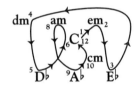

*Figure 39.6*

*Example 39.17*

Generally, it is useful to conceptualize the central six-key family as if it were a single extended key within which there is great freedom of motion—plus an exploratory fringe area available when the music becomes adventurous.

# Where Are We?

This might be a good time to review chapter 22, in which we were also talking about extended territory, but within a severe discipline. First of all, all chord progressions were harmonically continuous. Also, although Pythagorean and even whole-cadence relationships abounded, we were not thinking about tonicizing; our intent was to create cogent, balanced harmonic journeys. Nevertheless, it might be clarifying to recognize that the music we are making now is a complication of the music we were making then, complicated specifically by our new ability to be harmonically *discontinuous* within certain limits, as long as the driving energy is the perfect cadence. In other words, we can leap, but only within a circumscribed family and adhering to the strict cadential formulas. The more one combines harmonic leaping with extended territory, the more tonality becomes unstable, and the more deeply absorbing (and often puzzling) are the possibilities. As the territory increases, the more chances there are for occurrences of commas—more and more Didymic commas at first, rapidly followed by dieses and diaschismas—and the more precariously does the parent key organize and stabilize the harmonic flow. Yet historically we did flock toward this instability like lemmings, and our harmonic centers did begin to wobble, diffuse, and spin in sequences of new tonics. Harmonic models that demonstrate the many fascinating ways this can happen are presented in chapter 41. But even well within tonal boundaries there are a variety of leaping strategies, the most prolific of which involves the dominant seventh chord itself, as outlined below.

# A Conspiracy of Deceptions

All of the above modulatory events are predicated on the perception that the chord of the dominant seventh resolves to the tonic. Within the classical aesthetic, other resolutions are possible, but they are all considered more or less deceptions that must later be rectified. Both music and life are full of deceptions, but in music they are usually confined to the kind that lead to desirable twists in the plot. Of course, the too-frequent use of an agent of deception would soon lead us to *expect* deception, in which case the credibility of the agent would be diffused. This is what happened increasingly to the dominant seventh chord as the nineteenth century progressed: The clear through line of cadence-driven classical form was supplanted by musical impressionism, tone painting, and increasing tonal ambiguity. Although the $V^7$–I cadence still sounds perfect and right to us, we have learned to hear ways by which a dominant-seventh-type chord can progress to virtually any triad and still make sense in respect to some tonal context or other. What follows is a methodical look at $G^7$ resolving, or at least progressing cogently, to each of the twenty-four major and minor triads, listed chromatically beginning with C: $G^7$ to everywhere.

$G^7$ to Everywhere

1. $G^7$ to C major: $V^7$ to I in the key of C Major.

2. $G^7$ to C minor: $V^7$ to i in the key of C Minor.

3. $G^7$ to D♭, or D♭$^{aug6}$: $V^7$ to ♭II$^{aug6}$ in the key of C Major, constituting a Phrygianization of the key, especially in jazz (see chapter 37), but more conventionally as shown in example 39.18.

$V^7$    ♭II$^{♮6}$

*Example 39.18*

4. $G^7$ to C♯ minor: ♮VII to iii in A Major. Figure 39.7 shows the chord lattice. In the key of A MI/MA, $G^7$ to A represents perhaps the most attractive cadence (there is no major V); the rising whole step of the bass helps, as shown in example 39.19.

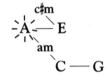

*Figure 39.7*

*Example 39.19*

Example 39.20 shows that by moving directly to C♯ minor, the progression circumvents the tonic and invokes a chromatic pair G/G♯, thus becoming at once elliptical, chromatic, and lovely.

*Example 39.20*

Example 39.21 gives a more complete context.

*Example 39.21*

5. G⁷ to D major or D⁷: IV⁷ to I in D Major blues, as example 39.22 shows.

*Example 39.22*

This harmony is also typically used to back-pedal in a cadence, as shown in example 39.23.

*Example 39.23*

6. G⁷ to D minor: IV⁷ to i in D Dorian.

Example 39.24 shows an alternative, less-obvious use directly involving a Didymic comma. In this case, G⁷ is VII⁷ of A Minor, and the progression moves (from the second beat of bar 2) VII⁷–iv–V⁷–i in A Minor. Figure 39.8 shows the lattice.

*Example 39.24*    *Figure 39.8* 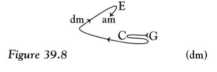    (dm)

7. G⁷ to E♭ major: V⁷/vi to I in E♭ Major. This is an especially evocative progression. Perceived in E♭, it is an ellipsis, progressing directly from the V⁷/vi to the I, thus omitting the vi, a backward kind of deceptive cadence. Perceived in C Minor, since the conventional deceptive cadence proceeds G⁷ to A♭, the E♭ triad is possibly heard as being a fifth too high, and it involves the chromatic pair B♮/B♭ besides. Figure 39.9 shows the lattice.

*Figure 39.9*

The preferred voice leading is given in example 39.25. Example 39.26 gives a more complete context.

*Example 39.25*

*Example 39.26*

8. $G^7$ to $E\flat$ minor: $V^7/ii$ to iv in $B\flat$. First, consider the unambiguous progression in
C Major shown in example 39.27.

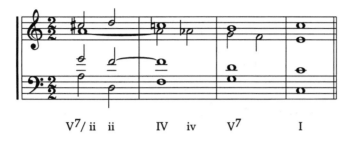

*Example 39.27*

$$V^7/ii \quad ii \qquad IV \quad iv \quad V^7 \qquad\qquad I$$

Omitting the second and third chords, the ear will follow the harmonic ellipses, which substitutes IV in place of ii and borrows iv from Minor, all in a single move, as shown in example 39.28.

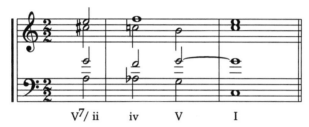

*Example 39.28*

$$V^7/ii \qquad iv \qquad V \qquad I$$

The sequence shown in example 39.29 will now be clear.

*Example 39.29*

The $G^7$, first heard as V of C Major, resolves (in a further ellipsis) to C minor, which becomes ii of $B\flat$. These ellipses may seem far out, and in a way they are, but they have sounded beautiful to us since late Medieval times. This particular sequence was much beloved by Bach.

The lattice of figure 39.10 reveals that the harmony does not sink into the Pythagorean west as one might suspect, but trails southeast. Notice that the ii pivot is the subdominant-associated 10:9 *re*.*

8a. (Bonus progression) $G^7$ = $G^{aug6}$ to $D\sharp$ minor: $\natural II^{aug6}$ to vi in $F\sharp$ Major. On the equal-tempered keyboard, $G^7$ can also function as $G^{aug6}$ in the Phrygian cadence shown in example 39.30.

*Figure 39.10*

*Challenge: Complete the sequence. Hint: Work it out part by part. (Example 41.36 may give some insight.)

*Example 39.30*

Omitting the I chord and progressing to vi creates the strangely elliptical deception of example 39.31.

*Example 39.31*

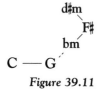

*Figure 39.11*

The lattice is shown in figure 39.11. A similar case (but in C) is shown at the end of example 38.18. Example 39.32 shows a jazzlike elaboration.

*Example 39.32*

The F/E♯ diaschisma makes the harmony work, of course, but still it is remarkable that progressions so distant can sound so gorgeous. Pathfinder has subtle powers. You will find, incidentally, that the more distant the harmony, the more rare are the possibilities for their artful expression. It takes extra patience and craft to squeeze all of the nutrients from weird harmonies, but, of course, that's one of the games we love to play.

9. G⁷ to E or E⁷: most simply, III to I in E Phrygian, as can be seen in example 39.33.

*Example 39.33*

But this harmony is also a congruence of the dominant of C and one of its secondary dominants, namely, V⁷/I to V⁷/vi. This latter use, shown in example 39.34, was common by the eighteenth century and is most familiar today. Figure 39.12 shows the lattice.

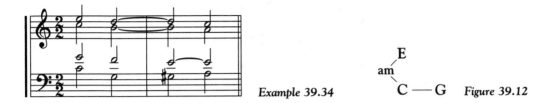

*Example 39.34*

*Figure 39.12*

10. G⁷ to E minor: V⁷ to iii in C Major, a bland but nonetheless surprising deception, shown in example 39.35.

*Example 39.35*

11. G⁷ to F major: V⁷ to IV in C. It is found when a progression momentarily backpedals, as example 39.36 demonstrates. (Compare with example 39.23.)

*Example 39.36*

This harmony can also function as V⁷/V to I⁶₄ in F Major, especially heard in the formula shown in example 39.37.

*Example 39.37*

It can also be heard as a simple ellipsis of the V chord, as shown in example 39.38.

*Example 39.38*

11a. G[7] to F can also be highly effective in the key of E♭ Major as the V[7]/vi progressing directly to V/V, as shown in example 39.39. Figure 39.13 shows the lattice.

*Example 39.39*

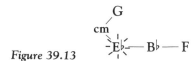

*Figure 39.13*

The F chord in this harmony is not the subdominant of C but its Didymic twin to the southeast. (Compare with the other three Didymic pairs of resolutions in this list: to D minor (number 6 above), and to A major and B♭ major (numbers 19 and 21 below).

12. G[7] to F minor: exactly as in examples 39.36 and 39.37, but substituting F-minor triads for F-major triads.

13. G[7] = G[aug6] to F♯ major: G[aug6] is ♮II in F♯, as shown in example 39.40.

*Example 39.40*

14. G[7] = G[aug6] to F♯ minor: as in number 13 above, but to F♯ minor.

15. G[7] to itself: G[7] or G. Within the blues style, equal temperament will reference the tonic septimal seventh. Blues played in G Major starts and ends on G[7].*

16. G[7] to G minor: this could happen easily in G modal music if the mode changed from, for instance, G Mixolydian to G Aeolian.

17. G[7] to A♭: V[7] to ♭VI in C Minor, a deceptive cadence. See chapter 38.

18. G[7] to A♭ minor. This harmony involves a built-in diesis between B♮ and C♭. G[7] is the V[7] of C Minor, which is the relative minor of the key of E♭ Major. A♭ minor is the iv of E♭. Example 39.41 demonstrates the harmony.

*Example 39.41*

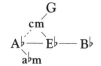

*Figure 39.14*

Compare this with the music demonstrating the B♮/C♭ diesis in chapter 31. Figure 39.14 shows the lattice.

*A special case of G[7] becoming its Didymic sibling is presented below under the heading "When the Pivot Involves a Comma," p. 423.

18a. (Bonus points) G⁷ to G♯ minor: G⁷ is III⁷ in E Phrygian, and G♯ minor is iii in the key of E Major. This is a remote and entirely *ga*-oriented example, but it makes delicious harmony nonetheless, as example 39.42 demonstrates. Figure 39.15 shows the lattice.

*Figure 39.15*

*Example 39.42*

19.  G⁷ to A major: VII⁷ to I in A MI/MA. The lattice is shown in figure 39.16.

19a. In a chain of dominant seventh chords falling toward C, G⁷ can progress to A and fill in the D, as shown in example 39.43.

*Figure 39.16*

*Example 39.43*

20. G⁷ to A minor: the deceptive cadence V⁷ to vi in C Major.

21. G⁷ to B♭ or B♭⁷: V⁷/vi to V⁷ in the key of E♭ Major. Example 39.44 shows a typical use.

*Example 39.44*

Figure 39.17 gives the lattice. Compare this harmony with example 39.35, of which it is a transposition in retrograde.

21a. G⁷ can also resolve to the B♭ that is the northwestern Didymic twin of number 21 above by leaping down three fifths and then climbing by fifths toward C, as shown in example 39.45. Figure 39.18 gives the lattice.

*Figure 39.17*

B♭ — F — C — G

*Figure 39.18*

*Example 39.45*

22. G[7] to B♭ minor: V[7]/V to iv in F Minor, as shown in example 39.46.

*Example 39.46*

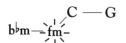

*Figure 39.19*

The lattice of figure 39.19 shows what is leapt over in this ellipsis.

22a. (Extra bonus) G[7] = G[aug6] to A♯ minor: ♮II[aug6] to iii in F♯ Major. Compare this with number 8a above, which progresses to vi; example 39.47 is an even more elliptical version of the same harmony.

23. G[7] = G[aug6] to B major: ♮VI[aug6] to I in the key of B Major. For a detailed discussion of the operation of the F/E♯ diaschisma in this progression, see chapter 32.

*Example 39.47*

24. G[7] = G[aug6] to B minor: as in number 23 above, but substituting B minor for B major.

This seems to be a reasonably complete list of chords to which G[7] (or G[aug6]) can progress, short of functioning as its own Didymic sibling (see the heading "When the Pivot Involves a Comma," below).

## A Map of the Domain of G[7]

The above material is presented chromatically for easy reference, but to get an overall picture of the domain of the G[7] (or G[aug6]) chord, a chord lattice of all the possible resolutions is presented in figure 39.20. The lattice is remarkably extensive. It is interesting to note that its center seems to lie between G and C, indicating that dominant seventh does indeed tend to pull downward, and lending credence to the supposition that the most prevalently perceived tuning of the seventh of the dominant is the 4:3 perfect fourth of the tonic.

$$\begin{array}{c}
\overset{4}{c\sharp m}\overset{18a}{—}g\sharp m\overset{8a}{—}d\sharp m\overset{22a}{—}a\sharp m \\
\overset{19}{A}\overset{9}{—}E\overset{23}{—}B\overset{13}{—}F\sharp \\
\overset{6a}{dm}\overset{20}{—}am\overset{10}{—}em\overset{24}{—}bm\overset{14}{—}f\sharp m \\
\overset{21a}{B\flat}\overset{11}{—}F\overset{1}{—}C\overset{15}{—}G\overset{5}{—}D\overset{19a}{—}A \\
\overset{22}{b\flat m}\overset{12}{—}fm\overset{2}{—}cm\overset{16}{—}gm\overset{6}{—}dm \\
\overset{3}{D\flat}\overset{17}{—}A\flat\overset{7}{—}E\flat\overset{21}{—}B\flat\overset{11a}{—}F \\
\overset{18}{a\flat m}\overset{8}{—}e\flat m
\end{array}$$

*Figure 39.20*

## How To Use the Conspiracy

These regularly resolving dominant seventh chords and irregularly resolving dominant-seventh-type chords we have been examining are not the only modulatory devices under the sun, of course (related augmented and diminished chords are given in chart form in chapter 31), but historically they have defined the evolution of tonal harmony, and they remain one of the sturdiest means of locomotion through tonal territory. Merely knowing that G⁷ (or what looks like it) can progress to twenty-four (plus 7) major and minor triads does not necessarily give you mobility in tonal harmony, but it does give insight as to how the tonal web is global, and how, with canny voice leading and a good sense of balance, you can go from anywhere to anywhere and still make harmonic sense.

My suggestion for harmonic practice using this material is, first, to hear well all of the examples given above, and then, selecting certain ones you are most attracted to, transpose to various keys. The process is like learning to navigate the streets of a city: A map is the first step, then you drive around a lot, then you begin to recognize where you are even though you've never been precisely in that place before.

## When the Pivot Involves a Comma

In the progression C–G⁷–C–Ami–Dmi–E⁷–Ami there is no ambiguity. The tuning of each chord—that is, its location on the lattice—is perfectly clear. The pivot chord is entirely unambiguous: It is the 10:9 ii in C Major, and it retains that tuning as the iv of A Minor. Pathfinder does not disintegrate, and the ground does not move. No one singing any part would have to adjust pitch in midstream by a comma. The center moves (from C to A), but the pitches stay put. The harmonic landscape is terra firma. This will be true for any matchstick progression, that is, any progression within the logic of continuous harmony.

Now consider example 39.48.

*Example 39.48*

The pivot in this case is the A-minor chord (don't be distracted by the passing G in the bass), but in just intonation the soprano must raise her pitch by the downbeat of bar 2, so we see that the pivot chord involves a Didymic comma on A. The change of tonal center (in this case C to G) is commingled with the ambiguity of a Didymic comma, and this combination of energies lends to the passage a particular affective quality.

A similar case, involving the dominant triad, occurs in the second bar of the Table of Didymic Triads (example 29.16). As first heard, the chord functions as V of C, but is then immediately recognized as the IV of the subdominant-associated ii; the second function lies a Didymic comma distant from the first. The dominant chord turns into its own Didymic sibling.

It is not an uncommon occurrence for the moment of modulation to be infused with one of the functional commas, thus giving the ear two simultaneous but distinct theaters in which to play out the loss and recovery of territorial certainty—the change of tonic and the navigation of a comma. Many examples of modulation coupled with comma phenomena have arisen in our study. The table of Didymic triads presents a forest of such cases wherein an entire chord functions as its own Didymic sibling. Many uses of the diaschismic tone are modulatory, and the pivot chord is often the point at which a diaschisma occurs (see chapter 32). The juiciest of the modulatory commas, however, involves the three-*ga* Great Diesis, and I would like to introduce additional exercises to facilitate its hands-on use.

# Great Diesis Practices

In chapters 30 and 31 we studied all the Great Diesis pairs that could be heard from the vantage point of the key of C. To learn diesis-driven harmony in every key, one needs, in order not to go *ga*-berserk, a friendly routine, a benign grabber. Dr. Overtone will present two such methods.

The objective of the first method is to become so thoroughly familiar with the harmonic territory *between* a pair of diesis tones that music can be composed or improvised confidently within that compass. To refresh your sense of this, review examples 30.28–32 and all the examples in chapter 31, paying special attention to the polarity of the flow. Then study the diagram shown in example 39.49.

*Example 39.49*

This is simply an adaptation of the lattice, with some octaves juggled. At the top and bottom we see the notes of the G♯/A♭ diesis; between them runs a central spine of thirds, the two middle notes of which (C and E) are left open. To the right is G, which completes the C-major triad; the A♭ associates with this chord as a selective borrowing from the minor mode of C—a reciprocal influx into the C Major matrix. To the left is A, which completes the A-minor triad; the G♯ associates with this chord as a selective borrowing from the major mode of A—an overtonal influx into the A Minor matrix. Although there are more notes and more chords that arise in evoking the G♯/A♭ diesis (E major and F minor especially), the ones shown constitute the core of the territory and can function as a shorthand while one is practicing in real time. In example 39.50, example 39.49 appears at the top of the circle and is transposed by ascending fifths clockwise and descending fifths counterclockwise.

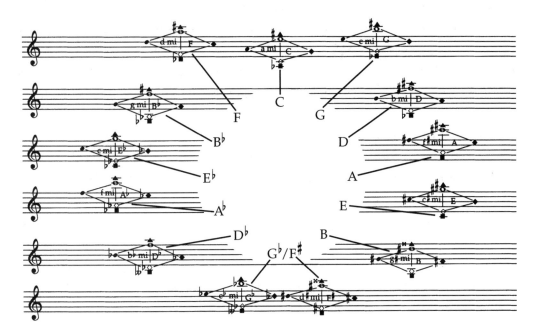

*Example 39.50*

It is not the object to go around the circle lickety-split; the best practice is to choose keys one at a time and eventually, through this form, become familiar with the diesis from every vantage point. (Especially attractive diesis-driven modulations are introduced in chapters 40 and 41.)

## An Opposite Method

The above method might be called the "inside out" method—that is, you stand at a center and look outward, surveying the territory bounded by the north-south diesis. But it is just as useful to be able to point to any tone on the keyboard and make it function as the diesis itself. It is as if you were surrounding the territory by having one foot on the northern boundary (G♯) and the other on the southern boundary (A♭) and from that vantage point looking down into the territory between. This might be called the "outside in" method. For instance, one can learn to recognize instantly that the black note between G and A can function as both the G♯ of A Minor and the A♭ of C Minor, and then to navigate convincingly between the two meanings. What about the white note below C? That's harder. (It's B♯/C♭.) What about the white note between C and E? (It's either C𝄪/D or E♭♭/D.) Crunch.

Example 39.51 features the same material we have just studied around the circle of fifths, but here it is arranged chromatically, beginning with the diesis pair F♯/G♭. Again, the object is not to play through every possibility at once, but to pick a note and try patiently to get it to behave like a diesis.

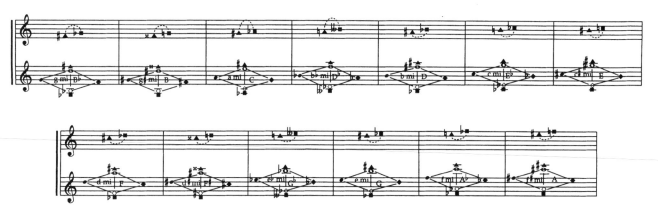

*Example 39.51*

# Full Diesis Practice

So far we have been using a span of only three major thirds (involving four spines). The full range of diesis harmony available from any given central tone, however, includes both an overtonal diesis pair and a reciprocal diesis pair, as outlined in chapter 31. The full diesis range from C is shown in example 39.52, using the conventional lattice notation and indicating the core triads.

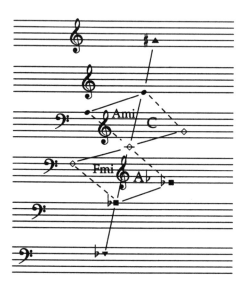

*Example 39.52*

Example 39.53 is an example of Great Diesis harmony that, centered on C, invokes in succession the overtonal G♯/A♭ diesis and the reciprocal E/F♭ diesis.

*Example 39.53*

For full credit toward your Ov.D., practice improvising your own version of the above in all twelve keys.

The exercises given in this chapter, though not exhaustive of every instance of modulation, do provide a practical guide for getting around the tonal web. Keep your ears wide open, of course, but use only as much brain as you need: Don't be afraid to turn it on and don't be afraid to turn it off. And try to do each exercise at least once before moving on.

# 40

# MODAL MODULATION

THE DOMINANT-SEVENTH-DRIVEN CADENCES we've been examining are the harmonic backbone of European classical music. They depend not only on the contractive force of the dominant seventh chord but also on a rigidly limited modal context. In the common practice period (roughly, from Bach to Brahms), there were only two available modes: Major and Minor. It is true that the Minor mode is somewhat mutable and mixed, and that other modes (not recognized in conventional theory) did come marginally into play, but the system of tonal harmony gained its modulatory force to a large extent by stripping down to the two most stable modes, and by retaining in all cases the major V triad: There is no Dorian in Beethoven. As early as Mozart, most touchingly in Chopin, and later in the Romantics up through Scriabin and beyond, you so often hear the longing to break the bonds of equal temperament and enter into the surviving resonances of the ancient village musics, the exotic modes of the gypsies and the sensuality of the Moors, but cultural pride and racial prejudice allowed the educated Western sensibility only to be titillated (and thereby "influenced") by "exotic" (read "primitive") music, never to actually embrace its practice, or the circumstances of its generation.

By the late nineteenth century, however, modal consciousness had begun to expand, and by the 1920s many composers had developed—as far as possible within the equal-tempered system—a modal sophistication. In modern times we have global access to music that has never lost its modal roots (as ours has for many centuries), and the vitality of modality is all around us. This runs both ways, of course: Non-Western musicians are rapidly becoming users of equal temperament. Consequently there has developed over the twentieth century a new kind of tonal harmony that is not dominant-seventh dependent and does allow the full panoply of modes expressible in equal temperament—not to mention those available in just intonation or "optimal tuning." This expanded system might be called *modulating modality*, or *modal modulation*; it means that one can potentially move from any mode in any key to any other mode in any other key. Some moves are better than others, of course, and this chapter is devoted to searching out the better ones.

Modulating modality was the route that Medieval and Renaissance music had embarked upon in a line of composers from Leonin through Machaut to Lassus and Gesualdo, before the Western ear, to fully realize its preoccupation with tonal modulation, narrowed down the possibilities to those within the two-mode system. By the late nineteenth century, when virtually every modulatory possibility in the Major/Minor system had been explored, Western music split into various camps. On one side of the river, Schoenberg and his followers were spurning the old language; out of its decay grew a new language of atonality, with a new grammar based on the unique powers of equal temperament. On the other bank, the Major/Minor system was evolving into the more diffuse but more extensive language of modal modulation. Shostakovich, Bartók, and Hovhannes are three among the myriad who have developed creative procedures for modal modulation; in more recent times Terry Riley (especially in *Salome Dances for Peace*) is a leading example. There is, most notably in contemporary Eastern Europe, a trend to incorporate ancient modal practice into modern composition, especially evidenced by the Bulgarian State Ensemble.

In developing discrimination in modulating modality there are two difficulties: First, the number of possibilities is staggering; second, to take advantage of those possibilities one must have a clear understanding of both modulation and modality. Understanding modulation means facility with commonly held harmonic territory, as well as with dominant-seventh-driven cadences. Understanding modality means, fundamentally, being able to sing in tune musically in a modal system of twelve or more tones. Our purpose here is not to present a complete pedagogy of modal modulation, but to present a practical hands-on method for creatively exploring the territory while analytically mapping it.

## A Way of Composing in Modulating Modality

Let's proceed by stringing together a series of modes that will serve as a harmonic template for composition. Then we'll compose a piece of piano music by allowing, as much as possible, the melodies, rhythms, textures, contrapuntal relationships, and other dimensions to arise from this template.

We'll presume that the piece begins and ends in the same mode of the same key. Let's be conservative and choose the pleasant and stable C Mixolydian. First, play the scale. Check out the available triads, four-tone chords, and cadences (see chapter 23). Remember your favorite collections; improvise something. The music need not be dronal, but it does need to sound as though C is the tonic. In other words, don't let the sense of center revert to, for instance, the more stable F Major, or the perhaps more beguiling A Phrygian, even though in equal temperament those modes comprise the same set of tones and are easy to evoke. To benefit from this particular method, you need to remain true to the mode and tonic you choose. By what criterion do you judge whether or not you have modulated out of C Mixolydian to some other set-related mode? The criterion is your ear. If you hear the music in C Mixolydian, that's what it's in.

Next, we need another mode in another key—not too close (since we want a sense of progression) and not too far (since we want a sense of continuity): Let's try A MA/MI.

To discover the relationship between the two modes, first notate C Mixolydian as in example 40.1.

*Example 40.1*

Notice that the first seven tones of the scale—the compass of its tonal content—is bracketed.

Next, notate the tones of the second scale directly below the first, taking care to line up vertically the notes with the same letter name. Bracket the first seven tones of A MA/MI. Additionally, tones that are common to both modes and *that lie within the C Mixolydian bracket* are then connected by a vertical line, as shown in example 40.2.

*Example 40.2*

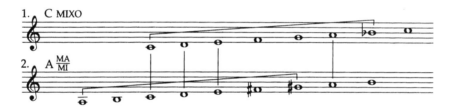

Notice that the A MA/MI scale is extended upward by a tone (to B). Here is the reason: While I am improvising in C Mixolydian I want to be able to read ahead. I need to be thinking in the "old" key while staking out the territory of the "new" key, to see the new key from the vantage point of the old key. While still in old territory, I need to know specifically which tones will stay the same and which will change. This allows me to prepare—in real time—for the immediate future. While playing in C Mixolydian I see that C, D, E, and A are going to be common tones, and that F, G, and B♭ will be changing tones. Through ear, eye and mind I lay my strategy and move ahead.

Example 40.3 demonstrates such a modulation.

*Example 40.3*

Within the first quarter note of bar 3, three common tones are sounding, but the B♮ of beat 2 signals a change, and the G♯ followed soon by F♯ help to define the new mode; the mild ii to i cadence from the end of bar 4 to the beginning of bar 5 further defines A as the new tonic.

The best way to grow into this subject is to practice improvising back and forth between the two modes, convincing yourself that you are evoking the qualities of each mode while discovering new conduits between them. Experiment, and remember the things you like.

For the next mode, I choose F Lydian, which cancels the *ga-ga* F♯ and G♯ of A MA/MI, though retaining the B. In the notation, I will again extend the material of the new scale so that all of its notes appear under the bracket of the old scale, as seen in example 40.4.

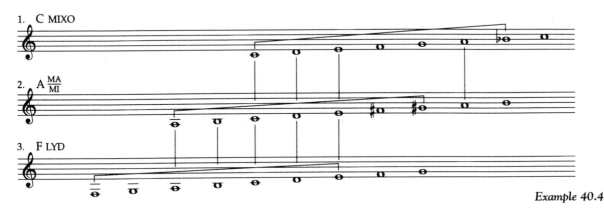

*Example 40.4*

Between scales 2 and 3 there are five common tones. Notice also that one of the changing tones is the new tonic (F♯ to F♮). Example 40.5 is a modulation from A MA/MI to F Lydian.

*Example 40.5*

Improvise your own modulations back and forth between the two modes, appreciating the appearance and disappearance of the *ga-ga* energy as you play.

For the next mode I choose B♭ Dorian—a safe way of introducing *ga*-below energy before returning finally to the original key and mode of C Mixolydian. I say "safe" partly because virtually any modal modulation is possible if the tonic changes by a fifth, a subject that is more fully discussed later in this chapter.

We now have a complete progression of keys and modes. If we agree to adopt the convention of using "key" to refer to both key *and* mode (as in "the key of C Major," by which is meant "the key of C and the mode of Major") then we can call our harmonic journey a chain of keys, or a *key chain*. Example 40.6 shows our completed key chain.

Notice that between F Lydian and B♭ Dorian there are only three common tones: F, G, and C. The four changing tones comprise the entire *ga*-spine of fifths of F Lydian, which polarizes to become the *ga*-below spine of fifths of B♭ Dorian. Example 40.7 shows such a modulation.

The moment of modulation (beat 3 of bar 3) is somewhat surprising in that the tenor

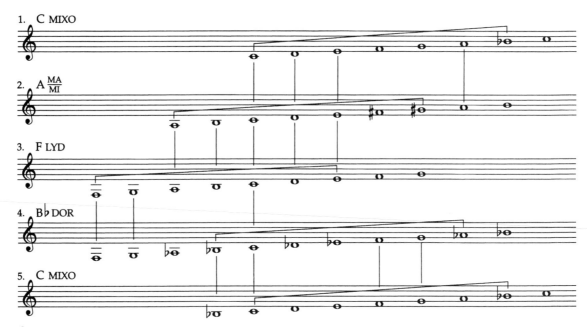

*Example 40.6*

*Example 40.7*

moves chromatically from D♮ to D♭, yet the harmony is strongly held together by the tones C and F, which are common to both modes. In bars 4 and 5 the remaining new notes (A♭, E♭, and B♭) are introduced more gradually.

Example 40.8 is a brief composition using all of the above material. Notice how the chromaticism at the moment of transition to final C Mixolydian (bar 19, beat 3), is even more surprising than the chromatic move in bar 15: since both the D♮ and the E♮ are introduced at the mildly dissonant interval of the major second. By itself this transition would not be very convincing, but in the context of the piece the ear is suddenly set down into territory it recognizes from the opening bars.

As you play the piece, zero in on the flavor of the modulations. You will find that—as will happen in short pieces like this—the modulations are closer to tonicizations: They move through territory rather than settle down into it. In longer pieces the modes can have more time to sink in; but neither way is better. This same key chain could just as easily generate a phrase lasting thirty seconds or a piece lasting ten minutes. In modulating modality, it's nice to keep moving and it's also nice to stand still.

A useful exercise is to follow what one might call the history of each note. Examine the key chain again (example 40.6), and track what happens to each letter-named note as it

*Example 40.8*

moves down the page. Both D and E remain natural except in B♭ Dorian, where they are flatted. F and G remain natural except in A MA/MI, where they are sharped. B♭ becomes B♮ at the first modulation and returns to B♭ at B♭ Dorian. Each note tells its own story.

It is important to have a general idea of where the modes fall on the lattice. This progression clearly rises to *ga-ga* land and then falls to *ga*-below land. But the ambiguities caused by the temperament's generation of Didymic commas persuades us not to draw too fine a line too soon in using positional analysis. Unless you need to know some particular harmonic detail in the process of composition, save the in-depth analysis for later, when you have become curious as to why your piece sounds so good. (Are the two D's in bar 8 and bar 9 separated by a Didymic comma? How does that affect the modulation?) The commas that result in a change of spelling are a more pressing matter: Since they generally involve a harmonic leap, they should be more consciously and deliberately employed (as we will soon discuss). The important thing at this point is to gain some keyboard facility in equal-tempered modal modulation, and to use the common-tone information as a basic guideline as you scroll down the progression of keys and modes.

## Composing from a Given Key Chain

Here is a longer key chain:

1. C Major
2. G Dorian
3. B♭ Mixolydian
4. D MA/MI
5. B Aeolian
6. G Lydian
7. C MA/MI
8. A♭ Lydian
9. C Major

First, play through the list simply as a series of scales. Next, make a chart modeled after the one on page 8. Then improvise your way down the chart, taking time to work out not only what sounds best to you in each new key and mode, but also some transitional possibilities. Then write a brief composition (between one and two pages—thirty to fifty bars) and learn to play it well. Finally, subject your piece to positional analysis. Unless you already know how, don't expect to do all this in less than a few hours. Twenty hours over two weeks would not be slow.

## Constructing Key Chains

After having composed at least one piece from a given template of modulating modes, let's consider the question of what makes a good template. Although this subject is probably more slippery to quantify than the history-sculpted procedures of the common practice period, it is nonetheless possible to point out guidelines according to at least two parameters: common tones between keys, and the relationship between tonics.

### COMMON TONES

The clearest example of mutually shared tones lies in what is often taught as the "church modes," or, thinking simply, the white notes on the piano. By repositioning the tonic we derive C Major, D Dorian, E Phrygian, F Lydian, G Mixolydian, and A Aeolian as a collection of modes that permutate freely among themselves. As mentioned in chapter 24, other types of modes have less prolific repositionings. Modes with four consecutive whole steps (like MA/MI) generate only four usable positions for the tonic; modes containing augmented seconds typically have only two usable positions.

As viewed from the keyboard, these repositionings *seem* to involve no change of set. But when viewed in the light of positional analysis, the distribution of the Didymic commas, and hence the overall harmonic and intervalic scheme, does indeed change. The D of C Major is not the D of A Aeolian, and so forth, as we have discussed in part 2 and elsewhere. Although it can be occasionally useful, retaining the set while repositioning the tonic is a fairly mild and not entirely satisfying move in equal temperament. It does, however, represent an extreme in mutuality, and one needs to have explored it. Here are three interesting examples. From the church modes: F Lydian to E Phrygian. From modes with four consecutive whole steps: F MIX/LYD to G MI/MA. From modes containing augmented seconds: C HAR.MI/MI.LYD to G HAR.MI/PHRYG.MA (C–D–E♭–F♯–G–A♭–B–C repositioned onto G).

## RELATIONSHIP BETWEEN TONICS

### Parallel modes: The tonic remains fixed

In the case of parallel modes, the tonic (and usually the fifth) remain fixed while the other degrees change, a subject we have studied throughout the first two sections of this book. In extreme cases, six tones can change, as, for instance, between C Lydian and C Locrian. In the less extreme case between C Lydian and C Phrygian, five tones change, and such progressions can be strong. Parallel modal modulation, which moves with a combination of rapid flexibility and grounded certainty, is the basis of much music. The extension of this concept is what we have called the Magic Mode or (for the less roseate-cheeked) the Omnimode, which simply means that all five chromatic pairs are simultaneously potentially active, and that a piece of modal music can flow freely among the various parallel modes of a given tonic (see the Magic Mode compositions at the end of part 2).

### Tonic Relation by the Various Intervals

To better understand the role that tonic relation has in modulation, let's first consider the simplest case by confining the discussion to the Major mode only. Compare the number of accidentals in C Major—zero sharps or flats—with the number of accidentals in every other major key, categorized by interval from C, as follows:

> up a minor second to D♭ Major: + 5 flats
> down a minor second to B Major: + 5 sharps
> up a major second to D Major: + 2 sharps
> down a major second to B♭ Major: + 2 flats
> up a minor third to E♭ Major: + 3 flats
> down a minor third to A Major: + 3 sharps
> up a major third to E Major: + 4 sharps
> down a major third to A♭ Major: + 4 flats
> up a perfect fourth (actually down a fifth) to F Major: + 1 flat
> down a perfect fourth (actually up a fifth) to G Major: + 1 sharp
> up an augmented fourth to F♯ major: + 6 sharps
> down an augmented fourth to G♭ Major: + 6 flats

This pure case—all Major modes—gives an idea of the general effect in equal temperament of each modulation solely by virtue of the intervalic relation between the various tonics. In actual music, both tonic and mode will typically change and affect one another mutually. Sometimes the change in mode and the change in tonic will tend to damp each other out: C Aeolian to E♭ Major for instance. On the other hand, the mutual effect can be additive. In the case of C Lydian to E♭ Aeolian, for instance, there are zero common tones. Although Lydian and Aeolian are both tame modes, and modulating up a minor third in cases of identical modes adds only three flats, this progression would probably not sound cogent unless it were balanced perfectly around some central harmonic territory (B♭ Major would serve). Zero common tones will usually break the harmonic thread.

Generally speaking, modal modulations work by balancing changes of tonic against changes of mode. Between two and five common tones (or one could say, between two and four changing tones) seems to work out best in most cases, but everything depends on how tonic and changes of mode affect one another, and on the context of the piece itself. After a certain amount of experimentation you will begin to develop an intuitive feel for these balances throughout the harmonic domain of an entire composition.

### Special case: The tonic moves by a perfect fifth

Perfect fifths are harmonically so closely bonded to one another that virtually any modulation is feasible when the tonics are a fifth distant. For instance, in moving from C Lydian to F Phrygian, six notes change, and the modal atmosphere goes entirely reciprocal, but the ear takes it all in, thanks to the fifth between the tonics. This method—not to be overused—is a safe and handy way of connecting even weird and disparate modes.


## BALANCE

It would be best to compose key chains containing between seven and ten keys, at least for now. Any number can be useful, of course, but the object here is to learn to construct balanced journeys. These key chains are the same in principle as the triadic odysseys we were constructing in chapter 22. The difference is that instead of triads generating modes, we now have modes generating entire families of triads and other less-consonant packages, allowing each new point of arrival on the lattice to reign over a more active and potentially wide domain. The game is the same, though, as it is in all of tonality: to remain tonally cogent and arrive home successfully. We will find ourselves preoccupied with dissolving the rules of that game later (in chapters 41 and 42), but for now, to learn the subject, it is best for your tonic progression to remain clearly unambiguous; that is, your beginning and ending tonics should be the same note on the lattice, not a comma distant. It is all too easy to overlook displacement by a Didymic comma; if you want to be sure not to do this, plot the tonic triads of your modes just as you learned to plot plain old triads. Returning home a Didymic comma distant will not wreck your life, or your piece, but it is extremely valuable to learn to be balanced as well as complex, and virtual harmonic balance is distinct from actual harmonic balance.

Let's have another look at the key chain on page 434. The key lattice notation of figure 40.1 shows the tonic triads. Start at 1 and follow the arrows. Notice how the progression moves through three quadrants: southeast to northeast to center to southwest to center. (For a more complete analysis you might draw a lattice showing all of the notes you need, and examine the domain of each mode as it arises, not only from the vantage point of its generating tonic, but also from that of the parent tone, C.)

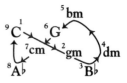

*Figure 40.1*

## CHROMATIC PAIRS

Modes often contain one or more chromatic pairs, thereby extending the domain of the mode and enriching the modulatory process. For example, C Mixolydian with two fourths (perfect and augmented) will progress nicely to A MA/MI with two sixths (major and minor), as shown in example 40.9.

*Example 40.9*

On the keyboard it appears that there are six common tones, and if we did not consider Didymic commas that would be true. However, you might be interested in checking out the difference not only between the two D's but also between the two F♯'s: The first, *tivra ma* in C, is 45:32; the second, the *dha* of *dha*, is a Didymic comma lower, and the difference in harmonic intention is quite sensible in this modulation. (Modes with more than one chromatic pair are discussed at the end of this chapter.)

## WHEN THE COMMON TONE INVOLVES A COMMA

Throughout parts 2 and 3 we have studied how each of the three functional commas can serve to catapult the harmonic energy from quadrant to quadrant within the domain of a parent key. The difference in this chapter is that the parent key is abandoned, at least temporarily. Nevertheless, the dynamics of commas when they are involved in modulation are exactly the same as when they stay centered around one tonic; they simply find themselves in a roving context. We'll use the Great Diesis as an example to demonstrate our key chain notation. Consider the two modes in example 40.10.

*Example 40.10*

The slanted line connecting C and B♯ is dotted, indicating that although the note is the same on the equal-tempered keyboard, the spelling and function have changed. (This harmony appears in example 40.12 below, between bars 12 and 13.)

The exercises at the end of chapter 39 under the heading "An Opposite Method" are especially valuable when roving the lattice. It is, perhaps, the epitome of harmonic craft to be able to turn any tone into any comma. Although the "opposite method" has been demonstrated for the diesis, the diaschisma can also play an active (though less frequent) role in modal modulation, and I urge the serious reader to invent his or her own strategy by which any tone on the keyboard can be perceived as a diaschisma. It is not difficult to see, for instance, that F♯, the augmented fourth of C Lydian Minor, could readily become G♭, the minor seventh of A♭ Mixolydian; but the obviousness fades (at least for me) when the example is transposed up a half step to the F𝄪/G diaschismic pair.

## The Composition

Consider the key chain of example 40.11 as a continuation of the keys we have just been examining.

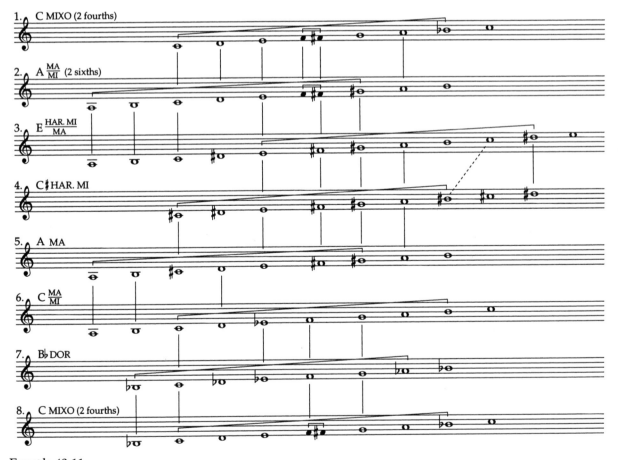

*Example 40.11*

Example 40.12 is a piece organized by the above progression of keys. It is a kind of extension of the harmonic material of example 40.8.

*Example 40.12*

Example 40.12
(continued)

Example 40.13

The first thing to do is to learn the piece well enough to play it through smoothly, if slowly. It may help to notice how often half steps in each mode are arranged to proceed from a minor ninth to a major seventh, as shown in example 40.13. When you can hear the flow of the piece, go back to its key chain chart (example 40.11) and follow the history of each note. Notice that no tone remains common throughout, and that the sharps (in this case) precede the flats. Figure 40.2 is a map of the tonic chords, shown in key lattice notation. The numbers show the order of keys.

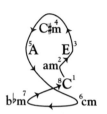

Let's go through the piece and look at a few things. We have already mentioned the difference in function between the F♯'s in bars 1 through 4 and the F♯'s in bars 6 on. The F♮ in the bass of bar 7 creates an augmented octave with the F♯'s in the upper voices on either side, allowing those two kinds of *dha* to float together in the same space like oil on water. On the last beat of bar 8, the D♯ of the E mode appears before the F♮ of the A mode is finished, mixing the two modes momentarily.

*Figure 40.2*

The C/B♯ diesis occurs between bars 12 and 13; notice that it is the C♯ in the tenor of bar 12 that effectively changes the mode, although the ear isn't at all certain of the modulation until the V⁷ function in the last half of bar 13. Likewise, A Major clarifies only as it goes along; it is fully clear by bar 16. C MA/MI, however, is immediately clear, forcing the changing tones by contrary motion, as shown in example 40.14.

Notice, however, how this sudden infusion of reciprocal energy requires some time to get used to: Nine bars are spent in C MA/MI—a long time for a piece this short—while the music rambles expansively through a new texture. This allows the three additional flats of B♭ Dorian to be more easily

*Example 40.14*

accepted in bar 26; the return to the parent key in bar 31 then sounds balanced.

# Hints for Composition

## KEY CHAIN FIRST

My advice for learning to compose, using these broad techniques of modal modulation, is to begin by writing a key chain that convinces you of its effectiveness as you improvise your way through it. Map your tonic triads on a chord lattice, which will serve as a kind of harmonic spell check.

As you first begin to compose, be absolutely faithful to your key chain, even if you have to put aside (not discard) ideas that sound great but are not part of the harmonic scheme. Gradually you will feel free to change your key chain in various ways as you flesh out your piece, and eventually the entire process becomes less linear and more holistic: It is, after all, a creative ideal that all dimensions of a work clarify themselves simultaneously as the work progresses. But for now, be disciplined in letting the harmony rule the content.

The question then becomes when to change the content. Sometimes the same material will endure through several modulations (for example, the first four keys in the above example); at other times a new key will signal new content (bar 17). How do you know when to change? In the case above, the infusion of flats was the trigger; but the answer is, you don't know, you find out. The entire point of fabricating a harmonic scheme prior to composing a piece is to discover the extent to which interesting and balanced harmonic motion is in itself creative. Under controlled conditions, harmony tells you what to do. It is a clear voice hidden in your ear, an abstruse but radiant guide. When you hear the voice of harmony, you realize that it is that same embodied intelligence that speaks unadorned through the tone-by-tone resonances of just intonation, but concealed and richly thickened by the simultaneously sounding tones of equal temperament. The discipline of composing according to a harmonic plan teaches you how contemporary composition can be a response to primal resonances. So, at least at first, let the harmony write the piece.

## A TEXT HELPS

An even more structured discipline is using the key chain method to set texts to music. Each line of a poem, or each phrase, can be used to suggest an appropriate mode in an appropriate key from which a singer's line can then arise. In this sense, the words write the harmony and the harmony writes the piece—an especially intuitive process conjoining the deepest meanings of both words and music.

## THE THREE FUNCTIONAL COMMAS COMPARED

From my point of view the three functional commas do not figure equally in the process of composition. I perceive them as follows:

Didymic commas I *notice*, from time to time, as they glide through. They are the least expressive and the most hidden of the commas, and they can stay hidden as far as I'm concerned, unless I need to know about them, which is usually only when I am trying to analyze myself out of an unbalanced or otherwise stuck place, and then I am thankful to know where they are.

Great Dieses I *use*, as a real-time tool. They are in my ear and in my hands, handy as a Swiss army knife. In the Great Opera of harmony they are active, special characters, always waiting patiently for their cues, often chiming in unbidden to produce serendipitous advances in the plot.

Diaschismas sometimes get pulled out of a hat, but more usually they show up as welcome—if surprising—visitors. Since the diaschisma is the least common comma, it is sometimes the most effective means of modulation.

## NONMODAL TONES

Because the modes used in modal modulation are usually not as stable as the major/minor grid of tonal harmony, tones that are not diatonic to the working mode can more easily disturb or destabilize precarious tonics. If tonal clarity is the object, nonmodal tones must be used cautiously. But the criterion is the same as always: If you hear the efficacy of the mode you are in, the mode is efficacious.

## TONAL CADENCES

There is nothing wrong with conventional tonal cadences, of course, but remember that they have become conventional because of their potency in focusing tonal gravity. Take care that the strong dominant-seventh-driven cadences of tonal harmony do not overpower the more pastel pushes and pulls of modal modulation.

# The Value of the Method

The contemporary composer and improvisor needs to find a way to make sense of a bewildering number of historical and global influences without getting tangled up in any of them. The key chain method is not an end in itself, but a way of developing a sophisticated harmonic language that is informed not only by a wide historical period, but also by the various manners and styles in the world's living music.

# The Modal Limit in Equal Temperament: The Modulating Magic Mode

We've seen how individual chromatic pairs figure in the process of modal modulation; we also know that some modes contain several chromatic pairs, and that with proper care, such modes can modulate. In fact, the Magic Mode, which contains all five chromatic pairs (or even more, if you include the Locrian and Super-Lydian options), can be made to modulate through any number of tonics. Does this mean that modal modulation can take the form of a series of Magic Modes progressing from tonic to tonic? Yes, indeed; one could even say that controlling the modulations and mutual influences of the twelve Magic Modes is the ultimate art of tonality. I say ultimate because lying at the edge of equal-tempered tonality is a boundary that separates intricate modal embroidery from finely spun chaos, deep wisdom from utter nonsense, and this boundary can be vanishingly small. One can only too easily find oneself on the unintended side of it. It would be fair to consider all of our labor up to now as an exercise in discerning this fine line.

When you feel you are ready, try your hand at composing a piece of modulating Magic Mode music. Compose many more than one—if not soon, then later. The possibilities of modulating Magic Mode music open themselves gradually over many years.

# 41

# A SYLLABUS OF CYCLIC SEQUENCES

## The Art of Virtual Return

A piece that begins in C Major and ends in D♭♭ Major results in a virtual return. In terms of the black and white notes on the equal-tempered keyboard, the piece appears to begin and end in the same key; if the piece is notated, there will be an enharmonic change of spelling at some point, and the music will appear on the page to have returned to the original key. But it has not (see chapter 34). A piece that begins in C Major and ends in the same C Major where it began undergoes an actual return. The difference in effect between a virtual return and an actual return is central to this book. So far, we have concentrated primarily on the limits and the mechanics of actual returns. By using the graphic metaphor of the five-limit lattice, we have seen how every actual return begins and ends at the same location. Now it is time to examine the various strategies of virtual return, all of which involve the lattice folding in such ways as to bring a distant location in contact with the original one. The cyclic sequences in this chapter are a collection of representative cases from every possible type of virtual return, that is, every possible type of folding using a five-limit lattice.

Unless you already are adept at keyboard harmony to some degree, I suggest that you reread (or at least scan) chapter 36 before plunging ahead. It contains a discussion of various diatonic sequences, most of which contain Didymic commas and result in a diatonic version of virtual return. The diatonic kind do not undergo a change of spelling; they are much stronger and more convincing to our Pathfinder nature than the cyclic sequences discussed here. The sequences of this chapter are chromatic; they involve all twelve equal tempered tones, they invariably invoke commas resulting in changes of spelling, and they leave Pathfinder in a swoon. In the course of studying these sequences and comparing them with the unambiguous progressions resulting in actual return (such as the progressions in chapter 22 and the cadences of chapter 38), a profound aesthetic law is demonstrated: The decay of a pure and wholesome simplicity can result in the rise of a sophisticated and useful complexity.

My grandmother Clara, born in 1876, was a great walker. She would rather walk several miles than take the trolley, thereby *earning* her destination step by step and concomitantly saving a dime. She stubbornly put off until the age of thirty-five the fretful moment of first stepping into an automobile—which she called a "machine"—and although she lived well into the 1960s she never did board an airplane. "If God had meant us to fly He would have given us wings," she reiterated over six decades, and perhaps, in a way, her intuition was right.

In 1705 Bach walked over two hundred miles, the legend says, to hear the organ playing of a composer he admired, Dietrich Buxtehude. Country kids of two generations ago would routinely walk several miles to school ("uphill both ways," they now recall). We moderns who hardly think twice about air travel have very nearly lost all sense of ground distance. Can you imagine with what intimacy hunter-gatherers knew (still know?) the earth beneath their feet, its buoyancy, its generosity in replenishing the walker? We buy our wings for a few dollars, then look down on chunks of the planet from thirty thousand feet up; but for these wings we have actually paid a high price.

In the special kind of travel afforded by harmonically complex equal-tempered music, we have learned the sophisticated mechanics of virtual return, and these have given our ears a kind of jet lag and our musical responses a loss of connectedness. But I don't think we should give up either our airplanes or our cyclic sequences. We should fly whenever we please *and* reclaim walking for ourselves; in music we should modulate in any conceivable virtual configuration *and* reclaim the ability to sing in tune over fixed, unmoving ground. The sequences that follow will teach you every looping design for escaping that fixed ground. They will give you the opportunity to consider from personal experience what is to be gained from such exotic flight. But I hope that, perhaps through their very complexity, they will also remind you of the need to balance earth and sky.

## Directional Organization of the Sequences

These sequences are organized according to ratios between their tonal centers. Sometimes the tonal centers are transient and suggested by only one chord; sometimes they are clearly established by cadential progressions.

The harmonic field contains the usual two dimensions: the triple nature of 3:2 perfect fifths and the pentamerous nature of 5:4 major thirds (see chapter 29, especially figure 29.5). Compass orientation allows motion by ascending 3:2 perfect fifths to be termed *3:2 east* (or Pythagorean east) or, if they are descending, *3:2 west* (or Pythagorean west), and allows purely pentamerous motion by ascending major thirds to be termed *5:4 north* (or pentamerous north) or, if descending, *5:4 south* (or pentamerous south). Consequently, any vector between horizontal pure fifths and vertical pure major thirds can unequivocally be termed by the compass points in between: northeast, southeast, southwest, and northwest. A complete chart appears at the end of this chapter (figure 41.37). It would be useful at this point to draw a chord lattice in compass orientation, as shown in figure 41.1, from memory. Using graph paper (two lines per inch is convenient) will insure the accuracy of the result.

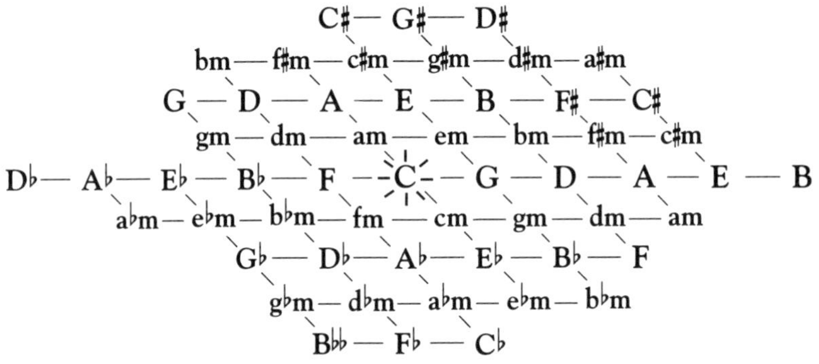

*Figure 41.1*

We will examine fifty-three cyclic sequences in all, beginning with perfect fifths descending.

## Movement by Fifths

### 3:2 WEST: PERFECT FIFTHS DESCENDING

Before studying the first cyclic sequence, here are some preliminary steps. Play the top C on the piano and descend by perfect fifths. Your thirteenth fifth should be the lowest C on the piano. Learn to play this descending arpeggio of fifths rapidly, as if to perceive all of the twelve tones at once.

Next, review the diatonic sequence of descending fifths (examples 36.6–15), including melodic discontinuities in the parts that result from their bicyclic arrangement. Then study the sequence in example 41.1, which begins on a G triad.

*Example 41.1*

On the chord lattice the direction is due west. Without an enharmonic change, the spelling of the chords would be as shown in figure 41.2.

$$D\flat\flat \leftarrow A\flat\flat \leftarrow E\flat\flat \leftarrow B\flat\flat \leftarrow F\flat \leftarrow C\flat \leftarrow G\flat \leftarrow D\flat \leftarrow A\flat \leftarrow E\flat \leftarrow B\flat \leftarrow F \leftarrow C$$

*Figure 41.2*

To visualize how equal temperament behaves in terms of the five-limit lattice, you must fold the D𝄫 over (left to right) so it touches the C; by courtesy of the temperament, the Pythagorean comma is distributed equally over the twelve moves so the first chord is identical to the thirteenth: a Pythagorean virtual return. What does the ear hear? You tell me.

The Pythagorean comma is typically shown by a circle of fifths, the most clear form of which is shown as figure 41.3a. Notice that the enharmonic change most practically occurs at F♯/G♭. Of course, any tone could be at the top, so perhaps figure 41.3b is the most useful configuration (you can spin it).

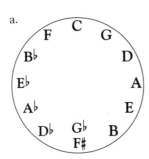
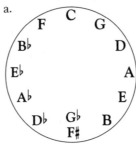

*Figure 41.3*

Although complete cycles of certain sequences appear in real music, complete cycles of major triads descending by fifths appear almost exclusively in music composed for pedagogical purposes. The Pythagorean comma is distributed in such tiny increments over so many chords, whose harmonic bond is so strong, that the ear cannot get much of a grip on its particular quality. However, parts of the sequence—six chords or more—are usual if not ubiquitous in real music, and for this reason—and because, generally, circle-of-fifth sequences teach you to think by fifths from any tonic—such sequences make excellent keyboard exercises.

Example 41.2 shows the same root motion, but with dominant-seventh-type chords. Notice that the fifth of every chord is omitted. Also, notice how the upper two parts alternate functions: If you were singing the soprano part, you would begin on the *third* of G⁷ (the tone B), then proceed to the *seventh* of C⁷ (B♭), then to the third of the next chord, then the seventh, and so on. If you were singing alto (try it) you would begin on the *seventh* of G⁷ (F), then proceed to the *third* of C⁷ (E), then the seventh, then the third, and so on. This is easy to understand, and easy to hear if you are singing; but it is not at all easy to hear both upper parts with equal effect while you are sitting quietly at the keyboard playing all the parts—and that is the recommended practice.

*Example 41.2*

The next step is to elaborate the sequence according to the suggestions in chapter 36. This is an important phase of learning keyboard harmony, and is recommended for most of the sequences that follow.

Example 41.3 shows the same sequence in four parts.

*Example 41.3*

Notice that only half the chords are in root position: Every other chord is in second inversion. Also notice that both the tenor and the bass progress exclusively by whole steps. You may know that there are only two available whole-tone scales in twelve-tone equal temperament; in this sequence, the tenor sings one while the bass sings the other. Why? (Hint: Each move in each part covers the territory of two fifths.)

Example 41.4 is a jazzlike version of the same sequence.

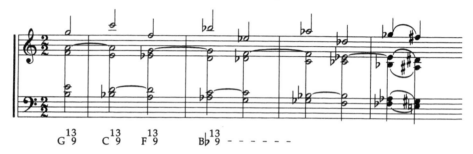

*Example 41.4*

The old bass of example 41.2 is the new soprano, and the old soprano is the new bass, which alternates function with the new middle part (starting on F). The fifths of each chord are again omitted. Meanwhile, the standing dissonances of the major ninth and the major thirteenth alternate function with one another. It is very useful, especially if you are learning to play jazz, to play the left hand as written around the circle and improvise (using either Mixolydian scales or "♯4♭7" scales above each root while emphasizing tonics and fifths), four beats per chord, from slow tempo at first to very rapid tempo.

## PYTHAGOREAN WEST: THE CIRCLE OF TWENTY-FOUR CHORDS

Play the top C of the piano, then descend by alternating minor thirds and major thirds: C, A, **F**, D, **B♭**, G, and so on. The italicized notes are the circle of fifths descending from C; if you thought of each of the italicized notes as roots generating a major triad, then the in-between notes could be considered as roots generating their relative minors: C, Ami, F, Dmi, and so on. Suitably octave-reduced, those tones become the bass of the sequence of twenty-four chords shown in example 41.5.

C  Ami  F  Dmi  B♭  Gmi  E♭  Cmi  A♭  Fmi  D♭  B♭mi  G♭  E♭mi = D♯mi  B  G♯mi  E  C♯mi  A  F♯mi  D  Bmi  G  Emi  C

*Example 41.5*

Although the most singable bass part results in jumping octaves every four notes (as we have done here), this is a tricyclic sequence and hence notated in triple meter.

The sequence falls by thirds and obeys the basic voice-leading mechanics of a diatonic sequence of falling thirds: One part at a time moves contrary to the bass (assuming the bass falls a third, as opposed to rising a sixth). But beyond that, the three upper parts display a most amazing pattern. To discover it, play each part solo. You will find that each comprises a "diminished scale," a symmetrical scale of alternating whole and half steps. (Symmetrical scales are discussed in detail in chapter 42.) Equal temperament allows the possibility of three such scales, and in this sequence, each of the three upper parts is singing one of them. How can this be? (Hint: A half step plus a whole step equals a minor third, which is also the interval—octave-reduced—covered by a stack of three perfect fifths. This is a tricyclic sequence. It took me decades to figure this out—why should you get it right away?)

The most useful graphic version of the circle of twenty-four chords takes its cue from the chord lattice, which describes a zigzag course moving west, as shown in figure 41.4.

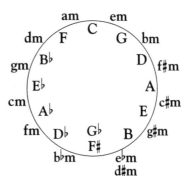

*Figure 41.4*

The circular version is shown in figure 41.5. This should be committed to photographic recall, and the sequence itself should be playable in your sleep—no kidding.

The following sequence is entirely dependent on fluency with the previous one. Beginning with the top C on the piano and descending stepwise, play the remainder of the notes in the upper tetrachord of C Major, namely, B, A, and G. Now play the upper tetrachord of F Major (F, E, D, C); next, the upper

*Figure 41.5*

tetrachord of B♭ Major, then of E♭ Major, and so on around the circle of descending fifths until you have played a special kind of scale that descends all the way to the lowest C on the piano. That scale is the bass line of example 41.6.

*Example 41.6*

Here, each of the twenty-four chords of the previous sequence is preceded by its dominant seventh, resulting in twenty-four pairs of chords, each pair comprising a dominant-to-tonic authentic cadence. In other words, the sequence tonicizes all twenty-four major and minor keys. On the chord lattice it describes a jagged pattern moving inexorably due west, as shown in figure 41.6.

Figure 41.6

Before you learn to play the sequence, be sure to play each part alone. You will notice that the upper three parts constitute a canon at the fifth below. To discover this, begin with the soprano of bar 1; the next entrance is the tenor of bar 2; the third entrance is the alto of bar 3 (which sounds at the fourth above instead of the fifth below). Also notice that each of the dominant seventh chords appears in second inversion and resolves to a tonic chord in root position.

The sequence should be practiced taking the upper three parts in the right hand. You may find it difficult at first to track twenty-four keys in one pass. But this is one of the most used and useful keyboard practices in all of tonal harmony, and it serves as a kind of initiation into a deeper knowledge of the subject. Any one who can play this sequence rapidly and smoothly (from memory, of course), hear the canon and follow the harmony at the same time, *and* develop the ability to elaborate upon it extemporaneously, can no longer not be serious. Following are some suggestions for improvising.

If we collapse the harmony so it's playable entirely in the left hand, the right hand becomes free to improvise melodically. Example 41.7 begins on G⁷.

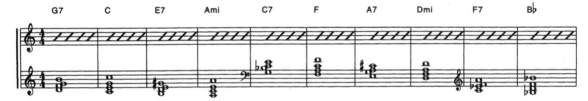

Example 41.7

Remember to think in terms of the approaching tonic (as outlined in chapter 37). When approaching minor tonics, you might use the Utility Minor exclusively in order to simplify the process; but the goal is to be able to use Full Minor for every minor key. You might also eventually consider discretionary borrowing from minor when approaching major keys. All of this will give you a practical cadential facility in all keys, and it's fun to play besides, especially if you play in time.

Example 41.8 is a jazz version of the above.

Example 41.8

## 3:2 EAST: PERFECT FIFTHS ASCENDING

Play the lowest C on the piano and ascend by fifths: The thirteenth note is the top C of the piano. That is the bass line for example 41.9.

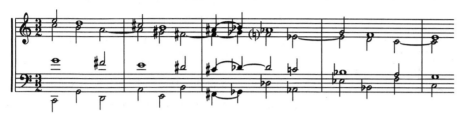

*Example 41.9*

The progression on the chord lattice is due west, as shown in figure 41.7. "Circle of fifths" harmony is usually taught as fifths descending.

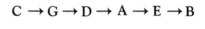

$$C \rightarrow G \rightarrow D \rightarrow A \rightarrow E \rightarrow B$$

*Figure 41.7*

When you hear the sequence of fifths ascending for the first time it sounds unfamiliar, yet at the same time entirely true. Notice that there is no melodic discontinuity in the upper parts as there was in the descending version (example 41.1) or its diatonic ancestors (example 36.8). To best understand how pianistically benign the upper three parts actually are, play them together in the right hand (without the bass), observing all ties; then add the bass in the left hand. When you can play the model smoothly from memory, try elaborating it according to the suggestions in chapter 36.

How does your ear hear the Pythagorean comma in this case? The comma is still distributed over too many strong moves for my ear to glean any characteristic affect from it, but, true to its yin roots, the ascending version of the sequence seems to have less stability and more mystery than the descending version, rendering the comma slightly less invisible, perhaps. In any case, of all virtual returns, this one seems to me least disquieting. My Pathfinder knows for sure that it is not the real Homebody pouring tea, but there seems to be an especially calm acceptance of the fact. Like sequences of descending fifths (and unlike pentamerous sequences that achieve a much more heightened affect with fewer, weaker moves) this sequence does not occur in complete form in actual music. Bits and pieces of it show up continually, of course.

When improvising over this sequence, the major scale of each chord will generate the most familiar-sounding passing tones. But there is another handy option: To better prepare for the upcoming key, you can Lydianize your scale *before* changing the harmony. For example, start with C Major, introduce the F♯ of C Lydian, *then* move to G Major (which has the same notes as C Lydian) for a moment, then G Lydian, then D Major, and so on.

Another option for elaboration of the above sequence is to use the tonic of the old key as a 4-3 suspension into the new key. Example 41.10 is the model.

*Example 41.10*

Again, learn the upper three parts in the right hand alone first, observing all ties and making a sweet legato. You will notice that only one part moves at a time. Solving the legato problem (without pedal, if possible) helps you internalize the harmony well enough to use it musically.

Root motion by ascending fifths is even more mysterious if every chord is minor, as shown in example 41.11.

*Example 41.11*

When improvising on this sequence, try using all Aeolian scales at first. Then, taking a cue from example 41.9 above, Dorianize as you go. In other words, play in C Aeolian, then, to prepare the next key, natural the A, thus playing in C Dorian, then move to G Aeolian (which contains the same notes as C Dorian), then play in G Dorian, and so on. You might try other flavors of Minor in various combinations; the goal, again, is to have the option of using the complete range of Full Minor for each new key.

The sequence in example 41.12a adds 4–3 suspensions to each triad.

*Example 41.12a*

It is not obvious why this sequence, even in its unelaborated model form, is so beautiful. Even though it sounds so transparent and nourishing to the ear, its use in real music is remarkably infrequent. Again, I don't think the beauty is in the evocation of the comma so much as in the sheer yin pleasure of ascending Pythagorean motion, combined with suspended minor triads. In any case, it is made for learning and enjoying. Example 41.12b is an elaboration of a complete cycle using Full Minor.

*Example 41.12b*

## CADENCES IN PYTHAGOREAN SEQUENCE

Following are two models that can help you learn certain cadences in all keys.

Example 41.13 is a sequence of full cadences descending by thirds through all twenty-four keys, with the IV and V triads in first inversion. The second chord of each bar can be heard simply as a repositioning of the tonic chord.

*Example 41.13*

Improvising on this sequence is much like improvising on example 41.6, but balanced by subdominant harmony in each key. The beauty of the first inversion chords inspires the improvisation.

Example 41.14 is the "Neapolitan sixth cadence" resolving to twelve minor keys ascending by fifths. We have studied this harmony as a "Phrygianization" of the approaching tonic; the value here is to feel the Phrygian energy of each key come into your fingers before it yields to conventional minor.

*Example 41.14*

## PYTHAGOREAN DISCONTINUITIES

Example 41.15 tonicizes twelve major keys, each with a perfect cadence.

*Example 41.15*

Notice that the roots ascend by fifths the way a trout moves upstream: down one fifth, up two fifths, down one, up two, and so on, thus making its way on the lattice due east. Every leap of two fifths is filled in by the root leapt over, weaving a taut cadential fabric. Notice also the two alternating versions of cadential voice leading.

In example 41.16 the roots leap up two fifths at a time with no back-filling.

*Example 41.16*

On the chord lattice the progression leapfrogs due east; the roots ascend at the ratio of 9:8. Because it takes only six chords for it to cycle around, the character of the comma seems faintly sensible to me: It is the single case of a functional Pythagorean comma that I know of. Although the roots describe a whole-tone scale in equal temperament, the placement of the major triads on the chord lattice is unambiguous. What do you hear? For the less compelling westward-bound version, play it backward. Then transpose it a half step to get at the other six major triads.

As we shall soon see, harmonic discontinuities more extreme than this, even within the relative safety of the central Pythagorean spine, give rise to tonal ambiguities.

Having completed our survey of "circle of fifths" sequences, we'll examine sequences based on what might be called the "circle of thirds."

# Movement by Major Thirds

## 5:4 SOUTH: MAJOR THIRDS DESCENDING

Figure 41.8 shows the chord lattice for major triads whose roots descend by major thirds. With an enharmonic change at every third triad, we have the sequence of example 41.17.

Example 41.17

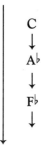

Figure 41.8

Example 41.18 shows the same sequence for minor triads.

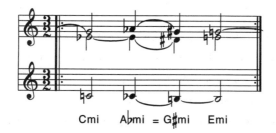

Example 41.18

The spelling makes the Great Diesis visible: Every third chord generates a diesis for each tone of the triad. Yet there *are* only three chords, and the original pitch—entirely sensible—does not move. Like a Mevlevi dervish, we sense both our spinning and our standing still. Such is the aesthetic of equal-tempered harmony: Are we whirling about in the world, or are we standing fixed while it whirls about us? Purely pentamerous harmony signals the endgame of tonality, and in these sequences of major thirds you can hear quite clearly the mechanics of tonal dissolution. And, just as in dervish whirling, there is an ecstacy in it, a kind of *ga*-cubed frenzy that gets inside of us and holds on. Play example 41.18 until you've had enough; then read some more.

Example 41.19 has the same tonal material, but now each chord is a dominant-seventh-type chord, and each has four positions (root position, first inversion, second inversion, and third inversion).

*Example 41.19*

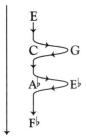

*Figure 41.9*

The standing dissonances soften the effect of the diesis, and the voice-leading pattern imposes an intriguing superficial pattern. (From here on, we'll no longer make visible every enharmonically equivalent spelling.)

Example 41.20 is a sequence that travels south with the aid of a Pythagorean shuttle, lending to its weird light a familiar comfort. Figure 41.9 shows the chord lattice.

*Example 41.20*

This progression is useful to know in all of its transpositions (there are three others—why three?) and makes an inspiring template for improvisation and composition.

Example 41.21 has a similar harmonic path but uses minor tonics.

*Example 41.21*

## 5:4 NORTH: MAJOR THIRDS ASCENDING

Example 41.22 shows major triads whose roots ascend by major thirds, moving due north on the lattice. Compare them with their polar compliments in example 41.17. Figure 41.10 shows the chord lattice.

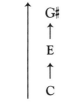

*Figure 41.10*

*Example 41.22*

C        E        G♯ = A♭

Example 41.23 shows minor triads moving due north. Compare with example 41.18.

*Example 41.23*

Cmi    Emi    G♯mi = A♭mi

Try using this progression as a kind of cyclic key chain employing the following two kinds of minor scales: Start with C U-MI, changing to C MA/MI, modulating smoothly to E U-MI (observing E♭ become D♯), changing to E MA/MI, modulating impeccably to G♯ U-MI (observing G become F✗). OK, now we think through the enharmonic change: G♯ U-MI = A♭ U-MI; now we proceed, changing A♭ U-MI to A♭ MA/MI, modulating to C U-MI (observing C♭ become B♮), and that brings us back. This is an especially attractive use of northward moving—northward *surging*—pentamerous energy, and worth practicing in the other three transpositions.

Example 41.24 is a four-part version of example 41.23, replete with a passing chord that demonstrates each diesis.

*Example 41.24*

In example 41.25 major triads move due north in tandem with their relative minors.

*Example 41.25*

Notice that each minor triad can be considered a pivot chord, the two functions of which are a major third distant: The vi of the old key (Ami in C Major) is the iv of the new key (Ami in E). Since vi and iv are a major third apart, a chord that pivots between the two functions causes a modulation to a key a major third distant. The chord lattice is shown in figure 41.11.

G♯
c♯m
E
am
C
fm
A♭

*Figure 41.11*

Example 41.26 is like the preceding sequence, with an added passing chord that weaves the Pythagorean/pentamerous woof/warp even tighter. Figure 41.12 shows the chord lattice.

*Example 41.26*

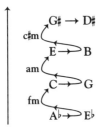

*Figure 41.12*

Example 41.27 adds more subtle passing chords: Now the old ii becomes the new ♭vii (a major third apart, incidentally), which then immediately becomes the new ♭II^aug6 (F^aug6 in E), and so on, as shown. The chord lattice is shown in figure 41.13.

*Example 41.27*

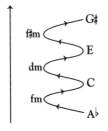

*Figure 41.13*

In example 41.28 the Pythagorean energy threatens to overwhelm the pentamerous energy, since two consecutive roots descend by fifths. The tonics ascend by major thirds, however, because the

*Example 41.28*

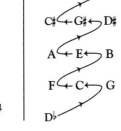

*Figure 41.14*

functions of the pivot chord are again a major third distant: The old IV (F in C Major) is the new ♭II (F in E Major), and IV is a major third above ♭II. The chord lattice is shown in figure 41.14.

# Movement by Minor Seconds

## 16:15 NORTHEAST: MINOR SECONDS DESCENDING

We'll now combine root motion of a perfect fifth ascending and a major third ascending. These two intervals compound to form a major seventh above, which can then invert to form a minor second below. Try it: Start with D♭; up a fifth to A♭; up a third to C; and now, because we don't want the basses to sing sequences full of major sevenths, down an octave to the C a minor second below D♭. Only pivot chords whose dual functions are a minor second distant can accomplish such a modulation; the two most workable are ♭II/I and ♭VI/V.

Play example 41.29.

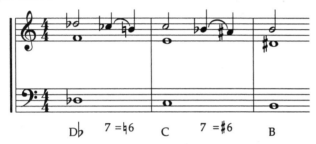

*Example 41.29*

The first chord of each bar is a tonic triad that immediately, by using a *ga-ga* diaschismic pair (see chapter 32), becomes the ♭II^aug6 of the approaching key. In figure 41.15, the lattice displays wild northeastern leaping.

Incidentally, the thirteenth bar will return to a tone twelve overtonal fifths plus twelve overtonal thirds distant from its gener-

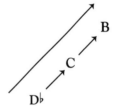

*Figure 41.15*

ating tone, that is, one Pythagorean comma plus *four* Great Dieses, resulting in a compound comma (as we will call it) for which there is certainly no name, and which clearly does not have a sensible affect. Now go back to our recent speculations about the Pythagorean comma, with its twelve moves (as compared with the three or four moves of the three "functional commas"). Could it be that commas with too many moves do not have a functional affect? Does *any* compound comma, as is $(\frac{16}{15})^{12}$, have a sensible affect?

Example 41.30 is a series of perfect cadences whose tonics descend by minor seconds in such a way that the old tonic (the second chord of each bar) is gracefully, thanks to its being in first inversion, the ♭II of the new tonic. The diaschisma is avoided. Figure 41.16 shows the chord lattice.

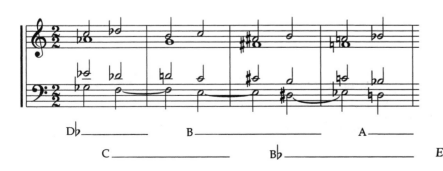

*Example 41.30*    *Figure 41.16*

Example 41.31 is a variation on the same material; its chord lattice is much the same.

*Example 41.31*

In example 41.32 the old V is the new ♭VI^aug6, with a *ga-ga* diaschismic pair each time. Figure 41.17 shows the chord lattice.

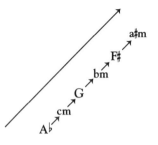

*Figure 41.17*

*Example 41.32*

Example 41.33 is a beautifully configured variation that uses Major keys instead of Minor.

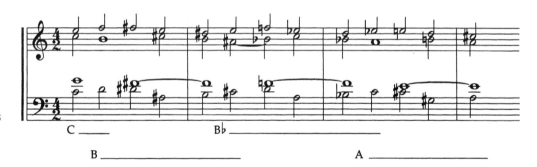

*Example 41.33*

## 16:15 Southwest: Minor Seconds Ascending

If the direction of the pivot chord in examples 41.32 and 41.33 is reversed (so that the old ♭VI is the new V), the tonics of the sequence will ascend by minor seconds, as seen in example 41.34. Figure 41.18 shows that on the chord lattice the progression falls southwest.

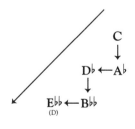

*Figure 41.18*

*Example 41.34*

The effect in Minor (example 41.35) is much more comfortable than in Major and could even be described as lush.

*Example 41.35*

# Movement by Minor Whole Tones

## 10:9 SOUTHEAST: MINOR WHOLE TONES DESCENDING

If you compound two fifths down with one major third up, the result, after octave reduction, is a 10:9 major second, also called a minor whole tone (to distinguish it from the 9:8 major whole tone). The class of sequences whose tonics progress by minor whole tones is of special interest because such progressions are easily confused with the stronger, more forthright Pythagorean progressions involving major whole tones. The distinction is both subtle and profound, and to appreciate it fully one must experience again the difference in quality between those two resonances in just intonation. (This subject was introduced in chapter 10 and developed in chapter 29). The most common *re*, for instance, is 9:8 with *sa;* in contrast, the most common *dha* is 10:9 with *pa* (both readily singable using the C and G drones of the equal-tempered keyboard). The act of internalizing such distinctions is the missing link in our culture's comprehension of harmony. If we had not lost the living experience of these resonances, our musical thought would be more lucid and our music might have attained an even more enduring vitality. As it turns out, the missing link is you—singing, feeling vitalized by the various resonances, and carrying this experience forward into equal-tempered music.

The sequence in example 41.36 blends Pythagorean energy and pentamerous energy in a particularly balanced way. Figure 41.19 presents the motion as it appears on the chord lattice.

*Figure 41.19*

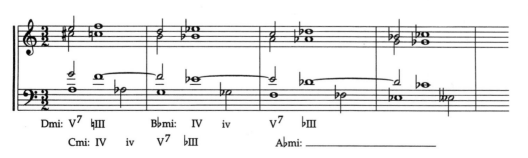

*Example 41.36*

Compare these with example 39.29 and figure 39.10.

Since the sequence involves a particular type of deceptive cadence ($V^7$ to $^\flat$III), the actual tonics are not sounded and appear on the lattice in parentheses. The actual root motions, represented by arrows, leap two fifths up and fall one major third down, followed by a mode change that allies the ear with reciprocal *ga* energy. The result describes a southeastern journey on the lattice that is a perfect vector between rising fifths (due east) and falling thirds (due south).

At first blush, the above sequence might seem to be some kind of descending Pythagorean harmony, since that is how we are conditioned to think about such chromatically descending sounds. To better appreciate the true mix, try playing example 41.16 (major triads ascending by 9:8), then example 41.18 (minor triads descending by 5:4), then alternating between those two several times, then finally playing example 41.36 again. What do you hear? When the sequence finally comes around to D$^{\flat\flat}$, incidentally, the compound comma is one overtonal Pythagorean comma (twelve fifths) minus two Great Dieses (six major thirds), again not a sensible compound comma. The harmony gains its quality essentially from its direction and its internal Didymic commas.

Why isn't the sequence in example 41.37 purely Pythagorean?

*Example 41.37*

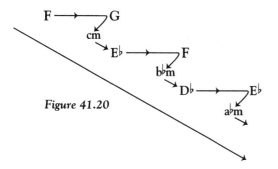

*Figure 41.20*

Figure 41.20 shows the chord lattice.

Example 41.37 does not simply descend by fifths. Rather, it ascends by fifths as it falls by major thirds: The second chord of each bar is unambiguously the $^\flat$III (that is, the relative major) of the minor tonic on the downbeat.

Example 41.38, with its resolution to a major tonic, opens into ambiguity.

*Example 41.38*

The ambiguity depends on how you hear ii$^7$–V$^7$–I harmony. If you hear the ii chord as having a subdominant quality (its primary historical role), the sequence describes a southeastern path, as shown in figure 41.21.

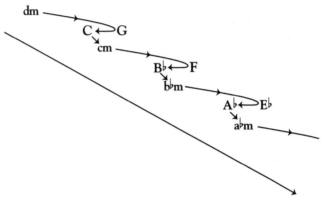

*Figure 41.21*

If you hear ii$^7$–V$^7$–I as falling fifths, then the ii chord would fill the role of the dominant of the dominant, which seems to occur with regularity within the root-position, falling-fifth progressions of jazz. The lattice path would then be inexorably west, as shown in figure 41.22.

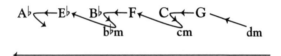

*Figure 41.22*

Which version do we hear? Maybe we hear both harmonic directions at once. What a concept!

## 10:9 NORTHWEST: MINOR WHOLE TONES ASCENDING

*Example 41.39*

Ascending sequences by minor whole tones are less common. Example 41.39 is one instance where the old I becomes the ♭VII of the new MI/MA mode (B♭$^7$ in C MI/MA). Figure 41.23 shows the northwestern direction on the chord lattice.

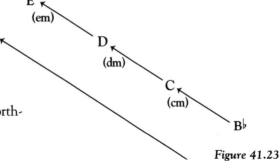

*Figure 41.23*

# Movement by Minor Thirds

## THE AMBIGUITY OF MINOR THIRDS: 6:5 VERSUS 32:27

Although cyclic sequences by definition set us spinning, the directionality and polarity of the sequences we have studied so far have been, for the most part, unambiguous. In some cases we do flirt with directional confusion, and in a few cases we are downright confounded. Now we come to a class of sequences that weaken the tonal bonds even further, allowing the fine, mesmerizing quality of symmetrical harmony to emerge fully as an inherent quality of the equal-tempered system. Let's begin by examining what could be thought of as a proto-typical progression by equal-tempered minor thirds.

## QUADRISECTIONS OF THE OCTAVE

If you divide the octave into four equal intervals, you will derive an equal-tempered diminished seventh chord. Because it is perfectly symmetrical, any of its four tones can function as its root, and it can resolve with equal effectiveness to any of four different tonics. This subject has already been introduced in the context of centered tonality (see chapter 31, page 311 and especially example 31.31). Now we will deal with the cyclic properties of diminished seventh chords.

Let's build a chord starting with the tone E. Go up three semitones to G, another three to B♭, and three more to D♭. Out of context, the tonality of this collection is so ambiguous that it has neither root nor proper spelling; we will call it the *x* chord. Tonal context will give the tones meaning, that is, function, and thus proper spelling. The four most available resolutions are as shown in example 41.40a (choosing minor tonics rather than major tonics).

*Example 41.40a.*
*The x chord*

Now start with D♯ and build a chord that quadrisects an octave. We'll call it the *y* chord. The four equally believable resolutions are shown in example 41.40b.

*Example 41.40b.*
*The y chord*

Now start with D; build a similar structure and call it the *z* chord. The resolutions are shown in example 41.40c.

*Example 41.40c.*
*The z chord*

Practice these twelve vii°⁷–i cadences until they become familiar to hand, eye, and ear. Try substituting the parallel major triads for the minor triads (F major instead of F minor).

Here is another way of approaching the same phenomena. Play the $x$ chord (E–G–B♭–D♭). Lower the soprano part a semitone (D♭ becomes C). The four tones now unequivocally form C⁷. Put the soprano back where it was and lower the alto a semitone (B♭ becomes A). The four tones are now E–G–A–C♯, or A⁷. Put the alto back where it was and lower the tenor: F♯⁷. Put the tenor back and lower the bass: E♭⁷. These four chords constitute a set of related dominant-seventh-type chords that are all harmonically equidistant from the same quadrisecting chord—in this case, the $x$ chord. There is another set for the $y$ chord and another for the $z$ chord, as shown below.

Example 41.40d shows all twelve dominant-seventh-type chords arranged according to the diminished-seventh-type chord from which they are equidistant. At first, simply repeat the four chords in each bar as a closed loop. Notice where the whole step (or minor seventh) falls within each chord, and how it travels. Also, the last chord of each set is related to the first chord of the next by a descending fifth, so the entire collection of twelve chords sounds quite remarkable when played straight through.

*Example 41.40d*

As you may have sensed, each closed set is exquisitely ambiguous. The minor third that connects each root to the next in its set can be heard either as the 32:27 (Pythagorean) type, or the 6:5 (pentamerous) type.

Let's examine one loop more closely for a moment: the $x$ chord loop. If it is Pythagorean, it travels due east in leaps, and look like figure 41.24 on the lattice.

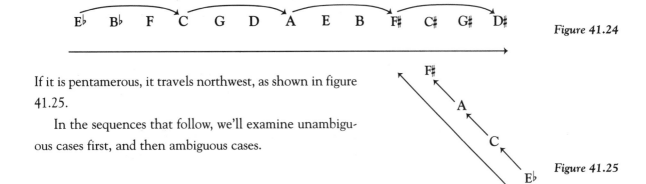

*Figure 41.24*

If it is pentamerous, it travels northwest, as shown in figure 41.25.

In the sequences that follow, we'll examine unambiguous cases first, and then ambiguous cases.

*Figure 41.25*

## 32:27 EAST: MINOR THIRDS DESCENDING

Example 41.41 presents an unambiguous Pythagorean pattern.

*Example 41.41*

C7   A7   D7   B7   E7   C♯7   F♯7 = G♭7   E♭7   A♭7   F7   B♭7   G7   C7

The roots of this endless stream of dominant-seventh-type chords leap up three fifths and backfill down one fifth. The path on the chord lattice is shown in figure 41.26.

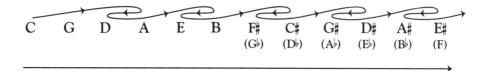

*Figure 41.26*

Example 41.42 is another configuration that results in the same harmonic path.

*Example 41.42*

## 6:5 NORTHWEST: MINOR THIRDS DESCENDING

Play example 41.43.

*Example 41.43*

In this sweet progression, the second chord of each group is merely a repositioning of the first. The third chord of each group is a pivot chord: It functions as both the ♭VII^aug6 of the chord preceding it and as the ♭II^aug6 of the approaching chord. Although it flirts with directional ambiguity, I think it continually leans northwest, that is, in the direction of the subdominant of the relative Minor (in C, for example, the 10:9 D minor).

The chord lattice appears in figure 41.27. The parenthesized chords show the equivalent dominant seventh chord for each ♭II.

The ♭VII operates differently in example 41.44 but results in the same northwesterly path. As in example 41.39, the ♭VII borrows from the approaching Minor; that is, B♭[7] to C evokes C MI/MA, and the B♭ is 9:5 in C. Figure 41.28 shows the lattice.

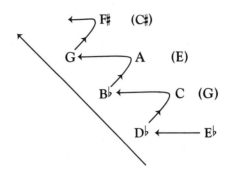

Figure 41.27

Example 41.44

Example 41.45 combines the two uses of the ♭VII chord that appear in 41.43 and 41.44 above. The chord lattice notation of figure 41.29 shows that the jagged harmonic path moves continually northwest. The arrow begins with the D♭[aug6] chord in the last full bar of the example.

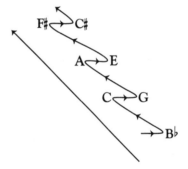

Figure 41.28

Example 41.45

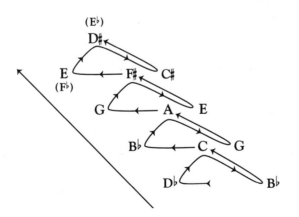

Figure 41.29

Example 41.46 is a jazz version (but starting a minor third higher).

*Example 41.46*

The sequence in example 41.47 is delightfully ambiguous.

*Example 41.47*

If you listen for the pentamerous energy, you can hear the tonal contexts emerge as marked. To check this, play the first three chords—D♭7–F♭7–B♭7—and then resolve to an E♭-major triad, which is the implied tonic. The actual tonics, shown in parentheses in figure 41.30, show how the progression zigzags northwest.

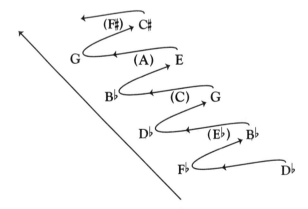

*Figure 41.30*

But you can also hear the purely Pythagorean motion of three fifths down alternating with six fifths up, as shown in figure 41.31.

*Figure 41.31*

The net result is a tonally flavored sequence of symmetrical harmony and veiled tonality boiling together in one pot.

## 27:16 WEST: MINOR THIRDS ASCENDING

Example 41.48 presents an unambiguous Pythagorean pattern, rising by one fifth and leaping down three fifths, eventually backfilling what is leapt over.

*Example 41.48*

Figure 41.32 shows the chord lattice.

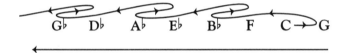

*Figure 41.32*

Compare this with example 41.41.

## 6:5 SOUTHEAST—MINOR THIRDS ASCENDING

Example 41.49 shows full cadences to four minor keys rising by minor thirds.

*Example 41.49*

The second chord of each full bar is the pivot, ♭VI of the old key and IV of the new key (the two functions are distant by a minor third). The chord lattice in figure 41.33 moves southeast, with a Pythagorean shuttle.

The sequence of example 41.50 also consists of four tonicizations, but its cadential mechanics are more mysterious. The progression oscillates around an unspoken tonic, shown on the chord

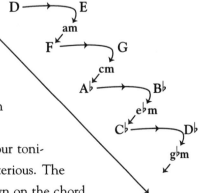

*Figure 41.33*

*Example 41.50*

Bmi: V    iv  ♭VI  ♭VII        Fmi: V    iv  ♭VI  ♭VII        C♭ mi:

Dmi: V    iv  ♭VI  ♭VII        A♭mi: _____

lattice in figure 41.34 in parentheses (in this it resembles example 41.47). Figure 41.34 shows the general progression southeast.

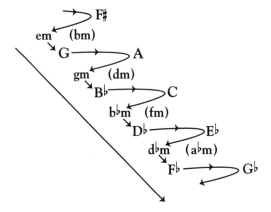

*Figure 41.34*

Example 41.50 contains essentially the same harmony as that in example 41.43, but reversed.

Example 41.51 is a progression full of pentamerous energy, and though it sounds for all the world like the reverse of example 41.45, it seems to move Pythagorean west. The tortuous harmonic path is revealed in figure 41.35.

*Example 41.51*

A:  ♭VII    I    ♭II    I    ♭II        E♭: ♭VII    I    ♭II    I

C:  ♭VII    I    ♭II    I    ♭II

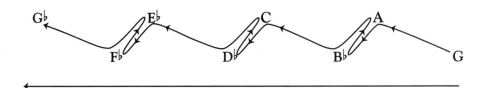

*Figure 41.35*

Example 41.52 is genuinely ambiguous.

*Example 41.52*

The actual roots simply fall by fifths, and the sequence, thus heard, would travel due west on the lattice. But, as in example 41.38, it all depends on how you hear the ii–V–I cadence. If the Didymic comma were in play, the motion would appear southeast on the lattice, as shown in figure 41.36.

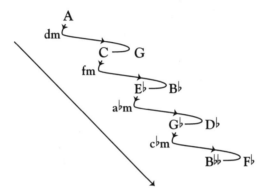

*Figure 41.36*

It's interesting to ponder how a progression that is so mind-splittingly ambiguous can feel so harmonically benign. Could it be that we like harmonic ambiguity? That we seek it? That it comforts us? That it mirrors a truth inexpressible by any other means?

I have left until last one of the most-used and perhaps the most-ambiguous of all the sequences, shown in example 41.53.

*Example 41.53*

Symmetry abounds in all directions. The top three parts seem to be an elaboration of a single diminished-seventh-type chord (the y chord, in this case). The bass line is a chromatic scale. Considering all four parts, the first and fourth beats of each bar form the closed loop of dominant-seventh-type chords that surround the y chord (see example 41.40d). This loop could be heard as traveling either Pythagorean east or pentamerous northwest, or as purely symmetrical. But there are other tonal seasonings in the stew as well. The first three chords, for instance, could be heard as part of a $\flat$VI$^{\text{aug6}}$ cadence centered on C minor; the next three chords, an identical cadence centered on A minor, and so on, traveling north-west. Furthermore, the sequence could be terminated at any time by treating any of the dom-inant-seventh-type chords as actual dominant sevenths: The downbeat of bar 2, for instance, could resolve the $F^7$ to a $B\flat{}^6_3$ chord. And finally, the sequence is fully as convinc-ing when it is played backward. (Its two transpositions elaborate in turn the *x* chord and the *z* chord.)

This harmony, which gives the ear so much choice at every turn, was much adored by late nineteenth-century and early twentieth-century Romantic composers, and learning to improvise on it will give valuable insight into that sensibility.

## A Graphic Summary of Cyclic Sequences

For reference and comparison, figure 41.37 shows all of the possible harmonic directions for cyclic sequences, displayed simultaneously on a simplified chord lattice. Harmony can travel in either direction along any of five straight lines:

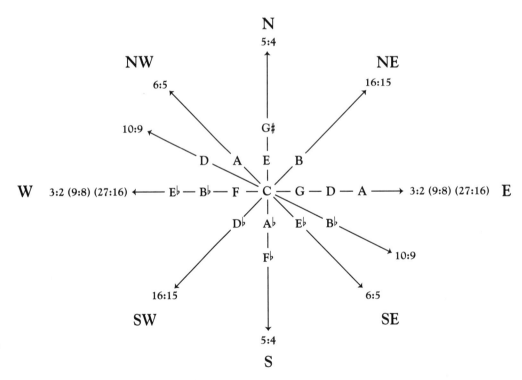

**Figure 41.37**

*N* and *S* 5:4

*NE* and *SW* 16:15

*E* and *W* 3:2 (also 9:8, 27:16, etc.)

*SE* and *NW* 10:9

*SE* and *NW* 6:5

Each of these lines represents a particular way the lattice can fold during a complete cyclic sequence. Each type of fold represents a particular variety of virtual return and involves its own specific comma or compound comma.

> *N/S 5:4* involves the Great Diesis.
> *NE/SW 16:15* involves a compound comma comprising one Pythagorean comma and four dieses.
> *E/W 3:2* involves the Pythagorean comma.
> *SE/NW 10:9* involves one Pythagorean comma and two dieses.
> *SE/NW 6:5* involves one diaschisma and one Great Diesis.

Of all these folds, only the Great Diesis operates in nonmodulating tonality (as we have discussed in part 3), and then only under the condition of extraordinary harmonic balance. In general, the folds serve as hidden mechanisms of virtual return. In table 41.1 they are organized by comma rather than by direction on the lattice.

| TABLE 41.1 | | | |
|---|---|---|---|
| 1 Pythagorean comma | folds over | 12 | 3:2 fifths |
| 1 Great Diesis | folds over | 3 | 5:4 thirds |
| 1 Pythagorean + 2 Dieses | folds over | 6 | 10:9 major seconds |
| 1 Pythagorean + 4 Dieses | folds over | 12 | 16:15 minor seconds |
| 1 Diaschisma + 1 Diesis | folds over | 4 | 6:5 minor thirds |

Anyone who wishes to investigate additional mathematical possibilities has Dr. Overtone's blessings, but he or she will soon recognize the musical constraints of such an exercise, beginning with the folds listed in table 41.2 and extending on into the night, moving toward even more complex tonic-related ratios that are even less sensible in equal temperament. The possibilities for just intonation, however, are intriguing, if not compelling. These are discussed in the afterword.

| TABLE 41.2 | | | |
|---|---|---|---|
| 1 Diaschisma | folds over | 2 | 45:32 augmented fourths |
| 1 Pythagorean + 8 Dieses | folds over | 12 | 25:24 augmented primes |
| 1 Diaschisma + 2 Dieses | folds over | 4 | 75:64 augmented seconds |

# Where Are We?

Although there are an infinite number of sequences and cadences possible in twelve-tone equal-tempered tonal harmony, I think we can now fairly claim to have studied examples from every useful nook and cranny of the diatonic and cyclic territory. What remains fades into symmetry; what we have not yet examined completely is the behavior of symmetrical scales and chords. A great many twentieth-century composers have been fascinated by the cusp between tonality and symmetry, and that will be our focus too, in the following chapter.

# 42

# SYMMETRICAL HARMONY AND THE DISSOLUTION OF TONALITY

THE ORIGINAL PURPOSE OF TWELVE-TONE EQUAL TEMPERAMENT was to make available a harmonic language of twelve equally useful tonal centers. The delights of ranging through this vast new field eventually outweighed the irritations of its tuning compromises, and over the course of the nineteenth century the Western ear fully explored and internalized the now-standard system of tuning. But I doubt if any musician alive in the mid-eighteenth century suspected that the new tuning harbored within itself an entirely new musical force.

## The Equal-Tempered Chromatic Scale

The new force arises from the ear's response to a succession of tones equidistant from one another. On the equal-tempered keyboard, play a chromatic scale evenly, without particularly choosing where you begin or end. The ear hears the even spacing between the pitches with the same kind of perception with which the eye sees the even spacing of a picket fence or the lines of type on the printed page.

In just intonation, no such thing occurs. A just chromatic scale is quite uneven, containing a wide variety of semitones depending on the tuning, potentially including not only the *ga*-blooded 16:15, 25:24, 135:128, and 27:25 but also the Pythagorean 256:243, as well as the septimal 28:27 and 21:20. To hear such chromatic scales played smoothly and rapidly sounds haphazard and unmusical; indeed, they have the cumulative effect of a poorly constructed picket fence. Even in the various unequal temperaments (including meantone and Bach's well temperaments), a chromatic scale has nothing of the smooth sheen ours possesses.

Before the days of equal temperament, the tones of a chromatic passage were heard in terms of their harmonic function. Revisit example 37.16 and sing each tone of the slowly rising scale in just intonation as a functional resonance (including the dissonant but compelling 45:32 F♯). The issue of equal distance is nowhere in sight. What we get is a cogently bonded melodic ascent accompanied by wildly divergent harmonic contrasts: rare, but dramatically useful when used in moderation. Likewise, if you tune a keyboard (electronic or acoustic) to some version of the just chromatic scale and play it slowly over the tonic or dominant, you can also hear the widely divergent harmonic effects; if you play the same just scale rapidly over several octaves but out of tonal context, the harmonic effect disappears and the melodic residue is simply uneven—in fact, it sounds out of tune. Now play the scale rapidly on the equal-tempered keyboard and hear how the various harmonic functions similarly disappear beneath the gloss of evenly spaced percussive events.

What are we actually hearing? In our earlier discussion of cents (the measurement of intervalic distance—see chapter 16), we saw that just resonances are expressed by rational, whole-integer ratios and equal-tempered intervals are expressed by irrational ratios, and that these two kinds of number are fundamentally different. The most common just semitone is the rational 16:15; the equal-tempered semitone is the irrational $\sqrt[12]{2}{:}1$, or $1.0594631\ldots{:}1$. Does this mean that just resonances are sane and equal-tempered intervals are crazy? No, because rational and irrational numbers are equally crazy. What it does mean is that the music these numbers express belongs to separate orders of experience.

An equal-tempered chromatic scale out of context is purely melodic and *merely* chromatic (see chapter 35); it has no tonal function and no proper spelling. It is difficult for the modern ear, which takes such things for granted, to imagine how the new aural artifact was heard by the eighteenth-century ear, but the surviving literature tells much of the story. Chromatic flourishes in Bach are rare (and usually appear in the context of descending diminished triads), but by Mozart's time, chromatic scales in cadenzas were common. Between 1750 and 1790, as equal temperament became more the rule than the exception in Europe, and as it became more familiar, composers and improvisors gradually began to respond to its newly available effects. By the early nineteenth century, chromatic scales were part of the compositional fabric.

Play an equal-tempered chromatic scale again, up and down several octaves in one hand, not too fast, and let your ear savor its regularity, its newfangled, manufactured, precisely measured *sameness*. Don't be bored, be fascinated, mesmerized. This sensibility opens the door for the more complex symmetrical forces hidden inside the Trojan horse of equal temperament.

## The Equal-Tempered Whole-Tone Scale

Someone—presumably by the mid-nineteenth century—had to be the first person to hear an equal-tempered whole-tone scale as a musical event. One day, no doubt seated at the piano, something new registered in that person's ear, a new possibility leapt from an old sound. Did that musical explorer exclaim? Frown? Smile and squint into the future?

Like chromatic scales, whole-tone scales have both tonal and symmetrical functions.

The term *symmetrical* refers to the precisely repeated patterns of intervals afforded by twelve-tone equal temperament. Symmetrical scales are organized by such patterns, and symmetrical harmony arises from them. The chromatic scale offers the simplest pattern: successive semitones. Before looking at the symmetrical effect of successive whole tones, let's first examine the harmonic function of whole-tone scales in just intonation.

## TONAL PROPERTIES OF THE WHOLE-TONE SCALE

Consider the passage in example 42.1.

*Example 42.1*

The scale in example 42.1 might be termed C MA/PHRYG (see chapter 24). The harmonic context renders unambiguous in equal temperament the five descending whole tones from B to D♭—they are respectively, the 15:8 major seventh, the 5:3 major sixth, the 3:2 perfect fifth, the 4:3 perfect fourth, the 6:5 minor third, and the 16:15 minor second.

Now consider the same tones played as shown in example 42.2.

*Example 42.2*

In place of the D♭ we have the augmented tonic, C♯, which is most immediately recognized as the augmented fourth above G, a tone we have named the super-Lydian (see chapter 32) and which makes, with the D♭ of the first example above, a diaschismic pair of tones spanning the Super-Lydian/Phrygian compass in the key of C.

## SYMMETRICAL PROPERTIES OF THE WHOLE-TONE SCALE

Now let's consider the same consecutive whole tones removed from any tonal context. They constitute a *sextatonic* (six-tone) symmetrical scale with no tonal center and no proper spelling. There are only two whole-tone scales, or *sets*, in twelve-tone equal temperament.*

---

*The French composer Olivier Messiaen called the whole-tone scale and the other scales examined in this chapter "modes of limited transposition." Unlike the usual diatonic scales, these scales cannot be transposed to twelve different tonal centers without repeating themselves. For instance, when either form of the whole-tone scale is transposed up or down a whole step, major third, or tritone, the resulting set is the same collection of tones—nothing changes. Experimentation with the other scales in this chapter will reveal which transpositions are redundant with the original scale. *Ed.*

The set we have been discussing is composed of the two grouped black notes plus the four white notes normally called F, G, A, and B; we'll call this the *alpha* set. The other is composed of the three grouped black notes plus the white notes normally called C, D, and E; this we'll call the *omega* set.

Play the alpha set as a scale, evenly and not too rapidly, in one hand over several octaves. As with a chromatic scale, appreciate the even spacing of the tones, the precision of the neverending sameness. We like it. Try the omega scale. We like it the same: two parallel, symmetrical six-tone universes.

Using the three-white, three-black omega set, try the harmonies in example 42.3.

*Example 42.3*

From the omega set alone, these combinations and many others can be derived, plus, of course, their transpositions to every other scale tone, since it is the nature of whole-tone symmetry that any intervalic structure built from one tone can be built from any other tone in the set. Example 42.4, for instance, shows the third chord of example 42.3 redistributed and transposed to every other tone in the omega scale.

*Example 42.4*

When you consider the possibility of transposing any combination to any tone and redistributing it to any octave in any rhythm, you can construct a freewheeling but consistently symmetrical music resembling, perhaps, example 42.5.

*Example 42.5*

Now try improvising using the alpha set. Then try the omega set. Then alternate between the two, switching back and forth with increasing frequency. Such music may seem slightly obvious to our generation, but in 1890 scarcely a soul had thought to hear this way. One can easily imagine the first hoots of derision: "ungrounded noise," "the annihilation of the known world," and so forth, but the enticing fluidity of whole-tone symmetry led a host of composers including Rimsky-Korsakoff, numerous French Impressionists, Vaughn Williams, and many others to routinely employ its shimmering, floating effect.

The "rules" for making music based on symmetrical scales seem both minimal and self-revealing: There are only a certain number of combinations; whatever can be constructed from one tone can be transposed to its symmetric equivalent; every combination is potentially useful; what sounds best *is* best. What interests us specifically in this study is the conjoining of tonal and symmetrical energies, their many intriguing ways of alternately grounding and vaporizing our Pathfinder sensibility.

## THE CUSP BETWEEN TONALITY AND WHOLE-TONE SYMMETRY

Consider again example 42.2. Realize that although the first bar functions as $V^7$ harmony, all of the notes in that bar are members of the same (alpha) whole-tone set. Only at the resolution, in the second bar, do members of the other set appear. Now, remembering that what is constructed from one tone of a whole-tone scale can be transposed to any tone, you can see how there are five other transpositions of the dominant function within the alpha set, as shown in example 42.6.

*Example 42.6*

The first three beats of each bar are members of the alpha set, which has been appropriately spelled according to the tonal context of each bar.

Now, to remind yourself of the floating nature of the symmetry without tonal context, play the alpha whole-tone scale up and down with your right hand against the nonresolving bass of example 42.7 in your left hand.

*Example 42.7*

Tonally, where are you? Without the resolutions you are on a spinning wheel, though you could choose to get off the wheel at any point. The whole-tone scale thus functions as a kind of *pivot scale* that, like pivot tones and pivot chords, looks simultaneously in more than one direction—in this case, in six directions. Such fluid symmetries bridge tonality and atonality much in the same way that water, as an intermediate state, bridges ice and steam.

Incidentally, if you want to experiment with a special kind of atonality generated by whole tone sets, try improvising with the alpha set in your right hand and the omega set in your left. Be sure to cross hands, and to interlock them as well.

## Diminished Scales

Another type of symmetrical scale arises from the alternation between whole tones and semitones, generating an eight-tone, or *octatonic*, scale, as shown in example 42.8.

*Example 42.8*

To better understand the place of such scales in the twelve-tone scheme of things, let's go back to the three diminished seventh chords—or octave quadrisections—of example 41.40d. Remember that there is no proper spelling for these events; we will use the *x*, *y*, and *z* nomenclature.

There are three diminished scales in twelve-tone equal temperament. One way to find them is to first play the *y* chord (up from C) in your right hand; then, placing your left over your right, play the *x* chord up from D♭, as shown in example 42.9.

*Example 42.9*

Now, starting with your left hand, arpeggiate the chords, alternating hands, as indicated in example 42.10.

*Example 42.10*

We will call this the *x* + *y* diminished scale.

Likewise, juxtapose the *x* chord in the left hand (up from G) and the *z* chord in the right hand (up from A♭) to produce the *x* + *z* diminished scale, as shown in example 42.11.

*Example 42.11*

Finally, juxtapose the $z$ chord in the left hand (up from F) with the $y$ chord in the right (up from G♭) to produce the $y + z$ diminished scale, as shown in example 42.12.

*Example 42.12*

I have given these scales with the initial pitches C, G, and F and begun each with the semitone. But the scales could begin on any pitch, and just as easily begin on the whole step. Any method you have of conceptualizing the three diminished scales and putting them into your hands is OK as long as it works. Although they fall easily under the fingers, diminished scales are hard to keep straight. Perhaps understanding the tonal uses will make them easier to grasp.

## THE TONAL PROPERTIES OF DIMINISHED SCALES

The diminished scale can have tonal meaning under several conditions. In example 42.13 the $x + y$ diminished scale functions as a MIXO/PHRYG-LYD with both forms of the third degree.

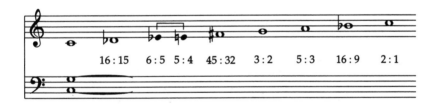

*Example 42.13*

If the tones are sung against a C-and-G drone, according to the simplest ratios of just intonation as indicated in the above example, a sweet, complex atmosphere arises. In dronal equal temperament, the harmonic possibilities are interesting; example 42.14, for instance, shows a cadence mixing Phrygian and Lydian.

*Example 42.14*

But also there lurks the latent augmented tonic, the 25:24 C♯, which suggests the parallel major of the relative minor, as shown in example 42.15.

*Example 42.15*

Trace this on the lattice of tones. (Hint: The F♯ is no longer 45:32.)

There is an even more available—perhaps even overly familiar—tonal use, however, involving dominant-seventh harmony. Examine the diatonic functions of each tone of the $x + z$ scale in example 42.16.

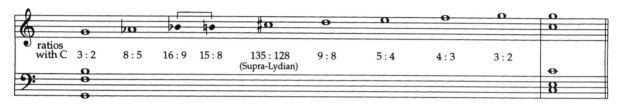

*Example 42.16*

The tonal function seems entirely unambiguous. Notice the odd mixture of Minor (the first four tones lie in the upper tetrachord of C U-MI) and Major. In fact, this mode could be described as a selective borrowing from Minor with a "Lydian-dominant" flavor, and best used (jazz players, please note) in targeting Major keys, not Minor keys. (It could sound at cross purposes to prepare the major third—E in this case—and then resolve to the minor third of the tonic minor triad.)

Example 42.17 shows a jazz use resolving to major.

*Example 42.17*

Example 42.18 is a more classical-sounding passage. Notice that the $y + z$ scale (which lies a perfect fifth higher than the $x + z$ scale) functions as the v̄ii̇/V with extremely evocative cadential effect.

The curious thing about these diminished-scale examples is that even though they *sound* unambiguously tonal in the given contexts, they *are* symmetrical on the equal-tempered keyboard. Their latent symmetrical properties, obscured here, lie waiting (from the historical viewpoint) for musicians to discover them.

*Example 42.18*

## SYMMETRICAL PROPERTIES OF DIMINISHED SCALES

Now we will consider diminished scales removed from tonal context. (Remember not to take harmonic cues from spelling—there is no proper spelling without tonality.) First, play the $x + y$ diminished scale up and down several octaves with one hand, appreciating the regularity of the pattern. This scale will generate not only the closed loop of dominant sevenths $E^{b7}$–$C^7$–$A^7$–$F^{\sharp 7}$ (see example 41.40d, bar 1) but also closed loops of other types of seventh: minor sevenths and, most notably, minor seventh ($b5$)s, as shown in example 42.19.

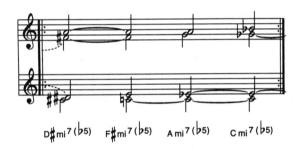

*Example 42.19*

Example 42.20 shows that whatever can be constructed from one tone can also be constructed a minor third away.

*Example 42.20*

Such octatonic symmetries generate a unique, identifiable harmony that has been used by twentieth-century composers with great artistry (e.g., Stravinsky in *Petrushka* and *Symphony of Psalms*). But octatonic harmony has become overly familiar in the entertainment industry. Beginning in the 1930s, composers for radio, films, and later, television used the quality of endless limbo peculiar to this harmony to keep audiences on the edge of their seats in fear and apprehension—to keep them, in a word, in suspense. The following scene, for which example 42.21 supplies the musical background, is typical of a 1940s radio script. The thirty-five-member studio orchestra is poised and ready to play. Quiet please. The red light is on.

*Narrator*: By the light of a flickering candle, Jessica can see only dimly the shifting shapes of cobwebs on the attic walls of her father's deserted mansion. With trembling hands she leafs through the yellowed photographs, peering at the all but forgotten faces from the ruins of her childhood. The faces move; they are whispering her name.

*Voice I*: Jessica, my sweet.

*Voice II*: Jessica, my dove.

(*The stairs creak.*)

*Jessica*: Who's there? Who *are* you?

(*Rapid footsteps*)

*Jessica*: (*screams*)

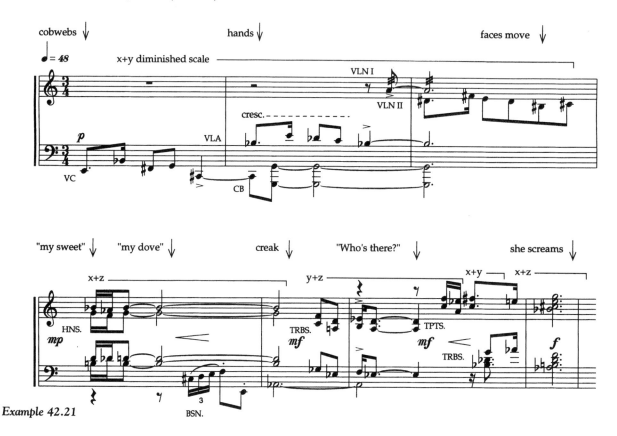

*Example 42.21*

Sound familiar?

## THE CUSP BETWEEN TONALITY AND OCTATONIC SYMMETRY

The most interesting and enduring use of symmetrical harmony seems to be when the listener can appreciate both the symmetrical and the tonal properties within the same context. The effect is something like having part of your consciousness in orbit while the other part is grounded on earth.

In example 42.22 the *x* + *z* diminished scale serves as a pivot scale between keys progressing by ascending minor thirds, moving southeast on the lattice of keys.

*Example 42.22*

Notice that the diminished scales are spelled, as much as possible, according to the upcoming key to which they resolve. Their tonal functions are sensed simultaneously with their symmetrical quality; the ear hears the spinning symmetry, but alights from the merry-go-round at specific points.

Example 42.23 is a less contrapuntal version that brings the symmetry farther forward (see also example 41.47).

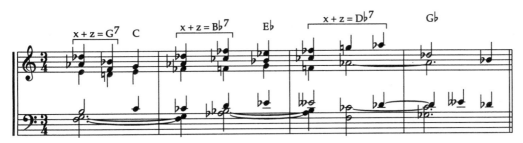

*Example 42.23*

# Augmented Scales

Just as diminished scales can be thought of as combinations of two interlocked diminished seventh chords, augmented scales can be thought of as two augmented chords. In equal temperament there are four augmented chords, each trisecting an octave. As symmetrical phenomena these chords have no proper spelling, so we will arbitrarily assign them the letters $m$, $n$, $p$, and $q$, as in example 42.24.

*Example 42.24*

Chords $m$ and $n$ combine to form the omega whole-tone scale; $p$ and $q$ combine to form the alpha whole-tone scale. The remaining two-chord combinations result in the new sextatonic symmetrical scales shown in example 42.25. Notice that these are all versions of the same scale, transposed to four pitch levels and starting with either a half step or an augmented second.

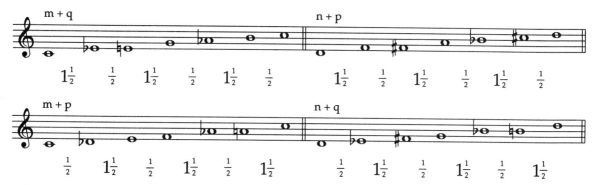

Example 42.25

It is also useful to combine any three augmented chords to construct a *nonatonic* (nine-tone) symmetrical scale. Since there are, in such cases, only three missing tones per scale, it is almost easier to keep track of what is left out rather than what is combined, as indicated in example 42.26.

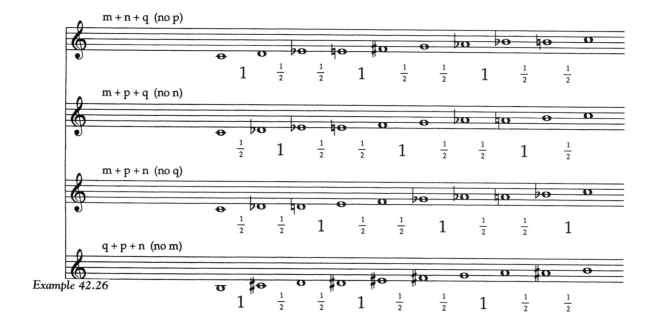

Example 42.26

## TONAL PROPERTIES OF AUGMENTED SCALES

The tonal properties of augmented scales are extremely intriguing, especially the sextatonic scales beginning with an augmented second (for example, *m* + *q*). The upper tetrachord is HAR.MI; the lower trichord (we will temporarily coin this word) simply alternates or combines major and minor thirds. The perfect fifth above the tonic offers tonal stability. The *m* + *p* and *n* + *q* versions reverse the positions of the tetrachord and the trichord, leaving only the perfect fourth above the tonic to give Pythagorean stability to the mode.

Try singing $m + q$ over a drone, using the tunings of example 42.27.

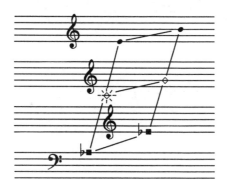

*Example 42.27*

In equal temperament, there is the possibility of ambiguity involving both the A♭/G♯ and the E♭/D♯ dieses, producing a harmonic texture of intense pentamerous longing, as demonstrated in example 42.28.

*Example 42.28*

## SYMMETRICAL PROPERTIES OF AUGMENTED SCALES

What is built from any tone of an augmented scale can also be built a major third away. Example 42.29 uses $m + q$; notice how the first chord of each bar transposes by a major third to produce the second and third chords.

*Example 42.29*

Nonatonic symmetry can be generated by the same method. Example 42.30 is based on the symmetrical properties of $m + n + q$.

*Example 42.30*

Notice that example 42.30 uses only one of the four possible combinations—one might say transpositions—shown in example 42.26. When transpositions are used, however, the listener is not expected to distinguish one transposition from another as one senses modulation in tonal music. Rather, symmetrical techniques, partly because of their spinning cyclic harmonies and partly because of their repeated intervalic patterns, can keep tonality evenly at bay with an unsettled, hovering, shimmering quality. The composer's harmonic skill often lies in controlling the consistency of that quality.

## THE CUSP BETWEEN TONALITY AND NONATONIC SYMMETRY

In comparison with tonality, symmetry is a weak force, by which I mean that the ear's perception of symmetrical intervalic patterning is easily submerged in and superseded by tonal gravity. One of the ideals of twentieth-century composition has been the development of a harmonic language wherein spinning symmetry and grounded tonality fade in and out of one another according to the dramatic needs of the music. As we have seen, it is not difficult to set modulatory harmony to spinning, nor is it difficult to evoke the various symmetrical properties of cyclic harmony. The art lies in the balance. To gain insight into the middle ground, it is operationally best to separate the two forces as much as possible. Learn your tonal and cyclic sequences. Learn the symmetrical properties of the temperament. Then you can experimentally discover your own sense of the interface between symmetry and tonality, and your musical research will have a personal slant to it and eventually become part of your individual style.

# Equal Temperaments with Other Than Twelve Tones

It comes as a great and usually delightful surprise to most musicians that there exist a large number of possible equal temperaments, some of which have novel and absorbing musical properties (most notably nineteen-tone equal temperament). I recommend the interested reader to the works of Easley Blackwood, the universally acknowledged maestro of and authority on this subject. Blackwood's CD *Microtonal Compositions* (Cedille CDR 90000 018) is a revelation of the musical potential of equal temperaments from thirteen to twenty-four tones per octave, and is most highly recommended. His book *The Structure of Recognizable Diatonic Tunings* (Princeton University Press, 1985) is devoted in part to a mathematical quantification of the theoretical possibilities of microtonality.

## QUARTER TONES

Musicians often use the term *microtone*, which means any small interval, when they mean *quarter tone*, which means half a semitone. The music in which quarter tones most usually occur is Arabic music, where typically they bisect major/minor chromatic pairs. It is most interesting to note that the tone located dead center between the 5:4 E and the 6:5 E♭ also exactly bisects the 3:2 perfect fifth C to G, and is thus $\sqrt{\frac{3}{2}}:1$. It is an equal-tempered tone in that it divides the perfect fifth into two equal parts. The astonishing thing about this tone is its affect, which functions strongly in both the rational and irrational worlds. We will call it the *quarter-tone third*; it is useful to look it up in the "Glossary of Singable Tones in Just Intonation" to better understand how it sits in the scheme of things.

The quarter-tone third is precisely centered between two strong internal norms, the just major and just minor thirds, that is, the most familiar overtonal and reciprocal pentamerous tones. From the point of view of resonance, the quarter-tone third has no inherent quality. Like the geographical center of the United States, it is not particularly interesting in itself; its position defines it. Consider the exact middle of a bridge that spans the yang shore and the yin shore; the midpoint is poised between extremes, at the place of balance. Similarly, the quarter-tone third is balanced between major and minor, equally pulled by two complimentary states.

As you can see from the "Glossary of Singable Tones," other fifths along the Pythagorean spine are similarly split: Midway between the Pythagorean B♭ and F lies the quarter-tone second (it splits the 16:15 D♭ and the 10:9 D); midway between the F and C lies the quarter-tone sixth (it splits the 5:3 A and the 8:5 A♭); midway between G and D lies the quarter-tone seventh (it splits the 9:5 B♭ and the 15:8 B); and midway between D and A lies the quarter-tone fourth (spitting the 45:32 F♯ the 27:20 F). It is not surprising that Arabic musicians, coming from a culture of great mathematical insight, were the ones to develop sensitivity to this class of tones.

How to hear these tones? Find some good Arabic music and listen up. My lifetime source is Hamza El Din, one of the greatest living musicians, emissary of Nubian Nile-hugging villages now flooded over by the Aswan Dam. From his music for oud and voice, the quarter tones, poised between lament and celebration for the tribal life of his childhood, pour out. Of all tones used in the music of the world, these are the ones I personally find most enigmatic. On a good day I can find, and use, the quarter-tone third; the others I consider works in progress.

## Beyond Tonality and Symmetry: Atonality

It is possible to annihilate tonality without deliberately using the force of symmetry as a reference. There have been many experiments in bitonality (two keys at once—for instance, C in the right hand and F♯ in the left) and even pantonality (twelve saxophone players improvising simultaneously, each in a different key). Many composers simply compose by ear, maintaining the chosen distance from tonality on a bar-by-bar basis, hoping that the cumulative effect achieves the desired balance. The line between developing a multitonal style and simply muddying the tonal waters is fine. At its worst, such ear music is a litany of "wrong notes"—things that are heard as sounding right because they wreck other things. At its best, the composer reveals a new kind of light. The task for each musician is to discover the most suitable vectors between modality, tonality, symmetry, and the ear's intuition. All music is, finally, ear music.

Music that has no tonal reference is called atonal, but so persistent is the force of tonality that one must go to special lengths (at least in twelve-tone equal temperament) to exorcise any perfect fifths or major or minor triads that could cue the ear toward a tonal center. Such a weeding out seems like a negative process to some, who term atonality "the music of avoidance."

This is not the book to describe the various techniques of dodecaphonic (twelve-tone) composition, although I'll mention two. The first might be called "fresh tone" technique: One simply keeps track of the tones that have been used in such a way that one may employ the least-used, or freshest, tone at any moment. The second, called serialism, arranges the twelve tones in a fixed order, or *twelve-tone row*. Each row has innate properties (including the possibility of symmetry and not precluding tonality) that suggest compositional direction and expansion. Schoenberg, in the early 1920s, was the first to articulate the discipline, which followers observed more or less strictly. By the 1940s Messiaen and others began to serialize additional dimensions, including rhythm and dynamics. Stravinsky shocked some by producing serial compositions in the 1950s (even though his interest in symmetry goes clear back to the Symphony No. 1 of 1905); by the 1980s the technique was becoming widely abjured by those who formerly espoused it.

The atonality of dodecaphonic music is the antithesis of the harmonic resonance of just intonation. It replaces the sensual correspondences of sound and psyche with intellectual perceptions of temporal order. Yet something entirely wonderful can occur in such music, a luminescence that is seen through no other window.

Dr. Overtone says: Learn everything. The jewel is everywhere. No one has a corner on the good music market.

# 43

# THE NOTATION OF POSITIONAL ANALYSIS

POSITIONAL ANALYSIS IS INTENDED not to supplant or supersede but to supplement traditional musical analysis. It is offered as an additional tool to clarify the intellect and nourish the senses. The primary purpose of this book is to guide you in developing your own working understanding of resonance; it cannot include detailed positional analysis of existing compositions. Nevertheless, this chapter presents brief demonstrations that may suggest models for future analytical work. But first, a brief summary of the notational conventions of positional analysis.

## The Three Lattices

There are three types of lattice, each of which corresponds to a separate order of musical magnitude. The *tone lattice* (or *lattice of tones*) can display in staff notation the derivation by perfect fifths and pure thirds of every tone used in a tonal composition. At the same time, it gives an immediate overview of the harmonic territory. The resulting configuration of the axes is called *staff orientation*. For visual ease in separating overtonal from reciprocal thirds, the diamond-shaped note heads of the central spine of fifths are left open; all others are filled in. Triangles may be drawn outlining the major and minor triads, using solid lines for perfect fifths and major thirds and dashed lines for minor thirds. Additionally, letters indicating the names of the triads may be placed in the center of each triangle, for instance C and Cmi (or cmi, lattices being the single acceptable context for the use of lowercase letters indicating minor triads). The details of constructing a tone lattice are revealed throughout part 1, especially chapters 10 and 16.

A *chord lattice* is an extrapolation of the tone lattice, a lower magnification of it, so to speak. The staff notation and the triangular boundaries are gone; what remains are the chord symbols. These then may be connected by solid lines along all the Pythagorean spines.

Additional solid lines may connect all relative and parallel pairs; dashed lines are used for additional mediants and submediants. Furthermore, to show all available contiguous harmony, lines may be drawn connecting all chords a fifth distant (see chapter 21, especially figure 21.3). If the purpose is to retain direct reference to the tone lattice, it is good to remain in staff orientation. However, when dealing with chordal motion through time (as in the cyclic sequences of chapter 41, for instance), it is best to align the axes perpendicularly in *compass orientation* (see chapter 29). Also, it is often clearer to omit chord symbols not under scrutiny by simply leaving a blank space (or a dot) where the letter name would have been.

The *key lattice* looks like a chord lattice, but its purpose is different. It represents only the tonic triad of each key through which the music modulates, and thus serves to condense an entire piece so it can be seen at a glance. Unused keys may be omitted, or shown by a dot only.

## Time-Related Notations for the Three Lattices

The three lattices are static; they show the harmonic territory, but they don't show progression through time. To show progression, there is a time-related notation for each lattice.

*Tone lattice notation* is a shape-note, real-time, staff notation showing the precise harmonic functions as well as the correct rhythms for each note. It is suitable for music with little or no harmonic ambiguity. We've already used shaped noteheads to display the extended tone lattice in scalar form (example 26.41) and to display the arrangement of comma siblings around a tonic (as in example 32.37). Now we'll use the same noteheads in the conventional manner to represent rhythmic differentiation; the result will be a real-time notation of just intonation. Let's begin by reviewing our spine-specific symbols. Figure 43.1 shows them in open noteheads.

△  *ga-ga* spine of fifths
𝘰  *ga* spine of fifths
◇  central spine of fifths
▢  *ga*-below spine of fifths
▽  *ga-ga*-below spine of fifths

*Figure 43.1*

It is valuable to become familiar at sight with certain configurations of noteheads. A typical major scale appears as in example 43.1. Example 43.2 shows a typical Phrygian scale.

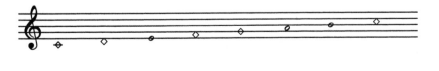

*Example 43.1*

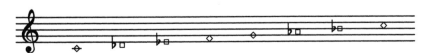

*Example 43.2*

Triads also have a special look: The fifths have same-shaped symbols, and the third is a representative from the spine above if the triad is major, or below if it is minor. Example 43.3 shows seven triads moving southwest with F major at the center. Their chord lattice is given for reference in figure 43.2. (This will be useful in the positional analysis of the Solage piece shown in example 43.7.)

*Example 43.3*

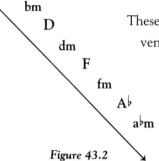

*Figure 43.2*

These noteheads can be filled in, and stems and flags and beams added according to conventional use, as the first few examples below will demonstrate.

*Chord lattice notation* looks like a chord lattice (usually in compass orientation), but with an arrow running through it. The arrow graphically represents the chordal sequence (including commas) through the harmonic territory. Bar numbers along the path of the arrow allow it to be read forward through time, but there is not sufficient detail for it to be read in real time.

*Key lattice notation* looks like a key lattice (usually in compass orientation)—that is, with only the functional tonic triads showing—but with an arrow running through it.

In both chord lattice and key lattice notation, a broken line (or some kind of hatching) can be used to indicate the "breaking" of a comma, as figures 43.6 and 43.8 below demonstrate.

In the following examples, existing music is analyzed with the aid of these various time-related lattice notations.

## *Raga* in Tone Lattice Notation

Example 43.4 is a passage from the *raga Bairov*, taken in dictation during a lesson with Pandit Pran Nath. It uses the 25:16 G♯ and the 25:24 C♯. The notation shows the tuning, the rhythm, and the *sargam*. Although it is only approximate in terms of the bending and gliding of the notes and does not show the subtlety of vowel inflections, the notation is precise in terms of the essential tuning of the passage.

*Example 43.4*

# Medieval Music in Tone Lattice Notation

Tone lattice notation is most suitable for music that can be performed with few or no Didymic commas, and the Medieval literature abounds with such pieces. *Fumeux fume* by Solage, a French composer who flourished in the late fourteenth century, is a remarkable mix of architectural subtlety and pentamerous sweetness. This rondeau was evidently composed for a "society of smokers"—possibly of opium or hashish—who no doubt delighted in the stylistic mixture of delicate whimsy and intricate design. The sense of the text is:

> *A smoker through smoke*
> *who smokes smoky ideas*
> *will find smoking to his liking*
> *if he keeps his head clear.*

The harmonic motion of Solage's piece is almost grotesquely extended, yet the journey through the vast territory is beautifully balanced and entirely believable. The net result is hardly caprice, but rather, deep satisfaction. A most wonderful thing is that there is no harmonic ambiguity. No singer or player needs to sing or play through a single comma, and each part has modal as well as melodic integrity. Positional analysis will demonstrate these various aspects.

Our reference recording* is performed by a countertenor and two vielles. The original text,† reduced to two staves in conventional notation, appears as example 43.5 (on p. 496).

Example 43.6 is the tone lattice, centered on F, of the tones used in the piece. Triads are shown for reference. The geographical center seems to lie between F and C in the Pythagorean dimension, but there are two overtonal *ga* spines and only one reciprocal *ga* spine.

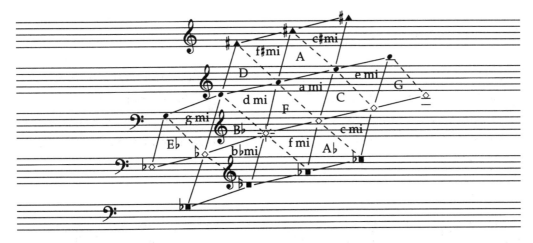

*Example 43.6*

---

*Ensemble PAN, *Ars Magis Subtiliter*, New Albion NA 021.

†From the Chantilly manuscript, transcribed in *French Secular Compositions of the Fourteenth Century*, ed. Willi Apel, Corpus Mensurabilis Musicae 53/1, ed. Aram Carapetyan (Rome: American Institute of Musicology, 1970).

*Example 43.5.*
*Solage, Fumeux fume*

Example 43.7 presents the piece as it looks in tone lattice notation.

*Example 43.7*

**Example 43.7**
**(continued)**

With a little practice, tone lattice notation will come to represent actual sounds in your ear. It helps to remember that when reading through a single part you are usually dealing with tones from adjacent spines of fifths. The general harmonic neighborhood is also clear from the page. *Fumeux fume* begins on the subdominant version of a ii chord, with the 10:9 *re* (G), located in the northwestern territory of relative minors and their overtonal *ga*'s. By bar 6 the music has gotten itself to the territory of parallel minors and their reciprocal *ga*'s, eventually cadencing strongly, in bar 8, on F.

The entire harmonic journey, all forty-three smoky bars of it, can be clarified by chord lattice notation. In the case of fourteenth-century music, however, letter names represent not so much fully expressed triads as more or less specific sites where the music alights. Because it is impossible to follow the chord-by-chord detail of such a long journey in one diagram, figure 43.3 shows the harmonic motion in twelve stages, vertically aligned. Reference bar numbers appear along the arrow's path.

Doesn't it even look a little like smoke? Yet the music never loses its harmonic inten-tion. It keeps its head clear and is to our liking. Of course, all this analysis has to be meticulously put together with the sound of the actual music.

It cannot be emphasized sufficiently that neither the composer nor the musicians of his time, nor the members of Ensemble PAN (who are exquisitely in tune), used our clever lattices to produce their music. The composer, working from his keen ear and vivid sense of style, did *not* have a well worked out, practical theory. He knew by intuition and experience what sounded agreeable. Likewise, the musicians worked out the best sounds intuitively, bar by bar. All praise to the compassionate intelligence that creates music prior to music theory.

And yet . . . now that we have come to a clearer understanding of the harmonic finery through graphic images of vital resonances, perhaps its beauty can become even more accessible to modern ears.

## Unambiguous Modality in Equal Temperament: The Magic Mode

Unambiguous modal music in equal temperament is also subject to positional analysis through tone lattice notation. Example 43.8 presents three excerpts from the earlier Magic Mode piece in C (example 26.42). Compare them with the original notation. Notice especially how the fifths (or fourths) of a triad—its Pythagorean aspect—show up as like-shaped symbols, and also how the general harmonic area can be ascertained at a glance. This points up the salient feature of tone lattice notation: It distinguishes between Pythagorean and pentamerous energy on a tone-by-tone basis.

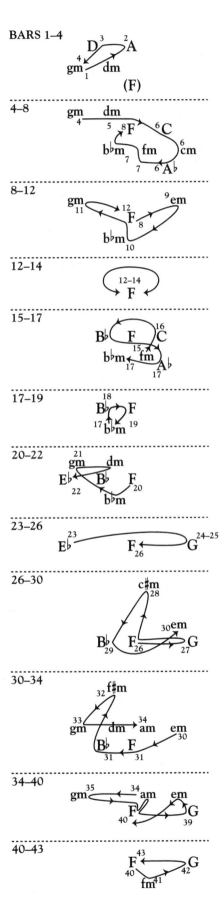

Figure 43.3

*Example 43.8*

# Bartók in Tone Lattice Notation

Twentieth-century literature abounds with equal-tempered modal composition, from Scriabin and Shostakovich to Stravinsky, Bartók, Hindemith, Copland, and many more. "In the Style of a Folk Song," a small piece from Bartók's *Microcosmos* (volume 4, no. 100) is well suited to tone lattice notation. The lattice of tones is shown in example 43.9. The numbers near the tones refer to the first appearance of that tone in the music. The first number is the bar number; the second refers to the note's position in the bar counting from left to right and bottom to top. For instance, in the second bar, A is 2,1; the next B is 2,2; the bass E is 2,3; C is 2,4; D♯ is 2,5; the B above it is 2,6; and so on.

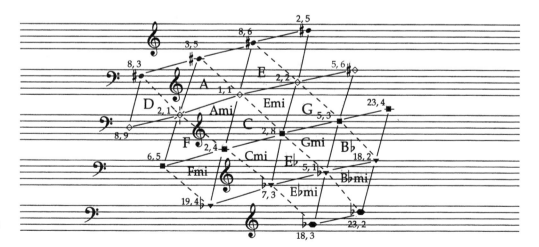

*Example 43.9*

Notice the addition of a new symbol in the southeast corner of the lattice; it represents tones on the *ga-ga-ga*-below spine of fifths. These tones represent a beautiful harmonic extreme introduced as a final burst of reciprocal energy just before the end of the piece. You may also notice that the territory encompasses four Didymic commas, three Great Dieses, and two instances of a new comma, the *superdiesis*. One of these latter is between G♭ and the *ga* F♯, the other is a fifth higher, between the D♭ and the *ga* C♯. The *superdiesis* spans the distance of a Great Diesis plus a Dydimic comma, or four pure thirds plus four perfect fifths. The piece is shown in tone lattice notation in example 43.10.

*Example 43.10.*
*Bartók, "In the Style*
*of a Folk Song"*

"In the Style of a Folk Song" never entirely leaves the tonal gravity of A. Arising from each of its three tonal centers—A, C, and E♭—is a mixed mode, with chromatic pairs for the third, fourth, and seventh degrees of each key; there is, in addition, a chromatic sixth in the tonic key of A. Example 43.11 presents the tones in tone lattice notation but viewed, for purposes of comparison, in key chain configuration; solid lines indicate common tones, dashed lines indicate Didymic commas, and dotted lines indicate dieses. There are no diaschismas. Notice that only two tones—C and G, neither of which has a comma sibling—are common to all three keys.*

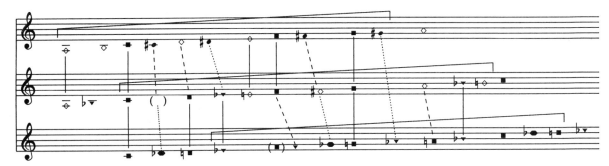

**Example 43.11**

Figure 43.2 is the key lattice notation, showing the temporal progression of keys. You can see at a glance the ever-deeper incursions into southeastern reciprocal territory.

To benefit most from all of this analysis, you need to learn the piece well enough to hear it clearly without playing it. (It's worth it.) Then, after comparing the various ways in which the tones have been analytically organized, read the tone lattice notation while sitting quietly. Then play the piece again at the equal-tempered keyboard. The analysis will help you appreciate the music; the music will help you understand the analysis.

One clear fact that emerges from all this is Bartók's immaculate modal sensibility—which is not surprising, since he was deeply devoted to the indigenous music of his culture. Also, as a speller of music his grade is A+: a perfect paper. Music such as this can guide us in bringing forward the deepest possibilities of modality and modal modulation in equal temperament.

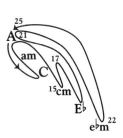

**Figure 43.4**

## Fauré in Chord Lattice Notation

Sometimes composers discover things that make other composers jealous. Maybe that is the real reason behind Dr. Overtone's tireless, ferretlike efforts. A composition student of mine, a connoisseur of fine harmony, showed up one day, flung a page from Gabriel Fauré's *Requiem* onto the music rack, and demanded, "What *is* this?" The passage occurs at rehearsal letter "E" of the "Agnus Dei." In example 43.12 I've reduced the harmony to four parts and transposed it up a major third to avoid enharmonic spelling changes.

The chord lattice notation of figure 43.5 shows how the passage ends a Didymic comma

---

*In example 43.11, notice that (a) each scale ascends as it moves to the right; (b) the scales are in order of increasing reciprocity as they move down the page; and (c) the broken lines all slant to the right downward. This means that the pitches of the comma siblings *rise* as they move downward toward increasingly reciprocal territory. Indeed, it may be generally said that a reciprocally positioned comma sibling is higher in pitch than its overtonal partner. This turns out to be more or less true for all comma siblings involving *ga* or *blu* blood. The single exception is the purely *pa*-blooded Pythagorean comma: The generating C is *lower* than the B♯ twelve fifths distant; but remember that the Pythagorean comma is rarely invoked in actual music in real time. So (save for the Pythagorean exception) the practical musician's guideline is: The pitch of comma siblings rises as you travel south on the lattice and falls as you travel north.

*Example 43.12.*
*Fauré, Requiem,*
*"Agnus Dei" (excerpt in*
*harmonic reduction)*

lower than it begins. In order to accurately represent the virtual return that occurs in equal temperament, one must ask: Where is the comma distributed? The hatch marks in figure 43.6 shows my interpretation: I think the Dmi—D♭ area between bars 3 and 4 is the most likely place, even though the music is sequential at that point.

*Figure 43.5*

*Figure 43.6*

In any case, the lattice not only shows the area over which the Didymic comma operates but also demonstrates how the southeasterly motion of the harmony is recovered by virtue of the temperament.

## Mozart in Positional and Traditional Analysis: Sonata in C, K.545

One of the most useful traditional analytical practices is the reduction of a score to a continuous progression of four-part chords that optimize the melodic and contrapuntal weave. The progressions are made to resemble harmonic models as much as possible. In such an analysis, the essential notes of the composer's bass are generally preserved intact (though not necessarily in their original octave), and all other aspects of the piece, including especially the tunes, are expunged for the purposes of perceiving the fleshless harmonic skeleton. The reduction is then played as rapidly as possible, as if to present the harmonic journey of the piece in one cogent moment. This practice, though requiring some skill, is the quickest, clearest route to understanding European classical music, not only in its formal aspect, but also in the deepest aspects of its interpretation. My purpose in discussing the traditional method here is to demonstrate how positional analysis is an extension of this practice—another antenna, so to speak, or a different frequency of light with which to examine the same object. I have chosen one of the best known (and also one of the best) pieces in the literature, the first movement of Mozart's Sonata in C, K. 545, composed in his full maturity, in 1788, when he was thirty-two.

First, get the piece from your shelf (or buy a copy, for heaven's sake) and play it (one more time), or review it in your head. Then play the reduction in example 43.13 smoothly, gracefully, musically, and as fast as possible.

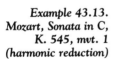

*Example 43.13.*
*Mozart, Sonata in C,*
*K. 545, mvt. 1*
*(harmonic reduction)*

If you know this piece well enough and can play the reduction at about ♩ = 144 (or better, in one, at 𝐨 = 72), you will experience in one long moment the formal structure of the harmony. It is like walking into a freshly built house and feeling the balance of its design sans paint, rugs, drapes, furniture, or even people. The truth is, a thousand entirely different perfect pieces could be created by fleshing out this skeleton, just as a thousand different interiors could furnish a beautifully made home.

Positional analysis examines the music on both greater and lesser orders of scale than traditional harmonic reduction. For the present, let's examine this already condensed harmonic

*Example 43.13.*
*Mozart, Sonata in*
*C, K. 545, mvt. 1*
*(harmonic reduction)*
*(continued)*

reduction by means of key lattice notation as if from an aerial view, so the entire scheme can be seen at once, as shown in figure 43.7.

The arrangement of keys forces a virtual return, a Didymic comma distant from the starting key. This may have contributed to Mozart's highly unusual choice of recapitulation in the key

*Figure 43.7*

of the subdominant, a tonic (F) that at least bends us westward after uninterrupted eastward travel. But there is another view. If we assume that the Didymic comma is absorbed somewhere

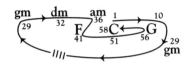

*Figure 43.8*

early in the development (between bars 29 and 38), the lattice shown in figure 43.8 appears more balanced.

Both views are interesting, especially in light of the other Didymic commas produced by the diatonic sequences within the piece. Together, they give the traditional harmonic reduction new perspective.

# Beethoven in Key Lattice Notation: Sonata in F Minor, Op. 57

The first movement of Beethoven's "Appassionata" Sonata is a travel guide to southern territory. As mentioned before (in chapter 34), it begins in F Minor and ends in A♭♭♭♭ Minor. How we do love flats. The key centers first travel due south through a Great Diesis, then southwest through a diaschisma. The entire construction appears in figure 43.9.

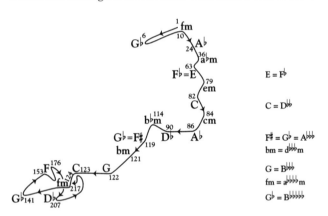

Notice how the piece falls south for 86 bars, takes only 40 more bars (to 124) to complete its virtual return to A♭♭♭♭ Minor, and then spends the next *140* bars (there are a total of 264 in the movement) turning in its old-new nest.

Again, this kind of analysis increases in value in proportion to how well you know the piece. Conversely, of course, it helps you know the piece better. I think its greatest value is for composers: a scope to draw a long bead on the Master.

*Figure 43.9*

# A Jazz Standard in Key Lattice Notation

The principal theoretical tool for jazz musicians is the concept known as "scales against chords," although, as we have discussed (in chapter 37), that concept would better serve as "scales against keys." To reiterate: It is critical to know the chord you are *on*, but it is crucial to know the key you are *in*.

Example 43.14 is a lead sheet for Jerome Kern's "All the Things You Are," one of the enduring jazz standards; its key lattice notation is shown in figure 43.10. If you are a jazz player, try consciously to hear your improvisations from the tonic as well as the root: In bar 5, for instance, think "A♭ Major positioned on D♭" (not D♭ Lydian); In bar 6, think "C U-MI positioned first on D and then on G" (not some weird D mode or G mode).

The last bar of the bridge (bar 24) is remarkable, incidentally, in that the melody is actu-

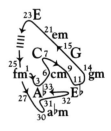

*Figure 43.10*

ally the G♯/A♭ Diesis pair, perfectly employed. A whole tone scale, effectively merging E⁷ with C⁷, is typically used for that bar.

*Example 43.14.*
*Kern, "All the Things You Are"*

# Harmony and Form

"Harmony is form" may seem like an extreme statement, but if we take harmony to mean the agreement among tones, from individual notes in a melody to chains of tonics in a symphonic movement, it is not difficult to see that the more the harmony is felt and understood, the clearer becomes the structure of music at every level. Positional analysis, along with its various graphic notations, can help make sensible the continuum of form and feeling from the smallest to the largest dimensions in music.

# 44

# REVIEW OF
# THE THEORY

HERE, FOR REFERENCE, IS A SUMMARY of the theory:

We recognize low-prime frequency ratios between tones as more than agreeable—they are affective in various ways. The primes two, three, five, and seven serve as norms that are both given by nature and internalized by experience: inner/internalized norms. The overtone series is only one incarnation of this, not the source. The primes three and five and their compounds and their reciprocals interweave, forming a lattice of tones and compound tones that can be displayed on a two-dimensional lattice, called a five-limit lattice, that confers on each tone a specific locus, or position, and imbues it with a sense of distance from and orientation to the center. By singing in just intonation against a drone we can experience in depth the pull of the tones and their affective nature. Tonality is the ear's ability to recognize and respond to the generating prime in a system of tones. Most of the world's modes are thus discrete selections from the five-limit lattice (plus a few seventh and even higher partials).

With the exception of the octave, none of the available harmonic combinations of twelve-tone equal temperament are tuned precisely to just intonation, yet its twelve tones can, under certain conditions, be heard as referring to, or *standing for*, the thirty-odd specific sites on the five-limit lattice. These references are most specific in the context of "matchstick" harmony and most of cadential harmony. The more specific and unambiguous this reference to low-prime ratios, the stronger the sense of tonality. As ambiguity increases, tonality weakens, resulting finally in the emergence of the affective force inherent but hidden in the tuning: its symmetry and ultimate atonality.

Ambiguity in equal temperament results from confusion between pairs of tones on the five-limit lattice that are near in pitch but distant in harmony, called comma siblings. In equal temperament, commas may be evoked instantaneously, or their force may be distributed over several beats. Each of the ambiguities that result from the various commas has its own mathematical quantification as well as its own qualitative affect, and all of the ambiguous harmony in equal temperament can be organized accordingly.

The Pythagorean comma (twelve fifths is not equal to seven octaves) is mathematically prior to all of the commas, but rarely functions in actual music.

The Didymic comma (four fifths is not equal to two octaves plus a major third) arises often in diatonic situations and in modulations to nearby keys.

The Great Diesis (three major thirds is not equal to an octave) arises from mixing overtonal and reciprocal thirds, a confounding of parallel and relative realms. Diesis harmony is either overtonally skewed (the overtonal family) or reciprocally skewed (the reciprocal family); in either case its three major thirds imbue it with the strongest affect of all the comma harmonies.

The diaschisma (four fifths plus two major thirds is not equal to three octaves) has a wider territory but a somewhat weaker affect than the Great Diesis. Again, there are two families: the *ga*-balanced family, and the *ga-ga* family, each producing an array of harmony.

There are, in addition, various quasi-functional and nonfunctional commas.

From these considerations, a shape for equal-tempered tonality emerges: Tonality is dynamic through time, by turns a two-dimensional plane (when unambiguous) and variously folded in a third dimension (when ambiguity evokes commas). Sometimes the ambiguity involves the central tone itself; a return to an ambiguous tonic (i.e., a pitch removed from the original tonic by one or more commas) is called a virtual return. It is possible to organize the various pathways of virtual return by an array of cyclic sequences, all of which are presented in positional analysis (the assignment of a piece's constituent tones to positions on the five-limit lattice). Positional analysis affords various notations that track the harmonic path of an entire piece through time.

Tonality in just intonation is an open system whose limits are defined by the capacity of the individual ear to relate compound tones to a generating tone. Tonality in equal temperament is an open system whose limits are defined by our sensitivity to the symmetric affect inherent in the tuning, which, at a certain point, becomes greater than the affect generated by the reference norms.

A précis of the summary: In equal temperament, everything tonal is composed of either unambiguous perfect fifths and major thirds or the quantifiable, sensible ambiguities among them, or is scattered by symmetry.


## The Value of the Theory

Assuming that you find the resonances of just intonation real, and that they serve as the norms of equal temperament, and that the inherent ambiguities of equal temperament result in a network of commas that are functional and affective for you, the theory and its consequent practices may be valuable in a variety of ways:

It draws unique distinctions. The theory allows you to draw subtle but real distinctions between harmonic values—especially between Pythagorean and pentamerous values—that have not heretofore been theoretically provided for.

It organizes tonal harmony. On the basis of these distinctions, all available tonal harmony in twelve-tone equal temperament can be organized and thus made more accessible for hands-on use.

It defines harmony as form. The affective qualities of perfect fifths and major thirds operate in tonal music over every musical order of magnitude, from tones to symphonies, from Medieval modality to twentieth-century cyclic harmony verging on atonality. The theory gives a handle on how the harmonic drama of centering and dispersing is played out at every level. It demonstrates how elemental harmonic principles are architectonic—that is, how their structure controls or directs other structures—and how this active, forming energy cuts both ways across the orders of magnitude, from tone lattices to key lattices. By this method, one begins to grasp the dialectic of extremes, that is, how the smallest elements and the largest formal shapes are mutually nourishing.

It promotes self-clarity. Because the work involved in learning these principles is so highly experiential, the theory throws you back onto your own perceptions, into your own hearing. Ultimately, one senses how the lattice is an expression of an inner working, and how harmony is the geography of the mind.

It gets you unstuck. Even though we learn music by imitation and are beholden to our teachers and our legacies, we don't want anything or anybody to stand between us and the source of sound. We want direct access. The theory allows you to track your stuck places back to the source, both conceptually and inspirationally, so your music can move forward.

It reveals a hidden gift. Although we began our work with a search for what is innate and ancient in human hearing, and were thereby led through an interior world of harmonic resonance, we eventually found ourselves in a forest of temperament, only to emerge with a realization that equal temperament, with its inherent lack of resonance, is nonetheless a radiantly beautiful gift, one of many from the musical gods.

## Flaws and Limits of the Theory

It is useful not to be too in love with one's own notions. The reason Dr. Overtone's profile can sometimes be observed well after midnight silhouetted against the spill of his reading lamp is that he is reflecting on the nature of music and music theory. Here are some of his nocturnal thoughts:

Anyone can create a subjective tautology. The notion that affective commas are the driving force behind equal-tempered harmony can never be objectively proved. What is presented in this book is an elaborate, operative system based on what is presumed to be the clear sensibilities of the investigator. No matter that you, the reader, are exhorted to be the true center of the investigation—the power of suggestion and the prose of a musical pen have swayed many a cynic. Anyone can claim inherent powers for any numbers $x$ and $y$ and construct a theory as neat as a pin. Subjective tautologies are easy to build and require little or no maintenance. What we may have here is an elaborate grammar for a made-up language.

Music is culturally determined. Music obviously changes dramatically across cultural boundaries, and even the most widespread popular music is not universal. Just as there is no universal language or grammar, there is no single unifying musical principle, no "one ear." Simply examine the world's music—the differences will convince you.

Aesthetic norms are wishful thinking. Since nothing is ever in tune anyway, and it is impossible to prove the existence of any harmonic norm, inner or outer, perhaps "approximations" don't approximate anything; maybe they are simply what is heard. Why can't things simply sound the way they do? Tunings fall where they fall, end of story. The tunings of Shona *mbiras* vary from village to village. Likewise, the tunings of Balinese gamelans change from tuner to tuner— in fact, each gamelan has its unique tuning. Even accurate-sounding European singers slide around incessantly like tobogganers. Under the circumstances, how can one ever distinguish the various "approximations" from one another, or the various commas from one another, or the approximations from the commas? We hear what we hear.

The theory is too shallow and too narrow. It is generally accepted that meaning, especially musical meaning, arises from many operations on many levels in the brain. A harmonic theory that places so much emphasis on the primacy of small-integer ratios would have to be part of a much larger picture taking into account more levels of perception. Furthermore, on the microend, the theory says nothing about the organization of waveforms themselves, or the electric signals triggered by them on the neuron level. The substantive answers would seem to depend on the analysis of brain activity involved in the decoding of those signals.

# The Doctor's Comfort

Now I'll tell you some of the thoughts that comfort the Doctor in the wee hours.

There are undoubtedly valid reservations about the efficacy of this modern theory of affects. But the work we do is art, not science; its subject is subjective experience, and its method is the self. The thinking reader must stop thinking, at least for a sufficient period, and sing. Ultimately, no single mode of activity sways us: We must sing, think, play, compare, reflect, listen to the world, and finally sort it all out for ourselves. In reply to written queries the Doctor sends a form letter: "Sing a few pure tones against a drone per day, and send me a post-card in a month."

There is a wonderful play by Bertolt Brecht called *The Life of Galileo*. In the first act, members of the Florentine ruling class, including the court mathemati-cian and the court philosopher, have come to Galileo's home ostensibly to view for themselves the newfangled, highly controversial telescope. Galileo entreats them to look through the instrument and observe for themselves the "Medicean stars," the satellites of Jupiter. "I fear things are not quite as simple as that," replies the philosopher, who, together with the mathematician, dispute their way beyond the necessity of observation. As they depart, Galileo runs after them, imploring, "But really, you need only look through the instrument!"

## Whose Theory Is It?

I would like to make the modest claim that neither I nor my comma sibling, Dr. Overtone, nor any of our lackeys, have created anything new. Speaking for myself, I think I did hap-pen to be standing at the right place at the right time (if you could describe the urge to pro-duce a nearly six-hundred-page book "right"). By this I mean that I grew up musically pri-marily through jazz, that my embrace of European pedagogy came later (in my twenties) and did not close me off from other music, that I had a natural proclivity for Indian and African music, and that I enjoyed the benefit of master teachers from many musics. That is to say, I was alive and well in America in the late twentieth century, and it was time for someone to love music sufficiently in a certain way *and* at the same time to have had a mediocre early training: I *had to know*, or I would never have developed as a musician. I am a stubborn man; if I deserve credit, it is for persevering until I heard what was true for me. Most of the ideas themselves were already in the air, waiting for someone to organize them and write them down, and under Dr. Overtone's stern gaze and mercurial smile, that is what I have tried to do.

# AFTERWORD

IN LIGHT OF THE EXPERIENCES AND DEFINITIONS that have arisen during the course of this study, I would like to make some comments about the way we make and teach music, especially composition. Also of special interest is the question of how music and brain form each other, and indeed, the mutuality of music with all of life.

Let's begin by reviewing the present limits of both equal temperament and just intonation, and then examine various ways of stretching those limits.

## The Limits of Twelve-Tone Equal Temperament

The most limiting aspect of twelve-tone equal temperament (other than its restriction to twelve tones) is that only the ratios 2:1 and 3:2 are close enough to their just norms to unequivocally represent them. Every pentamerous, septimal, or compounded event is an out-of-tune approximation that generates its tonal meaning by musical context. The system can be seen as a continuum of such situations whose ambiguity gradually increases until context no longer generates tonal meaning, at which point the inherent symmetry, with *its* limited number of possibilities, emerges. The twelve tones of equal temperament give a lot, but they also make the ear work overtime with little rest. The composer Mike Ellison, speaking of composing in equal temperament, once said, "Even when things are going well, the notes are never good enough." That seems true even when listening to Mozart on a good day: The ear gets tired and restless in twelve-tone equal temperament.

Historically, the systemic limits of twelve-tone equal temperament have long been reached and overreached. The trillions of combinations have all been sorted out many times over. That doesn't mean that there is no more equal-tempered music left to be made, of course, only that the language itself doesn't seem to have anywhere to grow without reaching over the fence. Nevertheless, here are three possible ways to transcend the limits:

*1. Greater sensitivity to the referent.* I say that everything has been discovered, and it has, but I think that as resonance revives in the West, more people will be able to use what is already known and used by a few. For instance, a musician especially sensitized to the 25:24 C♯ in just intonation will be able to evoke it reliably and creatively in equal temperament. The more frequently a culture physically experiences 25:24 as a resonance (and understands it through positional analysis), the more contexts for that tone will arise, and the more musicians will use them with sure footing and clear intention. If the cultural experience of just intonation were more cogent and conscious, there would be a more responsible use of extended modal and tonal harmony in equal temperament: that is to say, better music.

*2. More than twelve tones to the octave.* Much work has already been done in equal-tempered scales containing more than twelve tones to the octave, especially with nineteen-tone, thirty-one-tone, and fifty-three-tone equal. These scales generate extraordinary, fascinating new harmony, some of it quite musically compelling. The problem with such scales is that the difficulties in placing the pitch of twelve equal tones, already legion, are horribly magnified. Few players of variable-pitch instruments, and fewer singers, are willing or able to learn to accurately place the pitches of nineteen, much less thirty-one or more, equal-tempered tones per octave. Some promising fretboard instruments have been built,  but for the most part, these temperaments, fascinating as they are, depend on our symbiosis with electronic machines. This may not be all bad, but the inherent limit of twelve-tone equal temperament—that it is removed from the direct experience of resonance—is not transcended here, it is made more complex. Again, however, let me recommend Easley Blackwood's *12 Microtonal Etudes*, especially the nineteen-tone piece. Creasing the brain into nineteen tones turns out to be very seductive. (The tone [at 252.6 cents] that effectively splits a perfect fourth [at 505 cents] is definitely attractive; see his *Structure of Recognizable Diatonic Tunings*, chapter 12.)

By considering both headings above (greater sensitivity and more notes), one can begin to imagine the possibilities of extended modality in nineteen-tone or thirty-one-tone equal temperament. This is an open subject, a virgin field that composers will undoubtedly work as the musical quality of electronic instruments improves. Its great hope lies in retaining the balance between the just referent and the symmetrical aspects of the temperament.

*3. Cooperation with allied systems.* From its earliest use, equal temperament has, under certain circumstances, made friends with just intonation (see chapter 35). In modern times, these circumstances have grown in scope until equal-tempered keyboards and fretboards commonly combine with a wide array of just scales from around the world (including the overtonal Tuva singing of Mongolia), with results that are sometimes felicitous and sometimes obscene. What cures obscenity is empathy, which is precisely what just resonances, whose very essence is connectivity, bring forward in musicians. The more completely musicians are trained to be in tune, the more constructive become the alliances between the equal-tempered and the just-tuned worlds.

# The Limits of Just Intonation

The limits of just intonation are also clear: The farther you move from the center (or the more the center itself moves), the more territory is involved. More and more notes sprout up, and the system becomes increasingly complex, until the ear can no longer distinguish among its elements. How to transcend those limits?

*1. More singing.* There is a growing awareness of just intonation among composers, performers, designers of instruments (acoustic as well as electronic), and even market researchers, but not a commensurate increase in the number of folks who are experiencing the resonances for themselves. There is too much number crunching and future making in the air, and not enough resonance. Many people who write treatises on just intonation, and who design and program instruments intended for reproducing it, simply cannot sing in tune, as crazy as that sounds. The truth is that listening to music in just intonation is such a pure experiential hit that people become involved in the subject as listeners only, with the result that their responses are too easily intellectual. The nitty-gritty of singing in tune does not seem relevant for most, so it is not surprising that the treatises and instruments and programs are awkwardly off the mark. They come from concepts, not experiences.

So the first way of widening the meaning of just intonation is to learn to sing it, and then to teach others. The most efficient pedagogy of just intonation is probably well-taught North Indian music (which means *no equal-tempered harmoniums*), but that is hard to find in the West. This book suggests an alternative—the guitar-and-lattice approach—but there will arise other teaching methods as resonance revives. Notations that guide the singer and player may be of some help, but the ultimate answer lies with each musician, who has to demonstrate by his or her example the energy that just resonances open out into the world. Musical resonance is a lit torch that passes from one person to the next.

*2. More notes.* Many composers and theoreticians become fascinated with various arrays of increasingly complex ratios. These can be generated by two means: higher compounds and higher primes. In both cases, the pertinent issue is how far the ear can follow.

In the case of higher compounds, let's consider, for instance, compounds of the prime three. Is the Pythagorean major seventh ($3^5$, or 243:128) sensible? Evidently so, since it occurs widely in music that is sung and played by variable-pitch instruments. Is the Pythagorean augmented fourth ($3^6$, or 729:528) sensible? Can you sing it? I think I can, but I'm not sure. It shows up in Pythagorean systems. What about its reciprocal, the Pythagorean G♭? Or what about two fifths plus two thirds up, the 225:128 A♯? Dr. Overtone doesn't allow that one, but maybe you can find it and experience its affect. Would you use it even if you couldn't?

In the case of higher primes, much experimentation has been done with primes over seven. When these tones are limited to their noncompounded versions as they initially occur in the overtone series, the ear seems more easily to make sense of them. But taken individually, one must ask of each the critical question: Do you hear it well enough to sing it? The thirteenth partial seems to be at the cusp. Terry Riley says he knows where it is, hears it in extant music, and uses it; with Ben Johnston's help, I've recently learned to sing it and am now trying to figure out how to use it. But what about the higher primes: 17, 19, 23, 29, 31, 37? I am dubious that the ear distinguishes these, but they show up in computer-generated music as if it did.

Some composers feel that even though they can't reproduce a high prime or a complex compound vocally, when they tune it mechanically they are nonetheless registering its affect. In this way, huge compounds are generated, as well as their reciprocals—for instance, three perfect fifths below plus two septimal sevenths below: $1/3^3 \times 7^2$, or G, 2048:1323. A composer tunes the note mechanically, checks the inside of his skull, and says, "Yes, it has an affect," and proceeds to use it in his piece, or in his life's work, which is then regarded as mystical. Or, to consider an even more removed situation, a theoretician likes the look and feel of the numbers, and so includes the tone or tones in his system.

Is this a musical process? It all depends on your aesthetic slant. Maybe the perpetrators of such mentally led activity are fooling themselves, and us, with their alluring ideas. Maybe the detractors, the ones who say, "If you can't sing it, don't use it," are cutting themselves off from a vital part of their own responses (possibly because they have already been duped too many times by intellectually top-heavy art). Here is how to keep your sweet-talking, smooth-calculating, hungry-for-order mind from fooling you:

> Be wary of elegant systems and cosmic paradigms—they can be a lethal limit.
> Don't believe what you read until it goes well past the page. Print makes suckers
>   out of most of us.
> Wait patiently until an idea proves musical for you, and have the courage to test
>   its truth through the conscious experience of sounding music.

The best way to extend the possibilities of just intonation: tone by tone, resonance by resonance, ratio by ratio, tuning and singing your way through mazes and lattices of your own design.

## Why Is Just Intonation Not Taught?

Although musical resonance is passed individually from musician to musician, just intonation is rarely taught as a method in the West; indeed, there is resistance to teaching it. Why? Until very recently, most of its pedagogy has been more mathematical than musical, and its musical behaviors and applications have not been commonly understood. Consequently,  most teachers feel threatened by it. They have invested their lives in perceiving music a certain way, and of course, that is the way they have to teach. Even when new ways of perceiving the intuitive do arise, as is the present case with just intonation, the mechanics of transmitting them from teacher to student take time to develop. Furthermore, the West is not a humble culture. It took our ethnomusicology over a generation to shake off its paralyzing condescension, and European concert music, like an aging patriarchal bully, had to be well over half dead before it began to actually listen to its down-home neighbors (not to mention its own early history). Slowly but inevitably, the fact that equal-tempered music is only a slice of the global pie is being recognized less as a threat and more as a creative opportunity.

I hope that someday all ten-year-old kids will know the overtone series like they know their multiplication tables and that the singing of just resonances and the construction of just scales will be part of our sense of place in the natural world. Were that to come to pass, equal temperament and its musical domain would come into historical perspective. The distinction between what people ordinarily think of as "progress," in the sense of "breakthrough" (which is not necessarily continuous with the past), and "evolution" (which is) parallels the distinction between equal temperament as it is ordinarily perceived—that is, as being discontinuous with its dronal and modal roots—and the continuum of harmonic experience we have presented in this book. There is evolutionary value in demonstrating the acoustical basis of equal temperament because it presents equal temperament as a stage of development, not as an end in itself. We can now see equal temperament as part of the flow of history rather than as a radical separation from it. Just intonation is not some primitive, threatening voodoo but a generative source, both internal and external.

## Future Music and the Collective Ear

Currently there is a surge in the desire to hear through the collective ear, to grok the global sound of music, to use it, to earn the right to say, "There is only one pair of ears *and I can hear through them.*" Fabulous collections of world music, variously categorized and packaged, are being marketed and mass marketed, and more are coming. In light of this impulse, it is tempting to speculate on some future world music, some kind of musical Esperanto, or to envision great global endeavors.*

These foretellings may be exciting, but thinking about the future can be a trap if it takes you too far away from the work in front of you. Our first work as musicians is to take responsibility for our immediate soundscape, both inner and outer, to listen locally and hear globally, and to know what we hear. The real value of knowing what you hear is that it helps open yourself to the shared norms that unify the disparate dialects of the world's music, to feel at home with the prime language, the human core. That, in turn, leads to the realization that we already *have* a global music, and always have.

## Brain Harmony

According to one prevalent line of thought, the brain of the human fetus forms discrete configurations of synaptic circuits that are dedicated to specific tasks. By the time the fetus is a

*See "First World Piece" in my book *The Musical Life*.

living child, there are several hundred of these configurations, called dedicated maps, which become strengthened or weakened according to what happens in the environment. Parts of certain maps have a correspondence to parts of others—these are called parallel groups. Sensory stimuli combined with internal signals trigger synaptic firings between parallel groups, providing coherence to the system and integrating the brain's history.*

According to this model of layered, quasi-parallel maps, it is easy to see how music can influence the brain's mapmaking faculty through the excitation of inherent neural patterns. Indeed, recent experiments show that neural tissues dedicated to sound are enlarged in the brains of musically trained children. These children score considerably higher on tests in subjects parallel to music, such as spatial and temporal reasoning. Such findings certainly corroborate the subjective experience of most musicians, that music forms the brain as the brain forms music. Good music grows good brain. This may shed light on the mystery of the affect of musical harmony: Music and the brain are both maps through time. Motion through the harmonic lattice-map as it folds and unfolds through time helps to organize in specific ways the stacks of maps in the brain. Music can thus be seen as a kind of projected exterior brain that helps to align the interior one, a map of a map that the brain uses to orient and direct itself. Composers construct this artificial brain painstakingly, coordinate by coordinate, and then, as it proves authentic, performers scroll through it over and over again to keep the interior brain healthy.

When you study the historical development of music, you can observe the brain directing itself by evolving maps it can use. It both guides and is guided by the exterior acoustic world. The music that survives from generation to generation is the music that nourishes the brain in ways that it most needs to feel healthy.

In current brain research, sensory stimuli are presented to subjects whose brains are being monitored for blood flow, which is assumed to indicate brain activity, conscious or unconscious. We observe, in real time, specific sites in the brain as they are responding to specific stimuli: The brain map lights up. Exciting and promising as this is, neuroacoustics, a young and marginally funded science, has yet to ask certain central musical questions. What I would like to see with my own eyes are the neurological reactions to specific harmonic events. I want to see:

- What the brain looks like when it is hearing each of the singable tones of just intonation: 3:2, 5:4, 16:15, and so on. Is each one a discrete, observable state? That's how it feels.
- How cross-rhythms, such as three against two, compare with their parallel frequency ratios. Do they involve parallel neural networks?
- What the brain looks like when harmony moves from overtonal to reciprocal, and specifically through the various quadrants of the five-limit lattice. Is there any topographical correlation between the two-dimensional lattice on the page

---

*See "Dr. Edelman's Brain," by Steven Levy, *New Yorker*, May 2, 1994.

and the three-dimensional lattice in the brain?

- How the brain tracks compounds. How does it locate the *one* that unifies sounding pitches? How does it know where the tonic is? Is the tonic somehow physically central?
- What happens during the navigation through a comma in just intonation.
- How the physical responses, if any, to low-prime ratios compare to the responses to their equal-tempered analogues.
- What happens during the breaking of a comma in equal temperament, when the lattice on the page folds and becomes flat again. Is there a playing out of the drama of Homebody and Pathfinder in the electron world of the brain?
- The behavior of neural activity during symmetric and atonal harmony.

Of course, I experience these musical events internally, both affectively and cognitively, and on that level I know what is true. So why this fascination with visually observing the brain? Because I want to catch music and the brain *in the act* of forming one another. I want to see under one more new lens how inseparable we are from music, how purely we and music are aspects of one another.

## Music as a Model of Knowing

The brain isn't the only thing music maps. It helps us understand the entire body: the skeleton and the muscles as well as the subtle body. Consider how we create and respond to rhythms and cross-rhythms—how deeply we groove in duple, triple, and compound meters. Now remember how the cross-rhythms of macrotime parallel the harmonic ratios of microtime. We are familiar with the body that dances in macrotime, but what body responds to harmony? It is the neural, electric, etheric body. The way rhythm is a model for knowing the skeletal body, harmony is a model for knowing the subtle body. What you learn about your torso, arms, and legs when you play in rhythmic grooves and dance to them, you learn about your subtle body when you study harmony. You learn how enormously refined your sensibilities can become. You get small and you get fine.

You also get large. When you open yourself to the elemental wave patterns of music, you sense their innate intelligence, and by striving to understand how they organize into music, you recognize music's continuity with all forms, and the seamlessness from "dead" to "living." Being is alive, and it is musical. Every octave sings.

What I want most is for you to be able to connect what you are with what you hear so that there is no separation, no subject or object, only the state of mutuality between them. Music, especially the harmonic aspect of it, the "agreement" part, seems able to impart this way of knowing as a kind of effacement. When you know harmony, you see how it both is and is not you, and this generates a keen sense of inner authority and awakens wonder.

# What Music Stands For

When we listen to music, we are in a special zone of meaning that carries forward to the meaning of life itself. The specialness of life is made more present. Timbres and inflections invoke aspects of the human voice and of nature's voice. The undulations of melodies, the journeys to the harmonic quadrants, the rhythms, the textures, all combine to give a sense of displacement and return, a braided drama that serves as a sonic metaphor for real life. In this sense, music *stands for* real life. One can also say (I have said it) that music is self-contained, that it is itself only, and means itself only. Ultimately, however, nothing is itself only (with the exception of everything, of course).

When we listen to music, our absorption can be so complete that it seems to come into us from every dimension, from everywhere, and we feel contained within a larger Self. As long as the music is playing, it gives us that feeling of wholeness. We leap into the wholeness. Making that leap is what music is for. But when the music stops, we are discovered in the middle of real life, and music is not life. Life is life. Life is the way you are feeling right now as you read these words. Life is the health of your family, and your love energy, and your need for sleep, and the season's turning, and war and peace. Life can be lived musically, but what we call music is only a part of life that reflects and illumines it in a special way. When life is at its most intense—sudden danger, ecstatic orgasm, blind rage—there is no room or need for music. In the movies, yes. But in the real world, the music stops and life fills the sphere.

A metaphor is a transfer of sensibility from one realm to another. Consider, then, these realms that the music metaphor bridges:

- The resonances of just intonation stand for low-prime number relationships, thereby representing the pure realm of number in the sound world.
- The approximations of equal temperament stand for the resonances of just intonation, bringing the harmonic verities into a highly flexible system.
- Harmonic journeys through the lattice stand for real-life journeys. The tonic is our feet on the ground, while love- and soul-hungers sweep us off our feet and back again in endless configurations.
- The wholeness of music stands for the whole of life, each piece a birth and a death, a piece of one-ness.

Can we go farther than this? Does a person's life *stand for* something? Take the case of an isolated mystic. He has been praying in a mountain cave for sixty years. There are two explanations: (1) This is a disturbed individual, whom it takes sixty years of prayer to calm down. (2) This individual is dedicated to manifesting a sphere of protection around the planet by means of maximal refinement of his sensibilities. By the latter reckoning, one's life can stand for many. This leads to the image of the artist as the champion of humanity— Beethoven as the loner-savior, Bach as the composer-saint. But wait! We're going too far.

We've been talking all night, and we've passed all the signs and left the road. The crickets are silent, the clock is ticking, and what of our promise to play brilliantly in all twelve keys by morning?

## Some Parting Advice

Allow me to leave you with some parting advice:

> Immerse yourself deeply in musical experience, with special care to dip long and
> often into the realm of pure resonance.
> Respect the limits of theory while plunging into it headlong.
> Never forget how to not think, even when you are thinking.
> Be facile in keys.
> Invest in weird modes.
> Teach.
> Gain insight through your own resistances.

A very large number of musicians—all of them to date, in fact—have done perfectly well, and in many exemplary cases quite superlatively well, without the aid of this book. So why take it on? Why mess with the sacred?

This book will prove useful in proportion to how completely it is transcended. The great thirteenth-century poet Jelaluddin Rumi lived the normal life of a religious scholar until the age of thirty-seven, when, through the agency of a wandering mystic, Shams of Tabriz, he underwent a period of ecstatic, connective experiences. As the story goes, Shams "took Rumi's books, his intellectual brilliance, and threw them into a well to show him how he needed to live what he'd been reading."* Then his teacher disappeared, and Rumi became a master poet and musician, singing and whirling by the hour.

Someday I'll visit your house. "Where's my book?" I'll ask, eyebrows up. "Down the well," you'll say, and then I'll know you've earned your Overtone Doctorate.

---

*Coleman Barks, Introduction, *Unseen Rain: Quatrains of Rumi* (Putney, Vt.: Threshold Books, 1986).

# GLOSSARY OF TERMS

THIS GLOSSARY OMITS generally understood musical terms (such as *arpeggio, chord, polyphony, sonata, suspension*), which are the provenance of any music dictionary. It includes not only uncommon and coined terms but also common terms that have been redefined or particularized in this book, and is especially useful in clarifying distinctions within the following groups of terms:

- harmonic, melodic, chromatic
- pitch, tone, note
- bass, tonic, root
- relative, parallel
- key, mode, modality, modulation, tonal harmony

**affect (n):** an emotion, mood, or sensible psychological state.

**ambiguity, ambiguous:** tones, triads, or collections of tones that could be construed as having more than one harmonic meaning, that is, as having more than one position on the lattice.

**bass:** the lowest sounding tone; not to be confused with the root (of a chord), which may or may not be the bass.

***blu:*** the syllable used to identify the minor seventh derived from the seventh partial, 7:4.

***blu*-blooded:** compound tones whose ratios include seven as a factor.

***blu* spine:** the tones that stand in a 7:4 relation to the central spine of fifths, including primarily the 7:6 E♭, the 7:4 B♭, and the 21:16 F.

**bicyclic:** a coined term referring to harmonic sequences that alternate back and forth between two configurations.

**borrowing:** the temporary use of tones from a parallel mode before reestablishing the original mode. For instance, when in C Major, one can momentarily borrow the tone A♭ from C Minor before the final cadence in C Major.

**cadence:** the stabilizing or closing of a passage by harmonically centering on the tonic. A cadence that proceeds from V to I is called perfect or authentic. A cadence that proceeds IV to V to I is called a whole cadence. A half cadence pauses on V; a plagal cadence progresses IV to I. A deceptive cadence substitutes some other triad, usually the submediant, for the tonic triad.

**cent:** one hundredth of an equal-tempered semitone; one twelve-hundredth of an octave.

**chromatic:** generally, any instance where accidentals are used to indicate more than one form of a scale degree. Chromaticism is not a separate kind of tonal harmony, but rather a complexification of it.

**chromatic pairs:** two forms of a scale degree. For instance, in the key of C, the two forms of the seventh degree compose the chromatic pair B♮/B♭.

**collection (of tones):** any combination of two or more tones. In this book, triads are perceived as special collections.

**comma:** any very small interval between two tones near in pitch but disparate in harmonic generation.

**comma pair:** any two tones separated by a comma.

**comma sibling:** any two tones separated by a comma, but especially two tones of the same letter name separated by the Didymic comma.

**common practice period:** European classical music roughly from Bach to Brahms (1700–1900).

**common tone:** a tone shared by two chords, modes, or keys.

**compass orientation:** the configuration of a chord or key lattice when the fifths are drawn due east-west and the thirds are drawn due north-south; as distinct from staff orientation.

**compound tone:** a tone whose ratio with the generating tone involves the multiplication of a prime (higher than two) times itself or some other prime.

**contiguous ambiguity (between tonics):** tonal centers of equivalent strength that move about freely within a neighborhood of tones that are bonded on the lattice; noncontiguous ambiguity of tonics can result in a virtual return (*q.v.*).

**continuous harmony:** triads connected to one another by a single line on the lattice of chords, i.e., parallel pairs (C and C minor), relative pairs (C and A minor), mediant pairs (C and E minor), and all triads whose roots are distant by a perfect fifth.

**continuous voice leading:** the progression of each voice within its smallest possible melodic compass, avoiding parallel octaves or fifths with other voices.

*dha:* the sixth degree of the scale.

**diatonic:** in general use, *diatonic* refers to the tones within conventional major or minor heptatonic modes; a more narrow (and perhaps more useful) definition involves the construction "diatonic to . . . " and means "indigenous to a given key and mode"; for instance, the tone B♭ is diatonic to C Mixolydian.

**diaschisma:** the interval between three octaves and four perfect fifths plus two major thirds, or 2048:2025, about twenty cents.

**Didymic comma:** the interval between four perfect fifths and two octaves plus a pure third, 81:80, about twenty-two cents.

**Didymic pair of tones (or triads):** two tones (or triads) separated by a Didymic comma.

**Diesis:** *see* Great Diesis

**dodecaphonic:** a scale or system using twelve tones.

**Doctor Overtone:** don't ask.

**dominant:** the fifth degree of a scale.

**doppelgänger:** a double.

**dronal:** music played over a drone.

**dronality:** the system of dronal music.

**drone:** the sustained sounding of the tonic of a mode; may also include another tone, usually the dominant or the subdominant.

**equal temperament:** a system of tuning wherein the octave is divided into intervals of exactly equal size; twelve-tone equal temperament is the standard system of the Western world.

**elaborate (v):** to ornament or decorate; to elaborate a harmonic model is to flesh it out with added melodic and rhythmic content.

**ellipsis:** an expected event (in a series or a progression) that is omitted; a "filled-in" ellipsis subsequently supplies the missing element.

**five-limit system:** a system limited to tones derived by multiplying or dividing the frequency of a generating tone by the primes two, three, or five (namely, perfect octaves, perfect fifths, major thirds, and their compounds and reciprocals).

**fixed-pitch instruments:** instruments whose tuning cannot be altered during the act of playing.

**function:** the work, or job, or gig of an element of music.

**frequency:** the number of cycles per second an object vibrates to produce a tone.

***ga:*** generally, the third degree of the scale; as an adjective, *ga* refers to harmony generated by pure 5:4 thirds.

***ga*-blooded:** tones compounded from 5:4 major thirds (*ga*) and other pure harmonies.

***ga* dimension:** the aspect of music generated by 5:4 thirds.

***ga-ga:*** the result of compounding two pure thirds.

**grand-*pa*:** two perfect fifths compounded; specifically, the 9:8 *re*.

**Great Diesis:** as used in this book, the interval between one octave and three pure thirds, or 128:125, about 41 cents.

**harmonic (n):** an overtone.

**harmonic series:** the tones arising from an oscillating string (or other body) owing to its natural division into parts or segments.

**harmonic symmetry:** harmony generated by a balance between overtonal and reciprocal material; not to be confused with symmetrical harmony (*q.v.*).

**harmony:** refers primarily, in this book, to events that can be quantified by ratio, as opposed to events that can be measured by interval.

**heptatonic:** containing seven tones.

**Homebody:** a characterization of the ear's psychological desire to know and retain the generating tone of the harmony.

**interval:** a quantifier of the melodic distance between two tones, usually without specification as to their harmonic interaction, as distinct from ratio (*q.v.*).

**just intonation:** in some texts, the five-limit system of tuning; in this book, any system of tuning using low primes.

**key:** the tonic; in general use, the word often includes a designation of mode: *the key of C Minor*. This book attempts to retain the distinction between key and mode (*q.v.*) whenever possible.

**key chain:** a progression of keys and modes used as a harmonic template for improvisation or composition.

**komal:** flat; *ati komal:* a little more flat (usually by a comma).

**lattice:** a graphlike configuration where each axis is devoted to tones generated by a specific prime number; a two-dimensional lattice (i.e., on a page) is confined to a tuning system using two primes. A *lattice of tones* combines the graph principle with staff notation by skewing the direction of both axes. A *lattice of twelve notes* refers to the twelve most simply derived ratios; an *extended lattice* includes indefinitely more notes; a *chord lattice* abandons the staff notation and shows the major and minor triads by chord symbols only; in a *key lattice*, the symbols stand for keys.

**ma:** the fourth degree of the scale.

**Magic Mode:** an equal-tempered phenomenon according to which the twelve tones of an equal-tempered scale can refer unambiguously to twenty-eight tones on the five-limit lattice, depending on context. Also called the Omnimode.

**Magic Scale:** the tones of the Magic Mode arranged as a scale.

**major:** large; most narrowly, an adjective modifying a number, as in *major sixth*.

**major/minor pair:** two forms of one degree that stand to each other as 25:24; for instance, in the key of C, the 5:4 major third and the 6:5 minor third. The four scale degrees that have major/minor pairs are the second, third, sixth, and seventh.

**major whole tone:** the 9:8 major second.

**matchstick harmony:** *see* continuous harmony.

**melody:** refers in this book to the up-and-down aspect of music, that which is quantifiable by intervalic measurement; as distinct from harmony (*q.v.*).

**meend:** in Indian music, the sliding from resonance to resonance; the shaping of tones.

**minor:** small; most narrowly, an adjective modifying a number, as in minor third.

**minor whole tone:** 10:9.

**mode:** a chosen set of tones, usually comprising five or seven functional degrees of a scale.

**modality:** the quality of music within a mode. Most simply, the term refers to music that establishes clear choices of tones that relate to an unchanging tonic.

**modal modulation:** a change of tonic or mode or both, usually not driven by a conventional V to I cadence.

**modulation:** any convincing change of tonic; *see also* tonal modulation.

**ni:** the seventh degree of the scale.

**nonatonic:** containing nine tones.

**note:** the term is reserved for any tone (*q.v.*) that is related to notation. Generally, a tone sounds, a note is written, but the distinction is difficult to maintain.

**octatonic:** containing eight tones.

**octave reduction:** the transposition by octaves of intervals greater than an octave so that they lie within the compass of an octave; by octave reduction, a perfect twelfth becomes a perfect fifth, and a major seventeenth becomes a major third.

**Omnimode:** an alternative name for the Magic Mode.

**overtone, overtone series:** *see* harmonic series.

**overtonal:** quantifiable by the overtone series or its compounds; in this book, the result of the multiplication of low primes; in contradistinction to reciprocal (*q.v.*).

**pa:** the fifth degree of the scale; as an adjective, *pa* refers to harmony generated by the ratio 3:2.

**pa dimension:** the aspect of music generated by 3:2 fifths.

**parallel:** in counterpoint, parts moving in the same direction holding the same interval between them. Thus men and women singing the same melody an octave apart are said to be singing in parallel octaves. In harmony, the term refers to two modes with the same tonic but different tonal content. The parallel minor of C Major is C Minor; the parallel major of C Minor is C Major; as distinct from relative (*q.v.*).

**partial:** either a generating tone or one of its harmonics (*q.v.*). The generating tone is the first partial; the doubling of its frequency is the second partial (although it is the first harmonic); the tripling of the generating tone is the third partial (although it is the second harmonic), and so on. Because the multiplicand of the generating tone and the number of the partial are identical, the term is useful in mathematical discussions.

**Pathfinder:** a characterization of the ear's psychological desire to track its way cogently through the lattice of tonal harmony.

**perfect:** the quality assigned to 1:1 primes, 3:2 fifths, 4:3 fourths, and all octave expansions of these intervals.

**pentamerous:** harmony generated by the prime number five, that is, harmony characterized by the presence of 5:4 major thirds and their compounds and reciprocals.

**pentatonic:** containing five tones.

**ping-pong cadence:** a special configuration of a whole cadence intended to demonstrate its property of balance around a center.

**pitch:** the specific frequency of a tone; its precise tuning.

**pivot chord (or tone):** in modulation, a chord (or tone) that has one function in the old key and another in the new key.

**polar:** refers to the tendency of harmony, in its attraction to the central tone, to act in opposite directions. For example, in Pythagorean harmony, eastern (overtonal) harmony pulls westward back toward the center; western (reciprocal) harmony pulls eastward back toward the center. In pentamerous harmony, northern (overtonal) harmony pulls south; southern (reciprocal) harmony pulls north. Polarity thus refers to our sense of tension between opposites. A "polar flip in the *ga* dimension" refers to a sudden leap from north to south or vice versa, and its consequent reversal of pentamerous polarity.

**positional analysis:** the perception of tonal harmony as a series of positions or locations on a five-limit lattice, and the procedures and notations that consequently arise.

**prime number:** a positive whole number that has as factors only itself and unity.

**pure:** an interval with the lowest possible ratio. A pure prime is 1:1; a pure octave is 2:1; a pure fifth is 3:2; a pure fourth is 4:3; a pure major third is 5:4. Pure fifths and pure thirds are sometimes called "just fifths" and "just thirds."

**Pythagorean:** generally, having to do with the thought (or supposed thought) of Pythagoras. In this book, *Pythagorean* refers to a three-limit system, that is, a system confined to 2:1 octaves and 3:2 fifths, and their compounds and reciprocals.

**quadrisection (of an octave):** in equal temperament, the division of an octave into four equal parts.

***raga:*** in Indian music, a collection of tones, specifically tuned and shaped to evoke a mood, used as the basis for extended composition and improvisation.

**ratio:** the relationship between one frequency and another; the quantifier of harmonic space, as distinct from interval, (*q.v.*).

***re:*** the second degree of the scale.

**reciprocal:** the opposite of overtonal; the term as used in this book draws from the mathematical meaning "inverse." The reciprocal of the perfect fifth C up to G is thus the perfect fifth C down to F; the appropriate mathematical procedure is division instead of multiplication; the ratio of the upward fifth (3:2) is inverted to become its reciprocal (2:3). The concomitant adjective *reciprocity* conventionally implies mutuality, however, and is avoided here.

**reference norm:** in harmony, sensible low-prime ratios; metaphorically, specific locations on the lattice of just tones, which is a template of reference norms.

**relative:** conventionally, C Major is the relative Major of A Minor; A Minor is the relative Minor of C Major. But in a wider definition, any two modes sharing the same tonal content are said to be relative.

**resonance:** the conventional definition is the reinforcement of tones by synchronous or near-related vibration; as used in this book, the term refers to sensible (that is, singable) combinations of tones related by low-prime ratios.

**root:** the letter name of a chord, as distinct from both bass and tonic *(q.v.).*

*sa:* the tonic of a key or mode.

*sargam:* in Indian music, the names of the degrees of the scale, specifically, *sa, re, ga, ma, pa, dha,* and *ni,* abbreviated *s, r, g, m, p, d,* and *n.*

**scale:** the incrementally ascending or descending arrangement of the notes of a mode, or any set of tones. *Scalar* is the adjective.

**secondary dominant:** a major triad whose root is a fifth above that of any primary triad in a key (except the tonic triad).

**septimal:** involving the seventh partial.

**sequence:** a brief series of tones (melodic) or chords (harmonic) that repeats according to an intervalic pattern that is either diatonic or cyclic.

**set:** in music, a chosen group or collection of tones.

**sextatonic:** containing six tones.

**solfege:** any system of naming tones according to their scale degrees or letter names, usually by means of a system of phonemes. Generally used while singing.

**spine of fifths, of thirds:** on the lattice of tones, the *x* axis comprises tones separated by fifths and is called the central spine of fifths; the *y* axis is called the central spine of thirds. For the configuration of other spines of fifths and thirds see example 16.20, page 123.

**staff orientation:** the configuration of tones and chords that arises from the five-limit lattice of tones as portrayed on musical staves; as distinct from compass orientation *(q.v.).*

**subdominant:** the perfect fifth below the tonic.

**symmetrical harmony:** in equal temperament, harmony based on regularly recurring intervalic patterns; as distinct from harmonic symmetry *(q.v.).*

**temperament:** a method of tuning that defines a closed system of a finite set of tones (such as twelve), some or all of which are tuned in a prescribed deviation from their pure ratios (in contradistinction to just intonation, *q.v.*). In equal temperament *(q.v.)* all tones except the octave are tuned impure.

**tempered (of an interval):** intentionally tuned impure. Thus in twelve-tone equal temperament *(q.v.)* the major third is tempered fourteen cents wide of the 5:4 pure major third.

**tetrachord:** in this book, four consecutive tones of a heptatonic scale. Thus, in C Major, the lower tetrachord is C, D, E, and F; the upper tetrachord is G, A, B, and the octave C.

*tivra:* sharp.

**tonal harmony:** generally refers to modulating harmony with identifiable tonics. A more narrow definition refers to the dominant-seventh-driven harmony of the common practice period.

**tonal modulation:** the process of changing tonics in tonal harmony *(q.v.)*.

**tone:** any sustained, sensible frequency, but not necessarily octave-specific. For instance, "the tone C♯" means any C♯, or a certain C♯, depending on context. "The note *(q.v.)* C♯" refers (as much as possible) to one that is notated; *see also* pitch.

**tonic:** the generating tone, or key note, or home note of a piece.

**tonicization:** the temporary—often fleeting—establishment of a tonic.

**tricyclic:** a coined term referring to harmonic sequences that progress regularly through three configurations.

**unambiguous harmony:** any tones whose position on the lattice of just tones is discrete.

**variable-pitch instruments:** instruments whose tunings can be adjusted during the act of playing.

**virtual return:** the return to a tonic distant by one or more commas from the original tonic.

# GLOSSARY OF SINGABLE TONES IN JUST INTONATION

## (ACCORDING TO DOCTOR OVERTONE)

| CENTS* | PITCH | RATIO | DERIVATION |
|---|---|---|---|
| 0 | C | 1:1 | *sa* |
| 70 | C♯ | 25:24 | *ga* of *dha* |
| 85 | D♭ | 21:20 | *blu* of *komal ga* |
| 90 | D♭ | 256:243 | Pythagorean half step |
| 92 | C♯ | 135:128 | *ga* of great-grand*pa* |
| 100 -------- | C♯/D♭ -------------------------- | | equal-tempered half step |
| 112 | D♭ | 16:15 | *ga* below *pa* below; *komal re* |
| 147 | ¼ tone | | splits B♭ (8:9) and F (4:3) |
| 155 | D | 35:32 | *blu* of *ga*; *ga* of *blu* |
| 182 | D | 10:9 | *dha* of *ma*; minor whole tone |
| 200 -------- | D ------------------------------ | | equal-tempered whole step |
| 204 | D | 9:8 | *pa* of *pa*; *re* |
| 231 | D | 8:7 | *blu* below |
| 267 | E♭ | 7:6 | *blu* of *ma*; blues minor third |
| 274 | D♯ | 75:64 | *ga-ga* of *pa*; *ga* of *ni* |
| 294 | E♭ | 32:27 | Pythagorean minor third |
| 300 -------- | D♯/E♭ ------------------------ | | equal-tempered minor third |
| 316 | E♭ | 6:5 | *ga* below *pa*; *komal ga* |
| 351 | ¼ tone | | splits C (1:1) and G (3:2) |
| 386 | E | 5:4 | *ga*; fifth partial |
| 400 -------- | E ------------------------------ | | equal-tempered major third |
| 408 | E | 81:64 | Pythagorean major third |
| 428 | F♭ | 32:25 | *ga-ga* below |

*Cents are approximate except for equal-tempered reference tones.

| | | | |
|---|---|---|---|
| 471 | F | 21:16 | *blu* of *pa*; *blu ma* |
| 498 | F | 4:3 | *ma*; *pa* below |
| 500 -------- F ------------------------- | | | equal-tempered perfect fourth |
| 520 | F | 27:20 | great-grand*pa* of *ga* below |
| 551 | F♯ | 11:8 | eleventh partial |
| 555 | $\frac{1}{4}$ tone | | splits D (9:8) and A (27:16) |
| 568 | F♯ | 25:18 | *dha* of *dha*; *ga-ga* of grand*pa* below |
| 583 | G♭ | 7:5 | *blu* of *ga* below; *ga* below *blu* |
| 590 | F♯ | 45:32 | *tivra ma*; *ga* of grand*pa* |
| 600 -------- F♯/G♭ ----------------------- | | | equal-tempered tritone |
| 610 | G♭ | 64:45 | *ga* below grand*pa* below |
| 612 | F♯ | 729:512 | Pythagorean augmented fourth |
| 680 | G | 40:27 | *ga* of great-grand-*pa* below (wretched *pa*) |
| 700 -------- G ------------------------- | | | equal-tempered perfect fifth |
| 702 | G | 3:2 | *pa*; third partial |
| 738 | A♭ | 49:32 | *blu* of *blu* |
| 765 | A♭ | 14:9 | *blu* of grand-*pa* below |
| 772 | G♯ | 25:16 | *ga-ga* |
| 792 | A♭ | 128:81 | Pythagorean minor sixth |
| 800 -------- G♯/A♭ ----------------------- | | | equal-tempered augmented fifth/minor sixth |
| 814 | A♭ | 8:5 | *ga* below *sa*; *komal dha* |
| 841 | A♭ | 13:8 | 13th partial |
| 848 | $\frac{1}{4}$ tone | | splits F (4:3) and C (1:1) |
| 884 | A | 5:3 | *dha*; *pa* below *ga*; *ga* of *ma* |
| 900 -------- A ------------------------- | | | equal-tempered major sixth |
| 906 | A | 27:16 | Pythagorean major sixth |
| 969 | B♭ | 7:4 | seventh partial; *blu* |
| 996 | B♭ | 16:9 | grand-*pa* below |
| 1000 -------- B♭ ------------------------- | | | equal-tempered minor seventh |
| 1018 | B♭ | 9:5 | *ga* below grand-*pa*; *komal ni* |
| 1053 | $\frac{1}{4}$ tone | | splits G (3:2) and D (9:8) |
| 1088 | B | 15:8 | *ni*; *ga* of *pa* |
| 1100 -------- B ------------------------- | | | equal-tempered major seventh |
| 1110 | B | 243:128 | Pythagorean major seventh |
| 1200 | C | 2:1 | *sa* |

# SOURCES

## Books

What follows is not a proper bibliography or discography, but a recognition of some of the primary sources I have used for learning harmony and for writing this book. First, allow me to list my own books, which I had to write before writing this one.

*The Listening Book: Discovering Your Own Music.* Boston: Shambhala, 1991. This book for the general reader is meant to transform awareness of everyday sound into musical practice. It suggests ways to clarify the process of music practice and shows how to structure improvisatory practice.

*The Musical Life: What It Is and How to Live It.* Boston: Shambhala, 1994. Brief essays discuss the relation between psyche and muse. The book also contains a seventy-page section called "Sound Is the Teacher," which treats the overtone series experientially from its elemental nature to its larger harmonic meaning, and is recommended for readers of this book not familiar with the subject.

## HARMONIC THEORY

Blackwood, Easley. *The Structure of Recognizable Diatonic Tunings.* Princeton, NJ: Princeton University Press, 1985. An elegant alliance between perception (what is "recognizable") and number (its mathematical quantification). The book is essentially for theorists (and musicians) who are functional in algebra at the college level, which I am not, so I can follow it only so far. But what I do understand, including the tables and the gist of the text, has been of immense value in forming my own set of alliances.

Boomsliter, Paul, and Warren Creel. "Organization in Auditory Perception." An unpublished paper that may be available through some university libraries. It is the product of the authors' collaboration at the State University College in Albany, New York, in 1962; I first saw a photocopy of the manuscript in 1972. The authors were the first, I think, to intuit the physiology of the modal roots of modulating tonality. Specifically, they addressed the intricacies of compounding, which they called "extended reference"; they also articulated the pentamerous polarity between relative and parallel realms. They were pioneers, and their work, greatly admired by those who have benefited from it, is largely unrecognized.

Daniélou, Alain. *Music and the Power of Sound: The Influence of Tuning and Interval on Consciousness*. Rev. ed. Rochester, VT: Inner Traditions, 1995. First published as *Introduction to the Study of Musical Scales* in 1943, this is a brilliant, though biased, book. Brilliant because the author understood the universality of the harmonic generation of scales; biased because he dismissed equal temperament as a mistaken aberration leading only to decadence. Nevertheless, his book is wide in scope and thought-provoking.

Doty, David B. *The Just Intonation Primer*. 1993. Probably the most practical guide available for learning the subject. The text is clear, including explication of the math, and the definitions are precise. There are lattices (not in staff notation) and various other harmonic diagrams, ample discussion of higher primes, and a good discussion of just intonation played on "real instruments." The book is available through the Just Intonation Network, an organization of musicians devoted to the field; their address is 535 Stevenson Street, San Francisco, CA 94103.

Helmholtz, Hermann. *On the Sensation of Tone*. Translated by Alexander Ellis. Reprint. New York: Dover, 1954. Originally published in 1863 as *On the Sensations of Tone as a Physiological Basis for the Theory of Music*, and translated into English by Ellis in 1885. It endures not only as a seminal work but also as a most useful reference. Ellis made invaluable contributions in an appendix of 120 pages. He was the first, I believe, and possibly the most articulate, in describing the lattice of twelve notes, which he named the *harmonic duodene*, or the unit of modulation (on p. 461), although he did not use staff notation. The extended lattice he named the Duodenarium (p. 463). These concepts led eventually to present-day harmonic theory, including my own thinking.

Jorgensen, Owen. *Tuning: The Perfection of Eighteenth-Century Temperament, The Lost Art of Nineteenth-Century Temperament, and the Science of Equal Temperament*. East Lansing: Michigan State University Press, 1991. This book will tell you everything about the development of temperament that *Harmonic Experience* leaves out. Historically organized into 223 brief chapters, the text is clear, passionate, and wonderfully replete. Interspersed with liberal quotations from original sources are careful instructions for the tuning of each temperament discussed. Precise equal-tempered tuning was not fully accepted until the early twentieth century, and this volume gives a vivid picture of the dramatic transformations in musician's perceptions and tuner's craft that occurred along the way.

Levarie, Seigmund, and Ernst Levy. *Tone: A Study in Musical Acoustics*. Kent, OH: Kent State University Press, 1968. Like Ernst Levy's *A Theory of Harmony*, (Kent, OH: Kent

State University Press, 1985), this is a theoretical precursor to the present book, and I am indebted to the authors for many of their ideas. Although I disagree with much of their theory, they never lose sight of the interface between inner and outer worlds. Both books should be read by students interested in the development of contemporary music theory.

Makeig, Scott. "Affective versus Analytic Perception of Musical Intervals." In *Music, Mind, and Brain: The Neuropsychology of Music*, edited by Manfred Clynes. New York: Plenum Press, 1982. Makeig discusses "how the affective experience of tonal harmonies is linked to their objective structure"; he shows that harmony is highly structured by the compounding of small-integer frequency ratios according to "a small number of principles, and may be modelled spatially."

Partch, Harry. *Genesis of a Music*. 1949. Reprint. New York: Da Capo Press, 1974. A touchstone for musicians interested in eleven-limit just systems (especially Partch's), it has also become a primary reference as an overview of the subject of tuning, including synopses of the major contributions to the field. It is written with a cantankerous and engaging wit and, at least as much as Partch's music, keeps his creative spirit alive.

## ACOUSTICS

Benade, Arthur H. *Fundamentals of Musical Acoustics*. New York: Oxford University Press, 1976. The best college-level acoustics text I've seen.

## PRACTICUM

Blackwood, Easley. *A Practical Musician's Guide to Tonal Harmony*. An exceptionally thorough codification and expansion of Nadia Boulanger's pedagogy, which involves teaching tonal harmony through harmonic models learned at the keyboard. If you want to perceive tonal harmony the way it was perceived by the Europeans who developed it, this volume is an open window. Available through Blackwood Enterprises, 5300 South Shore Drive, Chicago, IL 60615.

Montfort, Matthew. *Ancient Traditions, Future Possibilities: Rhythmic Training through the Traditions of Africa, Bali, and India*. Mill Valley, CA: Panoramic Press, 1985. An extremely practical, hands-on guide, available through Ancient Future, P.O. Box 264, Kentfield, CA 94914.

## AESTHETICS, METAPHYSICS, AND POETRY

Barks, Coleman, trans. *The Essential Rumi*. San Francisco, CA: Harper San Francisco, 1995. A presentation of one of the most musical poets in the most musical English. Rumi's direct experience of the ecstatic is an inspiration for musicians seeking their musical truth. Here is a quatrain:

*I have lived on the lip*
*of insanity, wanting to know reasons,*
*knocking on a door. It opens.*
*I've been knocking from the inside!*

A catalog of the translations and other works of Mr. Barks is available through Maypop Books, 196 Westview Drive, Athens, GA 30606.

Bayles, David, and Ted Orlund. *Art and Fear*. Santa Barbara, CA: Capra Press, 1994. The best general book on the process of making art I have seen. It tells the hard truth in a warm way readers can use, discussing the monsters of failure, annihilation, pretending, academia, and money with clear eyes and direct language, and is especially appropriate for composers.

Dewey, John. *Art as Experience*. (Berkeley, CA: Berkeley Publications, 1959). Dewey develops a view of aesthetics on a vector between the subjective and the objective in art. This book was my first confirmation (in college) that it is useful and even proper to think about art from the inside out, and is thus a distant but direct ancestor of *Harmonic Experience*.

Khan, Hazrat Inayat. *The Mysticism of Sound*. Available in many editions under various titles, including *The Music of Life* (New Lebanon, NY: Omega Press, 1983), and most recently as *The Mysticism of Sound and Music* (Boston: Shambhala, 1996). Inayat Khan (1885–1927), in addition to being one of the great writers on spirituality, was also highly trained in North Indian music. He is the only holy man I know of who has articulated an authentic and inclusive spiritual message from the sensibilities of a master musician.

Schafer, R. Murray. *The Soundscape: Our Sonic Environment and the Tuning of the World*. Rochester, VT: Destiny Books, 1994. An impassioned, witty, and informed plea to the citizens of the world to take responsibility for its aural health.

Schwenk, Theodor. *Sensitive Chaos*. Fair Oaks, CA: Rudolf Steiner Press, 1963. Schwenk leads the reader to appreciate the creativity that exists at boundary surfaces. The author, a hydrodynamics engineer, spent a life "watching air and water with unprejudiced eyes" and came to a changed understanding of what is alive.

## REFERENCE

Goodwin, Joscelyn. *The Harmony of the Spheres: A Sourcebook of the Pythagorean Tradition in Music*. Rochester, VT: Inner Traditions, 1993. An excellent compendium of original sources.

Partridge, Eric. *Origins: A Short Etymological Dictionary of Modern English*. New York: Greenwich, 1983. An excellent etymological dictionary is indispensable, especially in a subject such as music theory, where the meanings of words have been muddied, eroded, or reversed over time. Also important is a handy desk dictionary, for which *The New Harvard Dictionary of Music* sets a decent standard.

Sadie, Stanley, ed. *The New Grove Dictionary of Music and Musicians*. London: Macmillan, 1980. Available in a twenty-volume paperback edition, this is probably more important than a new car.

# Recordings

## EARLY EUROPEAN MUSIC

Although there are a good number of excellent recordings of early European music, my purpose here is to list only a few that I have found most especially in tune, musical, and informative. Following are three groups that bring forward early sensibilities to an extraordinary degree.

- Sequentia, a group of three Americans living in Cologne, are especially empathetic to the medieval aesthetic and have recorded a considerable repertoire of medieval music (on Deutsche Harmonia Mundi), including the works of Hildegard von Bingen.
- Ensemble PAN (Project Ars Nova), a Boston-based consortium of virtuoso singers and instrumentalists, specialize in fourteenth-century polyphony, including Machaut, Landini, and Ciconia, which they perform with profoundly affective intonation and ideal musicianship. Their recordings are on New Albion.
- Ensemble Alcatraz, a San Francisco-based group specializing in medieval and early renaissance music, performs in perfect tune and with sensational verve, and has two recordings on Elektra/Nonesuch.

## WORLD MUSIC

There are so many recordings that testify to the vitality of music from around the globe that in order to familiarize yourself with the best without spending too much time and money you have to adopt a creative selection strategy. You could stand in front of the bins of a large record store and choose albums by intuition. You could seek out the discographies of books on relevant subjects. You could consult a reference that lists titles by country. You could keep your eye out for reviews (though that is risky). You could purchase a few collections of world music and proceed from there (a few are listed below). Perhaps the best method is to ask the advice of musicians whose taste you trust. I will list only a few recordings that have illuminated or amazed me, or influenced my compositional ear.

Perhaps the most astonishing music in the universe is produced collectively (and largely improvisationally) as a function of daily life by various tribes of Pygmies in central Africa. The music is modal, richly polyrhythmic and contrapuntal, and deeply joyous. One of the oldest and best collections is *Music of the Rain Forest Pygmies*, recorded in 1961 in the Ituri rain forest of Zaire by Colin M. Turnbull, and recently rereleased on Lyrichord (LYRCD 7157). A recent collection by Louis Sarno, Bayaka: *The Extraordinary Music of the Babenzele Pygmies* (Ellipsis Arts, 1995), contains a CD and a book by Sarno, who currently lives with the Babenzele in a resettled village he helped to found. Another release by Ellipsis Arts, *Echoes of the Forest,* contains music from both the Sarno and the Turnbull archives and comes with a smaller book including a good discography and bibliography.

Ellipsis Arts has released a number of collections that present various aspects of global music, among them *Voices of Forgotten Worlds* (an excellent two-disc compendium of vocal music), *Global Celebration* (music from festivals and celebratory rituals), *Planet Soup* (market-oriented cross-cultural collaborations) and, through their related firm, the Relaxation Company, *Global Meditation* (the music of sacred rituals).

Of special interest to those who want to hear the overtone series produced vocally with astonishing clarity is *Tuva: Voices from the Center of Asia* (Smithsonian/Folkways 40017).

The various Bulgarian state women's choirs have come into world prominence over the last two decades singing music that is elegantly composed (or arranged) but that arises from an ancient vocal style and technique. The music is not only powerfully moving but also possibly the most perfect demonstration of the relationship between ancient sensibilities and modern composition, and it presents the ideal in modal modulation: vibrantly in-tune singing throughout an extended harmonic lattice. Representative recordings are *Le Mystere des Voix Bulgares* (2 vols., Nonesuch/Explorer) and those of any choir conducted by Philip Koutev.

I will mention a few individual musicians. Hamza El-Din is a master troubadour, singing and playing (on oud) the songs of his Nubian homeland, long ago swallowed by the Aswan Dam. His music has been filtered through Asian, Middle Eastern, and European influences, and his tunings, impeccably just, are heavily accented with Arabic quarter tones. Any album is recommended; my current favorite is *Eclipse* (Ryko 0103).

If you have not investigated North Indian music you might begin with any recording by Pandit Pran Nath (voice), Ram Narayan (sarangi), and Lakshmi Shankar (voice).


# Contemporary Composition

Contemporary concert music is extremely diverse in style and intention, which seems to be a healthy state of affairs. I will not list my preferences, except to say that I think the works of Ben Johnston and Terry Riley are among the most intelligent and resonant of these times.

# ACKNOWLEDGMENTS

I WOULD FIRST LIKE TO ACKNOWLEDGE my teachers, Buddy Hiles, William Russo, Paul Sills, Easley Blackwood, Viola Spolin, Samuel Lewis, Pir Vilayat Khan, G. S. Sachdev, Terry Riley, Hamza El-Din, and Pandit Pran Nath, for allowing me to define myself and my work through their vision. Pandit Pran Nath, who passed away during the final preparation of this manuscript, has left behind through his recordings and through the voices of his students a golden legacy of transcendant music.

I give thanks also to my counselors Ben Johnston and Will Johnson for their timely support and pragmatic criticism. Many thanks to my students and friends Bob Fuller, Carol Frick, Jack Leissring, David Balakrishnan, Connie Coleman, Debra White, and Lori Levy for their grace and grit while I experimented on them—well, *through* them, perhaps.

I would like to thank the many people who have helped directly with the production of the book. Marie Carmichael and Francis Martineau read the manuscript and helped make it cogent. Dave Fraser helped develop many of the harmonic models. Kathleen Seidel procured the tapes of Mr. Creel and Dr. Boomsliter, as well as additional texts. Scott Makeig supplied copies of his own work as well as highly stimulating conversation. Marc Savage and Charlie Stevens provided invaluable assistance in compiling an index. And with the most profound generosity, Kirk Whipple supervised the production of over nine hundred musical examples, greatly improving their visual clarity and sustaining the highest standards of craft and musicality. Cory Gray aided us in this project with unflagging spirit, Virginia Cayton helped keep us organized, and Marilyn Morales provided us heartfelt and tactical support.

The editor of *Harmonic Experience*, Larry Hamberlin, has been not only its champion but also its fine-tuner, wetnurse, pilot, diplomat, and salesman, as well as its author's friend, and I thank him profoundly for all of these dimensions. Deep thanks also to Christine Sumner, Virginia Scott, and the staff of Inner Traditions International for their long patience and great resourcefulness.

And finally, to my three daughters, Athene, Lucy, and Amy, and to my wife, Devi, eternal gratitude.

# GENERAL INDEX

# INDEX OF RATIOS

In order of ascending value; see also Glossary of Singable Tones in Just Intonation, pp. 530–31

**1:1**, 17, 19, 96, 139
*See also sa*; unisons
**225:224**
and the *blu/ga-ga* comma, 339–40
**2048:2025**, 253
*See also* diaschisma
**81:80**, 250–51, 260
*See also* Didymic comma
**531441:524288**, 248
*See also* Pythagorean comma
**64:63**
and the septimal comma, 336–38
**128:125**, 251–52
*See also* Great Diesis
**36:35**
and the *blu/minor* commas, 338, 339
**25:24**, 57, 99, 121, 514
in the C♯/D♭ diesis, 300
cyclic properties of, in equal temperament, 473
major/minor chromatic pairs, 103, 106, 260
relation to **10:9**, 403
and *tivra sa*, 224
*See also* augmented octaves; augmented primes;
augmented tonic; chromatic pairs
**21:20**, 127
**256:243**, 98
**135:128**, 109, 119–20, 325
*See also* augmented primes; chromatic pairs
**16:15**, 59–61, 96, 225
in the C♯/D♭ diaschisma, 325
in the C♯/D♭ diesis, 300
and directionality in cyclic sequences, 472
as leading tone, 259–60

*See also komal re*; minor seconds
**10:9**, 97, 118–19
alternating with **9:8**, 118–19
compared with **9:8**, 266–67
compared with **9:8** in cyclic sequences, 461–63
and directionality in cyclic sequences, 472–73
in the Dorian mode, 190
in the Major (Ionian) mode, 185
in the relative minor, 155n
*See also* major seconds; minor whole tone; *re*
**9:8**, 96, 97, 98
alternating with **10:9**, 118–19
compared with **10:9**, 266–67
compared with **10:9** in cyclic sequences, 461–63
and directionality in cyclic sequences, 472–73
and the Didymic comma, 251
in the Dorian mode, 190
in the relative major, 155n
*See also* major seconds; major whole tone; *re*
**7:6**, 126–27
and the *blu/ga-ga* comma, 339–40
and the *blu/minor* comma, 338–39
*See also* minor thirds; septimal harmony
**75:64**
and the *blu/ga-ga* comma, 339–40
cyclic properties of in equal temperament, 473
*see also* augmented seconds
**32:27**, 97, 117
compared with **6:5** in cyclic sequences, 465–71
*See also* Pythagorean minor thirds
**6:5**, 54–57, 96, 97, 151
compared with **32:27** in cyclic sequences,
465–71
and directionality in cyclic sequences, 472
in the parallel minor, 156
*See also komal ga*; minor thirds

# Index of Most-Referenced Examples, Figures, and Tables

Correspondence with the author or requests for a catalog of his music should be directed to:

Cold Mountain Music
P.O. Box 912
Sebastopol, CA 95473